HANDBOOK ON THE SCIENCE OF LITERACY IN GRADES 3-8

Also Available

Developing Conceptual Knowledge
through Oral and Written Language:
Perspectives and Practices, PreK–12
edited by Melanie R. Kuhn and Mariam Jean Dreher

Developing Fluent Readers:
Teaching Fluency as a Foundational Skill
Melanie R. Kuhn and Lorell Levy

Handbook of Early Literacy Research, Volume 1
edited by Susan B. Neuman and David K. Dickinson

Handbook of Early Literacy Research, Volume 2
edited by David K. Dickinson and Susan B. Neuman

Handbook of Early Literacy Research, Volume 3
edited by Susan B. Neuman and David K. Dickinson

Handbook on the Science of Early Literacy
*edited by Sonia Q. Cabell, Susan B. Neuman,
and Nicole Patton Terry*

Knowledge Development in Early Childhood:
Sources of Learning and Classroom Implications
*edited by Ashley M. Pinkham, Tanya Kaefer,
and Susan B. Neuman*

Handbook on
THE SCIENCE OF LITERACY
in Grades 3–8

edited by
Susan B. Neuman
Melanie R. Kuhn

Foreword by Sharon Vaughn

THE GUILFORD PRESS
New York London

Copyright © 2025 The Guilford Press
A Division of Guilford Publications, Inc.
www.guilford.com

All rights reserved

No part of this book may be reproduced, translated, stored in a retrieval system, or transmitted, in any form or by any means, electronic, mechanical, photocopying, microfilming, recording, or otherwise, without written permission from the publisher.

Printed in the United States of America

This book is printed on acid-free paper.

For product and safety concerns within the EU, please contact GPSR@taylorandfrancis.com, Taylor & Francis Verlag GmbH, Kaufingerstraße 24, 80331 München, Germany.

Last digit is print number: 9 8 7 6 5 4 3 2 1

Library of Congress Cataloging-in-Publication Data

Names: Neuman, Susan B. editor | Kuhn, Melanie R. editor
Title: Handbook on the science of literacy in grades 3–8 / edited by Susan
  B. Neuman, Melanie R. Kuhn.
Description: New York : The Guilford Press, [2025] | Includes
  bibliographical references and index. |
Identifiers: LCCN 2025000703 | ISBN 9781462558018 cloth
Subjects: LCSH: Reading (Middle school) | Penmanship | Literacy | BISAC:
  LANGUAGE ARTS & DISCIPLINES / Literacy | EDUCATION / Schools / Levels /
  Elementary
Classification: LCC LB1573 .H17175 2025 | DDC 428.4071/2—dc23/eng/20250613
LC record available at https://lccn.loc.gov/2025000703

About the Editors

Susan B. Neuman, EdD, is Professor of Teaching and Learning at New York University. Previously, she was Professor at the University of Michigan and served as the U.S. Assistant Secretary for Elementary and Secondary Education, in which role she established the Early Reading First program and the Early Childhood Educator Professional Development Program and was responsible for all activities in Title I of the Elementary and Secondary Education Act. Dr. Neuman has served on the boards of directors of the International Literacy Association and numerous other nonprofit organizations, and as coeditor of *Reading Research Quarterly*. She has received two lifetime achievement awards for research in literacy development and is a member of the Reading Hall of Fame and a Fellow of the American Educational Research Association. She has published over 100 articles and numerous books.

Melanie R. Kuhn, PhD, is Professor and Jean Adamson Stanley Faculty Chair in Literacy at the Purdue University College of Education. Her primary focus has been on reading fluency and how best to support its development. In addition, her research interests include literacy instruction for struggling readers and comprehension and vocabulary development. Dr. Kuhn's instructional experience includes clinic work, directing reading interventions, and teaching in the Boston Public Schools. She served as a member of the Literacy Research Panel for the International Literacy Association and as a board member for the Literacy Research Association. Dr. Kuhn has written or edited several books, along with numerous journal articles and book chapters. She moderates the website *thereadingforum.com*.

Contributors

Steven J. Amendum, PhD, School of Education, University of Delaware, Newark, Delaware

Nina Bayer, MAT, Department of Educational Psychology, University of Connecticut, Storrs, Connecticut

Gina Biancarosa, EdD, Center on Teaching and Learning, University of Oregon, Eugene, Oregon

Jill Castek, PhD, Department of Teaching, Learning, and Sociocultural Studies, University of Arizona, Tucson, Arizona

Gina Cervetti, PhD, Marsal Family School of Education, University of Michigan, Ann Arbor, Michigan

Brennan Chandler, PhD, Department of Learning Sciences, Georgia State University, Atlanta, Georgia

Joanna A. Christodoulou, EdD, The Brain, Education, & Mind (BEAM) Lab, MGH Institute of Health Professions, Boston, Massachusetts

Huy Chung, PhD, UCI Writing Project, School of Education, University of California, Irvine, Irvine, California

Stephen Ciullo, PhD, Department of Curriculum and Instruction, Texas State University, San Marcos, Texas

Alyson A. Collins, PhD, Department of Curriculum and Instruction, Texas State University, San Marcos, Texas

Kristin Conradi Smith, PhD, Department of Curriculum and Instruction, William & Mary School of Education, Williamsburg, Virginia

Dennis S. Davis, PhD, Department of Teacher Education and Learning Sciences, North Carolina State University, Raleigh, North Carolina

Simone Gibson, PhD, Department of Teacher Education and Professional Development, Morgan State University, Baltimore, Maryland

Xiaoli Gong, MAT, Department of Teaching and Learning, Policy and Leadership, University of Maryland, College Park, Maryland

Amanda P. Goodwin, PhD, Department of Teaching and Learning, Vanderbilt University, Nashville, Tennessee

Megan Goss, EdD, Learning Design Group, University of California, Berkeley, Berkeley, California

Steve Graham, EdD, Mary Lou Fulton Teachers College, Arizona State University, Tempe, Arizona

Maughn Gregory, PhD, Department of Educational Foundations, Montclair State University, Montclair, New Jersey

Åste Mjelve Hagen, PhD, Department of Special Needs Education, University of Oslo, Oslo, Norway

Devin M. Kearns, PhD, Department of Teacher Education and Learning Sciences, North Carolina State University, Raleigh, North Carolina

Panayiota Kendeou, PhD, Department of Educational Psychology, College of Education and Human Development, University of Minnesota, Minneapolis, Minnesota

Rebecca Knoph, PhD, CREATE Center for Research on Equality in Education, University of Oslo, Oslo, Norway

Melanie R. Kuhn, PhD, Department of Curriculum and Instruction, Purdue University, West Lafayette, Indiana

Joshua Lawrence, EdD, Department of Education, University of Oslo, Oslo, Norway

Undraa Maamuujav, PhD, UCI Writing Project, School of Education, University of California, Irvine, Irvine, California

Anya Maloney, MS, The Brain, Education & Mind (BEAM) Lab, MGH Institute of Health Professions, Boston, Massachusetts

Meaghan McKenna, PhD, Department of Speech and Hearing Science, University of Illinois at Urbana–Champaign, Champaign, Illinois

Cheryl McLean, PhD, Department of Learning and Teaching, Rutgers–New Brunswick Graduate School of Education, New Brunswick, New Jersey

Kristen L. McMaster, PhD, Department of Educational Psychology, College of Education and Human Development, University of Minnesota, Minneapolis, Minnesota

Carol Booth Olson, PhD, UCI Writing Project, School of Education, University of California, Irvine, Irvine, California

Karen Omohundro, MS, Department of Counseling, Higher Education, and Special Education, University of Maryland, College Park, Maryland

Jeanne R. Paratore, EdD, Department of Literacy Education, Boston University, Boston, Massachusetts

C. Patrick Proctor, EdD, Department of Teaching, Curriculum, and Society, Boston College, Chestnut Hill, Massachusetts

Deborah K. Reed, PhD, Tennessee Reading Research Center, University of Tennessee Knoxville, Knoxville, Tennessee

Alina Reznitskaya, PhD, Department of Educational Foundations, Montclair State University, Montclair, New Jersey

Dana A. Robertson, EdD, Reading and Literacy Education Program, Virginia Tech, Blacksburg, Virginia

Aniqa Shah, PhD, Department of Teaching, Learning, and Sociocultural Studies, University of Arizona, Tucson, Arizona

Melissa Stalega, PhD, Department of Educational Psychology, University of Connecticut, Storrs, Connecticut

John Z. Strong, PhD, Graduate School of Education, University at Buffalo, State University of New York, Buffalo, New York

Ana Taboada Barber, PhD, Department of Counseling, Higher Education, and Special Education, University of Maryland, College Park, Maryland

Jessica R. Toste, PhD, Department of Special Education, The University of Texas at Austin, Austin, Texas

Jennifer D. Turner, PhD, Department of Teaching and Learning, Policy and Leadership, University of Maryland, College Park, Maryland

Margaret Vaughn, PhD, Department of Language, Literacy, and Technology, Washington State University, Pullman, Washington

Sharon Walpole, PhD, School of Education, University of Delaware, Newark, Delaware

Jade Wexler, PhD, Department of Counseling, Higher Education, and Special Education, University of Maryland, College Park, Maryland

Ian Wilkinson, PhD, Department of Teaching and Learning, The Ohio State University, Columbus, Ohio

Tanya Wright, PhD, Marsal Family School of Education, University of Michigan, Ann Arbor, Michigan

Foreword

The first time I met Susan Neuman (coeditor, with Melanie Kuhn, of this handbook), she was presenting her research at the Capitol building in Austin, Texas. It must have been about 1999 because it was before George W. Bush was president. She truly blew me away with her clear, purposeful, and unfiltered interpretation of the benefits of books in the classroom for preschoolers—books that were within their reach and thus accessible to them. Susan said lots of things that impressed me, but it was the clear, thoughtful, and direct way in which she said them that really captured my attention then and holds it today. The work collected in this *Handbook on the Science of Literacy in Grades 3–8* has those same qualities. I have no doubt you will agree that this book interprets the research related to language, vocabulary, complexity of text, and comprehension with solid evidence and applications for teaching and learning.

Like Susan Neuman, Melanie Kuhn has the mindset and proclivity to make research utilitarian to key stakeholders, with an emphasis on accurately interpreting research and making it approachable. Considering these two are the coeditors of this handbook, I suggest that you read it carefully, questioning your own assumptions and bolstering those that align with the evidence presented. There are too few opportunities to read about literacy practices that are both evidence based and useful in school settings. Don't miss this one!

Foreword technically means "before the word," and a solid foreword should help you decide that you want to read the book. There are so many pulls on our attention today. We have access to YouTube presentations, podcasts, and journal articles, just to name a few resources readily available to us. However, few of these accomplish the essential task of being both grounded in research and applicable to classroom implementation. The most important reason you should read this book is that you *deserve* it. You deserve to understand the research on literacy and to have it presented with the same unfiltered, direct way in which these editors communicate. You also deserve to better understand how to apply this research in your classroom or school setting. After reading this book, I bet you will understand why I am so encouraging.

SHARON VAUGHN, PhD
The University of Texas at Austin

Contents

Introduction   1
Melanie R. Kuhn and Susan B. Neuman

PART I
WHAT DOES THE RESEARCH SAY ABOUT LANGUAGE AND VOCABULARY?

1. Raising the Bar: Supporting Teachers in Engaging Students   11
   in Rigorous Argumentation
   Alina Reznitskaya, Ian Wilkinson, and Maughn Gregory

2. Multisyllabic Word-Reading Instruction in the Intermediate Grades   29
   Jessica R. Toste and Brennan Chandler

3. The Science of Reading: Morphology Matters   47
   Amanda P. Goodwin

4. Critical and Developmental Perspectives in Multilingual Literacy   62
   and Curriculum
   C. Patrick Proctor

5. The Language of Learning: Academic Vocabulary Development   80
   and Comprehension
   Joshua Lawrence, Rebecca Knoph, and Åste Mjelve Hagen

PART II
WHAT DOES THE RESEARCH SAY ABOUT TEXT COMPLEXITY AND COMPREHENSION?

6. Supporting Reading Comprehension in the Upper Elementary Grades — 99
   Kristen L. McMaster and Panayiota Kendeou

7. Complicating the Simple View of Reading — 115
   Gina Biancarosa

8. What Is Text Complexity and How Does It Affect Literacy Learning? — 135
   Steven J. Amendum and Kristin Conradi Smith

9. Readers' Motivation and Engagement in the Science of Literacy — 152
   Ana Taboada Barber and Xiaoli Gong

10. The Role of Knowledge in Text Comprehension — 168
    Gina Cervetti and Tanya Wright

PART III
WHAT DOES THE RESEARCH SAY ABOUT SUPPORTING STRUGGLING READERS?

11. Addressing Reading Achievement during Summer Vacation — 185
    Joanna A. Christodoulou and Anya Maloney

12. Multi-Tiered Systems of Support for Improving Literacy Outcomes for Students in Grades 3–8 — 204
    Devin M. Kearns, Nina Bayer, Melissa Stalega, and Meaghan McKenna

13. The Need for Schoolwide Literacy Models — 223
    Jade Wexler, Deborah K. Reed, and Karen Omohundro

14. Adaptive Teaching: A Critical Tool to Support Readers — 241
    Margaret Vaughn

15. Reading Fluency for Struggling Readers — 255
    Melanie R. Kuhn

PART IV
WHAT DOES THE RESEARCH SAY ABOUT WRITING INSTRUCTION?

16. Changing Writing Instruction in the Middle Grades — 275
    Steve Graham

17. Effective Writing Instruction for Students with Learning Disabilities in Grades 3–8 — 290
    Stephen Ciullo and Alyson A. Collins

18. A Cognitive Strategies Approach to Teaching Text-Based Argument Writing to English Learners — 307
    Carol Booth Olson, Undraa Maamuujav, and Huy Chung

19. Expansive Literacies for Middle Grade Learners — 326
    Jill Castek, Megan Goss, and Aniqa Shah

PART V
TEACHER KNOWLEDGE AND PROFESSIONAL DEVELOPMENT

20. Toward a Science of Professional Learning for Teachers of Grades 3–8 — 349
    Sharon Walpole and John Z. Strong

21. Discourse, Positioning, and Agency: A Relational Perspective on Literacy Coaching in the Upper Elementary and Middle Grades — 367
    Dana A. Robertson and Jeanne R. Paratore

22. Upper Elementary Teachers' Specialized Knowledge of the Components and Processes of Reading Comprehension — 383
    Dennis S. Davis

23. Black Futures Matter: Reimagining Science of Literacy Instruction for Black Students — 409
    Jennifer D. Turner and Simone Gibson

24. Beyond Words: Multimodal and Digital Literacies, Culture, and Identity in Learners' Lives — 428
    Cheryl A. McLean

Author Index — 439

Subject Index — 451

Introduction

Melanie R. Kuhn
Susan B. Neuman

We began collaborating on this volume in the midst of a renewed focus on research-based literacy instruction. At the time, the terms *science of reading* and *science of literacy* were being used as a shorthand for this research and its corresponding instructional practices. However, much of the research in these areas focuses on students in PreK–2. While this makes sense given the emphasis on literacy development and the role of mechanics in early literacy practice, we felt a pressing need to address upper elementary and middle grades as well. This book is meant to highlight research and instructional practices designed for grades 3–8, years that generally receive less attention than do the primary grades (e.g., Walpole et al., 2017).

One aspect of reading theory that we felt was particularly important to address is the notion that students first *learn to read*, and only then do they begin *reading to learn* (Chall, 1995). Critically, a substantial amount of research has shown that this is a false dichotomy (e.g., Cabell et al., 2023; Kuhn & Stahl, 2022). We now know that young children are capable of learning to read using a broad range of materials, including informational texts, and that they benefit from content-based instruction during their early years (Pearson et al., 2020).

At the same time, students in upper elementary and middle grades classrooms are responsible both for learning a greater amount of content and for reading an increased amount of text (e.g., Lupo et al., 2024). They are also expected to perform more complex tasks while interacting with increasingly difficult reading materials (National Governors Association Center for Best Practices & Council of Chief State School Officers, 2010a, 2010b). And while the divide would indicate students leave word learning behind in the primary grades, they in fact benefit from both multisyllabic word recognition and morphological development, often presented as part of their vocabulary learning.

Another area we feel is critical to reconsider is the notion of "reading wars" (Chall, 1992, p. 316). We agree with Jeanne Chall that rather than spending time arguing in the abstract, it is essential to ask two complementary questions when considering literacy learning: "Where's the evidence?" and "What does it mean for teaching?" (Adams, 2005). To determine what works, we need to look at the data. However, this involves considering all of the research rather than cherry-picking only that which supports our current views. This process requires looking at a broad range of research, that with which we agree, as well as that with which we disagree, through a critical lens. Does this method, approach, or theory work for some students in specific situations or can it be applied more broadly? Are we overgeneralizing what was learned in ways that are not supported by the data? Are we making assumptions that are not supported evidence?

We further contend that if we are to ensure effective literacy learning for all students, we must recognize the reciprocal role that language, writing, and reading play in this process. To do so, we need to consider what individual learners require at particular points in their development and how instruction can meet these needs—and not assume a "one size fits all" perspective. This book is designed to help achieve these goals.

Overview of This Handbook

Part I. What Does the Research Say about Language and Vocabulary?

Part I of this volume focuses on language and vocabulary development. In Chapter 1, Alina Reznitskaya, Ian Wilkinson, and Maughn Gregory address the importance of classroom dialogue in developing upper elementary students' disciplinary knowledge and argumentation skills. While there is recognition that discussion can be a major contributor to student learning, teachers often have difficulty integrating and evaluating these practices in their classrooms. The authors present an overview of elements that allow for more effective implementation of these practices, provide their readers with practical approaches to incorporate dialogue that promotes argumentation in the classroom, and suggest research directions that have the potential to make such discussions an integral part of student learning.

Chapters 2 and 3 focus on multisyllabic word recognition and morphology respectively. While most decoding instruction is undertaken during the primary grades, Jessica R. Toste and Brennan Chandler discuss the importance of being able to read complex words automatically for students in the upper elementary years and beyond. While vocabulary and content knowledge are critical to comprehending the increasingly complex material that students usually begin to encounter in the upper elementary grades, to do so, they must be able to decode the multisyllabic words that are central to such selections accurately. The authors present the challenges of multisyllabic word recognition, highlight critical aspects of its implementation, and provide readers with a research-based approach to classroom instruction. Amanda P. Goodwin then focuses on morphology instruction as a key to improving students' vocabulary learning in Chapter 3. She discusses the importance of assessing students' morphological knowledge and ways of integrating its explicit instruction into the classroom. This process is likely not only to increase students' ability to determine word meanings but also to have a positive impact on their comprehension more broadly.

Patrick Proctor expands the discussion of language in Chapter 4 by looking at research in multilingual literacy. Rather than posing this research as needing to take a developmental perspective *or* a critical perspective, he considers the potential for synthesizing the two. This process involves reviewing both critical and developmental perspectives, recognizing not only how they differ (e.g., theoretical orientation, analytical approaches), but also how they may be complementary. He then presents a language-based reading curriculum (Cultivating Linguistic Awareness for Voice and Equity in Schools) developed by himself and his colleagues and discusses how teachers can integrate these perspectives to improve student literacy. Joshua Lawrence, Rebecca Knoph, and Åste Hagen next consider the construct of academic vocabulary in Chapter 5. They explore vocabulary development across grades and then discuss the critical relationship between vocabulary and reading. The authors also critique the use of the term *academic vocabulary*, highlight issues surrounding vocabulary instruction, and provide an outline of the Word Generation approach, a systematic program that has been used successfully to increase word knowledge, classroom discussions, and student self-efficacy.

Part II. What Does the Research Say about Text Complexity and Comprehension?

Part II centers on text complexity, as well as comprehension. In Chapter 6, Kristen McMaster and Panayiota Kendeou begin by focusing on aligning research and practice to improve student reading comprehension. Comprehension is considered broadly, and the authors emphasize how to work effectively within the multi-tiered systems of support (MTSS) currently implemented in many schools to ensure student success. They further present ways in which technological advances can allow for individual tutoring across each of the tiers and technology's potential for differentiation within the classroom. Gina Biancarosa next considers the importance of both decoding and comprehension in her review of the simple view of reading (SVR) in Chapter 7. This process involves reflecting on how SVR is defined, as well as its influence on research and practice, especially as regards reading disabilities. She further explores ways in which the SVR may continue to provide a foundation for future theoretical models.

Steven J. Amendum and Kristin Conradi Smith next present the construct of text complexity in Chapter 8. While providing a historical review of the concept, they ground their broader discussion within the demands of various state and national standards and go on to explore the relationship between text difficulty and comprehension. This involves emphasizing the interaction between text complexity, reader characteristics, and instructional tasks. The authors conclude by considering ways to expand teacher knowledge of text complexity, along with instructional approaches and scaffolds that better ensure students' access to complex reading material.

In Chapter 9, Ana Taboada Barber and Xiaoli Gong focus on the role of motivation and engagement as a means of ensuring that learners become skilled readers. Rather than viewing these constructs as fixed, the authors emphasize how they can be fostered in the classroom. As part of this process, Taboada Barber and Gong review research on reading motivation, discuss the reading engagement model, present effective practices, and provide readers with a framework, Do SMILE, to highlight the principles that underlie these approaches. Next, Gina Cervetti and Tanya Wright discuss the critical role of knowledge in text comprehension in Chapter 10. They review both theoretical and empirical explanations of knowledge's contribution to reading comprehension. They then present research that is designed to build student knowledge through a series of conceptually coherent texts that emphasize vocabulary acquisition, reading comprehension, and higher-level reading processes. Such approaches can support not only reading to learn but also have the potential to support learning to read.

Part III. What Does the Research Say about Supporting Struggling Readers?

In Part III, the focus is on supports for struggling readers. Joanna A. Christodoulou and Anya Maloney begin in Chapter 11 by exploring the possibilities of using summer break as a time to provide reading support to students experiencing difficulties. They note that students in the upper elementary grades receive less reading instruction at a time when they face increased academic demands. Additionally, there are fewer resources available for reading instruction for older students than is the case for younger learners, even though more students are identified as experiencing difficulties in the later grades. By considering the research on effective practices, the authors argue that it is possible to create summer programs that positively affect students' literacy learning, as well as their social–emotional well-being.

Moving from summer to the traditional school year, Devin Kearns, Nina Bayer, Melissa Stalega, and Meaghan McKenna look at reading instruction within an MTSS framework as a means of supporting older students in Chapter 12. The authors identify practices that are evidence-based while simultaneously highlighting those that are commonly used but not supported by research. In addition to looking at instruction across the three tiers, they discuss data collection and analysis for students in each tier and factors, such as adequate resources and appropriate professional development, that are necessary to ensure student success. In Chapter 13, Jade Wexler, Deborah Reed, and Karen Omohundro look at the need for schoolwide literacy models for older students. As noted earlier, this is especially pressing given the increasing number of older students who experience difficulties with their literacy learning, coupled with the greater demands they face in their classes. The authors stress that effective models require both coordinated leadership and a reconsideration of school structure as the basis for increasing the amount of support provided in Tier 1 instructional settings and for ensuring effective supplemental interventions.

Next, Margaret Vaughn looks at adaptive teaching in Chapter 14. This approach facilitates the ability of teachers to meet student needs by modifying their instruction as necessary. Vaughn begins by discussing the theoretical foundations of adaptive teaching, presents common classroom adaptations and rationales for its use in the teaching of reading, and identifies teacher variables that help to ensure its successful implementation. In addition, Vaughn presents formative scales, such as the Adaptive Teaching Inventory, that can be used to improve adaptive instruction within a particular setting. This flexibility is critical to ensuring that teachers are not only able to plan appropriate literacy instruction for their students but also to respond effectively in real time to the varying requirements of the classroom.

In Chapter 15, Melanie R. Kuhn discusses the role of reading fluency for older readers. As part of this process, she looks at fluency's components, its role in the reading development of older readers, especially those experiencing reading difficulties, and the best ways to evaluate it in the upper elementary and middle grades. She further explores the notion of situational fluency in which readers experience more or less difficulty depending on the complexity of the text and their familiarity with the subject matter; this understanding moves us beyond the belief that fluency is an all-or-nothing skill and toward the recognition that it instead varies depending on a range of contextual factors. Finally, she highlights instructional approaches that make use of appropriate scaffolding as a means of better ensuring students' access to challenging text.

Part IV. What Does the Research Say about Writing Instruction?

Part IV considers the role of writing development and writing instruction in skilled literacy learning. In Chapter 16, Steve Graham discusses the importance of allocating a set amount of time daily for both writing instruction and students' practice of their writing skills. While recognizing the challenges of incorporating this time in an already crowded school day, he stresses that writing is not only an essential component of the literacy curriculum but also critical for students' success outside of their school lives. Graham further notes that even small changes in the classroom can increase student success, allowing teachers to make multiple adjustments over time rather than undertake an extensive shift all at once. The implementation of effective writing strategies has the potential to improve not only our instructional expertise but also students' competence.

Steven Ciullo and Alyson Collins consider effective writing instruction for students with learning disabilities, as well as striving writers. They begin Chapter 17 by reviewing theories of writing development and highlight challenges that students and teachers experience regarding writing and its instruction, respectively. Next, the authors provide a synthesis of the research on strategy instruction, as well as high-leverage teaching practices that have been shown to improve student writing. They further make recommendations for effective professional development and preservice preparation that can improve student learning in this area.

In Chapter 18, Carol Booth Olson, Undraa Maamuujar, and Huy Chung focus on a cognitive strategies approach for teaching text-based argument writing to English learners (ELs). The importance of this form of writing in comprehension and analytic thinking, and the disconnect that exists between ELs and their English-fluent peers in this skill, are highlighted. The authors then present research on the Pathway Project, a literacy intervention based on a cognitive strategies approach designed to prepare EL students and other students in high-needs schools to develop their analytic writing, as well as their strategic reading skill.

Jill Castek, Megan Goss, and Aniqa Shah explore the concept of expansive literacies and their role in middle school in Chapter 19. The authors emphasize the transformative potential of these literacies, their role in individual cognition, and their ability to connect learners through social processes. They also focus on the importance of digital and data literacies in incorporating meaningful connection points for all students. The authors draw from a range of research to provide readers with examples of culturally responsive teaching and learning in these modes, including engaged reading, a Socratic seminar sequence, multimodal writing, and digital inquiry learning. In this way, they remind us not only of the importance of new literacies in our schools but also of an expansive range of approaches that can be used to engage our students in their literacy learning.

Part V. Teacher Knowledge and Professional Development

Part V centers on teacher knowledge and professional development as a means of ensuring our students are receiving the best possible literacy instruction. Sharon Walpole and John Z. Strong discuss ways to develop a science of professional learning (PL) in Chapter 20. Centered around the importance of effective and efficient PL, the authors explore better ways to ensure this process leads to increases in student achievement. They highlight several elements with the potential to support better PL, including a focus on content (both subject matter and pedagogical), active learning, coherence, duration, and collective participation. While Walpole and Strong emphasize the need for further research in this area, their chapter can be used to strengthen the PL currently taking place. In Chapter 21, Dana Robertson and Jeanne R. Paratore expand the discussion around PL to focus on the role of literacy coaching. They note the mixed outcomes surrounding coaching to date and highlight those conditions that better ensure positive educational outcomes for students. In particular, the authors stress the importance of relational dynamics between coaches and teachers, emphasizing the role of coaches' talk-moves in this process, and highlight the need for coaches and teachers to interact as equitable partners if instructional supports are to be taken up in the classroom.

Chapter 22, by Dennis S. Davis, highlights the complexity of the teacher knowledge required for reading comprehension and its instruction in the upper elementary grades. The development of a clear knowledge base has been complicated by the lack of a precisely characterized domain regarding the content of reading. Despite obstacles, Davis synthesizes the research by first identifying the knowledge base that teachers currently encompass and then by discussing what they need to know if they are to teach reading comprehension to older elementary students effectively. He further provides his conceptualization of reading comprehension, along with an overview of the research on its instruction for both primary and upper elementary teachers, and considers multiple areas in need of further research.

In Chapter 23, Jennifer Turner and Simone Gibson consider ways of reimagining the science of literacy instruction to ensure the reaching and teaching of Black students. As part of this process, the authors provide a vignette discussing the structured literacy skills learned by male tutors from historically Black colleges and universities through the Literacy Brigade program. Rather than simply focusing on the instruction, the authors highlight the importance of connecting with the Black middle schoolers who are being tutored and maintaining their students' interest as an essential aspect of improving their literacy development. This process involves having open and honest conversations as part of their relationship building as well as understanding how this process serves as the basis of successful tutoring. The discussion in Turner and Gibson's chapter, along with its vignettes, better help readers understand the critical importance of creating a rich instructional model to increase equity in our literacy learning.

Finally, Cheryl McLean presents a praxis-oriented conception of multimodal and digital literacies and their connection to culture and identity in Chapter 24. She discusses how these modes of communication go beyond the printed word, as well as with students' ability to use them in meaningful ways within the classroom. She further argues that these literacies are central to children's lives and identities; as a result, it is essential that educators learn to integrate them into the curriculum. McLean next highlights ways in which social aspects of multimodal literacies influence students' identities as readers and writers, along with the role they play in learners' meaning-making processes. Finally, she provides the reader with examples of these literacies in learners' practices and experiences, reviews research on their role in the classroom, and describes challenges, implications, and future directions for research.

Conclusion

The overarching goal of this handbook is to explore the ways in which multiple components interact in the literacy development of students between grades 3 and 8. To do so, the contributing authors have not only highlighted the importance of reading-to-learn for older students but also the role of appropriate mechanics for upper elementary and middle grades students. The chapters also include ways in which a range of research-based approaches might best be applied in individual classrooms and across schools as a whole. Critically, they highlight how the research surrounding upper elementary and middle grades reading development and its components differs from that undertaken in primary grades. Our hope is that the reader will come away from this volume with a deeper recognition of the complexity of reading, writing, and oral language, how they interact with one another, and how this can be used to improve literacy instruction for our students.

REFERENCES

Adams, M. J. (2005, May). *A tribute to the work of Steven Stahl: Reading research into practice.* Paper presented at the annual meeting of the International Reading Association, San Antonio, TX.

Cabell, S. Q., Neuman, S. B., & Patton Terry, N. (Eds.). (2023). *Handbook on the science of early literacy.* Guilford Press.

Chall, J. S. (1992). The new reading debates: Evidence from science, art, and ideology. *Teachers College Record, 95*(2), 315–328.

Chall, J. S. (1995). *Stages of reading development* (2nd ed.). Harcourt Brace.

Kuhn, M. R., & Stahl, K. A. D. (2022). Teaching reading: Development and differentiation. *Kappan, 103*(8), 25–31.

Lupo, S. M., Reynolds, D., & Hardigree, C. (2024). *Tackling tough texts: A research-based guide to scaffolding learning in grades 6–12.* Guilford Press.

National Governors Association Center for Best Practices & Council of Chief State School Officers. (2010a). *Common Core State Standards for English language arts & literacy in history/social studies, science, and technical subjects.* Authors.

National Governors Association Center for Best Practices & Council of Chief State School Officers. (2010b). *Common Core State Standards for English language arts & literacy in history/social studies, science, and technical subjects. Appendix A: Research supporting key elements of the standards. Glossary of key terms.* Authors.

Pearson, P. D., Palincsar, A. S., Biancarosa, G., & Berman, A. I. (Eds.). (2020). *Reaping the rewards of the reading for understanding initiative.* National Academy of Education.

Walpole, S., Amendum, S., Pasquarella, A., Strong, J. Z., & McKenna, M. C. (2017). The promise of a literacy reform effort in the upper elementary grades. *Elementary School Journal, 118*(2), 257–280.

PART I
WHAT DOES THE RESEARCH SAY ABOUT LANGUAGE AND VOCABULARY?

CHAPTER 1

Raising the Bar
Supporting Teachers in Engaging Students in Rigorous Argumentation

Alina Reznitskaya
Ian Wilkinson
Maughn Gregory

More than a century ago, John Dewey (1910) wrote that the purpose of education was "to cultivate deep-seated and effective habits of discriminating tested beliefs from mere assertions, guesses, and opinions; to develop a lively, sincere, and open-minded preference for conclusions that are properly grounded, and to ingrain into the individual's working habits methods of inquiry and reasoning appropriate to the various problems that present themselves" (p. 28). In today's globalized, technologically advanced world, these habits of mind are both essential and in short supply (Barzilai & Chinn, 2020; Partnership for 21st Century Skills, 2012). Teaching students to construct, comprehend, and critically evaluate arguments is especially relevant in the current "epistemically complex" informational landscape, marked by a surge in misinformation, a diminishing trust in key societal institutions, and a growing disagreement about verifiable facts (Chinn et al., 2021; Kavanagh & Rich, 2018).

Argumentation is the process of generating and evaluating claims, as well as a type of discourse and a powerful tool for fostering knowledge and learning in every discipline (Asterhan & Schwarz, 2016; Erduran et al., 2004; Nussbaum & Edwards, 2011). The pedagogical benefits of engaging students in argumentation can be explained by constructivist theories. According to these theories, an internal mental conflict between existing ideas and new knowledge is a driving force that motivates learners to reexamine and revise their beliefs (Driver, 1995; Piaget & Inhelder, 1969), and language serves as a mechanism to support internalization of new ways of speaking, thinking, and acting (Vygotsky, 1968; Wells, 1999). Empirical studies confirm that engagement in argumentation improves students' reasoning and promotes deep understanding of content knowledge in different school subjects and grade levels (e.g., Gorard et al., 2015; Kuhn & Crowell, 2011).

Classroom *dialogue*, defined as the deliberative use of talk to advance students' learning, provides an ideal context for students to practice and learn argumentation (Kuhn & Moore, 2015; Resnick et al., 2015; Splitter & Sharp, 1996). However, not every dialogic engagement is or should be aimed at the construction and evaluation of ideas. Drawing on the work of Rosenblatt (1994), Chinn and colleagues (2001) proposed a taxonomy of three instructional stances used in dialogue about texts in language arts classes. The authors identified (1) an efferent stance, focused on acquiring information from the text; (2) an aesthetic stance, focused on personal reactions, associations, and feeling about the text; and (3) a critical-analytic stance, focused on reasoning about issues raised by the text. In this chapter, we discuss classroom dialogue that privileges a critical-analytic stance, as it is best aligned with the pedagogical goals of supporting argumentation and deep understanding of disciplinary knowledge.

Researchers whose work on dialogue-based pedagogy is explicitly or implicitly aligned with a critical-analytic stance have conducted numerous studies of classroom discourse in a variety of educational settings (for reviews, see Bouton & Asterhan, 2023; Hennessy et al., 2020; Howe et al., 2019; Reznitskaya & Gregory, 2013; Soter et al., 2008; Wilkinson et al., 2020). They have examined multiple models of "academically productive dialogue" (Bouton & Asterhan, 2023) that encompass different instructional goals, theoretical traditions, and disciplinary contexts. Despite the diversity of approaches, there is now an emerging consensus about the core features of productive talk: It focuses on open-ended, contestable questions and provides opportunities for students to offer elaborated explanations of their views, build on each other's ideas, and challenge perspectives presented by their peers.

In prior studies, researchers have also identified specific patterns of classroom discourse that are productive for student learning (e.g., Anderson et al., 2001; Hennessy et al., 2016; Mercer et al., 1999). For example, Michaels and O'Connor (2015) described "a family of talk moves (Can you say more? Say that again. Can you give us an example?) . . . intended to encourage students to elaborate on condensed, cryptic, or inexplicit utterances" (p. 348). Studies such as these have highlighted important differences between dialogue-based pedagogy and traditional instruction that limits opportunities for students to learn argumentation through dialogue (e.g., Mercer et al., 2004; Reznitskaya et al., 2012; Sedova et al., 2016). They have also revealed useful discursive patterns that, in turn, have informed professional development (PD) efforts to engage students in dialogue.

However, although certain discourse patterns can be productive for student learning, merely increasing the frequency of these practices is not the goal. Reflecting on decades-long research and teacher PD, Michaels and O'Connor (2015) concluded that "the simple deployment of talk moves does not ensure coherence in classroom discussions or robust student learning. To improve our PD with talk moves, we need to understand more about how to help teachers know when to use which moves in the service of deep conceptual understanding of core disciplinary ideas and practices" (p. 358).

Knowing when to use which moves is the principal challenge facing teachers who wish to facilitate dialogue with a critical-analytic stance because the choice of each teacher move needs to be informed by knowledge of discourse norms and practices of productive argumentation. "To invite students to articulate and explore their ideas . . . is to require that teachers hear those ideas, diagnose their virtues and weaknesses, and incorporate them into the substance of instruction. . . . This is a new role for teachers whose practice has been defined by traditional goals and methods, and it comes with different and strenuous intellectual demands" (Hammer & Schifter, 2001, p. 442).

In our work in elementary classrooms (e.g., Reznitskaya, 2012), we have observed teachers engaging students in discussions of controversial, authentic questions raised by the readings, but without utilizing any criteria for evaluating students' contributions. Students spent much of the discussion time sharing opinions, but they did not critically examine their own or others' viewpoints. Other research on teacher–student interactions has further confirmed an overemphasis on students' production of, rather than critique of, ideas during dialogue (Henderson et al., 2018; Rapanta, 2019). When interpreting the results of an observational study in the United Kingdom of 72 elementary classrooms, Howe (2023) concluded that "reasoned opposition" was rare during teacher-led discussions and that "the scarcity of opposition during teacher–student interaction may underpin the inconsequentiality of reasoned dialogue" for student learning (p. 33).

In this chapter, we describe our efforts to support teachers in conducting intellectually rigorous discussions, thus aiming to raise the bar on what typically occurs under the guise of classroom "argumentation." Our discussion is informed by a multiyear research project we conducted over 3 years at public schools in Ohio and New Jersey (Reznitskaya & Wilkinson, 2017; Wilkinson et al., 2023). The structure of this chapter is as follows. We begin by describing the classroom culture needed to support open exchange of ideas while also encouraging disciplinary critique of those ideas. We then present the normative dialogue and related epistemic commitments that underlie the development of sound judgments. To explain how we translated these theoretical assumptions into recommended classroom practices, we discuss instructional tools and activities we developed in collaboration with elementary school teachers. Here, we review evaluation criteria and facilitation practices teachers can use to enhance the quality of argumentation in their students' talk. We then take stock of the progress we made in raising the bar with teachers who participated in our PD. We focus on changes in teacher epistemic cognition and facilitation practices, and discuss improvements in student argumentation. We conclude by outlining directions for future research that can help to increase "reasoned opposition" in today's classrooms.

Theoretical Assumptions

Community of Inquiry

Classroom dialogue does not happen in a vacuum. It is situated within a culture, or a set of, often unstated, foundational assumptions about knowledge, authority, and roles and responsibilities of classroom members (Michaels et al., 2008; Windschitl, 2002). To define the normative culture in our studies, we drew on a variety of resources, including scholarship on dialogic teaching, argumentation, and epistemology (e.g., Alexander, 2017; Govier, 2010; Kuhn, 1991), as well as curriculum materials developed by the proponents of established educational models centered on argumentation (e.g., Dawes et al., 2004; Waggoner et al., 1995). However, our framing was most informed by the pedagogical literature from Philosophy for Children, an educational approach designed by philosophers with an explicit goal of supporting argumentation within a "community of inquiry" (Gregory, 2007a; Lipman et al., 1980; Splitter & Sharp, 1996).

Originally proposed by the American philosopher Charles Peirce, a *community of inquiry* is an epistemic environment designed to utilize the diverse perspectives and intellectual strengths a group may bring to an issue, and also to minimize the ever-present susceptibility of human thinking to error (for review, see Gregory, 2022). Inquiry transforms an undisciplined human activity into a self-correcting practice: "It generates rules, standards and criteria by means of which better results and procedures can be distinguished from worse" (Lipman, 1993, p. 291). And a community allows its members to learn from, build on, and critique each other's ideas (Gregory, 2022). "Individuals can and routinely do find reasons to refine, extend, and correct their own prior arguments; but a community can do so with incomparable efficacy. All the factors that make cognition fallible make it more difficult for us to recognize bias and error in our own thinking than in that of others" (Gregory, 2022, p. 6).

Constructing well-informed arguments and identifying errors in judgment within the community of inquiry hinges on a commitment to free speech and diversity of perspectives. "The community collects as many interesting hypotheses and arguments as it can find; in its search for new input, it allows just about anyone to say just about anything. Its guiding principle is freedom: free speech, free expression, diversity, pluralism. If the intake end of the system squelches ideas or silences speakers, it risks losing valuable insights and allowing errors to go unnoticed" (Rauch, 2021, p. 82). Further defending the freedom of speech, even for ideas that are offensive, Rauch (1995) explained that "the genius of intellectual pluralism lies not in doing away with prejudices and dogmas but in channeling them—making them socially productive by pitting prejudice against prejudice and dogma against dogma, exposing all to withering public criticism" (p. 38). And although public criticism does not need to be "withering," the idea of leveraging human fallibility to model and encourage disciplinary ways of knowing has clear relevance for education.

Unfortunately, freedom of speech is being increasingly threatened at our educational institutions and in the society at large (Lukianoff & Schlott, 2023; Mounk, 2023; Rauch, 2021). Today, attacks on freedom of speech come from both ends of the political spectrum and include demands for safe spaces and speech codes, censorship in the name of morality, and deplatforming (Lukianoff & Schlott, 2023; Mounk, 2023; Rauch, 2021). Moreover, opportunities for individuals to encounter opposing viewpoints are diminishing as our society becomes increasingly fragmented (e.g., Nguyen, 2020; Sunstein, 2009). Whether amplified by new machine algorithms or new ideologies, the natural human tendency toward tribalism based on group identity works to isolate individuals into impoverished intellectual environments, where bad ideas flourish.

The recent erosion of freedom of speech and diminished access to diverse perspectives in our society (Lukianoff & Schlott, 2023; Mounk, 2023; Rauch, 2021) underscores the need for a classroom culture to become an effective model of an open, democratic process that allows students to question and explore one another's ideas, to compare perspectives, and to talk freely about their disagreements. Deep understanding of any topic, whether ethical or scientific, comes not just from knowing why the right answers are right, but also from knowing why the wrong answers are wrong (Osborne, 2010). Teachers must hear students' ideas, no matter how misguided they are, in order to work with these ideas by both building on and challenging students' thinking.

Inquiry Dialogue

To further clarify how a classroom community should engage in discussions of controversial questions, we relied on the work of Gregory (2007b), who applied Walton's (1998) typology of dialogue types to education. According to Walton, dialogue types (e.g., inquiry, persuasion, negotiation) are characterized by distinct goals and methods and the assessment of dialogue quality needs to reflect these distinctions. Having compared different dialogue types, Gregory (2007b) concluded that *inquiry dialogue* is the normative type of discourse for engaging students in argumentation because it aims at finding the truth, or the most informed position according to available reasoning and evidence. This dialogue goal compels students not only to defend their own claims and critically examine those of others (as in persuasion), but also to give up or qualify their viewpoints in the face of previously overlooked evidence or faulty reasoning (Gregory, 2007b).

The truth-seeking nature of inquiry dialogue provides it with a much-needed direction that helps to mitigate against strong versions of relativist and standpoint epistemology (Gardner, 2015; Mounk, 2023). While relativists believe that truth is relative to (and different in) specific contexts, standpoint epistemology focuses on how individuals' social position, such as racial-ethnic or gender identity, influences what is known. Both relativism and standpoint epistemology emphasize individual contexts and perspectives, which are helpful for enriching our knowledge about the world. However, in their extreme versions, which are becoming widespread in educational contexts (Lukianoff & Schlott, 2023), these epistemic stances lead people to abandon the ideals of objectivity and deny a human capacity for mutual understanding, making it impossible to converge on a version of shared reality (Mounk, 2023; Rauch, 2021). When we advocate for the increased use of inquiry dialogue in the classroom, we do not assume that a single, unbiased truth will emerge from every episode of careful inquiry. Rather, we suggest that, at least for certain problems and questions, rigorous inquiry undertaken by a community will reduce bias and distinguish more reasonable from less reasonable results—as is the case in quality journalism, legal proceedings, and academic research.

Epistemic Stance

Within a community of inquiry, teachers, and eventually their students, need to adopt an epistemic stance that is aligned with the truth-seeking purpose of inquiry dialogue (Bråten et al., 2017). Here we rely on Kuhn's (1991) taxonomy of epistemic development, in which individuals at the most advanced, *evaluatist* level accept that knowledge is subjective, tentative, and influenced by contexts and perspectives, while also recognizing the possibility of engaging in a rational evaluation of different viewpoints and, as a result, judging some claims to be more reasonable than others.

We suggest that teachers who subscribe to an evaluatist stance are more likely to be effective facilitators of inquiry dialogue because they view knowledge as "the product of a continuing process of examination, comparison, evaluation, and judgment of different, sometimes competing, explanations and perspectives" (Kuhn, 1991, p. 202). Supporting the important role of epistemic cognition in teaching, research has shown that teachers' epistemic stances are typically aligned with their approaches to instruction, influencing power relations and interactional patterns in a classroom (Johnston et al., 2001; Richardson et al., 1991; Stipek et al., 2001).

To sum up, we maintain that inquiry dialogue helps to socialize students into discourse norms and practices that minimize errors in judgment and result in better conclusions. According to Gardner (2015), such dialogue should be neither teacher-centered, nor student-centered, "but centered on and controlled by the demands of truth. . . . Truth, however, is a hard taskmaster; it places severe restrictions on participants and puts exacting demands on the facilitator" (p. 75). Teachers facilitating inquiry dialogue need to learn how to evaluate arguments in student talk, notice missing perspectives, find flaws in reasoning, and address these problems with strategically chosen talk moves.

From Theory to Practice: Tools and Activities for Rigorous Argumentation

In this section, we describe how we translated our theoretical assumptions into classroom practice. The context was a 3-year project aimed at developing a PD program to support teachers in conducting intellectually rigorous discussions. A total of 49 fifth-grade language arts teachers in public schools in Ohio and New Jersey participated. Each year constituted a new iteration of the program. Each year, we worked collaboratively with a new cohort of teachers to identify and develop curriculum materials and activities that helped teachers engage students in argumentation about literary and informational texts. In the first and second years, we developed and trialed the materials and activities with teachers, collected data on their effectiveness, and made revisions for the next iteration. In the third year we tested the final version of the program. We implemented the PD using a combination of workshops, study group meetings, and individual coaching sessions with teachers. We videotaped discussions in all classrooms, tested the students on individual reading and writing tasks, and assessed teachers' epistemic stance.

We shared our curriculum materials, including lesson plans, instructional activities, and assessment tools in a book written for elementary school teachers (Reznitskaya & Wilkinson, 2017). Here, we discuss some of the strategies we found to be most productive for engaging students in collaborative and rigorous argumentation.

First, to promote a community of inquiry, teachers provided explicit discourse instructions to students at the beginning of the program, explaining the goals and expectations for their participation. One of the hallmarks of a community of inquiry is that students collectively share and critique each other's ideas, in order to garner multiple views on a topic, to encourage creativity in generating and formulating hypotheses, and to minimize bias and errors in individual thinking. To these ends, teachers worked with their students to establish ground rules for talk. Teachers listed the rules on an anchor chart on display in the classroom and continually revisited them over the year. Typical rules were as follows:

- We respect each other as thinkers.
- We are interested in other people's ideas.
- We support our positions with reasons and evidence.
- We connect our ideas to what others say.
- We build on and challenge each other's ideas.

Teachers also gave explicit discourse instructions to students prior to each discussion. Below is an example in which a teacher explained to students how to engage with each other in accordance with previously established ground rules:

"When *we* do this kind of talk, it's important that *we* are not just sharing. So, *our* job is not just to get *our* ideas out so that *everybody* can hear them. It's actually to offer ideas up in the hopes that the *group* can determine what the most reasonable answer is, the best answer, the most thought through. So, *our* job is not just to share *our* answers, but also to consider other people's answers. And that means that *we* have to build on each other's ideas and make connections. So, the idea is to test, test each other's ideas. *As a group, we* should be able to think better than *we* can by ourselves. Does that make sense? All right."

Note the use of plural pronouns (*we, our*) and other terms, italicized in the example, to emphasize the collaborative approach to argumentation. Note too, the way the teacher made mention of both the co-construction of ideas: ("*we* have to build on each other's ideas and make connections") as well as critical evaluation of ideas ("the idea is to test, test each other's ideas"). In this way, the teacher's language underscored the important cognitive, as well as social, moves students needed to use to constantly refine their thinking and make progress toward finding the truth.

Another recommended practice was to have students complete a checklist to help them reflect on what is meant by a community of inquiry (Reznitskaya & Wilkinson, 2017) (see Figure 1.1). Students completed the checklist either individually or as a class and discussed their answers. Although the "correct" answers may seem obvious, the questions provided students with a useful prompt to explore what they considered to be important characteristics of a community of inquiry.

To further help teachers facilitate inquiry dialogue and adopt an evaluatist stance, we identified four key criteria for rigorous argumentation, based on scholarship on logic, reasoning, and critical thinking (e.g., Ennis, 1996; Govier, 2010), and operationalized them in an instructional and assessment instrument called

What Do We Mean by Community of Inquiry?			
Decide whether the statements ARE or ARE NOT good things to do in a community of inquiry.			
	YES	NO	NOT SURE
1. Thinking about what you want to say more than listening to the person speaking.			
2. Noticing when only a few people are doing the talking and saying something about it.			
3. Giving reasons for your positions and explaining your thinking.			
4. Providing evidence from the text and other sources to support a position.			
5. Ignoring other people's positions when they are different from your own.			
6. Agreeing with your friend's ideas because you like your friend.			
7. Challenging someone else's position by questioning the reasons or by offering a different point of view.			
8. Working hard to "win" the argument to show that you are right.			
9. Building on the ideas of others in the group to support a position.			
10. Keeping your thoughts to yourself when you disagree with other people's ideas.			
11. Not responding to someone's idea because you don't understand what they mean.			
12. Being willing to change your position after listening to reasons given by others.			

FIGURE 1.1. Community of inquiry checklist. Adapted from Lipman and Sharp (1985).

the Argumentation Rating Tool (ART; Reznitskaya & Wilkinson, 2017, 2021). We formulated the criteria in a way that would be accessible to elementary school teachers and their students:

1. *Diversity of perspectives:* We explore different perspectives together.
2. *Clarity:* We are clear in the language and structure of our arguments.
3. *Acceptability:* We use reasons and evidence that are well examined and accurate.
4. *Logical validity:* We are logical in the way we connect our positions, reasons, and evidence.

We then connected the criteria to 11 facilitation practices that supported rigorous argumentation. To identify these facilitation practices, we again drew heavily on the pedagogy of Philosophy for Children (e.g., Gregory, 2007a; Splitter & Sharp, 1996). Additionally, we consulted research on classroom discourse in language arts settings (e.g., Nystrand et al., 2003; Soter et al., 2008) and teaching materials developed by proponents of established educational models centered on argumentation (e.g., Roberts & Billings, 2009; Waggoner et al., 1995). Figure 1.2 provides an overview of the ART.

To support teachers' facilitation, the ART also includes a 6-point rubric for each of the 11 facilitation strategies. The rubric measures teacher and student performance at three levels of proficiency—Advancing, Developing, and Not Yet—and it has been validated in our prior studies (Reznitskaya & Wilkinson, 2021). Figure 1.3 illustrates a portion of the ART, describing the facilitation practice of *Connecting Ideas* at the Advancing Level. As shown, the ART presents a general principle

Criterion	Description	Practice
1. Diversity of Perspectives	We explore different perspectives together.	1. Centering on Contestable Questions 2. Sharing Responsibilities 3. Discussing Alternatives
2. Clarity	We are clear in the language and structure of our arguments.	4. Clarifying Meaning 5. Connecting Ideas 6. Labeling Reasoning Processes and Parts of an Argument 7. Tracking the Line of Inquiry
3. Acceptability of Reasons and Evidence	We use reasons and evidence that are well examined and accurate.	8. Evaluating Facts 9. Evaluating Values
4. Logical Validity	We are logical in the way we connect our positions, reasons, and evidence.	10. Articulating Reasons 11. Evaluating Inferences

FIGURE 1.2. ART: Overview of four criteria and 11 practices.

guiding teacher performance and provides examples of specific talk moves teachers can use to enact a particular facilitation practice. Student performance is also measured in the ART because teacher facilitation needs to be contingent on the quality of students' arguments.

The ART differs from many other observational tools of classroom talk that are structured as lists of desirable practices (e.g., Accountable Talk Observation Rubric; Junker et al., 2006). Following Alexander (2008), we believe that teachers should be able to choose flexibly from a repertoire of discourse practices to achieve specific instructional goals for their students. The ART emphasizes connections between the function of talk (i.e., to encourage a given argumentation criterion) and its possible form. It aims to show teachers how to be strategic in using talk to enhance the quality of argumentation during inquiry dialogue.

We introduced teachers to the ART in the workshops and used it in study groups and coaching sessions. It became an important resource for us and the teachers during PD. We relied on the ART to operationalize recommended discourse practices, sequence PD, and support key instructional goals. Teachers used the ART to (1) review argumentation criteria and practices outlines in the ART when planning discussions, (2) choose relevant facilitation practices and talk moves when conducting discussions, and (3) engage in evaluation of their practice during coaching sessions following discussions. In addition, based on teacher recommendations, we developed an *ART for Kids* that students could use to rate the quality of their talk. Figure 1.4 shows the student version for the criterion of Clarity.

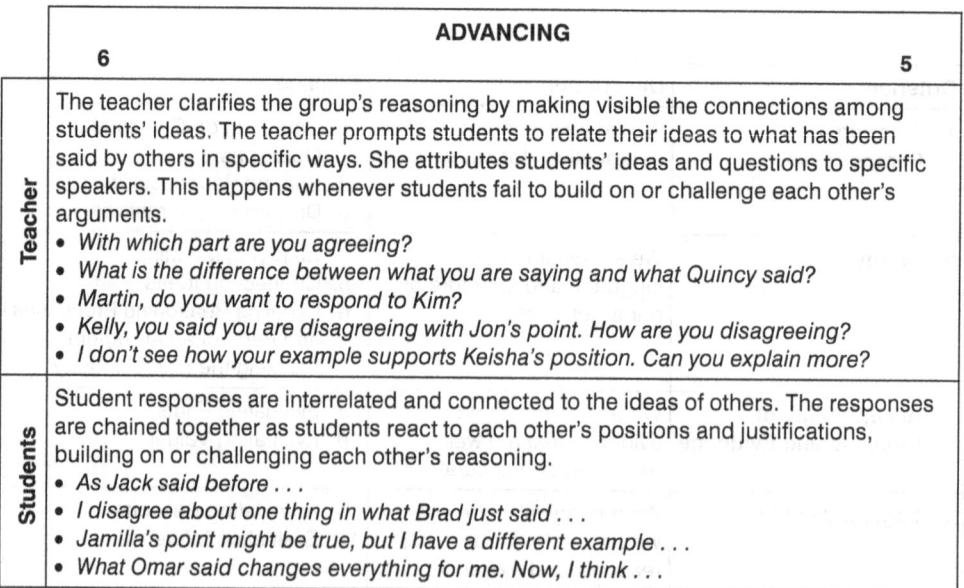

FIGURE 1.3. ART: Connecting ideas.

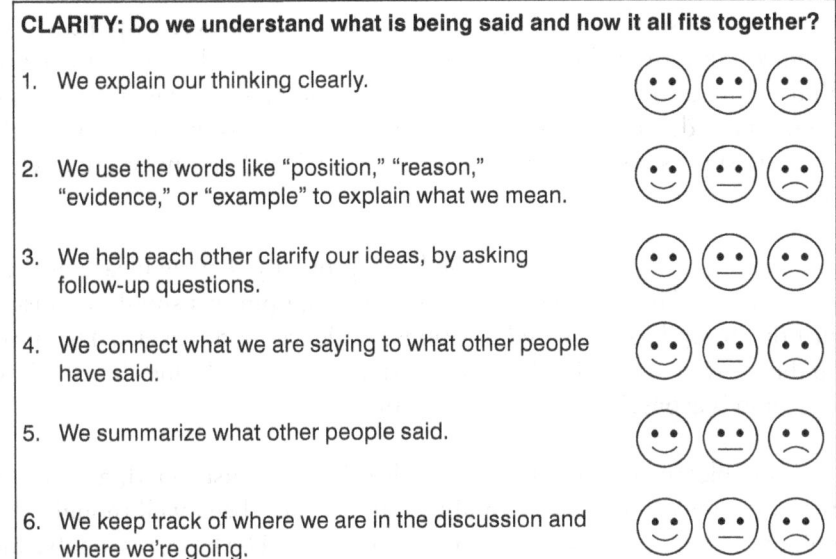

FIGURE 1.4. ART for Kids: Clarity.

Taking Stock of Progress

How well did we do? As a result of our yearlong PD, teachers and students made considerable progress in the quality of teacher facilitation and student argumentation. As measured by the ART, on a 6-point scale, teachers and students began the year with ratings of approximately 3.0 and ended the year with ratings of approximately 4.5. These gains in teacher facilitation and student argumentation correspond to effect sizes of 3.43 and 2.84, respectively—large gains by any measure. There were also indications that students whose teachers participated in the PD outperformed their peers who received business-as-usual instruction on individual argumentative reading and writing tasks given at the end of the year (Wilkinson et al., 2023).

Nonetheless, we doubt teachers ever reached the evaluatist end of the epistemological continuum described by Kuhn (1991). Scores of 6 on the ART, indicating the highest performance, remained elusive for most teachers. Consistent with this interpretation, when we conducted Reflective Judgment Interviews (King & Kitchener, 1994) with teachers to assess their epistemic stance at the beginning and end of the program, results showed little change. Teachers' epistemic stance remained at a multiplist (relativist) stage throughout the course of the program, suggesting that teachers continued to view all opinions as equally valid and regarded arguments and the use of reasons and evidence as idiosyncratic (i.e., there is no way of evaluating competing arguments).

On a more positive note, many of participating teachers responded in ways more aligned with an evaluatist epistemology when they discussed their practice as facilitators. In a focus group interview we conducted at the end of the year, we asked teachers to describe "What makes for the most reasonable answer?" Teachers' responses suggested they saw a need for critical evaluations of arguments. For example:

> "A most reasonable answer is reached by a group by sharing ideas with reasons and evidence. Through the discussion process, opinions should be suspended until the group has presented positions, evidence, and reasons. The most reasonable answer would be the position that the group decides has the best evidence and reasons." (focus group, Ohio)

> "A reasonable answer should be thoughtful, well-constructed, and able to be proved with evidence. All possibilities should have been well thought out and explored to ensure and strengthen the argument. The most reasonable answer should also relate to the Big Question or idea presented in the text." (focus group, New Jersey)

These responses are promising, but we believe there is room for teacher growth both in terms of their beliefs and practices. There is considerable agreement that teachers' epistemic beliefs are domain-specific, situated, and multidimensional (Buehl et al., 2002; Chinn et al., 2011; Cobb, 2002). Although teachers who took part in our program acquired new facilitation moves aimed at improving argumentation quality, our analysis of their experiences revealed that they found facilitation of argumentation quite challenging (Reznitskaya & Wilkinson, 2019). Thus, designing effective PD aimed to support teachers in engaging students in critical evaluation of competing views remains an important educational priority.

Future Directions

In this chapter, we sought to address an important problem in implementations of classroom dialogue: an overemphasis on students' production of, rather than critique of, ideas (Henderson et al., 2018; Rapanta, 2019). We presented our normative assumptions about a pedagogically rich environment that supports greater emphasis on critical evaluation of student ideas. We also shared instructional tools and activities developed as part of the research on teacher PD and reviewed related findings.

In our future studies, we plan to design and test additional materials for teachers that can further enhance their ability to model and support sound argumentation, as well as identify and address errors in students' arguments. For example, currently, the ART focuses on only domain-general evaluation criteria of argument quality, such as the need to support claims with acceptable reasons and evidence

(Govier, 2010). However, both domain-general and discipline-specific criteria and structures are important in argumentation (Fischer et al., 2018; Ford, 2008), and discussions of a given text often evoke distinct context-specific argument patterns. Walton and colleagues (2008) identified a variety of patterns that appear in scientific, legal, and everyday reasoning, called *argument schemes*, and developed evaluative questions, known as *critical questions*, attached to each scheme. For example, when encountering a scheme, "an argument from expert opinion," one can ask whether the expert is credible, whether the knowledge of the expert is in the relevant domain, and whether the expert's claim is supported by evidence (Walton, 2014). Argument schemes and critical questions have been effectively used to foster and assess argumentation in different disciplinary contexts (e.g., Nussbaum et al., 2021; Wissinger & De La Paz, 2016). They offer additional ways to enact facilitation practices beyond those currently shown in the ART. We plan to explore the use of Walton's schemes and critical questions to suggest context-specific evaluation criteria and talk moves that expand on those in the ART, thus providing teachers with both domain-general and context-specific resources to evaluate and scaffold students' argumentation.

At a more general level, we would also like to contribute to addressing a key challenge in the field of PD: scaling up effective pedagogy focused on argumentation (Alexander, 2015; Osborne, 2015). To date, most PD efforts focused on argumentation have involved small numbers of teachers, working in a small number of schools, in close collaboration with researchers. Our own project, for example, required a large investment of time and effort on our part working with, at most in any year, 14 teachers from six schools. As Howe and Mercer (2017) noted in commenting on PD in dialogue-based pedagogy, including our work, "Once more then, issues of scalability are raised; would any educational authority, anywhere in the world invest this amount in professional development?" (p. 88).

Fortunately, recent advancements in technology invite us to rethink future PD initiatives. For example, in our recent project, we aim to draw on prior research to develop an intelligent tutoring system to support teacher learning of facilitation. Using the system, teachers will facilitate argumentation during a simulated small-group discussion among student avatars. Teachers will learn how to evaluate the quality of argumentation, decide whether to intervene and, if so, what to say to their avatar students to provide instructional support. The automated system will provide formative feedback on the timing and content of teacher facilitation. We are cautiously optimistic about the potential of new technologies to change the landscape of teacher education, thus increasing opportunities for students to experience the challenges and joys of engaging in intellectually rigorous discussions about questions that matter.

REFERENCES

Alexander, R. (2008). *Essays on pedagogy*. Routledge.
Alexander, R. (2015). Dialogic pedagogy at scale: Oblique perspectives. In L. Resnick, C.

Asterhan, & S. N. Clarke (Eds.), *Socializing intelligence through academic talk and dialogue* (pp. 429–439). American Educational Research Association.

Alexander, R. J. (2017). *Towards dialogic teaching: Rethinking classroom talk* (5th ed.). Dialogos.

Anderson, R. C., Nguyen-Jahiel, K., McNurlen, B., Archodidou, A., Kim, S., Reznitskaya, A., . . . Gilbert, L. (2001). The snowball phenomenon: Spread of ways of talking and ways of thinking across groups of children. *Cognition and Instruction, 19*(1), 1–46.

Asterhan, C. S. C., & Schwarz, B. B. (2016). Argumentation for learning: Well-trodden paths and unexplored territories. *Educational Psychologist, 51*(2), 164–187.

Barzilai, S., & Chinn, C. A. (2020). A review of educational responses to the "post-truth" condition: Four lenses on "post-truth" problems. *Educational Psychologist, 55*(3), 107–119.

Bouton, E., & Asterhan, C. S. C. (2023). In pursuit of a more unified method to measuring classroom dialogue: The dialogue elements to compound constructs approach. *Learning, Culture and Social Interaction, 40*, Article 100717.

Bråten, I., Muis, K., & Reznitskaya, A. (2017). Teachers' epistemic cognition in the context of dialogic practice: A question of calibration? *Educational Psychologist, 52*(4), 253–269.

Buehl, M. M., Alexander, P. A., & Murphy, P. K. (2002). Beliefs about schooled knowledge: Domain specific or domain general? *Contemporary Educational Psychology, 27*(3), 415–449.

Chinn, C. A., Anderson, R. C., & Waggoner, M. A. (2001). Patterns of discourse in two kinds of literature discussion. *Reading Research Quarterly, 36*(4), 378–411.

Chinn, C. A., Buckland, L. A., & Samarapungavan, A. L. A. (2011). Expanding the dimensions of epistemic cognition: Arguments from philosophy and psychology. *Educational Psychologist, 46*(3), 141–167.

Chinn, C. A., Golan Duncan, R., & Av-Shalom, N. Y. (2021). Applying the grasp-of-evidence framework to design and evaluate epistemically complex learning environments. *Information and Technology in Education and Learning, 1*(1), Inv-p004.

Cobb, P. (2002). Epistemological world views, subject matter contexts, and the institutional setting of teaching. *Issues in Education, 8*(2), 149–158.

Dawes, L., Mercer, N., & Wegerif, R. (2004). *Thinking Together: A programme of activities for developing speaking, listening and thinking skills for children aged 8–11.* Imaginative Minds.

Dewey, J. (1910). *How we think.* D. C. Heath.

Driver, R. (1995). Constructivist approaches to science learning. In L. P. Steffe & J. Gale (Eds.), *Constructivism in education* (pp. 385–400). Erlbaum.

Ennis, R. (1996). *Critical thinking.* Prentice Hall.

Erduran, S., Simon, S., & Osborne, J. (2004). TAPping into argumentation: Developments in the application of Toulmin's argument pattern for studying science discourse. *Science Education, 88*(6), 915–933.

Fischer, F., Chinn, C. A., Engelmann, K., & Osborne, J. (Eds.). (2018). *Scientific reasoning and argumentation: The roles of domain-specific and domain-general knowledge.* Routledge.

Ford, M. (2008). Disciplinary authority and accountability in scientific practice and. *Science Education, 92*, 404–423.

Gardner, S. (2015). Commentary on "Inquiry is no mere conversation." *Journal of Philosophy in Schools, 2*(1), 71–91.

Gorard, S., Siddiqui, N., & See, B. H. (2015). *Philosophy for Children: Evaluation report and executive summary*. Education Endowment Foundation.

Govier, T. (2010). *A practical study of argument* (7th ed.). Wadsworth.

Gregory, M. (2007a). A framework for facilitating classroom dialogue. *Teaching Philosophy, 30*(1), 59–84.

Gregory, M. (2007b). Normative dialogue types in Philosophy for Children. *Gifted Education International, 22*, 160–171.

Gregory, M. (2022). Charles Peirce and the community of philosophical inquiry. *Analytic Teaching and Philosophical Praxis, 42*(1), 1–16.

Hammer, D., & Schifter, D. (2001). Practices of inquiry in teaching and research. *Cognition and Instruction, 19*(4), 441–478.

Henderson, J. B., McNeill, K. L., González-Howard, M., Close, K., & Evans, M. (2018). Key challenges and future directions for educational research on scientific argumentation. *Journal of Research in Science Teaching, 55*(1), 5–18.

Hennessy, S., Howe, C., Mercer, N., & Vrikki, M. (2020). Coding classroom dialogue: Methodological considerations for researchers. *Learning, Culture and Social Interaction, 25*, Article 100404.

Hennessy, S., Rojas-Drummond, S., Highama, R., Márquez, A., Maine, F., Ríos, R. M., ... Barrera, M. J. (2016). Developing a coding scheme for analysing classroom dialogue across educational contexts. *Learning, Culture and Social Interaction, 9*, 16–44.

Howe, C. (2023). Classroom interaction and student learning: Reasoned dialogue versus reasoned opposition. *Dialogic Pedagogy: An International Online Journal, 11*(3), A26–A41.

Howe, C., Hennessy, S., Mercer, N., Vrikki, M., & Wheatley, L. (2019). Teacher–student dialogue during classroom teaching: Does it really impact on student outcomes? *Journal of the Learning Sciences, 28*(4–5), 462–512.

Howe, C., & Mercer, N. (2017). Commentary on the papers. *Language and Education: An International Journal, 31*(1), 83–92.

Johnston, P., Woodside-Jiron, H., & Day, J. (2001). Teaching and learning literate epistemologies. *Journal of Educational Psychology, 93*(1), 223–233.

Junker, B. W., Wiesberg, J., Matsumura, L. C., Crosson, A., Wolf, M. K., Levison, A., & Resnick, L. (2006). *Overview of the instructional quality assessment*. University of California, National Center for Research on Evaluation, Standards, and Student Testing.

Kavanagh, J., & Rich, M. D. (2018). *Truth decay: An initial explorations of the diminishing role of facts and analysis in American public life*. RAND Corporation.

King, P. M., & Kitchener, K. S. (1994). *Developing reflective judgment: Understanding and promoting intellectual growth and critical thinking in adolescents and adults*. Jossey-Bass.

Kuhn, D. (1991). *The skills of argument*. Cambridge University Press.

Kuhn, D., & Crowell, A. (2011). Dialogic argumentation as a vehicle for developing young adolescents' thinking. *Psychological Science, 22*, 545–552.

Kuhn, D., & Moore, W. (2015). Argumentation as core curriculum. *Learning: Research and Practice, 1*(1), 66–78.

Lipman, M. (1993). Promoting better classroom thinking. *Educational Psychology, 13*(3–4), 291–304.

Lipman, M., Sharp, A. M., & Oscanyon, F. S. (1980). *Philosophy in the classroom* (2nd ed.). Temple University Press.

Lukianoff, G., & Schlott, R. (2023). *The canceling of the American mind: Cancel culture undermines trust and threatens us all—but there is a solution.* Simon & Schuster.

Mercer, N., Dawes, L., Wegerif, R., & Sams, C. (2004). Reasoning as a scientist: Ways of helping children to use language to learn science. *British Educational Research Journal, 30*(3), 359–377.

Mercer, N., Wegerif, R., & Dawes, L. (1999). Children's talk and the development of reasoning in the classroom. *British Educational Research Journal, 25*(1), 95–111.

Michaels, S., & O'Connor, C. (2015). Conceptualizing talk moves as tools: Professional development approaches for academically productive discussion. In L. B. Resnick, C. A. Asterhan, & S. N. Clarke (Eds.), *Socializing intelligence through academic talk and dialogue* (pp. 347–362). American Educational Research Association.

Michaels, S., O'Connor, C., & Resnick, L. B. (2008). Deliberative discourse idealized and realized: Accountable talk in the classroom and in civic life. *Studies in Philosophy and Education, 27*(4), 283–297.

Mounk, Y. (2023). *The identity trap: A story of ideas and power in our time.* Penguin Press.

Nguyen, C. T. (2020). Echo chambers and epistemic bubbles. *Episteme, 17*(2), 141–161.

Nussbaum, E. M., & Edwards, O. V. (2011). Critical questions and argument stratagems: A framework for enhancing and analyzing students' reasoning practices. *Journal of the Learning Sciences, 20*(3), 443–488.

Nussbaum, E. M., Van Winkle, M., Herrera, A., Putney, L. G., Huerta, M., & Dove, I. (2021). *"Their evidence is no good": How middle school English learners and students with low language scores successfully engaged in scientific argument critique.* Paper presented at the 15th International Conference of the Learning Sciences, Bloomington, IN.

Nystrand, M., Wu, L., Gamoran, A., Zeiser, S., & Long, D. A. (2003). Questions in time: Investigating the structure and dynamics of unfolding classroom discourse. *Discourse Processes, 35*(2), 135–198.

Osborne, J. (2010). Arguing to learn in science: The role of collaborative, critical discourse. *Science, 328*, 463–466.

Osborne, J. (2015). The challenge of scale. In L. Resnick, C. Asterhan, & S. N. Clarke (Eds.), *Socializing intelligence through academic talk and dialogue* (pp. 403–414). American Educational Research Association.

Partnership for 21st Century Skills. (2012). *A Framework for 21st Century Learning.* www.p21.org/index.php.

Piaget, J., & Inhelder, B. (1969). *The psychology of the child.* Basic Books.

Rapanta, C. (2019). Argumentation as critically oriented pedagogical dialogue. *Informal Logic, 39*(1), 1–31.

Rauch, J. (1995, May). In defense of prejudice: Why incendiary speech must be protected. *Harper's Magazine*, pp. 37–46.

Rauch, J. (2021). *The constitution of knowledge.* Brookings Institution Press.

Resnick, L. B., Asterhan, C. S. C., & Clarke, S. N. (2015). *Socializing intelligence through academic talk and dialogue.* American Educational Research Association.

Reznitskaya, A. (2012). Dialogic teaching: Rethinking language use during literature discussions. *Reading Teacher, 65*(7), 446–456.

Reznitskaya, A., Glina, M., Carolan, B., Michaud, O., Rogers, J., & Sequeira, L. (2012). Examining transfer effects from dialogic discussions to new tasks and contexts. *Contemporary Educational Psychology, 37*, 288–306.

Reznitskaya, A., & Gregory, M. (2013). Student thought and classroom language: Examining the mechanisms of change in dialogic teaching. *Educational Psychologist, 48*(2), 114–133.

Reznitskaya, A., & Wilkinson, I. A. G. (2017). *The most reasonable answer: Helping students build better arguments together.* Harvard Education Press.

Reznitskaya, A., & Wilkinson, I. A. G. (2019). Designing professional development to support teachers' facilitation of argumentation. In N. Mercer, R. Wegerif, & L. Major (Eds.), *The Routledge international handbook of research on dialogic education* (pp. 254–268). Routledge.

Reznitskaya, A., & Wilkinson, I. A. G. (2021). The Argumentation Rating Tool: Assessing and supporting teacher facilitation and student argumentation during text-based discussions. *Teaching and Teacher Education, 106,* Article 103464.

Richardson, V., Anders, P., Tidwell, D., & Lloyd, C. (1991). The relationship between teachers' beliefs and practices in reading comprehension instruction. *American Educational Research Journal, 28*(3), 559–586.

Roberts, T., & Billings, L. (2009). Speak up and Listen. *Phi Delta Kappan, 91*(2), 81–85.

Rosenblatt, L. M. (1994). *The reader. the text, the poem: The transactional theory of the literary work.* Southern Illinois University. (Original work published 1978)

Sedova, K., Sedlacek, M., & Svaricek, R. (2016). Teacher professional development as a means of transforming student classroom talk. *Teaching and Teacher Education, 57,* 14–25.

Soter, A., Wilkinson, I. A. G., Murphy, P. K., Rudge, L., Reninger, K., & Edwards, M. (2008). What the discourse tells us: Talk and indicators of high-level comprehension. *International Journal of Educational Research, 47,* 372–391.

Splitter, L. J., & Sharp, A. M. (1996). The practice of philosophy in the classroom. In A. M. Sharp & R. F. Reed (Eds.), *Studies in philosophy for children: Pixie* (pp. 285–314). Ediciones De La Torre.

Stipek, D. J., Givvin, K. B., Salmon, J. M., & MacGyvers, V. L. (2001). Teachers' beliefs and practices related to mathematics instruction. *Teaching and Teacher Education, 17*(2), 213–226.

Sunstein, C. R. (2009). *Going to extremes: How like minds unite and divide.* Oxford University Press.

Vygotsky, L. S. (1968). *Thought and language* (newly revised, translated, and edited by Alex Kozulin). MIT Press.

Waggoner, M., Chinn, C. A., Yi, H., & Anderson, R. C. (1995). Collaborative reasoning about stories. *Language Arts, 72,* 582–589.

Walton, D. (1998). *The new dialectic: Conversational contexts of argument.* University of Toronto Press.

Walton, D. (2014). On a razor's edge: Evaluating arguments from expert opinion. *Argument and Computation, 5*(2–3), 139–159.

Walton, D., Reed, C., & Macagno, F. (2008). *Argumentation schemes.* Cambridge University Press.

Wells, G. (1999). *Dialogic inquiry: Toward a sociocultural practice and theory of education.* Cambridge University Press.

Wilkinson, A. I. G., Soter, A., Murphy, P. K., & Lightner, S. C. (2020). Dialogue-intensive pedagogies for promoting iiterate thinking. In N. Mercer, R. Wegerif, & L. Major (Eds.), *The Routledge international handbook of research on dialogic education* (pp. 320–335). Routledge.

Wilkinson, I. A. G., Reznitskaya, A., & D'Agostino, J. V. (2023). Professional development in classroom discussion to improve argumentation: Teacher and student outcomes. *Learning and Instruction, 85,* Article 101732.

Windschitl, M. (2002). Framing constructivism in practice as the negotiation of dilemmas: An analysis of the conceptual, pedagogical, cultural, and political challenges facing teachers. *Review of Educational Research, 72*(2), 131–175.

Wissinger, D. R., & De La Paz, S. (2016). Effects of critical discussions on middle school students' written historical arguments. *Journal of Educational Psychology, 108*(1), 43–59.

CHAPTER 2

Multisyllabic Word-Reading Instruction in the Intermediate Grades

Jessica R. Toste
Brennan Chandler

By the time students reach middle school, they are expected to engage with complex texts and synthesize information across multiple sources (National Governors Association Center for Best Practices & Council of Chief State School Officers, 2010). Consider the following seventh-grade text from the *Core Knowledge Science Literacy* curriculum. What skills are necessary to access and understand this text? What are some of the challenges that students in the intermediate grades—upper elementary and middle school grades—may have with this text?

> **Anticancer Alkaloids.** *Medical scientists and pharmaceutical developers have looked to plants for many decades as a source of biologically active compounds that could fight diseases. The rosy periwinkle, native to Madagascar, was used in traditional healing to treat diabetes. Further experimentation showed that two alkaloids produced by the plant were effective at fighting several types of cancer. Since the 1950s, tens of thousands of cancer patients have benefited from drugs based on these compounds.* (Core Knowledge Foundation, 2019, CKSci 6–8 Unit 4: Matter Cycling and Photosynthesis)

Clearly, vocabulary knowledge is required to successfully engage with this text. Without knowing what *effective*, *patients*, or *compounds* mean, students may struggle to understand the key information being presented in this text—or may have to rely on context clues to infer meaning, which can limit their depth of understanding. Not only do students require general word knowledge but this text also relies on domain-specific vocabulary and background knowledge. Students must have some familiarity with the subject matter (e.g., science, plants, medicine), as well as knowledge of specialized terminology (e.g., *pharmaceutical*, *experimentation*) in order to make connections and comprehend the text. Perhaps prerequisite to engaging with word or text meaning, students must also be able to decode or pronounce the words written on the page. However, there is a steady increase in the number of complex words presented in text as students move into the upper elementary grades and beyond. As evident in the earlier sample, multisyllabic words are abundant in texts at this level, and they often carry the key meaning of the text. Students commonly skip or inaccurately read these words, which can leave a sentence or text essentially incomprehensible. While many students will have received instruction focused on word reading and decoding during their elementary years, it is essential to address ongoing development of proficient multisyllabic word reading (MWR) as text demands increase.

Reading comprehension—the goal of reading—is highly dependent on this skilled word reading. Indeed, theoretical frameworks posit that efficiency in reading words is central to advanced reading development (Gough & Tunmer, 1986; Kim, 2017; Perfetti & Hart, 2002). It is frequently assumed that students will be proficient in word reading by the upper elementary grades, but this is *not* often the case. Evidence suggests that over one-fourth of upper elementary students do not read words accurately or fluently (Cirino et al., 2013; Daane, 2005). This is of great concern, as it has been suggested that students who have not yet attained proficiency by fourth grade experience increasingly disparate educational outcomes (Brasseur-Hock et al., 2011; Dynarski et al., 2008; Francis et al., 1996). Yet there is decreased emphasis on word reading instruction through the intermediate grades (Vaughn et al., 2003), even though text demands increase and most new words introduced in text after third grade are multisyllabic. Meta-analytic reviews have reported that a limited number of programs focus on advanced word reading in the intermediate grades (e.g., Scammacca et al., 2015; Wanzek et al., 2010).

In a recent survey of reading legislation in the United States, Neuman and colleagues (2023) reported that 46 states had passed legislation since 2019 and 42 explicitly highlighted instruction for students beyond third grade. However, this legislation lacks specificity in programs, interventions, and supports. Consequently, schools are facing increased pressure to improve reading outcomes but have access to few programs for the intermediate grades and even fewer focusing on reading complex words. This chapter synthesizes the current research that helps address this gap in instructional knowledge.

We organize this chapter within three sections. First, we discuss the importance of word-reading efficiency and the unique challenges posed by multisyllabic words. Second, we outline important components of MWR instruction that benefit all readers. Finally, we describe the evidence and structure of a research-based MWR program, *Word Connections* (Toste et al., 2023). We highlight implementation resources and feedback from teachers who are using this program in the intermediate grades to support their students' advanced word reading skills.

Word-Reading Efficiency: Why It Matters

Across theories of reading development, there is agreement that word identification must be both accurate *and* rapid (e.g., Gough & Tunmer, 1986; Kim, 2017;

Perfetti & Stafura, 2014). Emerging readers often rely on serial decoding strategies while learning the alphabetic code. This is when a reader identifies graphemes and pronounces the corresponding phonemes to read a word in print. Decoding is undoubtedly an important step in learning to read in an alphabetic language, such as English. However, overreliance on serial decoding when reading connected text can become slow, cumbersome, and a strain on working memory resources (Maloney et al., 2009). Furthermore, almost half of words in the English language cannot be decoded solely through simple grapheme–phoneme correspondences (Hanna et al., 1966). Word-reading efficiency depends on readers moving from novice to expert and transitioning from decoding to rapid recognition of familiar words as these skills develop (Nation & Castles, 2017).

Rapid word identification reduces the need for compensatory word identification strategies often employed by less proficient readers and the cognitive burden of such strategies, which allows the reader to prioritize reading comprehension. Inaccurate identification of even one word in a sentence could lead to vastly different interpretations of a sentence. Rapid word identification also reduces the potential strain on a reader's working memory resources (Alloway, 2009). Words read accurately—but laboriously—through serial decoding strategies may be forgotten before it is possible to integrate them with other words and the remainder of the text. Moreover, cognitive resources used in extracting meaning from individual words are then inherently limited. The more cognitive resources the reader must allocate to word identification efforts, the fewer remain available to support their comprehension (Perfetti, 2007).

Furthermore, readers must continue to develop skills required to maintain word-reading efficiency as they move into intermediate grades and encounter increasingly complex words. For many students, the leap from decoding single-syllable words to efficiently reading multisyllabic words does not occur automatically. Ongoing, explicit word-reading instruction should extend beyond the primary grade, and MWR instruction is necessary for students to continue developing as proficient readers (Archer et al., 2003; Foorman et al., 2016; Vaughn et al., 2022). Premature cessation of word-level reading instruction leaves many students unprepared for the text demands in intermediate grades, which can negatively impact their overall reading comprehension and academic performance.

Multisyllabic Words

It is estimated that readers encounter more than 20,000 multisyllabic words in print per year (Hiebert et al., 2005; Kearns et al., 2016; Zeno et al., 1995). These words often carry the meaning of text. Note the number of multisyllabic words in the sample text shown at the start of this chapter. Not only are multisyllabic words abundant in intermediate grade-level texts, but they also often carry the key meaning of the text. So what makes multisyllabic words so complex?

In English, not only are multisyllabic words more challenging to decode simply because of the number of letters (Jared & Seidenberg, 1990), but also additional complexities come with this increased word length. Less predictable letter–sound correspondences, vowel stress reduction, and unclear syllable boundaries can complicate the process of reading multisyllabic words (Perry et al., 2010; Venezky, 1999). Let's consider some examples. The letters *lo* in the word *colonel* are pronounced as /ər/, or the letters *ch* in *chaos* are pronounced as /k/ (rather than /ch/, as students had likely learned during prior instruction). These irregularities in letter–sound correspondences introduce a layer of complexity to decoding. Vowel stress reduction is a linguistic phenomenon wherein vowel quality is neutralized, typically replaced with schwa /ə/ in English, to allow an unstressed syllable to be said more quickly as part of natural speech. We pronounce the letter *a* in *unbelievable* as /ə/ rather than /ă/, which can make it more challenging to decode because the neutralized vowel sound does not match the reader's expectation for the associated grapheme. Finally, ambiguity in syllable boundaries can complicate accurate pronunciation of a word. The word *different* might be pronounced as *dif/fer/ent* or *dif/frent* in more casual speech. There are many other instances in which the middle vowel is reduced or omitted: *every* reduced to *ev/ry*, *chocolate* reduced to *choc/lit*, or *camera* reduced to *cam/ra*. This can increase difficulty with determining the exact syllable boundaries and associated pronunciation of a printed word.

Another challenge is the multimorphemic nature of English orthography. Multisyllabic words often contain both *bound morphemes* (i.e., morphemes that are not words on their own but still have meaning) and *free morphemes* (i.e., base words). The word *international* contains two bound morphemes (*inter-* and *-al*) and one free morpheme (*nation*). Reading this word can be a challenge for many students, as they may struggle to realize that phonology of free morphemes in multimorphemic words often diverges, while spelling remains the same. For example, the free morpheme *nation* is pronounced /nā-shun/ but pronounced /nă-shun/ if the affix *-al* is attached—in *national* or *international*.

These examples help demonstrate why multisyllabic words are generally considered more complex or advanced. Accordingly, students require ongoing word-level reading instruction to support reading proficiency as they move through the upper elementary and middle school years (Apel, 2011). This instruction is even more critical for students who have reading or language difficulties, as they tend to have lower levels of morphological awareness compared to peers (Giazitzidou & Padeliadu, 2022; Siegel, 2008), which further impedes acquisition of fluent MWR skills. In the following section, we describe the key components of MWR instruction that have emerged from decades of reading research.

What to Know about MWR Instruction

MWR instruction can significantly enhance word recognition, reading fluency, and overall reading comprehension (Bhattacharya & Ehri, 2004; Diliberto et al., 2008; Toste et al., 2017, 2019). Meta-analytic findings have suggested that instruction focused on MWR is beneficial for all readers, but especially for students with reading or language difficulties, including emergent bilinguals and students with disabilities (Goodwin & Ahn, 2010, 2013). Across studies, these impactful practices share several guiding instructional principles: explicit instruction, immediate feedback, and cumulative practice.

Guiding Instructional Principles

Explicit instruction is characterized by clear, direct teaching of specific skills or concepts, step-by-step demonstrations and guided practice opportunities, as well as frequent and active student engagement (see Archer & Hughes, 2011). By briefly breaking down the decoding of complex words into manageable steps and routines, all students benefit, but especially those who may not pick up on these skills intuitively. Indeed, struggling readers often require more explicit and direct guidance to understand the morphological structure of words (Goodwin & Ahn, 2010).

However, explicit instruction alone is far from sufficient. While it helps to directly introduce students to important MWR concepts (i.e., the affix *pre-* means *before*), students also need extensive practice to consolidate and apply taught skills under the guidance of a teacher. Indeed, effective MWR programs consist mostly of brief explicit instruction coupled with extensive practice (e.g., Archer et al., 2003; Toste et al., 2023). Moreover, this practice should be paired with feedback, which can include immediate error correction from the teacher during MWR practice (e.g., "Not quite! That word is unmanageable. What word?"). Feedback in this context acts as a scaffold, supporting students as they build their reading proficiency.

While students should be provided with initial practice of taught MWR skills, such practice should also be distributed over time to enhance skill retention and mastery. Unlike massed practice, which involves intensive, short-term repetition, distributed practice spreads learning and practice sessions over time (Brown et al., 2014). A distributed approach can help students consolidate their learning, making it more durable and transferable to new contexts. By revisiting previously taught MWR skills regularly, students can better retain and apply their knowledge. This method is particularly effective for struggling readers and English learners in studies examining MWR instruction, as it allows for continuous reinforcement, ultimately leading to greater reading fluency and comprehension (Toste et al., 2017, 2019). Overall, the combination of explicit instruction with extensive, distributed practice and feedback can support students' reading proficiency and ease of access to multisyllabic words.

Key Components of Effective MWR Instruction

Researchers have investigated various instructional features taught to support development of MWR skills. This instruction inherently strengthens students' orthographic knowledge or the information stored in memory that tells readers how to represent spoken language in written form (Apel, 2011). Prior research has identified key components that can be leveraged by teachers. We focus on four components with the greatest instructional potential: review of essential skills, flexible syllabication, morphology, and oral reading fluency.

Review of Essential Skills

Due to the vowel heavy demands of multisyllabic words, it is vital to ensure that students can identify and pronounce multiple-letter vowel patterns, often referred to as *vowel teams*, before engaging in instruction focused solely on multisyllabic words. In English, vowel sounds (phonemes) are represented by various letters or letter combinations (graphemes). For instance, the long /ā/ sound in *alien* can be represented in printed words with the graphemes *a, ai, ay,* or *a_e*. Students must be able to accurately pronounce these vowel teams both in isolation and when encountered in an unfamiliar printed word (i.e., when they decode). For example, a student who does not recognize or have mastery of the vowel team *ea* and know its most common pronunciation might see the word *bread* and mistakenly identify *e* and *a* as separate graphemes, resulting in pronunciations like "bree-add" or "bray-add." Thus, the ability to identify and pronounce vowel teams is an essential precursor to the skills required for reading multisyllabic words.

Flexible Syllabication

Syllabication—the division of multisyllabic words into syllables—is a prominent feature in MWR instruction. Multisyllabic words in the English language contain ambiguous vowel pronunciations and syllable boundaries, which can hinder successful decoding. For example, single-letter vowel pronunciations in multisyllabic words can vary depending on the surrounding consonants. For example, the letter *a* is pronounced differently in *cat, later,* and *caramel*. While single-letter vowels have distinct short (e.g., /ĕ/ in *bed*) and long (e.g., /ē/ in *meet*) sounds, the schwa sound (i.e., "uh" sound or unstressed pronunciation of /ə/ in *sofa* or *pencil*) can be represented by any single-letter vowel. It is the most common vowel sound in English and is often found in the unstressed syllables of multisyllabic words. In these unstressed syllables, vowel sounds tend to be reduced to the schwa sound because unstressed syllables are pronounced more quickly and with less emphasis than stressed syllables. For example, in the word *sofa*, the first syllable is stressed (SO-fa) and the second is reduced (so-FUH). Therefore, it becomes important to support students in reading complex multisyllabic words.

While there are different approaches to syllabication instruction, researchers have found that instruction and extensive practice in the *flexible* decoding of multisyllabic words with a focus on alternate vowel pronunciations may be the most beneficial. This contrasts with a rules-based approach in which students are to memorize syllable types and rules for dividing syllables (e.g., *When a consonant is between two vowels, divide after the constant when the first vowel has a short sound*). Kearns (2020) found that these rules can be unreliable in the context of the English language. Indeed, the cited example rule only works for about one-third of vowel–consonant–vowel pattern words in a large corpus of common words.

To aid in the flexible decoding of multisyllabic words, teachers can provide instruction that helps students attend to syllables and complex vowels without the need for strict rules. To accomplish this, teachers can leverage an effective strategy used in reading interventions to help older students identify syllables and read multisyllabic words: ESHALOV (Every Syllable Has At Least One Vowel; O'Connor et al., 2015). In English, almost every syllable contains at least one vowel letter. Therefore, teachers can instruct students on dividing multisyllabic words into syllables, ensuring each syllable includes at least one vowel letter. To implement this strategy, the teacher guides students to underline all the vowels in a word and combine any vowel teams (e.g., *transportation*). Identifying the vowels helps segment the word into decodable parts. Next, students circle known affixes (e.g., *trans-*) and count the expected number of syllables based on the vowels (e.g., four). Finally, students break the word into syllables for decoding (e.g., *trans-por-ta-tion*) and attempt to read the entire word (e.g., *transportation*). If students mispronounce the word due to incorrect vowel pronunciations or misplaced syllable stress, teachers can provide immediate and corrective feedback.

Morphology

While there are various key ingredients in effective MWR instruction, researchers have found that clear attention to *morphology*—the study of the structure and form of words—plays a clear role in the efficacy of such instruction. Goodwin and Ahn (2010) conducted a meta-analysis of interventions focused on morphological instruction, which teaches students to identify and analyze units of meaning (i.e., affixes and roots). Across 17 studies, their findings indicated that morphological interventions significantly improved literacy achievement for students with reading difficulties. Specifically, instruction focused on morphology had a significant impact on various literacy outcomes, including phonological awareness, morphological awareness, vocabulary, reading comprehension, and spelling. Moreover, the authors found that this type of instruction was especially effective for children with reading, learning, or speech and language disabilities, as well as for English language learners and struggling readers, hinting at the potential role of morphological instruction in addressing phonological processing challenges.

Because most multisyllabic words are complex and are multimorphemic, a focus on morphology can help students not only decode these words but also understand their meaning. Common prefixes and suffixes (e.g., *in-, dis-, -ful, -less*) appear in many words and share meanings, aiding both word recognition and comprehension. Thus, teaching these common morphemes to students is beneficial. For example, consider the word *unhappiness*. Teaching students to recognize and understand the morphemes *un-, happy*, and *-ness* has multiple benefits. First, teaching students to break the word into these smaller parts makes it more manageable to read (*un-* + *happy* + *-ness*). Second, teaching the meanings of these parts helps students build word knowledge, understanding that "unhappiness" means the state of not being happy. Last, knowledge of and combining these morphemes helps with spelling, as students can develop the awareness to spell each part separately and then combine them to form the whole word. Another added benefit of morphologically focused instruction is that once students learn morphemes, they can use this learned knowledge to help decipher the pronunciation and meaning of new words.

Oral Reading Fluency

As students gain MWR knowledge and skills, it is vital to provide students with opportunities to read connected and authentic texts containing multisyllabic words in order to gain reading fluency. When students read fluently, they can shift their focus from decoding individual words to comprehending and making sense of text. Systematic reviews and meta-analyses examining reading fluency interventions have found that they are effective at improving reading fluency and comprehension for a wide range of learners, including elementary and secondary students with and without learning disabilities (Chard et al., 2009; Kim et al., 2017; Maki & Hammerschmidt-Snidarich, 2022; Stevens et al., 2017). Among the reviews, one intervention practice in particular—repeated reading—consistently demonstrated effectiveness for improving fluency and overall reading comprehension outcomes (Lee & Yoon, 2017).

Repeated reading is a structured and systematic practice that requires students to read the same passage several times (Therrien & Kubina, 2006). Multiple exposures to the same text allow students to achieve a level of automaticity during practice, enhancing their fluency with rapid multisyllabic word identification. Teachers can engage students in various oral reading practices during repeated reading: choral reading (e.g., teacher and students read aloud together), whisper reading (e.g., students read aloud softly), or echo reading (e.g., teacher reads and students repeat). If a student misreads a word or phrase, teachers can offer corrective feedback by providing the missing word(s). In addition to automaticity and reading speed, prosody (i.e., expression) is important in helping students understand what they are reading. Proficient oral reading prosody sounds much like speech with appropriate phrasing and stress, pausing, rise and fall patterns, and general expressiveness (Schwanenflugel et al., 2004). To support prosodic reading, explicit modeling and provision of opportunities to practice are vital.

Implementation

Each of these MWR instructional components is supported by research and has been shown to be important for promoting students' overall reading achievement. However, in practice, integrating these components can be challenging when planning for instruction.

Balancing and combining each component, ensuring a systematic scope and sequence, and allocating instructional time are common barriers to effective MWR implementation in the intermediate grades. Yet very few research-based MWR programs exist, which can make it difficult for teachers to overcome these barriers. In the following section, we provide an in-depth description of one research-based MWR program and highlight two others that have shown promising evidence for effectiveness.

Word Connections: A Research-Based MWR Program

Word Connections is a research-based program designed to improve MWR for students in third grade and above. It comprises 40 structured lessons, divided into four instructional units designed to enhance automaticity in reading multisyllabic words. Each lesson is intended for small groups of two to five students and can be completed in 30 to 40 minutes, three to four times per week. The program integrates multiple opportunities for word manipulation and reading, as opposed to relying solely on rule-based instruction. Indeed, the overall approach of Word Connections is rooted in the belief that automaticity in reading multisyllabic words is best achieved through judicious practice and application rather than through rule-based methods, which can overwhelm cognitive processing. Word Connections has been rated by What Works Clearinghouse as a program with "Promising Evidence" (Tier 3) for effectiveness based on a Toste and colleagues (2019) study that met standards without reservation.

To date, three randomized controlled trials have been conducted to test the efficacy of the Word Connections program—and all have demonstrated substantial gains in reading achievement for upper elementary students with or at-risk for reading disabilities who receive the intervention compared to those who do not. Toste and colleagues (2017) tested the intervention with third and fourth graders performing below the 37th percentile on a measure of word-reading efficiency (e.g., Test of Word Reading Efficiency—Second Edition [TOWRE-2]; Torgesen et al., 2012). Results indicated that students in treatment groups significantly outperformed those in the control group on measures of sight-word efficiency ($g = 0.73$), decoding efficiency ($g = 0.31$), word identification ($g = 0.29$), and decoding ($g = 0.30$). Toste and colleagues (2019) conducted a replication study with fourth and fifth graders performing below the 25th percentile on the TOWRE-2. The intervention had significant positive effects on measures of decoding ($g = 0.43$), sight-word efficiency ($g = 0.39$), word identification ($g = 0.29$), spelling ($g = 0.25$), reading comprehension ($g = 0.26$), and a proximal researcher-developed measure of MWR ($g = 0.90$).

Finally, Filderman and Toste (2022) investigated the differential effects of data use at two time points to intensify the Word Connections intervention for fourth and fifth graders who performed below the 25th percentile on the TOWRE-2. Students were randomized to one of three conditions: initial customization of the intervention (IC-only), initial customization with data-based decision making (IC+DBDM), or comparison control condition. Results indicated that students in the IC-only ($g = 0.47$) and IC+DBDM ($g = 1.12$) conditions both significantly outperformed those in the control condition on a researcher-designed mastery measure. The IC+DBDM condition had significant gains in decoding compared to control condition ($g = 0.87$); the IC-only condition also outperformed control, but the finding was not significant ($g = 0.26$). Taken together, research has demonstrated that the Word Connections program improves decoding, word reading, spelling, and reading comprehension outcomes for upper elementary students with reading difficulties.

Lesson Components

Each Word Connections lesson contains seven components with consistent instructional routines. While each lesson is scripted, these routines serve as a road map for teachers that provides students with a predictable and supportive learning environment. Below, we outline and describe each of the seven components used in program: warm-up, affix bank, word play, beat the clock, write word, speedy read, and text reading.

Warm-Up

The warm-up component of each lesson aims to review and reinforce common vowel patterns that serve as foundational anchors for reading multisyllabic words. Indeed, empirical evidence supports the regular review of vowel patterns to aid in the retention and automatic retrieval of these patterns during reading (Ehri, 2005). During this component, students engage in reading long-vowel patterns both in isolation and within nonsense words. The warm-up routine is phased out in the final lessons as students demonstrate mastery of common vowel patterns found in multisyllabic words.

Affix Bank

Following the warm-up, teachers introduce affixes during the affix bank routine. Knowledge of affixes is crucial for decoding multisyllabic words and understanding word structures, as research indicates that understanding affixes significantly enhances students' ability to decode and comprehend complex words (Nagy et al., 2014). The affix bank component involves a six-step process in which teachers introduce affixes, provide definitions, and guide students in generating sample words. Students record these affixes in a personal reference guide, with regular review to reinforce learning of previously taught affixes.

Word Play

Following explicit instruction of affixes, students engage in activities to practice assembling and reading multisyllabic words using learned affixes. This component provides engaging, repetitive practice of blending and reading these words, which can improve overall reading fluency (Adams, 1990). In this activity, teachers lead students through various games that involve attaching affixes to base words, reading word parts, and achieving fluent word reading. To maintain student engagement, there are five different word play games used throughout the program: Build-A-Word, Word Train, Quick Search, Elevator Words, and Spinner Words. While each game slightly differs in its format, all employ similar instructional routines that focus on the assembly and blending of word parts to automatically read words. The routines either begin with presenting base words and having students attach previously learned affixes, or having students sort previously learned

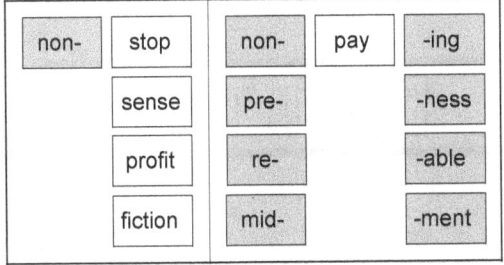

FIGURE 2.1. Word-building activity formats.

prefixes and suffixes then drag down a base word to attach to affixes (see Figure 2.1).

Beat the Clock

The beat the clock component focuses on enhancing accurate and fluent reading of multisyllabic words through timed practice. During this activity, students are given a list of multisyllabic words and are directed to circle affixes and then read the affixes chorally (see Figure 2.2). Following this, teachers prompt students to read the list of words aloud chorally. Following, all students are given two opportunities to complete two timed readings, trying to "Beat the Clock" the second time. During the first read, the teacher prompts the students to focus on word-reading accuracy, while the second read is focused on maintaining accuracy while increasing speed. While one student is reading, the teacher prompts others to follow along.

Write Word

In the write word component, students practice spelling multisyllabic words containing affixes learned in the program. This activity aims to develop spelling skills, which in turn enhance word analysis and reading abilities. Research highlights the strong connection between spelling practice and improved word-reading skills (Graham & Santangelo, 2014). Students practice spelling words by identifying syllables and combining word parts, reading the words aloud to determine whether they are real or nonsense words.

Speedy Read

To support word-reading fluency, students engage in timed reading of target word lists during the speedy read component. Fluent reading of both monosyllabic and multisyllabic words is key in building a mental lexicon that rapidly accesses words to comprehend text. Indeed, repeated and timed reading exercises have been shown to contribute to the development of a mental lexicon and fluent word recognition (LaBerge & Samuels, 1974). Each lesson, students are provided with a 40-word

LESSON 1

BEAT THE CLOCK

disrupt	invalid
reject	mistake
unwise	reject
rejoin	disgust
prewrite	prepare
decode	prevent
nonstick	mishap
unclear	invalid
dishonest	mistype
inhabit	nonmetal
injure	mislead
rename	subdue

Read 1 ☐   Read 2 ☐

FIGURE 2.2. Beat the Clock word list. This word list is found in the student materials for Lesson 1 of Word Connections. This image has been replicated with permission from the author (Toste et al., 2023).

list, and the teacher leads them in a choral reading of the words. Next, each student completes a 30-second timed reading of the list. Students engage in timed readings of word lists, receive corrective feedback, and track their progress in reading accuracy and speed.

Text Reading

The final component of each Word Connections lesson involves repeated reading of connected text. This practice is essential for upper elementary students to apply their MWR skills and develop reading fluency, as research indicates that reading connected text helps students generalize word-reading skills to broader reading contexts (Kim & Wagner, 2015). Initially, students read sentences, progressing to high-interest informational passages in later lessons. Teachers use various oral reading practices and comprehension checks to ensure understanding and engagement with the text.

Other Programs Targeting MWR

In addition to the Word Connections program, there are alternative programs teachers can use to support MWR. One such program—REWARDS (Archer et al., 2006)—is a research-based intervention designed to improve reading fluency and comprehension through systematic MWR instruction. Each lesson focuses on decoding multisyllabic words, identifying and understanding affixes, increasing word and passage reading fluency, and academic vocabulary instruction. Studies have demonstrated significant gains in reading fluency and comprehension among students who participate in REWARDS (Archer et al., 2006; Vaughn et al., 2010, 2015).

Another research-based program—PHAST—is available to support students' MWR. PHAST (Lovett et al., 2000) is a comprehensive multicomponent intervention program targeting decoding, word identification, and spelling skills in students with reading disabilities. Studies have shown that students with reading difficulties who participate in the PHAST program have shown substantial improvements in decoding and word-reading skills (Lovett et al., 2017, 2021).

Final Considerations and Future Directions

While developing foundational word-level reading skills is necessary for reading proficiency, this alone may not meet all students' needs. There are a range of student-level factors associated with reading achievement, including background knowledge, executive functions, motivation, and attention (e.g., Kim, 2017; Toste et al., 2020). Furthermore, opportunity gaps contribute to disparities in reading achievement across groups of learners (Pitre, 2014); that is, underachievement does not reflect students' lack of ability but rather a pervasive lack of opportunity. These opportunity gaps are often attributed to structural barriers that perpetuate differences in learning such as neighborhood, residential segregation, child care access, unequal distribution of resources, implicit biases of and interactions with teachers, and schooling experiences (e.g., Burchinal et al., 2011; Washington, 2001). There is a need for ongoing effort to fully understand these influences on student learning and achievement and integrate this understanding with existing knowledge of how to support student achievement.

It is also essential that the practices used for word-level reading instruction are both evidence-based and culturally responsive. For example, dialectical variation intersects with language and literacy development, which may influence interpretation of students' reading performance and delivery of effective instructional feedback for children who speak African American English (AAE; Gatlin-Nash et al., 2023). However, it has been suggested that there may not be a need for a differing theory of reading development for children who speak AAE—that the critical elements of instruction are consistent—but that the delivery of these elements must differ (Washington & Seidenberg, 2021). We acknowledge that gaps remain in the research regarding how these instructional methods can be optimized to meet the needs of all learners.

REFERENCES

Adams, M. J. (1990). *Beginning to read: Thinking and learning about print.* MIT Press.

Alloway, T. P. (2009). Working memory, but not IQ, predicts subsequent learning in children with learning difficulties. *European Journal of Psychological Assessment, 25*(2), 92–98.

Apel, K. (2011). What is orthographic knowledge? *Language, Speech, and Hearing Services in Schools, 42*(4), 592–603.

Archer, A. L., Gleason, M. M., & Vachon, V. L. (2003). Decoding and fluency: Foundation skills for struggling older readers. *Learning Disability Quarterly, 26,* 89–101.

Archer, A. L., Gleason, M., Vachon, V., King, J., & Pielaet, P. (2006). *REWARDS, Reading Excellence: Word Attack & Rate Development Strategies: Teacher's guide.* Sopris West Educational Services.

Archer, A. L., & Hughes, C. A. (2011). *Explicit instruction: Effective and efficient teaching.* Guilford Press.

Bhattacharya, A., & Ehri, L. C. (2004). Graphosyllabic analysis helps adolescent struggling readers read and spell words. *Journal of Learning Disabilities, 37*(4), 331–348.

Brasseur-Hock, I. F., Hock, M. F., Kieffer, M. J., Biancarosa, G., & Deshler, D. D. (2011). Adolescent struggling readers in urban schools: Results of a latent class analysis. *Learning and Individual Differences, 21*(4), 438–452.

Brown, P. C., Roediger, H. L. III, & McDaniel, M. A. (2014). *Make it stick: The science of successful learning.* Harvard University Press.

Burchinal, M., McCartney, K., Steinberg, L., Crosnoe, R., Friedman, S. L., McLoyd, V., . . . NICHD Early Child Care Research Network. (2011). Examining the Black–White achievement gap among low-income children using the NICHD study of early child care and youth development. *Child Development, 82*(5), 1404–1420.

Chard, D. J., Ketterlin-Geller, L. R., Baker, S. K., Doabler, C., & Apichatabutra, C. (2009). Repeated reading interventions for students with learning disabilities: Status of the evidence. *Exceptional Children, 75*(3), 263–281.

Cirino, P. T., Romain, M. A., Barth, A. E., Tolar, T. D., Fletcher, J. M., & Vaughn, S. (2013). Reading skill components and impairments in middle school struggling readers. *Reading and Writing, 26,* 1059–1086.

Core Knowledge Foundation. (2019). *Core knowledge science literacy (CKSci 6–8).* OpenSciEd.

Daane, M. C. (2005). *The nation's report card: Fourth-grade students reading aloud: NAEP 2002 special study of oral reading.* National Center for Education Statistics.

Diliberto, J. A., Beattie, J. R., Flowers, C. P., & Algozzine, R. F. (2008). Effects of teaching syllable skills instruction on reading achievement in struggling middle school readers. *Literacy Research and Instruction, 48*(1), 14–27.

Dynarski, M., Clarke, L., Cobb, B., Finn, J., Rumberger, R., & Smink, J. (2008). *Dropout Prevention* (IES Practice Guide. NCEE 2008-4025). National Center for Education Evaluation and Regional Assistance.

Ehri, L. C. (2005). Learning to read words: Theory, findings, and issues. *Scientific Studies of Reading, 9*(2), 167–188.

Filderman, M. J., & Toste, J. R. (2022). Effects of varying levels of data use to intensify a multisyllabic word reading intervention for upper elementary students with or at risk for reading disabilities. *Journal of Learning Disabilities, 55*(5), 393–407.

Foorman, B. R., Beyler, N., Anthony, J., Pollard-Durodola, S. D., Williams, K. J., & Sebastian, J. (2016). *Foundational skills to support reading for understanding in kindergarten through 3rd grade* (NCEE 2016-4008). National Center for Education Evaluation and Regional Assistance, Institute of Education Sciences, U.S. Department of Education. https://ies.ed.gov/ncee/wwc/docs/practiceguide/wwc_foundationalreading_040717.pdf.

Francis, D. J., Shaywitz, S. E., Stuebing, K. K., Shaywitz, B. A., & Fletcher, J. M. (1996). Developmental lag versus deficit models of reading disability: A longitudinal, individual growth curves analysis. *Journal of Educational Psychology, 88*(1), 3–17.

Gatlin-Nash, B., Chow, J. C., & Evans, I. (2023). Addressing the needs of nonmainstream dialect speakers with learning disabilities. *Intervention in School and Clinic, 59*(1), 20–28.

Giazitzidou, S., & Padeliadu, S. (2022). Contribution of morphological awareness to reading fluency of children with and without dyslexia: Evidence from a transparent orthography. *Annals of Dyslexia, 72*(3), 509–531.

Goodwin, A. P., & Ahn, S. (2010). A meta-analysis of morphological interventions: Effects on literacy achievement of children with literacy difficulties. *Annals of Dyslexia, 60*(2), 183–208.

Goodwin, A. P., & Ahn, S. (2013). A meta-analysis of morphological interventions in English: Effects on literacy outcomes for school-age children. *Scientific Studies of Reading, 17*(4), 257–285.

Gough, P. B., & Tunmer, W. E. (1986). Decoding, reading, and reading disability. *Remedial and Special Education, 7*(1), 6–10.

Graham, S., & Santangelo, T. (2014). Does spelling instruction make students better spellers, readers, and writers?: A meta-analytic review. *Reading and Writing, 27,* 1703–1743.

Hanna, P. R., Hanna, J. S., Hodges, R. E., & Rurorf, H. (1966). *Phoneme-grapheme correspondences as cues to spelling improvement.* U.S. Office of Education Cooperative Research. https://eric.ed.gov/?id=ED128835

Hiebert, E. H., Martin, L. A., & Menon, S. (2005). Are there alternatives in reading textbooks?: An examination of three beginning reading programs. *Reading and Writing Quarterly, 21*(1), 7–32.

Jared, D., & Seidenberg, M. S. (1990). Naming multisyllabic words. *Journal of Experimental Psychology: Human Perception and Performance, 16*(1), 92–105.

Kearns, D. M. (2020). Does English have useful syllable division patterns? *Reading Research Quarterly, 55*, S145–S160.

Kearns, D. M., Steacy, L. M., Compton, D. L., Gilbert, J. K., Goodwin, A. P., Cho, E., ... Collins, A. A. (2016). Modeling polymorphemic word recognition: Exploring differences among children with early-emerging and late-emerging word reading difficulty. *Journal of Learning Disabilities, 49*(4), 368–394.

Kim, M. K., Bryant, D. P., Bryant, B. R., & Park, Y. (2017). A synthesis of interventions for improving oral reading fluency of elementary students with learning disabilities. *Preventing School Failure: Alternative Education for Children and Youth, 61*(2), 116–125.

Kim, Y. S. G. (2017). Why the simple view of reading is not simplistic: Unpacking component skills of reading using a direct and indirect effect model of reading (DIER). *Scientific Studies of Reading, 21*(4), 310–333.

Kim, Y. S. G., & Wagner, R. K. (2015). Text (oral) reading fluency as a construct in reading development: An investigation of its mediating role for children from grades 1 to 4. *Scientific Studies of Reading, 19*(3), 224–242.

LaBerge, D., & Samuels, S. J. (1974). Towards a theory of automatic information processing in reading. *Cognitive Psychology, 6*, 293–323.

Lee, J., & Yoon, S. Y. (2017). The effects of repeated reading on reading fluency for students with reading disabilities: A meta-analysis. *Journal of Learning Disabilities, 50*(2), 213–224.

Lovett, M. W., Frijters, J. C., Steinbach, K. A., Sevcik, R. A., & Morris, R. D. (2021). Effective intervention for adolescents with reading disabilities: Combining reading and motivational remediation to improve outcomes. *Journal of Educational Psychology, 113*(4), 656–689.

Lovett, M. W., Frijters, J. C., Wolf, M., Steinbach, K. A., Sevcik, R. A., & Morris, R. D. (2017). Early intervention for children at risk for reading disabilities: The impact of grade at intervention and individual differences on intervention outcomes. *Journal of Educational Psychology, 109*(7), 889–914.

Lovett, M. W., Steinbach, K. A., & Frijters, J. C. (2000). Remediating the core deficits of developmental reading disability: A double-deficit perspective. *Journal of Learning Disabilities, 33*(4), 334–358.

Maki, K. E., & Hammerschmidt-Snidarich, S. (2022). Reading fluency intervention dosage: A novel meta-analysis and research synthesis. *Journal of School Psychology, 92*, 148–165.

Maloney, E., Risko, E. F., O'Malley, S., & Besner, D. (2009). Tracking the transition from sublexical to lexical processing: On the creation of orthographic and phonological lexical representations. *Quarterly Journal of Experimental Psychology, 62*(5), 858–867.

Nagy, W. E., Carlisle, J. F., & Goodwin, A. P. (2014). Morphological knowledge and literacy acquisition. *Journal of Learning Disabilities, 47*(1), 3–12.

Nation, K., & Castles, A. (2017). Putting the learning into orthographic learning. *Theories of Reading Development, 15*, 147–168.

National Governors Association Center for Best Practices & Council of Chief State School Officers. (2010). *Common Core State Standards.* Authors.

Neuman, S. B., Quintero, E., & Reist, K. (2023). Reading reform across America: A survey of state legislation. Albert Shanker Institute.

O'Connor, R. E., Beach, K. D., Sanchez, V. M., Bocian, K. M., & Flynn, L. J. (2015). Building BRIDGES: A design experiment to improve reading and United States history knowledge of poor readers in eighth grade. *Exceptional Children, 81*(4), 399–425.

Perfetti, C. (2007). Reading ability: Lexical quality to comprehension. *Scientific Studies of Reading, 11*(4), 357–383.

Perfetti, C. A., & Hart, L. (2002). The lexical quality hypothesis. In L. Verhoeven, C. Elbr, & P. Reitsma (Eds.), *Precursors of functional literacy* (pp. 189–212). John Benjamins.

Perfetti, C., & Stafura, J. (2014). Word knowledge in a theory of reading comprehension. *Scientific Studies of Reading, 18*(1), 22–37.

Perry, C., Ziegler, J. C., & Zorzi, M. (2010). Beyond single syllables: Large-scale modeling of reading aloud with the Connectionist Dual Process (CDP++) model. *Cognitive Psychology, 61*(2), 106–151.

Pitre, C. C. (2014). Improving African American student outcomes: Understanding educational achievement and strategies to close opportunity gaps. *Western Journal of Black Studies, 38*(4), 209–217.

Scammacca, N. K., Roberts, G., Vaughn, S., & Stuebing, K. K. (2015). A meta-analysis of interventions for struggling readers in grades 4–12: 1980–2011. *Journal of Learning Disabilities, 48*(4), 369–390.

Schwanenflugel, P. J., Hamilton, A. M., Kuhn, M. R., Wisenbaker, J. M., & Stahl, S. A. (2004). Becoming a fluent reader: Reading skill and prosodic features in the oral reading of young readers. *Journal of Educational Psychology, 96*(1), 119–129.

Siegel, L. S. (2008). Morphological awareness skills of English language learners and children with dyslexia. *Topics in Language Disorders, 28*(1), 15–27.

Stevens, E. A., Walker, M. A., & Vaughn, S. (2017). The effects of reading fluency interventions on the reading fluency and reading comprehension performance of elementary students with learning disabilities: A synthesis of the research from 2001 to 2014. *Journal of Learning Disabilities, 50*(5), 576–590.

Therrien, W. J., & Kubina, R. M., Jr. (2006). Developing reading fluency with repeated reading. *Intervention in School and Clinic, 41*(3), 156–160.

Torgesen, J. K., Wagner, R., & Rashotte, C. A. (2012). *Test of Word Reading Efficiency* (2nd ed). Pro-Ed.

Toste, J. R., Capin, P., Vaughn, S., Roberts, G. G., & Kearns, D. M. (2017). Multisyllabic word reading instruction with and without motivational beliefs training for struggling readers in the upper elementary grades: A pilot investigation. *Elementary School Journal, 117*(4), 593–615.

Toste, J. R., Capin, P., Williams, K. J., Cho, E., & Vaughn, S. (2019). Replication of an experimental study investigating the efficacy of a multisyllabic word reading intervention with and without motivational beliefs training for struggling readers. *Journal of Learning Disabilities, 52*(1), 45–58.

Toste, J. R., Capin, P., Williams, K. J., Kearns, D. M., & Vaughn, S. (2023). *Word Connections: A multisyllabic word reading program* (2nd ed.). figshare.

Toste, J. R., Didion, L., Peng, P., Filderman, M. J., & McClelland, A. M. (2020). A meta-analytic review of the relations between motivation and reading achievement for K–12 students. *Review of Educational Research, 90*(3), 420–456.

Vaughn, S., Cirino, P. T., Wanzek, J., Wexler, J., Fletcher, J. M., Denton, C. D., . . . Francis, D. J. (2010). Response to intervention for middle school students with reading difficulties: Effects of a primary and secondary intervention. *School Psychology Review, 39*(1), 3–21.

Vaughn, S., Gersten, R., Dimino, J., Taylor, M. J., Newman-Gonchar, R., Krowka, S., . . . Jayanthi, M. (2022). *Providing reading interventions for students in grades 4–9* (WWC 2022007). National Center for Education Evaluation and Regional Assistance (NCEE), Institute of Education Sciences, U.S. Department of Education. https://whatworks.ed.gov.

Vaughn, S., Linan-Thompson, S., Kouzekanani, K., Bryant, D. P., Dickson, S., & Blozis, S. A. (2003). Reading instruction grouping for students with reading difficulties. *Remedial and Special Education, 24,* 301–315.

Vaughn, S., Roberts, G., Wexler, J., Vaughn, M. G., Fall, A. M., & Schnakenberg, J. B. (2015). High school students with reading comprehension difficulties: Results of a randomized control trial of a two-year reading intervention. *Journal of Learning Disabilities, 48*(5), 546–558.

Venezky, R. L. (1999). *The American way of spelling: The structure and origins of American English orthography.* Guilford Press.

Wanzek, J., Wexler, J., Vaughn, S., & Ciullo, S. (2010). Reading interventions for struggling readers in the upper elementary grades: A synthesis of 20 years of research. *Reading and Writing, 23*(8), 889–912.

Washington, J. A. (2001). Early literacy skills in African American children: Research considerations. *Learning Disabilities Research and Practice, 16*(4), 213–221.

Washington, J. A., & Seidenberg, M. S. (2021). Teaching reading to African American children: When home and school language differ. *American Educator, 45*(2), 26–40.

Zeno, S., Ivens, S. H., Millard, R. T., & Duvvuri, R. (1995). *The educator's word frequency guide.* Touchstone Applied Science Associates.

CHAPTER 3

The Science of Reading
Morphology Matters

Amanda P. Goodwin

Students can have real difficulty learning vocabulary, something I often experienced as a fourth-grade teacher. Fortunately, a deeper understanding of morphology and morphological instruction can help create vocabulary instruction that is more supportive for students (for an overview of morphology, see Carlisle & Goodwin, 2013; Nagy et al., 2014; for overviews and specifics related to instruction, see Goodwin & Ahn, 2010, 2013; Goodwin & Perkins, 2015; Goodwin, Petscher, Jones, et al., 2020). Hence, in this chapter, I plan to provide the most important research-based takeaways regarding morphology, with the goal of bridging research and practice and helping teachers as they integrate the science of reading within their classroom instruction.

Classroom Contexts

As a classroom teacher, I supported my students by applying what I had learned in my teacher preparation programs. This involved listening to my students read, teaching vocabulary, questioning their comprehension, and providing extensive opportunities for reading and writing. However, when speaking with my students, I began to recognize the powerful role that word knowledge plays in reading and writing. In fact, I found that unfamiliarity with a word or phrase—from either a word reading or meaning perspective—served as a barrier to reading comprehension. This understanding motivated me to add extensive vocabulary instruction to my teaching, doubling both the number of words that were typically taught and tested, and the amount of time spent on word instruction.

Despite successfully learning targeted words, this increased vocabulary only allowed for the introduction of 210 unique words. Furthermore, my students continued to struggle with the multisyllabic, content-rich words that carry much of the meaning in complex texts, whether narrative or expository, which only touches the surface of the 200,000 words that comprise academic texts (Nagy & Anderson, 1984). Unfortunately, by leaving out root words, suffixes, and affixes, I had disregarded critical components for expanding word knowledge and helping ensure that my students had deep understandings of the code of English.

Research on Morphology

When I entered the research field, I wanted to find out about word-learning efficiency. English is *morphophonemic*, which means that meaning is conveyed through the written spelling of words (Chomsky & Halle, 1968; Henry, 1993). For example, the overlap in spelling between *know* and *knowledge* and *knowledgeable* conveys the link in meanings, so helping students attend to such links can highlight spelling, word reading, and meaning supports for many content specific, lower-frequency words (e.g., *governmental, nationalistic, transcontinental*), as well as the complex syntactical phrases in which such words are used (e.g., *the nationalistic principles of the governmental group*). Yet these links can often be hidden by spelling changes (e.g., *convene* and *convention*) or phonology changes (e.g., *magic* and *magician*), or changes in both phonology and orthography (e.g., *meter* and *biometric*). Given this, I set out to determine how morphological knowledge (i.e., how root words, prefixes, and suffixes combine to communicate meaning) links to literacy and how it might support different types of readers. This involved building understandings of not only morphology in general, but also how morphological instruction could add to and be integrated within classroom instruction to support literacy learning.

Morphology is an important answer to the challenges of students building word knowledge. In this chapter, I aggregate the findings from my research to share key principles related to morphology and the science of reading that can make word-learning instruction more efficient. I discuss the science of reading and then pull key principles from various studies to show important instructional insights. I end the chapter with a detailed discussion of the research that underlies these principles, with a focus on the ways in which morphology supports word reading, language comprehension, reading comprehension, and assessment.

Science of Reading

In the introductions of *Reading Research Quarterly*'s special issues on the science of reading (SOR), Bob Jimenez and I (2020, 2021) presented a range of definitions for the science of reading, pushing back on the narrow view that SOR solely emphasizes phonics and word reading. This broader understanding of SOR incorporates the biological, environmental, and cultural factors that influence reading and represents an interdisciplinary body of knowledge that informs best practices for reading instruction. Importantly, SOR includes a body of established truths that focus on phonics, phonological awareness, fluency, vocabulary, and comprehension (National Institute of Child Health and Human Development [NICHD], 2000).

However, the science of reading also highlights lesser-known topic areas as part of the constantly expanding body of research, adding nuance that can further improve learning. This includes research on morphology, as well as language comprehension, digital reading, and writing, among others. It also attends to subtleties that ensure instruction is more efficient and effective. For example, SOR considers various learner profiles, as well as continuums of word difficulties that inform sequences and intensity of instruction. Last, SOR in its most informative version considers bridges to practice such as instructional context. My focus here is on how morphology fits within the science of reading; specifically, I highlight the nuances that maximize the effectiveness of instruction.

Instructional Principles

My work points to four important principles that can support morphological instruction in this science of reading era. Below, I share those principles and some of the research that supports them. I prioritize instruction here because I hope these concepts will be helpful in bridging research to practice. With that said, I go into even further detail on the research in the next section of this chapter.

Assess Morphological Knowledge

One of the key things to emerge from my work is that teachers should assess students' morphological knowledge, not just vocabulary, fluency, word reading, or reading comprehension. This involves evaluating students' understanding of root words and their ability to manipulate and derive new words from these roots. This also involves assessing various aspects of morphological knowledge, including awareness of how combining root words and affixes works, and also knowledge of the syntactical, semantic, orthographic, and phonological information conveyed by morphemes. Importantly, morphological knowledge is not a single thing; hence, assessments need to involve different components, while also attending to different features of words, such as how frequent the root word or affix occurs, how large the morphological family is, and how transparently the units of meaning are put together (e.g., *fearful* is transparent because there are no spelling or sound changes when combining the units of meaning; *electrician* is less transparent because of the pronunciation change; *biometric* is even less transparent because of the spelling and pronunciation changes). Overall, assessment guides instruction; hence, assessing morphological knowledge and awareness can help inform nuanced and efficient instruction. There are various assessment choices (for more discussion on morphological assessment, see *www.worddetectives.com* or

Goodwin, Petscher, Jones, et al., 2020). My team has developed two assessments with our work showing that one of our morphological assessments (Monster, PI; see *www.worddetectives.com* or Goodwin, Petscher, Jones, et al., 2020) explains more than half the variance in reading comprehension for middle school students grades 5–8 (Goodwin, Petscher, & Reynolds, 2022), while the other assessment is under development. This confirms the importance of assessing different components of morphology to guide instruction as each additional morphological skill added understandings of reading comprehension.

Explicit Instruction in Morphological Analysis

My research has also suggested that incorporating explicit instruction on how to analyze and break down words into their morphemic components can support literacy. Here, we suggest using examples and non-examples to help students identify patterns and apply this knowledge to new words. It is helpful to attend to the morphological makeup of words, starting with those that are easier because of familiar units, big families, and transparent relations. Then move to more difficult words. In Goodwin (2016), we found that as few as four 30-minute sessions could introduce students to morphological analysis. Each of these sessions started with 5–10 minutes of explicit instruction where bigger principles were introduced and then reinforced through work within texts. For more information on how to combine explicit instruction within larger instruction, see *https://worddetectives.com/instructional-resources/#morph-intervention* and Goodwin (2016) and Goodwin and Perkins (2015).

Connect Morphological Instruction to Word-Reading, Vocabulary, and Syntax Instruction to Build Knowledge and Principles

Morphemes convey word reading, spelling, and meaning information. Hence, teachers should connect morphological instruction directly to these different components of reading. For instance, when teaching a new root word, also introduce its derived forms and use them in reading activities to reinforce understanding and application. Additionally, when teaching a vocabulary word, identify the root word and affixes, and connect that word to the larger morphological families. Morphology is often seen as connected to meaning, but instruction should also point out word-reading, spelling, and syntax supports. These can be specific (i.e., focusing on spelling the /shun/ sound as *ian* for a person or *ion* for a thing) or integrated across such that when learning a new word, the pronunciation, meaning, and spelling of the morphemes are discussed, and a larger morphological family is built. The research suggests that many of the phonics complexities that underlie multisyllabic word reading and spelling are morphological in nature. Similarly, figuring out the meaning of many academic words involves knowing the meaning of morphemes and morphological problem solving. Hence, identifying how morphology connects directly to word reading, spelling, and vocabulary can show how the code of language works and prevent students from just seeing morphemes as semantic supports.

Utilize Morphological Awareness Activities

A final, related instructional principle is to engage students in activities that build their morphological awareness, such as word sorting, word building, and morphological puzzles. These activities should encourage students to explore and manipulate the structure of words. An emphasis on word play and consideration of words as puzzles to be figured out via the code of language can empower students to do more than memorize words but instead understand and apply at scale the principles that underlie the word reading, spelling, and meaning within words. This work should include an emphasis on morphological problem solving (i.e., finding or using the parts known), which helps students deal with unfamiliar multisyllabic words. An example would be to help students find the parts they know within words such as *multinational*. Here, it is important not just to focus on the smaller units of meaning but also to emphasize the biggest parts focusing on *national* versus *ion*.

Further Discussion of the Research

Each of these instructional principles stems from bridging research to practice. I have been studying morphology for my career and have published more than 25 pieces on morphology with many colleagues. I have explored different aspects of morphology and have found that it is an important and underemphasized supporter of literacy.

Morphology: A Key Contributor to Literacy

My research has consistently demonstrated that morphological knowledge is a critical component of literacy development. As mentioned earlier, morphology, which the study of the structure and form of words or how root words and affixes are combined to convey meaning, plays a significant role in various aspects of literacy, including word reading, vocabulary acquisition, syntax, and reading comprehension (Carlisle, 2003). This is especially the case as texts get harder for readers. This is because many of the reasons texts are hard to read for young adolescents, including increased multisyllabic word reading and complex vocabulary and syntax demands, relate to morphology (Carlisle & Stone, 2005; Carlisle, Stone, & Katz, 2001; Gilbert et al., 2014; Kearns et al., 2016). My work shows that understanding morphology helps readers read, use, and interpret the low-frequency vocabulary words and phrases present in adolescent texts (Goodwin et al., 2014). In other words, understanding that a suffix is added to create *activation* to communicate a certain meaning helped students in ways that attending to letters, syllables, and individual words did not. Also, though, being able to recognize morphemes including low-frequency roots, root words, and affixes (e.g., *treelet*) is important to be able to apply morphological understandings (Anglin et al., 1993). Hence, integrating morphological instruction provides a helpful support to principles such as "sound it out" or "memorize the definition." Instead, understanding how words are built and put together shows the power of considering words as puzzles to be figured out via the code of language, and which can be taught and analyzed in meaningful sets (e.g., *act, active, activate, activation, reactivate*) that build high-quality lexical representations (i.e., deep understandings of words and their properties). For the purposes of this chapter, I highlight the ways my research suggests that morphological instruction can support two key areas of literacy highlighted by the simple view of reading (Hoover & Gough, 1990), including word reading and language comprehension. Because assessment should guide instruction, I conclude with a discussion of how a deeper understanding of morphology can guide assessment practices.

One thing to note is that this work builds on the work of others who have come before. How morphology has been studied in relation to reading has changed across time. For example, in the 1970s, researchers examined links between morphological awareness and general reading measures (Britain, 1970). In the 1980s, researchers determined the frequency of morphologically complex words in text (Nagy & Anderson, 1984) and how morphological awareness is acquired (Carlisle, 1988; Freyd & Baron, 1982; Tyler & Nagy, 1989). By the end of the 1980s, researchers contributed models of morphological stages of development (Templeton, 1989) and studies of morphological interventions (White et al., 1989; Wysocki & Jenkins, 1987). In the 1990s and 2000s, researchers examined how morphological processing supports vocabulary knowledge (Anglin et al., 1993) and used novel statistical models to determine how morphological awareness supports reading achievement beyond related linguistic dimensions such as phonological awareness (Carlisle, 1995; Carlisle & Nomanbhoy, 1993; Deacon & Kirby, 2004; Mahony et al., 2000; Nagy et al., 2006). During this time, researchers focused further on translating research understandings into effective morphological instruction (Bowers et al., 2010; Carlisle, 2010; Goodwin & Ahn, 2010, 2013; Goodwin et al., 2012; Henry, 1988).

During this period of important development of morphological research and bridges to practice, researchers and educators generally focused on the semantic meanings of morphemes (i.e., assessing or teaching *un* means *not* or that *undone* means *not done*). Often, a single assessment was used to relate morphological knowledge to literacy outcomes. In contrast, the most recent work on morphology, including my own, suggests a broader role for morphology that includes considering the various ways morphemes are combined (*fear* and *fearful*; *know* and *knowledge*; *activate* and *reactivation*), as well as the different types of information contained in morphemes, such as semantic, phonological (pronunciation, *-ing*), orthographic (spelling, *know*), and syntactic (grammar, *-ion* suggests a noun for *election*) information. In other words, the research on morphology is starting to highlight the multiple roles morphology plays in literacy. My work with colleagues suggests that focusing on any single area of morphology underestimates its impact on literacy (Goodwin, Petscher, & Reynolds, 2022).

Importantly, this focus on morphological awareness and different aspects of morphological knowledge (phonological, orthographic, semantic, and syntactic) extends understandings of a different area that the science of reading has shown to be particularly important to support of literacy learning: language comprehension. For language, in the past, researchers and educators have tended to default to assessing and teaching vocabulary, usually single definitions, often via a weekly list of words. As shown earlier, my work suggests that considering morphology in models of language comprehension can inform instruction in meaningful ways. For example, when considering vocabulary knowledge, one must consider knowledge of definitions, including definitions of the morphemes that make up the full word, relations to other words, including relations to other morphologically complex words with the word family, and also the ability to word-solve or figure out the meaning of unfamiliar words usually using morphology or context.

While I go into greater detail below, I emphasize that nuanced morphological understandings have moved the field forward in important ways. Multifaceted morphological and language knowledge has often taken a backseat to other reading-related skills such as phonological awareness, phonics, and even definition-focused vocabulary, because it is thought about in a narrow manner. The work described earlier and below extends the conceptualization of what it means to know a word by considering word parts and links to phrases. Hence, the information in this chapter contributes to the field and the science of reading by emphasizing that morphological knowledge extends beyond just semantic meanings of morphemes. This is important to remember when bridging to practice. For example, as a teacher, gaining a single score on morphology can be instructionally daunting, because I might not know which skill within morphology to work on. By assessing various components in morphology, teachers can gain more guidance on what to teach.

Morphology and Word Reading

According to the simple view of reading (Hoover & Gough, 1990), the two most critical components of reading are decoding (i.e., word reading) and language comprehension. Focusing on the decoding side of the equation, morphological knowledge and morphological awareness facilitate word reading by helping students recognize and decode morphologically complex words. By fourth grade, the majority of text comprises words that have more than one morpheme (Nagy & Anderson, 1984). Hence, a big part of the word-reading demands in upper elementary and secondary texts involve the multimorphemic words that students face. This can be overwhelming for readers, but three findings from my research make this a much more manageable problem space.

First, morphological knowledge and awareness can help with the fact that there are up to 200,000 words (Nagy & Anderson, 1984) that readers face when reading academic texts across their K–12 years. My work with colleagues Hiebert and Cervetti (Hiebert et al., 2018) showed that just 2,451 morphological families, averaging 4.61 members, make up the core vocabulary of school texts. In other words, knowing and understanding the morphological units in just 2,451 families can help readers figure out most words in text with these families making up 97.1% (grades K and 1) to 89.1% (grade 11 through college) of the total words in texts and 95.6% (grades K and 1) to 74.9% (grade 11 through college) of the unique words in texts. Here, the texts considered were the texts suggested by the Common Core State Standards in Appendix B (National Governors Association Center for Best Practices & Council of Chief State School Officers, 2010). This emphasizes the importance of teaching morphology as part of phonics instruction. Rather than teaching students to just sound out orthographic units in words, teaching students to use morphological units is likely to support their word reading.

Building on this, research can help guide teachers on *what words to teach* (i.e., start with more frequent words with frequent morphemes like *fearful* to highlight morphological relationships then move to words with more hidden morphological relationships that are less transparent and more opaque or have less frequent roots like *spectator*), what words might be hard (i.e., those with less frequent root words and less transparent morphological relationships), what morphological units to focus upon (i.e., root words especially), and for which readers these skills are particularly important (i.e., those with word-reading, vocabulary, or morphological knowledge weaknesses). For example, in Goodwin and colleagues (2013), we showed how morphological knowledge plays a critical role in adolescent word reading. Specifically, this study found that a reader's ability to read root words such as *govern* significantly predicted their ability to read related derived words such as *governmental*. Importantly, in terms of guiding what words to teach, this study showed that using root word knowledge was easier with root and derived words that are more frequent and transparent, such as *governmental* compared with less frequent roots and words such as *aquascape* or less transparent combinations such as *decision*. Additionally, readers who have higher levels of morphological and vocabulary knowledge are better able to apply these skills to reading multimorphemic words.

This study adds an important lens to the science of reading's emphasis on phonics and phonological awareness as word reading supports. Our study indicates that morphemes and morphological knowledge are important instructional tools to build advanced word-reading skills. In other words, instruction should focus on enhancing students' morphological knowledge and morphological awareness to improve their ability to read morphologically complex words. Teachers should also be aware of the challenges posed by certain multimorphemic words—especially those that are less frequent and are phonologically and orthographically opaque words—and provide targeted support to help students navigate these complexities, especially students with lower levels of morphological and vocabulary knowledge. Another study with a colleague, Gilbert and colleagues (2014), showed that morphological knowledge is particularly important for students with word-reading difficulties. This study showed that the interaction between word reading and morphological awareness explained significant additional variance in reading comprehension. In other words, the students who had more difficulties reading multisyllabic words seemed to need to use their morphological knowledge to read the challenging words to support their reading comprehension. These findings are backed up by two meta-analyses (Goodwin & Ahn, 2010, 2013) that indicated morphological instruction has a significant positive effect on word reading.

Overall, my research, along with that of others, shows that morphology can play an important role in word reading. By breaking down words into their root forms and affixes, students can apply their knowledge of morphemes to read unfamiliar words. This process not only aids in word recognition but also supports the development of fluency, as students become more adept at identifying and pronouncing morphologically complex words.

Morphology and Language Comprehension (Vocabulary and Syntax)

The second key component within the simple view of reading is language comprehension (Hoover & Gough, 1990). As mentioned previously, the National Reading Panel (NICHD, 2000) has emphasized the importance of teaching vocabulary, but missing from the discussion is the importance that the science of reading has shown for building language comprehension skills more broadly. This moves beyond the emphasis on learning words to instead learning how language works, within which morphology is a key player. Specifically, my work and the work of others, emphasizes the important role of morphology in vocabulary acquisition and in syntax. This is because, similar to word reading, knowing the meaning of roots, prefixes, and suffixes, and understanding how these units are put together in words and sentences allows students to access word meanings more efficiently (Perfetti, 2007), infer the meanings of new words successfully (Anglin et al., 1993; Pacheco & Goodwin, 2013), and then to also infer the meaning of complicated syntaxes (Goodwin, Petscher, & Reynolds, 2022). Knowing that *detect* can be adapted to *detection* to create a clause, *detection of the meaning*, gives students important clues to how academic language works (Nagy & Townsend, 2012). My research adds three important lenses to showing the importance of morphological knowledge and morphological instruction to both vocabulary and syntax.

First, many of my studies *emphasize the importance of morphological knowledge in vocabulary, especially in building high-quality lexical* representations. Here, the idea is to draw attention and teach the different linguistic information conveyed by the morphemes that make up words. For example, teaching students to identify root words such as *nation* within a larger word such as *nationalistic* and focusing on the meaning, decoding, and spelling of each part helps students build large networks of words and word parts. The lexical quality hypothesis suggests that readers are more efficiently able to access and use words for comprehension when readers have lexical representations of those words involving deep and consistent information about a word's orthographic, phonological, grammatical, and meaning-related properties (Perfetti, 2007). This means that the more a reader knows about a word, the more efficiently that reader can access the word and integrate it into the meaning of the text.

My work (Goodwin et al., 2014) and that of others (Reichle & Perfetti, 2003) suggests that the same principle applies to morphologically complex words and morphemes. In other words, the more a reader knows about the root words, prefixes, and suffixes that make up a word, the easier it is to access those units and the full word for meaning and comprehension. Here, Goodwin and colleagues (2014) showed that a reader's morphological knowledge of a root word (e.g., *isolate*) contributes to that reader's lexical representations (i.e., mental representation of form and meaning) of a related derived word (e.g., *isolation*). Readers who could read, spell, and know the meaning of the root word were more likely to know the meaning of the larger derived word. This is important to instruction because it means that the more teachers draw attention to the morphological makeup of the word, including the pronunciation, spelling, and meaning of the units that make up the word, the more students will know about the larger words they often come into contact with in the more complicated texts they read. One important finding from this study was that creating networks of morphologically related words seems additionally helpful. Here, being able to list the relatives of the root word (for *nation, national, nationalistic, international, nationally, transnationally*, etc.) resulted in higher quality lexical representations. Hence, adding morphological activities that emphasizes building of these networks within instruction is likely to support student learning. Ideas that include adding such activities to graphic organizers, playing games to produce as many related words as possible, and identifying morphologically complex words within text have been shown to be effective in research (see, e.g., Goodwin et al., 2012, 2016; Goodwin & Perkins, 2015; Pacheco & Goodwin, 2013).

The next key addition from my research involves showing that morphological instruction is effective in supporting vocabulary learning. Here, my research, along with that of colleagues, also suggests that attending to the morphological makeup of words can help guide which words are easier to learn versus which might be harder, providing another important lens to considering what words to teach and with what intensity. In terms of effectiveness of instruction, meta-analyses are research methods that look across a larger corpus of studies. My team has completed two meta-analyses (Goodwin & Ahn, 2010, 2013) indicating that morphological instruction builds vocabulary knowledge. Additionally, Goodwin and Ahn (2010) showed that morphological instruction is particularly effective for children with reading, learning, and speech and language disabilities, English language learners, and struggling readers. This fits with the earlier study by Gilbert and colleagues (2014), which found that morphological awareness is particularly helpful for poor word readers.

In terms of how morphological instruction supports vocabulary, one nuance shown involves considering different aspects of word knowledge. Here, one of my studies (Goodwin & Cho, 2016) indicated that overall, morphological learning activities support vocabulary learning for multiple aspects of word knowledge, including definitional knowledge, self-report knowledge, and also knowledge of morphological relatives. This links to the idea of building higher-quality lexical representations, because multiple aspects of word knowledge are considered. Also, the study showed that certain words are easier to learn for certain types of readers. Generally, words that have more morphological family members and words in which the morphological relationship is transparent were easier to learn. This work, similar to that discussed in the earlier section on word reading, emphasizes consideration of the morphological makeup of a word as a factor in word difficulty.

The final key lens that my research adds to understanding of the role of morphology in language comprehension involves syntax. Morphology is a key player in syntax, the set of rules that govern the structure of sentences. Knowledge of how words change form to express different grammatical relationships (e.g., tense, number, and possession) helps students understand and construct complex sentences. This syntactic awareness is crucial for both reading and writing, as it enables students to grasp the relationships between words in a sentence, thereby improving their overall language comprehension and production. One of the big additions of the science of reading is to emphasize the importance of language comprehension, especially for upper elementary and secondary students. Research consistently shows that by these ages, language comprehension measures explain more variance in reading comprehension than word reading. As mentioned, while vocabulary tends to be seen as the proxy for language comprehension, research also suggests the important and unique role of syntax in reading comprehension (see Goodwin, Petscher, & Reynolds, 2022). In terms of how morphology connects to syntax, with colleagues, we showed an important contribution of morphosyntax, which involves understanding of how suffixes convey grammatical information, as well as general syntax, which involves considering the ways that words and phrases are combined to convey meaning. This means that morphosyntactical understandings are additionally important beyond general syntax knowledge in supporting reading comprehension performance. Hence, as we consider morphological instruction, moving beyond attending to single words to include how those single words are used in larger phrases and sentences is likely to support additional literacy understandings.

Morphology and Assessment

As shown in the earlier parts of this chapter, the research is clear that morphological knowledge and morphological awareness supports word reading and language comprehension, including vocabulary and syntax. Yet, until recently, few options existed relative to morphological assessment. A final contribution of my work to the field and to the science of reading involves the development of multiple morphological assessments—one for third to fifth graders (see *https://education.ufl.edu/dimes/wordchomp*) and the other for fifth to eighth graders (see Goodwin, Petscher, Jones, et al., 2020; Goodwin, Petscher, Tock, et al., 2022; *www.word-detectives.com*). Each of these assessments shows that morphological knowledge is a multidimensional construct that can provide meaningful data to inform instruction. Each is computer adaptive, and while the assessment for third to fifth graders is still in development, Monster, PI has extensive research to back its validity and reliability (see Goodwin, Petscher, Jones, et al., 2022; Goodwin, Petscher, & Reynolds, 2022; Goodwin, Petscher, & Tock, 2020, 2021; Goodwin, Petscher, Tock, et al., 2022). Specifically, this work identifies four teachable morphological skills as described below:

1. Students can identify units of meaning—This skill focuses on students' awareness of morphemes in general and their ability to find them in words.
2. Students can use suffixes to gain syntactic information—This skill focuses on students' understanding of the syntactic properties of morphemes, that is, how they shift words' parts of speech.
3. Students can use morphology for meaning—This skill focuses on students' understanding of the semantic properties of morphemes, that is, what they mean.
4. Students can read and spell morphologically complex words—This skill focuses on students' understanding of the orthographic and phonological information conveyed by morphemes.

What is important from this work is that morphological assessments can provide data that can help educators unravel performance on skills that underlie many reading comprehension challenges and successes, but to do that, careful multidimensional assessment must occur rather than just seeing morphology as a single semantic skill. Additionally, part of this assessment involved the establishment of reader profiles, which suggests that it is important to look at groupings within assessment data to support more targeted instruction. Overall, an important contribution of my research is to emphasize the importance of using assessment data related to multiple morphological skills to tailor instruction, ensuring that all students receive appropriate support and challenges.

Conclusion

I started this chapter with classroom statements that highlight the potential of morphology to support classroom instruction. The research within the science of reading is clear that morphological instruction supports literacy learning. My research deepens understandings of how morphological instruction can support literacy learning, adding a lens to show that such instruction benefits all students but especially those with literacy learning difficulties. It also adds lenses to showcase a continuum of difficulty of words and word features to use for such instruction, as well as the importance of using assessment to guide instruction. My hope is that this chapter can help educators bridge research to practice and more effectively integrate teaching the code of language into instruction that is grounded in the science of reading.

REFERENCES

Anglin, J. M., Miller, G. A., & Wakefield, P. C. (1993). Vocabulary development: A morphological analysis. *Monographs of the Society for Research in Child Development, 58*(10), i–186.

Bowers, P. N., Kirby, J. R., & Deacon, S. H. (2010). The effects of morphological instruction on literacy skills: A systematic review of the literature. *Review of Educational Research, 80*(2), 144–179.

Britain, M. (1970). Inflectional performance and early reading achievement. *Reading Research Quarterly, 6,* 34–38.

Carlisle, J. F. (1988). Knowledge of derivational morphology and spelling ability in fourth, sixth, and eighth graders. *Applied Psycholinguistics, 9*(3), 247–266.

Carlisle, J. F. (1995). Morphological awareness and early reading achievement. In L. Feldman (Ed.), *Morphological aspects of language processing* (pp.131–154). Erlbaum.

Carlisle, J. F. (2003). Morphology matters in learning to read: A commentary. *Reading Psychology, 24*(3–4), 291–322.

Carlisle, J. F. (2010). Effects of instruction in morphological awareness on literacy achievement: An integrative review. *Reading Research Quarterly, 45*(4), 464–487.

Carlisle, J. F., & Goodwin, A. P. (2013). Morphemes matter: How morphological knowledge contributes to reading and writing. In C. A. Stone, E. R. Silliman, B. J. Ehren, & G. P. Wallach (Eds.), *Handbook of language and literacy: Development and disorders* (2nd ed., pp. 265–282). Guilford Press.

Carlisle, J. F., & Nomanbhoy, D. M. (1993). Phonological and morphological awareness in first graders. *Applied Psycholinguistics, 14,* 177–195.

Carlisle, J. F., & Stone, C. A. (2005). Exploring the role of morphemes in word reading. *Reading Research Quarterly, 40*(4), 428–449.

Carlisle, J. F., Stone, C. A., & Katz, L. A. (2001). The effects of phonological transparency on reading derived words. *Annals of Dyslexia, 51,* 249–274.

Chomsky, N., & Halle, M. (1968). *The sound pattern of English.* Harper & Row.

Deacon, S. H., & Kirby, J. R. (2004). Morphological awareness: Just "more phonological"?: The roles of morphological and phonological awareness in reading development. *Applied Psycholinguistics, 25,* 223–238.

Freyd, P., & Baron, J. (1982). Individual differences in acquisition of derivational morphology. *Journal of Verbal Learning and Verbal Behavior, 21*(3), 282–295.

Gilbert, J. K., Goodwin, A. P., Compton, D. L., & Kearns, D. M. (2014). Multisyllabic word reading as a moderator of morphological awareness and reading comprehension. *Journal of Learning Disabilities, 47*(1), 34–43.

Goodwin, A. P. (2016). Effectiveness of word solving: Integrating morphological problem solving within comprehension instruction for middle school students. *Reading and Writing, 29*(1), 91–116.

Goodwin, A. P., & Ahn, S. (2010). A meta-analysis of morphological interventions: Effects on literacy achievement of children with literacy difficulties. *Annals of Dyslexia, 60*(2), 183–208.

Goodwin, A. P., & Ahn, S. (2013). A meta-analysis of morphological interventions in English: Effects on literacy outcomes for school-age children. *Scientific Studies of Reading, 17*(4), 257–285.

Goodwin, A. P., & Cho, S. J. (2016). Unraveling word learning: Reader and item-level predictors of word learning within comprehension instruction for fifth and sixth graders. *Scientific Studies of Reading, 20*(6), 490–514.

Goodwin, A. P., Cho, S. J., & Nichols, S. (2016). Ways to "WIN" at vocabulary learning. *Reading Teacher, 70*(1), 93–97.

Goodwin, A. P., Gilbert, J. K., & Cho, S. J. (2013). Morphological contributions to adolescent word reading: An item response approach. *Reading Research Quarterly, 48*(1), 39–60.

Goodwin, A. P, Gilbert, J. K., Cho, S. J., & Kearns, D. M. (2014). Probing lexical representations: Simultaneous modeling of word and person contributions to multidimensional lexical representations. *Journal of Educational Psychology, 106*(2), 448–468.

Goodwin, A. P., & Jimenez, R. (2020). *The science of reading: Supports, critiques, and questions: An executive summary of the* Reading Research Quarterly *special issue.* https://literacyworldwide.org/docs/default-source/resource-documents/rrq-sor-executive-summary.pdf. (Also published in *Reading Research Quarterly, 55*(Suppl. 1), S7–S16)

Goodwin, A. P., & Jimenez, R. (2021). *The science of reading: Supports, critiques, and questions.* https://ila.onlinelibrary.wiley.com/doi/epdf/10.1002/rrq.416. (Also published in *Reading Research Quarterly, 56*(Suppl. 1), S7–S22)

Goodwin, A., Lipsky, M., & Ahn, S. (2012). Word Detectives: Using units of meaning to support literacy. *Reading Teacher, 65*(7), 461–470.

Goodwin, A. P., & Perkins, J. (2015). Word Detectives: Morphological instruction that supports academic language. *Reading Teacher, 68*(7), 504–517.

Goodwin, A. P., Petscher, Y., Jones, S., McFadden, S., Reynolds, D., & Lantos, T. (2020). The monster in the classroom: Assessing language to inform instruction. *Reading Teacher, 73*(5), 603–616.

Goodwin, A. P., Petscher, Y., & Reynolds, D. (2022). Unraveling adolescent language and reading comprehension: The monster's data. *Scientific Studies of Reading, 26*(4), 305–326.

Goodwin, A., Petscher, Y., Reynolds, D., Lantos, T., Hughes, K., & Jones, S. (2021). Monster, PI: Morphology assessment to guide instruction. In K. Ganske (Ed.), *Mindful of words: Spelling and vocabulary explorations, grades 4–8* (2nd ed., pp. 56–60). Guilford Press.

Goodwin, A. P., Petscher, Y., & Tock, J. (2020). Morphological supports: Investigating differences in how morphological knowledge supports reading comprehension for middle school students with limited reading vocabulary. *Language, Speech, and Hearing Services in Schools, 51*(3), 589–602.

Goodwin, A. P., Petscher, Y., & Tock, J. (2021). Multidimensional morphological assessment for middle school students. *Journal of Research in Reading, 44*(1), 70–89.

Goodwin, A. P., Petscher, Y., Tock, J., McFadden, S., Reynolds, D., Lantos, T., & Jones, S. (2022). Monster, PI: Validation evidence for an assessment of adolescent language that assesses vocabulary knowledge, morphological knowledge, and syntactical awareness. *Assessment for Effective Intervention, 47*(2), 89–100.

Henry, M. K. (1988). Beyond Phonics: Integrated decoding and spelling instruction based on word origin and structure. *Annals of Dyslexia, 38*(1), 259–275.

Henry, M. K. (1993). Morphological structure: Latin and Greek roots and affixes as upper grade code strategies. *Reading and Writing, 5*, 227–241.

Hiebert, E. H., Goodwin, A. P., & Cervetti, G. N. (2018). Core vocabulary: Its morphological content and presence in exemplar texts. *Reading Research Quarterly, 53*(1), 29–49.

Hoover, W. A., & Gough, P. B. (1990). The simple view of reading. *Reading and Writing, 2*, 127–160.

Kearns, D., Steacy, L., Compton, D., Gilbert, J., Goodwin, A., Cho, E., . . . Collins, A. (2016). Modeling polymorphemic word recognition: Exploring differences among children with early-emerging and late-emerging word reading difficulty. *Journal of Learning Disabilities, 49*, 368–394.

Mahony, D., Singson, M., & Mann, V. (2000). Reading ability and sensitivity to morphological relations. *Reading and Writing, 12*, 191–218.

Nagy, W., & Anderson, R. (1984). The number of words in printed school English. *Reading Research Quarterly, 19*, 304–330.

Nagy, W., Berninger, V., & Abbott, R. (2006). Contributions of morphology beyond phonology to literacy outcomes of upper elementary and middle school students. *Journal of Educational Psychology, 98*(1), 134–147.

Nagy, W., Carlisle, J. F., & Goodwin, A. P. (2014). Morphological knowledge and literacy acquisition. *Journal of Learning Disabilities, 47*(1), 3–12.

Nagy, W., & Townsend, D. (2012). Words as tools: Learning academic vocabulary as language acquisition. *Reading Research Quarterly, 47*(1), 91–108.

National Governors Association Center for Best Practices & Council of Chief State School Officers. (2010). *Common Core State Standards for English language arts and literacy in history/social studies, science, and technical subjects; Appendix B: Text exemplars and sample performance tasks.* Authors.

National Institute of Child Health and Human Development. (2000). *Report of the National Reading Panel. Teaching children to read: An evidence-based assessment of the scientific research literature on reading and its implications for reading instruction: Reports of the subgroups* (NIH Publication No. 00-4754). U.S. Government Printing Office. www.nichd.nih.gov/publications/product/247.

Pacheco, M. B., & Goodwin, A. P. (2013). Putting two and two together: Middle school students' morphological problem-solving strategies for unknown words. *Journal of Adolescent and Adult Literacy, 56*(7), 541–553.

Perfetti, C. (2007). Reading ability: Lexical quality to comprehension. *Scientific Studies of Reading, 11*(4), 357–383.

Reichle, E. D., & Perfetti, C. A. (2003). Morphology in word identification: A word-experience model that accounts for morpheme frequency effects. *Scientific Studies of Reading, 7*(3), 219–237.

Templeton, S. (1989). *Reading and spelling development: Stages and strategies.* In G. B. Schickendanz & D. R. Dickinson (Eds.), *Both art and science: A handbook for teachers of reading in the elementary grades* (pp. 156–176). International Reading Association.

Tyler, A., & Nagy, W. (1989). The acquisition of English derivational morphology. *Journal of Memory and Language, 28*(6), 649–667.

White, T. G., Sowell, J., & Yanagihara, A. (1989). Teaching elementary students to use word-part clues. *Reading Teacher, 42*(4), 302–308.

Wysocki, K., & Jenkins, J. R. (1987). Deriving word meanings through morphological generalization. *Reading Research Quarterly, 22*(1), 66–81.

CHAPTER 4

Critical and Developmental Perspectives in Multilingual Literacy and Curriculum

C. Patrick Proctor

There is no shortage of demographic information that describes the increasing linguistic diversity of the United States and its schools. The Migration Policy Institute (2021), for example, estimates that 33% of U.S. children under age 9 have at least one parent or guardian who speaks a language other than English at home. The National Education Association (2020) predicts that by 2025, 25% of students in U.S. classrooms will be ascribed the label of "English learner" by their school districts. These children and youth, who speak multiple named languages such as Spanish, Hmong, Mandarin, and many others, are, in today's educational parlance, "multilingual learners," a discursive shift that moves away from previous terminology, including "limited English proficient," "language minority," "bilingual," and a host of others.

Nomenclature aside, all of these terms suffer from the inevitable binary set up by their use. That is, the idea that one either is, or is not, a multilingual learner, reflects a kind of binary thinking (see Patel, 2023) that has driven a good deal of developmental literacy research over the years. However, labeling one student as multilingual (e.g., a Latinx Spanish–English bilingual fourth grader) and another as monolingual (e.g., a White "mainstream" English-speaking fourth grader) is arguably a manufactured distinction (Jones & Proctor, 2024). As such, critical language and literacy theorists (e.g., García & Wei, 2014) suggest that we are all multilingual, constantly making nuanced linguistic choices depending on context, expectations, and communicative intent. In my work as a language and literacy researcher, I have spent almost two decades navigating the schisms that emerge between developmental and critical perspectives.

Indeed, distinctions between critical and developmental literacy research extend well beyond labeling students and include fundamentally different epistemologies, theoretical orientations, methodological approaches, and reading audiences. But in my experience, there are more points of synergy than one might expect or have witnessed in literacy theory and practice. Given this, my goal in this chapter is to articulate the dialectic of developmental and critical perspectives (thesis and antithesis) on literacy, with synthesis of the two emerging through curriculum design and enactment in multilingual classroom contexts. To do this, I provide my own admittedly subjective and nonexhaustive characterizations of critical and developmental literacy perspectives with a multilingual lens. I then briefly describe how I, along with my colleagues, have attempted to merge these two perspectives through our own curriculum design work with multilingual students and their teachers.

A Brief and Subjective History of Multilingual Literacy

At the turn of the century, in 2003, Jill Fitzgerald wrote a short article for *Reading Research Quarterly* titled "Multilingual Reading Theory," in which she sought to briefly sketch out the need for what she called a "grand" theory of multilingual reading. In the article, Fitzgerald (2003) noted that multilingual reading research could be split into two theoretical "camps" operating independently of one another. The first camp comprised cognitive and psychological researchers who focused on the "individual psychology" of the reader, while the second camp was made up of "researchers who centered their work on social and cultural theories" (p. 120). In response to these encampments, Fitzgerald called for researchers to be mindful of the origins of their theoretical orientations, and, importantly, to actually talk with one another in an effort to recognize and integrate "interconnected webs of theories." Such interactions between different theories, she argued, would enhance our understanding about how multilingual literacy is context-dependent, which in turn might lead to sensible reading policy. More than two decades later, some progress has been made, but these two generalized camps still exist, with limited conversations between them, alongside reading policy that most certainly does not reflect the highly contextualized nature of multilingual reading (see Ascenzi-Moreno, 2024).

Surely a factor in Fitzgerald's (2003) commentary was the reality that research in the 20th century had not taught us much about the developmental processes of reading and literacy for multilingual children. At that time, reading researchers tended to exclude such learners from their studies because the linguistic profiles of multilingual children (often termed "English as a second language" students) were seen to introduce noise in their data for want of increased signal. As a result, two influential publications at that time were clear about that lack of information. Snow and colleagues (1998), in *Preventing Reading Difficulties in Young Children*, noted that "researchers and educators possess scant empirical guidance on how best to design literacy instruction . . . in either their primary language or English, much less in both" (p. 339). Two years later, the National Reading Panel (2000), arguably one of the most influential reviews of reading research, was more blunt: "The Panel also did not address issues relevant to second language learning" (pp. 1–3).

Given the lack of developmental information, the curriculum work of Carlo and colleagues (2004) within the domain of vocabulary instruction for multilingual learners stands out as particularly important. This seminal quasi-experimental study explored the effects of a targeted vocabulary intervention, in English, for Spanish–English bilingual students (and their monolingual English counterparts) in fifth grade. This "Vocabulary Improvement Project" was experimental, as much for its research design as for its instructional focus. Lacking information from the reading research community, Carlo and colleagues designed their vocabulary intervention drawing from research in English as a second or foreign language (often conducted with adult learners; e.g., Huckin et al., 1995), monolingual English vocabulary research with school-age children (e.g., Beck et al., 2013), and a nascent bilingual research base that explored the roles of cognates and strategy use in bilingual children's reading practices (e.g., Durgunoğlu et al., 1993; Jiménez et al., 1995, 1996). Results from Carlo and colleagues' study with 254 fifth graders (142 Spanish–English bilinguals) showed a significant effect on students' knowledge of words taught $\eta^2 = 0.19$) as well as a small but significant effect on a cloze measure of reading comprehension ($\eta^2 = 0.02$).

What was striking about this study was that it took a chance on vocabulary instruction as a driver of comprehension outcomes among bilingual students at a time when there was no established reading research base from which to draw. While it was obvious that vocabulary knowledge mattered for bilingual readers, the reading research base at the time was exclusionary. The two major summative publications that synthesized the "reliable" research base, *Preventing Reading Difficulties* (Snow et al., 1998) and the National Reading Panel (2000) report, not only reported on research that excluded bi- and multilingual students, but they also privileged a constrained set of epistemologies (cognition, developmentalism, psychology) and research methodologies (quantitative, correlational, experimental) that constrained study selection. So while the Carlo and colleagues' (2004) study was instructionally groundbreaking, it was methodologically aligned with developmental perspectives on literacy.

Here, more critical theorists began to openly take issue with reading research as overly White, monolingual, and methodologically constrained. One noteworthy clash between developmental and critical perspectives on literacy took place between 1999 and 2000, between James Gee and Catherine Snow in the pages of the *Journal of Literacy Research*. Snow, a developmentalist, was the lead author of *Preventing Reading Difficulties in Young Children*, while James Gee was well known for his critical theories around literacy as social practice, "new literacies," and a deep methodological expertise in discourse analysis. Gee (1999) was particularly critical of Snow and colleagues (1998) and argued that literacy (and literacies) is (are) inherently political, social, and cultural in nature. Gee thus lamented that the report ignored "an interdisciplinary effort that takes a sociocultural approach to language and literacy" (p. 355). Had such a focus been included in *Preventing Reading Difficulties in Young Children*, an entirely different report would have likely resulted. Snow (2000), for her part, responded that Gee had essentially misrepresented the purpose and exercise of the book, and his claims that all literacy was political was evident in "his frank misreadings of some aspects and improbable interpretations of other aspects of *Preventing Reading Difficulties*" (p. 119). This example is reminiscent of Fitzgerald's (2003) characterization of the disconnect between cognitive-psychological and sociocultural orientations in literacy research, with Snow and Gee hardly seeking to make connections between their adopted webs of theories.

It was during this time in the early 2000s that I was immersed in my own doctoral studies, focused on literacy and bilingualism. These types of disputes stuck out to me as interesting but largely unproductive, especially when the goal, ostensibly, was to improve literacy outcomes for children. It seemed to me that humans do in fact develop over time, and that development surely has included the skills, habits, and strategies that comprise literacies. But that development also occurs in specific intersectional contexts in which structural realities of racism, linguicism, sexism, and ableism interact with that development. While everyone seemed to essentially agree on this point in theory, disagreements were rampant when it came to how to study and operationalize domains and dimensions of literacy. It was truly perplexing. Since those early days, I have made it a priority to wrestle with those "interconnected webs of theories" that characterize both developmental and critical perspectives in literacy. The next sections provide overviews of both perspectives as they are applied to multilingual literacy contexts.

Critical Literacy Perspectives

Critical literacy perspectives are at least partially rooted in critical race theory (CRT) which emerged from the field of legal studies (Crenshaw, 1989) and subsequently made its way into education studies (Ladson-Billings & Tate, 1995). Those taking critical literacy perspectives are keen to acknowledge that race and racism are pervasive elements of U.S. life, including education and literacy. Lee and Lee (2020) provide a comprehensive review of CRT as it applies to literacy research, and articulate five core tenets that guide CRT: (1) centrality of race and racism, (2) Whiteness as property, (3) interest convergence, (4) the role of counternarratives in challenging majoritarian views and notions of neutrality, (5) centering the experiences of people of color in counternarratives, and (6) a commitment to justice and liberation (pp. 82–83). Jones and Proctor (2024) more broadly described criticality "as reflecting skills and dispositions necessary for problematizing and addressing sociocultural, political, and material realities manifested through languaging, language ideologies, and education" (p. 31). Relatedly, Thomas and colleagues (2020) refer specifically to critical literacy as an effort in "centering the margins" and to focus on expressions of power "because the idea of reading from a critical lens was first ignited by people from the margins—including children and youth—not represented within the official discourses and curricula of schooling itself" (p. 425). In my work on multilingual literacy, two critical perspectives have been particularly influential: the third space and translanguaging.

Third Space

At the same time when Gee (1999) and Snow (2000) were arguing over the ecological validity of *Preventing Reading Difficulties in Young Children*, Gutiérrez and colleagues (1999), building on Bhabha's (1994) location of culture, Vygotsky's (1978) zone of proximal development, and Engeström's (1987) cultural-historical activity theory, introduced the "third space" into the literacy world, where "hybrid language activity and language practices serve as triggers of transformation or expansion for literacy learning" (p. 289). In education, the third space exists as a place and a location in which participants achieve distance from the monolingual and standardized norms of typical schooling sites and practices. The third space can be planned or it can emerge unplanned. Either way, the third space is made manifest when students are engaged in contesting societal power relations, collective learning, and movement toward personal and intellectual transformation.

While Jones (2020) notes that most "literacy curricula, especially with bi/multilinguals, have often used models of explicit instruction that is teacher-centered and monologic in nature" (p. 99), third space theory has in fact been taken up in literacy and teacher education research, with explicit attention to multilingualism. Empirical depictions of the third space are exclusively qualitative in design, with few participants, and largely ethnographic data sources (i.e., interviews, observations, field notes, and artifacts), that use grounded and thematic approaches in service of theoretically rigorous analyses.

Despite the relatively low volume of empirical research, studies that engage third space theory include a broad developmental range. At early childhood, Levy (2008) used third space theory to explore how 4-year-old children constructed their own reading identities. The measures used were play and conversational interactions with children, which created empirical third spaces that allowed the researchers to center students' voices and funds of knowledge (Moll et al., 1992) to articulate their senses of self. At the elementary grades, Jones and Proctor (2025) described a design-based approach to developing a language-based reading curriculum through dialogic instruction, whose characteristics mapped to a third space in which two small groups of bilingual fourth and fifth graders engaged with rules, goals, tools, and divisions of labor (Greeno & Engström, 2014) that resulted in a unique third space of "critical metalinguistic engagement." Martínez and Morales (2014) operationalized the third space among sixth-grade Spanish–English bilingual students as "the creativity and skill embedded in bilingual Latin@ students' transgressive wordplay . . . as they make use of their full linguistic repertoires to construct particular identities within the context of social interaction" (pp. 337–338).

Research in third space has also focused on adolescent literacy (Benson, 2010; Gutiérrez, 2008; Moje et al., 2004). For example, Moje and colleagues (2004) applied third space pedagogy in their work with a group of Spanish–English bilingual middle school adolescents in a science curriculum development project. In identifying different forms of Discourse in the students' lives (specifically, family, community, peer, and popular culture) Moje and associates were able to examine when and where these overlapped within the science classroom. The findings suggested that third spaces can be fleeting or flimsy if left untended, and that teachers must make conscious efforts to foster them. Finally, Weippert and colleagues (2018) operationalized third space theory in an undergraduate teacher education course through an activity of cross-text comparisons of children's literature, and Flores and García (2013) merged third space theory with translanguaging (see below) to understand how two bilingual teachers created linguistic third spaces through their own translanguaging practices.

Translanguaging

Another significant critical multilingual literacy perspective that has received much empirical attention is translanguaging. A common misconception about translanguaging is that it is simply a new term for code-switching between two discrete languages, such as Spanish and English. While it is certainly accurate to note that such switching can be emblematic of translanguaging, the concept is much richer than simply moving between two languages.

Current understandings of translanguaging are derived from García and Wei's (2014) denominalization of the word *language*; that is, our common understanding of *language* is that it is a noun that can be counted and named such that a Spanish–English bilingual individual is considered to have two languages, learned either sequentially or simultaneously. García and Wei, however, proposed that we think of *language* as a verb that includes not just spoken and named written languages but also semiotic systems such as signing, gestures, media, and other nonverbal means of expression and representation. In this sense, we language multimodally, and as such, languaging becomes a strong reflection of who we are as individuals and social beings.

García and her colleagues over the years have worked to integrate languaging theory specifically into debates on bilingualism, contesting traditional views that treat languages as discrete psycholinguistic systems that share varying degrees of overlap depending on the languages in question (e.g., Cummins, 1979; Geva & Siegel, 2000; Proctor et al., 2010). To do this, they added the prefix *trans-* to the root *languaging*, which gets to *translanguaging*, which reflects how multilingual people "engage in selection of linguistic and other semiotic features within their repertoire in order to communicate effectively and not simply in the selection of two or more autonomous languages" (García, 2018, p. 884). In addition to multimodal communication, translanguaging is theorized as a distinctly critical phenomenon in that it exists to challenge majoritarian views of language, center the multilingual experience, and promote justice and liberation.

As an educational phenomenon, translanguaging has been, and continues to be, quite well studied. Ossa Parra and Proctor (2023) reviewed the extant literature on translanguaging and literacy, proposing a "translanguaging continuum." Their analysis focused on García and colleagues' (2017) notion of translanguaging as a linguistic *corriente*, which is the Spanish word for *current*. The *corriente* is a metaphor for "the underlying fluidity, resistance, and creativity in students' language practices as they draw from their full communicative repertoires to negotiate meaning and express understanding" (Ossa Parra & Proctor, 2023, p. 917). Ossa Parra and Proctor described three broad types of translanguaging literacy research vis-à-vis the *corriente*. On one end of the continuum, the most common type of translanguaging literacy research is labeled as "listening to the corriente," in which multilingual students' languages and cultures are documented as important components of classroom life. In the middle of the continuum, another commonly studied domain is "channeling the corriente," which documents how teachers "actively foster translanguaging practices to ensure that their multilingual students meet content and language curricular expectations" (p. 920). Many of these channeling studies apply ethnographic approaches in which researchers are embedded in classrooms over time. Finally, a less well-studied domain of translanguaging research is "flowing with the corriente." This line of research documents the deliberate design and implementation of curricula and instructional approaches that take multilingual students' languaging and cultures as the centerpieces of instructional design. In so doing, an explicit goal is the creation of linguistic third spaces "where students can experiment with language, bring their diverse sources of knowledge into the classroom, and develop their confidence and agency as active participants in the classroom community" (p. 921).

Developmental Perspectives

Developmental literacy research as it relates to multilingual learners treats language and teaching much differently than critical perspectives. Developmental literacy research tends to be grounded in psychological and cognitive orientations, such that the empirical concerns lie primarily "in the head," and center on the quantification of different processes and outcomes. Also, the word *literacy* tends to also have a more constrained meaning. While from a critical perspective we have gotten the plural, *literacies*, as a way to conceptualize how different forms of being in the world can constitute literacy, developmental literacy perspectives tend to taper down to reading and writing as outcomes and the measurable subcomponents that predict them.

Developmental perspectives are typically cross-sectional or longitudinal, the former tending to focus on a specific developmental time (e.g., fourth grade) and the latter seeking to describe and predict change over time (e.g., second through fifth grade) through repeated administrations of assessments that tap a given construct. Whereas critical perspectives tend to operationalize theory qualitatively, developmental perspectives tend to operationalize theory quantitatively. And while there exist quite a few developmental theories of literacy, the simple view of reading (SVR; Gough & Tumner, 1986; Hoover & Gough, 1990) has arguably been, and continues to be, the most influential in developmental reading research. The SVR is also noteworthy for its multilingual applications, having been applied in English, as well as in multiple other languages, in addition to having supported our understanding of cross-linguistic relations in multilingual literacy. No other developmental theory of literacy can claim to have had such an impact.

Simple versus Complex

One might convincingly argue that the SVR is empirically popular because it is easy to operationalize and manipulate. Characterizing reading comprehension (RC) as predicted by just two component parts—decoding (D) and linguistic comprehension (LC)—Gough and Tumner (1986) and Hoover and Gough (1990) introduced the enduring SVR equation: $RC = D \times LC$. Here, if either D or LC is equal to 0, then RC is also 0. If one cannot decode words (D = 0), then one cannot read for comprehension. Furthermore, one cannot read for comprehension if one has no proficiency in the language of the text (LC = 0). Scarborough (2001) took these three components and rendered them in developmental context, describing that, over time, young readers' D skills become increasingly automatic, while their LC skills become increasingly strategic so as to make sense of the growing linguistic demands of text in the upper elementary and secondary grades.

There is no doubt that other theories of reading are more comprehensive than the SVR. One such example is Kintsch's (2004) construction–integration (CI) model. Taking adequate decoding processes as a given, CI focuses on the ways in which a reader constructs a "situation model" (what is going on in a text) by attending to the micro- and macrostructures of a text (construction) and making sense of them as a whole (integration) to generate the situation model. Unlike the SVR, this model attends to the nature of the text itself (its micro- and macrostructure), as well as the reader of that text, including how background knowledge plays a role in the process. In construction, we see the reader engaging text-based (vocabulary, semantics, syntax) and knowledge-based (background knowledge stored in long-term memory) construction processes. At the point of integration, the text propositions have been aligned with the reader's existing knowledge base and combine to create a network synthesis that begets a final text representation (Kintsch & Welsh, 2013). The CI model is complex, indeed Chomskian, in its propositions and deconstructions of text as a means by which to enter into the theory. Thus, as Kinstch (2004) put it, "[t]he problems faced by the researcher trying to model the formation of situation models are formidable" (p. 1284).

When reading theories are as dense as those proposed by Kintsch and others, it becomes difficult, if not untenable, to pursue them empirically in a way that would result in a research corpus that could be reliably drawn upon for making generalizations about reading and literacy development. By contrast, a theory of reading that comprises just three psychologically measurable constructs becomes intriguing because it is easy to model through multiple regression techniques (see, e.g., Hoover & Gough, 1990), and is also usable as a baseline control model to explore other variables' impact on reading comprehension, including fluency (Silverman et al., 2013), motivation (Proctor, Daley, et al., 2014), and executive function (Kieffer et al., 2021), to name just three.

An example of the ubiquity of the SVR can be seen in a meta-analysis by Quinn and Wagner (2018), in which they used meta-analytic structural equation modeling to explore the relative contributions of D and LC to RC. Their results reinforced the developmental relationships between D, LC, and RC by drawing on a sample of selected studies that included more than 1 million students. One would be hard pressed to identify another developmental theory of literacy that has garnered such replicative attention, or one that has advanced developmental perspectives on multilingual literacy.

Cross-Linguistics in Multilingual Reading

The developmental relationships between D, LC, and RC with multilingual learners warrant multilingual linguistic considerations. In monolingual literacy contexts, with monoliterate readers, there is a singular linguistic expectation (typically English in U.S. literacy teaching and research). However, with multilingual people, one cannot ignore the fact that multiple linguistic repertoires are at play. This distinguishing characteristic has spawned a good deal of "cross-linguistic" research that takes the SVR's three constructs (D, LC, RC) and models them not monolingually (i.e., only in English or some other language) but rather bilingually, in which D, LC, and RC are measured in two languages, resulting in six rather than three variables, which are then covaried with one another in different correlational configurations.

Part of what makes these studies interesting is that while the constructs under study are consistent (i.e., D, LC, RC), the ways in which they are operationalized for modeling varies. Proctor and Louick (2018) and Proctor and Zhang-Wu (2019) reviewed the extant research on cross-linguistic literacy, finding that the large majority of studies have been conducted combining Spanish and English, but other correlational and causal literacy research has targeted English in combination with American Sign Language (Hoffmeister et al., 2022), Arabic (Abu-Rabia & Siegel, 2002), spoken Mandarin/written Chinese (Pasquarella et al., 2015; Wang, Cheng, et al., 2006), French (Côté et al., 2021), Hebrew (Bialystok et al., 2005), Kiswahili (Wawire & Zuilkowski, 2020), Korean (Kim, 2009; Wang, Park, et al., 2006), Malay and Tamil (Dixon et al., 2012), Samoan (Hemsley et al., 2013), and Turkish (Prevoo et al., 2015). D-oriented studies tend to focus on phonological and phonemic awareness, orthographic awareness and word reading. LC studies tend to target vocabulary (for an overview, see Proctor & Louick, 2018), morphological awareness, and sometimes syntax, while RC studies focus on how SVR component skills (D, LC, RC) in one language are associated with each other (Hoffmeister et al., 2022; Leider et al., 2013) or how D and LC in one language predict reading comprehension development in another (Lee & Schallert, 1997; Wawire & Zuilkowski, 2020). Across the extant cross-linguistic literature, variation in the ways D, LC, and RC are operationalized is considerable, with theoretical and empirical implications.

Theoretically, this line of work supports a set of cross-linguistic hypotheses that become relevant for thinking about literacy instruction. Geva and Siegel's (2000) "script dependence hypothesis" is supported by the research. Specifically, this hypothesis suggests an inverse relationship between the orthographic distance between a bilingual's two languages and the strength of the correlation between decoding in those two languages. D skills in a Spanish–English reader, for example, are more likely to overlap cross-linguistically given the common sound–symbol relationships, than they would with a Chinese–English reader, whose languages share is no orthographic overlap (see Bialystok et al., 2005).

Along LC lines, the enduring "linguistic interdependence" hypothesis (Cummins, 1979) also appears to hold. This hypothesis suggests that well developed language skills in one's first language (e.g., Spanish) are likely to positively affect development of language and literacy skills in their second language (e.g., English). For example, Spanish vocabulary knowledge has been shown to predict small amounts of variance in English RC (Nakamoto et al., 2008; Proctor et al., 2006), and cognate awareness is a vehicle for cross-linguistic associations when discrete languages (Spanish and English) have a base language (Latin) in common (Jiménez et al., 1995, 1996; Proctor & Mo, 2009).

As a matter of synthesis, Proctor and colleagues (2010) proposed the "interdependence continuum," a holistic model of bilingual reading in which the cross-linguistic associations between D, LC, and RC are theorized along a continuum in which more constrained skills (e.g., D) are likely to correlate cross-linguistically, especially if they share a common orthography. Simultaneously, LC skills are hypothesized to have relatively low cross-linguistic associations because language, unlike D, has no asymptote and is more multiply determined. However, if the languages in question share a linguistic family (e.g., Kanji, Latin), then there is more potential for cross-language associations. In comparison, RC combines both constrained (D) and unconstrained (LC) components. It also involves important competencies, such as applying reading strategies that are not linguistic but cognitive in nature, which makes it more robust to cross-linguistic overlap (Jiménez et al., 1995, 1996), particularly as language proficiency increases (Lee & Schallert, 1997). As such, RC is subject to factors that both promote and inhibit cross-linguistic covariance, and is thus hypothesized to reside in the middle of expected effects. The continuum of interdependence model was supported by Prevoo and colleagues (2015), who further suggested that the way in which a given construct is measured for study also has an effect on the relative strength or weakness of the cross-linguistic association.

Curriculum as Intersection

As the previous reviews suggest, critical and developmental perspectives differ in theoretical orientation, the nature and type of research questions asked, and the analytic approaches used to answer those questions. But the reality is that they can work well together, especially when it comes to thinking about multilingual learners and curriculum. While there has been some attention to merging the perspectives (e.g., Packer & Tappan, 2001), we rarely see critical and developmental literacy researchers coming together to contemplate, merge, and interrogate overlapping notions of criticality and developmentalism.

One noteworthy standout is the work of Jamaal Matthews and Francesca López (2020), who, as educational psychologists, work to infuse what they call "race reimaging" in educational psychology. In their empirical and editorial work, they urge developmentalists to move "beyond simply increasing the representation of disenfranchised people and groups and authentically honoring their experiences in our research . . . which ultimately supports greater precision in theory building, closer attention to nuance, culturally appropriate applications of psychological interventions in education, and stronger research-to-practice links" (p. 3). López (2017), for example, race-reimaged notions of teacher expectancies in predicting the reading performance of Latinx children, finding that teacher expectations in fact predicted reading outcomes, but those expectations were culturally derived such that the combination of teachers' critical consciousness along with high expectations revealed "a productive belief system that predicted increased reading achievement" (Matthews & López, 2020, p. 3).

In their work, Matthews and López (2020) speak specifically to "psychological interventions in education" (p. 3), but the same spirit applies to pedagogical interventions in literacy curricula. A rather sad reality these days is that publisher-created literacy curricula are in far more need of swift intervention than are the teachers and students who must endure them. In my experience, these curricula rarely attend to issues of developmentalism beyond monolingual views of language and literacy, and because the very notion of criticality is so politically scrutinized, it is all but absent from these curricula. In my work, I join practice-based researchers who are engaged in developmentally driven efforts to design curricula that attend to multilingual literacy (e.g., Jiménez et al., 2015; Lesaux et al., 2014; Snow et al., 2009), as well as my critical colleagues whose work recognizes that multilingual children (and their teachers) bring unique linguistic repertoires and identities to the receptive and expressive tasks of literacy instruction (Flores & García, 2013; García, 2020; Gutiérrez et al., 1999). The Cultivating Linguistic Awareness for Voice and Equity in Schools (CLAVES) curriculum represents my efforts, along with those of my long-term collaborators (Jones & Proctor, 2024; Proctor et al., 2020, 2021, 2023; Silverman et al., 2021), to integrate developmental and critical literacy perspectives into curriculum design and instructional research.

CLAVES

The intersection between criticality and developmentalism has informed the multilingual literacy curriculum work that my colleagues and I have undertaken in recent years. Specifically, from 2014 to 2017, we developed and evaluated a language-based reading curriculum called CLAVES (see *www.clavescurriculum.net*; Proctor, Silverman, et al., 2014) using tenets of both perspectives. CLAVES is Spanish for *keys* or *clues*.

Developmentally, we tapped a host of theory and research from literacy, bilingualism, and second-language acquisition that used correlational and experimental research designs to draw some clear conclusions around the importance of language components (vocabulary, morphology, syntax) in predicting RC for multilingual students (see Proctor et al., 2012, 2017; Silverman et al., 2015), along with the importance of implementing instructional approaches that leveraged not only language components but also how talk and argumentation can promote complex reasoning around text in schools (Clark et al., 2003). Theories of bilingual literacy (e.g., Cummins, 1979; Prevoo et al., 2015; Proctor et al., 2010) also informed our thinking about multilingualism and multilingual learners, and indeed at the time of conceptualizing CLAVES there existed good empirical evidence that supported the relationships between home language proficiency and second-language literacy outcomes among bilingual children (August & Shanahan, 2006).

Critically, we addressed Lee and Lee's (2020) tenets of critical race theory at the points of curriculum development and implementation—specifically, text selection, as well as unit and lesson design focused on the centrality of race in everyday life and on centering the experiences of multilingual people of color, with a commitment to themes of justice. This was addressed in part by carefully selecting texts that were representative of the students reading them, as well as issues and topics of race, language, environmental justice, and universal rights. In addition, CLAVES was designed as a small-group (four to six students per group) instructional model to promote dialogic interactions that centered student talk (Reznitskaya et al., 2009), allowed for fluid languaging practices (García & Wei, 2014), and focused on linguistic awareness (Beeman & Urow, 2013), as well as comprehension (Jiménez et al., 1995, 1996), all with the hope of creating something akin to linguistic third spaces (García & Flores, 2013; Guitérrez et al., 1999) that promoted students' language and literacy achievement.

In a quasi-experimental evaluation, the CLAVES curriculum was implemented by a group of 22 fourth- and fifth-grade teachers who taught CLAVES to small groups of students ($n = 119$), with a comparison "business as usual" (BAU) group ($n = 120$) that received typical small-group literacy instruction. Controlling for pretest performance, we found that CLAVES students outperformed their BAU counterparts on measures of reading comprehension and linguistic awareness (Hedges's $g = 0.166$ and 0.248, respectively; Proctor et al., 2020), as well as on features of argumentative writing, including argumentation and counterargumentation (effect sizes = 0.19 and 0.20, respectively; Silverman et al., 2021).

Toward a Critical Developmental Curriculum Framework

In conclusion, the nexus of critical and developmental perspectives in curriculum can function as a framework for designing or interrogating curricula. Key dimensions of such a framework, and questions to ask, include the following:

1. *Text selection.* Does the curriculum include representative texts that provide windows, mirrors, and sliding glass doors (Bishop, 1990; McNair & Edwards, 2021) that engage students in issues related to equity and justice?
2. *Attention to multilingualism.* Does the curriculum have an overt multilingual focus that recognizes language as varied and multifaceted, specifically

with respect to how it treats instruction around key components of literacy, such as foundational skills and language comprehension (Ascenzi-Moreno, 2024)?
3. *Dialogic instruction.* Does the curriculum include instructional and structural/grouping approaches that seek to leverage student talk and build community around selected texts, with an understanding that "talk" is varied and multifaceted (Gutiérrez, 2008; Gutiérrez et al., 1999; Ossa Parra et al., 2016)?
4. *Multimodality.* Does the curriculum seek to leverage multiple modalities, beyond printed text, that provide alternative entrées into knowledge building and expression of ideas (Proctor et al., 2021)?

These four domains of inquiry can help us better create and adopt literacy curricula that respect and engage critical and developmental perspectives in multilingual literacy. As student multilingualism continues to flourish across the United States, we need to be in a state of active cultivation of language to foster literacy and identity, and push curriculum to keep pace with the strength and brilliance of the students we aim to serve.

REFERENCES

Abu-Rabia, S., & Siegel, L. S. (2002). Reading, syntactic, orthographic, and working memory skills of bilingual Arabic-English speaking Canadian children. *Journal of Psycholinguistic Research, 31,* 661–678.

Ascenzi-Moreno, L. (2024). Toward a multilingual perspective on reading: Aligning emergent bilinguals' resources with theories of reading and implications for instruction. *Reading Teacher, 77*(6), 918–926.

August, D., & Shanahan, T. (Eds.). (2006). *Developing literacy in second-language learners: Report of the national literacy panel on language minority children and youth.* Erlbaum.

Beck, I. L., McKeown, M. G., & Kucan, L. (2013). *Bringing words to life: Robust vocabulary instruction.* Guilford Press.

Beeman, K., & Urow, C. (2013). *Teaching for biliteracy: Strengthening bridges between languages.* Caslon.

Benson, S. (2010). "I don't know if that'd be English or not": Third space theory and literacy instruction. *Journal of Adolescent and Adult Literacy, 53*(7), 555–563.

Bhabha, H. (1994). *The location of culture.* Routledge.

Bialystok, E., Luk, G., & Kwan, E. (2005). Bilingualism, biliteracy, and learning to read: Interactions among languages and writing systems. *Scientific Studies of Reading, 9*(1), 43–61.

Bishop, R. S. (1990). Mirrors, windows, and sliding glass doors. *Perspectives, 6*(3), ix–xi.

Carlo, M. S., August, D., McLaughlin, B., Snow, C. E., Dressler, C., Lippman, D. N., . . . White, C. E. (2004). Closing the gap: Addressing the vocabulary needs of English-language learners in bilingual and mainstream classrooms. *Reading Research Quarterly, 39*(2), 188–215.

Clark, A. M., Anderson, R. C., Kuo, L. J., Kim, I. H., Archodidou, A., & Nguyen-Jahiel,

K. (2003). Collaborative reasoning: Expanding ways for children to talk and think in school. *Educational Psychology Review, 15*, 181–198.

Côté, M. F., Savage, R., & Petscher, Y. (2021). Cross linguistic transfer of literacy skills between English and French among grade 1 students attending French immersion programs. *Scientific Studies of Reading, 25*(5), 383–396.

Crenshaw, K. (1989). *Demarginalizing the intersection of race and sex: A black feminist critique of antidiscrimination doctrine, feminist theory, and antiracist politics.* University of Chicago Legal Forum.

Cummins, J. (1979). Linguistic interdependence and the educational development of bilingual children. *Review of Educational Research, 49*(2), 222–251.

Dixon, L. Q., Chuang, H. K., & Quiroz, B. (2012). English phonological awareness in bilinguals: A cross-linguistic study of Tamil, Malay and Chinese English-language learners. *Journal of Research in Reading, 35*(4), 372–392.

Durgunoğlu, A. Y., Nagy, W. E., & Hancin-Bhatt, B. J. (1993). Cross-language transfer of phonological awareness. *Journal of Educational Psychology, 85*(3), 453–465.

Engeström, Y. (1987). *Learning by expanding* (2nd ed.). Cambridge University Press.

Fitzgerald, J. (2003). Multilingual reading theory. *Reading Research Quarterly, 38*(1), 118–122.

Flores, N., & García, O. (2013). Linguistic third spaces in education: Teachers' translanguaging across the bilingual continuum. In D. Little, C. Leung, & P. Van Avermaet (Eds.), *Managing diversity in education: Key issues and some responses* (pp. 243–256). Multilingual Matters.

García, O. (2018). The multiplicities of multilingual interaction. *International Journal of Bilingual Education and Bilingualism, 21*(7), 881–891.

García, O. (2020). Translanguaging and Latinx bilingual readers. *Reading Teacher, 73*(5), 557–562.

García, O., Ibarra Johnson, S., & Seltzer, K. (2017). *The translanguaging classroom: Leveraging bilingualism for learning.* Caslon.

García, O., & Wei, L. (2014). *Translanguaging: Language, bilingualism, and education.* Palgrave Macmillan.

Gee, J. P. (1999). Critical issues: Reading and the new literacy studies: Reframing the national academy of sciences report on reading. *Journal of Literacy Research, 31*(3), 355–374.

Geva, E., & Siegel, L. S. (2000). Orthographic and cognitive factors in the concurrent development of basic reading skills in two languages. *Reading and Writing, 12*, 1–30.

Gough, P. B., & Tunmer, W. E. (1986). Decoding, reading, and reading disability. *Remedial and Special Education, 7*(1), 6–10.

Greeno, J. G., & Engeström, Y. (2014). Learning in activity. In R. K. Sawyer (Ed.), *The Cambridge handbook of the learning sciences* (pp. 128–150). Cambridge University Press.

Gutiérrez, K. D. (2008). Developing a sociocritical literacy in the third space. *Reading Research Quarterly, 43*(2), 148–164.

Gutiérrez, K., Baquedano-López, P., & Tejeda, C. (1999). Rethinking diversity: Hybridity and hybrid language practices in the third space. *Mind, Culture, and Activity, 6*, 286–303.

Hemsley, G., Holm, A., & Dodd, B. (2013). Conceptual distance and word learning: Patterns of acquisition in Samoan–English bilingual children. *Journal of Child Language, 40*(4), 799–820.

Hoffmeister, R., Henner, J., Caldwell-Harris, C., & Novogrodsky, R. (2022). Deaf children's ASL vocabulary and ASL syntax knowledge supports English knowledge. *Journal of Deaf Studies and Deaf Education, 27*(1), 37–47.

Hoover, W. A., & Gough, P. B. (1990). The simple view of reading. *Reading and Writing, 2*, 127–160.

Huckin, T., Haynes, M., & Coady, J. (Eds.). (1995). *Second language reading and vocabulary learning.* Ablex.

Jiménez, R. T., David, S., Fagan, K., Risko, V. J., Pacheco, M., Pray, L., & Gonzales, M. (2015). Using translation to drive conceptual development for students becoming literate in English as an additional language. *Research in the Teaching of English, 49*(3), 248–271.

Jiménez, R. T., García, G. E., & Pearson, P. D. (1995). Three children, two languages, and strategic reading: Case studies in bilingual/monolingualreading. *American Educational Research Journal, 32*, 31–61.

Jiménez, R. T., García, G. E., & Pearson, P. D. (1996). The reading strategies of bilingual Latina/o students who are successful English readers: Opportunities and obstacles. *Reading Research Quarterly, 31*(1), 90–112.

Jones, R. L. (2020). *(Meta)Languaging: Exploring metalinguistic engagement within a language-based reading intervention for upper elementary bi/multilingual students.* Unpublished doctoral dissertation, Boston College.

Jones, R. L., & Proctor, C. P. (2024). Pursuing language through critical metalinguistic engagement. *Harvard Educational Review, 94*(1), 25–54.

Jones, R. L., & Proctor, C. P. (2025). *Pursuing language and metalinguistics in K–12 classrooms: A framework for critical engagement.* Routledge.

Kieffer, M. J., Mancilla-Martinez, J., & Logan, J. K. (2021). Executive functions and English reading comprehension growth in Spanish–English bilingual adolescents. *Journal of Applied Developmental Psychology, 73*, Article 101238.

Kim, Y. S. (2009). Crosslinguistic influence on phonological awareness for Korean–English bilingual children. *Reading and Writing, 22*, 843–861.

Kintsch, W. (2004). The construction–integration model of text comprehension and its implications for instruction. *Theoretical Models and Processes of Reading, 5*, 1270–1328.

Kintsch, W., & Welsch, D. M. (2013). The construction–integration model: A framework for studying memory for text. In W. E. Hockley & S. Lewandowsky (Eds.), *Relating theory and data* (pp. 381–400). Psychology Press.

Ladson-Billings, G., & Tate, W. (1995). Toward a critical race theory of education. *Teachers College Record, 97*(1), 47–67.

Lee, A. Y., & Lee, A. J. (2020). Critical race methodologies. In M. H. Mallette & N. K. Duke (Eds.), *Literacy research methodologies* (3rd ed., pp. 81–101). Guilford Press.

Lee, J. W., & Schallert, D. L. (1997). The relative contribution of L2 language proficiency and L1 reading ability to L2 reading performance: A test of the threshold hypothesis in an EFL context. *TESOL Quarterly, 31*(4), 713–739.

Leider, C. M., Proctor, C. P., Silverman, R. D., & Harring, J. R. (2013). Examining the role of vocabulary depth, cross-linguistic transfer, and types of reading measures on the reading comprehension of Latino bilinguals in elementary school. *Reading and Writing, 26*, 1459–1485.

Lesaux, N. K., Kieffer, M. J., Kelley, J. G., & Harris, J. R. (2014). Effects of academic vocabulary instruction for linguistically diverse adolescents: Evidence from a randomized field trial. *American Educational Research Journal, 51*(6), 1159–1194.

Levy, R. (2008). "Third spaces" are interesting places: Applying "third space theory" to nursery-aged children's constructions of themselves as readers. *Journal of Early Childhood Literacy, 8*(1), 43–66.

López, F. A. (2017). Altering the trajectory of the self-fulfilling prophecy: Asset-based pedagogy and classroom dynamics. *Journal of Teacher Education, 68*(2), 193–212.

Martínez, R. A., & Morales, P. Z. (2014). ¿Puras Groserías?: Rethinking the role of profanity and graphic humor in Latin@ students' bilingual wordplay. *Anthropology and Education Quarterly, 45*(4), 337–354.

Matthews, J. S., & López, F. (2020). Race-reimaging educational psychology research: Investigating constructs through the lens of race and culture. *Contemporary Educational Psychology, 61*, Article 101878.

McNair, J. C., & Edwards, P. A. (2021). The lasting legacy of Rudine Sims Bishop: Mirrors, windows, sliding glass doors, and more. *Literacy Research: Theory, Method, and Practice, 70*(1), 202–212.

Migration Policy Institute. (2021). *Young dual language learners in the United States and by state.* www.migrationpolicy.org/programs/data-hub/charts/us-state-profiles-young-dlls.

Moje, E. B., Ciechanowski, K. M., Kramer, K., Ellis, L., Carrillo, R., & Collazo, T. (2004). Working toward third space in content area literacy: An examination of everyday funds of knowledge and discourse. *Reading Research Quarterly, 39*(1), 38–70.

Moll, L., Amanti, C., Neff, D., & Gonzalez, N. (1992). Funds of knowledge for teaching: Using a qualitative approach to connect homes and classrooms. In N. Gonzalez, L. C. Moll, & C. Amanti (Eds.), *Funds of knowledge: Theorizing practices in households, communities, and classrooms* (pp. 71–87). Routledge.

Nakamoto, J., Lindsey, K. A., & Manis, F. R. (2008). A cross-linguistic investigation of English language learners' reading comprehension in English and Spanish. *Scientific Studies of Reading, 12*(4), 351–371.

National Education Association. (2020, July). *English language learners.* www.nea.org/resource-library/english-language-learners.

National Reading Panel, National Institute of Child Health and Human Development. (2000). *Teaching children to read: An evidence-based assessment of the scientific research literature on reading and its implications for reading instruction: Reports of the subgroups.* National Institute of Child Health and Human Development, National Institutes of Health.

Ossa Parra, M., & Proctor, C. P. (2023). The translanguaging pedagogies continuum. *Journal of Education, 203*(4), 917–924.

Ossa Parra, M., Wagner, C., Proctor, C. P., Leighton, C. M., Robertson, D. A., Paratore, J. R., & Ford-Connors, E. (2016). Dialogic reasoning: Supporting emergent bilingual students' language and literacy development. In C. P. Proctor, A. Boardman, & E. Hiebert (Eds.), *Teaching emergent bilingual students: Flexible approaches in an era of new standards* (pp. 119–137). Guilford Press.

Packer, M. J., & Tappan, M. B. (Eds.). (2001). *Cultural and critical perspectives on human development.* State University of New York Press.

Pasquarella, A., Chen, X., Gottardo, A., & Geva, E. (2015). Cross-language transfer of word reading accuracy and word reading fluency in Spanish-English and Chinese-English bilinguals: Script-universal and script-specific processes. *Journal of Educational Psychology, 107*(1), 96–110.

Patel, L. (2023, September 25). *What I learned from debating the Science of Reading more than 20 years ago is still true.* https://decolonizing.net/2023/09/25/what-i-learned-from-debating-the-science-of-reading-more-than-20-years-ago-is-still-true.

Prevoo, M. J., Malda, M., Emmen, R. A., Yeniad, N., & Mesman, J. (2015). A context-dependent view on the linguistic interdependence hypothesis: Language use and SES as potential moderators. *Language Learning, 65*(2), 449–469.

Proctor, C. P., August, D., Carlo, M. S., & Snow, C. (2006). The intriguing role of Spanish language vocabulary knowledge in predicting English reading comprehension. *Journal of Educational Psychology, 98*(1), 159–169.

Proctor, C. P., August, D., Snow, C., & Barr, C. D. (2010). The interdependence continuum: A perspective on the nature of Spanish–English bilingual reading comprehension. *Bilingual Research Journal, 33*(1), 5–20.

Proctor, C. P., Daley, S., Louick, R., Leider, C. M., & Gardner, G. L. (2014). How motivation and engagement predict reading comprehension among native English-speaking and English-learning middle school students with disabilities in a remedial reading curriculum. *Learning and Individual Differences, 36*, 76–83.

Proctor, C. P., Harring, J. R., & Silverman, R. D. (2017). Linguistic interdependence between Spanish language and English language and reading: A longitudinal exploration from second through fifth grade. *Bilingual Research Journal, 40*, 372–391.

Proctor, C. P., Kieffer, M. J., Silverman, R. D., Coleman, A., & Yu, Q. (2023, April 15). *Same curriculum, different approach: Case studies of teachers' implementation of a language-based reading curriculum for multilingual learners.* Paper presented at the annual meeting of the American Education Research Association, Chicago.

Proctor, C. P., & Louick, R. (2018). Development of vocabulary knowledge and its relationship with reading comprehension among emergent bilingual children: An overview. In A. Bar-On & D. Ravid (Eds.), *Handbook of communication disorders: Theoretical, empirical, and applied linguistics perspectives* (pp. 643–666). De Gruyter Mouton.

Proctor, C. P., & Mo, E. (2009). The relationship between cognate awareness and English comprehension among Spanish–English bilingual fourth grade students. *TESOL Quarterly, 43*(1), 126–136.

Proctor, C. P., Silverman, R. D., & Harring, J. R. (2014). *The CLAVES Intervention Project: Developing a supplemental intervention for comprehension, linguistic awareness, and vocabulary in English for Spanish speakers* (Award #R305A140114). Institute of Education Sciences.

Proctor, C. P., Silverman, R. D., Harring, J. R., Jones, R. L., & Hartranft, A. M. (2020). Teaching bilingual learners: Effects of a language-based reading intervention on academic language and reading comprehension in grades 4 and 5. *Reading Research Quarterly, 55*, 95–122.

Proctor, C. P., Silverman, R. D., Harring, J. R., & Montecillo, C. (2012). The role of vocabulary depth in predicting reading comprehension among English monolingual and Spanish–English bilingual children in elementary school. *Reading and Writing, 25*, 1635–1664.

Proctor, C. P., Silverman, R. D., & Jones, R. L. (2021). Centering language and student voice in multilingual literacy instruction. *Reading Teacher, 75*, 255–267.

Proctor, C. P. & Zhang-Wu, Q. (2019). Cross-linguistic relations among bilingual and biliterate learners: Interdisciplinary perspectives and convergences. In V. Grøver, P. Uccelli, M. Rowe, & E. Lieven (Eds.), *Learning through language: Toward an educationally informed theory of language learning* (pp. 218–234). Cambridge University Press.

Quinn, J. M., & Wagner, R. K. (2018). Using meta-analytic structural equation modeling to study developmental change in relations between language and literacy. *Child Development, 89*(6), 1956–1969.

Reznitskaya, A., Kuo, L. J., Clark, A. M., Miller, B., Jadallah, M., Anderson, R. C., & Nguyen-Jahiel, K. (2009). Collaborative reasoning: A dialogic approach to group discussions. *Cambridge Journal of Education, 39*(1), 29–48.

Scarborough, H. S. (2001). Connecting early language and literacy to later reading (dis)abilities: Evidence, theory, and practice. In S. B. Neuman & D. K. Dickinson (Eds.), *Handbook of early literacy research* (Vol. 1, pp. 97–110). Guilford Press.

Silverman, R. D., Proctor, C. P., Harring, J. R., Hartranft, A. M., Doyle, B., & Zelinke, S. B. (2015). Language skills and reading comprehension in English monolingual and Spanish-English bilingual children in grades 2–5. *Reading and Writing, 28*, 1381–1405.

Silverman, R. D. Proctor, C. P., Harring, J. R., Taylor, K. S., Johnson, E. M., Jones, R. L., & Lee, Y. (2021). The effect of a language and literacy intervention on upper elementary bilingual students' argumentative writing. *Elementary School Journal, 122*, 208–232.

Silverman, R. D., Speece, D. L., Harring, J. R., & Ritchey, K. D. (2013). Fluency has a role in the simple view of reading. *Scientific Studies of Reading, 17*(2), 108–133.

Snow, C. E. (2000). On the limits of reframing: Rereading the National Academy of Sciences report on reading. *Journal of Literacy Research, 32*(1), 113–120.

Snow, C. E., Burns, M. S., & Griffin, P. (1998). *Preventing reading difficulties in young children*. National Research Council.

Snow, C. E., Lawrence, J. F., & White, C. (2009). Generating knowledge of academic language among urban middle school students. *Journal of Research on Educational Effectiveness, 2*(4), 325–344.

Thomas, E. E., Bean-Folkes, J., & Coleman, J. J. (2020). Restorying critical literacies. In E. B. Moje, P. P. Afflerbach, P. Enciso, & N. K. Lesaux (Eds.), *Handbook of reading research* (Vol. V, pp. 424–435). Routledge.

Vygotsky, L. S. (1978). *Mind in society: The development of higher psychological processes*. Harvard University Press.

Wang, M., Cheng, C., & Chen, S. W. (2006). Contribution of morphological awareness to Chinese-English biliteracy acquisition. *Journal of Educational Psychology, 98*(3), 542–553.

Wang, M., Park, Y., & Lee, K. R. (2006). Korean-English biliteracy acquisition: Cross-language phonological and orthographic transfer. *Journal of Educational Psychology, 98*(1), 148–158.

Wawire, B. A., & Zuilkowski, S. S. (2020). The role of vocabulary and decoding language skills in reading comprehension: A cross-linguistic perspective. *International Multilingual Research Journal, 15*(1), 23–42.

Weippert, T. L., Domke, L. M., & Apol, L. (2018). Creating a third space through intertextuality: Using children's literature to develop prospective teachers' critical literacy. *Journal of Language and Literacy Education, 14*(2), Article n2.

CHAPTER 5

The Language of Learning
Academic Vocabulary Development and Comprehension

Joshua Lawrence
Rebecca Knoph
Åste Mjelve Hagen

In this chapter, we present a broad conceptualization of the language of learning and connect it to the literature on academic vocabulary and ongoing research within our research team. First, we use recent empirical advances to outline which words are learned at different ages. Next, we review work on the relationship between vocabulary and reading development. Last, we review research on vocabulary instruction and the difficulties associated with learning different kinds of words. Along the way, we explore the connection between vocabulary and reading development, and identify the types of words that facilitate learning increasingly complex content. Additionally, we discuss key arguments that there are significant structures in vocabulary development that can guide us in identifying important words and how best to support their learning.

Vocabulary knowledge is one of the best predictors of student reading comprehension (Cromley & Azevedo, 2007; Quinn et al., 2015), correlates with content-area reading (Townsend et al., 2012), and is at the heart of prominent models of reading (Perfetti & Hart, 2002). In a foundational series of studies, Beck, Perfetti, and McKeown (1982) and McKeown, Beck, Omanson, and Perfetti (1983) showed that robust, long-term vocabulary instruction significantly improved students' reading comprehension. Despite the widespread evidence of its importance, supporting vocabulary development so students can learn from text is not at all simple. One reason vocabulary is an interesting and challenging area to support is the seemingly incomprehensible variety of words and how they are used. Grammar may be governed by a consistent set of rules, but there does not seem to be much rhyme or reason as to why particular meanings are mapped onto particular phonological representations. For instance, why does the sound /kat/ refer to a four-legged mammal? Despite the dizzying variety of words to be learned, there are generalities that apply to the lexicon, and these are important for understanding and supporting skilled reading and learning. For example, across historically unrelated languages, there is a recurrent use of certain sounds (like /ma/, /pa/) to refer to parents (Passmore et al., 2023). One explanation for this consistency is that these sounds are easy for infants to produce, and the lexicon actually accommodates learners' needs. The intuition that the *lexicon*, the set of words in a language, is related to the developmental needs of learners has broad implications.

For example, the distribution of phonologically simple words ensures that young learners easily learn and employ sets of easy-to-pronounce high-utility words (Zipf, 1949). Zipf (1949) noticed that languages seem to have a word frequency distribution that balances efficiency for learning (which favors the ability to learn a few phonologically simple words and use them widely) and efficiency for hearers (who need clear and precise language to understand new or complex ideas efficiently). According to Zipf, across languages, high-frequency words are *much* more frequent than might be expected, which means that a new learner of the language can learn a set of simple high-frequency words and express a wide range of meanings. Unfortunately, there is a trade-off for hearers: they may need to work quite hard to contextualize and disambiguate the meanings of words used by young children. Zipf argues that all languages balance the needs of speakers (who want to be maximally communicative while learning the fewest number of words) with the needs of hearers (who want the maximum amount of precision of meaning and the minimum amount of ambiguity). Research has demonstrated that frequency distributions change as children get older (Ferrer I Cancho & Solé, 2001): Words used in child-directed speech get more lexically complex and precise as children age.

The Language of Learning

In this chapter, we show that as children age, the words they learn tend to be more orthographically complex, less frequent, and have fewer meanings on average. Words like these allow students to communicate new and abstract ideas clearly and precisely. We call this *the language of learning*. These words tend to be less phonologically considerate or efficient and include precise terms that are used (relatively) rarely. Learning a large number of relatively rare words facilitates precise communication of detailed information. Providing clear and precise communication is particularly important when communicating to an audience that lacks a clear grasp of the content or contexts: This is why we refer to this as the language of learning. The greater range of meanings and terms available to the speaker allows them to communicate in a way that ensures that the hearer or reader does not get confused or need to work hard to disambiguate the meanings of multiple words. This kind of language could support teaching about edible foods in the Amazon, how to guide your ship by the stars, or how to break down a defense in basketball or on the battlefield. In each case, there is a need for specific terms that denote objects, processes, and relationships that need to be communicated clearly and precisely to a learner. Being an expert communicator and an expert learner requires knowing many words and how to employ them correctly in many contexts.

We argue that academic vocabulary is just a special case of the language of learning: These are words that are helpful for learning new information in school disciplines such as math, science, history, and law. Previous research has used corpus analysis to identify words that are encountered regularly across a range of undergraduate academic texts (Coxhead, 2000). Coxhead's work has been instrumental in identifying sets of words for research interventions and emphasizing the importance of contextual diversity in word selection. Her use of corpus analysis has essentially identified sets of words proposed in well-known instructional heuristics (i.e., Tier Two words; Beck et al., 2002). These general academic words—such as *justify*, *interpret*, or *indicate*—are exactly the kinds of words that Beck, McKeown, and Kucan (2002) have identified as critical for helping students articulate more nuanced ideas. McKeown and colleagues emphasize that such words rarely appear in casual conversation and must therefore be taught directly and robustly, especially to students who may not acquire them incidentally through exposure. However, identifying specific sets of words as *academic* may place undue emphasis on the words themselves rather than on the purposes children have for using them. This might lead to a misunderstanding of the importance of vocabulary learning at all ages. After all, studies of science talk in preschools (Henrichs & Leseman, 2014) and elementary classrooms (Gotwals et al., 2022) demonstrate that young children and their adult interlocutors express complex ideas, and we know that language demands change as children age (Baixeries et al., 2013). While we feel Coxhead's academic word list and other instructional lists derived from corpus analysis have had a positive impact on research and practice, we posit that this approach threatens to overemphasize the words rather than the goals, needs, and existing competencies of students. Indeed, McKeown (1985) showed that even when academic words appeared in context, students often failed to learn them without explicit instruction, especially those from lower-ability groups. Students across all ages and contexts are on a journey to develop the language of learning, and our goal should be to understand where they are in the journey and support them to gain precision, so that they can expand their use of language to support their goals and explore contexts in which they are interested. Relatedly, we worry that the term *academic* might be taken to contrast with technical, career, or other vocabulary, even though the Zipfian trends have been demonstrated across languages, and the developmental trends we describe here apply broadly to domains where language precision is needed. There is no evidence to suggest that the kinds of words identified as *academic vocabulary* in word lists or as conceptualized by educational researchers (Nagy & Townsend, 2012) are not equally useful tools in these domains. Indeed, researchers are clear that academic language may be quite as useful for communicating in other contexts as it is in communicating within the four walls of the school.

Developmental Trends in Vocabulary

To present a bird's-eye view of children's vocabulary, we use a set of estimates of when during childhood people learned sets of words (Kuperman et al., 2012). Kuperman created the Age of Acquisition (AoA) measures by gathering ratings from 1,960 participants using Amazon Mechanical Turk, resulting in a total of 842,438 ratings for various words. To test the quality of these estimates, they applied criteria such as excluding invalid responses and correlating participant ratings with established norms. They found strong correlations between the AoA estimates and other well-known measures. For instance, they found an $r = .93$ ($N = 50, p < .001$) between the AoA measures and the Bristol norms for acquisition (Stadthagen-Gonzalez & Davis, 2006). While there is no reason to believe that the sample used to obtain AoA ratings is representative of a full range of learners that we try to support in our schools and represent in our research, we believe these ratings are useful to illustrate broad developmental trends and allow us to give specific examples of words that children might learn at different ages.

Since word part of speech has a strong effect on all other aspects of word use, we begin with a cursory look at word learning trends across early childhood (age 2–4), later childhood (age 4–6), elementary school (age 6–12), middle school (age 12–14), and high school and beyond (age 14–21) in Table 5.1. The data show that in early childhood, the majority of words children learn are nouns. As children age, the percentage of nouns and verbs they learn decreases while the percentage

TABLE 5.1. Distribution of Parts of Speech of Words Learned at Each Age Band

	Nouns	Adjectives	Verbs	Adverbs	Other	Total
Early childhood	3,325	792	688	128	132	5,091
	65%	15.56%	13.51%	2.51%	2.59%	100%
Later childhood	2,975	1,212	608	32	16	4,866
	61.14%	24.91%	12.49%	0.66%	0.33%	100%
Elementary	2,713	1,248	604	19	6	4,621
	58.71%	27.01%	13.07%	0.41%	0.13%	100%
Middle school	2,395	1,150	505	9	5	4,098
	58.44%	28.06%	12.32%	0.22%	0.12%	100%
High school	1,872	954	380	4	0	3,252
	57.56%	29.34%	11.69%	0.12%	0%	100%
Adulthood	1,044	494	117	1	0	1,678
	62.22%	29.44%	6.97%	0.06%	0%	100%
Total	14,324	5,850	2,902	193	159	23,606
	60.68%	24.78%	12.29%	0.82%	0.67%	100%

of adjectives increases. Because parts of speech have such a strong influence on empirical measures, we decided to focus on nouns in this chapter to simplify and clarify the trends.

Words can be measured in terms of how much they are used in texts, when they were first introduced into English, how many meanings they have, and in many other ways. To try to understand the foundational dimensions of words, Knoph and colleagues (2024) searched for empirical, nonbehavioral measures of words to understand the fundamental dimensions of vocabulary that underlie separate measures; an analysis of 22 empirical measures demonstrated that five key factors explain variability in word features. Here, we list each factor and give the citation for one of the variables that loads on it as an example.

- *Frequency* describes how often a word is encountered in language use, which makes frequently seen or heard words easier to learn and recognize (Davies, 2008); for example, *the* is high frequency while *vortex* is low frequency.
- *Complexity* measures how complicated a word is based on its length, number of syllables, and morphological structure, with longer words being generally more complex; for example, *a* is low complexity while *indistinguishableness* is high complexity.
- *Proximity* looks at how similar a word is to other words, including the number of similar-sounding or similar-looking words, which often makes words with many "neighbors" easier to remember (Yarkoni et al., 2008); for example, *cat* has high proximity while *doozy* has low proximity.
- *Polysemy* involves the number of different meanings a word can have, making words with multiple meanings not only more challenging to learn but also more flexible in use (Parks et al., n.d.); for example, *run* has a high polysemy rating while *hypothyroidism* has a low rating.
- *Diversity* assesses the range of contexts in which a word can appear, with words used in various situations and texts being more versatile in language use (Zeno et al., 1995); for example, *cell* is highly diverse while *perjury* scores low in diversity.

We found that these five key factors can explain 67–74% of the variability across the 22 lexical measures. Ongoing research indicates that these key factors can predict differences in behavioral measures, such as item difficulty (Lawrence et al., 2022) and reaction time (Knoph et al., 2024). To illustrate what kinds of words children acquire and how they develop the language of learning, we present the means and standard deviations on the five factors for the nouns in Table 5.1 ($n = 5,580$) split into six equal age bands ($n = 930$ each) in Figure 5.1.

At every age band, the words being learned tend to be less frequent, less polysemous, and more complex. That is to say, they are used less frequently, have fewer meanings, and are harder to say or read. We might say that children are learning words that support their ability to communicate and understand increasingly complex ideas and articulate them precisely. The cognitive downside is that learners

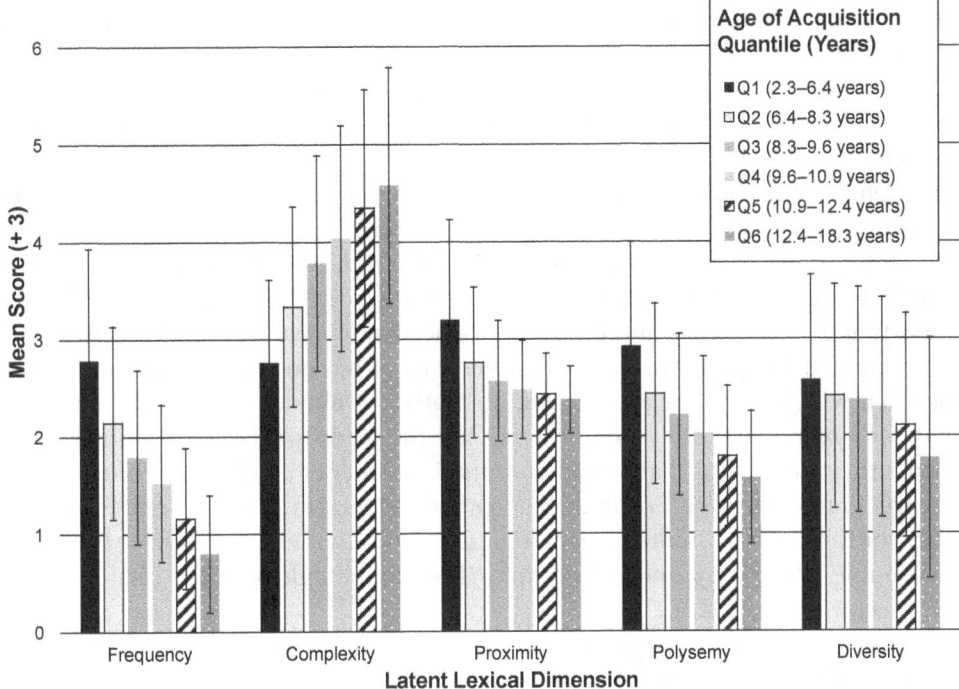

FIGURE 5.1. Mean lexical dimension scores by quantile.

need to master increasingly difficult phonetics, and the words they learn can only be used in narrow contexts.

The darkest bars represent the word characteristics for words learned from age 2 to 6.5 years. During this time, children are learning words needed for communication in daily life, which tend to be high-frequency (shown in the first grouping of bars). The sequence of vocabulary learning is relatively stable and rapid (Biemiller & Slonim, 2001). Words tend to be phonologically and orthographically simple (the second set of bars) and proximate to one another. For instance, if a *cat* and a *bat* are near neighbors, you only need to change one letter to convert one of these words to another. Teaching and learning words at this age range in groupings such as rhymes can facilitate both learning the meanings of new words and phonological awareness, which aids in mastering early reading (Bryant & Goswami, 1987). These high-frequency words also tend to have many meanings and senses (high polysemy rating) and can be used in many contexts (high diversity rating). These words are powerful tools for the early learner, but the trade-off is that caregivers, family members, and teachers may be challenged to understand exactly what a child intends sometimes (e.g., "give me that *thing*"). Among the words that were easier to learn and apply broadly at this age were words such as *house*, *name*, *side*, *life*, *day*, and *case*. During this same time period, children are learning words that are more complex, more precise, and less frequent: words such as *dishtowel*, *inchworm*, *hippopotamus*, *sandcastle*, and *bathmat*. These words were not as easy to learn, or as frequently used, but they provide the ability to communicate and understand language with far greater precision.

From ages 6–8, children are even more focused on learning to read. Of course, during this period, children are learning to map phonological components to sound symbols (Nation, 2019), and these skills are essential for early reading comprehension (Hoover & Gough, 1990). At the same time, children continue to learn new base words and learn to combine words. Some high-frequency, more orthographically simple words that children learn during this time include *form*, *charge*, *power*, *post*, *law*, *war*, *sense*, *rate*, and *support*. Note that these words have important general senses and more precise academic meanings that children may not encounter for many years. For example, *power* has precise and different meanings that will, in time, be encountered in math and physics classes. We might say that early representations of these words are the seeds for the more mature set of usages that these words have in adult texts (Landauer et al., 2011). Word learning in early grades is critical for later academic development, as is the understanding that words often have multiple meanings and senses that may or may not be related in meaning, phonology, and orthography (Booton, Hodgkiss, et al., 2022; Booton, Wonnacott, et al., 2022).

Interestingly, at this age, children are relatively strict with their interpretations of words and less inclined to use common metaphorical structures to interpret the meanings of words (Köder & Falkum, 2020). We can see this trend in the abundance of literal compounds that children use at this age, in words like *gemstone*, *joyfulness*, *weightlifter*, and *tablespoon*. These are general words that allow for greater precision and experience with more advanced morphology and lexical compounding. Given the important role of understanding word meanings and vocabulary as a predictor of reading proficiency in later adolescence, it is clear that the language of learning in early grades will be a critical driver of advanced comprehension in later years. These descriptives do not suggest clear demarcation in the kinds of words children learn across childhood and adolescence. Rather, the trends are consistent and move toward language that is more difficult to learn but provides more precise expression.

As students enter grade 3 (Figure 5.1: ages 7.9–10.6), they continue to grow their vocabulary by leveraging new meanings of idioms and novel uses of words (Anglin et al., 1993). A multiword expression is a sequence of words used together frequently in a discourse (Biber et al., 2004; Hyland, 2012). They are also known as idioms, lexical bundles, collocations, and formulaic expressions, among others, in linguistics and corpus linguistics. Multiword expressions come in different forms (Hyland, 2012). Some multiword expressions, such as idioms, have two or more words coined together and have nontransparent, distinct meanings (e.g., "once in a blue moon"; Nippold & Taylor, 2002). In other multiword expressions, such as prepositional phrases, two or more words occur concurrently more frequently than what would be expected by chance and have more transparent meanings (e.g., "paralyzed with fear"). Knowing different kinds of multiword expressions has been found to enhance children's reading comprehension (Cain et al., 2005; Levorato et al., 2004). In their research, Conklin and Schmitt (2008) found that students were able to process multiword expressions more quickly and read passages more efficiently, which led to better reading comprehension. Similar results have also been found with second-language learners (Conklin & Schmitt, 2008; Martinez & Murphy, 2011). The development of the ability to use these expressions seems to directly support word learning by extending the novel ways that words can be used and is also related to reading comprehension possibly as a proxy for other general verbal and metalinguistic skills. The increasing creativity that early elementary students have in stretching meanings in compounds and multiword expressions is connected to their extended skills in making pragmatic inferences that require them to go beyond the literal meanings of the linguistic forms and use common word extension strategies (Köder & Falkum, 2020; Pouscoulous & Pouscoulous, 2014).

The words children learn in upper elementary school are less frequent and more precise, reflecting the broader range of words encountered in text (Hiebert & Fisher, 2005) that have more narrow academic meanings. We can see these trends in prototypical words learned at this age. Examples of high-frequency words with many meanings include *system*, *shift*, *design*, *sex*, *source*, *tax*, *cell*, *credit*, and *union*. The most common meaning of these words may be heard in dinner conversations in some homes. In other homes, some of these words might be used less frequently; there is likely to be higher variability in student baseline knowledge of these words. Relatedly, some of the key meanings of these words, such as *tax* or *cell*, are central to some academic domains.

The more complex and precise words learned during this time include *whippersnapper*, *inappropriateness*, *mercifulness*, and *enormousness*. Notice that these words represent the most morphologically complex words that children have learned. Mastering these words requires robust morphological parsing skills (Carlisle & Stone, 2005). Recent studies have demonstrated how important morphological skills are for word learning and, ultimately, reading comprehension during this age range (Deacon & Levesque, 2024; Levesque & Deacon, 2022). For instance, Deacon and Levesque (2024) highlight that children's awareness of morphemes significantly influences their reading comprehension by enabling them to read and understand words, a process referred to as *morphological decoding and analysis*. The study's longitudinal data, analyzed through structural equation modeling, revealed that while both mechanisms are enhanced by morphological awareness, only morphological analysis mediates the relationship between morphological awareness and reading comprehension gains from grades 3–5, underscoring its critical role in developing strong reading comprehension skills and guiding effective classroom instruction. Tong and colleagues (2011) demonstrated that poor morphological awareness significantly contributed to reading comprehension difficulties in third and fifth graders. Children with lower morphological skills showed poorer reading comprehension outcomes despite similar phonological awareness, naming speed, and orthographic processing abilities compared to children without reading difficulties. Moreover, the study suggests that children with different reading comprehension profiles may acquire morphological skills at varying rates, affecting their reading comprehension over time.

Language learning through later elementary school forms the foundation for more disciplinary learning. In middle and high school, children begin to attend content-area classes and read and write increasingly specific disciplinary texts, such as moving from a picture book about bugs, to a textbook chapter about insects, to deciphering an insect field guide. Disciplinary texts convey key information about approaches to studying the world through mathematics, science, literature, social sciences, arts, and many other important disciplines. There are important differences in the kinds of structures and words used in these disciplines, but also similarities in the language used across academic texts. For example, all disciplines represent the accumulation of formal processes for exploring and sharing information about the world. As such, they are built on a bedrock of precise language, allowing for the clear communication of powerful ideas to a community of scholars and practitioners. One class of words that helps to communicate complicated ideas precisely is *connectives*: functional words that help make connections between arguments and texts.

Connectives are words that signal specific relationships between ideas. As basic examples, *and* connects two similar ideas, while *but* connects two opposing ideas. These basic words are related to a much more extensive class of words that students encounter and use (Andreev & Uccelli, 2024). As students encounter increasingly complex texts and argumentative discussions, understanding how a range of connectives function can aid in comprehension (Crosson & Lesaux, 2013; Uccelli, Barr, et al., 2015; Uccelli, Galloway, et al., 2015) and support cohesion across passages of text. There are several major categories of connectives (Halliday & Hasan, 1976). The category of additive connectives includes words or phrases such as *furthermore* or *in addition*. Adversative connectives include examples such as *nevertheless*, *however*, or *despite*. Causal connectives include *consequently*, *therefore*, and *as a result*. Finally, temporal connectives include *then*, *after that*, *finally* (Halliday & Hasan, 1976).

Knowledge of connectives is related to student ability to produce advanced arguments in writing. Taylor and colleagues (2019) studied argumentative reasoning in the writing of middle school students. They coded connectives in student writing and, while generally infrequent in student writing, the usage patterns of different types of connectives were related to the quality of student argumentation. Specifically, they discovered that the use of adversative connectives (*nevertheless*, *however*, *despite*) was positively correlated with the overall quality of argumentation in essays. A set of resources developed by our team (available at *https://readingways.org/blog/argumentative-writing*) integrate organizers for argumentative writing with support for specific adversative and other connectives.

Students at this age often take content-area classes and learn words that help them master new and challenging content. Less complex and more polysemous words acquired at ages 10–12 include *firm, process, mold, survey, transfer, evidence*, and *void*. Considering these words from the perspective of the functional roles in which they are likely to be encountered, it is easy to understand why an emphasis on these words might be important. When students encounter the word *evidence*, it is typically in the context of learning potentially contested facts about the world. For instance, one may be presented with evidence about plate tectonics or evidence about the interpretation of a poem. In either case, the reader's attention is (we hope) occupied with understanding new content. In such circumstances, struggling with understanding the meaning of a word like *evidence* (which is meant to facilitate clear understanding), could result in a complete comprehension breakdown.

That is to say, these words facilitate mastery of increasingly complex content by offering a precision of language that allows for the communication of complex ideas to a new learner. Not surprisingly, these words appear on academic word lists derived from corpus linguistics analysis. Words such as *evidence* can be used across disciplines and can therefore be very useful for second-language learners in university settings (Coxhead, 2000). However, it is noteworthy that the approach we used to identify words for this chapter did not rely on identifying a normative sample of academic texts. Rather, we used the lexical dimensions to identify words that are useful for learning and in communicating precisely.

In our discussion of early word learning we mentioned the word *power*. According to WordNet (Fellbaum, 1998) there are 10 noun meanings and one verbal meaning of the orthographic word form *power*. The most common and general meaning (the one that children will have learned at a young age) means something related to "possession of a controlling influence" as in "the power of his love saved her." In middle and high school, students encounter and need to master other meanings, including the rate of doing work (measured in watts = joules/second), the designated and legal scope of action in an official capacity (the power of the president), and the exponent of a base term (indicating the times a quantity is multiplied by itself). Our innate and astounding ability to distinguish word meanings masks the extent and importance of polysemous sense disambiguation in our reading lives. In our analysis of WordNet, we found that nouns ($M = 2.9$, $SD = 2.4$) and versions ($M = 4.3$, $SD = 4.5$) had multiple senses and meanings. Controlling for pretest scores, the number of target word meanings predicted posttest knowledge better than word frequency measures (Cervetti, Hiebert, Pearson, & McClung, 2015). In contrast, Hiebert, Scott, Castaneda, and Spichtig (2019) found no link between target word knowledge and the number of word senses and meanings in students in grades 2–12. We examined academic vocabulary assessment data from middle school students ($N = 1,747$) to see how word frequency, complexity, proximity, polysemy, and diversity related to students' knowledge of target words across ability levels using explanatory item response theory models. We found that polysemy was the only significant predictor of correct responses to word knowledge items: Words with more meanings were easier to understand than those with fewer meanings (beta = 0.35, $SE = 0.13$, $p < .01$; Lawrence et al., 2022). We suggested that to learn new word usages, learners must first recognize the novelty of the usage by comparing it with their existing knowledge and the context's semantic constraints. They must then update their understanding of the word to include the new meaning. This process enhances their word knowledge, especially when encounters are staggered and explicit. Hiebert (2019) has amplified calls for instructors to be explicit in teaching multiple meanings (Beck et al., 2002) by providing specific routines for teachers to support *remixing* (when a word takes a new meaning) and *recycling* (combining words in novel ways).

Supporting Vocabulary Development in Schools

Experimental evaluations of programs meant to support academic vocabulary show a measurable, albeit limited, success. Stahl and Fairbanks's (1986) review of various vocabulary interventions found that the most effective programs facilitated the learning of approximately 300 words per academic year. The National Reading Panel (National Institute of Child Health and Human Development, 2000) identified 47 studies with reliable results from experimental or quasi-experimental research. However, few vocabulary interventions are designed for postprimary urban schools serving many language-minority students (e.g., Carlo et al., 2004; Lesaux, Kieffer, Faller, & Kelley, 2010). These effective programs share key design elements: a limited number of high-utility words, presentation within meaningful texts rather than isolated lists, student-friendly definitions, and explicit teaching of word analysis tools such as etymology, morphology, and cognates.

We have a history of collaboration with the Strategic Education Research Partnership (*www.serpinstitute.org*) to understand the impacts of one vocabulary program, the Word Generation program. Word Generation, an interdisciplinary academic language program aimed at middle school students, has grown to include a diverse family of programs, such as Word Generation Weekly. Each week, Word Generation Weekly introduces five new vocabulary words, such as *relevant*, *advocate*, *presume*, *justify*, and *indicate*, that have been identified as the kinds of learning words that are needed by middle school students in discussions and learning that involve constructing positions, weighing ideas, and evaluating arguments. Throughout the week, students engage with the weekly vocabulary by reading, talking, and writing about a central topic in their English language arts, math, science, and social studies classes. This cross-disciplinary approach involves a grade-level teaching team rather than a single teacher, complicating the analysis of classroom-level predictors on student outcomes. The program includes 24 week-long units, covering topics from immediate student interests, for example, "Should you be able to rent a pet?", to broader civic issues, such as "Should there be federal funding for stem cell research?" Activities in each unit are designed for various content-area classrooms, providing opportunities for academic discussions from different disciplinary perspectives.

Over the course of decades, our research into the effects of systematic vocabulary instruction on high-leverage words has yielded some key findings. First, it is clear that a structured focus on these words can result in improved knowledge of target words (Snow et al., 2009). Second, we found that, although ostensibly a vocabulary program, the program's design around controversial social issues resulted in improved classroom discussions, which moderated the effect of program treatment on word learning (Lawrence et al., 2015). Importantly, we found that program participation enhanced students' self-efficacy in discussing controversial political and societal issues (Lin et al., 2015). The Word Generation program has also helped us better understand how important school- and student-level variability are in estimating treatment effects (Lawrence et al., 2017) and to inform our development of approaches that support academic language by using more collaborative professional learning and curriculum development models (Snow & Lawrence, 2024).

Although now stretching slightly beyond the target range of this chapter, we would be remiss if we did not mention the increasing importance of domain- or context-specific words in later middle school, high school, and beyond. At this age, the more complex and semantically narrow terms that children learn tend to be words used in some specific contexts or domains, but not others. For instance, words like *campaign, node, parallelogram, multimillionaire, agriculturalist,* and *oversimplification* are learned during this time. Many of these words, like *parallelogram*, have meanings that tend to be used in one or more technical, professional, or academic domains; that is, while knowledge of the word *parallelogram* will likely be correlated with overall vocabulary and reading ability (as would knowledge of any word), the precise knowledge of that word could have a critical instrumental relationship with the ability of a student to understand a specific math text. One of the challenges our content-area teachers face in teaching this class of words is understanding which words are the most important. O'Reilly and colleagues (2019) showed that knowledge of some words (e.g., *ecosystem* and *habitat*) are more strongly related to content knowledge than others (e.g., *predation* and *fauna*). The particular words that need instruction will change across topics and student age, but these results strongly suggest that strategic word selection for instructional focus is likely to make a difference in how well our students master content knowledge. It should be noted that the words strongly connected to explained variance in knowledge were key to the discipline's overarching concepts (in this case, ecology). Research has demonstrated how important thinking and reading are across disciplines (Goldman et al., 2016; Ippolito et al., 2019), and suggests strongly that what constitutes knowledge of words may vary across disciplines. If so, we should support word-learning strategies that help students build word knowledge of topic- and content-specific words in disciplinary-specific ways. For instance, key events might be usefully organized in a time line in a history class. Shapes may be usefully present in conceptual organizers in a math class. Processes related to sedimentary rock formation might be usefully learned through a process chart or word wall. The point is, since the key reason for learning these words is to apply them in the context of a discipline, it is appropriate and probably helpful that they be learned in ways that emphasize lexical and conceptual relationships that are germane to those contexts.

Conclusion

This chapter has underscored the intricate and multifaceted nature of vocabulary development, emphasizing the crucial role that a well-rounded vocabulary plays in reading comprehension and overall academic success. We have discussed the gradual progression from learning high-frequency, phonologically simple words in early childhood to mastering complex, precise, and less frequent words that enable clear communication of sophisticated ideas. This progression is pivotal in fostering the language of learning, which we argue is essential for success across various disciplines in academic and other contexts. By framing academic vocabulary as a subset of the broader language of learning, we aim to shift the focus from mere word acquisition to cultivating precise and effective communication skills. Our research and interventions, such as the Word Generation program, demonstrate that systematic vocabulary instruction can enhance not only word knowledge but also classroom discussions and student self-efficacy. Ultimately, the goal is to provide learners with the linguistic tools necessary for critical thinking, learning, and communication in academic, technical, career, and personal pursuits.

REFERENCES

Andreev, L., & Uccelli, P. (2024). The secret life of connectives: A taxonomy to study individual differences in mid-adolescents' use of connectives in writing to persuade. *Reading and Writing, 37*(1), 173–204.

Anglin, J. M., Miller, G. A., & Wakefield, P. C. (1993). Vocabulary development: A morphological analysis. *Monographs of the Society for Research in Child Development, 58*(10), i–186.

Baixeries, J., Elvevåg, B., & Ferrer-i-Cancho, R. (2013). The evolution of the exponent of Zipf's law in language ontogeny. *PLoS ONE, 8*(3), Article e53227.

Beck, I., McKeown, M. G., & Kucan, L. (2002). *Bringing words to life: Robust vocabulary instruction.* Guilford Press.

Beck, I., Perfetti, C. A., & McKeown, M. (1982). Effects of long-term vocabulary instruction on lexical access and reading comprehension. *Journal of Educational Psychology, 74*(4), 506–521.

Biber, D., Conrad, S., & Cortes, V. (2004). If you look at . . . : Lexical bundles in university teaching and textbooks. *Applied Linguistics, 25*(3), 371–405.

Biemiller, A., & Slonim, N. (2001). Estimating root word vocabulary growth in normative and advantaged populations: Evidence for a common sequence of vocabulary acquisition. *Journal of Educational Psychology, 93*(3), 498–520.

Booton, S. A., Hodgkiss, A., Mathers, S., & Murphy, V. A. (2022). Measuring knowledge of multiple word meanings in children with English as a first and an additional language and the relationship to reading comprehension. *Journal of Child Language, 49*(1), 164–196.

Booton, S. A., Wonnacott, E., Hodgkiss, A., Mathers, S., & Murphy, V. A. (2022). Children's knowledge of multiple word meanings: Which factors count and for whom? *Applied Linguistics, 43*(2), 293–315.

Bryant, P., & Goswami, U. (1987). Beyond grapheme–phoneme correspondence. *Cahiers de Psychologie Cognitive/Current Psychology of Cognition, 7*(5), 439–443.

Cain, K., Oakhill, J., & Lemmon, K. (2005). The relation between children's reading comprehension level and their comprehension of idioms. *Journal of Experimental Child Psychology, 90*(1), 65–87.

Carlo, M. S., August, D., McLaughlin, B., Snow, C. E., Dressler, C., Lippman, D. N., ... White, C. E. (2004). Closing the gap: Addressing the vocabulary needs of English-language learners in bilingual and mainstream classrooms. *Reading Research Quarterly, 39*(2), 188–215.

Carlisle, J. F., & Stone, C. A. (2005). Exploring the role of morphemes in word reading. *Reading Research Quarterly, 40*(4), 428–449.

Cervetti, G. N., Hiebert, E. H., Pearson, P. D., & McClung, N. A. (2015). Factors that influence the difficulty of science words. *Journal of Literacy Research, 47*(2), 153–185.

Conklin, K., & Schmitt, N. (2008). Formulaic sequences: Are they processed more quickly than nonformulaic language by native and nonnative speakers? *Applied Linguistics, 29*(1), 72–89.

Coxhead, A. (2000). A new academic word list. *TESOL Quarterly, 34*(2), 213–238.

Cromley, J. G., & Azevedo, R. (2007). Testing and refining the direct and inferential mediation model of reading comprehension. *Journal of Educational Psychology, 99*(2), 311–325.

Crosson, A. C., & Lesaux, N. K. (2013). Does knowledge of connectives play a unique role in the reading comprehension of English learners and English-only students? *Journal of Research in Reading, 36*(3), 241–260.

Davies, M. (2008). *The corpus of contemporary American English: 520 million words, 1990–present.* http://corpus.byu.edu/coca.

Deacon, S. H., & Levesque, K. (2024). Mechanisms in the relation between morphological awareness and the development of reading comprehension. *Journal of Educational Psychology, 16*(6), 1052–1069.

Fellbaum, C. (Ed.). (1998). *WordNet: An electronic lexical database.* MIT Press.

Ferrer-i-Cancho, R., & Solé, R. V. (2001). Two regimes in the frequency of words and the origins of complex lexicons: Zipf's law revisited. *Journal of Quantitative Linguistics, 8*(3), 165–173.

Goldman, S. R., Britt, M. A., Brown, W., Cribb, G., George, M., Greenleaf, C., ... Project READI. (2016). Disciplinary Literacies and learning to read for understanding: A conceptual framework for disciplinary literacy. *Educational Psychologist, 51*(2), 219–246.

Gotwals, A. W., Wright, T. S., Domke, L., & Anderson, B. (2022). Science talk in elementary classrooms: A synthesis of the literature. *Elementary School Journal, 122*(4), 642–673.

Halliday, M. A. K., & Hasan, R. (1976). *Cohesion in English.* Longman.

Henrichs, L. F., & Leseman, P. P. M. (2014). Early science instruction and academic language development can go hand in hand: The promising effects of a low-intensity teacher-focused intervention. *International Journal of Science Education, 36*(17), 2978–2995.

Hiebert, E. H. (2019). *teaching words and how they work: Small changes for big vocabulary results.* Teachers College Press.

Hiebert, E. H., & Fisher, C. W. (2005). A review of the National Reading Panel's studies on fluency: The role of text. *Elementary School Journal, 105*(5), 443–460.

Hiebert, E. H., Scott, J. A., Castaneda, R., & Spichtig, A. (2019). An analysis of the features of words that influence vocabulary difficulty. *Education Sciences, 9*(1), 8.

Hoover, W. A., & Gough, P. B. (1990). The simple view of reading. *Reading and Writing, 2*(2), 127–160.

Hyland, K. (2012). Bundles in academic discourse. *Annual Review of Applied Linguistics, 32,* 150–169.

Ippolito, J., Dobbs, C. L., & Charner-Laird, M. (2019). *Disciplinary literacy: Inquiry and instruction.* Learning Sciences.

Knoph, R. (2024, November). *Latent lexical dimensions are robust predictors in lexical decision reaction times and improve interpretability.* Poster presentation at the Psychonomic Society 65th Annual Meeting, New York.

Knoph, R. E., Lawrence, J. F., & Francis, D. J. (2024). The dimensionality of lexical features in general, academic, and disciplinary vocabulary. *Scientific Studies of Reading, 28*(2), 142–166.

Köder, F., & Falkum, I. L. (2020). Children's metonymy comprehension: Evidence from eye-tracking and picture selection. *Journal of Pragmatics, 156,* 191–205.

Kuperman, V., Stadthagen-Gonzalez, H., & Brysbaert, M. (2012). Age-of-acquisition ratings for 30,000 English words. *Behavior Research Methods, 44*(4), 978–990.

Landauer, T. K., Kireyev, K., & Panaccione, C. (2011). Word maturity: A new metric for word knowledge. *Scientific Studies of Reading, 15*(1), 92–108.

Lawrence, J. F., Crosson, A. C., Paré-Blagoev, E. J., & Snow, C. E. (2015). Word Generation randomized trial: Discussion mediates the impact of program treatment on academic word learning. *American Educational Research Journal, 52*(4), 750–786.

Lawrence, J. F., Francis, D., & Snow, C. E. (2017). The poor get richer: Heterogeneity in the efficacy of a school-level intervention for academic language. *Journal of Research on Educational Effectiveness, 10*(4), 767–794.

Lawrence, J. F., Knoph, R., McIlraith, A., Kulesz, P. A., & Francis, D. J. (2022). Reading comprehension and academic vocabulary: Exploring relations of item features and reading proficiency. *Reading Research Quarterly, 57*(2), 669–690.

Lesaux, N. K., Kieffer, M. J., Faller, E., & Kelley, J. (2010). The effectiveness and ease of implementation of an academic vocabulary intervention for linguistically diverse students in urban middle schools. *Reading Research Quarterly, 45*(2), 196–228.

Levesque, K. C., & Deacon, S. H. (2022). Clarifying links to literacy: How does morphological awareness support children's word reading development? *Applied Psycholinguistics, 43*(4), 921–943.

Levorato, M. C., Nesi, B., & Cacciari, C. (2004). Reading comprehension and understanding idiomatic expressions: A developmental study. *Brain and Language, 91*(3), 303–314.

Lin, A. R., Lawrence, J. F., & Snow, C. E. (2015). Teaching urban youth about controversial issues: Pathways to becoming active and informed citizens. *Citizenship, Social and Economics Education, 14*(2), 103–119.

Martinez, R., & Murphy, V. A. (2011). Effect of frequency and idiomaticity on second language reading comprehension. *TESOL Quarterly, 45*(2), 267–290.

McKeown, M. G. (1985). The acquisition of word meaning from context by children of high and low ability. *Reading Research Quarterly, 20*(4), 482–496.

McKeown, M. G., Beck, I. L., Omanson, R. C., & Perfetti, C. A. (1983). The effects of long-term vocabulary instruction on reading comprehension: A replication. *Journal of Reading Behavior, 15*(1), 3–18.

Nagy, W., & Townsend, D. (2012). Words as tools: Learning academic vocabulary as language acquisition. *Reading Research Quarterly, 47*(1), 91–108.

Nation, K. (2019). Children's reading difficulties, language, and reflections on the simple view of reading. *Australian Journal of Learning Difficulties, 24*(1), 47–73.

National Institute of Child Health and Human Development (NICHD). (2000). *Report of the National Reading Panel. Teaching children to read: An evidence-based assessment of the scientific research literature on reading and its implications for reading instruction.* U.S. Government Printing Office.

Nippold, M. A., & Taylor, C. L. (2002). Judgments of idiom familiarity and transparency: A comparison of children and adolescents. *Journal of Speech, Language, and Hearing Research, 45*(2), 384–391.

O'Reilly, T., Wang, Z., & Sabatini, J. (2019). How much knowledge is too little?: When a lack of knowledge becomes a barrier to comprehension. *Psychological Science, 30*(9), 1344–1351.

Parks, R., Ray, J., & Bland, S. (n.d.). *Wordsmyth English dictionary–thesaurus.* www.wordsmyth.net.

Passmore, S., Barth, W., Greenhill, S. J., Quinn, K., Sheard, C., Argyriou, P., . . . Jordan, F. M. (2023). Kinbank: A global database of kinship terminology. *PLoS ONE, 18*(5), Article e0283218.

Perfetti, C., & Hart, L. (2002). The lexical quality hypothesis. In L. Verhoeven, C. Elbro, & P. Reitsma (Eds.), *Precursors of functional literacy* (pp. 189–213). John Benjamins.

Pouscoulous, N., & Pouscoulous, N. (2014). "The elevator's buttocks": Metaphorical abilities children. In D. Matthews (Ed.), *Pragmatic development first language acquisition* (pp. 239–259). John Benjamins.

Quinn, J. M., Wagner, R. K., Petscher, Y., & Lopez, D. (2015). Developmental relations between vocabulary knowledge and reading comprehension: A latent change score modeling study. *Child Development, 86*(1), 159–175.

Snow, C., & Lawrence, J. F. (2024). Opportunities to learn and intersubjectivity. In O. Erstad, B. E. Hagtvet, & J. Wertch (Eds.), *Education and dialogue in polarized societies: Dialogic perspectives in times of change.* Oxford University Press.

Snow, C. E., Lawrence, J. F., & White, C. (2009). Generating knowledge of academic language among urban middle school students. *Journal of Research on Educational Effectiveness, 2*(4), 325–344.

Stadthagen-Gonzalez, H., & Davis, C. J. (2006). The Bristol norms for age of acquisition, imageability, and familiarity. *Behavior Research Methods, 38*(4), 598–605.

Stahl, S. A., & Fairbanks, M. M. (1986). The effects of vocabulary instruction: A model-based meta-analysis. *Review of Educational Research, 56*(1), 72–110.

Taylor, K. S., Lawrence, J. F., Connor, C. M., & Snow, C. E. (2019). Cognitive and linguistic features of adolescent argumentative writing: Do connectives signal more complex reasoning? *Reading and Writing, 32*(4), 983–1007.

Tong, X., Deacon, S. H., Kirby, J. R., Cain, K., & Parrila, R. (2011). Morphological awareness: A key to understanding poor reading comprehension in English. *Journal of Educational Psychology, 103*(3), 523–534.

Townsend, D., Filippini, A., Collins, P., & Biancarosa, G. (2012). Evidence for the importance of academic word knowledge for the academic achievement of diverse middle school students. *Elementary School Journal, 112*(3), 497–518.

Uccelli, P., Barr, C. D., Dobbs, C. L., Galloway, E. P., Meneses, A., & Sánchez, E. (2015). Core academic language skills: An expanded operational construct and a novel instrument to chart school-relevant language proficiency in preadolescent and adolescent learners. *Applied Psycholinguistics, 36*(5), 1077–1109.

Uccelli, P., Galloway, E. P., & Barr, C. D. (2015). Beyond vocabulary: Exploring cross-disciplinary academic-language proficiency and its association with reading comprehension. *Reading Research Quarterly, 50*(3), 337–356.

Yarkoni, T., Balota, D., & Yap, M. (2008). Moving beyond Coltheart's N: A new measure of orthographic similarity. *Psychonomic Bulletin and Review, 15*(5), 971–979.

Zeno, S. Z., Ivens, S. H., & Duvvuri, M. R. (1995). *The educators word frequency guide.* Touchstone Applied Science Associates.

Zipf, G. K. (1949). *Human behavior and the principle of least effort.* Addison-Wesley.

PART II
WHAT DOES THE RESEARCH SAY ABOUT TEXT COMPLEXITY AND COMPREHENSION?

CHAPTER 6

Supporting Reading Comprehension in the Upper Elementary Grades

Kristen L. McMaster
Panayiota Kendeou

In this chapter, we discuss our attempts to bridge the science of literacy research and practice in ways intended to have a meaningful, sustainable, positive impact on students' reading comprehension. First, we discuss why we focus on reading comprehension, the importance of aligning theory to practice, and how we strive to do so within current educational service delivery models (i.e., multi-tiered systems of support [MTSS]). Then, we provide examples of our work at the upper elementary levels designed for implementation at Tiers 1 and 2, along with efforts to develop a personalized intelligent tutoring system that may be implemented across tiers using innovative technology tools. We end with implications for practice and directions for future research aimed at improving reading comprehension using the best scientific evidence available.

Why Reading Comprehension?

Supporting students' successful development of the skills needed to comprehend and learn from a wide array of complex and challenging texts is an educational imperative. Few would dispute that reading comprehension is essential for success in school and beyond—indeed, our information-driven society can only thrive if its citizens can engage with, understand, use, and respond to various texts. Success in doing so has become increasingly challenging at a time when people are inundated with information and *mis*information that can (and does) have dire consequences for key societal functions, including education, public health, government, and even democracy as we know it (Ecker et al., 2022; Kendeou & Johnson, 2024).

For many learners, successful reading comprehension does not simply arise from the development of fluent word recognition skills but requires intentionally designed teaching and learning opportunities. Thus, researchers and practitioners have exerted extensive efforts to understand the complex and multidimensional processes involved in reading comprehension (Kendeou et al., 2024), to develop and test theories that describe these processes (van den Broek & Kendeou, 2022), and to design instruction and interventions to support reading comprehension. Indeed, decades of research have been devoted to developing and evaluating ways to teach reading comprehension skills and strategies (e.g., Snow, 2002), including for readers who experience difficulties (see Filderman et al., 2022, for a recent meta-analysis).

While the importance of this work cannot be overstated, national assessment data suggest that even these efforts have not been sufficient. High proportions of students continue to perform below proficient levels of reading; in fact, for decades, a persistent one-third of elementary-level schoolchildren have not reached proficiency on the National Assessment of Educational Progress (U.S. Department of Education, 2022). Moreover, alarming gaps persist for historically marginalized students, including Black and Brown students and children living in poverty (Terry, 2021), multilingual learners (Choi et al., 2025), and students with disabilities (Choi et al., 2025; Gilmour et al., 2019). It is clear that continued, concerted effort is needed to close these gaps and to find ways to ensure that all students have opportunities to achieve success in reading.

Aligning Theory to Practice

We, along with other scholars, have argued that the seemingly intractable high rates of below-proficient levels of reading are likely due, in part, to gaps between theory, empirical research, and practice (McMaster & Kendeou, 2023); that is, the teaching of reading (including instruction, intervention, and assessment) does not always reflect what we know to be "evidence based," and even research-based practices do not always connect directly to theory. Yet a stronger alignment of theory to teaching practices should lead to more robust and sustained student outcomes—as theory can help specify and explain the processes involved in reading and why they might break down for some readers, as well as the conditions that need to be in place to support these processes to achieve successful reading.

In our work, we have attempted to bridge theory and teaching practices by drawing from a cognitive view of reading comprehension to design instruction and interventions that are directly aligned to processes central to successful reading comprehension. According to this perspective, successful comprehension requires the reader to construct a coherent representation of text in memory (Kintsch, 1988), thereby building a *situation model* (Kintsch & Van Dijk, 1978). Readers construct this situation model by forming a network of semantic (meaningful) relations between text elements and prior knowledge as they progress through a text. Readers make a variety of such connections during reading; in our work, we focus specifically on *causal* connections, as these are central to comprehension (Oakhill & Cain, 2007).

Causal connections help link events or ideas within text, and between the text and prior knowledge (e.g., connecting a character's actions to their motivation to achieve a goal). Forming such connections often requires readers to make *inferences*—or to fill in gaps that are not explicitly stated in the text. Readers often seem to make inferences automatically, with little conscious thought, but at times they must make inferences *strategically* by actively searching and connecting parts of the text with each other or with background knowledge to fill in those gaps (Rapp & van den Broek, 2005; van den Broek et al., 2005). For example, consider the following two phrases from a popular children's book, *If You Give a Pig a Pancake*, by L. J. Numeroff (1998):

If you give a pig a pancake, she'll want some syrup to go with it.

Some readers automatically draw the inference needed to understand the connection between these two phrases (in fact, you might have done so and not realized that you made an inference). These readers most likely have knowledge of, or experience with, eating pancakes as a sweet breakfast treat, and understand that syrup is often poured on top. Other readers need to strategically search for the connection between the two phrases. Readers who are accustomed to eating pancakes as a savory dish with meat or vegetables might not automatically associate syrup with pancakes. These readers might need to actively search the text and/or their background knowledge for more information to meaningfully connect the two phrases. This example is intended to illustrate how creating a network of semantic relations involves a combination of automatic and strategic processes, and that the extent to which these processes are automatic or strategic depends to some degree on the reader's prior knowledge (Compton et al., 2014); of course, readers often encounter much longer and more complex texts that require them to engage in such processes to a much greater extent than in the example.

Two additional factors influence the reader's ability to create a semantic network: (1) the reader's general inference-making ability (Cain & Oakhill, 2006, 2012; Oakhill & Cain, 2007; van den Broek et al., 2009) and (2) the reader's standards of coherence. *Standards of coherence* refers to the extent to which the reader aspires to maintain coherence while reading (Todaro et al., 2010; van den Broek et al., 1995). An individual reader's standards of coherence influence the extent to which they implement strategies to maintain overall comprehension of a text (Oakhill & Cain, 2012). For example, some readers who did not understand the connection between pancakes and syrup might try to figure out the relation, while others might decide to continue to read without trying to understand the connection.

In summary, a cognitive view of reading comprehension suggests that readers must engage in actively building networks of semantic relations between text information and prior knowledge to form a coherent representation of the text, and that the construction of this network depends on both automatic and strategic processes. Furthermore, some readers have more difficulty than others in constructing this network, and readers vary in their standards of coherence. Our work is motivated by this view, which leads to questions regarding whether and how readers can be taught to engage in these processes in ways that lead to improved reading comprehension.

Research has revealed that one factor that is central to such improvement is inference making. Inference making is a two-stage process that involves the *activation* and *integration* of information from text and from prior knowledge (Kintsch, 1988). Key findings from research provide guidance for developing reading instruction that promotes inference making, including that inference making (1) is a general skill that develops and transfers across media (Kendeou et al., 2009), (2) can be prompted with questioning (to prompt the necessary *activation* and *integration* of information) and facilitated with scaffolding and feedback (McMaster et al., 2012, 2014), and (3) can be facilitated by leveraging media affordances—that is, the supports that technology can offer such as audio and video, interactive features, and ways to automate and personalize various functions (Kendeou et al., 2020). We return to these key findings in our description of relevant work later in this chapter.

Multi-Tiered Systems of Support

In addition to aligning with theory, our work is situated within a framework known as MTSS. Many U.S. school districts have adopted an MTSS framework to meet students' diverse learning needs in an equitable, inclusive, and resource-efficient way. MTSS is intended to be an integrated framework for educational service delivery that draws on evidence-based practices to address all students' academic, behavioral, and social–emotional needs. This framework is prioritized in U.S. educational policy (Every Student Succeeds Act, 2015).

Although the implementation of MTSS varies, it typically comprises several common key components: (1) universal screening and progress monitoring, (2) increasingly intensive "tiers" of instruction and intervention, and (3) data-based decision making to identify students in need of more intensive instruction and to evaluate the effectiveness of that instruction (Burns et al., 2016). MTSS is driven by the assumption that the vast majority (approximately 80%) of students will benefit from core instruction (Tier 1) provided by the general education teacher. Some (around 15%) will require additional support, usually in the form of Tier 2 research-based, standard interventions delivered by a qualified interventionist to small groups of students. Creating such groups relies on reliable and valid assessment data that can be obtained in a timely manner. For example, in reading, assessment data might indicate several students in a class need more targeted support in learning to make inferences to comprehend text; these students might be grouped together to receive Tier 2 instruction. This approach reserves Tier 3, the most resource-intensive, individualized instruction, for a small number of students (around 5%) who are most likely to benefit from specialized instruction tailored to their specific needs.

Inference-Making Instruction and Intervention

Our research teams have worked to develop reading comprehension instruction and interventions that align with cognitive theory and are designed to be implemented within MTSS frameworks. This work has focused primarily on supporting inferencing and the use of other core strategies to promote overall reading comprehension in upper elementary schoolchildren. In this section, we describe work that aligns with Tiers 1 and 2 of MTSS, as well as technology-based instruction that can be personalized to fit the needs of individual learners.

Tier 1 Instruction

In 2004, we, along with other researchers at the University of Minnesota, initiated a comprehensive program of research that aimed to (1) describe the reading processes and products of elementary- and secondary-level students and the extent to which these processes and products differed for readers with varying skill levels and (2) use insights gained from that research to develop instructional approaches that would support reading comprehension development. This work was conducted in the context of core instruction provided to all students within the general education classroom, thus aligning with Tier 1 in MTSS frameworks. Here we focus on the work conducted with upper elementary (fourth-grade) students.

To meet the first aim of this research, we administered behavioral measures of reading (using eye-tracking methodology) and think-aloud protocols to assess the reading *processes* that students engaged in, along with an extensive battery of reading- and cognitive-focused measures to assess the *products* of students' reading, as well as characteristics that might contribute to their reading outcomes (see Rapp et al., 2007). First, fourth graders were asked to read four grade-level texts (two narrative and two expository) that varied in difficulty level (easy vs. hard) based on the overall coherence of each text. Their eye movements were tracked while they read these texts on a screen. Eye-tracking data showed the points in the text where readers fixated their eye gaze, for how long, and both within and across sentences, as they proceeded through each text. These data enabled us to deduce the processes in which readers engaged as they read, such as whether they were drawing particular inferences (e.g., by looking back at key points in text needed to make connections) or experiencing difficulties (e.g., by slowing down) at different points in the text (Rayner et al., 2006). We noticed that readers identified as more highly skilled based on traditional reading assessments tended to proceed more quickly through the text than those identified as lower skilled, and showed patterns consistent with strategic reading (e.g., looking back at specific points needed to generate inferences vs. fixating on difficult words).

Whereas eye-tracking data gave us some insights into specific behaviors in which readers of different skill-levels engaged, such insights were indirect and required us to make assumptions about readers' specific processes. Thus, we complemented the eye-tracking data with think-aloud protocols. Think-aloud methods have a long history in cognitive research as a way to learn what individuals are thinking about as they read texts (Ericsson & Simon, 1984). During think-alouds, we asked readers to read new grade-level texts (two narrative, two expository, which again varied in difficulty level) line-by-line, pausing after each sentence to state what they were thinking. Responses were transcribed and coded to provide insight into the processes in which readers engaged as they read. For example, readers paraphrased or repeated text, called on background knowledge to fill in missing information in the text (i.e., explanatory inferences), predicted what might happen next in the text (i.e., predictive inferences), related what they were reading to their own lives (i.e., associations), and engaged in other types of processes.

Whereas results from think-alouds revealed that readers of all skill levels engaged in a variety of processes, one particularly interesting finding emerged. We hypothesized that those readers identified as lower skilled were a heterogeneous group (i.e., that they encountered difficulties for a variety of reasons), so we conducted a cluster analysis to see if we could detect subgroups of readers whose difficulties might be related to different patterns of processing during reading. Sure enough, this analysis revealed two specific subgroups—one that pervasively relied on paraphrasing and repeating text during the think-aloud activity (and thus we referred to them as "paraphrasers"), and one that engaged in a high proportion of elaborative inferences (in which they attempted to connect the text to their background knowledge; thus dubbed "elaborators"). Although paraphrasing and elaborative inferences are often useful processes that support comprehension (McNamara, 2004), it seemed that lower-skilled readers were using these processes to the exclusion of others that might also be helpful—and sometimes in inaccurate or ineffective ways (e.g., they might connect the text to background knowledge that was irrelevant to the content they were reading). Upon examination of these subgroups' performance on standardized cognitive and reading assessments, we found that paraphrasers and elaborators did not differ on listening or reading comprehension, oral reading fluency, decoding and word recognition, vocabulary, general intelligence, motivation, or working memory.

Our findings from eye-tracking and think-aloud methodologies led us to two important conclusions; first, that evidence from "online" or in-the-moment assessments of reading—obtained during the actual reading *process*—provided different information from "offline" assessments obtained after the fact (i.e., the *product* of reading, such as responses to multiple-choice questions answered after reading a passage); second, that such insight into readers' *processes* might be instructionally useful—that is, it might provide guidance as to what to focus on during reading instruction and how to support readers' engagement in processes that lead to successful comprehension.

This latter conclusion motivated the next stage of our research, which was to design instructional protocols to support readers' comprehension in the context of whole-class (Tier 1) instruction and determine whether students at different skill levels or profiles (paraphrasers and elaborators) would respond differently to different questioning approaches (see McMaster et al., 2012). In line with our cognitive view of reading comprehension, we designed questioning approaches to prompt students to make connections in text to support inference making. We compared three different questioning approaches to test (1) whether questions designed to promote inference making would lead to stronger comprehension than simply asking literal "who," "what," "where," and "when" ("Wh") questions about text and (2) whether questions designed to elucidate causal relations in text ("causal" questions) would lead to stronger comprehension than questions designed to prompt the reader to make any kind of connections ("general" questions). Furthermore, we examined whether students identified as paraphrasers versus elaborators (using think-alouds) would respond differently to the different questioning approaches.

To develop causal questions, we analyzed grade-level narrative texts according to their causal structure, identified places where an inference was needed to support the reader's construction of a coherent representation of the text, and inserted a specific "why" or "how" question to prompt a text-based inference. "Wh" questions were also specific to the text and inserted in the same places as the causal questions but were literal rather than inferential in nature. General questions consisted of prompts (again, in the same locations as the causal and "Wh" questions) for the reader to "Connect it!" during reading—in other words, to connect the current sentence to earlier parts of the text. This approach was designed to provide readers with a generic strategy that they could apply to any text that they read.

Participating fourth graders ($n = 246$) were identified as struggling, average, or good readers based on performance on a standardized, norm-referenced reading test and curriculum-based reading measures. Furthermore, struggling readers were identified as "paraphrasers" or "elaborators" using think-aloud protocols. Students were stratified by skill level and assigned randomly to instructional groups (causal, general, or "Wh" questioning). Classroom teachers delivered the instruction in a classwide peer tutoring format for 20–30 minutes, two to four times per week, for 9 weeks. Specifically, students worked in pairs to read the texts together, and when they came to the questions inserted in the text, they prompted each other to answer them.

On average, students in all three questioning conditions made significant pre- to posttest growth; however, there were no reliable differences among the three conditions on readers' recall of central events in stories they read at posttest, regardless of their skill level. However, further analyses revealed that subgroups of struggling readers responded differently to the different questioning approaches. Specifically, those identified as "elaborators" outperformed "paraphrasers" in the causal condition ($d = 0.86$), paraphrasers outperformed elaborators in the general condition ($d = 1.46$), and paraphrasers in the general condition outperformed paraphrasers in the causal condition ($d = 1.52$). These findings tentatively supported our hypothesis that the two subgroups would respond differently to the different questioning approaches. Theoretically, the differential responses made sense: Elaborators likely benefited from prompts to connect information within the text rather than relying on background knowledge that might or might not be relevant. Paraphrasers may have benefited from prompts to make any kind of connection, rather than simply paraphrasing or repeating what they read.

Tier 2 Intervention

Intrigued by our initial finding that different instructional approaches might have varying effects for different types of struggling comprehenders, our research team further developed and tested the questioning approaches described earlier. We decided to focus specifically on students identified as experiencing comprehension difficulties and designed a more intensive intervention (to be delivered in small groups by a trained interventionist as a supplemental "Tier 2" intervention). We worked in partnership with classroom teachers to ensure that the intervention would be both feasible for classroom use and responsive to the needs of subgroups of struggling readers. Similar to McMaster and colleagues (2012), we developed narrative texts (fiction and biographical nonfiction) with questions inserted where inferences were needed for the reader to generate a coherent representation of the text.

Again, we developed specific causal ("why" and "how") questions, to be compared to the more generic prompt to "Connect it." With input from classroom teachers, we also developed versions in which questions would be asked "online," or during the reading process, versus "offline," or after reading the complete text. We did so to address the question of whether prompting inferencing *during* reading would actually change the reading process in a way that would positively impact the reading outcome, or whether such an approach would be too disruptive (in which case, asking questions *after* reading might be more effective).

After development of the intervention with extensive input and feedback from teacher partners, we identified 60 fourth graders performing at the bottom 25th percentile in reading comprehension (but not decoding), and further identified them as "elaborators" and "paraphrasers," once again using a think-aloud task (see McMaster et al., 2014, 2015). We assigned groups of three to five students randomly to Causal or General questioning conditions; all readers responded to questions asked *during* or *after* reading, in counterbalanced order. Highly trained tutors delivered intervention to the groups for 20–30 minutes, three times per week, for 18 sessions. Similar to McMaster and colleagues (2012), there were no reliable main effects of questioning approach on students' text recalls or oral reading fluency, although students made significant pre- to posttest growth in both conditions. An effect size of $d = 0.88$ for the proportion of gist story units recalled, though not statistically significant, favored the Causal questioning approach. Also, quantitative results suggested no meaningful difference between asking questions during versus after reading, though feedback from tutors indicated that asking them during reading was more feasible. Additionally, and in contrast to previous findings, there were no differential effects for elaborators versus paraphrasers (McMaster et al., 2014).

Results of this study led us to conclude that (1) asking causal questions during reading emerged as having the most promise when triangulating theory, evidence, and practical considerations and (2) this conclusion held true for both paraphrasers and elaborators. We hypothesized that the two subgroups did not respond differently to the two different questioning approaches because they worked in small groups that included both types of readers (unlike in McMaster et al., 2012, in which they worked in pairs), which meant they were not only exposed to a variety of responses to the questions but also received specific feedback from the tutor that addressed their specific learning needs.

In fact, as we further refined the intervention, we developed scaffolding and feedback options that tutors could use in response to individual readers' answers to questions (e.g., feedback that directed them either to make text-based connections when they overrelied on irrelevant background knowledge or to make an inference instead of simply paraphrasing). In this way, the scaffolding and feedback served as the means of differentiating instruction. In a final study in which we assigned 59 students randomly to receive the final version of the intervention or to serve as a business-as-usual control, we observed a positive effect ($d = 0.20$) favoring the intervention on the Multiple-Choice Online Cloze Comprehension Assessment (MOCCA; Carlson et al., 2014), demonstrating the promise of this intervention to improving outcomes for readers with comprehension difficulties.

Personalized Learning Using Technology

Even though supplemental interventions can effectively support comprehension, many students would likely benefit from more personalized reading instruction than can be offered in large or small groups. Such instruction can be adapted to the specific strengths and needs of the student, offering opportunities for both targeted instruction and deliberate practice. However, teachers have limited time to provide one-to-one or small-group personalized instruction, offer practice opportunities, and provide personalized feedback (McCarthy & Yan, 2024).

Given these classroom and time constraints, educational technology and specifically intelligent tutoring systems (ITSs) are uniquely positioned to fill a role for developing reading comprehension strategies. ITSs with fully automated adaptive responses provide the opportunity for personalized instruction and practice that would not otherwise be possible in the classroom. Using natural language processing (NLP), ITSs can provide immediate, automated feedback on learners' use of reading strategies. Such ITSs can also supplement reading classroom instruction, offering more intensive opportunities for instruction and practice.

Recognizing the promise of ITSs, McNamara and colleagues (2006) designed and tested a series of theories based ITSs to support the development of reading comprehension strategies called iSTART (Interactive Strategy Training for Active Reading and Thinking). iSTART combined self-explanation, a means to externalize students' strategy use, with comprehension strategy instruction (McNamara,

2004). Specifically, students learn how to explain challenging texts with instruction on how to use effective strategies such as paraphrasing, making bridging inferences, and elaborating using prior knowledge. iSTART has a strong evidence base, showing efficacy to improve comprehension for middle school (McNamara et al., 2007), high school (O'Reilly et al., 2004), and college students (Magliano et al., 2005).

These effects, though, do not mean that using this exact system would be appropriate or effective for younger students. Therefore, together we recently developed iSTART–Early (Kendeou et al., 2022; Watanabe et al., 2024) to address the needs of students in upper elementary school, by building and expanding on the latest version of iSTART (McNamara, Arner, et al., 2023). In iSTART–Early, upper elementary school students learn five comprehension strategies drawing on the self-explanation reading strategy training model (McNamara, 2004), in addition to question asking and summarization through video lessons, guided demonstration, and game-based practice (Jackson & McNamara, 2013). These strategies were adapted specifically for upper elementary school and include *ask*, *reword*, *find*, *explain*, and *summarize*.

Ask focuses on comprehension monitoring and question asking, facilitating better regulation and comprehension (McCarthy et al., 2018). *Reword* focuses on paraphrasing, an important part of the comprehension process because it helps readers to build on and draw inferences (McNamara, Newton, et al., 2023). *Find* focuses on identifying important sentences in the text, an effective strategy to improve comprehension performance (Butterfuss et al., 2024). *Explain* enables students to generate inferences that connect ideas in the text (bridging) and with background knowledge (elaborations). Finally, *summarize* helps readers reduce the text to its core ideas and integrate it better with their background knowledge (McNamara et al., 2004).

Most importantly, three major technological advances were incorporated into iSTART–Early to make it developmentally appropriate for upper elementary school students (Balyan et al., 2022). The first advance is automated speech recognition technology, which enables easy interaction with the system, without the need for the students to type in responses. The second advance is the expansion of NLP algorithms, which enable more precision in the assessment of less structured or syntactically incorrect phrases typical for this age group. The third advance is text-to-speech, which enables the option to have the text read-aloud by a pedagogical agent. Incorporating these advances allows iSTART–Early to provide automated reading strategy training to a younger age group more effectively. With these core components and advanced features, iSTART–Early provides explicit instruction for comprehension strategies, with grade-level informational texts, so that students can build relevant background knowledge while learning reading strategies. Immediate feedback, gamification, and deliberate practice are designed to enhance student motivation and self-regulation. Based on our initial pilot studies and prior work, iSTART–Early is usable and feasible for school implementation, also showing initial promise to improve comprehension (Butterfuss et al., 2024; Kendeou et al., 2022; McNamara, Arner, et al., 2023; Watanabe et al., 2024). It is important to note that we view such technology as a promising and innovative way to *supplement* the broader literacy curriculum, and that the expert role of the teacher in making critical instructional decisions to meet students' needs will likely remain paramount to their success.

Implications of This Work

The work described in this chapter has several important implications for bridging science and practices that focus on improving reading comprehension for students in upper elementary grades. First, our work underscores the importance of aligning practice with theory. We have built reading comprehension instructional approaches that draw from cognitive theories that help us understand reading processes and ways those processes might support (and sometimes detract from) successful comprehension. Our work builds on existing research that shows that promotion of inference making and the use of other core strategies can improve outcomes for readers with a range of skill levels, and that we can optimize the effects of such instructional approaches through timing, scaffolding and feedback, and a variety of technological advances.

Second, our work highlights the importance of asking questions regarding "for whom" and "under what conditions" instruction and interventions are most likely to be effective. Given that readers who experience comprehension difficulties are not a homogeneous group, but rather struggle in different ways for different reasons, it is important to gather information about their specific strengths and needs and align instruction to those strengths and needs. Effects of such instruction might vary depending on the instructional context (e.g., whether instruction is delivered to the whole class vs. a small group)—which is a highly relevant consideration in the context of MTSS, in which students have opportunities to receive instruction at varying tiers of intensity depending on their needs. Related to this point is a third important implication: that technology offers a promising way to personalize instruction, which might ultimately lead to greater efficiency and efficacy in the way that instruction is delivered across tiers.

Future Directions

Much of the work described in this chapter shows the *promise* of practices designed to promote successful comprehension for readers in upper elementary grades. Further work is needed to continue to develop instructional materials that are culturally appropriate and motivating for diverse learners, to establish the *efficacy* of these approaches for samples of students who are representative of diverse learners in our schools (including students of historically marginalized racial and ethnic backgrounds, multilingual learners, and those with disabilities), and ultimately to determine whether they are effective when implemented at scale.

Another critical direction for future research is the ongoing need for theory- and intervention-aligned assessment. One of the challenges we have encountered in this work is the limited availability of assessments of reading comprehension processes that have evidence of strong psychometric properties (e.g., reliability and validity), are sensitive to students' growth in response to instruction, and can help identify relevant subgroups of readers in an efficient and instructionally useful way. Some existing measures have shown promise to do so (e.g., the MOCCA; Carlson et al., 2014); however, further research is needed to show how such assessments can be used seamlessly to inform instruction and intervention within MTSS.

Finally, ongoing development of educational technology is a critical direction for future research. A considerable amount of evidence suggests that technology such as games, interactive applications, and ITSs improves a variety of student-level outcomes, such as motivation, engagement, and learning (e.g., Jackson & McNamara, 2013). With the introduction of large language models via chatbot systems (e.g., ChatGPT), the automatic evaluation of reading strategies in systems such as iSTART–Early may be further improved, significantly influencing learner experience, as well as scalability of these personalized systems (Nicula et al., 2023). Advances in artificial intelligence (AI) offer opportunities to evaluate learner strengths and needs via stealth assessments (McNamara, Arner, et al., 2023) that in turn can be used to tailor feedback and adaptivity in the system (McCarthy & Yan, 2024). With generative AI, content can also be tailored to student needs and interests far more effectively and at scale. Given that AI systems are inherently susceptible to algorithmic bias, it is important to be cautious and continue to push for theory- and evidence-based application in education that is also responsible, ethical, and human-centered (Allen & Kendeou, 2024).

Conclusion

In this chapter, we have described how we designed instructional practices to promote reading comprehension in upper elementary students, including examples of our work using whole-classroom instruction, small-group intervention, and personalized learning. Our work underscores the importance of aligning theory with practice, as well as attending to questions regarding *for whom* and *under what conditions* such practices will be most effective. Ongoing research is needed to continue to address these questions, to align assessments with theory and instruction, and to leverage technology to create personalized learning systems that show initial promise to improve a variety of outcomes for diverse learners.

ACKNOWLEDGMENTS

The research reported here was supported in part by the Institute of Education Sciences, U.S. Department of Education, through Grant Nos. R305G040021, R324A110046, R305A190050, and R305A220107 to the University of Minnesota. The opinions expressed are those of the authors and do not represent views of the Institute or the U.S. Department of Education.

REFERENCES

Allen, L. K., & Kendeou, P. (2024). ED-AI Lit: An interdisciplinary framework for AI literacy in education. *Policy Insights from the Behavioral and Brain Sciences, 11*(1), 3–10.

Balyan, R. Arner, T., Li, T., Orcutt, E., Butterfuss, R., Kendeou, P., & McNamara, D. (2022). (2022). Integrating speech technology into the iSTART–Early Intelligent Tutoring System. In S. Crossley & E. Popescu (Eds.), *International conference on intelligent tutoring systems* (pp. 362–370). Springer International.

Burns, M. K., Jimerson, S. R., VanDerHeyden, A. M., & Deno, S. L. (2016). Toward a unified response-to-intervention model: Multi-tiered systems of support. In S. R. Jimerson, M. K. Burns, & A. M. VanDerHeyden (Eds.), *Handbook of response to intervention: The science and practice of multi-tiered systems of support* (2nd ed., pp. 719–732). Springer.

Butterfuss, R., McCarthy, K. S., Orcutt, E., Kendeou, P., & McNamara, D. S. (2024). Identification of main ideas in expository texts: Selection versus deletion. *Reading and Writing, 37*(3), 757–785.

Cain, K., & Oakhill, J. (2006). Profiles of children with specific reading comprehension difficulties. *British Journal of Educational Psychology, 76*, 683–696.

Cain, K., & Oakhill, J. (2012). Reading comprehension development from seven to fourteen years: Implications for assessment. In J. P. Sabatini, E. R. Albro, & T. O'Reilly (Eds.), *Measuring up: Advances in how we assess reading ability* (pp. 59–76). Rowan & Littlefield Education.

Carlson, S. E., Seipel, B., & McMaster, K. (2014). Development of a new reading comprehension assessment: Identifying comprehension differences among readers. *Learning and Individual Differences, 32*, 40–53.

Choi, S., Bak, M. Y. S., & McMaster, K. L. (2025). *Reading development of multilingual and English-monolingual students with and without disabilities in response to intervention: An exploratory study.* Manuscript under review.

Compton, D. L., Miller, A. C., Elleman, A. M., & Steacy, L. M. (2014). Have we forsaken reading theory in the name of "quick fix" interventions for children with reading disability? *Scientific Studies of Reading, 18*, 55–73.

Ecker, U., Lewandowsky, S., Cook, J., Schmid, P., Fazio, L., Brashier, N., . . . Amazeen, M. (2022). Drivers of misinformation belief and its resistance to correction. *Nature Reviews Psychology, 1*, 13–29.

Ericsson, K. A., & Simon, H. A. (1984). *Protocol analysis: Verbal reports as data.* MIT Press.

Every Student Succeeds Act, 20 U.S.C. § 6301 (2015). *www.congress.gov/bill/114th-congress/senate-bill/1177.*

Filderman, M. J., Austin, C. R., Boucher, A. N., O'Donnell, K., & Swanson, E. A. (2022). A meta-analysis of the effects of reading comprehension interventions on the reading comprehension outcomes of struggling readers in third through 12th grades. *Exceptional Children, 88*(2), 163–184.

Gilmour, A. F., Fuchs, D., & Wehby, J. H. (2019). Are students with disabilities accessing the curriculum?: A meta-analysis of the reading achievement gap between students with and without disabilities. *Exceptional Children, 85*(3), 329–346.

Jackson, J. G., & McNamara, D. S. (2013). Motivation and performance in a game-based intelligent tutoring system. *Journal of Educational Psychology, 105*, 1036–1049.

Kendeou, P., & Johnson, V. (2024). The nature of misinformation in education. *Current Opinion in Psychology, 55*, Article 101734.

Kendeou, P., McMaster, K., Butterfuss, R., Kim, J., Bresina, B., & Wagner, K. (2020). The Inferential Language Comprehension (*iLC*) framework. *Topics in Cognitive Science, 12*, 256–273.

Kendeou, P., McMaster, K., McNamara, D. S., & Wilke, B. C. (2024). Literacy. In P. A. Schutz & K. R. Muis (Eds.), *Handbook of educational psychology* (4th ed., pp. 553–575). Routledge.

Kendeou, P., Orcutt, E., Arner, T., Li, T., Balyan, R., Butterfuss, R., Watanabe, M., & McNamara, D. (2022). iSTART-Early: Interactive strategy training for early readers. In S. Crossley & E. Popescu (Eds.), *International conference on intelligent tutoring systems* (pp. 371–379). Springer International.

Kendeou, P., van den Broek, P., White, M. J., & Lynch, J. S. (2009). Predicting reading comprehension in early elementary school: The independent contributions of oral language and decoding skills. *Journal of Educational Psychology, 101*(4), 765–778.

Kintsch, W. (1988). The use of knowledge in discourse processing: A construction-integration model. *Psychological Review, 95*, 163–182.

Kintsch, W., & Van Dijk, T. A. (1978). Toward a model of text comprehension and production. *Psychological Review, 85*(5), 363–394.

Magliano, J. P., Todaro, S., Millis, K. K., Wiemer-Hastings, K., Kim, H. J., & McNamara, D. S. (2005). Changes in reading strategies as a function of reading training: A comparison of live and computerized training. *Journal of Educational Computing Research, 32*, 185–208.

McCarthy, K. S., Likens, A. D., Johnson, A. M., Guerrero, T. A., & McNamara, D. S. (2018). Metacognitive overload!: Positive and negative effects of metacognitive prompts in an intelligent tutoring system. *International Journal of Artificial Intelligence in Education, 28*, 420–438.

McCarthy, K. S., & Yan, E. F. (2024). Reading comprehension and constructive learning: Policy considerations in the age of artificial intelligence. *Policy Insights from the Behavioral and Brain Sciences, 11*(1), 19–26.

McMaster, K. L., Espin, C. A., & van den Broek, P. (2014). Making connections: Linking cognitive psychology and intervention research to improve comprehension of struggling readers. *Learning Disabilities Research and Practice, 29*(1), 17–24.

McMaster, K. L., & Kendeou, P. (2023). Refocusing reading comprehension: Aligning theory with assessment and intervention. *Learning and Individual Differences, 102*, Article 102256.

McMaster, K. L., van den Broek, P., Espin, C. A., Pinto, V., Janda, B., Lam, E., . . . van Boekel, M. (2015). Developing a reading comprehension intervention: Translating cognitive theory to educational practice. *Contemporary Educational Psychology, 40*, 28–40.

McMaster, K. L., van den Broek, P. A., Espin, C., White, M. J., Rapp, D. N., Kendeou, P., . . . Carlson, S. (2012). Making the right connections: Differential effects of reading intervention for subgroups of comprehenders. *Learning and Individual Differences, 22*(1), 100–111.

McNamara, D. S. (2004). SERT: Self-explanation reading training. *Discourse Processes, 38*, 1–30.

McNamara, D. S., Arner, T., Butterfuss, R., Fang, Y., Watanabe, M., Newton, N., . . . Roscoe, R. D. (2023). iSTART: Adaptive comprehension strategy training and stealth literacy assessment. *International Journal of Human–Computer Interaction, 39*(11), 2239-2252.

McNamara, D. S., Levinstein, I. B., & Boonthum, C. (2004). iSTART: Interactive strategy training for active reading and thinking. *Behavior Research Methods, Instruments, and Computers, 36*(2), 222–233.

McNamara, D. S., Newton, N., Christhilf, K., McCarthy, K. S., Magliano, J. P., & Allen, L. K. (2023). Anchoring your bridge: The importance of paraphrasing to inference making in self-explanations. *Discourse Processes, 60*(4–5), 337–362.

McNamara, D. S., O'Reilly, T. P., Best, R. M., & Ozuru, Y. (2006). Improving adolescent students' reading comprehension with iSTART. *Journal of Educational Computing Research, 34*, 147–171.

McNamara, D. S., O'Reilly, T. P., Rowe, M., Boonthu, C., & Levinstein, I. B. (2007). iSTART: A web based tutor that teaches self-explanation and metacognitive reading strategies. In D. S. McNamara (Ed.), *Reading comprehension strategies: Theories, interventions, and technologies* (pp. 397–421). Psychology Press.

Nicula, B., Dascalu, M., Arner, T., Balyan, R., & McNamara, D. S. (2023). Automated assessment of comprehension strategies from self-explanations using LLMs. *Information, 14*(10), Article 567.

Numeroff, L. J. (1998). *If you give a pig a pancake*. HarperCollins.

Oakhill, J., & Cain, K. (2007). Issues of causality in children's reading comprehension. In D. S. McNamara (Ed.), *Reading comprehension strategies: Theories, interventions, and technologies* (pp. 47–71). Erlbaum.

Oakhill, J., & Cain, K. (2012). The precursors of reading ability in young readers: Evidence from a four-year longitudinal study. *Scientific Studies of Reading, 16*, 91–121.

O'Reilly, T. P., Sinclair, G. P., McNamara, D. S. (2004). iSTART: A web-based reading strategy intervention that improves students' science comprehension. In *Proceedings of the IADIS International Conference Cognition and Exploratory Learning in the Digital Age, Lisbon, Portugal* (pp. 173–180). IADIS Press.

Rapp, D., & van den Broek, P. (2005). Dynamic text comprehension: An integrative view of reading. *Current Directions in Psychological Science, 14*, 276–279.

Rapp, D. N., van den Broek, P., McMaster, K. L., Kendeou, P., & Espin, C. A. (2007). Higher-order comprehension processes in struggling readers: A perspective for research and intervention. *Scientific Studies of Reading, 11*(4), 289–312.

Rayner, K., Chace, K. H., Slattery, T. J., & Ashby, J. (2006). Eye movements as reflections of comprehension processes in reading. *Scientific Studies of Reading, 10*(3), 241–255.

Snow, C. E. (2002). *Reading for understanding: Toward an R&D program in reading comprehension*. RAND Corporation.

Terry, N. P. (2021). Delivering on the promise of the science of reading for all children. *Reading Teacher, 75*(1), 83–90.

Todaro, S., Millis, K., & Dandotkar, S. (2010). The impact of semantic and causal relatedness and reading skill on standards of coherence. *Discourse Processes, 47*, 421–446.

U.S. Department of Education. Institute of Education Sciences, National Center for Education Statistics. (2022). *National Assessment of Educational Progress 2022 Reading Assessment*. www.nationsreportcard.gov/highlights/reading/2022.

van den Broek, P., & Kendeou, P. (2022). Discourse comprehension: Inferences and mental representations. In M. Snowling, C. Hulme, & K. Nation (Eds.), *The science of reading: A handbook* (2nd ed., pp. 239–261). Wiley.

van den Broek, P., Rapp, D. N., & Kendeou, P. (2005). Integrating memory-based and constructionist processes in accounts of reading comprehension. *Discourse Processes, 39*, 299–316.

van den Broek, P., Risden, K., & Husebye-Hartman, E. (1995). The role of readers' standards of coherence in the generation of inferences during reading. In R. F. Lorch, Jr.

& E. J. O'Brien (Eds.), *Sources of coherence in text comprehension* (pp. 353–373). Erlbaum.

van den Broek, P., White, M. J., Kendeou, P., & Carlson, S. (2009). Reading between the lines: Developmental and individual differences in cognitive processes in reading comprehension. In R. K. Wagner, C. Schatschneider, & C. Phythian-Sence (Eds.), *Beyond decoding: The behavioral and biological foundations of reading comprehension.* (pp. 107–123). Guilford Press.

Watanabe, M., Arner, T., & McNamara, D. (2024). iSTART–Early and now I can read: Effective reading strategies for young readers. *Reading Teacher, 77*(4), 533–540.

CHAPTER 7

Complicating the Simple View of Reading

Gina Biancarosa

The simple view of reading (SVR) was introduced by Gough and Tunmer (1986) nearly four decades ago. Ever since, it has served, as intended, as a useful heuristic for broadly conceptualizing two distinct contributors to reading: decoding and comprehension. It has subsequently become a central theory in the field of reading, informing a wide range of research and fueling debates about what reading instruction should entail (e.g., Cervetti et al., 2020; Duke & Cartwright, 2021). This chapter reviews the SVR, including its definition and implications for the definition of reading disabilities. It further elaborates how its use has both informed and confounded research and practice and concludes with recommendations regarding its future.

Overview of the SVR

Gough and Tunmer (1986) explicitly aimed for the SVR to serve as a heuristic for understanding the role of decoding in the reading process rather than as a complete explanation of reading. Indeed, they stated that their intended audience included those who doubted decoding played a role in the skilled reading process at all (e.g., Goodman, 1973). They defined decoding not as "sounding out" words but as fast and accurate word recognition out of context, perhaps best exemplified by nonsense word recognition (p. 7). Furthermore, they acknowledged that understanding letter–sound correspondence is necessary but insufficient for decoding. Nonetheless, its necessity results in strong covariance between letter–sound correspondence knowledge and decoding skill.

With this definition in place, they then explicated the SVR as meaning that reading (R) is quite literally the product of decoding (D) and comprehension (C). The use of the term *product* was deliberate, in that they equated their definition with a mathematical equation, $R = D \times C$, such that a total lack of skill, conceptualized as a zero, for either ingredient would necessarily result in an inability to read. They also stressed that the C in their equation was linguistic comprehension and not reading comprehension, which has led many to equate their R with reading comprehension. In other words, accurate decoding with no linguistic comprehension would not be considered reading any more than linguistic comprehension in the absence of decoding would.

Implications of the SVR

Originally published in *Remedial and Special Education*, more than half of the original SVR article (Gough & Tunmer, 1986) focused on implications for conceptions of reading disability. The authors grouped struggling readers into three disability categories: dyslexia, hyperlexia, and "garden-variety" difficulties. Students with dyslexia were those who struggled with the decoding side of the SVR equation. Students with hyperlexia, often termed *word callers*, were defined by their successful decoding but poor linguistic comprehension. Garden-variety struggling readers struggled with both decoding and linguistic comprehension. These readers are termed *garden variety* because decoding and linguistic comprehension are positively correlated in the same manner as in the general population, whereas among hyperlexic and dyslexic readers, this correlation is negative.

Despite elaborating on these three origins of poor reading, Gough and Tunmer (1986) did not pay much attention to their instructional implications. Subsequent publications have focused on not only how the SVR produces testable hypotheses and predictions but also how it can inform practice (e.g., Gough et al., 1996; Hoover, 2024; Hoover & Gough, 1990; Hoover & Tunmer, 2018). For example, while the SVR predicts readers with dyslexia, hyperlexia, and garden-variety difficulties, it can predict neither readers who decode well and have excellent linguistic comprehension but cannot read nor readers who excel solely in one component of the model but can read well. To find such readers would be evidence that the SVR was invalid, or at least had shortcomings (Gough & Tunmer, 1986). Hoover and Gough (1990) tested the hypotheses generated by the SVR, with reading operationalized as reading comprehension, and found results to be consistent with the SVR and further outlined instructional implications. They noted that linguistic comprehension develops "naturally," while decoding does not (p. 151), but they maintained that instruction in decoding and in linguistic comprehension should each contribute to improvements in reading comprehension. They also noted that given the contrasting nature of development in linguistic comprehension and decoding, students with hyperlexia would be rarer than those with dyslexia. Indeed, the relatively more common occurrence of dyslexia led Gough (1996) to claim that instruction in sight-word recognition and phonics was inadequate for preventing dyslexia and to recommend instruction in phonemic awareness for all in kindergarten.

Complicating the SVR

The simplicity of the SVR and its implications as drawn by Gough and colleagues (Gough, 1996; Gough et al., 1996; Hoover, 2024; Hoover & Gough, 1990; Hoover & Tunmer, 2018) has long fascinated the field of reading research. A quick search via Google Scholar for the phrase reveals it is cited in thousands of articles, with over 200 including the SVR in their title. Many have questioned whether the SVR is too simple and excludes too much, whereas others have questioned its applicability to shallower orthographies than English. Still others have accepted the SVR but have interrogated the dimensionality of its ingredients. In the subsequent sections, I explore the literature that seeks to complicate the SVR in various ways.

Ingredients of the SVR

Several researchers have sought to expand on the SVR in various ways. In what follows, I summarize some of the most popular candidates for missing ingredients of the SVR.

Processing Speed, Fluency, and Decoding

Processing speed and fluency have been prime candidates for separate or mediating factors in the SVR. Joshi and Aaron (2000) found that processing speed, as measured by a letter-naming task, contributed significant and substantial additional unique explained variance in reading comprehension in a sample of 40 third-grade readers. Working with a somewhat larger sample of third-grade students followed through fifth grade, Johnston and Kirby (2006) found that processing speed, as measured by a picture-naming task, explained significant but modest additional unique variance in reading comprehension in fourth and fifth grade, but not in third grade. Processing speed, as measured by speed of identifying two identical doodles in a series of seven, predicted decoding but not reading ability among typically developing Swedish fourth-grade students (Gustafson et al., 2013). The variability in results across studies may be due in part to differences in how processing speed was measured.

When processing speed is measured specifically as oral reading fluency (i.e., processing speed for text), a number of additional studies contribute to understanding its role in the SVR. For example, Adlof and colleagues (2006) followed children from second through eighth grade and measured oral reading fluency using lists of words and nonsense words, as well as connected texts. At second grade, all of the variance in oral reading fluency was shared with decoding. In both fourth and eighth grade, fluency was separable from decoding but did not significantly predict reading. By contrast, in a cross-sectional study of first- through 10th-grade readers, Cutting and Scarborough (2006) found that reading speed of connected text but not processing speed, as measured by a composite of serial naming measures, predicted unique variance in reading comprehension above and beyond what decoding and linguistic comprehension explained. In another cross-sectional study of fourth-, seventh-, and ninth-grade readers (Tilstra et al., 2009), fluency in reading connected text aloud contributed significant additional unique variance when added to a model representing the SVR. Expanding on the Adlof and colleagues' (2006) use of multiple fluency measures, Silverman and colleagues (2012) used measures of word list and connected text oral reading fluency plus a measure of rapid naming (i.e., processing speed) and found that fluency was separable from but highly correlated with decoding. Moreover, when fluency was included in the prediction of reading, decoding no longer significantly predicted reading comprehension. In fact, fluency entirely mediated the relation between decoding and reading comprehension in their sample of fourth-grade students.

Interestingly, in a cross-sectional sample of third-, seventh-, and 10th-grade students, Kershaw and Schatschneider (2012) measured decoding with word list reading fluency measures and found that the SVR did not hold for seventh- and 10th-grade students, in that decoding did not significantly predict reading comprehension, but fluency, as measured by oral reading of connected texts, did. They did not, however, test for whether fluency mediated the effects of decoding. Kim and Wagner (2015) working with a younger longitudinal sample from first through fourth grade and using similar measures to those of Kershaw and Schatschneider, did test for mediation and, similar to Silverman and colleagues (2012), found that fluency, as measured by oral reading of connected texts, did mediate the relationship between decoding and reading comprehension in every grade but first grade, in which decoding also had a direct relation to reading comprehension. These results are complemented by those of the Language and Reading Research Consortium (LARRC; 2015), which found that both accuracy and fluency in word reading predicted reading comprehension, but that the magnitude and significance of those relationships differed across grades 1–3 with accuracy as the significant predictor in grades 1 and 2, but fluency as the significant predictor in grade 3.

Across these studies, it is clear that processing speed, at least as measured by the reading of text aloud, does contribute to the explanation of reading comprehension beyond what decoding and linguistic comprehension do. The implications of these results suggest that measurement of reading fluency can productively predict reading comprehension outcomes across most, if not all, grades studied in the foregoing research (i.e., first through 10th grade). These results also suggest that, like decoding and linguistic comprehension, fluency may be a promising mechanism for improving reading comprehension.

Vocabulary and Linguistic Comprehension

Vocabulary has traditionally been considered part of the linguistic comprehension side of the SVR equation, but more recently, researchers have posited a crosscutting role for vocabulary. Before delving into this role, it must be acknowledged that vocabulary is part of linguistic comprehension. Tunmer and Chapman (2012) raised the fair criticism that in much SVR research, linguistic comprehension is equated with listening comprehension, whereas in the original theory, it was defined more broadly to include understanding at word, sentence, and discourse levels. Thus, to some degree, separating vocabulary from other measures of linguistic comprehension is at odds with the original conceptualization of how linguistic comprehension is defined.

That acknowledged, Tunmer and Chapman (2012) are among those who have sought to refine the role of vocabulary. Using multiple analytic approaches, they sought to determine whether vocabulary contributed to the prediction of reading comprehension above and beyond a measure of listening comprehension. Using hierarchical regression and exploratory factor analysis, they found that it did not. Once they employed structural equation modeling, however, and allowed for reciprocal indirect effects of linguistic comprehension, including vocabulary, via decoding and vice versa, they found that linguistic comprehension contributed both directly and indirectly to reading comprehension, while decoding only did so directly. This result is consistent with research suggesting that vocabulary specifically has a facilitative role in the development of decoding (e.g., Ouellette & Beers, 2010; Perfetti, 2010; Tunmer & Chapman, 2012).

Wagner and colleagues (2015) offered an important critique of analyses by Tunmer and Chapman (2012) and argued that properly fitted structural models indeed yielded a relationship between decoding and linguistic comprehension, but that the relationship was not directional other than in theory. Indeed, much SVR-inspired research that does not make directional assumptions has demonstrated a large amount of shared variance between linguistic comprehension and decoding (e.g., Cutting & Scarborough, 2006; Foorman et al., 2018, 2020). Subsequent studies focusing on the role of vocabulary thus far have nonetheless found evidence of mediation. Specifically, the LARRC (2015) found that vocabulary was fully mediated by listening comprehension and decoding across multiple grades, but, as the authors noted, the influence of vocabulary was stronger for listening comprehension than for decoding. In contrast, Florit and colleagues (2022) found that vocabulary was only mediated by listening comprehension. Further complicating the picture, Protopapas and colleagues (2013) found the opposite: that listening comprehension was mediated by vocabulary.

Others have questioned the attempt to separate vocabulary from linguistic comprehension at all. Lonigan and Milburn (2017) examined the dimensionality of linguistic comprehension by administering to almost 2,000 children in preschool through fifth grade three or more measures of six theoretical dimensions of linguistic comprehension: receptive vocabulary, expressive vocabulary, depth of vocabulary, receptive syntax and grammar, expressive syntax and grammar, and listening comprehension. Despite testing a wide range of factor-analytic models, they found that a two-factor model best fit the data across grades, although the two factors shared over 80% of their variance also across grades. The two factors aligned to a vocabulary factor and what they labeled as a syntax factor, but which included measures of syntax, grammar, and listening comprehension (e.g., syntactic understanding, grammaticality, morphology, following directions, oral comprehension). The authors argued that their results suggest that those interested in adequately covering the linguistic comprehension construct would do best to include measures of both word-level knowledge (i.e., vocabulary) and sentence- and discourse-level understanding.

Clearly questions remain as to the role of vocabulary in the influence of linguistic comprehension on reading comprehension. More research using designs that enable causal inference, as suggested by Wagner and colleagues (2015), as well as more comprehensive measurement approaches, as suggested by Lonigan and Milburn (2017), is needed to settle the matter.

Beyond Decoding and Linguistic Comprehension

Beyond debating the definition, dimensionality, and sufficiency of decoding and linguistic comprehension as predictors in the SVR, many researchers have looked outside the constructs most closely associated with reading for additional factors that contribute to reading comprehension. Among these factors are constructs such as motivation (Cartwright et al., 2015, 2019; Duke & Cartwright, 2021), texts and context (Francis et al., 2018), and executive functioning (EF). While processing speed can be thought of as an EF factor, it was discussed earlier due to its overlap with reading fluency in how it is often measured in studies. Discussion in this section, therefore, turns to other global cognitive skills that may contribute to reading comprehension beyond their influence on decoding and linguistic comprehension, namely EF.

Research has shown that EF relates to reading comprehension (e.g., Cain et al., 2004), and SVR investigations have delved into a diverse array of EF candidates, from attentional control (Conners, 2009) and performance, or nonverbal, intelligence (Conners, 2009; Kershaw & Schatschneider, 2012; van Wingerden et al., 2018) to critical thinking (Paige et al., 2024), but the following discussion is constrained to a brief consideration of a commonly investigated candidate: working memory. Working memory has had mixed results for complicating the SVR. Some studies have found both direct and indirect effects of working memory among students in a wide range of grades. Nouwens and colleagues (2021) found that among fourth-grade students, working memory directly predicted reading comprehension after researchers controlled for decoding and linguistic comprehension, as well as indirectly predicted it via decoding. Taboada Barber and colleagues (2021) also found that working memory contributed indirectly via decoding and via oral language but did not contribute directly among second- to fourth-grade English bilingual students; however, among their English-monolingual peers, only the indirect contribution through linguistic comprehension was significant. Yet Kershaw and Schatschneider (2012) did not find similar results in their third-grade sample; working memory did not contribute directly to the prediction of reading comprehension. Importantly, however, they did not investigate indirect contributions in their study. Morris and Lonigan (2022) did examine both direct and indirect relations of working memory and only found evidence for indirect relations in a sample of third- to fifth-grade students. Among first- through 10th-grade students, Cutting and Scarborough (2006) did not find that working memory contributed as an addition to the SVR. In contrast, Spencer and colleagues (2020) found no direct effect but did find an indirect effect for working memory via both decoding and oral language. Finally, among undergraduate students, Cartwright and colleagues (2019) found that working memory contributed both directly and indirectly to reading comprehension, and that indirect effects were again mediated by both decoding and linguistic comprehension.

In a recent and comprehensive meta-analysis, Peng and colleagues (2018) shed additional light on the potential role of working memory in the SVR. They found only five studies that provided a correlation table sufficient to support the meta-analysis, but these studies yielded 126 correlations. Using these correlations, they assessed whether working memory contributed to reading comprehension after both decoding and linguistic comprehension, measured as vocabulary, and results showed that working memory was not a significant contributor. Despite the temptation to take this meta-analytic result as definitive, five is a relatively low number of studies on which to determine the role of working memory conclusively. Peng and colleagues did not include the more recent studies discussed earlier, nor did they investigate indirect associations, which were more commonly found in the studies summarized earlier. Taken together, these results suggest that working memory most likely serves as an ability underpinning linguistic comprehension and/or decoding, but not as a third direct ingredient to reading comprehension.

Applicability of the SVR

The previous section reviewed select candidate factors that have been investigated as potentially complicating the SVR, but other attempts to complicate the SVR have focused on its applicability to different populations and different contexts. The earlier discussion mainly ignored differences in sampling, languages, and orthographies, which are the focus of this section.

Applicability to Students with Disabilities

One point of contention in the literature seeking to complicate the SVR has been its applicability for students with disabilities. Disabilities that have been investigated include those with attention-deficit/hyperactivity disorder (ADHD; Cole et al., 2023), who are hard of hearing or deaf (Wauters et al., 2021), and with intellectual disabilities (ID; Nilsson et al., 2021; Roch & Levorato, 2009; van Wingerden et al., 2018), with the bulk of these studies being conducted in European countries. Among 8- to 13-year-old children, the SVR worked, in that decoding and linguistic comprehension explained the bulk of variance (i.e., well over 90%) among both those children with and without an ADHD diagnosis (Cole et al., 2023). Working with Dutch adults who were deaf or hard of hearing, Wauters and colleagues (2021) also found that the SVR applied, although substantially less variance was explained in reading comprehension (i.e., 48%). Additionally, similar to developmental studies of the SVR, they found that linguistic comprehension was the stronger predictor among those with more skill in decoding.

In a sample of Swedish adolescents with nonspecific ID, Nilsson and colleagues (2021) found that the SVR did not fit the data well when an interaction between decoding and linguistic comprehension was included in their model, but it did fit well when that term was excluded, which is how the SVR is typically modeled, thus suggesting that contrary to the authors' conclusions, the SVR applies to this population.[1] Similarly, among Dutch children with nonspecific ID, van Wingerden and colleagues (2018) found that the SVR fit well. Complicating the SVR, though, they found that nonverbal IQ improved prediction of reading comprehension, suggesting that factor as an additional ingredient to the SVR for this population. Working in Italy with 11- to 18-year-old children with Down syndrome and a small comparison sample of typically developing first-grade children, Roch and Levorato (2009) also found that the SVR functioned well. Nonetheless, they pointed to the stronger predictive power of linguistic comprehension for students with Down syndrome compared to typically developing first graders. Across these studies, the SVR generally fits well, but differences in fit, explanatory power, the relative contributions of SVR ingredients, and the contribution of additional predictors suggest that further investigation is merited. Indeed, the bulk of the research into the applicability of the SVR for students with disabilities has been conducted in European countries in languages other than English, leaving a gap as to whether results would be consistent in English or outside of Europe.

Applicability across Languages and Orthographies

Given the English origins of the SVR, another strong line of inquiry has focused on the degree to which the SVR applies to different languages with different orthographies. European investigations have found the SVR applies in European Portuguese (Cadime et al., 2017), European Spanish (Montesinos et al., 2022), Finnish (Torppa et al., 2016), French (Massonnie et al., 2019), Greek (Kendeou et al., 2013; Protopapas et al., 2013), Italian (Florit et al., 2022; Tobia & Bonifacci, 2015), Norwegian (Hjetland et al., 2019), and Swedish (Gustafson et al., 2013), to name just a few. So many investigations existed by 2011 that Florit and Cain were able to conduct a meta-analysis comparing the fit of the SVR in English to a range of European languages with more transparent orthographies. They found that in English decoding related more strongly earlier in development, and linguistic comprehension became stronger later in development, but that in more transparent orthographies, linguistic comprehension was a strong predictor regardless of developmental stage, and the relative contributions of decoding were weaker, though not null, in these languages.[2]

Investigations beyond Europe have included work with Kiswahili in Kenya (Wawire et al., 2021), Spanish in the Dominican Republic (Sanchez-Vincitore et al., 2022), Portuguese in Brazil (Oliverira et al., 2020), Hebrew in Israel (Joshi et al., 2015), and Arabic using both its transparent (i.e., vowelized) and deep orthographic forms in Israel (Asadi & Ibrahim, 2018), and results consistently supported the SVR. Chinese has been an especially popular language due to the unique qualities of its orthography, so much so that Peng and colleagues (2021) were able to conduct a meta-analysis with over 200 studies from which to draw. Despite the differences between English and Chinese orthography, the SVR fit the data well, with a metalinguistic factor being fully mediated via linguistic comprehension and decoding. Even more striking, they found that, similar to patterns in English, the influence of decoding on reading comprehension was significant in earlier grades (i.e., grade 2 or earlier) but not so in later grades.

Applicability for Students with Diverse Backgrounds

Questions of applicability have also focused on students with diverse ethnic and linguistic backgrounds. In a group of English-speaking First Nations children who also received some instruction in Cree, Georgiou and colleagues (2009) found that, using English measures, the SVR fit well but only explained about 45% of variance in reading comprehension. Taboada Barber and colleagues (2021) examined the SVR among second- to fourth-grade readers, including emergent bilingual learners, defined as those eligible for English for speakers of other languages services and over 90% of whom spoke Spanish at home. Assessing the SVR in English, they found that the SVR fit well for both groups of students, but a larger proportion of unexplained variance remained for the emergent bilinguals (27%) compared to their monolingual English-speaking peers (12%). Kieffer and colleagues (2013) investigated the SVR among Spanish-speaking language-minority learners, a term that includes both English-dominant and Spanish-dominant speakers of Spanish at home and does not require eligibility for English language services. Studying the SVR in English, they found that while the SVR applied to this population, both passage-reading fluency and morphological awareness served as additional direct predictors of reading comprehension and that morphological awareness also had indirect, mediated effects via vocabulary. Working with grade 4 students in Singapore, Zhang and Ke (2019) examined the applicability of the SVR with three different groups of bilingual learners: ethnically Malay students who spoke Malay and English and ethnically Chinese students who spoke Chinese (i.e., Mandarin, Cantonese, or other varieties) and English and were either English-dominant or Chinese-dominant. They examined the SVR in English and found decoding had no direct contribution to reading comprehension, but rather was fully mediated by morphological decoding fluency for all three groups. The role of linguistic comprehension, measured as vocabulary, was direct for all three groups, but was also partially mediated by morphology for the English-dominant Chinese students and the Malay students. Finally, Huo and colleagues (2021) examined the SVR in French among English-speaking children attending a French immersion school and found that the SVR again held, although their model accounted for accuracy and fluency separately, with both contributing significantly to the explanation of reading comprehension in grades 1 and 2.

In a recent meta-analysis that examined the sufficiency of the SVR for students learning to read in a second language (Lee et al., 2022), the first language spoken by learners varied widely, as did the second language. While English was the most common second language and the United States the most common context, studies included Dutch, French, Hebrew, and Japanese among second languages and contexts ranging from Canada and the United Kingdom to Belgium, Israel, Japan, the Netherlands, and Norway. Results again supported the SVR in second-language reading. Interesting additional findings included that the relationship between decoding and reading comprehension was not significant for adolescent or adult readers and that the proximity of first and second languages in terms of their linguistic origins did not moderate the SVR.

Summary

That the SVR has robust support from a wide range of researchers and investigations cannot be denied. The preceding review neglects far more than it covers due to the breadth of the literature. Yet attempts to complicate the SVR have been decidedly mixed. What then are we to make of all this? Ought the SVR to be left alone? Ought it to be complicated? The answer, I would argue, is both.

Importantly, almost from the very start, Gough and his colleagues (1996, p. 1) acknowledged that reading is complex: "Only a fool would deny that reading is complex. Reading clearly involves many subprocesses, and those subprocesses must be skillfully coordinated." In the original article, which appeared in *Remedial and Special Education*, Gough and Tunmer (1986) proposed the SVR predominantly as a means of understanding the role of decoding in reading and as a means of delineating the major potential causes of reading disability. Thus, the beauty of the SVR lies not in its ability to explain reading comprehension fully in its myriad manifestations, but precisely in its aims: identifying the importance of decoding and linguistic comprehension as the most proximal causes of reading comprehension and the three main ways that reading comprehension can be compromised (i.e., due to decoding insufficiencies, linguistic comprehension insufficiencies, or both; Ebert & Scott, 2016).

The mixed results for additional direct and indirect influences on reading comprehension can be explained in at least three ways. First, the choice of analytic method varies widely across studies. Older studies relied heavily on hierarchical regression analyses (e.g., Chen & Vellutino, 1997), while newer studies have increasingly relied on structural equation modeling and latent measurement models (e.g., Kershaw & Schatscneider, 2012), as well as meta-analytic methods (Peng et al., 2018, 2021). With more advanced modeling approaches, however, comes increased opportunity for model misspecification (e.g., Wagner et al., 2015). Studies varied, too, in the degree to which their analyses operationalized decoding, linguistic comprehension, and reading comprehension as observed or latent variables (Cutting & Scarborough, 2006; Kershaw & Schatschneider, 2012; Snow, 2018). Indeed, Catts (2018) argued that a primary reason for conflicting results regarding whether vocabulary serves as a separate predictor of linguistic comprehension or a constituent of it is due to variation in whether or not linguistic comprehension is measured as a latent factor. Perhaps more importantly, the constituent variables for latent factors in more complex models can vary widely, yet another explanation for mixed results.

The second explanation is that studies examining additional candidate proximal causes and mediated factors varied widely in how they measured decoding and even more so in how they measured linguistic comprehension. As noted in the section on processing speed and fluency, some researchers used fluency measures as part of the decoding construct (e.g., LARRC & Chiu, 2018), while others treat them separately (e.g., Silverman et al., 2012), and still others treat fluency for reading words and nonsense words as distinct from fluency in reading passages (e.g., Kershaw & Schatschneider, 2012). Apel (2022) offers an excellent review of the numerous ways that linguistic comprehension has been defined and measured across studies, ranging from a constellation of measures (e.g., LARRC, 2015) to a lone vocabulary measure (e.g., Carver, 1998). As is obvious from the preceding review, others separated vocabulary out from linguistic comprehension, seeking an independent role for it (e.g., Florit et al., 2022). This variability in how the central constructs of the SVR are conceptualized and measured makes synthesis across studies difficult because differences in results may be a function of measurement choices (Cutting & Scarborough, 2006; Kershaw & Schatschneider, 2012; Lonigan & Burgess, 2017).

The third explanation is that studies varied widely in the ages and grades under examination. The SVR predicts that as decoding is mastered, presumably in the early grades for typically developing readers, linguistic comprehension will increasingly drive reading comprehension and decoding decreasingly so (see Gough et al., 1996, for a discussion). In other words, differences in the age or grade of a sample should yield differences in the strength and significance of the components of the SVR. Taken together with variability in analytic methods and measurement choices, it is no wonder that study results have been somewhat contradictory.

Despite all this variability, studies that examine mediation of underlying and component skills for decoding and linguistic comprehension offer the most promise for exposing additional malleable factors that can be capitalized on for intervention. From the preceding selective review, candidate malleable factors include, but are not limited to, processing speed, fluency, vocabulary, and working memory. As noted earlier, many other candidates exist in the literature, including but not limited to morphological awareness (e.g., Kieffer et al., 2013; Oliverira et al., 2020; Verhoeven et al., 2019), motivation (Cartwright et al., 2015, 2019), attentional control (Conners, 2009), intelligence (Conners, 2009; Kershaw & Schatschneider, 2012; van Wingerden et al., 2018), critical thinking (Paige et al., 2024), perspective taking (Kim, 2020; La Russo et al., 2016; Snow, 2018), and texts and context (Francis et al., 2018). The limitation that most of these studies share is their correlational nature. Few examined relationships longitudinally.

The Long View of the SVR

Indeed, one relatively underinvestigated avenue for future investigations of the SVR and the mechanisms by which reading comprehension might be improved is longitudinal analysis. This avenue seems the most promising in that it can provide time-course information about how development in SVR components and other candidates inform reading comprehension over time rather than simply for one point in time. While a great deal of longitudinal research of reading exists, few studies are framed by their authors as directly addressing the SVR.

Several studies have examined how well the SVR explains reading over the early school years using a structural equation modeling analytic approach (Hjetland et al., 2019; Kendeou et al., 2009; LARRC & Chiu, 2018; Torppa et al., 2016). Two studies have tracked the sufficiency of the SVR from preschool into the late elementary grades (Hjetland et al., 2019; LARRC & Chiu, 2018). LARRC and Chiu (2018) tracked 420 predominantly White monolingual U.S. students from preschool to third grade and found that preschool linguistic comprehension- and decoding-related skills strongly but indirectly predicted grade 3 reading comprehension via grade 3 linguistic comprehension and decoding, with decoding being the stronger direct predictor. Hjetland and colleagues (2019) tracked preschool monolingual Norwegian students through fourth grade. Specifically, they examined how preschool linguistic comprehension and decoding predicted growth in reading comprehension from grade 2 to grade 4. They found that while decoding-related skills in preschool predicted decoding in grades 1 and 2, decoding only predicted initial reading comprehension in grade 2 and did not predict growth to grade 4. In contrast, preschool linguistic comprehension predicted grade 2 linguistic comprehension, which in turn predicted both initial status and growth in reading comprehension from grade 2 to 4. The difference in the role of decoding in these two studies may be due to differences in modeling, but also related to the greater transparency of Norwegian orthography.

An additional two studies evaluated the sufficiency of the SVR from kindergarten through the elementary grades (Kendeou et al., 2009; Torppa et al., 2016). Kendeou and colleagues (2009) followed predominantly White U.S. students from kindergarten to grade 2 and found that while kindergarten decoding strongly predicted grade 2 decoding, kindergarten linguistic comprehension was less strongly predictive of grade 2 linguistic comprehension, yet grade 2 linguistic comprehension was more strongly related to grade 2 reading comprehension than was grade 2 decoding. Working in Finnish, another transparent orthography, Torppa and colleagues (2016) followed children from kindergarten through grade 3 and found that kindergarten vocabulary directly predicted grade 1 linguistic comprehension, decoding, and reading comprehension, while decoding-related skills in kindergarten only predicted grade 1 decoding and reading comprehension. Moreover, similar to Hjetland and colleagues (2019), they found the influence of decoding on reading comprehension faded by grade 2, whereas the influence of linguistic comprehension did not and persisted through grade 3. These findings suggest that across the earliest years of schooling, linguistic comprehension is the better long-term predictor of later reading comprehension, at least among monolingual U.S. students and monolingual European students reading in transparent orthographies.

Far fewer studies have explored the SVR longitudinally among older readers (Foorman et al., 2020; Mancilla-Martinez et al., 2011). In a relatively small sample of students, Mancilla-Martinez and colleagues (2011) used hierarchical linear growth modeling to examine growth from grades 5 to 7 among predominantly

Latine U.S. students, about half of whom were formerly limited English proficient. They found that decoding was a stronger predictor than linguistic comprehension of initial reading comprehension in grade 5 but that neither predicted growth in reading comprehension. Given the relatively small and homogeneous sample, it may be that there was not enough variance in student growth rates for decoding and linguistic comprehension to explain; alternatively, though, it may be that by the intermediate and middle school grades, other factors are driving growth. Foorman and colleagues (2020) used structural equation modeling to explore growth in three cohorts of students that started in grades 5, 7, and 9 and were followed to grades 6, 8, and 10, respectively. Their sample was larger and more diverse than that of Mancilla-Martinez and colleagues, with one-fourth of students identified as White, another one-fourth as Latine, one-third as Black, and the rest split among other racial and ethnic categories; their sample also had 20, 17, and 8% limited-English-proficient students in each respective cohort. In their sample, fifth-grade decoding and linguistic comprehension both predicted sixth-grade reading comprehension strongly, as did their interaction. For the seventh- and ninth-grade cohorts, the importance of decoding was reduced in strength and was no longer significant for the oldest cohort, while for both cohorts, the importance of linguistic comprehension increased in strength, and the interaction of decoding and linguistic comprehension was not significant.

Of note across these studies is that the importance of linguistic comprehension relative to decoding holds with the SVR, which posits that as decoding is mastered, linguistic comprehension carries increased weight in the prediction of reading comprehension. Interestingly, the bulk of these studies used a structural equation modeling approach that did not estimate growth specifically, with the exceptions being Mancilla-Martinez and colleagues (2011) and Hjetland and colleagues (2019). While Hjetland and associates found that linguistic comprehension but not decoding predicted growth in reading comprehension in a younger sample, Mancilla-Martinez and colleagues found that neither decoding nor linguistic comprehension predicted growth trajectories in their older sample. More research is obviously needed to determine the degree to which these findings reflect a developmental trend versus other factors in which the studies differed (e.g., language, orthographic depth, measures of the key constructs, analysis methods). Nonetheless, what these studies add is the possibility of identifying the degree to which linguistic comprehension and decoding explain reading comprehension not only at a concurrent point in time or even predictively from one time to another, but also growth across multiple time points, thereby potentially suggesting mechanisms for changing growth and candidates for instruction.

In 2018, Hoover and Tunmer updated their claims about the SVR, noting that its intentions were to explain status and never growth:

> The SVR is a concurrent or static model, describing reading at a single point in time. It is not, by itself, a model of reading development, though certain aspects of reading development can be captured as successive changes in the relative strengths of its two component skills at distinct points in time. Thus, the SVR

does not state *how* reading develops over time (i.e., what and when component skills change), only that the level of development attained at *any* point in time will depend *entirely and only* on the multiplicative combination of the levels of the two components. (p. 306)

Thus, to some extent, all the studies reviewed in this section go beyond the original claims for the SVR theory, which was also never intended to inform instruction absolutely. Nonetheless, if we return to one of the original purposes of the SVR—to explicate the predominant types of reading difficulties readers might experience (Gough & Tunmer, 1986)—it is worth considering how the delineation of sources of disability naturally implies those sources are levers by which to improve reading; hence, the drive to use the SVR as a means of understanding development.

If nothing else, the preceding literature review in its totality suggests the importance of the SVR for understanding reading. Regardless of the original intent of the SVR, it has served well as a common heuristic for those seeking to explore the complexities of reading comprehension whether concurrently or over time. Indeed, the SVR is one of the most influential theories in reading research and can be construed as the theory that launched a thousand studies. In the last two decades, it has also launched new theories that build off it. Scarborough (2001) created the Reading Rope, which breaks both decoding and linguistic comprehension into constituent components and conveys that while decoding becomes increasingly automatic with development, linguistic comprehension becomes increasingly strategic. The direct and inferential mediation model (DIME) of reading comprehension (Ahmed et al., 2016) sought to complicate the SVR specifically for older readers, where decoding is more commonly mastered. While it includes decoding, it also decomposes linguistic comprehension, seeking distinct roles for background knowledge, vocabulary, and inferencing, and invokes reading strategies as a separate construct. In the complete view of reading (CVRi), Francis and colleagues (2018) sought to complicate the SVR for middle school readers, but less by debating component skills than by adding passage characteristics as predictors of variance in reading comprehension. The CVRi allows for not only the distinct influence of person and text characteristics but also their interactions, thereby providing a means of understanding how the effects of one depend on the effects of the other. Similar to DIME, Kim's (2020) direct and indirect effects model of reading (DIER) also includes decoding and decomposes linguistic comprehension but has been explored with second- and fourth-grade students and is unique in its inclusion of working memory and attention as domain-general cognitive factors influencing both decoding and linguistic comprehension. DIER is also distinguished by its inclusion of three meta-cognitive factors: inferencing, comprehension monitoring, and theory of mind. Duke and Cartwright's (2021; Burns et al., 2023) active view of reading dissects both linguistic comprehension and decoding into component skills; moreover, it specifies bridging processes—factors that influence both decoding and linguistic comprehension, as well as reading comprehension—and a role for self-regulation, which encompasses motivation, engagement, strategic processes, and EF. Finally, the lattice model of the development of reading comprehension (Conner, 2016) takes a distinctly longitudinal view of the SVR and incorporates a role for instruction. Specifically, the model holds a place for decoding and other text-specific processes, for linguistic comprehension and processes, and for social, cognitive, and regulatory processes, and provides a cross-lagged conceptualization of how these factors influence each other over time with intervening instruction.

What each of these models shares, besides inspiration from the SVR, is a more explicit purpose to identify malleable factors by which reading may be actively improved. Contrary to the SVR, they overtly seek to bring instruction and its impacts into the equation. Along with the longitudinal studies summarized earlier, they take a long view of reading; that is, while it is good to explain reading at a given point in time, the more promising aim at this stage in the field is to pursue avenues for advancing reading achievement. As Burns and colleagues (2023) point out, inequality in reading outcomes is one the most pressing social justice issues of our time, and moving beyond simply describing the problem requires looking beyond the SVR.

NOTES

1. There are numerous studies beyond Nilsson et al. (2021) investigating whether the interaction of decoding and linguistic comprehension, which is viewed as the essence of the SVR, significantly adds to the explanation of reading comprehension beyond their main effects (e.g., Chen & Vellutino, 1997; Foorman et al., 2020; Georgiou et al., 2009; Hoover & Gough, 1990; Savage, 2006). These studies are not discussed in depth here due to space limitations.

2. An important additional finding outside the scope of this discussion but relevant to the discussion of fluency in the preceding sections is that among decoding measures, fluency was generally a stronger predictor than accuracy.

REFERENCES

Adlof, S. M., Catts, H. W., & Little, T. D. (2006). Should the simple view of reading include a fluency component? *Reading and Writing, 19,* 933–958.

Ahmed, Y., Francis, D. J., York, M., Fletcher, J. M., & Barnes, M. (2016). Validation of the direct and inferential mediation (DIME) model of reading comprehension in grades 7 through 12. *Contemporary Educational Psychology, 44-45,* 68–82.

Apel, K. (2022). A different view on the simple view of reading. *Remedial and Special Education, 43*(6), 434–447.

Asadi, I. A., & Ibrahim, R. (2018). The simple view of reading model in the transparent and deep versions of Arabic orthography. *Reading Psychology, 39*(6), 537–552.

Burns, M. K., Duke, N. K., & Cartwright, K. B. (2023). Evaluating components of the active view of reading as intervention targets: Implications for social justice. *School Psychology, 38*(1), 30–41.

Cadime, I., Rodrigues, B., Santos, S., Viana, F. L., Chaves-Sousa, S., Cosme, M. d. C., & Ribeiro, I. (2017). The role of word recognition, oral reading fluency and listening comprehension in the simple view of reading: A study in an intermediate depth orthography. *Reading and Writing, 30*, 591–611.

Cain, K., Oakhill, J., & Bryant, P. (2004). Children's reading comprehension ability: Concurrent prediction by working memory, verbal ability, and component skills. *Journal of Educational Psychology, 96*(1), 31–42.

Cartwright, K. B., Lee, S. A., Taboada Barber, A., DeWyngaert, L. U., Lane, A. B., & Singleton, T. (2019). Contributions of executive function and cognitive intrinsic motivation to university students' reading comprehension. *Reading Research Quarterly, 55*(3), 345–369.

Cartwright, K. B., Marshall, T. R., & Wray, E. (2015). A longitudinal study of the role of reading motivation in primary students' reading comprehension: Implications for a less simple view of reading. *Reading Psychology, 37*, 55–91.

Carver, R. P. (1998). Predicting reading level in grades 1 to 6 from listening level and decoding level: Testing theory relevant to the simple view of reading. *Reading and Writing, 10*, 121–154.

Catts, H. W. (2018). The simple view of reading: Advancements and false impressions. *Remedial and Special Education, 39*(5), 317–323.

Cervetti, G. N., Pearson, P. D., Palincsar, A. S., Afflerbach, P., Kendeou, P., Bincarosa, G., . . . Berman, A. I. (2020). How the Reading for Understanding Initiative's research complicates the simple view of reading invoked in the science of reading. *Reading Research Quarterly, 55*(S1), S161–S172.

Chen, R. S., & Vellutino, F. R. (1997). Prediction of reading ability: A cross-validation study of the simple view of reading. *Journal of Literacy Research, 29*(1), 1–24.

Cole, A. M., Chan, E. S. M., Gaye, F., Spiegel, J. A., Soto, E. F., & Kofler, M. J. (2023). Evaluating the simple view of reading for children with attention-deficit/hyperactivity disorder. *Journal of Educational Psychology, 115*(5), 700–714.

Conner, C. M. D. (2016). A lattice model of the development of reading comprehension. *Child Development Perspectives, 10*(4), 269–274.

Conners, F. A. (2009). Attentional control and the simple view of reading. *Reading and Writing, 22*, 591–613.

Cutting, L. E., & Scarborough, H. S. (2006). Prediction of reading comprehension: Relative contributions of word recognition, language proficiency, and other cognitive skills can depend on how comprehension is measured. *Scientific Studies of Reading, 10*(3), 277–299.

Duke, N. K., & Cartwright, K. B. (2021). The science of reading progresses: Communicating advances beyond the simple view of reading. *Reading Research Quarterly, 56*(1), 525–544.

Ebert, K. D., & Scott, C. M. (2016). Bring the simple view of reading to the clinic: Relationships between oral and written language skills in a clinical sample. *Journal of Communication Disorders, 62*, 147–160.

Florit, E., & Cain, K. (2011). The simple view of reading: Is it valid for different types of alphabetic orthographies? *Educational Psychology Review, 23*, 553–576.

Florit, E., Roch, M., Dicataldo, R., & Levorato, M. C. (2022). The simple view of reading in Italian beginner readers: Converging evidence and open debates on the role of the main components. *Learning and Individual Differences, 93*, Article 101961.

Foorman, B. R., Petscher, Y., & Herrera, S. (2018). Unique and common effects of decoding and language factors in predicting reading comprehension in grades 1–10. *Learning and Individual Differences, 63*, 12–23.

Foorman, B. R., Wu, Y.-C., Quinn, J. M., & Petscher, Y. (2020). How do latent decoding and language predict latent reading comprehension: Across two years in grades 5, 7, and 9? *Reading & Writing, 33,* 2281–2309.

Francis, D. J., Kulesz, P. A., & Benoit, J. S. (2018). Extending the simple view of reading to account for variation within readers and across texts: The complete view of reading (CVRi). *Remedial and Special Education, 39*(5), 274–288.

Georgiou, G. K., Das, J. P., & Hayward, D. (2009). Revisiting the "simple view of reading" in a group of children with poor reading comprehension. *Journal of Learning Disabilities, 42*(1), 76–84.

Goodman, K. S. (1973). The 13th easy way to make learning to read difficult: A reaction to Gleitman and Rozin. *Reading Research Quarterly, 8*(4), 484–493.

Gough, P. B. (1996). How children learn to read and why they fail. *Annals of Dyslexia, 46,* 3–20.

Gough, P. B., Hoover, W. A., & Peterson, C. L. (1996). Some observations on a simple view of reading. In C. Cornoldi & J. Oakhill (Eds.), *Reading Comprehension Difficulties: Processes and Intervention* (pp. 1–13). Erlbaum.

Gough, P. B., & Tunmer, W. E. (1986). Decoding, reading, and reading disability. *Remedial and Special Education, 7*(1), 6–10.

Gustafson, S., Samuelsson, C., Johansson, E., & Wallmann, J. (2013). How simple is the simple view of reading? *Scandinavian Journal of Educational Research, 57*(3), 292–308.

Hjetland, H. N., Lervag, A., Lyster, S.-A. H., Hagtvet, B. E., & Hulme, C. (2019). Pathways to reading comprehension: A longitudinal study from 4 to 9 years of age. *Journal of Educational Psychology, 111,* 751–763.

Hoover, W. (2024). The simple view of reading and its broad types of reading difficulties. *Reading and Writing, 37,* 2277–2298.

Hoover, W. A., & Gough, P. B. (1990). The simple view of reading. *Reading and Writing, 2,* 127–160.

Hoover, W. A., & Tunmer, W. E. (2018). The simple view of reading: Three assessments of its adequacy. *Remedial and Special Education, 39*(5), 304–312.

Huo, M. R. Y., Koh, P. W., Cheng, Y., Marinova-Todd, S. H., & Chen, X. (2021). The simple view of reading in French second language learners. *Learning and Individual Differences, 92,* Article 102082.

Johnston, T. C., & Kirby, J. R. (2006). The contribution of naming speed to the simple view of reading. *Reading and Writing, 19,* 339–361.

Joshi, R. M., & Aaron, P. G. (2000). The component model of reading: Simple view of reading made a little more complex. *Reading Psychology, 21,* 85–97.

Joshi, R. M., Ji, X. R., Breznitz, Z., Amiel, M., & Yulia, A. (2015). Validation of the simple view of reading in Hebrew—a Semitic language. *Scientific Studies of Reading, 19*(3), 243–252.

Kendeou, P., Papadopoulos, T. C., & Kotzapoulou, M. (2013). Evidence for the early emergence of the simple view of reading in a transparent orthography. *Reading and Writing, 26,* 189–204.

Kendeou, P., van den Broek, P., White, M. J., & Lynch, J. S. (2009). Predicting reading comprehension in early elementary school: The independent contributions of oral language and decoding skills. *Journal of Educational Psychology, 101*(4), 765–778.

Kershaw, S., & Schatschneider, C. (2012). A latent variable approach to the simple view of reading. *Reading and Writing, 25,* 433–464.

Kieffer, M. J., Biancarosa, G., & Mancilla-Martinez, J. (2013). Roles of morphological awareness in the reading comprehension of Spanish-speaking language minority learners: Exploring partial mediation by vocabulary and reading fluency. *Applied Psycholinguistics, 34,* 697–725.

Kim, Y.-S. G. (2020). Hierarchical and dynamic relations of language and cognitive skills to reading comprehension: Testing the direct and indirect effects model of reading (DIER). *Journal of Educational Psychology, 112*(4), 667–684.

Kim, Y.-S. G., & Wagner, R. K. (2015). Text (oral) reading fluency as a construct in reading development: An investigation of its mediating role for children from grades 1 to 4. *Scientific Studies of Reading, 19*(3), 224–242.

Language and Reading Research Consortium. (2015). Learning to read: Should we keep things simple? *Reading Research Quarterly, 50*(2), 151–169.

Language and Reading Research Consortium, & Chiu, Y. D. (2018). The simple view of reading across development: Prediction of grade 3 reading comprehension from pre-kindergarten skills. *Remedial and Special Education, 39*(5), 289–303.

LaRusso, M., Kim, H. Y., Selman, R., Uccelli, P., Dawson, T., Jones, S., . . . Snow, C. (2016). Contributions of academic language, perspective taking, and complex reasoning to deep reading comprehension. *Journal of Research on Educational Effectiveness, 9*(2), 201–222.

Lee, H., Jung, G., & Lee, J. H. (2022). Simple view of second language reading: A meta-analytic structural equation modeling approach. *Scientific Studies of Reading, 26*(6), 585–603.

Lonigan, C. J., & Burgess, S. R. (2017). Dimensionality of reading skills with elementary-school-age children. *Scientific Studies of Reading, 21*(3), 239–253.

Lonigan, C. J., & Milburn, T. F. (2017). Identifying the dimensionality of oral language skills of children with typical development in preschool through fifth grade. *Journal of Speech, Language, and Hearing Research, 60,* 2185–2198.

Mancilla-Martinez, J., Kieffer, M. J., Biancarosa, G., Christodoulou, J. A., & Snow, C. E. (2011). Investigating English reading comprehension growth in adolescent language minority learners: Some insights from the simple view. *Reading and Writing, 24,* 339–354.

Massonnie, J., Bianco, M., Lima, L., & Bressoux, P. (2019). Longitudinal predictors of reading comprehension in French at first grade: Unpacking the oral component of the simple view. *Learning and Instruction, 60,* 166–179.

Montesinos, M. M. T., Salceda, J. C. R., Alonso, G. A., & Joshi, R M. (2022). Simple view of reading in Spanish: A longitudinal study. *Revista de Logopedia, Foniatría y Audiología, 42,* 214–226.

Morris, B. M., & Lonigan, C. J. (2022). What components of working memory are associated with children's reading skills? *Learning and Individual Differences, 95,* Article 102114.

Nilsson, K., Danielsson, H., Elwer, A., Messer, D., Henry, L., & Samuelsson, S. (2021). Investigating reading comprehension in adolescents with intellectual disabilities: Evaluating the simple view of reading. *Journal of Cognition, 4*(1), Article 56.

Nouwens, S., Groen, M. A., Kleemans, T., & Verhoeven, L. (2021). How executive functions contribute to reading comprehension. *British Journal of Educational Psychology, 91,* 169–192.

Oliverira, M., Levesque, K. C., Deacon, S. H., & da Mota, M. M. P. E. (2020). Evaluating models of how morphological awareness connects to reading comprehension: A study in Portuguese. *Journal of Research in Reading, 43*(2), 161–179.

Ouellette, G., & Beers, A. (2010). A not-so-simple view of reading: How oral vocabulary and visual-word recognition complicate the story. *Reading and Writing, 23,* 189–208.

Paige, D., Rupley, W. H., & Ziglari, L. (2024). Critical thinking in reading comprehension: Fine tuning the simple view of reading. *Education Sciences, 14*, 225.

Peng, P., Barnes, M., Wang, C. C., Wang, W., Li, S., Swanson, H. L., . . . Tao, S. (2018). A meta-analysis on the relation between reading and working memory. *Psychological Bulletin, 144*(1), 48–76.

Peng, P., Lee, K., Luo, J., Li, S., Joshi, R. M., & Tao, S. (2021). Simple view of reading in Chinese: A one-stage meta-analytic structural equation modeling. *Review of Educational Research, 91*(1), 3–33.

Perfetti, C. (2010). Decoding, vocabulary, and comprehension. In M. G. McKeown & L. Kucan (Eds.), *Bringing reading research to life* (pp. 291–303). Guilford Press.

Protopapas, A., Mouzaki, A., Sideridis, G. D., Kotsokakou, A., & Simos, P. G. (2013). The role of vocabulary in the context of the simple view of reading. *Reading and Writing Quarterly, 29*, 168–202.

Roch, M., & Levorato, M. C. (2009). Simple view of reading in Down's syndrome: The role of listening comprehension and reading skills. *International Journal of Language and Communication Disorders, 44*(2), 206–223.

Sanchez-Vincitore, L. V., Veras, C., Mencia-Ripley, A., Ruiz-Matuk, C. B., & Cubilla-Bonnetier, D. (2022). Reading comprehension precursors: Evidence of the simple view of reading in a transparent orthography. *Frontiers in Education, 7*, Article 914414.

Savage, R. (2006). Reading comprehension is not always the product of nonsense word decoding and linguistic comprehension: Evidence from teenagers who are extremely poor readers. *Scientific Studies of Reading, 10*(2), 143–164.

Scarborough, H. S. (2001). Connecting early language and literacy to later reading (dis) abilities: Evidence, theory, and practice. In S. Neuman & D. Dickinson (Eds.), *Handbook of early literacy research* (Vol. 1, pp. 97–110). Guilford Press.

Silverman, R. D., Speece, D. L., Harring, J. R., & Ritchey, K. D. (2012). Fluency has a role in the simple view of reading. *Scientific Studies of Reading, 17*(2), 108–133.

Snow, C. E. (2018). Simple and not-so-simple views of reading. *Remedial and Special Education, 39*(5), 313–316.

Spencer, M., Richmond, M. C., & Cutting, L. E. (2020). Considering the role of executive function in reading comprehension: A structural equation modeling approach. *Scientific Studies of Reading, 24*(3), 179–199.

Taboada-Barber, A., Cartwright, K. B., Hancock, G. R., & Klauda, S. L. (2021). Beyond the simple view of reading: The role of executive functions in emergent bilinguals' and English monolinguals' reading comprehension. *Reading Research Quarterly, 56*(Suppl. 1), S45–S64.

Tilstra, J., McMaster, K., van den Broek, P., Kendeou, P., & Rapp, D. (2009). Simple but complex: Components of the simple view of reading across grade levels. *Journal of Research in Reading, 32*(4), 383–401.

Tobia, V., & Bonifacci, P. (2015). The simple view of reading in a transparent orthography: The stronger role of oral comprehension. *Reading and Writing, 28*, 939–957.

Torppa, M., Georgiou, G. K., Lerkkanen, M.-K., Niemi, P., Poikkeus, A.-M., & Nurmi, J.-E. (2016). Examining the simple view of reading in a transparent orthography: A longitudinal study from kindergarten to grade 3. *Merrill–Palmer Quarterly, 62*(2), 179–206.

Tunmer, W. E., & Chapman, J. W. (2012). The simple view of reading redux: Vocabulary knowledge and the independent components hypothesis. *Journal of Learning Disabilities, 45*(5), 453–466.

van Wingerden, E., Segers, E., van Balkom, H., & Verhoeven, L. (2018). Cognitive constraints on the simple view of reading: A longitudinal study in children with intellectual disabilities. *Scientific Studies of Reading, 22*(4), 321–334.

Verhoeven, L., Voeten, M., & Vermeer, A. (2019). Beyond the simple view of early first and second language reading: The impact of lexical quality. *Journal of Neurolinguistics, 50,* 28–36.

Wagner, R. K., Herrera, S. K., Spencer, M., & Quinn, J. M. (2015). Reconsidering the simple view of reading in an intriguing case of equivalent models: Commentary on Tunmer and Chapman (2012). *Journal of Learning Disabilities, 48*(2), 115–119.

Wauters, L., van Gelder, H., & Tijsseling, C. (2021). Simple view of reading in deaf and hard-of-hearing adults. *Journal of Deaf Studies and Deaf Education, 26*(4), 535–545.

Wawire, B. A., Piper, B., & Liang, X. (2021). Examining the simple view of reading in Kiswahili: Longitudinal evidence from Kenya. *Learning and Individual Differences, 90,* Article 102044.

Zhang, D., & Ke, S. (2019). The simple view of reading made complex by morphological decoding fluency in bilingual fourth-grade readers of English. *Reading Research Quarterly, 55*(2), 311–329.

CHAPTER 8

What Is Text Complexity and How Does It Affect Literacy Learning?

Steven J. Amendum
Kristin Conradi Smith

Twenty years ago, a handbook such as this one likely would not have contained a chapter on text complexity and literacy learning. Instead, text complexity was a construct addressed by specific readability formulas to estimate the level of a particular text. Various text-leveling processes were used to match readers with texts, from the McGuffy readers in the 1800s to Fountas and Pinnell's (2013) Guided Reading leveling system designed to match readers to particular text levels.

However, the 2010 introduction of the Common Core State Standards (CCSS; National Governors Association Center for Best Practices & Council of Chief State School Officers [NGA & CCSSO], 2010) and other state standards ushered in a new era related to text complexity. The Standards provided text complexity benchmarks by grade-level bands that students would be required to achieve to be college and career ready. Moreover, the CCSS provided an appendix that included background on text complexity, a three-pronged model for measuring text complexity, and a description of quantitative and qualitative measures of text complexity. Given the sudden elevated status of text complexity, Fisher and colleagues (2012, p. 1) noted that "text complexity is the new black."

Once text complexity was elevated as a concept in practice, an additional flurry of research followed. Researchers addressed features of texts themselves (e.g., Graesser et al., 2014), text complexity and reader characteristics (e.g., Northrop & Kelly, 2019), and text complexity and instructional tasks (e.g., Valencia et al., 2014). In this chapter our aim is to address what text complexity is and how it affects literacy learning in grades 3–8. We begin with a brief history and definitions, then consider relevant theoretical frameworks. We then shift to what is known from the text complexity research and move to how this knowledge can guide educators' actions. We end with a brief discussion of additional work needed.

What Is Text Complexity?

Traditionally, text complexity has been viewed through the lens of readability (Benjamin, 2012). This perspective emphasizes characteristics inherent to the text itself, such as word difficulty, sentence length, and cohesion, as factors that contribute to complexity. For instance, a text about soccer with specific characteristics might be classified as a fourth-grade-level text based on quantitative measures such as those listed earlier.

However, an alternative perspective emphasizes the interaction between reader characteristics and text features (Burns, 2024; Fountas & Pinnell, 1996). From this perspective, a student's prior knowledge may significantly influence perceived complexity. For example, a student with extensive knowledge of soccer might find the same text about a particular historical soccer game less complex, despite the presence of technical vocabulary, than a student with limited background knowledge of soccer.

Further complicating conceptualizations of text complexity is the potential mediating role of teacher instruction (Valencia et al., 2014). Pedagogical strategies such as preteaching vocabulary, choral reading, or using graphic organizers can scaffold student comprehension and make complex texts accessible to students. Thus, a text initially considered too difficult can become more accessible through targeted instructional support.

Quantitative Measurement of Text Complexity

Educators and curriculum developers have historically relied on readability formulas for determining what makes one text more or less difficult than another (Benjamin, 2012). These tools (e.g., Fry, Dale–Chall, Lexile Framework), often categorized as first-generation or second-generation tools, typically analyze a limited set of surface-level features such as word frequency and sentence length (Benjamin, 2012; Tortorelli, 2020). The conventional assumption of these readability formulas was that texts containing a greater number of longer words and sentences were more complex and difficult for students to read and comprehend (Benjamin, 2012).

More recent third-generation tools include text complexity measurement across multiple dimensions. Coh-Metrix (Graesser et al., 2004) evaluates text on multiple measures of cohesion, language, and readability using components from computational linguistics. TextEvaluator (Sheehan et al., 2014) approximates text complexity based on multiple dimensions (academic vocabulary, syntactic complexity, word concreteness, word unfamiliarity, interactive/conversational style, degree of narrativity, lexical cohesion, and argumentation). The Lexile Framework for Reading, which is explicitly used and referenced in the CCSS (NGA & CCSSO,

2010), includes the Lexile Early Literacy Indicators. These indicators effectively differentiate between emergent reader texts with similar Lexile scores, for example, those high in decodability versus predictability (Fitzgerald et al., 2016; Smith & Turner, 2017). However, their usefulness diminishes for more conventional texts encountered by students in second grade and beyond (Fitzgerald et al., 2016). The Lexile Framework beyond the early literacy indicators correlates with other text-leveling systems (Hiebert & Pearson, 2010); however, they have been criticized for lacking comprehensiveness (e.g., Benjamin, 2012) and failing to accurately predict student performance (e.g., Cunningham et al., 2018), particularly with online texts (Ardoin et al., 2010).

Qualitative Measurement of Text Complexity

Though newer generations of quantitative text measures have allowed for advances in our understanding of text complexity, some aspects of text complexity are less quantifiable and measurable only by an "attentive human reader" (CCSS, 2010; NGA & CCSSO, 2010, p. 4, Appendix A). The CCSS identifies four qualitative dimensions of text complexity worth considering. These dimensions include levels of meaning, text structure, language conventionality and clarity, and knowledge demands. In Appendix A, they offer some description of these components, which have been further elaborated in articles for teachers (see Fisher & Frey, 2014; Strong et al., 2018). In short, the addition of these qualitative dimensions conveys that quantitative factors, alone, may fail to capture what makes a text complex. Moving beyond sentence and word length and word familiarity, how texts are written and organized—and the language and text demands of a text—can further contribute to its complexity.

Levels of meaning refers both to the macro-level purpose of the text (literary or informational) and whether the text includes a singular or multiple meanings for the reader to unpack and infer. The text's structure addresses aspects of the text's organization, such as whether the author used language or features to help simplify the reading, or whether the author employed flashbacks or other literary devices that render the reading more difficult. The dimension of language conventionality and clarity suggests the familiarity of dialect used, along with the considerations of both general academic and domain-specific vocabulary, can contribute to a text's complexity. Finally, the knowledge demands of a given text—whether in terms of cultural knowledge, content knowledge, or otherwise—can contribute to its complexity. All readers have different "funds of knowledge" (Moll et al., 2013), but texts often make assumptions about the types of knowledge that readers should know or bring to the text before reading.

Operationalizing Text Complexity

The term *text complexity* is used to encompass qualitative aspects of texts, quantitative aspects of texts, and reader and task considerations, and even broader contexts. For example, with the adoption of CCSS text complexity grade-level bands, at times, *grade-level text* began to be used synonymously with *complex text*. Given that multiple factors contribute to the broad concept of text complexity—and that various terms are often used interchangeably in the literature—the multidimensional nature of this construct necessitates a clear distinction between the different terms. Mesmer and colleagues (2012) provide a helpful framework, defining *text complexity* as inherent properties of a text itself, independent of reader characteristics or task. Conversely, *text difficulty* reflects the ease or hardship a particular text presents for a specific reader. Thus, *complexity* is judged comparatively across texts, while *difficulty* is reader-centric (and potentially task-dependent; see Figure 8.1).

If we revisit our earlier soccer example, a measure of text complexity might consider the vocabulary and syntactic demands of the text and deem a specific passage about soccer to be at a fifth-grade level of complexity. Whether the text is *difficult* for fifth graders, however, depends on their reading ability and the knowledge about soccer they bring to the text. If the student still struggles with word recognition or fluency, the text will likely prove difficult. The text might also prove difficult depending on the (lack of) background knowledge readers bring, regardless of their fluency skills. Readers who lack knowledge of soccer may struggle to navigate the text's vocabulary, make inferences, and thus construct an accurate understanding of the text.

Within a conceptualization that prioritizes text *difficulty*, students are viewed as active participants (Duke & Cartwright, 2021) in the reading process. Any text can be challenging for some readers based on their individual characteristics or the required task (RAND Reading Study Group, 2002). Such a prioritization requires consideration of texts for particular students within specific instructional contexts. Individual differences in student characteristics affect reading outcomes (e.g., Sparapani et al., 2016), and instructional tasks in which teachers engage students also have the potential to affect outcomes such as reading motivation

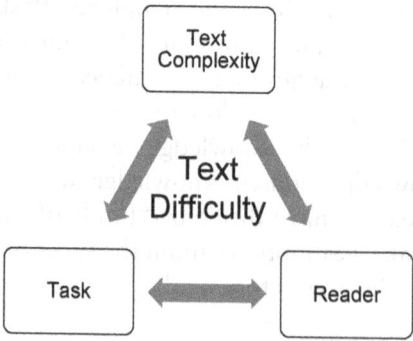

FIGURE 8.1. Conceptualization of text difficulty. Based on RAND Reading Study Group (2000), the National Governors Association Center for Best Practices and the Council of Chief State School Officers (2010), and Mesmer and colleagues (2012).

and achievement (e.g., Guthrie et al., 2012). Aligned with research emphasizing comprehension (Valencia et al., 2014), in this chapter we prioritize *text difficulty* as our central focus. As shown in Figure 8.1, we operationalize text difficulty as Mesmer and colleagues (2012) suggested: Text difficulty lies at the intersection of text complexity, reader characteristics, and instructional tasks.

Theoretical Framework(s)

Given our focus on text difficulty, a review of guiding theoretical frameworks proves obligatory. A number of theoretical frameworks can inform our understanding of students' meaning making. There is a convergence of evidence suggesting that reading is an active, meaning-making process, dependent on a number of skills (Burns et al., 2023). Theories guiding our understanding of *how* students make sense of texts vary in terms of their focus and breadth. We know that successful reading depends on both foundational code-level and language skills (Gough & Tunmer, 1986), but more recent research argues for a broader view of the complexity of reading; this "active view of reading" includes factors such as motivation and executive functioning skills (Duke & Cartwright, 2021). Comprehension-specific theories further assert the importance of what a reader brings to the text—how the relevant knowledge they have facilitates their ability to construct mental representations of the text they are reading (Kintsch, 1998) and how this transaction is ultimately dependent on their purpose for reading (Rosenblatt, 1978).

The aforementioned theories tend to center the *reader*, without giving due attention to the instructional context, which, of course, includes the texts being read. A broader guiding framework posited by the RAND model (RAND Reading Study Group, 2002) suggests reading comprehension is "the process of simultaneously constructing and extracting meaning through *interaction and involvement with written language*" (p. xiii; emphasis added). By defining comprehension as a process intertwined with print, this model acknowledges the key role of the text in the comprehension process. It further situates comprehension within a sociocultural context and suggests that for it to occur, in addition to considerations of the reader, we must also attend to the text and the activity.

Though the RAND model of comprehension comprises readers, texts, activities, and context, it lacks specificity. Missing from the field is a framework that captures the adaptive behaviors readers make when encountering texts of varying complexity. Such a framework, in turn, could further inform the necessary dynamic pedagogical moves teachers might include to scaffold learning.

What Do We Know?

As previously described, the CCSS (NGA & CCSSO, 2010) shocked the field of education with the publication of the Standards and the appendix related to text complexity. Prior to the CCSS, most state standards lacked explicit requirements for students to encounter increasingly complex texts across their K–12 education. Specifically, in Appendix A, the CCSS laid out a model of complexity—a three-pronged approach: qualitative evaluation of text, quantitative evaluation of text, and matching reader to text and task (Common Core State Standards Initiative, 2021). The CCSS approach, along with the grade-level bands that set benchmarks for text complexity, also set a new framework for considering text complexity.

Hiebert and Mesmer (2013) examined the CCSS text complexity standards and argued that whereas the focus on complex texts is commendable, the CCSS implementation had weaknesses. They noted that although the CCSS defines text complexity through a combination of qualitative, quantitative, and reader–task analyses, specific guidelines are only provided for the quantitative analysis using Lexile scores. In addition, they criticized the heavy reliance on quantitative measures because they fail to account for factors like student engagement and content-area background knowledge. They also argued that the research cited by the CCSS to justify an acceleration of text complexity in grades 2–3 did not support the assumption that primary-level texts had become less complex. They concluded that there were potential negative consequences of the CCSS text complexity implementation, including decreased reading fluency, motivation, and teacher efficacy. The article concludes by calling for further research to investigate the impact of the CCSS text complexity standards, particularly for primary grade students.

In 2014, *Elementary School Journal* published a special edition on text complexity. The special issue addressed the three-pronged model of text complexity outlined in Appendix A of the CCSS, which served as the foundation for the articles provided in the special issue. Articles aligned with the three prongs of the model, addressing (1) qualitative features best analyzed by human readers, (2) quantitative characteristics typically measured by software, and (3) reader–task considerations requiring teacher expertise in student needs and subject matter.

Qualitative Features

Human expertise plays a vital role in analyzing qualitative features, which include aspects of the text such as text structure, vocabulary, and the presence of figurative language (Pearson & Hiebert, 2014). These features can significantly impact comprehension but are challenging to quantify automatically with software. For instance, a text with a seemingly simple average sentence length might contain complex sentence structures or dense technical vocabulary, preventing understanding. Qualitative analysis allows educators to identify these intricacies and tailor instruction accordingly (Pearson & Hiebert, 2014).

Quantitative Characteristics

Software such as TextEvaluator (Sheehan et al., 2014) or Coh-Metrix (Graesser et al., 2014) can efficiently analyze quantitative features such as word frequency, sentence length, and lexical density. While these factors offer valuable insights, they also have limitations. High readability scores based on quantitative measures do not guarantee comprehension (Cunningham & Mesmer, 2014). The content itself may be conceptually challenging, highlighting the need to consider qualitative aspects alongside quantitative ones. However, text analysis systems such as Coh-Metrix (Graesser et al., 2014) offer a more advanced analysis of language and discourse measures, which provides a more comprehensive picture than traditional readability formulas.

Reader-Task Considerations

Reader–task considerations emphasize the critical role of readers' background knowledge, experiences, and assigned tasks in influencing comprehension (Sheehan et al., 2014). Given teachers' expertise in knowledge of their students and grade-level content, they are likely best positioned to consider these factors (Sheehan et al., 2014). For instance, a student with a strong science background might find a complex science text manageable, while another student who lacks that specific background knowledge might struggle. Similarly, the task itself—partner reading for fun or independent synthesis across texts—will influence how students approach the text (Sheehan et al., 2014). While Williamson and colleagues (2014) focus on historical student reading growth trends, their work underscores the importance of considering individual student characteristics when teaching reading aligned with CCSS text-complexity standards.

Our Review

Based on calls for additional research, we conducted a systematic review on the relationships between text complexity and reading fluency and comprehension (see Amendum et al., 2018). Our findings from the review indicate that text complexity matters in important ways. In the simplest form, more difficult texts are negatively related to fluency, and either negatively related, or unrelated, to comprehension. In a more sophisticated form, the difficulty of a text is best captured by the interaction of the reader's characteristics and the complexity of the text, and is likely further moderated by the context of the task or activity in which the reader–text interaction occurs (Valencia et al., 2014).

Text Complexity and Fluency

Our study investigated the relationship between text difficulty and reading fluency, with a particular focus on how reader skill level may play into this relationship. Consistent with prior research, our findings revealed that increased text difficulty generally led to decreased accuracy and reading rate, especially for less skilled readers. This effect held true for all aspects of fluency: accuracy, rate, and prosody. However, for skilled readers, the relationship between text difficulty and prosody differed from the pattern observed for accuracy and rate. One study (Benjamin & Schwanenflugel, 2010) suggested that prosody might actually improve for skilled readers when encountering more complex texts given the presence of longer sentences and more complex phrasing, which provide opportunities for richer prosodic expression. The researchers suggest that skilled readers may even "marshal prosodic resources" (p. 399) to effectively navigate these complexities.

The conceptualization and measurement of text difficulty also influenced fluency outcomes (e.g., Compton et al., 2004). For instance, Compton and colleagues (2004) found that improved reading rates were associated with easier texts, defined by a higher proportion of high-frequency or decodable words. Furthermore, the level of support provided during reading played a role in fluency (cf. O'Connor et al., 2010). Reading aloud to a supportive adult, reading after a teacher's reading, or engaging in repeated readings all demonstrated a positive influence on fluency, suggesting that increased scaffolding generally benefits students' reading fluency.

To summarize, our prior review highlights the complex interplay between text difficulty, reader skill, and reading fluency. While increased difficulty generally presents challenges for less skilled readers, skilled readers may leverage prosodic resources to navigate complex texts. Additionally, the definition of text difficulty and the level of support provided during reading can influence fluency outcomes.

Text Complexity and Comprehension

Our findings revealed a primarily negative or nonsignificant relationship between text difficulty and comprehension. No studies demonstrated improved comprehension with increased text difficulty. However, the magnitude of an increase in difficulty might be a critical factor; one study found a moderate increase beneficial to students, but students still struggled with highly challenging texts (Topping et al., 2008).

Measurement limitations were a notable concern. Comprehension is a multifaceted construct that evolves over time (Paris, 2005) and the measures often used might not fully capture the nuances of students' reading comprehension (Sabatini et al., 2012). The wide range of comprehension assessments (Pearson & Hamm, 2005) further complicates interpretation of the findings related to comprehension, as studies have shown significant variation in student performance depending on the measure used (Keenan et al., 2008). However, advancements in comprehension measurement (e.g., Sabatini et al., 2020) offer an opportunity to further our understanding of the relationship between text difficulty and reading comprehension.

Selected Additional Research

More recent research related to text complexity has highlighted the complex interactions among text characteristics, students' cognitive skills, and reading performance. Several studies have continued to highlight the limitations of traditional readability formulas that solely rely on surface-level features (Nguyen et al., 2020; Tortorelli, 2020). Tortorelli (2020) emphasizes the importance of semantic complexity and text cohesion for young readers, while Nguyen and colleagues (2020) point out that text complexity can influence student errors during oral reading. Liceralde and colleagues (2022) additionally note the concept of "production-related effects" that are inherent to a text's structure and can impact reading rate independent of complexity. Together these findings suggest a need for more nuanced measures of text complexity that capture these diverse dimensions.

Results from recent studies also underscore the critical role of students' cognitive skills in reading comprehension. For example, relationships exist between executive functions (EF) and self-correction behavior during oral reading fluency measures, particularly when dealing with complex texts (Nguyen et al., 2020). In fact, a range of cognitive skills have been identified as predictors of performance across different reading outcomes (e.g., Spencer et al., 2019), further emphasizing the importance of cognitive skills for successful comprehension.

The impact of text difficulty on reading outcomes is complicated. While Spencer and colleagues (2019) found a negative effect of text complexity on oral reading fluency and free recall, Trottier Brown and colleagues (2018) report that assisted readers in dyads, who read chorally with stronger readers from an above-grade-level text for 15 minutes a day, outperformed control students when using above-grade-level texts. These findings suggest that instructional supports may mitigate comprehension challenges posed by difficult texts. Moreover, researchers demonstrated an interactive effect of readability and cohesion on comprehension, highlighting the importance of considering both factors when selecting instructional texts (Reed & Kershaw-Herrera, 2016).

What Can We Do about It?

Building Teacher Knowledge of Text Complexity

Given the importance of understanding the factors that make texts complex, our first recommendation for the field is to build teacher knowledge of text complexity. Though a number of studies have focused on the importance of teacher knowledge of reading foundations (cf. Hudson et al., 2021), fewer studies have directly examined teacher knowledge of *text complexity*. Of those that have, it is clear that teachers' understanding varies considerably. Less than half of respondents in one small survey were able to provide a well-rounded definition for text complexity, and those who were most skilled at recognizing factors tended to be secondary English teachers (Hodgkinson & Small, 2018). In other studies that have considered teachers' knowledge or behaviors around text complexity, it is clear that teachers are skilled at evaluating some aspects of text complexity but ignore others. Lammert and colleagues (2023), for example, examined preservice teachers' knowledge and found that teachers failed to consider the role of text structure as it relates to a text's complexity. Though text complexity was an indirect aspect of the study, in a descriptive study examining teacher supports of comprehension-based discussions, participants were quick to note how specialized vocabulary might contribute to text complexity—but this sometimes led to the exclusion of other areas (Kucan et al., 2011). Given that previous research highlights the important role that factors such as text structure and syntax do play in contributing to a text's complexity, preservice educators and professional development should focus on building teachers' knowledge.

Fluency and Comprehension Supports and Routines

As states adopt language sponsoring the use of more complex texts, it is critical to address the pedagogical supports that can aid in this endeavor. These supports are multilayered and often need to address the text's complexity at both at the word and the text level.

Addressing Foundational Needs

It is important to underscore first that for students for whom accurate reading of the text remains difficult, priority ought to be given to shoring up students' word knowledge and word-level skills. A deficit in foundational skills impedes students' accurate rendering of the text. A number of research studies highlight the efficaciousness of such interventions with students who are beyond the primary grades (Metsala & David, 2022; Toste et al., 2017).

An additional word-level intervention that facilitates the reading of more complex text involves addressing students' morphological knowledge. Studies have acknowledged the complexity of vocabulary and language in texts as students move through school (Hiebert et al., 2018; Lane et al., 2019). These studies note the abundance of Latin and Greek words, along with the presence of nominalizations in disciplinary texts, thus rendering morphological awareness instruction suitable. Though direct effects on fluency have not been established (Goodwin & Ahn, 2013), morphology instruction has been shown to improve students' word reading and vocabulary (Carlisle, 2010)—two factors that certainly matter for the reading of complex text.

Fluency Supports

Beyond work at sublexical and lexical levels, a number of fluency supports can be put into place to support the reading of connected text. One common fluency scaffold includes having the student read the text alongside a more skilled reader, like a teacher or tutor (Kuhn, 2020; Trottier Brown et al., 2018). Another is to encourage multiple readings of the same text (Kuhn, 2020). The benefits of repeated readings have been consistently demonstrated. For example, Fluency-Oriented Reading Instruction (FORI; Stahl & Heubach, 2005) engages students in scaffolded reading of a grade-level text. As a 5-day routine, the students read the text multiple times, and the teacher gradually provides less support over the course of the week. Students who have engaged in FORI have made considerable gains (Kuhn et al., 2006), as have students who engaged in a variation, Wide FORI, in which students read three different texts over the 5 days, rather than just one.

Multicomponent Supports

Walpole and McKenna drew on FORI in the development of the shared reading block in their open-access curriculum (Walpole et al., 2017). This 45-minute block engages all students in a grade-level tradebook. Following a teacher-led choral reading of the text alongside explicit vocabulary instruction and addressing text structure, students are strategically paired up to read the text a second time, with partners providing support and feedback for one another. Schools using the curriculum have made gains compared to schools not using it (see May et al., 2024).

In a recent Institute for Education Sciences practice guide, similar recommendations are made for supporting students in "stretch" texts (see Vaughn et al., 2022). They define *stretch texts* as texts above students' independent reading level and at, or just below, students' grade level. These involve first previewing the text to prepare for the lesson and identify areas that might need clarification that would benefit from discussion, and to identify vocabulary words that need to be pretaught. Before actually reading the text with students, they recommend teaching two to three essential vocabulary words, reviewing the proper nouns in the text, and reading through any difficult multisyllabic words. Then during reading, they recommend a variety of approaches—ranging from reading aloud and having students follow along to alternating reading with the students, to choral reading the text together. Additionally, they recommend stopping throughout to clarify and discuss the text and to ask and answer questions. Finally, after students have had significant practice with the stretch text, Vaughn and colleagues recommend providing students the opportunity to read the text on their own, but with some electronic supports to aid with vocabulary.

Reynolds (2021) has conducted a number of studies examining the benefits of scaffolding with complex texts. In an experimental design, he demonstrated that the use of scaffolds led to comprehension gains for high school students and that syntax and text structure scaffolds were the most effective. In a descriptive study with fifth- and sixth-grade students, he found that tutors tend to use one of three types of scaffolds—vocabulary, fluency, and comprehension—with the latter being the most commonly used, both in general and specifically with students more inclined to struggle (Reynolds & Goodwin, 2016a). Though scaffolds with complex text proved effective, he asserts that teachers or tutors need to be flexible and consistent, and that the chosen scaffolds need to align with the overall lesson objective and purpose.

Additional Supports

Finally, some work developed for practitioners (and not yet tested empirically) suggests providing *text scaffolds* to support the reading of complex texts. For example, Quad Text Sets, advanced by Lewis and colleagues (2014) and expanded and described in papers by Lupo and colleagues (2018), suggest that teachers develop a coherent set of texts in service of supporting the reading and engagement of a complex text. The idea behind Quad Text Sets is that by providing simpler texts as foots in the door—texts that not only engage students but also build background knowledge—students will have some content knowledge and interest in the topic prior to reading the more challenging text.

In their study with fifth- and sixth-grade students using complex texts, Reynolds and Goodwin (2016b) found that *motivational scaffolds* predicted growth. These motivational scaffolds included using time limits, building in some competition for students (e.g., "Who can do the most? How many can you do?"; p. 13), using incentives, and including nonverbal and verbal praise. The authors attribute the success of the scaffolds to building an engaging routine and environment for working with the complex texts.

Similarly, intervention work with struggling readers suggests there is value in addressing students' sense of competence alongside the foundational work (e.g., Toste et al., 2017). As teachers work with students on complex texts, they build in efficacy statements that focus on students' beliefs that they can be successful. This is particularly important given that research on middle school students reveals that perception of difficulty relates to steeper declines (Fulmer & Tulis, 2013).

Future Research Directions

Understanding factors that contribute to text difficulty remains an ongoing endeavor. To move the field forward, we advocate for a cohesive research agenda that further explores the following areas: conceptual clarification and coherence, refined theoretical frameworks, and connections to policy and practice.

A crucial first step involves agreements on precise definitions and operationalization of key terms. This includes providing greater clarity around *text complexity*, *text difficulty*, and related constructs such as *tasks* and *reader characteristics*. Movement to greater clarity and coherence has the potential to foster increased collaboration and consistency across research efforts and facilitate connections to practice.

In addition, future research should be firmly anchored within a refined theoretical framework or frameworks. Cognitive and sociocultural theories each offer valuable lenses for examining how readers interact with complex texts. While perspectives from each of these paradigms may not often align with respect to text complexity, an integrated perspective is likely to be most informative. Development of such theoretical perspectives to guide both research and practice would provide a major contribution to the field.

Future research on text difficulty must also inform policy and educational practice. Given the flat or declining trajectory of recent National Assessment of Educational Progress scores (National Center for Education Statistics, 2025), researchers should examine state policies, including state standards and recent reading-related legislation to consider the effects of these policies on students' reading achievement, particularly across subgroups of students by race/ethnicity, socioeconomic status, special education status, and multilingual learner status. Bridging policy and practice, future research on curriculum materials and instructional approaches must be conducted to evaluate their effects on the diverse needs of learners. Crucially, research efforts must move beyond manipulation of isolated instructional practices or specific texts and examine the effectiveness of entire instructional packages that integrate high-quality curriculum materials with evidence-based routines (e.g., May et al., 2024). Rigorous evaluations of curricular packages are essential to ensure their efficacy in promoting students' achievement.

Finally, we note the importance of continued research on promising instructional practices related to reading difficult text with additional nuances such as when, for whom, and under what conditions the practices are most helpful. Promising directions that warrant further exploration include the following:

- *Building teacher knowledge of text complexity:* Equipping teachers with a deeper understanding of text complexity empowers them to make informed text selection decisions and tailor instruction to address specific challenges within texts.
- *Fluency and comprehension:* Research is needed to explore how effective fluency and comprehension instruction can be effectively integrated within classrooms using high-quality curriculum materials.
- *Stretch texts:* The concept of "stretch texts"—materials that push students beyond their independent reading level—holds promise for promoting growth. Further research is necessary to determine the optimal characteristics of stretch texts and how to best support students in navigating their complexities.
- *Text scaffolds and knowledge building:* Investigating the effectiveness of various text scaffolds (e.g., graphic organizers, preteaching vocabulary, text sets) and knowledge-building activities in facilitating reading of difficult text is crucial.
- *Motivational principles:* Understanding how motivational principles can be harnessed to engage students with challenging texts is vital. Research should explore how to foster and cultivate motivation for students' reading of difficult materials.

REFERENCES

Amendum, S. J., Conradi, K., & Hiebert, E. H. (2018). Does text complexity matter in the elementary grades?: A research synthesis of text difficulty and elementary students' reading fluency and comprehension. *Educational Psychology Review, 30*(1), 121–151.

Ardoin, S. P., Williams, J. C., Christ, T. J., Klubnik, C., & Wellborn, C. (2010). Examining readability estimates' predictions of students' oral reading rate: Spache, Lexile, and Forcast. *School Psychology Review, 39*(2), 277–285.

Benjamin, R. G. (2012). Reconstructing readability: Recent developments and recommendations in the analysis of text difficulty. *Educational Psychology Review, 24*, 63–88.

Benjamin, R. G., & Schwanenflugel, P. J. (2010). Test complexity and oral reading prosody in young readers. *Reading Research Quarterly, 45*, 388–404.

Burns, M. K. (2024). Assessing an instructional level during reading fluency interventions: A meta-analysis of the effects on reading. *Assessment for Effective Intervention, 49*(4), 214–224.

Burns, M. K., Duke, N. K., & Cartwright, K. B. (2023). Evaluating components of the active view of reading as intervention targets: Implications for social justice. *School Psychology, 38*(1), 30–41.

Carlisle, J. F. (2010). Effects of instruction in morphological awareness on literacy achievement: An integrative review. *Reading Research Quarterly, 45*(4), 464–487.

Common Core State Standards Initiative. (2021). *English Language Arts Standards? » Standard 10: Range, Quality, & Complexity?» Measuring text complexity: Three factors.* Common Core State Standards Initiative. *www.thecorestandards.org/ela-literacy/standard-10-range-quality-complexity/measuring-text-complexity-three-factors.*

Compton, D. L., Appleton, A. C., & Hosp, M. K. (2004). Exploring the relationship between text-leveling systems and reading accuracy and fluency in second-grade students who are average and poor decoders. *Learning Disabilities Research and Practice, 19*, 176–184.

Cunningham, J. W., Hiebert, E. H., & Mesmer, H. A. E. (2018). Investigating the validity of two widely used quantitative text tools. *Reading and Writing, 31*, 813–833.

Cunningham, J. W., & Mesmer, H. A. E. (2014). Quantitative measurement of text difficulty: What's the use? *Elementary School Journal, 115*(2), 255–269.

Duke, N. K., & Cartwright, K. B. (2021). The science of reading progresses: Communicating advances beyond the Simple View of Reading. *Reading Research Quarterly, 56*(S1), S25–S44.

Fisher, D., & Frey, N. (2014). Contingency teaching during close reading. *Reading Teacher, 68*, 277–286.

Fisher, D., Frey, N., & Lapp, D. (2012). *Text complexity: Raising rigor in reading.* International Reading Association.

Fitzgerald, J., Elmore, J., Hiebert, E. H., Koons, H. H., Bowen, K., Sanford-Moore, E. E., & Stenner, A. J. (2016). Examining text complexity in the early grades. *Phi Delta Kappan, 97*(8), 60–65.

Fountas, I. C., & Pinnell, G. S. (1996). *Guided reading: Good first teaching for all children.* Heinemann.

Fountas, I. C., & Pinnell, G. S. (2013). *The Fountas and Pinnell leveled book list K–8+* (Vol. 1) (2013–2015 ed.). Heinemann Educational Books.

Fulmer, S. M., & Tulis, M. (2013). Changes in interest and affect during a difficult reading task: Relationships with perceived difficulty and reading fluency. *Learning and Instruction, 27*, 11–20.

Goodwin, A. P., & Ahn, S. (2013). A meta-analysis of morphological interventions in English: Effects on literacy outcomes for school-age children. *Scientific Studies of Reading, 17*(4), 257–285.

Gough, P. B., & Tunmer, W. E. (1986). Decoding, reading, and reading disability. *Remedial and Special Education, 7*(1), 6–10.

Graesser, A. C., McNamara, D. S., Cai, Z., Conley, M. W., Li, H., & Pennebaker, J. (2014). Coh-Metrix measures text characteristics at multiple levels of language and discourse. *Elementary School Journal, 115*, 210–229.

Graesser, A. C., McNamara, D. S., Louwerse, M. M., & Cai, Z. (2004). Coh-Metrix: Analysis of text on cohesion and language. *Behavior Research Methods, Instruments, and Computers, 36*(2), 193–202.

Guthrie, J. T., Wigfield, A., & You, W. (2012). Instructional contexts for engagement and achievement in reading. In S. L. Christenson, A. L. Reschly, & C. Wylie (Eds.), *Handbook of research on student engagement* (pp. 601–634). Springer.

Hiebert, E. H., Goodwin, A. P., & Cervetti, G. N. (2018). Core vocabulary: Its morphological content and presence in exemplar texts. *Reading Research Quarterly, 53*(1), 29–49.

Hiebert, E. H., & Mesmer, H. A. E. (2013). Upping the ante of text complexity in the Common Core State Standards: Examining its potential impact on young readers. *Educational Researcher, 42,* 44–51.

Hiebert, E. H., & Pearson, P. D. (2010). *An examination of current text difficulty indices with early reading texts* (Reading Research Report 10–01). TextProject. https://files.eric.ed.gov/fulltext/ed518046.pdf.

Hodgkinson, T., & Small, D. (2018). Orienting the map: Where K to 12 teachers stand in relation to text complexity. *Literacy Research and Instruction, 57*(4), 369–386.

Hudson, A. K., Moore, K. A., Han, B., Wee Koh, P., Binks-Cantrell, E., & Malatesha Joshi, R. (2021). Elementary teachers' knowledge of foundational literacy skills: A critical piece of the puzzle in the science of reading. *Reading Research Quarterly, 56*(Suppl. 1), S287–S315.

Keenan, J. M., Betjemann, R. S., & Olson, R. K. (2008). Reading comprehension tests vary in the skills they assess: Differential dependence on decoding and oral comprehension. *Scientific Studies of Reading, 12,* 281–300.

Kintsch, W. (1998). *Comprehension: A paradigm for cognition.* Cambridge University Press.

Kucan, L., Hapgood, S., & Sullivan Palincsar, A. (2011). Teachers' specialized knowledge for supporting student comprehension in text-based discussions. *Elementary School Journal, 112*(1), 61–82.

Kuhn, M. R. (2020). Whole class or small group fluency instruction: A tutorial of four effective approaches. *Education Sciences, 10,* 1–11.

Kuhn, M. R., Schwanenflugel, P. J., Morris, R. D., Morrow, L. M., Woo, D. G., Meisinger, E. B., . . . Stahl, S. A. (2006). Teaching children to become fluent and automatic readers. *Journal of Literacy Research, 38,* 357–387.

Lammert, C., DeJulio, S. R., & Hiebert, E. H. (2023). "Batting" around ideas: A design/development study of preservice teachers' knowledge of text difficulty and text complexity. *Reading Psychology, 44*(5), 484–513.

Lane, H. B., Gutlohn, L., & van Dijk, W. (2019). Morpheme frequency in academic words: Identifying high-utility morphemes for instruction. *Literacy Research and Instruction, 58*(3), 184–209.

Lewis, W. E., Walpole, S., & McKenna, M. C. (2014). *Cracking the Common Core: Choosing and using texts in grades 6–12.* Guilford Press.

Liceralde, V. R. T., Loukina, A., Beigman Klebanov, B., & Lockwood, J. R. (2022). Beyond text complexity: Production-related sources of text-based variability in oral reading fluency. *Journal of Educational Psychology, 114*(1), 16–36.

Lupo, S. M., Strong, J. Z., Lewis, W., Walpole, S., & McKenna, M. C. (2018). Building background knowledge through reading: Rethinking text sets. *Journal of Adolescent & Adult Literacy, 61,* 433–444.

May, H., Strong, J. Z., & Walpole, S. (2024). The effects of Bookworms literacy curriculum on student achievement in grades 2–5. *Scientific Studies of Reading, 28*(3), 321–344.

Mesmer, H. A. E., Cunningham, J. W., & Hiebert, E. H. (2012). Toward a theoretical model of text complexity for the early grades: Learning from the past, anticipating the future. *Reading Research Quarterly, 47*, 235–258.

Metsala, J. L., & David, M. D. (2022). Improving English reading fluency and comprehension for children with reading fluency disabilities. *Dyslexia, 28*(1), 79–96.

Moll, L. C., Soto-Santiago, S. L., & Schwartz, L. (2013). Funds of knowledge in changing communities. In K. Hall, T. Cremin, B. Comber, & L. C. Moll (Eds.), *International handbook of research on children's literacy, learning and culture* (pp. 172–183). Wiley-Blackwell.

National Center for Education Statistics. (2025). *Nation's report card. 2024 NAEP Report Card: Reading. Performance by student group.* https://www.nationsreportcard.gov/reports/reading/2024/g4_8/performance-by-student-group/?grade=4#student-group-scores.

National Governors Association Center for Best Practices & Council of Chief State School Officers. (2010). *Common Core State Standards for English Language Arts.* www.corestandards.org/wp-content/uploads/ela_standards.pdf.

Nguyen, T. Q., Pickren, S. E., Saha, N. M., & Cutting, L. E. (2020). Executive functions and components of oral reading fluency through the lens of text complexity. *Reading and Writing, 33*(4), 1037–1073.

Northrop, L., & Kelly, S. (2019). Who gets to read what?: Tracking, instructional practices, and text complexity for middle school struggling readers. *Reading Research Quarterly, 54*(3), 339–361.

O'Connor, R. E., Swanson, H. L., & Geraghty, C. (2010). Improvement in reading rate under independent and difficult text levels: Influences on word and comprehension skills. *Journal of Educational Psychology, 102*, 1–19.

Paris, S. G. (2005). Reinterpreting the development of reading skills. *Reading Research Quarterly, 40*, 184–202.

Pearson, P. D., & Hamm, D. N. (2005). The assessment of reading comprehension: A review of practices—Past, present, and future. In S. G. Paris & S. A. Stahl (Eds.), *Children's reading comprehension and assessment* (pp. 13–69). Erlbaum.

Pearson, P. D., & Hiebert, E. H. (2014). The state of the field: Qualitative analyses of text complexity. *Elementary School Journal, 115*(2), 161–183.

RAND Reading Study Group. (2002). *Reading for understanding: Toward an R&D program in reading comprehension.* RAND.

Reed, D. K., & Kershaw-Herrera, S. (2016). An examination of text complexity as characterized by readability and cohesion. *Journal of Experimental Education, 84*(1), 75–97.

Reynolds, D. (2021). Scaffolding the academic language of complex text: An intervention for late secondary students. *Journal of Research in Reading, 44*(3), 508–528.

Reynolds, D., & Goodwin, A. P. (2016a). Making complex texts a reality for all students: Dynamic scaffolding that bridges the gaps between student and text. *Voices from the Middle, 23*(4), 25–31.

Reynolds, D., & Goodwin, A. (2016b). Supporting students reading complex texts: Evidence for motivational scaffolding. *AERA Open, 2*(4).

Rosenblatt, L. M. (1978). *The reader, the text, the poem: The transactional theory of the literary work.* Southern Illinois University Press.

Sabatini, J., Albro, E., & O'Reilly, T. (2012). *Measuring up: Advances in how we assess reading ability.* Rowman & Littlefield Education.

Sabatini, J., O'Reilly, T., Weeks, J., & Wang, Z. (2020). Engineering a twenty-first century reading comprehension assessment system utilizing scenario-based assessment techniques. *International Journal of Testing, 20*(1), 1–23.

Sheehan, K. M., Kostin, I., Napolitano, D., & Flor, M. (2014). The TextEvaluator Tool: Helping teachers and test developers select texts for use in instruction and assessment. *Elementary School Journal, 115*(2), 184–209.

Smith, M., & Turner, J. (2017). *Neglected no more: Addressing text complexity in the early grades* (MetaMetrics Research Brief). MetaMetrics.

Sparapani, N., Connor, C. M., Day, S., Wood, T., Ingebrand, S., McLean, L., & Phillips, B. (2016). Profiles of foundational learning skills among first graders. *Learning and Individual Differences, 70*, 216–227.

Spencer, M., Gilmour, A. F., Miller, A. C., Emerson, A. M., Saha, N. M., & Cutting, L. E. (2019). Understanding the influence of text complexity and question type on reading outcomes. *Reading and Writing, 32*(3), 603–637.

Stahl, S. A., & Heubach, K. M. (2005). Fluency-oriented reading instruction. *Journal of Literacy Research, 37*, 25–60.

Strong, J. Z., Amendum, S. J., & Conradi Smith, K. (2018). Supporting elementary students' reading of difficult texts. *Reading Teacher, 72*(2), 201–212.

Topping, K. J., Samuels, J., & Paul, T. (2008). Independent reading: The relationship of challenge, non-fiction and gender to achievement. *British Educational Research Journal, 34*, 505–524.

Tortorelli, L. S. (2020). Beyond first grade: Examining word, sentence, and discourse text factors associated with oral reading rate in informational text in second grade. *Reading and Writing, 33*(1), 143–170.

Toste, J. R., Capin, P., Vaughn, S., Roberts, G. J., & Kearns, D. M. (2017). Multisyllabic word-reading instruction with and without motivational beliefs training for struggling readers in the upper elementary grades: A pilot investigation. *Elementary School Journal, 117*(4), 593–615.

Trottier Brown, L., Mohr, K. A. J., Wilcox, B. R., & Barrett, T. S. (2018). The effects of dyad reading and text difficulty on third-graders' reading achievement. *Journal of Educational Research, 111*(5), 541–553.

Valencia, S. W., Wixson, K. K., & Pearson, P. D. (2014). Putting text complexity in context: Refocusing on comprehension of complex text. *Elementary School Journal, 115*, 270–289.

Vaughn, S., Jayanthi, M., Gersten, R., Dimino, J., Taylor, M. J., Newman-Gonchar, R., . . . Wavell, S. (2022). *Providing reading interventions for students in grades 4–9* (WWC 2022007). National Center for Education Evaluation and Regional Assistance (NCEE), Institute of Education Sciences, U.S. Department of Education.

Walpole, S., McKenna, M. C., Amendum, S., Pasquarella, A., & Strong, J. Z. (2017). The promise of a literacy reform effort in the upper elementary grades. *Elementary School Journal, 118*(2), 257–280.

Williamson, G. L., Fitzgerald, J., & Stenner, A. J. (2014). Student reading growth illuminates the Common Core text-complexity standard: Raising both bars. *Elementary School Journal, 115*(2), 230–254.

CHAPTER 9

Readers' Motivation and Engagement in the Science of Literacy

Ana Taboada Barber
Xiaoli Gong

Learning to read well is a long-term developmental process. When we think about proficient readers, we usually have in mind people who can read a variety of materials with ease and interest, read for multiple purposes, and read with comprehension even when the text materials are neither personally interesting nor easy to understand (RAND, 2002). As a former teacher of elementary school, I (ATB) think back three decades and recall observing my first graders bursting with enthusiasm and curiosity about the world and thinking, "I bet Maria will be a great reader in a few years . . ." or "Mmmhh, Juanca, not so much. He is likely to struggle with reading and push books aside." What made me think that way early on, when these young learners were only beginning to decode, or map sounds to letters? I could not help wondering, "Why did I 'categorize' them that way early in their learning and development?"

Years later, as a graduate student and, even later, as a researcher on reading motivation and reading engagement, I realized that in my first years of teaching I thought of reading skills and dispositions as "traits," that is, as fixed characteristics that were rather stable and difficult to change over time. In Carol Dweck's (2006) framework, I had a fixed mindset for reading development. That probably does not sound very good for a teacher! If anything, many of us choose to become teachers precisely because we view students' cognitive abilities, skills, and dispositions as malleable and capable of improvement through effort—or under a "growth mindset" (Dweck, 2006). Thinking back, I realize that as a new teacher, I did not believe that my instructional practices could influence students' reading engagement, and that engagement, in turn, could improve their reading comprehension over time. Nowadays, the science of literacy and the access of data-driven information (in seconds!) offer us many capabilities as teachers. One of them is the ability to understand the complexity and the *malleability* of reading comprehension.

However, many of us still think of reading comprehension as mostly a cognitive skill. We would like to suggest that one way of thinking about the malleability of reading comprehension is to draw from motivation theory and the reading engagement framework.

In this chapter, we, a former and a current teacher, propose that if we are to look into evidence-driven instructional practices that seek to improve or foster reading comprehension, we need to bring to the science of literacy the science of reading motivation and reading engagement. We organize our chapter by first sharing seminal and current research on reading motivation dimensions and practices. We then move onto the reading engagement model, to finally present a set of instructional practices based on empirical research and the engagement framework using the acronym Do SMILE, to capture the essence of these practices.

The Science of Reading Motivation

Motivation, broadly, refers to the energization and direction of human behavior (Pintrich, 2003). *Reading motivation* refers to an individual's goals, values, and beliefs about the topics, processes, and outcomes of reading (Guthrie & Wigfield, 2000). There is wide agreement that both motivation *and* reading motivation are multidimensional constructs (e.g., Schiefele et al., 2012). In part, this leads to the overlap of certain terms and ideas (e.g., Conradi et al., 2014); however, these can still be distinguished from each other. Let's tackle each of these dimensions of reading motivation.

Goals

Goals or *goal orientation* refers to an individual's habitual approaches toward reading and the intentions they set related to their reading actions. Simply put, reading goals are defined as readers' purposes for reading (Baker & Wigfield, 1999). Reading goals are related to whether the reader is driven by intrinsic or extrinsic motivation. *Intrinsic motivation for reading* refers to taking up reading to meet the intrinsic needs of the readers versus gaining external rewards or grades (Ryan & Deci, 2000). Intrinsically motivated readers generally have learning goal orientations and set purposes for reading that are driven by curiosity, reading involvement, and importance. *Curiosity* is defined as the desire to read about the reader's specific topics of interest and, as such, curiosity is closely related to the literature on reading interest (Baker & Wigfield, 1999). Curious readers have specific topics of interest, they enjoy learning through their reading, and they have an overall positive disposition toward reading whether it is to learn facts or develop insights about the world (Baker & Wigfield, 1999; Schiefele et al., 2012). The third grader who seeks to read about warm-weather insects to develop deep knowledge they believe will be useful when their family (finally) goes camping is likely an intrinsically motivated reader—their interest and curiosity might be short term or long lived, but their purpose for reading is intrinsically driven. At the same time, the knowledge about insects in warm climates might serve a concrete purpose—to deal with insect bites during camping; this increasing knowledge about mosquitoes, ticks, and ants might also become the child's purpose for reading avidly on the topic. Becoming knowledgeable about a topic can be motivating!

Extrinsically driven goals for reading—competition and recognition—are well known in most school systems. Teachers know these incentives too well and are aware that these are prevalent in many children and adults alike. The *extrinsic dimension of competition* refers to reading to do better than others. Competitive readers are driven to read because they derive satisfaction in doing better than their peers (Guthrie et al., 1996; Wigfield & Guthrie, 1997). Recognition, the other extrinsic dimension, implies reading to receive praise from others—mostly teachers and other adults. Recognition-driven readers feel encouraged to read more when others acknowledge and compliment their reading (Guthrie et al., 1996; Wigfield & Guthrie, 1997)

Beliefs about the Topics, Processes, and Outcomes of Reading

Beliefs in the field of reading motivation refer to (1) beliefs about self—students' perceptions and judgments related to their competence, abilities, and capacity (e.g., self-efficacy, self-concept, agency) and (2) beliefs about reading tasks and reading activities, as well as experiences with reading (expectancy, value). Teachers know well that students who struggle with reading have experienced more instances of failure and frustration with reading-related tasks.

In terms of beliefs about self, *self-efficacy beliefs* refer to one's perceptions about succeeding at tasks. Within social-cognitive theory (Bandura, 1997) self-efficacy refers to beliefs about an one's capabilities to learn or carry out behaviors at specific levels of a task (Schunk, Meece & Pintrich, 2014). Efficacious students persevere longer in the face of difficulties, participate more readily, and tend to achieve at higher levels than students who lack self-efficacy. This is why efficacious readers believe they are capable of succeeding at reading activities, have confidence in their reading skills, and are willing to attempt more challenging texts (Guthrie et al., 2009). Self-efficacy for reading has been operationalized as students' perceptions of competent reading, or their beliefs regarding their ability and skill in reading tasks (Chapman & Tunmer, 1995).

Reading self-efficacy has consistently been found to correlate or predict different dimensions of reading across grades, race, and ethnic backgrounds. For example, in their seminal study on reading self-efficacy, Chapman and Tunmer (1995) looked at the perceptions of competence of a 5-year-old child in performing reading tasks and their perceived difficulty with reading activities. They found that initial-reading experiences in school are closely associated with students' self-efficacy beliefs and their self-concepts as readers, concluding that early stages of formal reading instruction are critical for students' development as readers both cognitive and motivationally (Chapman & Tunmer, 1995). In another early study on efficacy beliefs, Baker and Wigfield (1999) found that reading self-efficacy was strongly related with fifth and sixth graders' frequency of reading and reading for fun. Decades later, several other studies have supported the predictive role of reading self-efficacy in relation to reading attitudes, other motivations, or cognitive dimensions of reading (Guthrie et al., 2009; Ho & Guthrie, 2013; Taboada Barber et al., 2018).

Importantly, what these studies suggest is that self-efficacy beliefs are malleable and susceptible to being influenced by targeted classroom practices. For example, our team examined the combined impact of cognitive (e.g., comprehension strategy use) and motivation practices (e.g., support for self-efficacy and involved reading) within a social studies literacy intervention (United States History for Engaged Reading [USHER]) for sixth-grade students (45% of whom were Spanish-speaking emergent bilinguals). We found that all students, irrespective of home language background, improved their reading comprehension of history texts, their reading engagement, and their self-efficacy as readers. Important to note is that in the USHER intervention program, reading self-efficacy beliefs were supported for specific reading tasks in social studies and assessed accordingly (e.g., scale items to assess students' reading self-efficacy included "I am completely certain I can learn about social studies by reading books" and "I am completely certain that I can find supporting details for a main idea on a page in a social studies book"; Taboada Barber et al., 2018, p. 86).

Despite students' positive beliefs in relation to achievement, it is also the case that middle schoolers' *negative beliefs* about reading, such as *perceived difficulty* with reading tasks (i.e., students' perception that reading tasks are difficult for them to perform) turned out to be a stronger motivational belief in reading outcomes than self-efficacy (Guthrie et al., 2009). In fact, undermining motivations—such as avoidance of reading and peers devaluing reading—along with negative beliefs, predict seventh graders' reading comprehension more strongly than students' affirming motivations (Ho & Guthrie, 2013). Collectively, these findings indicate that teachers and other reading professionals need to focus on affirming reading related beliefs—such as reading efficacy, increasing the value of reading—more so than aiming to reduce the devaluation or perceived difficulty of reading (Ho & Guthrie, 2013).

The Science of Reading Engagement

Both motivation and engagement play crucial roles in literacy development and in reading comprehension. However, the two are often confounded, and for good reasons: The two constructs are highly related and correlated, and they overlap in their nature. However, they do not overlap completely, which warrants separating them in research and instructional practice. Recent literature reviews posit that both motivation (e.g., Katzir et al., 2009; Retelsdorf et al., 2011; Taboada et al., 2009; Toste et al., 2020; Wang & Guthrie, 2004) and engagement (e.g., Taboada Barber et al., 2015; Wantchekon & Kim, 2019; Wigfield et al., 2008) explain children's reading performance across ages beyond academic and cognitive skills. However, given that motivation and engagement are distinct constructs, teachers benefit from understanding their relations in promoting their students' literacy development and long-term reading engagement.

Reading motivation captures individuals' thoughts, feelings, and beliefs, whereas *reading engagement* refers to individuals' involvement in reading, as manifested in behavior, affect, and/or cognition (Guthrie et al., 2012) in accord with domain-general conceptualizations of academic engagement (e.g., Fredricks et al., 2004; Reeve, 2012). Motivation and its more internal nature can be thought of as an antecedent of reading engagement. As such, teachers, reading specialists, librarians, and parents can impact reading engagement through motivation. For example, *cognitive engagement* may appear in a child's sustained attention while reading. Attention is a key feature of cognitive engagement. In fact, *deep reading* (Wolf, 2018) or the set of cognitive processes that drive deep text comprehension, such as inferencing, deductive reasoning, and analogical skills, all rely on attention. Deep reading relies on engaged reading and vice versa.

Affective engagement may be apparent from a child's facial expression and body language in discussing a topic of interest. When a child can't wait to jump in to share their opinion or expand on a teacher's read-aloud, they are engaged in reading. *Behavioral engagement* may also be described as cognitive and affective indicators, since these require behavioral manifestations, whether by focused attention during independent reading or by raising an insistent hand during a read-aloud. *Behavioral engagement* can also take the form of social engagement, when a child wants to share the latest information on venomous snakes or tsunamis with their classmates. Cognitive and social engagement also manifest in sharing and applying knowledge learned from text. When students get into a lively discussion about the Greek gods and the influence of mythology in ancient Greek society or the powers of the demigods or half-bloods after reading *Percy Jackson* books, engagement is at play. The time invested and attention to text details are also indicators of cognitive engagement. The social, behavioral, cognitive, and affective dimensions of reading engagement might overlap at times, but they can be observed, inferred, and, most importantly, learned by teachers who want to foster engaged reading in their classrooms.

Within the reading engagement model (Guthrie & Klauda, 2016), reading motivation (whether this is fully intrinsic and/or supported by teachers in some fashion) engenders reading engagement, which in turn promotes reading achievement, often in the form of reading comprehension; that is, when students set reading goals, value reading, and believe in themselves as readers (all dimensions of reading motivation), and when they have the cognitive skills necessary to build meaning from text, they will more willingly and fully engage in reading-related activities and tasks. The manifestations of reading engagement can be overtly noted through behavioral engagement, as well as cognitive, social, and affective engagement (e.g., De Naeghel et al., 2012; Taboada Barber et al., 2009).

How Engaged Reading Improves Reading Comprehension

In the rest of this chapter, we aim to share instructional practices and policies that facilitate *sustained* reading engagement as an enduring attribute or an individual characteristic, rather than short-lived instruction (Guthrie & Wigfield,

2017; Taboada Barber & Klauda, 2020). Like other educational psychologists with expertise in reading engagement (e.g., Guthrie & Wigfield, 2017), we believe that when teachers implement the recommended practices and policies in a consistent and integrated manner, students gradually develop the habits, attitudes, and dispositions that enable meaningful engagement in the long term, with the texts they need to or wish to read (Guthrie & Klauda, 2016; Hidi & Harackiewicz, 2000). We limit our recommendations to four motivation dimensions, as well as engagement itself, because they are clearly malleable and amenable to teachers' adaptation of the recommended practice both for students and their literacy instruction.

We also believe that the recommendations we make below are useful for researchers who are interested in translational research and in how the implementation of these practices could impact students' reading comprehension, knowledge building from text, and motivation to read. Furthermore, when making these recommendations, we take into account the diversity of the student population in the various contexts of the United States—and abroad—becoming fully aware that the adaptation of these practices to specific readers and contexts is ultimately up to teachers. We follow the call to spread the acronym SMILE—sharing; me; importance; liking; engagement—to represent these dimensions (Guthrie & Wigfield, 2017; Taboada Barber & Klauda, 2020). To the existent SMILE acronym, we add "do" to represent the importance we give to "deep reading-oriented instruction" and to emphasize the close connection between deep and engaged reading.

Do SMILE to Nurture Motivated, Engaged Readers

Do: Deep Reading-Oriented Instruction

The D captures "deep reading," which is described as a set of cognitive processes that drive text comprehension, including formation of images as we read (imagery), taking another person's perspective (empathy), integrating new information with our background knowledge (internalized knowledge), analogical and inferential thinking, and critical analysis (Wolf, 2018). Wolf (2018) says that deep reading employs all these processes simultaneously, while the reader is immersed in text. The immersive experience of reading evokes the characteristics of engaged reading because it underscores that *how* we read can become as important as to *what* we read. Motivated readers might not always read deeply, but engaged reading relies on deep reading, and vice versa.

S: Sharing

The S in SMILE represents student-to-student sharing of ideas, details, or conceptual understandings relevant to a reading task. According to self-determination theory (SDT; Ryan & Deci, 2000), relatedness to others is one of three basic psychological needs in human development that motivates individuals.

Positive interactions with others at school shapes students' academic dispositions and success (Eccles & Wang, 2012). When teachers encourage frequent and structured collaboration around literacy activities, they meet the needs for social engagement. High-quality and well-structured student collaboration and idea sharing allows students to tap into each other's intellectual resources and enable the emergence of knowledge building from text; in fact, these connections may not happen for certain students with sustained individual reading alone. Student collaboration around literacy tasks has long been established to promote cognitive investment in the reading tasks (Klingner et al., 1998). As we know from studies on reading comprehension reported in the National Reading Panel (National Institute of Child Health and Human Development, 2000) more than two decades ago, student collaboration in small groups, coupled with teacher-scaffolded comprehension strategy instruction enables not only the practice of reading comprehension strategies but also, more importantly, the sharing of ideas that emerge from text. As experienced reading teachers know, cognitive comprehension strategies (i.e., text questioning, graphically organizing information, summarizing) are tools in the service of text comprehension. We would argue that strategy use in itself is not motivating. However, when students have an authentic reading purpose for communicating information and viewpoints about text with others, then the use of comprehension strategies with optimally challenging texts ensure they are motivated to read text more closely and think deeper about new understandings (Rozendaal et al., 2005). There are many authentic reading purposes: from communicating knowledge to a new audience to applying new knowledge from text to a specific context or scenario. As such, authentic reading purposes are content-based, such as finding supporting details to a key idea in a social studies unit, or related to students' personal interests around a theme, such as exploring how bird nests are built (e.g., Guthrie et al., 1996) or how barnacles adapt to life in the changing waters of the Pacific Ocean on the coast of Chile (Taboada Barber, 2021).

Recent research evidence from longitudinal studies shows that collaborative research activities in social studies and science classes helped first and second graders develop expertise in topics such as Arctic animals (student choice of snowy owls, Arctic foxes, narwhals) or dinosaurs (student choice of *Tyrannosaurus rex*, oviraptor, megalosaurus). In this program, small-group collaboration allowed for the in-depth study of the chosen animals, such that students became experts on a topic and organized themselves into team to read, write, and discuss self-selected topics with their peers (Kim et al., 2023). As such, these collaborative content-driven activities provided students with autonomy (an important motivator) to make choices, perform authentic tasks, and sustain attention on completing optimally challenging tasks (Guthrie et al., 2007). Students were also provided with the opportunity to read newspaper and magazine articles on their chosen animals and write words and concepts about their topics. Key to these collaborative activities was the contextualization within thematic units that were taught over a sustained period of time (10 weeks), allowing students' knowledge to develop over time. Similar collaborative literacy activities led sixth and seventh graders to engage with U.S. history texts and read within the same overall topic (e.g., Native Americans) while developing expertise on specific subthemes—in this case, tribes (e.g., the Iroquois, Sioux, and Lakota). The responsibility to report on a specific tribe, while responding to classmates' questions on it, fostered a sense of ownership, as well as a collaborative effort within and across student groups. Within each "tribe" group, students had different roles, such as the reporter, the question asker, the summarizer, and the illustrator (Taboada Barber et al., 2018).

Although student small-group collaboration was just one of the ways in which student engagement was supported, it was a key to sustaining student-motivated reading. Additionally, building knowledge of topic-specific schemas in both grade 1 science and social studies lessons and scaffolding wide reading through choice of reader-level matched, informational books "were critical levers for impacting domain-general reading comprehension" (Kim et al., 2023, p. 91). When students collaborate in reading tasks that have authentic purposes for reading, they may not only learn content from each other but also get inklings on how their peers view and value reading. Peer attitudes toward reading can affirm or undermine reading and its value and, as such, influence reading motivation and engagement (Guthrie et al., 2012).

How can teachers leverage the power of social engagement through meaningful small-group collaboration that promotes not only specific-tasks engagement but also sustained, cognitive, social, and affective reading engagement? Experienced teachers are aware of research-supported collaboration approaches such as reciprocal teaching (Palincsar & Brown, 1986) or collaborative reasoning (Chinn, Anderson, & Waggoner, 2001), which provide defined structures and guidance for working together around meaningful tasks and to comprehend texts. For instance, in reciprocal teaching groups, students take specific roles such as the question generator, clarifier, predictor or summarizer. Similarly, later instantiations of reciprocal teaching have recommended providing guidance for structured discussions of texts in which students take roles in clarifying specific vocabulary for each other, discuss confusing details, and encourage the group to arrive at both factual and conceptual understandings of text-based content (Klingner et al., 1998). Shared literacy activities will mostly support engaged reading when they are structured around knowledge goals, that is, meaningful opportunities for students to build knowledge from text in a *sustained* way over time, such as think-pair activities, inference generation for specific text excerpts (Guthrie & Klauda, 2016), or building a team poster on a 3-week-long project that seeks to answer a specific conceptual question in science or social studies (e.g., Taboada Barber et al., 2018). Indeed, sustained thematic content literacy lessons (e.g., Guthrie et al., 2004; Kim et al., 2023; Taboada Barber et al., 2018) coupled with small-group collaboration and specific cognitive comprehension supports are likely to impact content reading comprehension in the elementary and middle school grades, as well as knowledge transfer (Kim et al., 2023), reading engagement, and content reading in the middle grades (Taboada Barber et al., 2018).

M: Me

The *M* in SMILE stands for students' perception of "me" as a self-efficacious reader. As we discussed earlier in the chapter, self-efficacy beliefs play a pivotal role in one's inclination and motivation to read. In a recent metanalysis of 132 studies of the relationship between reading outcomes and the motivation beliefs about one's reading ability, self-efficacy beliefs stood out as having the strongest correlation with reading outcomes ($r = .28$, confidence interval [0.24, 0.32]) compared to five other motivations, such as expectancy about reading (i.e., expectation for success in reading), value of reading (i.e., beneficial, important, and pleasurable), attitudes (i.e., feelings about reading and how they steer one to engage in reading or avoid it), and interest (i.e., one's inclination to read certain topics) (Conradi et al., 2014, as cited in Toste et al., 2020). Readers formulate their own self-efficacy in reading based on their ability to read words, to understand vocabulary, their frequency of reading (Klauda et al., 2020), or their ability to comprehend. Indeed, there is substantial evidence that beliefs in one's reading ability (e.g., belief that I can do well in reading) is positively and moderately correlated with both code-focused reading outcomes (e.g., phonemic awareness and word decoding) and reading comprehension (Abbott et al., 2017; Toste et al., 2020).

So, how can teachers support readers' self-efficacy and elevate the "me" in reading? We know from research that reading self-efficacy can mean different things to students at different ages. For instance, third to fifth graders formulate their efficacy for reading based on their judgments of their abilities to read words fluently, understand vocabulary, and the frequency of their reading (Klauda et al., 2020), whereas for 5-year-old students, reading self-efficacy has been positively and moderately related to code-focused reading outcomes such as phonemic awareness (i.e., phoneme deletion), word decoding, and letter identification skills (e.g., Chapman, Tunmer, & Prochnow, 2000). Similarly, for fourth and fifth graders who qualify as having reading difficulties, including struggling emergent bilingual readers, self-efficacy beliefs were more strongly related to their word reading than to their reading comprehension skills (Cho et al., 2018). Evidence seems to indicate that competence in word recognition is seen as a prevalent component in determining self-efficacy in struggling readers and in children in the early grades—when foundational skills are taught or emphasized. However, there is a shift toward self-efficacy for comprehending and the ability to build meaning from text in the later elementary grades and middle school—and that this varies for different kinds of reading genres (e.g., informational texts vs. narrative texts; Ho & Guthrie, 2013). Children's literacy development and the emphasis placed on the different instructional dimensions of reading (e.g., code focus vs. meaning focus) therefore relate to students' efficacy for reading. Teachers' awareness of this variability is important to their supports of students' reading self-efficacy.

Because self-efficacy development depends on students' performing well in reading and on their awareness of that performance, teachers' attention to key instructional practices for promoting success in reading that are linked to positive achievement outcomes will strengthen students' reading self-efficacy. Teachers can use evidence-based practices for the *cognitive* as well as for the *motivational* dimensions of literacy development. For instance, one long-standing practice, derived from goal setting within self-efficacy theory (Schunk & Zimmerman, 2007) is for teachers to set reachable, yet increasingly challenging, goals for students' reading.

These goals can be related to mastery skills for reading, such as use of cognitive comprehension strategies that aid students with deep reading (e.g., ask two factual and two conceptual questions about the water cycle described in the next two pages). Reachable but increasingly challenging goals can also be related to the content of the texts within a thematic unit—for example, "Let's solve the mysterious function of the 'terrible claw' of deinonychus had for evolution." As students see themselves meeting each new goal, their self-efficacy grows and their sense of success in reading does as well.

I: Importance

The *I* in SMILE represents the "importance" or value of reading. Readers who value reading and think reading is important read more frequently (Baker & Wigfield, 1999). Across several studies, frequency of reading in students in grades K–12 was strongly related to their perceived value of reading (Toste et al., 2020). Value of reading stems from expectancy–value theory (EVT; Eccles & Wigfield, 2002), which posits four dimensions of valuing academic task; two of these are reading's importance and usefulness. Teachers and caregivers can provide value for reading by simply modeling reading time and making it habitual, as well as by providing verbal or written rationales for reading. The latter can be done by asking students to reflect on and write about the benefits that may come from readings. For example, when earlier in this section we discussed the immersive nature of deep reading (Wolf, 2018), and the need for carving the time out for it, we were assigning value to the act of reading. The value or the importance of reading is also conveyed by caretakers and by making the time for reading at home. Often, teachers can emphasize the value of reading by emphasizing meaningful, authentic activities—third and fourth graders' buddy reading to kindergarteners can provide the older students with a sense of value and meaningfulness for the reading task that they had not discovered before.

L: Liking

The *L* in SMILE refers to "liking"—capturing the enjoyment or pleasure of reading or being intrinsically motivated to read (Cox & Guthrie, 2001). Intrinsic motivation refers to conducting an activity "for its inherent satisfactions rather than for some separable consequences" (Ryan & Deci, 2000, p. 56). Engaged readers have a true liking or enjoyment of reading in a sustained way as an individual characteristic, regardless of the specific context. The child who is intrinsically motivated to read tends to view reading as a means of experiencing joy as well as an end in itself—recognizing that there are generally feelings of pleasure and involvement in reading. Intrinsic reading motivation has been found consistently to be related to general reading outcomes, as well as to reading comprehension (Rettig & Schiefele, 2023; Schaffner & Schiefele, 2013; Schiefele & Löweke, 2017; Toste et al., 2020). By contrast, extrinsic reading motivation, or the desire to read for external rewards (Ryan & Deci, 2000) such as competition, better grades, or recognition from teachers, tends not to be associated with improved reading outcomes (Rettig & Schiefele, 2023; Schaffner & Schiefele, 2007; Schiefele & Löweke, 2017).

The construct of intrinsic motivation has its roots both in SDT (Ryan & Deci, 2000) and EVT (Eccles & Wigfield, 2002). Within SDT, feeling in control of the outcomes of an activity enhances an individual's intrinsic motivation, whereas perceiving the proximal environment as controlling the activity tends to diminish it (Deci et al., 1989). For readers who feel in control of outcomes of their reading, or feel a sense of autonomy toward reading tasks, reading itself is enjoyable, exciting, and interesting, such that they routinely approach reading as a way to explore their interests and satisfy their curiosity. This, in turn, leads to a sense of autonomy in relation to reading tasks and activities, and fosters intrinsic motivation for reading. Conversely, classroom structures lacking in autonomy support, in which teachers provide mostly or exclusively extrinsic rewards for making progress toward goals, tend to weaken intrinsic motivation (Assor et al., 2005; Jang et al., 2010).

Although students may be intrinsically motivated to read, and teachers and caregivers may think of intrinsic motivation as a "trait," or an individual, stable characteristic, experiences that nurture the perception of autonomous learning through reading have immediate and long-term impact on reading itself (Guthrie & Wigfield, 2017). One practice that has been studied within autonomy-supportive teacher behaviors is the affordance of choices. Even though many studies within the motivation field suggest that choice is a powerful motivator, *how* choices are offered can create minimum or no effect on motivation and performance (e.g., Patall et al., 2010; Reeve, 2003). For example, when students have a choice of homework, the chances of homework completion are better than when homework is simply assigned by the teacher. However, the impact of choice on perceived competence, interest, and performance is stronger when choices are accompanied by other teacher autonomy-supportive behaviors such as using noncontrolling language or allowing students to express opinions (Patall, 2016; Patall et al., 2010). Choices also need to be meaningful—a choice of color for an illustration is rather meaningless because it does not foster a true sense of autonomous learning. However, a choice of how to convey or share newly learned knowledge about a specific animal within a thematic unit—via a poster, video making, or a booklet—carries more significance and latitude, affording a sense of meaningful choice and autonomous learning. Reasonable choices that are aligned with students' development or familiarity with the activity are appropriate (Wigfield et al., 2014). When the task is appropriate for choosing, and choices are reasonable and meaningful, students are prepared to choose, and teachers can unlock student motivation to learn (Patall, 2016).

E: Engagement

Reading *engagement* represents the E in SMILE. *Engagement*, or active involvement in reading, is the direct product of motivation—values, goals, and beliefs. When students *value* reading as important to their lives, both as learners and for their future, set *goals* for their reading, *perceive themselves as efficacious* readers, and feel inherently *interested* in reading in a sustained way, they are more likely to be engaged in reading (Wigfield et al., 2008). Aside from the four motivations listed in the preceding statement, another key consideration for teachers and caretakers is—simply—time spent reading (Taboada Barber et al., 2020). The support of motivation through teachers' efforts becomes meaningful—and we argue viable—if teachers can afford in their busy schedules the time for sustained reading. We believe that as necessary as cognitive strategies are for comprehension, time spent practicing discrete reading comprehension skills such as identifying main ideas in short paragraphs or making summary statements of texts that are disconnected from content learning are not conducive to the immersive experience in the same way that deep, engaged reading is. Reading engagement has a social dimension, as we discussed earlier, but it also has a cognitive and affective one. The immersive experience of deep reading that integrates new information into our schemas, uses analogical and inferential thinking, and fosters critical analyses of text (Wolf, 2018)—all manifestations of cognitive engagement—requires sustained, involved reading for deep comprehension of text to take place (Guthrie & Wigfield, 2017).

Conclusion

Implementing motivation-supporting practices as a coordinated set is important for fully supporting students' development into engaged readers. It is unlikely that a single practice, by itself, will be conducive to sustained reading engagement. In today's world of artificial intelligence (AI), when we google and skim most of the information we need, children and adolescents need time for deep, focused, sustained reading across days and weeks. But students also need teachers who create school environments that foster motivated reading in a coordinated, persistent way. Instilling one single motivation practice (e.g., choice) without a broader classroom environment that supports reading motivation is likely to leave us with short-lived engaged reading or limited reading achievement.

When I (ATB) queried ChatGPT-3.5 on the instructional practices that foster engaged reading, the generated list was comprehensive and quite relevant to current science (e.g., recommendations included choice in reading materials, discussion and collaboration, making connections, questioning strategies). AI has been here for a while, and language processors are ready to transform learning, teaching, and a lot of the work that we do. Yet, AI language processors can only generate the information (in milliseconds and with high levels of precision, for sure!) that human-generated data (both supervised and unsupervised) can feed into them. What AI language processors cannot give us is the nuanced understanding, the craft that goes into fusing empirically driven practices with teacher behaviors that are empathetic, thoughtful, and critically necessary for students to learn. When it comes to engaged reading, it is the panoply of motivation practices and teachers' increasing and nuanced knowledge, as well as their trial and error of motivation supports, that will engender engaged, deep reading in our learners.

REFERENCES

Abbott, R., Mickail, T., Richards, T., Renninger, K. A., Hidi, S. E., Beers, S., & Berninger, V. (2017). Understanding interest and self-efficacy in the reading and writing of students with persisting specific learning disabilities during middle childhood and early adolescence. *International Journal of Educational Methodology, 3*(1), 41–64.

Assor, A., Kaplan, H., Kanat-Maymon, Y., & Roth, G. (2005). Directly controlling teacher behaviors as predictors of poor motivation and engagement in girls and boys: The role of anger and anxiety. *Learning and Instruction, 15*(5), 397–413.

Baker, L., & Wigfield, A. (1999). Dimensions of children's motivation for reading and their relations to reading activity and reading achievement. *Reading Research Quarterly, 34*(4), 452–477.

Bandura, A. (1997). *Self-efficacy: The exercise of control.* Freeman.

Chapman, J. W., Tunmer, W. E., & Prochnow, J. E. (2000). Early reading-related skills and performance, reading self-concept, and the development of academic self-concept: A longitudinal study. *Journal of Educational Psychology, 92*(4), 703–708.

Chinn, C. A., Anderson, R. C., & Waggoner, M. A. (2001). Patterns of discourse in two kinds of literature discussion. *Reading Research Quarterly, 36*(4), 378–411.

Cho, E., Lee, M., & Toste, J. R. (2018). Does perceived competence serve as a protective mechanism against performance goals for struggling readers?: Path analysis of contextual antecedents and reading outcomes. *Learning and Individual Differences, 65,* 135–147.

Conradi, K., Jang, B. G., & McKenna, M. C. (2014). Motivation terminology in reading research: A conceptual review. *Educational Psychology Review, 26*(1), 127–164.

Cox, K. E., & Guthrie, J. T. (2001). Motivational and cognitive contributions to students' amount of reading. *Contemporary Educational Psychology, 26*(1), 116–131.

Deci, E. L., Connell, J. P., & Ryan, R. M. (1989). Self-determination in a work organization. *Journal of Applied Psychology, 74,* 580–590.

De Naeghel, J., Van Keer, H., Vansteenkiste, M., & Rosseel, Y. (2012). The relation between elementary students' recreational and academic reading motivation, reading frequency, engagement, and comprehension: A self-determination theory perspective. *Journal of Educational Psychology, 104,* 1006–1021.

Dweck, C. S. (2006). *Mindset: The new psychology of success.* Random House.

Eccles, J. S., & Wang, M. (2012). Part I commentary: So what is student engagement anyway? In S. Christensen, A. Reschly, & C. Wylie (Eds.), *Handbook of research on student engagement* (pp. 133–149). Springer.

Eccles, J. S., & Wigfield, A. (2002). Motivational beliefs, values, and goals. *Annual Review of Psychology, 53,* 109–132.

Fredricks, J. A., Blumenfeld, P. C., & Paris, A. H. (2004). School engagement: Potential of the concept, state of the evidence. *Review of Educational Research, 74*(1), 59–109.

Guthrie, J. T., Coddington, C. S., & Wigfield, A. (2009). Profiles of reading motivation among African American and Caucasian students. *Journal of Literacy Research, 41*(3), 317–353.

Guthrie, J. T., & Klauda, S. L. (2016). Engagement and motivational processes in reading. In P. Afflerbach (Ed.), *Individual differences in reading* (pp. 41–53). Routledge.

Guthrie, J. T., Van Meter, P., McCann, A. D., Wigfield, A., Bennett, L., Poundstone, C. C., . . . Mitchell, A. M. (1996). Growth of literacy engagement: Changes in motivations and strategies during concept-oriented reading instruction. *Reading Research Quarterly, 31*(3), 306–332.

Guthrie, J. T., Wigfield, A., & You, W. (2012). Instructional contexts for engagement and achievement in reading. In S. Christensen, A. Reschly, & C. Wylie (Eds.), *Handbook of research on student engagement* (pp. 133–149). Springer.

Guthrie, J. T., Hoa, A. L. W., Wigfield, A., Tonks, S. M., Humenick, N. M., & Littles, E. (2007). Reading motivation and reading comprehension growth in the later elementary years. *Contemporary Educational Psychology, 32*, 282–313.

Guthrie, J. T., & Wigfield, A. (2000). Engagement and motivation in reading. In M. L. Kamil, P. B. Mosenthal, P. D. Pearson, & R. Barr (Eds.), *Reading research handbook* (Vol. 3, pp. 403–424). Erlbaum.

Guthrie, J. T., & Wigfield, A. (2017). Literacy engagement and motivation: Rationale, research, teaching, and assessment. In D. Lapp & D. Fisher (Eds.), *Handbook of research on teaching the English language arts* (pp. 57–84). Routledge.

Guthrie, J. T., Wigfield, A., Barbosa, P., Perencevich, K. C., Taboada, A., Davis, M., Scaffidi, N., & Tonks., S. (2004). Increasing reading comprehension and engagement through concept-oriented reading instruction. *Journal of Educational Psychology, 96* (3), 1–21.

Hidi, S., & Harackiewicz, J. M. (2000). Motivating the academically unmotivated: A critical issue for the 21st century. *Review of Educational Research, 70*, 151–179.

Ho, A. N., & Guthrie, J. T. (2013). Patterns of association among multiple motivations and aspects of achievement in reading. *Reading Psychology, 34*(2), 101–147.

Jang, H., Reeve, J., & Deci, E. L. (2010). Engaging students in learning activities: It is not autonomy support or structure but autonomy support and structure. *Journal of Educational Psychology, 102*(3), 588–600.

Katzir, T., Lesaux, N. K., & Kim, Y. S. (2009). The role of reading self-concept and home literacy practices in fourth grade reading comprehension. *Reading and Writing, 22*(3), 261–276.

Kim, J. S., Burkhauser, M. A., Relyea, J. E., Gilbert, J. B., Scherer, E., Fitzgerald, J., . . . McIntyre, J. (2023). A longitudinal randomized trial of a sustained content literacy intervention from first to second grade: Transfer effects on students' reading comprehension. *Journal of Educational Psychology, 115*(1), 73–98.

Klauda, S. L., Taboada Barber, A., & McAllen, E. B. (2020). Reading motivation in Spanish-speaking dual language learners: Comparing two types of student report. *Reading Psychology, 41*(6), 605–630.

Klingner, J. K., Vaughn, S., & Schumm, J. S. (1998). Collaborative strategic reading during social studies in heterogeneous fourth-grade classrooms. *Elementary School Journal, 99*(1), 3–22.

National Institute of Child Health and Human Development. (2000). *Report of the National Reading Panel: Teaching children to read: An evidence-based assessment of the scientific research literature on reading and its implications for reading instruction: Reports of the subgroups* (NIH Publication No. 00-4754). U.S. Government Printing Office. www.nichd.nih.gov/sites/default/files/publications/pubs/nrp/documents/report.pdf.

Palincsar, A. S., & Brown, A. L. (1986). Interactive teaching to promote independent learning from text. *Reading Teacher, 39*(8), 771–777.

Patall, E. A. (2016, April). *Division C Early Career Award Address: The promise and peril of choice provision as a motivational strategy*. Paper presented at a symposium conducted at the annual meeting of the American Educational Research Association, Washington, DC.

Patall, E. A., Cooper, H., & Wynn, S. R. (2010). The effectiveness and relative importance of choice in the classroom. *Journal of Educational Psychology, 102*(4), 896–915.

Pintrich, P. R. (2003). Motivation and classroom learning. In W. M. Reynolds & G. E. Miller (Eds.), *Handbook of psychology: Educational psychology*, Vol. 7, pp. 103–122). Wiley.

Reeve, J. (2012). A self-determination theory perspective on student engagement. In S. Christensen, A. Reschly, & C. Wylie (Eds.), *Handbook of research on student engagement* (pp. 149–173). Springer.

Reeve, J., Nix, G., & Hamm, D. (2003). Testing models of the experience of self-determination in intrinsic motivation and the conundrum of choice. *Journal of Educational Psychology, 95*(2), 375–392.

Retelsdorf, J., Köller, O., & Möller, J. (2011). On the effects of motivation on reading performance growth in secondary school. *Learning and Instruction, 21*(4), 550–559.

Rettig, A., & Schiefele, U. (2023). Relations between reading motivation and reading efficiency—Evidence from a longitudinal eye-tracking study. *Reading Research Quarterly, 58*(4), 685–709.

Rozendaal, J. S., Minnaert, A., & Boekaerts, M. (2005). The influence of teacher perceived administration of self-regulated learning on students' motivation and information processing. *Learning and Instruction, 15*(2), 141–160.

Ryan, R. M., & Deci, E. L. (2000). Intrinsic and extrinsic motivations: Classic definitions and new directions. *Contemporary Educational Psychology, 25*, 54–67.

Schaffner, E., & Schiefele, U. (2007). Auswirkungen habitueller lesemotivation auf die situative textreprasentation [Effects of habitual reading motivation on the situational representation of text]. *Psychologie in Erziehung und Unterricht, 54*, 268–286.

Schaffner, E., & Schiefele, U. (2013). The prediction of reading comprehension by cognitive and motivational factors: Does text accessibility during comprehension testing make a difference? *Learning and Individual Differences, 26*, 42–54.

Schiefele, U., & Löweke, S. (2017). The nature, development, and effects of elementary students' reading motivation profiles. *Reading Research Quarterly, 53*(4), 405–421.

Schiefele, U., Schaffner, E., Möller, J., & Wigfield, A. (2012). Dimensions of reading motivation and their relation to reading behavior and competence. *Reading Research Quarterly, 47*(4), 427–463.

Schunk, D. H., Meece, J. L., & Pintrich, P. R. (2014). *Motivation in education: Theory, research, and applications* (4th ed.). Pearson.

Schunk, D. H., & Zimmerman, B. J. (2007). Influencing children's self-efficacy and self-regulation of reading and writing through modeling. *Reading and Writing Quarterly, 23*(1), 7–25.

Snow, C. E. (2002). *Reading for understanding: Toward a research and development program in reading comprehension*. RAND Reading Study Group.

Taboada, A., Tonks, S. M., Wigfield, A., & Guthrie, J. T. (2009). Effects of motivational and cognitive variables on reading comprehension. *Reading and Writing, 22*(1), 85–106.

Taboada Barber, A. (2021, August). *Motivando y comprometiendo a los estudiantes con la lectura* [Motivating and engaging students with reading]. Paper presented at Aprendizaje de la lectura [The learning of reading]: Fundación Educacional Seminarium, Santiago de Chile, Chile.

Taboada Barber, A., Buehl, M. M., Beck, J. S., Ramirez, E. M., Gallagher, M., Richey Nuland, L. N., & Archer, C. J. (2018). Literacy in social studies: The influence of cognitive and motivational practices on the reading comprehension of English learners and non-English learners. *Reading and Writing Quarterly: Overcoming Learning Difficulties, 34*(1), 79–97.

Taboada Barber, A., Buehl, M. M., Kidd, J. K., Sturtevant, E. G., Richey Nuland, L., & Beck, J. (2015). Reading engagement in social studies: Exploring the role of a social studies literacy intervention on reading comprehension, reading self-efficacy, and engagement in middle school students with different language backgrounds. *Reading Psychology, 36*(1), 31–85.

Taboada Barber, A., & Lutz Klauda, S. (2020). How reading motivation and engagement enable reading achievement: Policy implications. *Policy Insights from the Behavioral and Brain Sciences, 7*(1), 27–34.

Toste, J. R., Didion, L., Peng, P., Filderman, M. J., & McClelland, A. M. (2020). A meta-analytic review of the relations between motivation and reading achievement for K–12 students. *Review of Educational Research, 90*(3), 420–456.

Wang, J. H. Y., & Guthrie, J. T. (2004). Modeling the effects of intrinsic motivation, extrinsic motivation, amount of reading, and past reading achievement on text comprehension between US and Chinese students. *Reading Research Quarterly, 39*(2), 162–186.

Wantchekon, K., & Kim, J. S. (2019). Exploring heterogeneity in the relationship between reading engagement and reading comprehension by achievement level. *Reading and Writing Quarterly, 35*(6), 539–555.

Wigfield, A., & Guthrie, J. T. (1997). Relations of children's motivation for reading to the amount and breadth of their reading. *Journal of Educational Psychology, 89*(3), 420–432.

Wigfield, A., Guthrie, J. T., Perencevich, K. C., Taboada, A., Lutz, S., McRae, A., & Barbosa, P. (2008). Role of reading engagement in mediating the effects of instruction on reading outcomes. *Psychology in the Schools, 45*(5), 432–445.

Wigfield, A., Mason-Singh, A., Ho, A. N., & Guthrie, J. T. (2014). Intervening to improve children's reading motivation and comprehension: Concept-oriented reading instruction. In S. A. Karabenick & T. C. Urdan (Eds.), *Advances in motivation and achievement: Vol. 18. Motivational interventions* (pp. 37–70). Emerald Group.

Wolf, M. (2018). *Reader come home: The reading brain in a digital world.* HarperCollins.

CHAPTER 10

The Role of Knowledge in Text Comprehension

Gina Cervetti
Tanya Wright

Research on Knowledge and Comprehension

The impact of domain and topic knowledge on text comprehension is far reaching—across readers of different age levels and across texts of different genres (Cervetti & Wright, 2020). Knowledge is a significant predictor of reading comprehension among monolingual and emerging bilingual learners (Davis et al., 2017). Knowledge predicts not only reading comprehension of a particular text, but having a great deal of knowledge about school-relevant topics also predicts reading growth over time. For example, Hwang and colleagues (2023) found a positive relationship between science domain knowledge and growth in reading across the elementary years. The significance of knowledge is well documented across a large body of studies and is one of the most important and robust research-based insights about reading comprehension.

These understandings about the impact of knowledge on comprehension led to a host of interventions that taught readers strategies for activating and leveraging prior knowledge (Pearson & Cervetti, 2017). Although there was some evidence that building knowledge might also have important impacts on students' reading development, supporting their learning and use of reading strategies, their acquisition of word knowledge, and their reading comprehension, the research was sparse. In this chapter, we discuss our efforts to investigate the potential of knowledge building through reading in a series of studies with elementary-age readers.

We begin by describing theoretical and empirical explanations of how knowledge contributes to comprehension and research on knowledge building before describing three studies in which we explored the potential of knowledge building through conceptually coherent reading—reading a series of texts designed to build conceptual understandings—on students' vocabulary acquisition, reading comprehension, and use of higher-level reading processes.

Theoretical and Empirical Models of Knowledge and Comprehension

Over the last century, prominent theoretical models of reading comprehension have attempted to document and explain the role of knowledge in the process of reading comprehension (see Pearson & Cervetti, 2015, for a review). For instance, schema theory (Anderson, 1984), a psychological theory regarding how knowledge is stored in memory, was widely applied to describe the process of reading comprehension in the 1970s and 1980s. The thrust of this theory is that the knowledge and experiences readers bring to text provide a kind of "ideational scaffolding" for the interpretation and assimilation of information encountered in text, guiding attention, enabling inferences, and influencing how readers remember the text. Construction–integration models have offered a detailed depiction of the process by which existing knowledge interacts with the text in reading comprehension. In Kintsch's (1998) account, knowledge plays different and important roles at each stage of representing the text. Readers use knowledge to recognize words, understand individual propositions, and add semantic richness to the text. In these models, knowledge constrains possible meanings by activating relevant meanings in the text and deactivating irrelevant meanings in what would otherwise be a flood of possible connections and interpretations. Although the depictions of the interactions between prior knowledge and textual information differ across these accounts, knowledge is consistently conceptualized as shaping meaning making by informing, guiding, and constraining possible interpretations of text.

More recently, models built from analyses of predictors of comprehension, including the direct inferential mediation model in adolescence (Cromley & Azevedo, 2007), have offered empirical evidence of the role that knowledge plays in relation to other predictors of comprehension. In a study of ninth-grade students, Cromley and Azevedo found that background knowledge has direct and indirect influences on comprehension and, along with vocabulary, makes the largest contributions to reading comprehension among a set of variables that also includes word reading and strategy use.

Knowledge Building for Reading and Learning from Text

Although we have long understood the positive impact of having knowledge on comprehending text, only recently has knowledge-building been considered as having a more pedagogical role in English language arts (ELA). Many instructional routines and models—including K-W-L (Know, Want to Know, Learned; Ogle, 1996), the directed reading–thinking activity (Stauffer, 1969), and Guided Reading (Fountas & Pinnell, 1996)—have included activities that call on students to activate, or surface, their prior knowledge related to a text. However, knowledge activation is unlikely to support comprehension if students are encountering texts on unfamiliar topics (Kaefer, 2020). Working to build knowledge through and for reading has received far less attention, although a few studies have investigated the possibility of briefly preteaching knowledge related to a text.

Studies involving brief preteaching of knowledge related to a text have had mixed results. Stahl and Jacobson (1986) found that briefly preteaching knowledge improved sixth graders' comprehension of a text on an unfamiliar topic, but the preteaching was not powerful enough to overcome the challenge of reading a text with many unfamiliar vocabulary words. Kaefer (2020) found that brief preteaching of knowledge was insufficient to support kindergartener's comprehension of an unfamiliar text.

More complex and longer-term interventions involving knowledge-enriching and content-area instruction have suggested that knowledge development may be a powerful ingredient in interventions designed to improve students' reading comprehension. For example, across the intervention studies conducted under the federal Reading for Understanding initiative, the three programs that showed significant impacts on listening or reading comprehension at the early and elementary levels situated reading instruction in knowledge-enriching units. The Let's Know program (Lo & Xu, 2022) for prekindergarten and kindergarten students included instruction related to grammar, vocabulary, inferencing, comprehension monitoring, and text-structure knowledge in units focused on topics such as animals and earth materials. In a large experimental trial, the researchers documented impacts on curriculum aligned measures, including comprehension of expository text.

The second program, Content-Area Literacy Instruction (CALI), was a comprehensive intervention designed for use with children in kindergarten through fourth grade (Connor et al., 2017). CALI developed students' content-area knowledge in social studies and science, while building higher-order comprehension skills, use of comprehension strategies, and expository writing skills. In CALI, students read about topics in science and social studies, engaged in firsthand science experiences, and maintained notebooks with observational notes, graphic organizers, and written responses to question prompts. Compared with students in a business-as-usual control condition, third- and fourth-grade students who participated in CALI gained more knowledge of social studies and science topics and made greater gains in passage comprehension. The third program, Word Generation, involved word learning, discussion, debate, and writing around topics in science and social studies. In an experimental evaluation of the program, positive impacts included reading comprehension in grades 4–7 (Jones et al., 2019).

More recently, Kim and colleagues (2021) engaged first-grade students in a Model of Reading Engagement (MORE) intervention involving a 10-lesson unit on the topic of Arctic animal survival. The children read informational texts and used concept mapping to organize the science words in the texts, received instruction on science words, and engaged in activities to work with the new concepts being introduced in the books. Toward the end of the unit, students produced an argumentative response to an open-ended question related to the key concepts in the unit. The authors found that the science-literacy intervention had positive impacts on first graders' proximal science vocabulary knowledge, listening comprehension, and argumentative writing. In addition, students in the MORE intervention outperformed those in a traditional instruction condition on a distal measure of reading comprehension. The groups performed similarly on measures of reading engagement.

Additional evidence for the efficacy of knowledge-focused interventions for literacy development comes from a recent meta-analysis of the effectiveness of comprehension strategy instruction for students who were identified as "struggling readers" in grades 3–12. Peng and colleagues (2024) found that comprehension strategy instruction was only effective when combined with instruction in background knowledge. Teaching strategies, such as inferencing, and strategy combinations, such as main idea, text structure, and retelling were found to be effective in improving students' reading comprehension only along with building background knowledge. Earlier research had shown that teaching strategies using texts about which students had knowledge were more effective than using texts with novel topics (Gaultney, 1995). These studies suggest there is a powerful interaction between strategy instruction and knowledge building.

The series of studies we describe in this chapter were intended to help us better understand how knowledge building through reading conceptually rich and conceptually connected texts supports reading and vocabulary development. When we initiated this series of studies, ELA instruction included a focus on knowledge activation as a reading comprehension strategy, but not on knowledge building. Also, while ELA programs were often organized by broad themes, knowledge development was not an explicit goal, and there was limited focus on the concepts that children were expected to learn. Finally, there seemed to be increased attention to providing students with informational texts; however, this was often done in the context of an informational text unit, in which the focus was primarily on learning the structure of this type of text and not on using informational texts for the purpose of building knowledge in a coherent and meaningful way.

Guided by existing models of reading comprehension, we theorized that careful attention to knowledge development through explanation, elaboration, and repetition of connected concepts could help readers develop a kind of cognitive architecture or connected web of knowledge. We further hypothesized that this connected web would support comprehension of related texts and memory of the information in those texts by enabling students to fill in information and form connections. Finally, we hypothesized that the connected web of knowledge would increase readers' incidental acquisition of new vocabulary knowledge by informing interpretations of unknown words and enabling connections between the new words and familiar concepts.

By using highly controlled experimental designs, in which only the content of the texts varied—conceptually connected or conceptually diverse—we have been able to acquire insights into the questions of whether readers build usable knowledge from reading, how that knowledge impacts their comprehension, and whether this kind of reading can have other benefits, such as incidental acquisition of vocabulary knowledge from reading. We have examined these questions with students in the early and middle elementary grades, and the differing results have also offered insights into these questions.

Study 1: Conceptually Coherent Reading, Comprehension, and Vocabulary Acquisition

In addition to building knowledge and supporting comprehension, we were curious about the additional benefits that may accrue when students read a set of conceptually coherent (CC) texts. In particular, we wondered whether creating a text set that focused on knowledge building might support students' incidental vocabulary learning. Anderson and Freebody (1981) theorized that the well-documented relationship between vocabulary and comprehension (see Wright & Cervetti, 2017, for a review) may be a reflection of the reader's underlying knowledge related to the text. In other words, a person who has knowledge of a particular topic or subject area also likely knows the meaning of words associated with that topic. Therefore, as readers build their conceptual knowledge, they are also likely to learn associated vocabulary.

More knowledge may also free up attention, so that readers can make better inferences about the meaning of unknown words in the text. For example, studies with adult second-language learners had shown that readers with more knowledge of a text's topic had higher rates of incidental vocabulary learning during reading compared to readers with less background knowledge (Pulido, 2003). In this first study (Cervetti et al., 2016), we wondered whether knowledge built through reading might be robust enough to support comprehension of related texts in the short term. We also wondered whether this knowledge might support incidental acquisition of word learning by associating word learning with conceptual development and by easing comprehension, thus freeing up attention to notice and acquire information about unfamiliar words.

Fourth-grade students in a CC condition read six books designed to build their knowledge of concepts related to birds—for example, that different birds use a wide variety of materials and structures to make nests. Students in the comparison nonconceptually coherent (NCC) condition read six books about a variety of topics, including wolves, glaciers, and the sun. In addition to building concepts through the books, we embedded a set of target words within each set of texts. Five were unique concept words related to each text set (e.g., *fledgling*, *incubate*, and *molt* for the CC set) and five were more general academic words that appeared across both sets (e.g., *attribute* and *dependent*). All books averaged 700 words in length and had a similar readability score using the Flesch–Kincaid Grade Level reading formula.

Participants read the texts independently and engaged in a scripted small-group discussion of the texts led by a teacher. Before and after the invention, students were given an open-ended assessment of the concepts presented in the CC text set ("Tell me everything you know about birds") and knowledge of target concept-related and general academic words (What does the word *molt* mean?"). After the intervention, students also read a brief passage about birds and both retold the passage and answered questions about it. Students in the CC condition acquired more knowledge of bird concepts. They also acquired more knowledge of the concept words in the texts they read than did the comparison students of the words in their texts. The students in the CC condition also seemed to acquire more knowledge of the academic words that appeared across both sets of texts. Scores on the comprehension questions were not different across groups, but the CC students had stronger retelling scores based on the number of idea units they recalled.

These results not only reflected earlier research that had documented an association between prior topic knowledge and reading comprehension but also extended that research in important ways. It provided some evidence that even a brief knowledge-building intervention could positively influence comprehension of related texts. The findings further confirmed that reading in this way supported incidental word learning. The study offered some evidence that the concepts students developed through reading made new information and unfamiliar words more meaningful and memorable. In other words, the study documented positive impacts of attending to *what* students were learning as they read (content), in addition to *how* they were reading (skills).

Study 2: CC Read-Alouds

Although the first study showed promising results for building knowledge to support incidental vocabulary development and text comprehension (i.e., retelling), it included a small sample of students at only one grade level. For our next study (Wright et al., 2022), we asked whether CC text sets would support similar outcomes for younger children who engage with the texts through participation in read-alouds. In this study, we asked whether building children's knowledge through read-alouds of CC texts would support incidental vocabulary building, both for conceptually central vocabulary and for other general academic vocabulary words in the CC texts. We also asked whether read-alouds of CC texts might support listening comprehension of related texts for young children in the primary grades.

For this study, participants included first- and second-grade students from 11 classrooms in a rural school district. Classrooms were randomly assigned to either the CC treatment group or to an NCC comparison group. In total, 48 first-grade and 57 second-grade students participated in the CC group, and 35 first-grade and 55 second-grade students participated in the NCC group. All classrooms participated in read-alouds and discussion of six texts over 3 days. Similarly to our first study, the CC group participated in read-alouds of texts that included a set of concepts related to birds. The children in the NCC group participated in read-alouds of six unrelated texts. We also included vocabulary using a similar structure to the first study. Each text set included five concept words that related to the concepts in the texts (i.e., related to the bird concepts for the CC group and related to the range of concepts in the NCC group), and five general academic words were included in both sets of texts. All participants experienced the same number of exposures to the conceptually central words in their texts and to the general academic words that were embedded across both sets of texts.

Children were assessed on their word knowledge for all 15 target words and on two of three listening comprehension passages. One passage (concepts-only) was conceptually related to birds but did not contain any target words from the

CC texts, another passage was conceptually related to birds and included the CC treatment target words (concepts + vocabulary), and the final passage was unrelated to birds but included the CC treatment target words (vocabulary only).

We found that all children learned concept words from the texts to which they were exposed compared to the words to which they were not exposed, replicating findings from previous research that young children can learn words incidentally as they engage with read-alouds. However, the children in the CC read-aloud condition learned more about their concept words than the children in the NCC condition. In contrast to our first study, we found no differences between the treatment groups in incidental learning of general academic words. However, we found no differences between the NCC and CC groups on comprehension, and because treatment was assigned at the classroom level and we did not pretest the children, it was unclear whether the treatment groups were comparable at the outset of the study. Within-group comparisons revealed no differences in the NCC group's comprehension of the three different types of comprehension texts; however, the CC participants at both grade levels demonstrated significantly higher comprehension of the concepts + vocabulary passage compared to either the concepts-only or vocabulary-only passages. Together these findings suggest that CC text read-alouds are a supportive context for incidental learning of conceptually central vocabulary for young children. Also, young children can bring the combination of knowledge and vocabulary they build through participation in CC read-alouds to support their comprehension of novel texts that include words and concepts from the text set. We hypothesize that young children may have more limited "knowledge networks" than their upper elementary-grade peers. Therefore, vocabulary knowledge or conceptual knowledge alone may not be enough to support listening comprehension of a novel text. Rather, it may be that building a combination of both vocabulary and conceptual knowledge is necessary to support comprehension for younger learners.

Study 3: Knowledge-Building and the Use of Higher-Level Processing

In the third study in this series (Cervetti et al., 2023), our goal was to understand more about how and why building knowledge through CC reading might support elementary students' vocabulary learning and comprehension of new texts on closely related topics. In particular, we asked whether building knowledge through reading would change the ways that children process the new texts, inviting the use of more higher-level processes.

A significant body of research has documented that readers who have higher scores on standardized reading assessments use processes such as making connections (inferring and elaborating) and questioning as they read (Carlson et al., 2022; McMaster et al., 2014; Pressley & Harris, 2006). Young readers who are less skilled at reading comprehension tend to use lower-level processes, such as paraphrasing a text (Kraal et al., 2018). In one of these studies, Carlson and colleagues

(2022) found that readers who were skilled comprehenders in grades 3–5 generated more correct connections within narrative texts and made more relevant connections to background knowledge as they read. Existing research also suggested that one consequence of skilled reading was higher rates of incidental acquisition of vocabulary knowledge (Swanborn & De Glopper, 1999). We asked whether the knowledge students were building from reading CC texts was, in effect, helping students process texts more like skilled readers, and whether this might be responsible for the effects we observed in the earlier studies.

To investigate these issues, we conducted an experimental study in which 21 fourth graders were randomly assigned to independently read a set of eight CC informational texts about oceans or a set of unrelated informational texts on things such as bees and chocolate. The CC books were designed to provide repeated exposure to a set of ideas about the ocean, such as "Healthy oceans are essential for all life on earth, but human activities are harming the ocean," and a set of related words, such as *terrain*, *plankton*, and *safeguard*. Students read the books over the course of 2 weeks and completed a brief activity following the reading of each text. For example, after reading a book about how scientists consider the Earth as having only a single global ocean, students planned a boat journey around the world using a map. Control students completed analogous activities based on the concepts in their books. After reading the set of texts, students took an assessment of ocean concepts and vocabulary and engaged in think-alouds and retellings with new ocean texts. In the think-alouds, students read two texts about the ocean and were asked to describe their thinking at predetermined stopping points. After reading each text, they were asked to retell the text as if the assessor had not heard it before.

Unsurprisingly, the students who read the CC texts gained more knowledge and vocabulary about the ocean concepts from their reading than students who read informational texts on a variety of topics. More germane to the central concern of this study were the results of the think-alouds and retellings. When students read the new texts about the ocean, those who had participated in the CC reading condition engaged in significantly more higher-level processing compared with students who had read the unrelated texts. Higher-level processes included inference making, monitoring, predicting, proposing, evaluating, questioning and wondering, visualizing, and sharing feelings. Students in the comparison groups used more low-level processes, such as repeating and paraphrasing the text, though the difference between groups in use of lower-level strategies fell below the threshold of statistical significance. In addition, the students who had participated in the CC treatment included more correct statements about the texts in their retellings.

Even in the short time frame of the study, students in the treatment condition built enough knowledge about the texts to show different text processing behaviors and stronger retelling outcomes than children who read the unrelated texts. The question remains as to whether this kind of instruction can create enduring impacts on readers' processing, vocabulary acquisition, and reading comprehension over time—particularly on transfer texts and when implemented over a longer term.

What Does All of This Mean?: Implications for Instruction

This set of studies adds to evidence about how building knowledge through reading texts can support vocabulary development, text processing, and text comprehension in the elementary grades. We have long understood that knowledge supports comprehension of related texts. The studies reported in this chapter suggest that having knowledge also makes new information—new words and new ideas—more meaningful and more memorable, producing higher rates of learning from reading. We found that when readers are engaged in building knowledge through CC reading, they pick up more vocabulary knowledge incidentally as they read. Although the amount of vocabulary knowledge gained from any particular text is probably small, knowledge-enriching reading could result in substantial gains in vocabulary knowledge over time.

We also found that readers who built knowledge through reading the CC texts used higher-level processes when reading new, related texts than did readers in the comparison group. Higher-level processes included inferring, visualizing, and evaluating. This may help to explain the compensatory effect of knowledge documented in previous research—the finding that learners who generally have less skill in reading comprehension can often read with comprehension similar to more skilled readers if they bring knowledge to the text (O'Reilly & McNamara, 2007; Recht & Leslie, 1988).

Duke and colleagues (2011) refer to these benefits as part of a "virtuous cycle" in which having knowledge leads to better comprehension of and more learning from reading, and that learning becomes the knowledge that supports comprehension of the next text and so on (p. 53). What the studies in this chapter show is that knowledge-enriching reading might accrue other benefits—vocabulary learning and practice with higher-level cognitive processing—that also contribute to this virtuous cycle. Building knowledge and bringing that knowledge to reading may make every experience with text just a little more powerful.

When we initiated these studies, we were involved in projects that integrated literacy learning and content-area instruction (e.g., Cervetti et al., 2012; Wright & Gotwals, 2017). In the context of these projects, we observed the benefits of moving beyond reading individual informational texts to dive deeply into understanding ideas and phenomena through a combination of reading and firsthand involvement in investigations and problem solving. In addition to hopeful research findings in efficacy trials of these curricula, our informal observations persuaded us that in-depth study was supporting students in reading and writing more sophisticated texts and in acquiring new vocabulary knowledge.

This led us to wonder whether elementary ELA instruction that focused on building skills and strategies missed the opportunity to develop the knowledge that students would need to engage in the increasingly complex content-area texts they would encounter as they moved through school. Even when students were reading informational texts in ELA or engaging in informational units, there seemed to be insufficient attention to the question of what students would understand as a result. It also led us to wonder whether in-depth study of concepts might offer other kinds of benefits. The studies reported in this chapter provide some insight about these potential benefits. Our findings show that even a limited focus (six to eight books) on using texts to build students' understanding of a set of interrelated concepts produced more word learning and opportunities for higher-level processing compared with the instruction that is typical in elementary ELA classrooms.

Although we do not have a firm explanation of these effects, it is likely that building knowledge supports learning from text in at least two ways. First, knowledge may offer attentional benefits. Readers have limited attention to devote to the range of meaning-making processes that are required for successful reading. Bringing knowledge to reading makes comprehension a little easier and may free up attention for problem solving, using cognitive processes, and figuring out new words. Second, knowledge may offer a kind of scaffolding—a cognitive web of understanding that supports sense making and makes it possible to catch and hold new ideas and words.

These studies do not represent the kind of instruction we hope to see in ELA classrooms; they are experiments designed to test theories about the relationship between knowledge and reading. Nevertheless, they do add to evidence that students may benefit from ELA instruction that is designed to build students' skills and strategies while simultaneously supporting knowledge building.

Future Research

As we consider the ways that CC text sets can be used in ELA instruction, it will be critical to combine reading of these text sets with high-quality reading instruction. In our studies, teachers did not provide instructional support because we were attempting to isolate, as far as possible, the contribution of the CC texts as proof of the concept that organizing texts in a way that focuses on knowledge building contributes to students' vocabulary and comprehension development. However, there is substantial evidence (e.g., Shanahan et al., 2010) that teaching comprehension strategies and supporting text-based discussion also promotes students' comprehension. And, for students with reading difficulties, combining these comprehension supports with attention to background knowledge is more effective than strategy instruction alone for supporting comprehension (Peng et al., 2024). As such, future research should continue to examine how best to combine texts that are structured to support knowledge building with other effective components of comprehension instruction for a range of student populations and across different instructional contexts.

In addition, we need studies of longitudinal impacts. For example, if students regularly read CC text sets as part of instruction in the early grades, would they be less likely to experience comprehension challenges later in their schooling? If we spend time using texts to build young students' webs of knowledge, will this help them to more effectively catch on to new ideas when they read new texts or are exposed to new concepts during content area instruction? These questions still need to be answered with empirical evidence.

The idea that literacy instruction is made more powerful through conceptual coherence needs more research with texts focused on a broader range of types of knowledge. In our studies, we tested this idea with concepts about birds and oceans. However, text sets could include academic knowledge that complements content-area learning or opportunities for revisiting or extending important ideas about the natural, social, creative, and cultural worlds. In particular, it is important to understand how text sets might be used to connect to students' interests, their communities, and their experiences in the world. In addition, a focus on making connections between texts and students' lived experiences may have added benefits associated with meeting students where they are and building on their networks of existing knowledge.

Because we were interested in building knowledge through reading, we focused primarily on considering how knowledge building with CC texts may be supportive during ELA instruction. However, there are other lines of research that consider the ways that text can be brought into content-area instruction to support disciplinary learning and disciplinary literacy (e.g., Cervetti et al., 2006; Guthrie et al., 2004). Therefore, using texts to build knowledge during ELA and integrating literacy into content-area learning are not either–or instructional recommendations. Rather, future research should consider exactly how best to support knowledge building across the school day. Students also need opportunities to engage in the practices of other disciplines that are not primarily text based (e.g., planning and carrying out investigations in science instruction; NGSS [Next Generation Science Standards] Lead States, 2013). Therefore, in future studies that examine the idea of knowledge building in ELA, researchers should consider how to build knowledge that supplements but does not supplant the learning that students gain in other subject areas.

Finally, our studies begin to explore the benefits for vocabulary development and text processing that are associated with reading CC texts. However, there may be additional benefits to building knowledge through reading that we have not yet explored. For example, how might a focus on reading CC texts support students as writers? Could reading CC texts be particularly supportive for students who are reading below grade level? Could reading CC texts support students to engage in more sophisticated text-based discussions?

There are still many questions that remain to be answered, but, overall, we believe that the line of work described in this chapter suggests that attention to knowledge building in the elementary grades supports students' vocabulary development, text processing, and text comprehension. While the idea that students should "learn to read before they read to learn" is still commonplace, these studies add to a growing body of evidence indicating that reading to learn may be a powerful way to support learning to read.

REFERENCES

Anderson, R. C. (1984). Role of readers' schema in comprehension, learning and memory. In R. Anderson, J. Osbourne, & R. Tierney (Eds.), *Learning to read in American schools: Basal readers and content text* (pp. 243–258). Erlbaum.

Anderson, R. C., & Freebody, P. (1981). Vocabulary knowledge. In J. T. Guthrie (Ed.), *Comprehension and teaching: Research reviews* (pp. 77–117). International Reading Association.

Carlson, S. E., van den Broek, P., & McMaster, K. L. (2022). Factors that influence skilled and less-skilled comprehenders' inferential processing during and after reading: Exploring how readers maintain coherence and develop a mental representation of a text. *Elementary School Journal, 122*(4), 475–501.

Cervetti, G. N., Barber, J., Dorph, R., Pearson, P. D., & Goldschmidt, P. (2012). The impact of an integrated approach to science and literacy in elementary school classrooms. *Journal of Research in Science Teaching, 49*(5), 631–658.

Cervetti, G. N., Fitzgerald, M. S., Wright, T. S., & Anderson, B. (2023, December). *Conceptually connected reading: Supporting knowledge and vocabulary*. Paper presented at the annual meeting of the Literacy Research Association, Atlanta, GA.

Cervetti, G. N., Pearson, P. D., Bravo, M. A., & Barber, J. (2006). Reading and writing in the service of inquiry-based science. In R. Douglas, M. Klentschy, & K. Worth (Eds.), *Linking science and literacy in the K–8 classroom* (pp. 221–244). National Science Teaching Association.

Cervetti, G. N., & Wright, T. S. (2020). The role of knowledge in understanding and learning from text. In E. B. Moje, P. Afflerbach, P. Enciso, & N. K. Lesaux (Eds.), *Handbook of reading research* (Vol. V, pp. 237–260). Routledge.

Cervetti, G. N., Wright, T. S., & Hwang, H. (2016). Conceptual coherence, comprehension, and vocabulary acquisition: A knowledge effect? *Reading and Writing, 29*, 761–779.

Connor, C. M., Dombek, J., Crowe, E. C., Spencer, M., Tighe, E. L., Coffinger, S., . . . Petscher, Y. (2017). Acquiring science and social studies knowledge in kindergarten through fourth grade: Conceptualization, design, implementation, and efficacy testing of content-area literacy instruction (CALI). *Journal of Educational Psychology, 109*(3), 301–320.

Cromley, J. G., & Azevedo, R. (2007). Testing and refining the direct and inferential mediation model of reading comprehension. *Journal of Educational Psychology, 99*(2), 311–325.

Davis, D. S., Huang, B., & Yi, T. (2017). Making sense of science texts: A mixed-methods examination of predictors and processes of multiple-text comprehension. *Reading Research Quarterly, 52*(2), 227–252.

Duke, N. D., Pearson, P. D., Strachan, S. L., Billman, A. K. (2011). Essential elements of fostering and teaching reading comprehension. In S. J. Samuels & A. Farstrup (Eds.). *What research has to say about reading instruction* (4th ed., pp. 51–93). International Reading Association.

Fountas, I. C., & Pinnell, G. S. (1996). *Guided reading: Good first teaching for all children*. Heinemann.

Gaultney, J. F. (1995). The effect of prior knowledge and metacognition on the acquisition of a reading comprehension strategy. *Journal of Experimental Child Psychology, 59*(1), 142–163.

Guthrie, J. T., Wigfield, A., Barbosa, P., Perencevich, K. C., Taboada, A., Davis, M. H., . . . Tonks, S. (2004). Increasing reading comprehension and engagement through concept-oriented reading instruction. *Journal of Educational Psychology, 96*(3), 403–423.

Hwang, H., McMaster, K. L., & Kendeou, P. (2023). A longitudinal investigation of directional relations between domain knowledge and reading in the elementary years. *Reading Research Quarterly, 58*(1), 59–77.

Jones, S. M., LaRusso, M., Kim, J., Yeon Kim, H., Selman, R., Uccelli, P., . . . Snow, C. (2019). Experimental effects of word generation on vocabulary, academic language, perspective taking, and reading comprehension in high-poverty schools. *Journal of Research on Educational Effectiveness, 12*(3), 448–483.

Kaefer, T. (2020). When did you learn it?: How background knowledge impacts attention and comprehension in read-aloud activities. *Reading Research Quarterly, 55*(Suppl. 1), 173–183.

Kim, J. S., Burkhauser, M. A., Mesite, L. M., Asher, C. A., Relyea, J. E., Fitzgerald, J., & Elmore, J. (2021). Improving reading comprehension, science domain knowledge, and reading engagement through a first-grade content literacy intervention. *Journal of Educational Psychology, 113*(1), 3–26.

Kintsch, W. (1998). *Comprehension: A paradigm for cognition*. Cambridge University Press.

Kraal, A., Koornneef, A. W., Saab, N., & van den Broek, P. W. (2018). Processing of expository and narrative texts by low- and high-comprehending children. *Reading and Writing, 31*(9), 2017–2040.

Lo, M., & Xu, M. (2022). Impacts of the Let's Know! curriculum on the language and comprehension-related skills of prekindergarten and kindergarten children. *Journal of Educational Psychology, 114*(6), 1205–1224.

McMaster, K. L., Espin, C. A., & Van Den Broek, P. (2014). Making connections: Linking cognitive psychology and intervention research to improve comprehension of struggling readers. *Learning Disabilities Research and Practice, 29*(1), 17–24.

NGSS Lead States. (2013). *Next Generation Science Standards: For states, by states*. National Academies Press.

Ogle, D. M. (1996). K-W-L: A teaching model that develops active reading of expository text. *Reading Teacher, 12*, 564–570.

O'Reilly, T., & McNamara, D. S. (2007). Reversing the reverse cohesion effect: Good texts can be better for strategic, high-knowledge readers. *Discourse Processes, 43*(2), 121–152.

Pearson, P. D., & Cervetti, G. N., (2015). Fifty years of reading comprehension theory and practice. In P. D. Pearson & E. H. Hiebert (Eds.), *Research-based practices for Common Core literacy* (pp. 1–24). Teachers College Press.

Pearson, P. D., & Cervetti, G. N. (2017). The roots of reading comprehension instruction. In S. Israel (Ed.), *Handbook of research on reading comprehension* (2nd ed., pp. 12–56). Guilford Press.

Peng, P., Wang, W., Filderman, M. J., Zhang, W., & Lin, L. (2024). The active ingredient in reading comprehension strategy intervention for struggling readers: A Bayesian network meta-analysis. *Review of Educational Research, 94*(2), 228–267.

Pressley, M., & Harris, K. R. (2006). Cognitive strategies instruction: From basic research to classroom instruction. In P. A. Alexander & P. H. Winne (Eds.), *Handbook of educational psychology* (pp. 265–286). Erlbaum.

Pulido, D. (2003). Modeling the role of second language proficiency and topic familiarity in second language incidental vocabulary acquisition through reading. *Language Learning, 53,* 233–284.

Recht, D. R., & Leslie, L. (1988). Effect of prior knowledge on good and poor readers' memory of text. *Journal of Educational Psychology, 80*(1), 16–20.

Shanahan, T., Callison, K., Carriere, C., Duke, N. K., Pearson, P. D., Schatschneider, C., & Torgesen, J. (2010). *Improving reading comprehension in kindergarten through 3rd grade* (IES Practice Guide, NCEE 2010-4038). What Works Clearinghouse.

Stahl, S. A., & Jacobson, M. G. (1986). Vocabulary difficulty, prior knowledge, and text comprehension. *Journal of Reading Behavior, 18*(4), 309–323.

Stauffer, R. G. (1969). *Directing reading maturity as a cognitive process.* Harper & Row.

Swanborn, M. S., & De Glopper, K. (1999). Incidental word learning while reading: A meta-analysis. *Review of Educational Research, 69,* 261–285.

Wright, T. S., & Cervetti, G. N. (2017). A systematic review of the research on vocabulary instruction that impacts text comprehension. *Reading Research Quarterly, 52*(2), 203–226.

Wright, T. S., Cervetti, G. N., Wise, C, & McClung, N. A. (2022). The impact of knowledge-building through conceptually-coherent read alouds on vocabulary and listening comprehension. *Reading Psychology, 43*(1), 70–84.

Wright, T. S., & Gotwals, A. W. (2017). Supporting kindergartners' science talk in the context of an integrated science and disciplinary literacy curriculum. *Elementary School Journal, 117*(3), 513–537.

PART III
WHAT DOES THE RESEARCH SAY ABOUT SUPPORTING STRUGGLING READERS?

CHAPTER 11

Addressing Reading Achievement during Summer Vacation

Joanna A. Christodoulou
Anya Maloney

Summer vacation from school is an extended period during which students can selectively foster academic skills based on needs and/or interests, if given the opportunity to do so. This window may be especially important to consider for vulnerable learners, here conceptualized as students experiencing reading difficulties/disabilities (RD). We explore this topic for students advancing into grades 3–8 to extend the ample work that has addressed the importance of harnessing summer opportunities for vulnerable learners during *early* elementary school grades. We also highlight two contrasts specific to students in later elementary school: (1) the amount of direct reading instruction decreases and academic skill demands increase and (2) more reading resources are available in early elementary school years, but more students are routed to services through identification with RD in later grades. These challenges can limit the progress of struggling readers during the academic year; for older vulnerable readers to make appreciable gains on reading skills, summer vacation can offer a period of flexibility and opportunity.

Students advancing into upper elementary through middle school grades have often completed the most intensive years of foundational formal reading instruction. During early elementary school, curricula are dedicated to the acquisition of the alphabetic principle, decoding, word reading, and building semantic networks and background knowledge, as well as other aspects of morphosyntactic, semantic, phonological, orthographic, and pragmatic processing (Wolf, 2007). In grades 3–8 and beyond, increasing academic demands and content-area learning are built on the foundation of language and literacy established earlier. Yet students who struggle with reading acquisition face the double challenge of expanding their learning of content-area knowledge through print while also needing to establish foundational literacy competencies. Students are expected to read and analyze complex texts that include more sophisticated academic vocabulary and longer, more complex sentences (Nippold, 2017). Older students with RD often continue to lag in decoding, struggle with reading fluency, and exhibit weak vocabulary, poor reading comprehension, and/or underdeveloped written expression skills. Without proficient literacy skills necessary to access material in content-areas classes, these students face the risk of persistent academic and socioemotional burdens (Wanzek et al., 2010). Students in middle school are more likely to experience challenging externalizing and internalizing behaviors, as well as issues with attention, self-control, and task engagement, when they struggle academically in early elementary school grades (Lin et al., 2013; Morgan et al., 2011).

Older students with RD often require greater intensity of services outside of their classes to accelerate their learning and to narrow achievement gaps. More instructional time can be accessed by using existing school time more effectively (e.g., minimizing interruptions), adding school days, or having longer school days (Kraft & Novicoff, 2024), which are valuable pathways to consider. However, school year constraints on time and other resources can limit the feasibility of implementing activities that may be easier to accommodate during the summer break. Tutoring programs have also been impactful for reading (Nickow et al., 2024), as they provide more time-on-task for text exposure and reading experiences. In this vein, summer vacation can be designed to provide impactful reading opportunities that yield more time-on-task that is also structured and targeted. While many efforts to address the learning needs of readers with RD are available within school walls, we focus on the opportunities that are possible through summer learning to promote reading progress. These efforts have the potential to provide proactive instruction for students with RD that does not compete with school year agendas, but rather maintains or accelerates learning momentum.

Reading Difficulties and Disabilities

RD, the most common learning disability, impacts an estimated 5–10% of school-age students in the United States. The most common type of RD is developmental dyslexia—difficulty with reading words accurately and/or fluently (Lyon et al., 2003). Disability in reading comprehension is similarly a major challenge for students (Snowling & Hulme, 2012), both as a primary disability and as a consequence of dyslexia. Correlates of RD include academic challenges, negative psychosocial factors, such as increased incarceration rates and co-occurrence with related conditions, including oral language, writing, math, attention, and executive function challenges (Al Dahhan et al., 2022; Humphrey & Mullins, 2002). Among the estimated 50% of U.S. students who qualify for special education services based on a specific learning disability (SLD), about 85% demonstrate primary oral and/or written language challenges (Moats & Dakin, 2008). Importantly, reading can be an issue for students outside of RD identification, including those with other developmental disorders (e.g., attention-deficit/hyperactivity disorder [ADHD], autism

TABLE 11.1. Number and Percentage of Students with SLD with an IEP across Elementary School Grades

Grade	N	% by Grade	Cumulative %
Kindergarten	20	4	4
1st grade	70	9	13
2nd grade	160	17	30
3rd grade	290	23	53
4th grade	380	17	70
5th grade	540	30	100

Note. All N's rounded to the nearest 10. Data from ECLS-K:2011 (Tourangeau et al., 2019); adapted from Marks et al. (2025).

spectrum disorder) or acquired difficulties (e.g., after brain surgery) (Christodoulou, 2018; Perazzo et al., 2022).

SLDs in reading negatively impact the acquisition of language and literacy skills, but access to special education services is most common after the primary reading instruction years. During elementary school, 70% of children with SLD receive their first individualized education program/plan (IEP) between grades 3 and 5, in contrast to just 30% during grades K–2 (see Table 11.1) (Marks et al., 2025). A fraction of children with IEPs are offered services during the summer under the provision of "extended school year" special education instruction, often contingent on risk of skill regression determined with a wide range of approaches (Christodoulou et al., 2023). We also highlight that the time between a child's struggles with reading being recognized and the time that IEP-based changes to the child's education are implemented is, on average, 13.5 months (Al Dahhan et al., 2021). The prolonged access window between recognition of academic difficulty and receipt of services, as well as shifts in general education away from formal reading instruction, can all compound the challenges older struggling students can experience.

Reading Outcomes during School and Summer Vacation

Research on reading trajectories converges on several key points. First, literacy-related skills during kindergarten are already significantly lower in students who will later be identified with SLD (Marks et al., 2025). Second, the (achievement–opportunity) gap evident at school entry persists throughout primary and secondary school years between students with and without SLD (Marks et al., 2025). Third, struggling readers have strong potential to accelerate growth through beneficial experiences (Johnson & Barker, 2021). This work, *focused predominantly on school year progress*, elevates the importance of considering reading trajectories throughout the calendar year, including the summer months. While the value proposition can range from aiming to close achievement gaps to having struggling readers reach the average range of performance (or make measurable progress), summer opportunities remain an invaluable period to enhance reading performance.

Few researchers have studied summer reading trajectories; fewer still include older students (who also have RD). Selected studies have focused on summer reading outcomes using large scale datasets of U.S. schoolchildren. One study, using the Northwest Evaluation Association's (NWEA) Measures of Academic Progress (MAP) growth assessments dataset with over 17 million students in grades 1–8, reported that summer lags accumulate to the same students, with an estimated 40% of their total school-year gains "attriting," or weakening, during the intervening summers (Atteberry & McEachin, 2021). A relatively smaller sample of the NWEA MAP dataset (about 4,000 students) was used to analyze summer reading outcomes of students from kindergarten to fourth grade who had ever (or never) received special education services (Johnson & Barker, 2021). Achievement gaps already evident at kindergarten grew through fourth grade, driven by greater decreases in summer reading outcomes for students receiving special education services, despite selected academic years of their faster growth in reading. Although neither analysis focuses on students with RD specifically, this evidence highlights that vulnerable students show differential summer reading outcomes that persist and accumulate disproportionately.

Students with RD show significant summer reading score decreases in the absence of intervention (Christodoulou et al., 2017). This finding is based on a randomized controlled trial of struggling readers who had completed grade 1 or grade 2 and were assigned to an intensive summer reading intervention group or to a waiting control (business as usual) group. While there was no comparison group of unimpaired readers, the decrease in standard scores (equivalent to 2.25 months of learning) across several reading measures from the start to end of summer impacting the nonintervention RD group stresses the importance of attending to reading outcomes for RD students early, often, and onward as they advance into late elementary school years and beyond.

Mechanisms of Summer Activities' Impact on Reading Outcomes

While limited research differentiates the nature of summer reading outcomes by RD status, reading level, or grade, there is consensus among community members that summer opportunities can enrich reading skills, and that is through access to, and benefit of, summer literacy resources. The Matthew effect (ME) is one of the most common frameworks describing the impact of reading experiences generally (not specifically related to out-of-school time): The gap between struggling readers and their peers is tied to a virtuous cycle for skilled readers, in which more reading is associated with more learning from text, and enjoyment of the process, while the contrasting cycle for struggling readers is characterized by reading less, learning less, enjoying the process less (Stanovich, 1986).

An extension of the ME is that skills are prone to requiring more capacity to "reactivate" without consistent practice. This conceptualization is framed within the *dynamic skills framework*, which describes a flexible learning system that tracks nonlinear skill progress based on available instruction, support, and experience (De Bot et al., 2007; Fischer & Bidell, 2006). This theory lends a systematic expectation for skill fading among students lacking sufficient skill, practice, and/or resources for reading acquisition. Reading outcomes during the summer have included trajectories of slower growth to score decreases, with the decreases suggestive of skill attrition that has been described as summer learning loss, regression, setback, and slide. An underexplored topic is the speed of "bounce back" following attrition, especially important for older students who often have an established baseline of skill to "reactivate."

Dynamic performance is similarly captured in cognitive neuroscience research on summer reading outcomes in the broader framework of neuroplasticity, here conceptualized as the capacity of the brain to modify activity via changes in structure, function, or connectivity in response to intrinsic or extrinsic stimuli (Mateos-Aparicio & Rodríguez-Moreno, 2019). Many studies on reading intervention for struggling readers report modifications in brain structure, function, and connectivity associated with reading performance *improvements* (Barquero et al., 2014; Perdue et al., 2022). Yet, as summer outcomes have most saliently evidenced, dynamic performance in reading outcomes can present as score increase, decrease, or maintenance. Our work investigated brain structure (white matter) and reading performance at the start and end of the summer across participants with and without RD. Summer reading outcomes ranged from increases (mostly for students with RD who participated in summer reading intervention and for non-RD peers) to decreases (mostly for students with RD not participating in intensive summer programming). Reading score changes were associated with neuroplasticity in two white-matter tracts important for reading, with brain changes accounting for 9–16% of score variance in reading (Meisler et al., 2024). This finding is notable for capturing the full range of reading score changes (positive to negative)—across students with and without RD—and showcasing brain structure correlates associated with score *increase* and *decrease* across a continuum. Future work should address potential interactions of puberty with contributors to reading performance such as executive function and/or ADHD (Porter, Roe, Mitchell, & Church, 2024; Wright & Zecker, 2004).

Summer Reading Programs

Research examining summer reading programs has predominantly focused on summer reading interventions for vulnerable students in the context of lower socioeconomic backgrounds; less research has examined interventions for older students (and those with RD). Overall, summer reading programs demonstrate positive impacts on struggling readers in upper elementary and middle school grades. Drawing on this work, we highlight principles of impactful summer programming for learners who continue to struggle with literacy skills in the context of adolescence.

Research on summer reading programs has spanned settings that are home-based, at school, small-group, or 1:1 (Borman & Dowling, 2006; Contesse et al., 2021; Kim et al., 2016; Kim & Quinn, 2013; McCombs et al., 2019; Reed et al., 2023). While school-based summer programs, which are designed to be implemented by educators and researchers, aim to provide remediation to maintain or boost academic skills, home-based interventions generally aim to foster more equitable access to resources and learning experiences for striving readers from low-income families primarily in an effort to increase vocabulary and reading comprehension via wide reading (Allington, 2024; Kim & Quinn, 2013). Research on summer interventions typically includes students from a wide range of grades, only lower elementary grades, or students who are struggling readers due to myriad reasons; limited research focuses on older students with RDs (Contesse et al., 2021; Reed et al., 2016).

Home-Based Summer Reading Interventions

Summer vacation can offer a valuable opportunity to implement programs targeting academic interventions and recreational enrichment activities that foster positive academic outcomes. A meta-analysis of 41 experimental and quasi-experimental summer reading intervention studies developed for low-income students in grades K–8 (Kim & Quinn, 2014) revealed positive impacts of home-based ($d = 0.12$) and classroom-based ($d = 0.09$) interventions on total reading achievement outcomes, including impact on reading comprehension ($d = 0.23$) and on fluency and decoding combined ($d = 0.24$).

Home-based interventions designed for use during summer vacation have largely emerged to foster more equitable access to resources and enriching activities for striving readers from low-income families. These interventions were developed in light of research showing that children from low-income and working-class families had fewer books at home, read less than their affluent counterparts outside of school, and engaged in fewer book-related discussions with their caretakers compared to peers from middle-income families (Allington & McGill-Franzen, 2013; Burkam et al., 2004). Importantly, while underresourced home literacy environments are tied to weaker oral language and literacy skills, many home literacy features can be strengthened via impactful activities and practices (Romeo et al., 2022) to positively impact language and literacy outcomes.

Research studies on summer book distribution as home-based reading interventions for students in grades 3 and 4 provide a mixed picture of their effectiveness. Kim and Guryan (2010) found no statistically significant difference in reading performance between children in grade 4 who received books tailored to their reading level and interests for one summer and children in a control group (effect size [ES] = 0.02). White and colleagues (2014) supplied third graders from high-poverty schools with books to read and found significant effects on reading comprehension for students from high-poverty schools (ES = 0.08 and 0.11) but not for students from moderate-poverty schools (ES = −0.11 and −0.12). On the other hand, in another study that examined the effectiveness of a book-distribution-only condition compared with summer tutoring (about 40 hours; group size of 15 or less) for economically disadvantaged students in grades 1–7 who read below grade-level, Bell and colleagues (2020) found that students in both conditions improved their word-reading fluency and connected-text reading fluency, though neither group improved in reading comprehension. While the ESs of home-based book-distribution were small to moderate, increasing access to books can support low-income students' reading development over the summer months as a cost-effective alternative to intensive school-based reading programs that can be expensive due to the human and material resources required.

Home-Based Summer Programs with Teacher and Parent Scaffolding

Recruiting parents and caretakers in implementing a summer reading intervention at home, in addition to teacher scaffolding, can have a positive impact on reading outcomes for vulnerable readers from high-poverty schools, as well as struggling readers from mixed income backgrounds. Several large-scale randomized controlled trials examined the short- and long-term impacts of a home-based literacy instruction called READS for Summer Learning that was provided by parents who were trained in researcher-developed reading routines (Kim, 2006; Kim & Guryan, 2010; Kim et al., 2016; Kim & White, 2008; Stein, 2017; White et al., 2014). For these studies, teachers provided explicit reading comprehension lessons over 6 days in the final weeks of school to struggling readers from predominantly lower-socioeconomic-status backgrounds. Students were provided with books for the summer that matched their interests and reading levels. Their parents and guardians were taught routines to facilitate high-quality reading interactions to support reading comprehension, and they engaged their children in reading activities and discussions during summer vacation. Trials of this program demonstrated statistically significant, though small, improvements in both short- and long-term reading comprehension outcomes (ES = 0.06 and 0.09, respectively). These findings emphasize the importance of teacher and parent scaffolding to optimize home-based literacy success.

A randomized controlled trial home-based intervention study that recruited parents as reading partners for children from mixed economic backgrounds also reported positive effects on reading outcomes for students in third and fifth grade with low-average expressive vocabulary and reading comprehension (Pagan & Sénéchal, 2014). Parents were taught to model and to encourage the use of evidence-based strategies, including paired reading, reciprocal teaching, repeated reading, and vocabulary enhancement strategies, to improve children's reading comprehension, reading fluency, and vocabulary. The children received books that were matched to their interests and reading levels, and read them with their parents for 15 minutes every day over 8 weeks during the summer. Children were also encouraged to read independently. At the end of the summer months, children who participated in the intervention group made significantly greater gains than the children in the control group in reading comprehension (Cohen's d = 0.30), reading fluency (Cohen's d = 0.44), and receptive vocabulary (Cohen's d = 0.29). Based on studies of home-based summer reading interventions, when paired with parent coaching, increased access to books and voluntary reading has the potential to foster children's reading comprehension, fluency, and vocabulary outside of the classroom and to reduce potential summer setback.

Though limited, research on home-based summer interventions indicates that book distribution during the summer, combined with teacher scaffolding and parent-led interventions, can be a cost-effective approach for fostering summer reading skills for both younger and older children, particularly those from low-income families. A book fair model is another way to provide an opportunity for students to self-select books they are interested in reading—a critical active ingredient for increasing the likelihood that children will read more over the summer (in addition to having books at the appropriate reading level) (Allington & McGill-Franzen, 2013). Researchers suggest distributing as many as 12–15 books to children in grades 1–4 or as few as 5 or 6 books for sixth graders (Allington & McGill-Franzen, 2013; Kim, 2004), paired with training for both students and parents in comprehension routines (Kim et al., 2017, 2016; Pagan & Sénéchal, 2014).

Home-based reading interventions have focused primarily on increasing reading volume as a mechanism for increasing children's vocabulary, background knowledge, and reading fluency, which are critical for improving overall reading comprehension. For older students who continue to struggle with foundational reading skills, such as grapheme–phoneme correspondence, word reading, and spelling, home-based summer book-distribution programs with a focus on increasing student's engagement with books may not translate to the same gains seen for readers from lower socioeconomic backgrounds. Older students with reading disorders who have weak foundational literacy skills require more formal and structured literacy instruction to make gains, addressed in the next two sections.

School-Based Summer Programs

In terms of school-based summer reading interventions for vulnerable readers from disadvantaged communities, just 35% of the classroom-based summer interventions report using research-based instruction identified in the National Reading Panel Report (Kim & Quinn, 2013). The National Reading Panel Report (National Institute of Child Health and Human Development, 2000) describes five critical components for literacy instruction to address: phonemic awareness, phonics, fluency, vocabulary, and comprehension. Programs incorporating research-based instruction yielded moderate to large ESs on students' reading scores (d = 0.25 to d = 0.63), while interventions that did not report inclusion of research-based strategies yielded smaller effects ($d \leq 0.18$). More intensive studies (i.e., studies that had fewer than 13 students per class, provided 4–8 hours of instruction each day, and provided a total of 70–175 hours of total instruction) had a greater effect on total reading achievement ($d = 0.25$) than studies that did not have that level of instructional intensity ($d = 0.03$). This meta-analytic synthesis points to the positive effects of intensive and evidence-based summer reading interventions that were most impactful for struggling readers from lower-socioeconomic-status households.

Focus on curricular elements must be balanced with consideration of student attendance at summer programs, as both are requisites for progress to increase time-on-task for reading. Efforts to improve summer outcomes through nonobligatory programs are often limited by student absences. For example, high no-show rates severely limited evaluation of a rigorous randomized controlled trial that was otherwise scientifically robust—large-scale, longitudinal study of voluntary summer school aimed at providing academic, recreational, and social–emotional enrichment for disadvantaged students in urban areas at no cost (Augustine et al., 2016; McCombs et al., 2020). Students who received at least 34 hours of language arts instruction scored higher on assessments in the fall after the first summer program (ES = 0.05) and in the fall after the second summer program (ES = 0.09) compared with students who had less summer instruction. Though students with high attendance rates the second summer of the program made modest gains in language arts (ES = 0.08) that were also demonstrated on a state assessment test the following spring, interpretation of the program was complicated by both program improvements and cumulative challenges with summer attendance.

While several school-based summer programs have been shown to be effective in ameliorating summer reading loss, that outcome is not guaranteed. School-based summer programs vary widely across schools and classrooms, instructional time, the experience of teachers with teaching struggling readers, and the extent to which they provide explicit, systematic reading instruction tailored to students' needs (Folsom et al., 2019; Reed et al., 2023). Recommendations for increasing the effectiveness of a summer-based reading program for older struggling readers include the following:

- *Year-round planning.* In addition to establishing budgets, hiring personnel, and acquiring curricular materials, planning for summer programming in advance is especially helpful for recruiting staff and students early, which allows for preparation, including student grouping based on needs (McCombs et al., 2020; Reed & Gates, 2020).

- *High-quality instruction.* Delivery of high-quality instruction depends on informed instructors who are well supported. Teachers (during the summer *and* the school year) can strengthen their impact by being provided with professional development; alternatively, summer programs can hire teachers with specialized qualifications for delivering high-quality, evidence-based instruction (Folsom et al., 2019; McCombs et al., 2011). Summer program curricula should center around evidence-based practices, align/integrate with the academic-year curriculum, and be data-driven, based on the specific needs of individual students.

- *Alignment between summer and academic-year approaches.* Continuity of learning goals is supported by compelling evidence of the benefits of providing additional opportunities to practice targeted skills with prompt teacher feedback when intervention instruction and content-class instruction are aligned. In a study comparing Tier 2 intervention that was aligned with Tier 1 instructional strategies for vocabulary and reading comprehension to a comparison condition of non-aligned Tier 1 and Tier 2 instruction, statistically significant and positive effects were found in favor of the aligned condition on proximal outcome measures, though not on standardized measures of reading comprehension and vocabulary (Stevens et al., 2020). A caveat is that not all reading programs during the school year warrant replication/continuation during the summer when considering the program focus, the target population, the cost, and so forth.

- *Pre- and posttesting.* Students should be assessed at the end of the school year as close to the start of the summer program as possible to group them appropriately into homogeneous groups based on their current needs. Students should also be posttested at the end of the program or in the first 2–3 weeks of the academic year to determine the effectiveness of the summer intervention program (Reed & Gates, 2020). Standard progress monitoring schedules may accommodate summer purposes to minimize extra testing burden.

- *Homogeneous groups.* Grouping students based on their profile of strengths and weaknesses can increase intervention intensity by targeting intervention on the students' specific areas of need (Al Otaiba et al., 2016; Coolong & Wagner, 2015).

- *Small class size.* Smaller group instruction of about four to seven students can offer more differentiated and intensive intervention for foundational reading skills (Cooper et al., 2000; Folsom et al., 2019) and groups as small as one or two students show greater effects on reading comprehension outcomes (Donegan & Wanzek, 2021).

- *Maximize attendance.* To curb attrition rates, which average around 20% in summer programs (Kim et al., 2017; Reed et al., 2019) it is recommended to provide enrichment activities and fun experiences in addition to academic blocks to increase student motivation to participate in summer programming.

- *Sufficient duration.* Successful summer reading programs have ranged from 3 to 8 weeks (Donnelly et al., 2019; Lara-Cinisomo et al., 2020; Reed & Gates, 2020). McCombs and colleagues (2020) recommend that a school-based program last at least 5 weeks, with at least 80 hours or more of reading intervention to increase intensity of time-on-task. Studies with younger elementary students that provided over 88.5 hours of intervention demonstrated the highest ESs (Christodoulou et al., 2017; Denton et al., 2010).

For specific details and monthly checklists for how to prepare for a school-administered summer reading intervention program, we recommend Reed and Gates (2020).

Intensive Summer Reading Interventions

The constellation of strengths and weaknesses among readers is essential to understand; by grades 3–8, students have well-established patterns of reading performance, with areas warranting remediation and skills serving compensatory roles. However, most research to date has focused on vulnerabilities during reading acquisition. Older struggling readers can have deficits in one or more aspects of literacy, including phonemic awareness, decoding, spelling, reading fluency, vocabulary, reading comprehension, and writing (Daniel et al., 2024; Flynn et al., 2012). In addition, these students face more challenging academic content and increasingly longer and more complex reading assignments. The required texts include dense and abstract language, morphologically complex words, sophisticated disciplinary vocabulary, syntactically more complex sentences, and abstract ideas (Nippold, 2017). Because older struggling readers face the dual challenge of needing to improve their basic reading skills while trying to keep pace with grade-level assignments in their content classes in which reading is the vehicle for learning, many of these students will require intensive instructional support beyond what can be delivered during the typical school day (Wanzek et al., 2020). Also, the cumulative burden of struggling with literacy can weigh heavily on students as they advance to higher grades. The summer months offer a window of time during which both the intensity of the instruction and the focus on specific skills can be better tailored to older students' needs.

Intervention research studies for students in upper elementary and middle school grades have demonstrated that students with the most severe RD may require smaller groups and longer, more intensive intervention throughout the academic year in order to accelerate their rate of reading growth (Donegan et al., 2020; Torgesen et al., 2001; Vaughn et al., 2010). Instructional intensity can be increased by (1) forming homogeneous, same-ability, small groups of three to five students; (2) increasing the frequency and time of intervention sessions to provide extended opportunities to practice skills with teacher feedback; (3) providing targeted instruction that is explicit and systematic and tailored to students' specific literacy needs; (4) providing intervention instruction and strategies that are closely aligned with the academic year curriculum; and (5) increasing the duration of the intervention (i.e., number of weeks or months it is provided) (Vaughn et al., 2010). Students with severe RD, who may still be developing foundational reading skills, may require more tailored, one-on-one instruction, with a greater number of opportunities to practice specific reading skills with teacher support and feedback.

Few studies have evaluated intensive summer reading interventions that included upper elementary and middle school students. One study examined an intensive 3-week, school-based summer intervention program with an additional benefit of more intensive one-on-one tutoring on the reading outcomes of students in grades 1–5 who still struggled with basic reading skills (Contesse et al., 2021). Some, but not all, of the students were diagnosed with dyslexia or identified with an SLD in reading. Students who scored above a grade-specific oral reading fluency cutoff score received 4 hours of evidence-based reading instruction daily in a whole-group or small-group setting, while those below the cutoff score received

1 hour of one-on-one tutoring and participated in the whole-group and small-group activities the remainder of the day (3 hours per day). All students received 60 hours of evidence-based reading instruction. Tutoring sessions included explicit and systematic instruction in decoding and encoding skills, multisensory instructional methods, and followed a specified scope and sequence for introducing key concepts of written language, including phoneme–grapheme correspondences, syllable types, syllable division patterns, and basic spelling rules. The one-on-one format of the tutoring condition provided students with many opportunities to practice, respond, and receive feedback. Students made progress in their decoding skills, specifically decoding of r-controlled words (ES = 0.71) and words with short vowels and consonant blends (ES = 0.54). Overall, students made statistically significant growth on criterion-referenced reading measures of word reading (i.e., CORE Phonics Survey) but not on standardized measures of word-reading fluency or on measures of connected text fluency. While this study demonstrated that upper elementary students can benefit from explicit and intensive evidence-based reading instruction, additional support is necessary to improve reading fluency.

Principles of Effective Literacy Instruction for Older Struggling Readers

Effective summer practices for older students with RD can be gleaned from intervention studies implemented during the academic school year (Flynn et al., 2012; Scammacca et al., 2015; Torgesen, 2002; Vaughn et al., 2010). Several meta-analyses focus on intervention research for older students with RD (Donegan & Wanzek, 2021; Flynn et al., 2012; Scammacca et al., 2015; Wanzek et al., 2013). Across these analyses, researchers reported positive effects on student reading outcomes for older students with RD. ESs for interventions focusing on reading comprehension ranged from 0.10 (Wanzek et al., 2013) to 0.73 (Flynn et al., 2012). Regarding reading fluency, ESs of intervention ranged from –0.29 (Flynn et al., 2012) to 0.16 (Wanzek et al., 2013). ESs on foundational reading skills, such as decoding, ranged from 0.09 (Donegan & Wanzek, 2021) to 0.15 (Wanzek et al., 2013). The analyzed studies included a wide range of grade levels, including both lower elementary grades and high school grades; thus, upper elementary and middle school grades were represented in these meta-analyses, but the results are not specific to these grade levels. Furthermore, the interventions synthesized in these meta-analyses were implemented during the academic school year. In this context, we offer extrapolated principles of effective literacy instruction for older students with persistent RD.

When it comes to struggling readers in upper elementary and middle school grades, Flynn and colleagues (2012) found that studies with moderate positive ESs typically incorporated explicit and systematic literacy instruction. According to Donegan and Wanzek (2021), groups of four to seven students showed higher effects in developing foundational reading skills compared to larger groups or smaller groups of one or two students. However, for comprehension outcomes, smaller groups of one or two students had higher effects. Interventions that were standardized, rather than tailored based on student progress, yielded better results for both foundational and comprehension outcomes. Moreover, interventions lasting 30 hours or more significantly improved comprehension outcomes. Donegan and Wanzek's meta-analysis also indicated that multicomponent interventions, which addressed both word-level and text-level instruction, are particularly beneficial for older students with RD. More specifically, studies show positive reading outcomes for older students when explicit instruction is provided in strategies for decoding polysyllabic and morphologically complex words, explicit vocabulary instruction plus generative word-meaning strategies for deriving the meanings of unknown words, targeted reading-fluency interventions (repeated reading and continuous reading), and comprehension strategy instruction, namely, strategies that target identification of main ideas, question generation, and summarizing (Bowers & Kirby, 2010; Edmonds et al., 2009; Scammacca et al., 2007; Toste et al., 2017; Wanzek et al., 2010). Given the potential heterogeneity of older students who lack proficient reading skills and their diverse needs, intervention should aim to match each student's specific areas of need (i.e., foundational skills, comprehension, or both).

When working with adolescents with persistent reading and learning challenges, it is important to keep in mind that these students may have developed negative self-perceptions and attitudes toward reading and may struggle with engagement, motivation, and/or anxiety (Grills-Taquechel et al., 2012; Pennell, 2020; Vaughn et al., 2022). When developing literacy interventions for older students, researchers and educators should consider their social–emotional needs, as these difficulties can emerge or intensify in students who face long-term academic struggles. Evidence indicates that RD can lead to heightened anxiety levels, which in turn can negatively impact children's responses to reading intervention (Grills-Taquechel et al., 2012; Vaughn et al., 2022). Research shows that addressing anxiety within reading intervention yields positive results in both areas. Vaughn and colleagues (2022) demonstrated that combining evidence-based reading interventions together with cognitive-behavioral anxiety management techniques led to positive outcomes for students in grades 3 and 4 over a 2-year period. Upper elementary students who took part in this combined intervention made statistically significant gains in reading comprehension compared to the business-as-usual control group. They also achieved larger ESs than the group receiving reading and math intervention, which provided the same reading intervention but did not include anxiety management strategies. These encouraging findings suggest that such interventions can enhance both reading proficiency and the overall social and emotional well-being of students.

Conclusion

Older students (in grades 3–8) who struggle with reading are often left without sufficient resources during the school year and summer; research can, and should, guide summer reading programming opportunities for this group. Concern for reading progress is elevated for students with RD during the summer when formal schooling is largely suspended (Menard & Wilson, 2014). The summer itself offers a window within which effective programming, resources, structure, and content can be designed for struggling readers. High-quality summer programming can positively impact neurocognitive reading systems, reading performance, and social–emotional well-being of struggling readers.

REFERENCES

Al Dahhan, N. Z., Halverson, K., Peek, C. P., Wilmot, D., D'Mello, A., Romeo, R. R., ... Christodoulou, J. A. (2022). Dissociating executive function and ADHD influences on reading ability in children with dyslexia. *Cortex, 153*, 126–142.

Al Dahhan, N. Z., Mesite, L., Feller, M. J., & Christodoulou, J. A. (2021). Identifying reading disabilities: A survey of practitioners. *Learning Disability Quarterly, 44*, 235–247.

Allington, R. L. (2024). Free books to close the reading achievement gap. *Phi Delta Kappan, 105*, 48–51.

Allington, R. L., & McGill-Franzen, A. (2013). Eliminating summer reading setback: How we can close the rich/poor reading achievement gap. *Reading Today, 30*, 10–11.

Al Otaiba, S., Allor, J., Ortiz, M., Greulich, L., Wanzek, J., & Torgesen, J. (2016). Tier 3 primary grade reading interventions: Can we distinguish necessary from sufficient? In S. R. Jimerson, M. K. Burns, & A. M. VanDerHeyden (Eds.), *Handbook of response to intervention* (pp. 389–404). Springer.

Atteberry, A., & McEachin, A. (2021). School's out: The role of summers in understanding achievement disparities. *American Educational Research Journal, 58*, 239–282.

Augustine, C. H., McCombs, J. S., Pane, J. F., Schwartz, H. L., Schweig, J., McEachin, A., & Siler-Evans, K. (2016). *Learning from summer: Effects of voluntary summer learning programs on low-income urban youth*. RAND.

Barquero, L. A., Davis, N., & Cutting, L. E. (2014). Neuroimaging of reading intervention: A systematic review and activation likelihood estimate meta-analysis. *PLoS ONE, 9*, Article e83668.

Bell, S. M., Park, Y., Martin, M., Smith, J., McCallum, R. S., Smyth, K., & Mingo, M. (2020). Preventing summer reading loss for students in poverty: A comparison of tutoring and access to books. *Educational Studies, 46*(4), 440–457.

Borman, G. D., & Dowling, N. M. (2006). Longitudinal achievement effects of multiyear summer school: Evidence from the Teach Baltimore randomized field trial. *Educational Evaluation and Policy Analysis, 28*, 25–48.

Bowers, P. N., & Kirby, J. R. (2010). Effects of morphological instruction on vocabulary acquisition. *Reading and Writing, 23*, 515–537.

Burkam, D. T., Ready, D. D., Lee, V. E., & LoGerfo, L. F. (2004). Social-class differences in summer learning between kindergarten and first grade: Model specification and estimation. *Sociology of Education, 77*, 1–31.

Christodoulou, J. A. (2018). Reading: Insights on a common skill from uncommon cases. In M. Schwartz & E. Paré-Blagoev (Eds.), *Research in mind, brain, and education* (pp. 133–152). Routledge/Taylor & Francis Group.

Christodoulou, J. A., Azor, A. M., & Marks, R. A. (2023). Reaching students with reading disabilities during the summer. *Policy Insights from the Behavioral and Brain Sciences, 11*, 67–75.

Christodoulou, J. A., Cyr, A., Murtagh, J., Chang, P., Lin, J., Guarino, A. J., . . . Gabrieli, J. D. E. (2017). Impact of intensive summer reading intervention for children with reading disabilities and difficulties in early elementary school. *Journal of Learning Disabilities, 50*, 115–127.

Contesse, V. A., Campese, T., Kaplan, R., Mullen, D., Pico, D. L., Gage, N. A., & Lane, H. B. (2021). The effects of an intensive summer literacy intervention on reader development. *Reading and Writing Quarterly, 37*, 221–239.

Coolong, C. M., & Wagner, D. (2015). Using brief experimental analysis to intensify Tier 3 reading interventions. *Learning Disabilities Research and Practice, 30*, 193–200.

Cooper, H. M., Charlton, K., & Valentine, J. C. (2000). Making the most of summer school: A meta-analytic and narrative review. *Monographs of the Society for Research in Child Development, 65*, 1–117.

Daniel, J., Barth, A., & Ankrum, E. (2024). Multicomponent reading intervention: A practitioner's guide. *Reading Teacher, 77*, 473–484.

De Bot, K., Lowie, W., & Verspoor, M. (2007). A dynamic systems theory approach to second language acquisition. *Bilingualism: Language and Cognition, 10*, 7–21.

Denton, C. A., Nimon, K., Mathes, P. G., Swanson, E. A., Kethley, C., Kurz, T. B., & Shih, M. (2010). Effectiveness of a supplemental early reading intervention scaled up in multiple schools. *Exceptional Children, 76*, 394–416.

Donegan, R. E., & Wanzek, J. (2021). Effects of reading interventions implemented for upper elementary struggling readers: A look at recent research. *Reading and Writing, 34*, 1943–1977.

Donegan, R. E., Wanzek, J., & Al Otaiba, S. (2020). Effects of a reading intervention implemented at differing intensities for upper elementary students. *Learning Disabilities Research and Practice, 35*, 62–71.

Donnelly, P. M., Huber, E., & Yeatman, J. D. (2019). Intensive summer intervention drives linear growth of reading skill in struggling readers. *Frontiers in Psychology, 10*, Article 1900.

Edmonds, M. S., Vaughn, S., Wexler, J., Reutebuch, C., Cable, A., Tackett, K. K., & Schnakenberg, J. W. (2009). A synthesis of reading interventions and effects on reading comprehension outcomes for older struggling readers. *Review of Educational Research, 79*, 262–300.

Fischer, K. W., & Bidell, T. R. (2006). Dynamic development of action, thought, and emotion. In W. Damon & R. M. Lerner (Eds.), *Handbook of child psychology: Vol. 1. Theoretical models of human development* (6th ed., pp. 313–399). Wiley.

Flynn, L. J., Zheng, X., & Swanson, H. L. (2012). Instructing struggling older readers: A selective meta?analysis of intervention research. *Learning Disabilities Research and Practice, 27*, 21–32.

Folsom, J. S., Reed, D. K., Aloe, A. M., & Schmitz, S. (2019). Instruction in district-designed intensive summer reading programs. *Learning Disability Quarterly, 42*, 147–160.

Grills-Taquechel, A. E., Fletcher, J. M., Vaughn, S. R., & Stuebing, K. K. (2012). Anxiety and reading difficulties in early elementary school: Evidence for unidirectional- or bi-directional relations? *Child Psychiatry and Human Development, 43*, 35–47.

Humphrey, N., & Mullins, P. M. (2002). Self?concept and self?esteem in developmental dyslexia. *Journal of Research in Special Educational Needs, 2*(2).

Johnson, A., & Barker, E. (2021). *Understanding differential growth during school years and summers for students in special education* (Research Brief, Center for School and Student Progress at NWEA). Northwest Evaluation Association.

Kim, J. S. (2004). Summer reading and the ethnic achievement gap. *Journal of Education of Students at Risk, 9,* 169–189.

Kim, J. S. (2006). Effects of a voluntary summer reading intervention on reading achievement: Results from a randomized field trial. *Educational Evaluation and Policy Analysis, 28,* 335–355.

Kim, J. S., Burkhauser, M. B., Quinn, D. M., Guryan, J., Kingston, H. C., & Aleman, K. (2017). Effectiveness of structured teacher adaptations to an evidence-based summer literacy program. *Reading Research Quarterly, 52,* 443–468.

Kim, J. S., & Guryan, J. (2010). The efficacy of a voluntary summer book reading intervention for low-income Latino children from language minority families. *Journal of Educational Psychology, 102,* 20–31.

Kim, J. S., Guryan, J., White, T. G., Quinn, D. M., Capotosto, L., & Kingston, H. C. (2016). Delayed effects of a low-cost and large-scale summer reading intervention on elementary school children's reading comprehension. *Journal of Research on Educational Effectiveness, 9,* 1–22.

Kim, J. S., & Quinn, D. M. (2013). The effects of summer reading on low-income children's literacy achievement from kindergarten to grade 8: A meta-analysis of classroom and home interventions. *Review of Educational Research, 83,* 386–431.

Kim, J. S., & White, T. G. (2008). Scaffolding voluntary summer reading for children in grades 3 to 5: An experimental study. *Scientific Studies of Reading, 12,* 1–23.

Kraft, M. A., & Novicoff, S. (2024). Time in School: A conceptual framework, synthesis of the causal research, and empirical exploration. *American Educational Research Journal, 61*(4), 724–766.

Lara-Cinisomo, S., Taylor, D. B., & Medina, A. L. (2020). Summer reading program with benefits for at-risk children: Results from a freedom school program. *Reading and Writing Quarterly, 36,* 211–224.

Lin, Y.-C., Morgan, P. L., Hillemeier, M., Cook, M., Maczuga, S., & Farkas, G. (2013). Reading, mathematics, and behavioral difficulties interrelate: Evidence from a cross-lagged panel design and population-based sample of US upper elementary students. *Behavioral Disorders, 38,* 212–227.

Lyon, G. R., Shaywitz, S. E., & Shaywitz, B. A. (2003). A definition of dyslexia. *Annals of Dyslexia, 53,* 1–14.

Marks, R., Mesite, L., Fox, A., & Christodoulou, J. A. (2025). *Early reading and math developmental trajectories: Examining influences of specific learning disabilities and socioeconomic status.* Manuscript under review.

Mateos-Aparicio, P., & Rodríguez-Moreno, A. (2019). The impact of studying brain plasticity. *Frontiers in Cellular Neuroscience, 13,* Article 66.

McCombs, J. S., Augustine, C. H., Pane, J. F., & Schweig, J. D. (2020). *Every summer counts: A longitudinal analysis of outcomes from the National Summer Learning Project.* RAND.

McCombs, J. S., Augustine, C. H., Schwartz, H. L., Bodilly, S. J., McInnis, B., Lichter, D. S., & Cross, A. B. (2011). *Making summer count: How summer programs can boost children's learning.* www.rand.org/content/dam/rand/pubs/monographs/2011/RAND_MG1120.pdf.

McCombs, J. S., Augustine, C. H., Unlu, F., Ziol-Guest, K. M., Naftel, S., Gomez, C. J., . . . Todd, I. (2019). *Investing in successful summer programs: A review of evidence under the Every Student Succeeds Act.* RAND.

Meisler, S. L., Gabrieli, J. D. E., & Christodoulou, J. A. (2024). White matter microstructural plasticity associated with educational intervention in reading disability. *Imaging Neuroscience, 2*, 1–18.

Menard, J., & Wilson, A. M. (2014). Summer learning loss among elementary school children with reading disabilities. *Exceptionality Education International, 23*(1), 72–85.

Moats, L., & Dakin, K. (2008). *Basic facts about dyslexia and other reading problems.* International Dyslexia Association.

Morgan, P. L., Farkas, G., & Wu, Q. (2011). Kindergarten children's growth trajectories in reading and mathematics: Who falls increasingly behind? *Journal of Learning Disabilities, 44*, 472–488.

National Institute of Child Health and Human Development. (2000). *Report of the National Reading Panel: Teaching Children to Read: Reports of the Subgroups* (00-4754). U.S. Government Printing Office.

Nickow, A., Oreopoulos, P., & Quan, V. (2024). The promise of tutoring for preK–12 learning: A systematic review and meta-analysis of the experimental evidence. *American Educational Research Journal, 61*, 74–107.

Nippold, M. A. (2017). Reading comprehension deficits in adolescents: Addressing underlying language abilities. *Language, Speech, and Hearing Services in Schools, 48*, 125–131.

Pagan, S., & Sénéchal, M. (2014). Involving parents in a summer book reading program to promote reading comprehension, fluency, and vocabulary in grade 3 and grade 5 children. *Canadian Journal of Education, 37*, 1–31.

Pennell, C. (2020). Summer school for middle school readers labeled as struggling: Lessons learned and pathways forward. *Clearing House: A Journal of Educational Strategies, Issues and Ideas, 93*, 142–147.

Perazzo, D., Moore, R., Kasparian, N. A., Rodts, M., Horowitz-Kraus, T., Crosby, L., ... Hutton, J. (2022). Chronic pediatric diseases and risk for reading difficulties: A narrative review with recommendations. *Pediatric Research, 92*, 966–978.

Perdue, M. V., Mahaffy, K., Vlahcevic, K., Wolfman, E., Erbeli, F., Richlan, F., & Landi, N. (2022). Reading intervention and neuroplasticity: A systematic review and meta-analysis of brain changes associated with reading intervention. *Neuroscience and Biobehavioral Reviews, 132*, 465–494.

Porter, B. M., Roe, M. A., Mitchell, M. E., & Church, J. A. (2024). A longitudinal examination of executive function abilities, attention?deficit/hyperactivity disorder, and puberty in adolescence. *Child Development, 95*, 1076–1091.

Reed, D. K., Aloe, A. M., Reeger, A. J., & Folsom, J. S. (2019). Defining summer gain among elementary students with or at risk for reading disabilities. *Exceptional Children, 85*, 413–431.

Reed, D. K., & Gates, C. (2020). Don't fail to plan for summer reading interventions. *Preventing School Failure: Alternative Education for Children and Youth, 64*, 223–229.

Reed, D. K., Meginnis, T., Park, S., & Gibbs, A. (2023). Surveying elementary schools summer reading interventions in a state policy context. *Remedial and Special Education, 44*, 16–27.

Reed, D. K., Schmitz, S., Aloe, A. M., & Folsom, J. S. (2016). *Report of the 2016 Intensive Summer Reading Program (ISRP) study.* Iowa Reading Research Center, University of Iowa.

Romeo, R. R., Uchida, L., & Christodoulou, J. A. (2022). Socioeconomic status and reading outcomes: Neurobiological and behavioral correlates. *New Directions for Child and Adolescent Development, 2022*, 57–70.

Scammacca, N., Roberts, G., Vaughn, S., Edmonds, M., Wexler, J., Reutebuch, C. K., & Torgesen, J. K. (2007). *Interventions for adolescent struggling readers: A meta-analysis with implications for practice.* RMC Research Corp, Center on Instruction.

Scammacca, N., Roberts, G., Vaughn, S., & Stuebing, K. (2015). A meta-analysis of interventions for struggling readers in grades 4–12: 1980–2011. *Journal of Learning Disabilities, 48,* 369–390.

Snowling, M. J., & Hulme, C. (2012). Annual Research Review: The nature and classification of reading disorders—a commentary on proposals for DSM-5: DSM-5 reading disorders. *Journal of Child Psychology and Psychiatry, 53,* 593–607.

Stanovich, K. E. (1986). Matthew effects in reading: Some consequences of individual differences in the acquisition of literacy. *Reading Research Quarterly, 21,* 360–407.

Stein, M. L. (2017). Supporting the summer reading of urban youth. *Education and Urban Society, 49,* 29–52.

Stevens, E. A., Vaughn, S., Swanson, E., & Scammacca, N. (2020). Examining the effects of a Tier 2 reading comprehension intervention aligned to Tier 1 instruction for fourth-grade struggling readers. *Exceptional Children, 86,* 430–448.

Torgesen, J. K. (2002). The prevention of reading difficulties. *Journal of School Psychology, 40,* 7–26.

Torgesen, J. K., Alexander, A. W., Wagner, R. K., Rashotte, C. A., Voeller, K. K. S., & Conway, T. (2001). Intensive remedial instruction for children with severe reading disabilities: Immediate and long-term outcomes from two instructional approaches. *Journal of Learning Disabilities, 34,* 33–58.

Toste, J. R., Capin, P., Vaughn, S., Roberts, G. J., & Kearns, D. M. (2017). Multisyllabic word-reading instruction with and without motivational beliefs training for struggling readers in the upper elementary grades: A pilot investigation. *Elementary School Journal, 117,* 593–615.

Tourangeau, K., Nord, C., Lê, T., Wallner-Allen, K., Vaden-Kiernan, N., Blaker, L., & Najarian, M. (2019). *Early Childhood Longitudinal Study, Kindergarten Class of 2010-11 (ECLS-K:2011): User's manual for the ECLS-K:2011 kindergarten-fifth grade data file and electronic codebook, public version.* National Center for Education Statistics, Institute of Education Sciences, U.S. Department of Education.

Vaughn, S., Denton, C. A., & Fletcher, J. M. (2010). Why intensive interventions are necessary for students with severe reading difficulties. *Psychology in the Schools, 47,* 432–444.

Vaughn, S., Grills, A. E., Capin, P., Roberts, G., Fall, A.-M., & Daniel, J. (2022). Examining the effects of integrating anxiety management instruction within a reading intervention for upper elementary students with reading difficulties. *Journal of Learning Disabilities, 55,* 408–426.

Wanzek, J., Al Otaiba, S., Schatschneider, C., Donegan, R. E., Rivas, B., Jones, F., & Petscher, Y. (2020). Intensive intervention for upper elementary students with severe reading comprehension difficulties. *Journal of Research on Educational Effectiveness, 13,* 408–429.

Wanzek, J., Vaughn, S., Scammacca, N. K., Metz, K., Murray, C. S., Roberts, G., & Danielson, L. (2013). Extensive reading interventions for students with reading difficulties after grade 3. *Review of Educational Research, 83,* 163–195.

Wanzek, J., Wexler, J., Vaughn, S., & Ciullo, S. (2010). Reading interventions for struggling readers in the upper elementary grades: A synthesis of 20 years of research. *Reading and Writing, 23,* 889–912.

White, T. G., Kim, J. S., Kingston, H. C., & Foster, L. (2014). Replicating the effects of a teacher-scaffolded voluntary summer reading program: The role of poverty. *Reading Research Quarterly, 49,* 5–30.

Wolf, M. (2007). *Proust and the squid: The story and science of the reading brain.* HarperCollins.

Wright, B. A., & Zecker, S. G. (2004). Learning problems, delayed development, and puberty. *Proceedings of the National Academy of Sciences USA, 101,* 9942–9946.

CHAPTER 12

Multi-Tiered Systems of Support for Improving Literacy Outcomes for Students in Grades 3–8

Devin M. Kearns
Nina Bayer
Melissa Stalega
Meaghan McKenna

Multi-tiered systems of support (MTSS) is a term to describe a way of providing the level of support necessary for all students to maximize students' academic growth. The term is inclusive of supports directly related to the academic content area (in this chapter, reading) and behavior supports that create a positive learning environment. Our purpose in this chapter is to focus on the reading-specific aspects of MTSS. *Response to intervention* (RTI) was the term originally used to describe MTSS, but it was used mostly by researchers and educators focused on academic outcomes. The term MTSS is now used to emphasize the importance of integrating academic and behavior supports.

Summary of Key Components of MTSS

A typical MTSS system has three tiers. Each tier comprises two components: (1) an instructional program or set of instructional practices and (2) a system for monitoring students' response to instruction. Each of the following three sections describes these tiers in greater detail. In brief, here is a general description of each tier. Tier 1 is general education instruction provided for all students following grade-level standards. These students are screened at least twice a year to identify students at-risk for long-term reading difficulties. Students who fall below benchmark (i.e., score cut points) are recommended to receive additional instruction in Tier 2 and/or Tier 3. About 20% of students who do not respond to Tier 1 instruction will receive small group support in Tier 2. Instruction in Tier 2 includes focus on foundational skills according to grade-level expectations. These students are progress monitored on a regular basis to track growth. Even with Tier 2 supports, about 15% of those students will need intensive support in Tier 3. Tier 3 instruction meets students where they are at (i.e., instructional level) and includes adaptations based directly on individual need. A comparison of assessments across each tier is described in Table 12.1.

This Chapter

Our purpose in this chapter is to disambiguate evidence-based practices from those that are common but not supported by empirical research. In each of the following three sections, we examine practices for each of the tiers. Each section has two parts, the first about instructional programs and practices and the second about data collection and analysis. We describe within each section widely used MTSS practices with evidentiary support and those without it. The final section of the chapter addresses the contextual factors that may or may not lead to success in implementing MTSS.

Tier 1 Practices: What Is Evidence Based?

Instruction

In Tier 1, the resources for teaching the content and strategies frequently come from a *core program*, a locally designed curriculum, or a local curriculum paired with a supplemental program used for a specific purpose (e.g., teaching word recognition skills). A core program includes enough content to last an entire year and a set of grade-appropriate strategies the student learns to use. Most core curricula are commercial products that are evaluated and approved by state education agencies; more than 70% of schools use these (Dewitz et al., 2009).

A locally designed curriculum includes resources created by educators at the classroom, school, or district level. In most cases, these curricula describe the content and strategies to be taught, along with resources to support individual lessons, but without the instructional guidance and materials needed for a single lesson. A supplemental program includes the daily detail expected of a core program for certain skills but locally designed curriculum for others.

MTSS begins with core (Tier 1) instruction. While nationally marketed core reading programs are used in 73% of U.S. elementary schools (Dewitz et al., 2009), an awareness of research, policy, and evidence-based practice is needed for delivery of robust core instruction that is responsive to the strengths and needs of the diverse group of children attending schools across the nation. Research-based high-impact features (Clay et al., 2021; Tomlinson, 2017) of Tier 1 include the following:

- Implementing a master schedule.
- Supplementing or adapting the core program to include culturally responsive instruction and supports for multilingual learners, as needed.

TABLE 12.1. Comparison of Assessments across Tiers

Assessment type	Frequency of administration	Purpose	Psychometric validation required?	Example
Formative/instructional	Daily	Evaluate response to instruction provided	No	Spelling assessment; exit ticket
Screening/universal screening	Multiple (three to four) times per year	Identify students at risk of long-term reading difficulty if their performance falls below a certain level of performance	Yes (primary measure) No (secondary measure selected by teacher or mandated by district)	Assessment of phoneme segmentation fluency, letter-sound fluency, word recognition fluency, pseudoword (nonsense) word fluency, oral reading fluency, or cloze fluency (ability to identify one of multiple options for filling in missing words in a passage)
Progress monitoring (PM)/curriculum-based measurement (CBM)—general outcome measure	Weekly (Tier 3) Every 2–4 weeks (Tier 2)	Evaluate overall response to instruction over a period of weeks using a measure of that indexes overall grade-level performance	Yes	Assessment of phoneme segmentation fluency, letter-sound fluency, word recognition fluency, pseudoword (nonsense) word fluency, oral reading fluency, or cloze fluency (ability to identify one of multiple options for filling in missing words in a passage)
PM/CBM—mastery measurement	Weekly (Tier 3) Every 2–4 weeks (Tier 2)	Evaluate overall response to instruction over a period of weeks using a measure of that aligns with the standards covered over a period of weeks	No (teachers must develop multiple parallel forms that have different items in different orders)	High-frequency word fluency, consonant–vowel–consonant—consonant word-reading fluency
Summative assessment	Annually or following an instructional unit, or as part of an evaluation of overall skill (e.g., for special education identification or reevaluation)	Evaluate overall performance on grade-level skills using a measure that covers a wide range of grade-appropriate (standards-based skills) or that has evidence of differentiating levels of student performance	Yes (overall evaluation) No (unit- or district-mandated annual assessment)	State standards assessment; comprehensive academic assessment published by a commercial testing company
Diagnostic assessment	As needed; from other assessments listed here	Identify the reasons a student may continue to experience difficulty after a period of instruction	Yes, if relevant for understanding difficulty with a particular skill No, as relevant for understanding difficulty with a skill	Formative assessments; screenings; PM measurement; summative assessments as relevant scores on recently administered spelling assessment such as a spelling inventory; scores on universal screening

- Conducting administrator walk-throughs and quality teaching rounds.
- Providing ongoing professional learning.

Implementing a Master Schedule

To ensure that all children have access to core instruction, time for delivery needs to be allocated within a master schedule (Clay et al., 2021). A master schedule includes how time is used during a school day, in addition to guidance for how to spend time during each instructional block. This includes allocating time for direct instruction with modeling and guided practice in multiple settings and opportunities for independent practice. The emphasis on teacher-led instruction versus independent practice and word recognition skills versus language comprehension skills varies based on instructional need (Connor et al., 2005). Effective master schedules include time for teachers to differentiate instruction (Tomlinson, 2017)—that is, small-group lessons to help all students meet or exceed grade-level standards. They also include time for teachers to provide individualized instruction that differs from the core curriculum, sometimes termed an *intervention block* or *"What I Need" (WIN) time*. Differentiated instruction occurs in small groups during the teacher's core program instructional time, not during "What I Need" time.

Supplementing Core Instruction to Ensure Cultural and Linguistic Responsiveness

Integration of linguistic and culturally responsive practices is essential (e.g., Gay, 2002). This involves ensuring that students' cultural experiences are considered assets and are integrated within the school's reading program, frequently by ensuring representation in core texts, selecting supplemental texts that relate to the local community, and including students' home languages within the curriculum when it is not English. Multilingual learners require supports for learning that extend beyond the information in the core program. This may include preteaching of vocabulary, providing syntactic language frames, and using visual supports to aid language development.

Conducting Administrative Walk-Throughs and Quality Teaching Rounds

Administrators must regard themselves as instructional leaders. Researchers have shown that effective administrative leadership involves monitoring instruction (Hallinger et al., 2020; Spillane et al., 2004). Administrative walk-throughs heighten leadership visibility on campus (Fisher, 2013) and allow for an increased familiarity with the daily activity in a classroom (Stout et al., 2010). Walk-throughs are brief (no more than 15 minutes), informal, often unannounced, and nonevaluative. Rather, walk-throughs are conducted to better understand implementation of teaching practices or school programs, and to gather information to improve teaching and learning practices (Garza et al., 2016). Walk-throughs have been conducted in many different ways, such as providing teachers with performance feedback and collaboratively developing action plans (e.g., Calvin et al., 2009), using an observational protocol to allow for reflection (e.g., Downey et al., 2004), and focusing in on delivery of an instructional practices (e.g., Allen & Topolka-Jorissen, 2014). The outcomes of walk-throughs should be used to plan for professional development activities because they have proved to be ineffective without proper follow up and follow through (Grissom et al., 2013).

Research also indicates that quality teaching occurs when teachers participate in professional learning and subsequent professional learning communities. The professional learning communities component involves discussion of readings directly relevant to instructional practice, observation of all classrooms for all members of the professional learning communities, and subsequent discussion of the degree to which practices aligned with features of the Quality Teaching Framework (Gore et al., 2017). A randomized controlled trial by Gore and colleagues (2021) showed a small positive effect for this process on student achievement.

Providing Ongoing Professional Learning

To successfully implement evidence-based practices, ongoing professional learning is needed. A professional learning plan for MTSS may consist of several approaches. Joyce and Showers (2002) propose providing the theory/rationale, modeling of practices, and opportunities to apply learning and collaboratively reflect. Professional learning can also be job-embedded, allowing educational professionals to apply practices during the workday, which increases the likelihood of uptake (Franke & Kazemi, 2001). This often involves coaching, which facilitates the accuracy of application of practices within the appropriate context and the adaptation of these practices to apply to other contexts as well (Freeman et al., 2017). The combination of inservice professional learning along with regular visits during the academic year (Jacob et al., 2017) has the potential to have an impact on teacher practice (Benedict et al., 2021) *and* student achievement for students with and without reading difficulty (Brownell et al., 2017). Additionally, professional learning communities increase the likelihood that new practices are applied accurately and smoothly, in the appropriate context and over time, and adapted as contexts vary.

Data Collection and Data Analysis

Targeted instruction based on data has been shown to positively affect students' reading performance (e.g., Connor et al., 2009). Schools are increasingly expected to use data to assess student response to instruction (Bondie et al., 2019). To obtain data that can be used for data-based decision making (DBDM), various assessments are administered as described in Table 12.1. In this section, we discuss three assessment types: universal screening, formative assessments, and summative assessments (see Table 12.1 for further description) used for determining response to core instruction.

Universal screening is conducted by schools three to four times per year to determine present levels of student performance. Performance is quantified in terms of students' results on the universal screening assessment. The screening is a psychometrically validated assessment that includes cutoff points to identify risk and is usually commercially available. The cutoff point recommendations provided by the assessment developer typically reflect whether students will experience difficulty in reading at a later date (e.g., in 2–3 years). In other words, the cutoff point is based on an estimate of long-term risk. Long-term risk is often identified conservatively, such that many students whose scores fall below the cutoff point may not have long-term difficulty. State departments of education, districts, and schools may establish their own risk cutoff points. Districts must choose between many possible assessment options based on evidence of whether it will provide reliable and validated data for local students (i.e., evidence indicates that they work for the district's demographic population) as well as practical considerations such as requirements to implement new data systems or cost (e.g., Bao et al., 2024; National Center on Intensive Intervention, 2021). The screening tools considered most valuable to districts are those that accurately identify students (Johnson et al., 2010).

Decisions about local cutoff points may also depend on school and district capacity to provide support for students. Developers' cutoff points are typically set around the 35th–40th percentile, but researchers often recommend providing additional support for students whose scores fall below the 25th percentile. Districts may set an even lower cutoff point if they have limited capacity to support the number of students whose scores fall below the developer's cutoff point. Figure 12.1 illustrates the distribution of need under different scenarios. Schools and districts also use screening data to identify possible challenges with Tier 1 instruction. The challenge might be pervasive (all schools have low scores) or vary by school or classroom (specific schools or teachers have especially low scores). Should a school match the Example C distribution of need in Figure 12.1, the district will run out of time, money, space, and staff resources; in this case, the district must

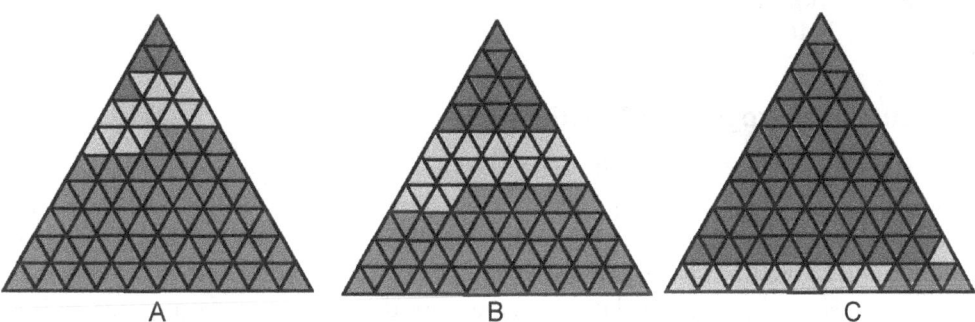

FIGURE 12.1. Examples of screening results. In these examples, there are 100 small triangles, each representing 1% of the students who take the universal screening. Example A represents the expected distribution of need, with 20% of students requiring additional support; B represents the distribution of students if the 40th percentile is used to identify risk for Tier 2 and the 16th percentile for Tier 3; and C represents the reverse of A, in which 80% of students require additional support.

change its approach to Tier 1 for fewer students to demonstrate need for Tier 2 or Tier 3. Regardless of the scope of the Tier 1 problem, districts must evaluate how to address this instructional issue, even as they consider how to provide additional supports for students with difficulty.

Tier 2: What Is Evidence Based?

Students who receive Tier 2 supports have difficulty with skills foundational to their current grade level. In the upper elementary and secondary grades, the definition of a foundational skill is more expansive than it is in the lower grades. Specifically, older students frequently require support for increasing their language comprehension. In models of adolescent literacy, literacy skills can be classified as *basic, intermediate,* or *disciplinary* (Shanahan & Shanahan, 2012). Intermediate literacy involves the kinds of skills that are essential to comprehension of texts across disciplines. Some of the most common essential areas of need for intermediate literacy are summarizing, retelling, and understanding (Peng et al., 2024). Many older students also have word recognition difficulties (Stanovich, 1986), even if these are not as serious as their language comprehension difficulties. As a result, Tier 2 instruction in most cases involves support for word recognition and language comprehension.

Tier 2 reading intervention supports students whose data suggest they are at risk of, or struggling to, access the core reading curriculum at their grade level, despite differentiation in the classroom. Tier 2 intervention is a systematic approach to engage students with additional targeted reading instruction. Data are collected and analyzed over the intervention cycle and used to evaluate the student's RTI. Tier 2 can be a springboard: Data-based decisions, drawn from more robust evidence, are made into action plans to identify a student's need for special education evaluation or intensive Tier 3 intervention, or to verify that the instructional boost allowed enough progress to warrant exiting the student from intervention (Wanzek et al., 2016).

Instructional Program or Practices

Evidence-based Tier 2 intervention has two essential features: (1) it addresses skills immediately foundational to grade level and Tier 2 instruction should provide students with additional practice that can fill holes in their knowledge and provide a more solid foundation for grade-level content and (2) it involves use of a program—when one is available. In the late elementary grades, a variety of programs address skills just below grade level. At the middle school level, there are fewer programs—but some are available (e.g., Kim et al., 2016). There are also structured strategy approaches that show evidence of improving student outcomes (e.g., Vaughn et al., 2024). In general, programs provide benefits to teachers. Some are practical: Teaching a program involves less planning and collection of materials than creating lessons. Others relate to essential features of Tier 2 programs: systematicity, explicitness, feasibility, and the completeness of content.

Systematicity

Systematic foundational reading programs, regardless of the tier they are used in, include a scope, the range and depth of topics and content, and a sequence—an order of instruction that is logical and cumulative in terms of content and complexity. The scope and sequence allow a bird's-eye view of a program's content and how it is intended to unfold over the course of instruction. In reading, systematicity for word recognition describes an order for introducing sound–spelling correspondences (also called sound–symbol or grapheme–phoneme correspondences) based on their frequency. For language comprehension, there is no clear order in which skills should be taught, but data indicate that retelling or paraphrasing, summarizing, making inferences, identifying and mapping text structure, and comprehension monitoring are important components of effective comprehension instruction (Cervetti et al., 2020; Pearson et al., 2020).

Tier 2 intervention may be especially effective when aligned with Tier 1—using the same reading strategies, techniques, and instructional language but with a difference in the level of content (e.g., Fien et al., 2015). For example, a teacher using a Tier 1-aligned program during Tier 2 intervention may be prompted to introduce a skill in isolation and then integrate it with other skills for students to generalize (Gersten et al., 2009). Misalignment across tiers (e.g., use of different terms, sequence, pace, skills, and content) is common in practice but not a research-based practice (Stevens et al., 2024). Misalignment between tiers increases student difficulty to connect and generalize, skills that support comprehension and strategy application across tiers (Capin et al., 2023). Although more research is needed, students with reading and attention difficulty who participated in aligned intervention and core programs compared to business as usual and non-aligned programs made significant gains in comprehension skills and vocabulary acquisition outcomes (Stevens et al., 2024). At the secondary level especially, evidence supports that vocabulary and comprehension practices used in Tier 2 intervention align with Tier 1 core instruction (Vaughn et al., 2022).

Evidence-based programs include guidance for teachers to follow regarding the duration, repetitions, and order of activities.

Summary of Evidence-Based Practices: Program Systematicity

- Foundational reading intervention programs include a scope and sequence of grapheme–phoneme correspondences and foundational skills across the entire program.
  - Following the scope and sequence with fidelity is an evidence-based practice.
  - An evidence-based practice during Tier 2 instruction is to introduce a skill in isolation, then integrate it with other skills to encourage generalization.
- Secondary reading intervention programs do not always include a scope and sequence. Instead, they may include instructional methods (i.e., a structured set of practices), curricula (program includes materials: text, lessons and supporting materials), and/or lesson packages (lessons that can be implemented as a supplement or within another curriculum).

Explicitness

In addition to a systematic scope and sequence, evidence supports the use of structured, systematic lessons and instructional strategies. Some evidence supports the understanding that receiving systematic and explicit instruction on word recognition skill acquisition is more important relative to the alignment with the core program (Gersten et al., 2009). This may be particularly true when the core program does not include explicit, systematic decoding instruction.

Explicit instruction is structured, follows a pattern, and is briskly paced. To teach explicitly, an instructor (1) has a clear objective limited to one or two foci, (2) models examples and non-examples with concise explanations, (3) incorporates guided practice with frequent student opportunities to respond (OTRs) (e.g., choral, whole-class OTRs with scaffolded support), (4) includes independent OTRs while monitoring accuracy and providing specific feedback, and (5) includes review and closure to the lesson. It is evidence-based practice, during Tier 2 instruction, to exponentially increase teacher-student interaction, especially in terms of student OTRs paired with specific teacher feedback. This includes modeling metacognitive strategies, for example thinking aloud, and building them into student practice (Gersten et al., 2009).

Explicit instruction is key to programs used for Tier 2 intervention at the elementary and secondary levels. A summary of research over a recent 20-year period notes the inclusion of explicit instruction in two-thirds of all studies that yielded positive outcomes from adolescents who received tiered intervention, and routines were practiced in half of those that did not formally include explicit instruction (Herrera et al., 2016). However, some features of explicit instruction pan out differently in elementary versus secondary instructional settings. For instance, it is an evidence-based practice in secondary Tier 2 intervention programs to include more collaborative/peer-to-peer engagement (Herrera et al., 2016; Vaughn et al., 2022). Tier 2 intervention for elementary-age students, in comparison, includes more choral practice during guided instruction.

Feasibility

Tier 2 interventions must be feasible in real school settings. The What Works Clearinghouse recommends at least 5 weeks of Tier 2 intervention, three to five times weekly, in 20- to 40-minute sessions (Gersten et al., 2009). Evidence suggests time spent on targeted skills is more significant than total instructional time.

Prolonged Tier 2 intervention is not supported by evidence. Instead, it is important to collect and analyze data during defined cycles to inform decisions about increasing intensity or decreasing support. Students should be grouped based on instructional needs (Gersten et al., 2009), which influences dosage decisions. Students with similar needs can be grouped across classes and grades (Gersten et al., 2009). Secondary-level groups vary more in size and setting, ranging from whole-class to individual tutoring (Herrera et al., 2016).

For elementary students, the instructor's role (specialist, teacher, paraprofessional) matters less than content delivered given appropriate training (Wanzek et al., 2016). At the secondary level, teacher certification may relate to student progress (Herrera et al., 2016). Stability, consistency, and adequate resources are crucial for Tier 2 interventions.

Tier 2 Content

ELEMENTARY

Some research supports targeting only foundational word recognition skills (phonological awareness, phonics), while multicomponent approaches show smaller effects (Wanzek et al., 2016). Experts recommend a strategic multicomponent approach when possible, covering three to four core skills. Evidence-based comprehension instruction includes literal comprehension activities, general strategies (e.g., summarizing), and listening comprehension. Vocabulary and inferential comprehension are more effective in Tier 1 (Wanzek et al., 2016).

SECONDARY

Strong evidence supports explicit instruction in polysyllabic–polymorphemic word reading and fluency building (Vaughn et al., 2022). Programs should develop students' spelling skills, expose students to varied text genres, and provide extensive reading practice. Comprehension strategies include word (vocabulary) and world (background knowledge) work, text navigation, summarizing, and supporting ideas with evidence. Moderate evidence suggests including "stretch texts" slightly above students' independent level, with more teacher support (Vaughn et al., 2022).

Progress Monitoring

DBDM requires formal and informal progress monitoring (Hamilton et al., 2009, and Mandinach & Jackson, 2012, as cited in Crone et al., 2016). Collect data at the start, midcycle (e.g., week 4 in an 8- to 9-week cycle), and end of intervention. Monthly monitoring is sufficient for Tier 2, unlike Tier 3 (Gersten et al., 2009). Secondary students may need less frequent monitoring over longer periods due to slower progress (Filderman et al., 2019). The Middle School Intervention Project found disparities between self-reported and observed practices in data use (Crone et al., 2016). Evidence-based practices include specific time lines for data-team meetings, follow-up procedures to monitor action plans, capacity building, and use of multiple data sources for decisions.

Tier 3: What Is Evidence Based?

Tier 3, also referred to as intensive intervention, involves highly individualized instruction for students who are not making adequate progress in Tier 2, have very low academic achievement and/or with disabilities, and are not making adequate progress in meeting the goals of their individualized education plans. The key characteristics of intensive intervention are that (1) it is a *process* and not a quick solution, (2) it is *individualized* to specific student need based on *data analysis* and *problem solving* (i.e., it is not a program or manual), (3) it is *intensive* both in content and teaching practice (i.e., it is not more of the same Tier 1 or Tier 2 instruction), and (4) it involves frequent *progress monitoring.*

Data-based individualization (DBI; National Center on Intensive Intervention; *www.intensiveintervention.org*) is a research-based intensive intervention that follows a multistep approach to adapt and individualize instruction to accelerate stagnant academic growth (Lemons et al., 2014; see Figure 12.2). The process begins with (1) an examination of diagnostic data. The data are analyzed by the school team to determine the student's specific skills area of need. Then, (2) an evidence-based program is identified, based on what the team thinks will best target those skills. After about 6 weeks, (3) progress monitoring data are examined to decide whether the student has made adequate progress and (4) the teacher either continues with implementation or reexamines student data and (5) makes an adaptation. This is an iterative process that continuously cycles through progress monitoring, data evaluation, and adaptation (i.e., steps 4–6), until the team members have

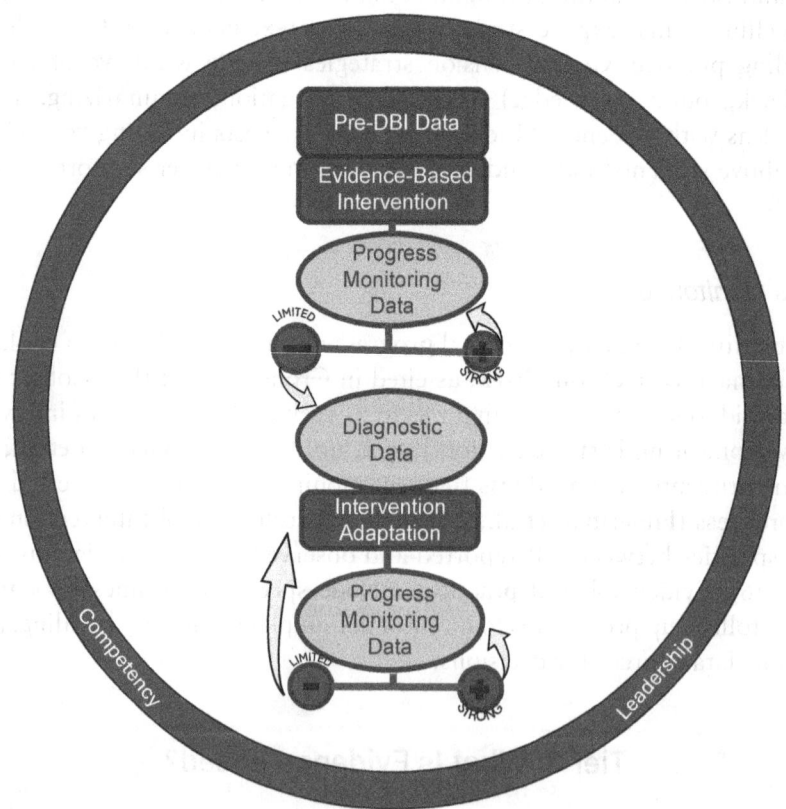

FIGURE 12.2. Data-based individualization model.

determined that they have identified the type of instruction that is leading to adequate growth for the student.

There is evidence that intensive intervention can accelerate the rate of improvement in struggling readers' comprehension across time (Roberts et al., 2013) compared to typical readers or struggling readers who do not receive intensive intervention and that it is especially effective for students with significant reading disabilities (Vaughn & Fletcher, 2012). However, there are specific practices and conditions that must be in place to foster the benefits of DBI.

Critical Conditions for DBI Success

The successful implementation of DBI relies on three critical conditions: competency, organization, and leadership. These "implementation drivers," as identified by Fixsen and colleagues (2005), are essential for sustaining effective interventions.

Competency in DBI requires educators to have a solid grasp of explicit reading instruction, the ability to identify students needing intervention, proficiency in administering progress monitoring tools, and skill in analyzing data to determine student progress (Bean & Lillenstein, 2012). However, research has shown that many educators lack a comprehensive understanding of reading instruction (Moats & Foorman, 2003; Spear-Swerling et al., 2005; Spear-Swerling & Cheesman, 2012) and assessment administration (McCombes-Tolis & Feinn, 2008). This gap underscores the crucial need for ongoing professional development (Fuchs et al., 2021; Stormont et al., 2011). Incorporating such training within intensive intervention programs has been shown to enhance teachers' knowledge of foundational reading skills (Hudson et al., 2023; Podhajski et al., 2009).

Organizational systems play a vital role in supporting intensive intervention. These systems should foster communication and work to identify and remove implementation barriers. At the heart of this organizational structure are professional learning communities (Brown & Poortman, 2018). Successful collaboration hinges on shared goals, joint decision-making responsibility, accountability, and the exchange of expertise (Friend & Cook, 2003). Evidence suggests that increased collaboration between general and special education teachers, as well as with speech–language pathologists, leads to improved student outcomes (Chow, 2023; Murawski & Swanson, 2001).

Leadership, though often overlooked, is a critical component of successful DBI implementation (Choi et al., 2023; Lemons et al., 2019). It operates on two levels: District-level leadership (e.g., superintendents, directors of pupil services) provides essential resources such as evidence-based programs and professional development, while building-level leadership (e.g., principals) offers daily support, manages scheduling, and facilitates DBI meetings. When leadership is actively involved, it fosters greater educator buy-in, enhances collaboration, and improves the ability to meet student needs. District-level leadership, in particular, has been shown to increase DBI fidelity and shift thinking about intensive intervention (Kearns et al., 2022).

Despite these critical conditions, educators face significant barriers, chief among them being time limitations (Poch et al., 2020). This often results in quick, informal collaborations rather than structured, in-depth discussions. When student progress is limited, educators must examine diagnostic data to form hypotheses, typically falling into categories such as dosage, alignment, attention to transfer, use of explicit instruction principles, and behavior support (Fuchs et al., 2017). The path to effective DBI implementation is complex, but focusing on these critical conditions—competency, organization, and leadership—can significantly enhance the success of intensive interventions and, ultimately, improve student outcomes.

Evidence-Limited Practices

Research on educational interventions for students with learning disabilities reveals several areas in which evidence is mixed or inconclusive:

- Collaboration between general and special education teachers has been recommended, but its impact on academic outcomes is unclear (van Garderen et al., 2012). Some researchers suggest that systems alignment, such as coordinating MTSS and DBI teams, may be more crucial than collaboration alone (Bailey et al., 2019).
- Waiting for students to complete Tier 2 instruction before starting intensive intervention (Tier 3) may not always be necessary. Delaying intensive intervention could hinder progress for students with significant needs, especially those in grade 3 and above reading well below grade level (Vaughn et al., 2010; Vaughn & Wanzek, 2014).
- Intensive interventions appear less effective in grades 4–12 compared to early elementary grades. More research is needed to understand the factors contributing to this difference (Vaughn & Wanzek, 2014).
- Evidence regarding the importance of group size in upper elementary interventions is mixed (Vaughn & Wanzek, 2014).
- There is insufficient evidence supporting highly individualized instruction over standardized, research-based programs. Some studies suggest students with learning disabilities may benefit more from standardized instruction in word reading and comprehension skills at the upper elementary level (Vaughn et al., 2011; Vaughn & Wanzek, 2014).

These findings highlight the need for continued research to refine intervention practices. Educators and policymakers should remain open to evidence that challenges conventional wisdom and be willing to adapt practices based on current research.

Data Collection and Data Analysis

Intensive intervention relies on two primary data sources: (1) progress monitoring and (2) diagnostic data. Generally, a school team will meet to examine progress

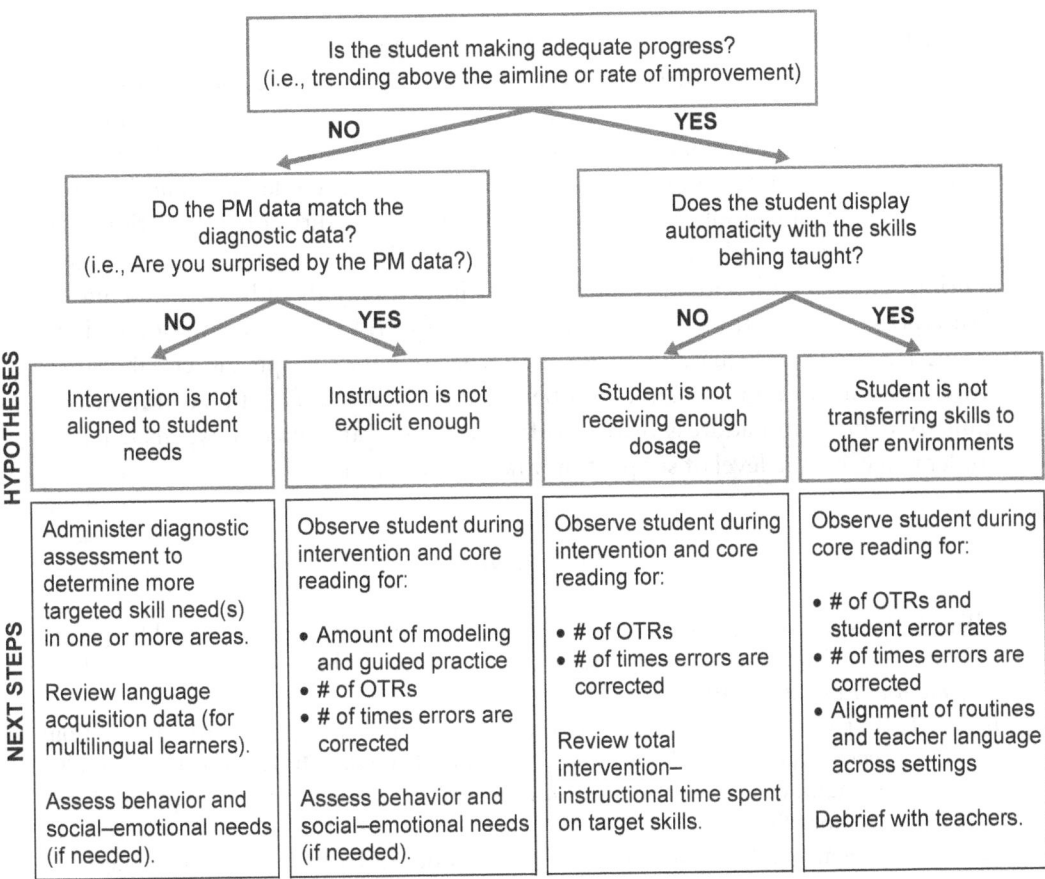

FIGURE 12.3. Making data-based decisions. Adapted with permission from Potter (2024). Copyright © 2024 National Center on Intensive Intervention at the American Institutes for Research.

monitoring data every 6 weeks to determine whether a student is making adequate growth. If the student's growth is flat (i.e., scores do not change week to week) or minimal (i.e., scores change below the average rate of improvement for other students at that instructional level), the data predict that without making any change to instruction, the student is unlikely to reach their goal. Therefore, progress monitoring data provide an indication that an adaptation needs to be made. Diagnostic data help guide educators in deciding what type of adaptation to make. An example of how to make decisions based on data is depicted in Figure 12.3.

Conclusion

MTSS involve a comprehensive approach to providing appropriate levels of academic and behavioral support for all students; our focus here has been on reading instruction. It comprises three tiers of increasing intensity: Tier 1 (core instruction for all students), Tier 2 (targeted intervention for students not responding adequately to Tier 1), and Tier 3 (intensive, individualized intervention for students with persistent difficulties). Key components across all tiers include evidence-based instruction, regular screening and progress monitoring, data-based decision making, and collaborative problem solving. Tier 1 emphasizes high-quality core instruction with universal screening and differentiation. Tier 2 provides small-group, targeted interventions aligned with core instruction. Tier 3 involves highly individualized, intensive support using a DBI process. Success factors for MTSS implementation include strong leadership, adequate resources and professional development, collaborative teams, and integrated academic and behavioral supports. This tiered framework aims to identify and address reading difficulties early and effectively, ensuring all students receive the level of support they need to succeed.

REFERENCES

Allen, A. S., & Topolka-Jorissen, K. (2014). Using teacher learning walks to build capacity in a rural elementary school: Repurposing a supervisory tool. *Professional Development in Education, 40*(5), 822–837.

Bailey, T. R., Chan, G. A. I. L., & Lembke, E. S. (2019). Aligning intensive intervention and special education with multi-tiered systems of support. In R. Zumeta Edmonds, A. G. Gandhi, & L. Danielson (Eds.), *Essentials of intensive intervention* (pp. 136–156). Guilford Press.

Bao, R., & Chen, J. (2024). Everyone matters: A multimodal learning analysis framework based on individual time series. *Technology, Knowledge and Learning.*

Bean, R., & Lillenstein, J. (2012). Response to Intervention and the changing roles of schoolwide personnel. *Reading Teacher, 65*(7), 491–501.

Benedict, A. E., Brownell, M., Bettini, E., & Sohn, H. (2021). Learning together: Teachers' evolving understanding of coordinated word study instruction within an RTI framework. *Teacher Education and Special Education, 44*(2), 134–159.

Bondie, R. S., Dahnke, C., & Zusho, A. (2019). How does changing "one-size-fits-all" to differentiated instruction affect teaching? *Review of Research in Education, 43*(1), 336–362.

Brown, C., & Poortman, C. (Eds.). (2018). *Networks for learning: Effective collaboration for teacher, school and system improvement.* Routledge.

Brownell, M., Kiely, M. T., Haager, D., Boardman, A., Corbett, N., Algina, J., . . . Urbach, J. (2017). Literacy learning cohorts: Content-focused approach to improving special education teachers' reading instruction. *Exceptional Children, 83*(2), 143–164.

Calvin, G., Flannery, K. B., Sugai, G., & Monegan, J. (2009). Using observational data to provide performance feedback to teachers: A high school case study. *Preventing School Failure, 53*(2), 95–104.

Capin, P., Stevens, E. A., & Vaughn, S. (2023). Self-regulation and reading comprehension: Integrating and aligning to improve reading outcomes. *Mind, Brain, and Education, 17*(4), 362–372.

Cervetti, G. N., Pearson, P. D., Palincsar, A. S., Afflerbach, P., Kendeou, P., Biancarosa, G., . . . Berman, A. I. (2020). How the reading for understanding initiative's research complicates the simple view of reading invoked in the science of reading. *Reading Research Quarterly, 55,* S161–S172.

Choi, S., Shanahan, E., Casey-Wilke, B., An, J., & Johnson, L. (2023). Implementation drivers of data-based instruction for students with intensive learning needs: A systematic review. *Journal of Learning Disabilities, 57*(5), 291–302.

Chow, J. C. (2023). Collaboration to support language and learning outcomes for students with disabilities. *Intervention in School and Clinic, 58*(3), 143–145.

Clay, A., Chu, E., Altieri, A., Deane, Y., Lis-Perlis, A., Lizarraga, A., . . . Wolters, M. (2021). *About time: Master scheduling and equity.* Center for Public Research and Leadership at Columbia University.

Connor, C. M., Lara J. J., Crowe, E. C., & Meadows, J. G. (2009). Instruction, student engagement, and reading skill growth in reading first classrooms. *Elementary School Journal, 109*(3), 221–250.

Connor, C. M., Son, S. H., Hindman, A. H., & Morrison, F. J. (2005). Teacher qualifications, classroom practices, family characteristics, and preschool experience: Complex effects on first graders' vocabulary and early reading outcomes. *Journal of School Psychology, 43*(4), 343–375.

Crone, D. A., Carlson, S. E., Haack, M. K., Kennedy, P. C., Baker, S. K., & Fien, H. (2016). Data-based decision-making teams in middle school: Observations and implications from the Middle School Intervention Project. *Assessment for Effective Intervention, 41*(2), 79–93.

Dewitz, P., Jones, J., & Leahy, S. (2009). Comprehension strategy instruction in core reading programs. *Reading Research Quarterly, 44*(2), 102–126.

Downey, C., Steffy, B. E., English, F. W., Frase, L. E., & Poston, W. K., Jr. (2004). *Changing school supervisory practices one teacher at the time: The three-minute classroom walkthrough.* Corwin Press.

Fien, H., Smith, J. L. M., Smolkowski, K., Baker, S. K., Nelson, N. J., & Chaparro, E. (2015). An examination of the efficacy of a multitiered intervention on early reading outcomes for first grade students at risk for reading difficulties. *Journal of Learning Disabilities, 48*(6), 602–621.

Filderman, M. J., Austin, C. R., & Toste, J. R. (2019). Data-based decision making for struggling readers in the secondary grades. *Intervention in School and Clinic, 55*(1), 3–12.

Fisher, J. (2013). *Starting from the child: Teaching and learning in the foundation stage: Teaching and learning from 4–8.* McGraw-Hill Education.

Fixsen, D. L., Naoom, S. F., Blase, K. A., Friedman, R. M., & Wallace, F. (2005). *Implementation research: A synthesis of the literature.* National Implementation Research Network.

Franke, M. L., & Kazemi, E. (2001). Learning to teach mathematics: Focus on student thinking. *Theory Into Practice, 40*(2), 102–109.

Freeman, J., Sugai, G., Simonsen, B., & Everett, S. (2017). MTSS coaching: Bridging knowing to doing. *Theory Into Practice, 56*(1), 29–37.

Friend, M., & Cook, L. (2003). *Interactions: Collaboration skills for school professionals* (4th ed.). Allyn & Bacon.

Fuchs, L. S., Fuchs, D., Hamlett, C. L., & Stecker, P. M. (2021). Bringing data-based individualization to scale: A call for the next-generation technology of teacher supports. *Journal of Learning Disabilities, 54*(5), 319–333.

Fuchs, L. S., Fuchs, D., & Malone, A. S. (2017). The taxonomy of intervention intensity. *Teaching Exceptional Children, 50*(1), 35–43.

Garza, R., Ovando, M., & O'Doherty, A. (2016). Aspiring school leaders' perceptions of the walkthrough observations. *International Journal of Educational Leadership Preparation, 11*(1). www.ncpeapublications.org/index.php/volume-11-number-1-spring-2016.

Gay, G. (2002). Preparing for culturally responsive teaching. *Journal of Teacher Education, 53*(2), 106–116.

Gersten, R., Compton, D., Connor, C. M., Dimino, J., Santoro, L., Linan-Thompson, S., & Tilly, W. D. (2009). *Assisting students struggling with reading: Response to Intervention and multi-tier intervention for reading in the primary grades. A practice guide* (NCEE 2009-4045). National Center for Education Evaluation and Regional Assistance, Institute of Education Sciences, U.S. Department of Education.

Gore, J., Lloyd, A., Smith, M., Bowe, J., Ellis, H., & Lubans, D. (2017). Effects of professional development on the quality of teaching: Results from a randomised controlled trial of Quality Teaching Rounds. *Teaching and Teacher Education, 68*, 99–113.

Gore, J. M., Miller, A., Fray, L., Harris, J., & Prieto, E. (2021). Improving student achievement through professional development: Results from a randomised controlled trial of Quality Teaching Rounds. *Teaching and Teacher Education, 101*, Article 103297.

Grissom, J. A., Loeb, S., & Master, B. (2013). Effective instructional time use for school leaders: Longitudinal evidence from observations of principals. *Educational Researcher, 42*(8), 433–444.

Hallinger, P., Gümüş, S., & Bellibaş, M. Ş. (2020). "Are principals instructional leaders yet?": A science map of the knowledge base on instructional leadership, 1940–2018. *Scientometrics, 122*(3), 1629–1650.

Herrera, S., Truckenmiller, A. J., & Foorman, B. R. (2016). *Summary of 20 years of research on the effectiveness of adolescent literacy programs and practices* (REL 2016-178). Regional Educational Laboratory Southeast.

Hudson, A. K., Lambright, K., Zhang, S., Wijekumar, K., Owens, J., & McKeown, D. (2023). Professional development in a pandemic: Transforming teacher knowledge of reading comprehension instruction. *Education Technology Research and Development, 71*, 1965–1991.

Jacob, R., Hill, H., & Corey, D. (2017). The impact of a professional development program on teachers' mathematical knowledge for teaching, instruction, and student achievement. *Journal of Research on Educational Effectiveness, 10*(2), 379–407.

Johnson, E. S., Jenkins, J. R., & Petscher, Y. (2010). Improving the accuracy of a direct route screening process. *Assessment for Effective Intervention, 35*(3), 131–140.

Joyce, B. R., & Showers, B. (2002). *Student achievement through staff development* (Vol. 3). Association for Supervision and Curriculum Development.

Kearns, D. M., Walker, M. A., Borges, J. C., & Duffy, M. E. (2022). Can reading practitioners and researchers improve intensive reading support systems in a large urban school system? *Journal of Research in Reading, 45*(3), 488–516.

Kim, J., Hemphill, L., Troyer, M., Jones, S., LaRusso, M., Kim, H. Y., . . . Snow, C. (2016). *The experimental effects of the Strategic Adolescent Reading Intervention (STARI) on a scenarios-based reading comprehension assessment.* Society for Research on Educational Effectiveness.

Lemons, C. J., Kearns, D. M., & Davidson, K. A. (2014). Data-based individualization in reading: Intensifying interventions for students with significant reading disabilities. *TEACHING Exceptional Children, 46*(4), 20–29.

Lemons, C. J., Sinclair, A. C., Gesel, S., Gandhi, A. G., & Danielson, L. (2019). Integrating intensive intervention into special education services: Guidance for special education administrators. *Journal of Special Education Leadership, 32*(1), 29–38.

McCombes-Tolis, J., & Feinn, R. (2008). Comparing teachers' literacy-related knowledge to their state's standards for reading. *Reading Psychology, 29*(3), 236–265.

Moats, L. C., & Foorman, B. R. (2003). Measuring Teachers' content knowledge of language and reading. *Annals of Dyslexia, 53*(1), 23–45.

Murawski, W. W., & Swanson, H. L. (2001). A meta-analysis of co-teaching research: Where are the data? *Remedial and Special Education, 22*(5), 258–267.

National Center on Intensive Intervention & Center on Multi-Tiered System of Supports. (2021). *Selecting an MTSS data system.* American Institutes for Research.

Pearson, P. D., Palincsar, A. S., Biancarosa, G., & Berman, A. I. (2020). *Reaping the rewards of the Reading for Understanding Initiative.* National Academy of Education.

Peng, P., Wang, W., Filderman, M. J., Zhang, W., & Lin, L. (2024). The active ingredient in reading comprehension strategy intervention for struggling readers: A Bayesian network meta-analysis. *Review of Educational Research, 94*(2), 228–267.

Poch, A. L., McMaster, K. L., & Lembke, E. S. (2020). Usability and feasibility of data-based instruction for students with intensive writing needs. *Elementary School Journal, 121*(2), 197–223.

Podhajski, B., Mather, N., Nathan, J., & Sammons, J. (2009). Professional development in scientifically based reading instruction: Teacher knowledge and reading outcomes. *Journal of Learning Disabilities, 42*(5), 403–417.

Potter, J. (2024). *Problem analysis roadmap: Moving from hypothesis to plan.* National Center on Intensive Intervention at the American Institutes for Research.

Roberts, G., Vaughn, S., Fletcher, J. M., Stuebing, K. K., & Barth, A. E. (2013). Effects of a response-based, tiered framework for intervening with struggling readers in middle school. *Reading Research Quarterly, 48*(3), 237–254.

Shanahan, T., & Shanahan, C. (2012). What is disciplinary literacy and why does it matter? *Topics in Language Disorders, 32*(1), 7–18.

Spear-Swerling, L., Brucker, P. O., & Alfano, M. P. (2005). Teachers' literacy-related knowledge and self-perceptions in relation to preparation and experience. *Annals of Dyslexia, 55*, 266–296.

Spear-Swerling, L., & Cheesman, E. (2012). Teachers' knowledge base for implementing response-to-intervention models in reading. *Reading and Writing, 25*, 1691–1723.

Spillane, J. P., Halverson, R., & Diamond, J. B. (2004). Towards a theory of leadership practice: A distributed perspective. *Journal of Curriculum Studies, 36*(1), 3–34.

Stanovich, K. E. (1986). Matthew effects in reading: Some consequences of individual differences in the acquisition of literacy. *Reading Research Quarterly, 22*, 360–407.

Stevens, E. A., Stewart, A., Vaughn, S., Lee, Y. R., Scammacca, N., & Swanson, E. (2024). The effects of a Tier 2 reading comprehension intervention aligned to Tier 1 instruction for fourth graders with inattention and reading difficulties. *Journal of School Psychology, 105*, Article 101320.

Stormont, M., Reinke, W., & Herman, K. (2011). Teachers' knowledge of evidence-based interventions and available school resources for children with emotional and behavioral problems. *Journal of Behavioral Education, 20*, 138–147.

Stout, J., Kachur, D. S., & Edwards, C. (2010). *Classroom walkthroughs to improve teaching and learning.* Routledge.

Tomlinson, C. A. (2017). *Fundamentals of gifted education.* Routledge. www.thecenterforcharters.org/wp-content/uploads/2016/09/differentiation-article-by-tomlinson.pdf.

van Garderen, D., Stormont, M., & Goel, N. (2012). Collaboration between general and special educators and student outcomes: A need for more research. *Psychology in the Schools, 49*(5), 483–497.

Vaughn, S., Boardman, A., & Klingner, J. K. (2024). *Teaching reading comprehension to students with learning difficulties.* Guilford Press.

Vaughn, A., Denton, C. A., & Fletcher, J. M. (2010). Why intensive interventions are necessary for students with severe reading difficulties. *Psychology in the Schools, 47*(5), 432–444.

Vaughn, S., & Fletcher, J. M. (2012). Response to intervention with secondary students with reading difficulties. *Journal of Learning Disabilities, 45,* 241–253.

Vaughn, S., Kieffer, M. J., McKeown, M., Reed, D. K., Sanchez, M., St Martin, K., . . . Yañez, A. (2022). *Providing reading interventions for students in grades 4–9* (Educator's Practice Guide WWC 2022007). What Works Clearinghouse.

Vaughn, S., & Wanzek, J. (2014). Intensive Interventions in Reading for Students with Reading Disabilities: Meaningful Impacts. *Learning Disabilities Research and Practice, 29*(2), 46–53.

Vaughn, S., Wexler, J., Roberts, G., Barth, A. A., Cirino, P. T., Romain, M. A., . . . Denton, C. A. (2011). Effects of individualized and standardized interventions on middle school students with reading disabilities. *Exceptional Children, 77*(4), 391–407.

Wanzek, J., Vaughn, S., Scammacca, N., Gatlin, B., Walker, M. A., & Capin, P. (2016). Meta-analyses of the effects of Tier 2 type reading interventions in grades K–3. *Educational Psychology Review, 28,* 551–576.

CHAPTER 13

The Need for Schoolwide Literacy Models

Jade Wexler
Deborah K. Reed
Karen Omohundro

Students in upper elementary and secondary schools, regardless of reading ability, spend a majority of their instructional day in the Tier 1 content-area setting (i.e., English language arts [ELA], science, social studies, math; National Center for Education Statistics [NCES], 2023). Students also take elective classes (e.g., art), and some receive supplemental reading intervention, typically in place of an elective class (Reed et al., 2012). Considering the multitude of students who struggle with reading at the secondary level (U.S. Department of Education, [USDOE], 2022), it is important to consider the need for implementing schoolwide literacy models that incorporate and align evidence-based instruction and intervention in these settings.

Converging evidence supports the need to provide intervention for secondary students who have intensive needs in the supplemental intervention setting. For example, in 2012, Vaughn and colleagues conducted a seminal study investigating the effects of a yearlong, intensive, researcher-implemented supplemental reading intervention for eighth-grade students with serious reading difficulties who demonstrated low response to intervention in grades 6 and 7.[1] Students in the intervention condition demonstrated significantly higher scores than comparison students on standardized measures of comprehension (effect size [ES] = 1.20) and word identification (ES = 0.49).

A subsequent study, led by some of the same researchers, also lends support for providing intensive supplemental reading intervention for students—this time for high school students with disabilities (Vaughn, Roberts, Wexler, et al., 2015). In this study, the authors implemented a reading intervention in place of each student's elective class (e.g., art) for students with disabilities who met criteria for low reading comprehension. Students received researcher-implemented intervention in a 50-minute reading class in place of an elective every day for 2 years. Notably, the students who were provided reading intervention demonstrated significant gains on reading comprehension compared with their peers who qualified for the intervention but were randomly assigned to a business-as-usual typical-instruction comparison group.

Although these studies lend support for providing supplemental intervention for students who require intensive support, we know that this type of intervention support alone is not necessarily sufficient to close the gap with students' typically developing peers. In fact, in the Vaughn and colleagues (2012) study described earlier, students with persistent reading difficulties had promising outcomes after participation in multiyear supplemental intensive intervention. Nevertheless, students in the intervention classes did not close the gap with their typically developing peers, and therefore continued to lack grade-level proficiency in reading despite 3 years of intervention. Furthermore, in a meta-analysis conducted on extensive interventions (i.e., 75 sessions or more and not part of the general education curriculum) for students in grades 4–12, authors reported a small effect (ES = 0.10–0.16) on reading comprehension, reading fluency, word reading, word-reading fluency, and spelling outcomes (Wanzek et al., 2013). On a positive note, these small effects on standardized measures do undergird the idea that older students can make small gains through extensive interventions. However, when compared to the earlier grades (see Wanzek & Vaughn, 2007), it is clear that accelerating growth in the upper grades remains challenging, even when implementing extensive interventions.

It is important to highlight that the primary focus of the studies discussed earlier was on the supplemental intervention setting (i.e., not part of the general education setting). However, students' reading performance also is linked to their achievement in content-area classes (Reed et al., 2017), suggesting that integrating evidence-based comprehension building practices into content-area instruction could serve an important role in reinforcing intervention practices, while supporting students in building content knowledge. This highlights the need to focus on all tiers in which students are expected to learn and use reading and writing skills, thus creating a comprehensive schoolwide literacy model that integrates literacy and knowledge-building approaches. In fact, in addition to our knowledge about the benefits of providing supplemental intervention to students who need it, we also have evidence that Tier 1 instruction can be improved by integrating evidence-based literacy practices. Swanson, Stevens, and colleagues (2017) meta-analyzed the effects of literacy instructional practices within the Tier 1 content-area setting on reading outcomes for students in grades 4–12, reporting an average ES across 25 studies of $g = 0.09$—a small but statistically significant effect. They also synthesized results from a subset of 10 studies that focused on students with and at risk for reading disabilities, reporting that reading comprehension, vocabulary, and multicomponent interventions delivered in the Tier 1 setting positively impacted reading outcomes for students with or at risk for disabilities—with ESs ranging from −0.02 to 0.54 on standardized reading comprehension outcomes and 0.26 to 2.12 on proximal vocabulary outcomes.

Tier 1 also can be intensified by capitalizing on existing service delivery models. For example, in many secondary schools, co-teaching is a prevalent service delivery model in the Tier 1 setting (Cook et al., 2017). Co-teaching occurs when a special education and general education teacher work together to provide instruction to students with and without disabilities in a general education classroom (Cook & Friend, 1995). In theory, this service delivery model affords teachers the opportunity to provide more specialized instruction to students who struggle with the demands of the secondary setting (e.g., complex text; Cook & McDuffie-Landrum, 2020). While this commonly implemented model makes sense in theory, systematic observation study research has revealed that co-teachers do not always implement the model in its intended form (e.g., shared instructional responsibilities during a station teaching lesson; Wexler et al., 2018). In response to this, researchers sought to develop Project CALI (Content-Area Literacy Instruction), a professional development (PD) model designed to improve content-area literacy instruction in Tier 1 co-taught classrooms (Wexler et al., 2022). After a multi-year development phase, the research team tested the efficacy of Project CALI in a randomized controlled trial. CALI teachers demonstrated significantly higher scores than comparison teachers at posttest on a measure of knowledge and skills, perceived personal effectiveness, and perceived co-teachers' effectiveness. Furthermore, students in the CALI classrooms demonstrated significant gains on a researcher-developed measure of comprehension. Results provided initial support for a PD model that provides teachers with guidance on how to strengthen literacy instruction for students in the Tier 1 co-taught setting.

There is another more practical reason that it is important to provide Tier 1 literacy instruction: Many schools struggle to serve the excessive number of students who are in need of supplemental intervention due to a variety of reasons (e.g., lack of trained personnel; O'Connor et al., 2017). When the percentage of students who *cannot* read and understand grade-level text with proficiency reflects the majority, schools likely will lack sufficient resources (e.g., trained personnel) and time to provide supplemental support to all those who need it. In other words, although it seems intuitive to advocate for schools to provide more intensive intervention time to students experiencing difficulties (Fuchs et al., 2014), this effort may be futile. The national trends in student reading performance noted earlier (USDOE, 2022) suggest that many secondary schools across the nation face such a phenomenon, making it critical to consider strengthening Tier 1. Given that supplemental intervention alone is not always enough to close the gap (and may not even be possible), it is important that we provide an integrated literacy and knowledge-building approach in the Tier 1 setting to increase the dosage and strength of literacy instruction for all students.

Implementing schoolwide literacy models is not easy, requiring us to consider factors that make this type of model successful (e.g., school-level supports; Wexler et al., 2022). One important factor is the school structure and supports that need to be in place to make instruction and intervention possible. For example, expecting teachers to implement evidence-based literacy practices in various Tier 1 content areas and in intervention settings necessitates the provision of professional learning opportunities, like those provided in Project CALI, to ensure that all teachers have the skills to implement the practices with fidelity. We know that PD can lead to improved knowledge and skills, leading to change in practice (Kennedy, 2014), and ultimately improvement in student outcomes (Kennedy, 2016; Wexler et al., 2022). Because Part V in this volume addresses teacher knowledge and PD, we do not discuss this topic in depth here.

Another consideration is what practices should be implemented and how they should be implemented in a schoolwide model, the focus of this chapter. Therefore, we next provide an overview of evidence-based practices appropriate for implementation in the Tier 1 and supplemental intervention settings. We then provide considerations for how to implement these practices and, finally, directions for future investigation and consideration.

What Works?

Practices for Tier 1 Content-Area Classes

In 2008, Kamil led a panel of adolescent literacy experts to provide a set of coherent evidence-based recommendations for educators to use to improve literacy achievement among adolescents in upper elementary, middle, and high schools. The recommendations, published in a USDOE Institute of Education Sciences (IES) Practice Guide, are drawn from findings from studies that meet the highest standards for rigorous experimental research, supporting the use of the practices presented in the guide. The recommendations also are subject to rigorous external peer review, and authors provide recommendations about the quality of evidence that supports each recommendation. Because all students, regardless of reading ability, spend a majority of their day in the Tier 1 content-area setting (NCES, 2023), we first address the practices that are appropriate for that setting.

Recommendations supported by strong evidence include providing direct and explicit vocabulary and comprehension strategy instruction. First, several meta-analyses have reported that vocabulary instruction produces an effect on reading comprehension measures (e.g., Elleman et al., 2009; Wright & Cervetti, 2017). Although students learn the meaning of some words incidentally through context, this is not sufficient for learning all of the words needed to understand the complex texts they are expected to read and understand. Thus, explicit instruction in word meanings and instruction in strategies to promote independent word meaning acquisition (e.g., context clues) is necessary. Second, because vocabulary knowledge is correlated with but does not cause comprehension (Elleman et al., 2009), many students require explicit comprehension strategy instruction (e.g., summarization) and an understanding of when to use the strategies. These routines can help students make sense of text (Stevens et al., 2019), thereby acquiring content knowledge.

A third recommendation, supported by moderate evidence, is to ensure that students are engaged in frequent text-based discussion. In fact, it is troublesome that many teachers spend an excessive amount of time talking *to* students instead of engaging students in text-based discussion (Swanson et al., 2016) given that this type of content-based approach can result in improved reading comprehension *and* content knowledge (McKeown et al., 2009; Swanson et al., 2019; Vaughn, Swanson, et al., 2013). Finally, because correlational evidence suggests that students' motivation to read and engage in text declines as students reach the upper grades (Toste et al., 2020), a fourth recommendation supported by moderate evidence is for educators to consider ways to increase student motivation and engagement in literacy learning (e.g., build in goal setting; Wigfield et al., 2016).

Although the IES Practice Guide (Kamil et al., 2008) is over 15 years old now, findings from more recent syntheses (e.g., Peng et al., 2024; Swanson et al., 2017) continue to align with the recommendations. Also, subsequent large-scale rigorous intervention research investigating the efficacy of these practices, both separately and in combination, has shed light on how to implement the recommended practices. For example, in an 18-week randomized controlled trial with fourth graders, researchers compared the effects of two approaches recommended by the 2008 IES Practice Guide: multiple cognitive strategies intended to help students independently comprehend text and a multicomponent vocabulary acquisition routine (Simmons et al., 2010). Forty-eight teachers were randomly assigned by school to content vocabulary, content reading comprehension, or typical practice. Researchers were interested in understanding the individual effects of each approach to building knowledge and comprehension. Results indicated statistically significant differences on a social studies content measure, favoring the two strategy conditions over typical practice. Students in the vocabulary intervention also outperformed typical practice peers on a measure of taught vocabulary. Effects of the comprehension and vocabulary conditions were otherwise comparable.

Considering that comprehension and knowledge acquisition often require application of multiple reading approaches (Francis et al., 2006), the research team also was interested in whether combining the vocabulary and comprehension practices would lead to greater impact. Thus, a subsequent IES-funded study addressed the effects of the combined Strategies for Teaching Reading, Information, and Vocabulary Effectively (STRIVE; Swanson, Vaughn, & Roberts, 2015). This involved a distributed PD model designed to help teachers implement reading comprehension and vocabulary practices in fourth-grade social studies classes. Eighty-one schools were randomly assigned to one of three conditions: researcher-led PD, school-led PD, or a business-as-usual condition. Findings revealed significant effects for both treatment conditions when compared to the business-as-usual condition for content knowledge ($g = 0.51$–0.55), vocabulary learning ($g = 0.49$), and reading comprehension in content ($g = 0.16$–0.26; Swanson et al., 2023).

The school-led PD condition statistically significantly outperformed the business-as-usual condition on a distal measure of vocabulary, and all groups performed equally well on a distal measure of comprehension ($g = 0.04$–0.06). This study made three contributions to the field. First, it demonstrated that PD models can support the efficacious implementation of recommended literacy practices. Second, it showed the benefits of *combining* vocabulary and reading comprehension strategies. Third, it offered evidence that helping social studies teachers implement the strategies can enable students to benefit and more fully engage in a content approach to improving knowledge and reading comprehension.

Tier 1 Example

To illustrate how the 2008 IES Practice Guide recommendations can be implemented schoolwide, we next provide an example from several federally funded studies that focused on improving Tier 1 instruction. A literacy model demonstration project titled Promoting Adolescents' Comprehension of Text Plus (PACT Plus; Vaughn, Swanson, Wexler, 2015; Vaughn, Wexler, & Swanson, 2020) funded by the USDOE Office of Special Education Programs, aimed to improve reading among sixth- through eighth-grade students by providing teachers with PD and instructional coaching on a curriculum- and content-agnostic, multicomponent, integrated literacy and knowledge-building routine designed to equip students with evidence-based vocabulary and comprehension support. Researchers provided teachers in four middle schools in an urban area with PD and follow-up instructional coaching support using a scaffolded approach that included more intensive to less intensive support over several years.[2]

The PACT practices were originally designed to be implemented in social studies classes across two-week units that included infusing comprehension building practices (i.e., building background and vocabulary knowledge, critical reading of text with text-based discussion, and team-based learning) in content learning.[3] Three independent randomized controlled trials in Tier 1 settings found that eighth-grade students in treatment classes consistently demonstrated statistically significantly higher scores in content vocabulary and content knowledge (ES = 0.17–0.40), reading comprehension in the content area (ES = 0.29), and broad reading comprehension (ES = 0.20; Vaughn, Roberts, Swanson, et al., 2015; Vaughn, Swanson, et al., 2013; Vaughn et al., 2017). PACT also was tested within the Tier 1 setting on outcomes for students with disabilities (SWDs). Results (Swanson, Wanzek, et al., 2015, 2017; Wanzek et al., 2016) indicated statistically significant differences in favor of SWDs who received PACT on measures of content acquisition (ES = 0.26–0.51) and content reading comprehension (ES = 0.04–0.34), in addition to higher (but not statistically significant) scores on a distal measure of reading comprehension (ES = 0.02–0.09).

During the PACT Plus model demonstration project, PACT was implemented as part of a schoolwide literacy model. The research team adapted the practices, so that they were no longer unit-based in social studies but were now a text-based content- and curriculum-agnostic approach. In other words, teachers could implement the vocabulary- and comprehension-building practices with any text that they were required to teach or with text that supplemented their curriculum. The PACT practices included Comprehension Canopy (i.e., providing background knowledge on a text prior to students reading the text; IES Recommendation 4), Essential Words (i.e., providing vocabulary instruction on a text prior to students reading the text; IES Recommendation 2), and Critical Reading of Text (i.e., engaging in a peer mediated reading routine that included opportunities for text-based discussion; IES Recommendations 3 and 4). Teachers were expected to use the practices twice per week.

Although the team intended to integrate the practices into the supplemental intervention settings, this became challenging because (1) these classes were sparse and (2) in the buildings where these settings did exist, the school already had adopted a published program. This and the fact that the students with reading difficulties typically spent most of their day in the Tier 1 setting compelled the research team to focus on enhancing instruction across ELA, science, and social studies—the classes with the most opportunities for text reading. Despite facing several implementation challenges (e.g., teacher turnover), the research team was able to conduct an exploratory multiple-case study investigating teachers' adoption and sustained use of the practices across the Tier 1 setting with two administrators and seven teachers who sustained implementation of the PACT Plus practices beyond 1 year of researcher support. Analyses revealed factors about the practices themselves and the school-level supports that influenced teachers' sustained use of PACT Plus. For example, the team found that teachers who sustained the use of PACT Plus perceived that the practices had a simple and routine-like format to use, which encouraged uptake. This allowed teachers to routinely implement the practices and frequently observe their students engaged in the practices. Ultimately, this provided feedback to the teachers that encouraged their sustained use of the practices.

As identified in the PACT Plus case study, school-level supports that were tailored to teachers' variety of needs (i.e., skill and will) were necessary to foster teachers' implementation of the practices. Thus, in a subsequent Development and Innovation project funded by the IES (Wexler et al., 2020), the research team developed and rigorously evaluated an adaptive intervention literacy coaching model (AIM Coaching).[4] Aligned with lessons from the Swanson, Wanzek, and colleagues (2015) study, AIM Coaching empowered school-based coaches to implement the model to support the evidence-based PACT Plus literacy practices. In addition, because many students in the Tier 1 classes were in need of supplemental intervention support but were not provided this support, we offered an intensified version of the practices. In this version, the Critical Reading routine was infused with an explicit version of Get the Gist, an evidence-based strategy that provides students with systematic guidance on how to generate a main idea of the text (Klingner et al., 2004). In other words, we conceptualized this option as a way for teachers to provide a strategy approach in service of a content approach.

To make Get the Gist more explicit, the research team offered "gist pointers" for students to use and teachers to demonstrate through think-alouds. For example, instead of asking students to identify the "who" or "what" a section of text was about, we offered pointers such as "Is anyone or anything mentioned most frequently?" Although teachers in both conditions reported about the same amount of dosage of PACT Plus literacy instruction, teachers in AIM Coaching schools demonstrated significantly higher levels of fidelity of implementation (i.e., adherence) when implementing PACT Plus during the spring semester (ES = 1.37). Furthermore, students of those teachers receiving the AIM Coaching demonstrated practically important effects on standardized and researcher-developed measures of reading comprehension.

Together, these studies highlight the critical need for Tier 1 content-area courses to implement comprehension-building practices that align with the 2008 IES Practice Guide recommendations and to couple those practices with ongoing, targeted teacher support. In addition, it is important to provide some students with supplemental support to improve reading comprehension and content knowledge, the fifth recommendation in the 2008 IES Practice Guide. Next, we provide an overview of the practices that are important to implement in an intervention setting.

Practices for Supplemental Intervention Classes

Integrating literacy and content instruction is necessary but not sufficient for ensuring the success of students in grades 4 and above who exhibit reading difficulties (Vaughn et al., 2012). This is because many students need instruction in below-grade-level literacy skills (e.g., letter–sound correspondences), and all need more intensive intervention in the strategies that can support their comprehension of complex text (Vaughn et al., 2019). An IES Practice Guide that reviewed supplemental interventions for students in grades 4–9 found strong evidence for building students' multisyllabic word-reading skills, effortless reading, and the ability to make sense of texts (Vaughn et al., 2022). In addition, there was moderate evidence supporting the use of challenging text to give students access to more sophisticated vocabulary and concepts than typically are included in below-level text (Lupo et al., 2019). Critically, the Vaughn and colleagues (2022) IES Practice Guide recommendations should not be implemented linearly or in isolation. Rather, they should be used in complementary fashion. For example, studies of morphology instruction find that it supports both word-based and meaning-based skills because it can help students break down big words, pronounce parts that might be inconsistent with typical phonological patterns, and gain access to the meaning of those words (Dawson et al., 2018; Levesque et al., 2017). Similarly, students can reread a variety of texts for multiple reasons, such as practicing prosody, learning new words, and asking and answering questions to monitor their comprehension (Vaughn et al., 2022).

Tier 2 Example

It is important to note that our understanding of how to design and deliver supplemental interventions for older readers has come from scientifically-based research—both previous studies provide evidence of effectiveness and ongoing work that seeks to advance the field. For example, for many years, having students with reading difficulties repeatedly read the same text under timed conditions was considered an evidence-based practice, but meta-analytic findings suggested the improvements to the rate and accuracy of reading an assigned text did not commonly generalize to unrehearsed texts (Lee & Yoon, 2017). Thus, one research team has been investigating a new approach that retains what is beneficial about repetitive reading, while addressing its limitations and improving the integration with other reading skills beyond reading rate and accuracy. As the contrast to repeated reading, the team calls this approach varied practice reading (VPR; Reed et al., 2019). It presents students with sets of passages that are written to provide an 85% overlap of the unique words within a set, so that students get the benefit of multiple practice opportunities. In addition, the sets gradually increase in complexity from below- to on-grade-level text in order to scaffold students' success with the kinds of material they are expected to read in their content-area classes. As they read, students are directed to focus on their prosody and make their reading "sound like talking." An initial investigation with fourth-grade students at a range of ability levels found that the intervention was not only statistically significantly more effective than repeated reading (ES = 0.133 on a measure of transfer), but also most effective for students in need of a Tier 2 intervention (Reed et al., 2019).

To capitalize on the limited intervention time in middle schools (O'Connor et al., 2017), the next phase of the research involved writing the passage sets to target the science and social studies vocabulary and concepts that students would encounter in their content-area classes. In addition, the sets provided a balance of fictional and informational text that allowed for including comprehension questions and writing prompts targeting ELA standards for both genres. Thus, the intervention integrates the fluency, comprehension, and challenging text recommendations of the Vaughn and colleagues (2022) IES Practice Guide and simultaneously provides connections to what students must do outside of their supplemental intervention class. In a proof-of-concept study, seventh graders in the VPR intervention experienced the greatest pre-to-posttest improvement on standardized measures of science (ES = 1.128), vocabulary (ES = 0.721), and social studies (ES = 0.425; Reed & Aloe, 2020). An ongoing federally funded study will determine VPR's promise as an effective intervention when compared to what is typically offered for Tier 2 in grades 6–8.[5]

How to Implement the Practices

In addition to considering *what* practices teachers should implement in a schoolwide literacy model, we also need to consider *how* teachers should implement the practices. Next, we provide an overview of the need to implement evidence-based literacy practices using explicit instruction, creating alignment between tiers (i.e., instruction and intervention settings), and ensuring that teachers implement practices with fidelity while allowing for an element of customization.

Use Explicit Instruction

Explicit instruction has been characterized as systematic, direct, engaging, and success-oriented (Archer & Hughes, 2010), and has been considered the "gold-standard" method of instruction for over four decades (Becker et al., 1981).

Providing this type of instruction includes establishing a purpose for learning before a lesson and providing modeling, guided practice, and independent practice, as well as frequent opportunities for students to engage in practice that allows for immediate, corrective feedback. This type of instruction has had a large effect on outcomes for students with disabilities ($d = 0.76$), students without disabilities ($d = 1.27$), younger students ($d = 0.87$), and older students ($d = 1.50$; Adams & Engleman, 1996). Importantly, it has outperformed discovery-based approaches ($d = .39$; Alfieri et al., 2011).

Teachers can use explicit instruction to intensify instruction for students within Tier 1 and in supplemental intervention settings. For example, when introducing a new skill, teachers can model with a think-aloud (i.e., the "I do" phase of instruction), provide prompts as students work alongside the teacher (i.e., the "we do," or guided practice phase), and then work independently with teacher feedback (i.e., the "you do" phase). During this gradual release of responsibility, teachers might stay longer in modeling and guided practice to provide more intensive support. They also can increase the intensity of support with smaller group sizes, so that students receive additional opportunities to practice and receive feedback. Throughout the phases of instruction, teachers maintain a brisk pace and provide specific feedback that helps students understand what they are doing that supports their learning and what they need to refine in order to improve their performance (Reed, 2023).

Create Alignment between Tiers

It is important to consider alternative ways to intensify instruction and intervention beyond the use of explicit instruction. One way is to create an alignment between the two settings, leading to a symbiotic system of supports for students that encourages a schoolwide approach to literacy instruction. For example, intervention teachers can use text and topics derived directly from students' Tier 1 curriculum to reinforce content. In addition, Tier 1 teachers can reinforce the same comprehension-building practices students are learning in their intervention setting (e.g., using an evidence-based routine for providing vocabulary instruction). This can promote generalization of these practices, so that students have explicit modeling about how practices can be applied within and across content areas, increasing the chances they eventually apply them on their own.

Creating an alignment between tiers is supported by several studies. For example, in a meta-analysis of Tier 2 and Tier 3 reading interventions delivered using social studies content (Swanson et al., 2014), students with disabilities performed well on reading outcomes (average ES = 1.02). We also have evidence that when we align Tier 1 with supplemental intervention, we can build a strong platform upon which intervention can be supported, thus improving outcomes for students with disabilities. For example, Stevens and colleagues (2020) implemented a study examining the effects of three different conditions (Tier 2 intervention aligned to Tier 1 instruction, nonaligned Tier 2 intervention, and business as usual) on the content knowledge, vocabulary, and reading outcomes of upper elementary students with reading difficulties. In the aligned condition, teachers integrated evidence-based literacy practices several times a week into their typical social studies instruction, while the students with reading difficulties from these classes received an additional dose of instruction and feedback in small-group intervention aligned to those practices. In the nonaligned condition, students with reading difficulties received the same small-group intervention but they were not provided the same literacy instruction during their social studies instruction. Finally, students in the comparison condition received typical social studies instruction and intervention.

Results yielded statistically significant, positive effects in favor of the aligned condition on proximal measures of content knowledge and vocabulary but no significant differences on standardized measures of reading comprehension and vocabulary (Stevens et al., 2020). The authors hypothesized that students derived benefits from having instruction front-loaded through Tier 2 prior to being taught in Tier 1. Thus, this study provided initial support for the benefits of aligning Tier 1 and Tier 2 instruction for students with reading difficulty in the upper grades.

Implement Practices with Fidelity that Allows for Customization

Knowing what evidence-based practices to teach and how to implement them is critical, as reviewed earlier. It is equally critical to understand conditions that can enhance adoption, implementation, and sustainability of such practices (Durlak, 2010). This is especially important in the secondary setting, considering the variety of needs our secondary students *and* teachers have (e.g., skill and will).

Fidelity of implementation, or implementing practices as they were designed, is an important aspect of ensuring the practices will be successful and achieve the goal of improved student outcomes (Sanetti & Luh, 2019). For example, using fidelity data from 19 U.S. history teachers implementing PACT, researchers wanted to know the relation between fidelity and student knowledge acquisition (Vaughn, Roberts, Swanson, et al., 2015). In other words, they wanted to know empirically—does fidelity matter? Results indicated that content knowledge developed along a continuum: When fidelity was low, students did not gain much content knowledge. However, when teachers implemented PACT with high levels of fidelity, their students gained a great deal of content knowledge. Furthermore, findings from a study examining the effects of collaborative strategic reading, a multicomponent approach to teaching reading comprehension strategies, demonstrated a similar positive association between fidelity and student reading comprehension, as measured by a standardized reading comprehension measure (Vaughn, Roberts, Klingner, et al., 2013).

Although fidelity is related to the effectiveness of interventions (Fixsen et al., 2005), we also know that interventions often are implemented in a modified way during daily classroom instruction (Harn et al., 2013). Some may perceive this as concerning. In fact, reasonable adaptations made to evidence-based practices, based on the needs of practitioners and students, actually has the potential to increase the efficacy of the intervention (Webster-Stratton et al., 2008). This is because the way in which practitioners perceive and implement an intervention can provide valuable insight into its potential acceptability, feasibility, usability, and sustainability (Rademaker et al., 2021). Some adaptations to interventions might be appropriate in order to individualize the procedures and ensure a better fit within the classroom (Carter et al., 2019), but substantial adaptations may inadvertently negate the effectiveness of interventions (Domitrovich et al., 2008).

Therefore, it is crucial for researchers to work with school-based practitioners to develop a shared understanding of what the "non-negotiable" (i.e., essential) aspects of the intervention are and which "negotiable" aspects can be customized according to school and classroom needs (Webster-Statton et al., 2008). Based on this knowledge, researchers and practitioners can develop fidelity measures that capture these "active ingredients" but allow for an element of customization. A shared understanding of the criteria for fidelity of interventions can increase the likelihood that interventions are implemented and sustained (Durlak, 2010). These considerations are even more critical when implementing schoolwide literacy models at the secondary level, due to the variety of disciplines involved.

School-based instructional coaches can help ensure that teachers understand the negotiables and non-negotiables of an intervention. Evidence indicates that instructional coaching supports and sustains teacher learning and improves student outcomes (Kraft et al., 2018). Coaches can increase teachers' access to resources and enable quality implementation of evidence-based practices (Kretlow & Bartholomew, 2010). In the AIM Coaching project described earlier (Wexler et al., 2020), researchers identified the empirically validated literacy practices that coaches would support (i.e., PACT Plus) but soon saw the need to allow for customization of the practices to encourage adoption and sustained implementation. Through an iterative process, literacy coaches and teachers provided insights into how some of the components of the evidence-based practices could be adapted to fit the local curriculum and target the needs of students in the local context.

Seventeen teachers participated in semistructured interviews which shed light on ways that customization influenced teachers' uptake of the PACT Plus practices. Teachers explained that they engaged in iterative and varied adaptations to the PACT Plus practices in order to support their students and address challenges in their specific context. For example, to combat perceived postpandemic anxiety in students, many teachers noted that they implemented flexible grouping structures during the peer-mediated portions of the PACT Plus routines. This work exemplifies the need to match interventions to the contextual variables that exist in the educational environment as a key factor to ensuring evidence-based practices are successfully implemented and sustained (Von Hippel, 2005).

Future Directions

Despite the importance of reading ability to students' performance on content-area achievement tests (Reed et al., 2017), many teachers reportedly avoid text-based assignments (Swanson et al., 2016). Nevertheless, research has not yet established the optimal amount of time that students should spend reading or the particular practices that are the most feasible and effective to integrate into different disciplinary courses (e.g., history vs. geography, biology vs. chemistry) or in different school structures (e.g., scheduling configurations, class sizes, reliance on technology). School structures also impact the provision of supplemental intervention, with many middle schools confronting limited options to balance instructional time in core academic, enrichment, and intervention courses (Reed, 2023). This can mean that students may not have access to a needed literacy intervention or that they receive less intervention time than recommended.

Thus, research necessarily is ongoing, and the literature base known as the "science of reading" is ever evolving. This includes research on the best ways to offer schoolwide support for teachers and leaders (Wexler et al., 2022). The essential role of school- and district-level leadership in making systemic changes to literacy instruction should not be overlooked (Redding & Nguyen, 2020; Woulfin & Gabriel, 2020). Without coordinated leadership, teachers are not likely to feel the efforts are important or to persist through the implementation challenges (Reed, 2023). However, research is needed to identify effective approaches for strengthening middle and high school administrators' abilities to lead the implementation of literacy instruction across the core academic and supplemental intervention classes.

Even though research has not definitively answered all questions about literacy instruction in upper elementary and secondary schools, it is unacceptable to delay acting on the best available knowledge about promising and best practices. Older students with reading difficulties do not have time to lose, so, at a minimum, focused instruction and efficient use of class time are critical. No intervention or Tier 1 strategy would be powerful enough to make a difference if pacing were too slow or class time wasted, such that students end up with half the amount of instruction they otherwise could have. In particular, teachers and school leaders need to take intervention seriously; otherwise, the opportunity cost of putting students into these supplemental courses instead of some other class is too great. There are potentially devastating long-term consequences for older students with reading difficulties (Livingston et al., 2018), so students deserve having high expectations set for their learning, as well as for the teaching and leadership in their schools.

ACKNOWLEDGMENTS

The research reported here was supported by the following: Institute of Education Sciences, U.S. Department of Education, Grant No. R324A200012 to the University of Maryland (Jade Wexler, Principal Investigator) and the University of Texas at Austin (Elizabeth Swanson and Greg Roberts, Co-Principal Investigators); Grant No. R324A220269 to the University of Tennessee (Deborah K. Reed, Principal Investigator); and the Office of Special Education, U.S. Department of Education, Grant No. H326M200015 to the University of Maryland (Jade Wexler, Principal Investigator) and the University of Texas at Austin (Colleen Reutebuch and Greg Roberts, Co-Principal Investigators). The opinions expressed are those of the authors and do not represent views of the Institute of Education Sciences, the Office of Special Education Programs, or the U.S. Department of Education.

NOTES

1. See *www.texasldcenter.org*.
2. See *https://meadowscenter.org/project/pact-plus* for more information.
3. See *https://meadowscenter.org/project/promoting-adolescents-comprehension-of-text*.
4. See *www.aimcoaching.org*.
5. See *https://trrc.utk.edu/research-projects/varied-practice-reading*.

REFERENCES

Adams, G. L., & Engelmann, S. (1996). *Research on direct instruction: 25 years beyond DISTAR*. Educational Achievement Systems.

Alfieri, L., Brooks, P. J., Aldrich, N. J., & Tenenbaum, H. R. (2011). Does discovery-based instruction enhance learning? *Journal of Educational Psychology, 103*(1), 1–18.

Archer, A. L., & Hughes, C. A. (2010). *Explicit instruction: Effective and efficient teaching*. Guilford Press.

Becker, W. C., Engelmann, S., Carnine, D. W., & Rhine, R. (1981). The direct instruction model. In R. Rhine (Ed.), *Making schools more effective: New directions from "Follow Through"* (pp. 95–154). Academic Press.

Carter, E. W., Dykstra Steinbrenner, J. R., & Hall, L. J. (2019). Exploring feasibility and fit: Peer-mediated interventions for high school students with autism spectrum disorders. *School Psychology Review, 48*(2), 157–169.

Cook, L., & Friend, M. (1995). Co-teaching: Guidelines for creating effective practices. *Focus on Exceptional Children, 28*(3), 1–12.

Cook, S. C., & McDuffie-Landrum, K. A. (2020). Integrating effective practices into co-teaching: Increasing outcomes for students with disabilities. *Intervention in School and Clinic, 55*(4), 221–229.

Cook, S. C., McDuffie-Landrum, K. A., Oshita, L., & Cook, B. G. (2017). Co-teaching for students with disabilities: A critical and updated analysis of the empirical literature. In J. M. Kauffman, D. P. Hallahan, & P. C. Pullen (Eds.), *The handbook of special education* (2nd ed., pp. 233–248). Routledge.

Dawson, N., Rastle, K., & Ricketts, J. (2018). Morphological effects in visual word recognition: Children, adolescents, and adults. *Journal of Experimental Psychology: Learning, Memory, and Cognition, 44*(4), 645–654.

Domitrovich, C. E., Bradshaw, C. P., Poduska, J. M., Hoagwood, K., Buckley, J. A., Olin, S., . . . Ialongo, N. S. (2008). Maximizing the implementation quality of evidence-based preventive interventions in schools: A conceptual framework. *Advances in School Mental Health Promotion, 1*(3), 6–28.

Durlak, J. A. (2010). The importance of doing well in whatever you do: A commentary on the special section, "Implementation Research in Early Childhood Education." *Early Childhood Research Quarterly, 25*(3), 348–357.

Elleman, A. M., Lindo, E. J., Morphy, P., & Compton, D. L. (2009). The impact of vocabulary instruction on passage-level comprehension of school-age children: A meta-analysis. *Journal of Research on Educational Effectiveness, 2*(1), 1–44.

Fixsen, D. L., Naoom, S. F., Blase, K. A., Friedman, R. M., & Wallace, F. (2005). *Implementation research: A synthesis of the literature*. University of South Florida, Louis de la Parte Florida Mental Health Institute, National Implementation Research Network. https://nirn.fpg.unc.edu/resources/implementation-research-synthesis-literature.

Francis, D. J., Rivera, M., Lesaux, N., Kieffer, M., & Rivera, H. (2006). *Practical guidelines for the education of English language learners: Research-based recommendations for instruction and academic interventions.* RMC Research Corporation, Center on Instruction.

Fuchs, D., Fuchs, L. S., & Vaughn, S. (2014). What is intensive instruction and why is it important? *Teaching Exceptional Children, 46*(4), 13–18.

Harn, B., Parisi, D., & Stoolmiller, M. (2013). Balancing fidelity with flexibility and fit: What do we really know about fidelity of implementation in schools? *Exceptional Children, 79*(3), 181–193.

Kamil, M. L., Borman, G. D., Dole, J., Kral, C. C., Salinger, T., & Torgesen, J. (2008). *Improving adolescent literacy: Effective classroom practices: A practice guide* (NCEE No. 2008-4027). National Center for Education Evaluation and Regional Assistance.

Kennedy, A. (2014). Understanding continuing professional development: The need for theory to impact on policy and practice. *Professional Development in Education, 40*(5), 688–697.

Kennedy, M. M. (2016). How does professional development improve teaching? *Review of Educational Research, 86*(4), 945–980.

Klingner, J. K., Vaughn, S., Arguelles, M. E., Tejero Hughes, M., & Ahwee Leftwich, S. (2004). Collaborative strategic reading: "Real-world" lessons from classroom teachers. *Remedial and Special Education, 25*(5), 291–302.

Kraft, M. A., Blazar, D., & Hogan, D. (2018). The effect of teacher coaching on instruction and achievement: A meta-analysis of the causal evidence. *Review of Educational Research, 88*(4), 547–588.

Kretlow, A. G., & Bartholomew, C. C. (2010). Using coaching to improve the fidelity of evidence-based practices: A review of studies. *Teacher Education and Special Education, 33*(4), 279–299.

Lee, J., & Yoon, S. Y. (2017). The effects of repeated reading on reading fluency for students with reading disabilities: A meta-analysis. *Journal of Learning Disabilities, 50*(2), 213–224.

Levesque, K. C., Kieffer, M. J., & Deacon, S. H. (2017). Morphological awareness and reading comprehension: Examining mediating factors. *Journal of Experimental Child Psychology, 160,* 1–20.

Livingston, E. M., Siegel, L. S., & Ribary, U. (2018). Developmental dyslexia: Emotional impact and consequences. *Australian Journal of Learning Difficulties, 23*(2), 107–135.

Lupo, S. M., Tortorelli, L., Invernizzi, M., Ryoo, J. H., & Strong, J. Z. (2019). An exploration of text difficulty and knowledge support on adolescents' comprehension. *Reading Research Quarterly, 54*(4), 457–479.

McKeown, M. G., Beck, I. L., & Blake, R. G. (2009). Rethinking reading comprehension instruction: A comparison of instruction for strategies and content approaches. *Reading Research Quarterly, 44*(3), 218–253.

National Center for Education Statistics. (2023). *Students with disabilities: Condition of education.* U.S. Department of Education, Institute of Education Sciences. https://nces.ed.gov/programs/coe/indicator/cgg.

O'Connor, R. E., Sanchez, V., Beach, K. D., & Bocian, K. M. (2017). Special education teachers integrating reading with eighth grade U.S. history content. *Learning Disabilities Research and Practice, 32*(2), 99–11.

Peng, P., Wang, W., Filderman, M. J., Zhang, W., & Lin, L. (2024). The active ingredient in reading comprehension strategy intervention for struggling readers: A Bayesian network meta-analysis. *Review of Educational Research, 94*(2), 228–267.

Rademaker, F., de Boer, A., Kupers, E., & Minnaert, A. (2021). It also takes teachers to tango: Using social validity assessment to refine an intervention design. *International Journal of Educational Research, 107*, Article 101749.

Redding, C., & Nguyen, T. D. (2020). The relationship between school turnaround and student outcomes: A meta-analysis. *Educational Evaluation and Policy Analysis, 42*(4), 493–519.

Reed, D. K. (2023) Reading intervention in middle schools: Challenges and suggested approaches. *Middle School Journal, 54*(5), 42–51.

Reed, D. K., & Aloe, A. M. (2020). *Evaluation of the Varied Practice Reading intervention in Evans Middle School.* Iowa Reading Research Center.

Reed, D. K., Petscher, Y., & Truckenmiller, A. J. (2017). The contribution of general reading ability to science achievement. *Reading Research Quarterly, 52*(2), 253–266.

Reed, D. K., Wexler, J., & Vaughn, S. (2012). *RTI for reading at the secondary level: Recommended literacy practices and remaining questions.* Guilford Press.

Reed, D. K., Zimmermann, L., Reeger, A. J., & Aloe, A. M. (2019). The effects of varied practice on the oral reading fluency of fourth-grade students. *Journal of School Psychology, 77*, 24–35.

Sanetti, L. M. H., & Luh, H. J. (2019). Fidelity of implementation in the field of learning disabilities. *Learning Disability Quarterly, 42*(4), 204–216.

Simmons, D., Hairrell, A., Edmonds, M., Vaughn, S., Larsen, R., Willson, V., . . . Byrns, G. (2010). A comparison of multiple-strategy methods: Effects on fourth-grade students' general and content-specific reading comprehension and vocabulary development. *Journal of Research on Educational Effectiveness, 3*(2), 121–156.

Stevens, E. A., Park, S., & Vaughn, S. (2019). A review of summarizing and main idea interventions for struggling readers in grades 3 through 12: 1978–2016. *Remedial and Special Education, 40*(2), 131–149.

Stevens, E. A., Vaughn, S., Swanson, E., & Scammacca, N. (2020). Examining the effects of a Tier 2 reading comprehension intervention aligned to Tier 1 instruction for fourth-grade struggling readers. *Exceptional Children, 86*(4), 430–448.

Swanson, E., Hairrell, A., Kent, S., Ciullo, S., Wanzek, J. A., & Vaughn, S. (2014). A synthesis and meta-analysis of reading interventions using social studies content for students with learning disabilities. *Journal of Learning Disabilities, 47*(2), 178–195.

Swanson, E., Stevens, E. A., Scammacca, N. K., Capin, P., Stewart, A. A., & Austin, C. R. (2017). The impact of Tier 1 reading instruction on reading outcomes for students in grades 4–12: A meta-analysis. *Reading and Writing, 30*, 1639–1665.

Swanson, E., Stevens, E. A., & Wexler, J. (2019). Engaging students with disabilities in text-based discussions: Guidance for general education social studies classrooms. *Teaching Exceptional Children, 51*(4), 305–312.

Swanson, E., Stewart, A. A., Stevens, E. A., Scammacca, N. K., Capin, P., Bhat, B. H., . . . Vaughn, S. (2023). The efficacy of two models of professional development mediated by fidelity on fourth grade student reading outcomes. *Journal of Research on Educational Effectiveness, 17*(2), 288–317.

Swanson, E., Vaughn, S., & Roberts, G. (2015). *Examining the efficacy of differential levels of professional development for teaching content area reading strategies (Project STRIVE)* (Grant No. R305A150407). Institute of Education Sciences, U.S. Department of Education.

Swanson, E., Wanzek, J., McCulley, L., Stillman-Spisak, S., Vaughn, S., Simmons, D., . . . Hairrell, A. (2016). Literacy and text reading in middle and high school social studies and English language arts classrooms. *Reading and Writing Quarterly, 32*(3), 199–222.

Swanson, E., Wanzek, J., Vaughn, S., Fall, A. M., Roberts, G., Hall, C., & Miller, V. L. (2017). Middle school reading comprehension and content learning intervention for below-average readers. *Reading and Writing Quarterly, 33*(1), 37–53.

Swanson, E., Wanzek, J., Vaughn, S., Roberts, G., & Fall, A. M. (2015). Improving reading comprehension and social studies knowledge among middle school students with disabilities. *Exceptional Children, 81*(4), 426–442.

Toste, J. R., Didion, L., Peng, P., Filderman, M. J., & McClelland, A. M. (2020). A meta-analytic review of the relations between motivation and reading achievement for K–12 students. *Review of Educational Research, 90*(3), 420–456.

U.S. Department of Education, Institute of Education Sciences, National Center for Education Statistics. (2022). *National Assessment of Educational Progress (NAEP) 2022 Reading Assessment.* https://nces.ed.gov/nationsreportcard/reading.

Vaughn, S., Gersten, R., Dimino, J., Taylor, M. J., Newman-Gonchar, R., Krowka, S., . . . Jayanthi, M. (2022). *Providing reading interventions for students in grades 4–9* (WWC 2022007). National Center for Education Evaluation and Regional Assistance, Institute of Education Sciences, U.S. Department of Education.

Vaughn, S., Martinez, L. R., Wanzek, J., Roberts, G., Swanson, E., & Fall, A. M. (2017). Improving content knowledge and comprehension for English language learners: Findings from a randomized control trial. *Journal of Educational Psychology, 109*(1), 22–34.

Vaughn, S., Roberts, G., Klingner, J. K., Swanson, E. A., Boardman, A., Stillman-Spisak, S. J., . . . Leroux, A. J. (2013). Collaborative strategic reading: Findings from experienced implementers. *Journal of Research on Educational Effectiveness, 6*(2), 137–163.

Vaughn, S., Roberts, G. J., Miciak, J., Taylor, P., & Fletcher, J. M. (2019). Efficacy of a word- and text-based intervention for students with significant reading difficulties. *Journal of Learning Disabilities, 52*(1), 31–44.

Vaughn, S., Roberts, G., Swanson, E. A., Wanzek, J., Fall, A. M., & Stillman-Spisak, S. J. (2015). Improving middle-school students' knowledge and comprehension in social studies: A replication. *Educational Psychology Review, 27*(1), 31–50.

Vaughn, S., Roberts, G., Wexler, J., Vaughn, M. G., Fall, A. M., & Schnakenberg, J. B. (2015). High school students with reading comprehension difficulties: Results of a randomized control trial of a two-year reading intervention. *Journal of Learning Disabilities, 48*(5), 546–558.

Vaughn, S., Swanson, E. A., Roberts, G., Wanzek, J., Stillman-Spisak, S. J., Solis, M., & Simmons, D. (2013). Improving reading comprehension and social studies knowledge in middle school. *Reading Research Quarterly, 48*(1), 77–93.

Vaughn, S., Swanson, E., Wexler, J., (2015). *Promoting adolescent comprehension of Text Plus.* (Grant No. H326M150016). Office of Special Education Programs, U.S. Department of Education.

Vaughn, S., Wexler, J., Leroux, A., Roberts, G., Denton, C., Barth, A., & Fletcher, J. (2012). Effects of intensive reading intervention for eighth-grade students with persistently inadequate response to intervention. *Journal of Learning Disabilities, 45*(6), 515–525.

Vaughn, S., Wexler, J., & Swanson, E. (2020). *Promoting Adolescents' Comprehension of Text Plus (PACT Plus)* (Grant No. H326M150016). Office of Special Education Programs, U.S. Department of Education.

Von Hippel, E. (2005). *Democratizing innovation.* MIT Press.

Wanzek, J., Swanson, E., Vaughn, S., Roberts, G., & Fall, A. M. (2016). English learner and non-English learner students with disabilities: Content acquisition and comprehension. *Exceptional Children, 82*(4), 428–442.

Wanzek, J., & Vaughn, S. (2007). Research-based implications from extensive early reading interventions. *School Psychology Review, 36*(4), 541–561.

Wanzek, J., Vaughn, S., Scammacca, N. K., Metz, K., Murray, C. S., Roberts, G., & Danielson, L. (2013). Extensive reading interventions for students with reading difficulties after grade 3. *Review of Educational Research, 83*(2), 163–195.

Webster-Stratton, C., Reid, M. J., & Stoolmiller, M. (2008). Preventing conduct problems and improving school readiness: Evaluation of the Incredible Years teacher and child training programs in high-risk schools. *Journal of Child Psychology and Psychiatry, 49*(5), 471–488.

Wexler, J., Kearns, D. M., Lemons, C. J., Mitchell, M., Clancy, E., Davidson, K. A., . . . Wei, Y. (2018). Reading comprehension and co-teaching practices in middle school English language arts classrooms. *Exceptional Children, 84*(4), 384–402.

Wexler, J., Kearns, D. M., Lemons, C. J., Shelton, A., Pollack, M. S., Stapleton, L. M., . . . Lyon, C. (2022). Improving literacy instruction in co-taught middle school classrooms to support reading comprehension. *Contemporary Educational Psychology, 68,* Article 102040.

Wexler, J., Swanson, E., & Roberts, G. (2020). *Developing an instructional leader adaptive intervention model (AIM) for supporting teachers as they integrate evidence-based adolescent literacy practices school-wide (Project AIM)* (Grant No. R324A200012). Institute of Education Sciences, U.S. Department of Education.

Wigfield, A., Gladstone, J. R., & Turci, L. (2016). Beyond cognition: Reading motivation and reading comprehension. *Child Development Perspectives, 10*(3), 190–195.

Woulfin, S., & Gabriel, R. E. (2020). Interconnected infrastructure for improving reading instruction. *Reading Research Quarterly, 55*(Suppl. 1), S109–S117.

Wright, T. S., & Cervetti, G. N. (2017). A systematic review of the research on vocabulary instruction that impacts text comprehension. *Reading Research Quarterly, 52*(2), 203–226.

CHAPTER 14

Adaptive Teaching
A Critical Tool to Support Readers

Margaret Vaughn

Adaptive teaching is an instructional approach to teaching in which educators construct adaptations or unplanned modifications during the lesson to support students' instructional needs (Duffy, 2005). Effective literacy teachers are adaptive as they make a variety of instructional adjustments in the moment to support student literacy learning (Gambrell et al., 2011; Pearson & Hoffman, 2011; Purcell-Gates et al., 2016; Taylor et al., 2011). In nationwide studies of exemplary first- and fourth-grade teachers, Pressley and colleagues (2001) recognized that the most effective teachers of literacy instruction applied a flexible approach to teaching literacy based on student needs. Rather than adopting a singular theory or approach to literacy instruction, these teachers were "on alert for opportune moments to intervene and prompt" (p. 17) and made a variety of adjustments ranging from explicitly reteaching literacy skills and providing challenging tasks to developing mini-lessons as needed based on student cues.

In a review of empirical research spanning 1975–2014, scholars identified how adaptability afforded educators the ability to question, assess, and challenge their students (Parsons et al., 2018) and concluded what Williams and Baumann (2008) found in their research synthesis, that excellent teachers possess "an ability to adjust their instructional practices to meet individual student needs . . . [and are] able to sense and respond to diverse students and changing needs" (p. 367).

While the concept of adaptability is not necessarily new (e.g., Dewey (1938) emphasized that classroom environments should be experiential and that teachers should adopt a flexible stance in their teaching), over the last two decades, high-profile educational policies that have sought to mitigate the nation's widening achievement gap in literacy have restricted teachers' ability to adapt the curriculum, particularly during reading instruction (Coburn et al., 2011). High-stakes accountability reform mandates emphasized teaching with mandated, prescribed literacy curricula without deviation or adjustments (Woulfin, 2015). However, a singular approach to teaching literacy does not meet the diverse and individual needs of students (Duffy et al., 2008). Instead, teachers must adapt their instructional approaches to scaffold students' background knowledge and support students' linguistic, instructional, and social–emotional needs.

An adaptive approach to teaching literacy instruction is indeed vital given the increased demands in schools today. Recent National Assessment of Educational Progress (National Center for Education Statistics [NCES], 2022) scores indicate that over two-thirds of students in grades 4 and 8 are not reading at a proficient level. This means that a majority of upper elementary and middle school students in the nation are struggling to integrate details to support their opinions, locate relationships between concepts in a text, or adequately comprehend what they read. In fact, students in grades 4 and 8, in the bottom 10th and 25th percentiles, have scores in reading that have decreased or remained stagnant since 2009 (NCES, 2022). These findings, coupled with the influx of immigrants in the United States, given natural disasters, political unrest, and economic uncertainties (Russell & Mantilla-Blanco, 2022), signal the critical need for an adaptive approach to teaching reading to meet the varied instructional, linguistic, cultural, and social–emotional needs of today's ever-changing, diverse student populations.

In the context of supporting struggling readers in the upper elementary grades' literature, there is an emphasis on students' lack of foundational skills that are typically taught in early childhood classrooms. These foundational skills, outlined by the National Reading Panel (2000), highlight the skills learners need to build to navigate and interact with texts (e.g., phonemic awareness, phonics, vocabulary, fluency, and comprehension). Students in higher grades who have not mastered these foundational skills experience a variety of hurdles when reading (e.g., limited vocabulary, inaccurate comprehension, fluency) and as a result experience frustration when reading and may avoid reading altogether (Ackerman & Dyckman, 1996). Without the necessary knowledge of vocabulary, their motivation to read decreases, and as Allington (1977, 2009) in his critical work on struggling readers cautions, "If they don't read much, how they ever gonna get good?" This, coupled with alarming trends of how students are continually unmotivated to read, particularly as they progress in upper elementary grades (Eccles et al., 1993; Wigfield et al., 2021), presents a dismal portrait of the hurdles upper elementary literacy teachers face when teaching reading.

However, one productive pathway forward in efforts to support teaching underperforming third- through eighth-grade readers is with adaptive teaching. Given that effective literacy teaching highlights adaptability as an essential aspect of classroom teaching (Allington & Johnston, 2002; Dozier & Rutten, 2005; Fairbanks et al., 2010), the focus of this chapter is on examining adaptive teaching as a tool to support underperforming readers in grades 3–8. First, the theoretical foundation of adaptability is discussed. Then, common adaptations and teacher rationales for adaptations are explored in relation to teaching reading. Finally, teacher variables that are needed to cultivate an adaptive learning environment are identified, with important implications for future research directions about ways to support students' literacy learning—particularly for students who are considered underperforming.

Theoretical Alignment

Adaptive teaching is theoretically aligned within theories of social constructivism and teacher metacognition. Along the theoretical base of constructivism, social constructivism highlights the ways in which students and teachers are situated in learning environments within dynamic social settings (Vygotsky, 1978). Adaptive teachers notice and use instructional contexts, tools, and resources (e.g., students' linguistic repertoires, background knowledge), and scaffolds to modify their instruction in the moment, depending on students' varied contributions and needs within a lesson. In this way, student learning is socially constructed and (re)shaped during these interactions (Israel et al., 2005). Students and teachers are in a dialogic relationship in adaptive classrooms.

Teachers situate students as active contributors in the learning process, full of agency and intentionality with goals and purpose (Vaughn, 2020). These classrooms seek to support students' construction of knowledge through interactive and dynamic modes of learning. Sawyer (2004) conceptualizes these learning environments as "a collaborative improvisation among the students [and teacher], with the goal of guiding them [students] toward the social construction of their own knowledge" (p. 15). Given this flexibility, adaptability requires teachers to engage in metacognition (Flavell, 1976) and deep reflection as they act on the specific context they face to notice and modify their instruction in the moment.

Applied to instructional contexts, teacher metacognition encourages educators to critically analyze their thinking, evaluate their knowledge of effective pedagogy, and assess students' needs in the moment (Duffy et al., 2009). Duffy and Roehler (1987) found that teachers who were responsive in practice were, in fact, adaptive in their approach and understood the necessary professional knowledge needed to support students' literacy needs. Borko and Livingston (1989) outlined how adaptability requires teachers to examine knowledge, routines, and patterns, and apply actions in a responsive manner to fit individual student characteristics and needs. Shulman and Shulman (2004) pointed out that effective teachers take adaptive actions to use a variety of knowledge learned to respond to the situational variables and apply to practice.

In classrooms and across various grouping structures (i.e., small group, one-on-one tutoring, whole class) in which teachers engage in metacognitive thought processes, they continually assess, monitor, and apply knowledge to craft specialized decisions to support and engage students. Teachers' adaptations to meet student needs are anchored in myriad knowledge categories, from knowledge of students, families, and communities, to content, assessment, and pedagogical practices (Grossman, 1990; Shulman, 1987). As teachers enact instructional adaptations, they contribute to the social dynamics of the classroom environment to enhance student learning opportunities.

Critical to these adaptations is the role of teacher reflection. Schon's (1983) reflection in action emphasizes how teachers engage in reflection in the moment, to frame and solve problems on the spot, considering student responses, cues, the instructional and emotional context present in the classroom, and other situational variables. Teachers also reflect on action (Schön, 1983) by considering students' needs after a lesson to structure plans for subsequent lessons. As a result, adaptive teachers reflect and learn from experiences that prepare them for future classroom interactions. Social constructivism and teacher metacognition connect how adaptive learning environments are shaped by teachers and their students in complex learning systems.

Common Adaptations and Rationales

Adaptability highlights the innovative actions teachers can take to support students' reading difficulties. From scaffolding students with targeted comprehension questions based on their understandings of a text or supporting students with strategies to expand on their word-level knowledge (Athanases & de Oliveria, 2014), syntactic knowledge, and morphemic knowledge (Griffith & Lacina, 2018), adaptive teachers structure learning opportunities in which students' instructional needs are met and expanded. In these classrooms, students' literacy learning is maximized, as teachers use knowledge of reading acquisition and differentiation to structure instructional actions embedded within students' instructional needs, cultures, backgrounds, and languages (Pearson & Hoffman, 2011).

Illustratively, during a reading lesson, in Ms. Hill's third-grade class, the lesson objective was for students to read an informational passage on humpback whales and locate important facts. As students worked in pairs to read aloud sentences and then determine whether the facts were important to include in their graphic organizer, Ms. Hill listened to students' conversations as one group shared, "Why do whales have scars (the correct word in the passage was *scarce*)?" After listening to students' discussions about the text, Ms. Hill called the groups together. She invited students to pull out words they thought were tricky in the text and write them on Post-its. She first wrote the word *scarce*, and students added words such as *endanger* and *infrequent* to the list.

Then, Ms. Hill conducted a whole-group mini-lesson on multisyllabic words. For example, she began the lesson with the word family *ar* and asked students to write words that had this similar word family pattern on their whiteboards. Ms. Hill explicitly taught a variety of word patterns. She modeled common syllable division principles (vc/cv, v/cv, vc/v, vc/ccv, or vcc/cv, and consonant-*le*), and then the class created a chart on which they broke down words from the text that had prefixes and suffixes. Students wrote down the words *endanger, return, nonexistent, barely,* and *extinction*. They worked in small groups and discussed the meaning of the prefixes and suffixes. Students analyzed the parts of the words, made definitions of the words, and drew pictures to explain their definitions. Because Ms. Hill knew that students' comprehension was breaking down in the lesson, she inserted this mini-lesson to provide the support students needed to be successful and fully comprehend what they were reading.

Using knowledge of her students and analyzing students' responses, Ms. Hill then planned for additional lessons focused on reading nonfiction passages and pertinent information to support reading comprehension. In the next lesson, Ms. Hill explicitly modeled how to find and locate facts and evidence from the text, and then encouraged students to work in pairs to read aloud sentences and then determine if the facts were important to include in their graphic organizer on the impact of the environment on endangered animals. As students read aloud their passages, Ms. Hill informally assessed students' fluency and listened to discussions about important facts in the texts. Adaptive teachers like Ms. Hill view students' contributions as a critical component of effective literacy instruction. Rather than strictly adhering to the lesson plan outlined in the curricular program, she adapted her instruction by inserting mini-lessons throughout her instruction to continually scaffold and support student learning.

Across research with colleagues in over 70 classrooms and schools across the nation, with over 300 observations, my colleagues and I have found that adaptive teachers modify their instruction to support students' instructional needs and interests, while viewing students as co-collaborators in the classroom (e.g., Ankrum et al., 2020; Parsons et al., 2010; Vaughn, 2019).

As Table 14.1 illustrates, from across this research, there are common adaptations and rationales effective teachers make during literacy instruction to support students' learning needs. For example, in the previous example, Ms. Hill's adaptation is considered "inserting a mini-lesson" and her rationale was to "address student misunderstanding." Understanding these common adaptations and teacher rationales for adapting is critical when planning to support underperforming

TABLE 14.1. Common Adaptations

Teacher rationales for adapting
- Address student misunderstanding
- Challenge, elaborate, or enhance student understanding
- Teach a specific strategy or skill
- Help students make connections
- Use knowledge of student(s) to alter instruction
- Anticipate upcoming difficulty
- Manage time or behavior
- Promote student engagement or involvement
- Follow student interest, curiosity, or inquiry

Teacher adaptations
- Introduces new content
- Inserts a new activity
- Omits a planned activity
- Provides a resource or example
- Models a skill or inserts a mini-lesson
- Suggests a different perspective to students
- Pulls a small group, conducts an individual conference, or changes grouping structure

readers because it makes visible the thought process adaptive teachers engage in to support students as they struggle to understand texts, decode words, and comprehend. This information can guide teachers as they plan for instruction and as they reflect on decision-making practices during reading instruction to support and scaffold readers.

In addition to utilizing whole-group structures when adapting instruction, adaptive teachers make adaptations in small-group and during one-on-one tutoring interactions with students. Teachers use patterns of observation and assessment to guide their adaptations that are rooted in supporting what specific students need in the moment and as they are reading. For example, during small-group reading instruction in a fourth-grade class, Mr. Wrigs observed a small group of students who were struggling with comprehension while reading the book *Crenshaw* (Applegate, 2015). There were two students who struggled to recall important events in the text. Mr. Wrigs intervened and provided these students with a graphic outlining plot structure, and modeled for students how critical it is when reading to identify important events and notice characters' actions.

Necessary to adapting his instruction were the various knowledge categories that Mr. Wrigs accessed—knowledge of students, knowledge of foundational skills of reading (i.e., comprehension), as well as knowledge of how to effectively motivate and engage students in the learning process. Because he knew that these particular students were good friends and enjoyed visiting and talking with one another, he capitalized on this knowledge and structured focused discussion and time for the students to critically talk and analyze the texts with guided support. For example, he modeled for the two students how authors intentionally structure events to help with character dynamics, the structure of the story, and make visible various dimensions (i.e., conflicts, themes, mood). After every three to four pages, Mr. Wrigs encouraged the two students to talk together about essential questions (e.g., who, what, why, and what might happen next based on knowledge from the text) and to write down what each had shared in response to these questions on Post-its to document their thinking. Then, he modeled for the students how to critically listen for important facts when discussing texts with a partner. He informally assessed the students by listening to how they responded and answered the questions, reviewing their responses on Post-its, and monitoring their levels of engagement throughout the discussion. At any point, he was ready to readjust the lesson further to support the skills needed during the interaction. To further extend the lesson, Mr. Wrigs asked the students targeted comprehension questions at the end of their discussion and asked them to write a summary of important events using the knowledge from the graphic organizer and from their discussions.

Given that Mr. Wrigs knew his students well through careful observation of their discussions, he was able to explicitly teach a variety of scaffolds using a variety of resources (i.e., graphic organizer, discussion, and question frames) to support students' comprehension of the text. Mr. Wrigs was aware that although these students were reading fluently, they struggled to comprehend the text fully. He made a note to monitor and assess these students over the next several weeks to see if they progressed in their ability to identify events and think critically about the story elements.

Consider another adaptive instructional opportunity during a one-on-one tutoring lesson with, Marcus, a fifth grader in Ms. Palmer's class, who struggled with fluency when reading texts, which ultimately limited his comprehension. As Ms. Palmer knows, students who are proficient readers read with expression (i.e., prosody) in addition to reading individual words with automaticity (Kuhn & Stahl, 2003). During one lesson, while Marcus was reading out loud a page from *The Magic Finger* (Dahl, 2013), Ms. Palmer listened as Marcus struggled to read fluently. Although Marcus was able to decode and had the morphological awareness (knowledge of words and morphemes) needed to read the words on the page, he struggled with reading the passages fluently and with expression. To support Marcus as he struggled with reading fluently, Ms. Palmer incorporated the poem "The Ogre and the Giant" (Hoberman, 2015), which had highlighted passages for partner reading. She asked Marcus to identify words that he thought would stop him from reading fluently and then conducted a brief mini-lesson on those words (i.e., *trembled, breezy*) and modeled how fluent readers read as if they were in a conversation together. What resulted was a back-and-forth reading of the poem in which Marcus could see firsthand how fluent readers use reading in phrases as a critical step toward reading fluently.

Much like teachers during whole-group instruction, when teachers adapt their instruction as they notice student discussion and student cues within smaller groups and during individual interactions (i.e., one-on-one tutoring), teachers craft individualized adaptations focused on supporting students' varied learning needs. Essentially, the grouping structure may vary in adaptive classrooms when teaching reading, but the ways in which teachers respond to students' learning needs follows a similar pattern—the teacher has a goal and objective in mind in the lesson as it pertains to teaching targeted reading skills, and as students participate in the lesson, through reading, writing, and/or manipulating sounds/words, adaptive teachers are responsive to what skills students need in-the-moment based on student feedback, cues, and interactions.

Consider another example from across research in schools. Mr. Jenks, a sixth-grade teacher, while listening to students' discussions during literature circles using nonfiction passages, noticed that his students were struggling with identifying the author's point of view and thinking critically about information (Vaughn, 2019). To engage students, Mr. Jenks, stopped the literature circle discussions and shared the letters to the editor posted online in the local newspaper. The letters to the editor focused on community members' reactions to the depletion of water in the aquifers in the region. In part, given the lack of snow and rainfall throughout the previous season, the area was experiencing an increase in frequency of forest fires.

The prevalence of forest fires had a direct impact on students and families who were farmers and were restricted in their outdoor activities such as camping and hunting. As the area had many local farmers, as well as researchers from the neighboring universities, conversation about how to mitigate the impact of the declining water levels in the aquafers was a continual topic of interest in the local newspaper. To engage his students, Mr. Jenks redirected the class away from their literature circle readings, and had students read the letters and identify the position of each letter. One author wrote that there simply wasn't a problem and cited the lack of evidence presented by the city. Another wrote about the continued water usage in the local water park and other city-owned parks, and the high use of sprinklers in the area. Yet another wrote about the research conducted across the two local universities on forest fires and the relationship to groundwater, and the critical impact of the low water levels in relation to developing infrastructure to support the aquifers.

Across these three letters, students identified each author's position, then wrote additional questions about each author's argument. To extend the learning, after seeing students' interest and engagement, Mr. Jenks expanded this lesson into an integrated science unit on water resources and conversation. When asked why he decided to veer away from the planned lesson of having students discuss passages in their literature circles, he shared:

> "Students needed to be engaged in what they were reading—and they just weren't with what they had. So, I decided to use the letters in the moment—mainly because I knew there would be strong opinions from various sides. I've really been focusing a lot on considering that author's point of view in a situation . . . looking at who is writing the material and why they are writing. These are real-world skills. And then at the objectivity of things and looking at the points of view of the authors, there's so much information out there nowadays so when reading, thinking about how students read, and really supporting their ability to think critically about what they are reading."

Adaptive teachers reflect like this about their instructional adaptations. They self-assess, critically analyze their decisions, and then adjust their instructional actions before, during, and after their instruction to better support their students' needs. As Mr. Jenks assessed student engagement and interest during this lesson, he deviated from his original planned lesson to create an opportunity in which students could read about something of interest to their lives. He accomplished the same goal of having his students identify the author's purpose but used different materials to reach his goal. In this way, Mr. Jenks "provide[d] a resource or example" to engage his students (see Table 14.1). Adaptive teachers like Mr. Jenks modify their instruction and thoughtfully adapt curricular components in standardized literacy programs given the wide variety of learning needs in their classroom. In adaptive classroom settings, teachers view students with a sense of agency in their decision-making capabilities and as a result, students identify as someone capable of reading, writing, and accomplishing tasks (Johnston et al., 2016).

Characteristics of Adaptive Teachers of Reading

There are several teacher characteristics that may appear invisible when teachers teach adaptively during reading instruction. For example, adaptive teachers possess a variety of knowledge that they masterfully craft in the moment to structure effective adaptations during reading instruction. These teachers have the necessary knowledge of foundational aspects of reading and literacy instruction, knowledge of students' backgrounds, cultures, and linguistic strengths, as well as knowledge of the critical role of assessment as it pertains to supporting and developing skilled readers.

As Figure 14.1 indicates, adaptive teachers of reading possess knowledge of how to teach the foundational skills of reading (i.e., phonemic awareness, phonics, fluency, vocabulary, and comprehension) (National Reading Panel, 2000). In addition, these teachers possess knowledge of how students learn and the instructional strategies needed to adapt and modify instructional opportunities to support and scaffold students' reading abilities. To understand how to support their students, adaptive teachers have a comprehensive understanding of their students. They seek knowledge to learn about their students to craft meaningful adaptations reflective of students' linguistic repertoires and racial, gendered, and cultural identities.

Adaptive teachers use assessment and understand the vital role of affective dimensions of learning (motivation, agency, etc.) to support intrinsic motivation and the value of reading, as well as the need for fostering social aspects of reading (Guthrie & Wigfield, 2023). In this way, students envision what it is they want to accomplish when it comes to their reading goals and pursue learning interests with the goal of enhancing or supporting their individual or collective learning pursuits. Johnston and colleagues (2016) emphasize how adaptability allows students to imagine possibilities as teachers use language that is invitational and supports an environment in which individual and self-correction are welcome.

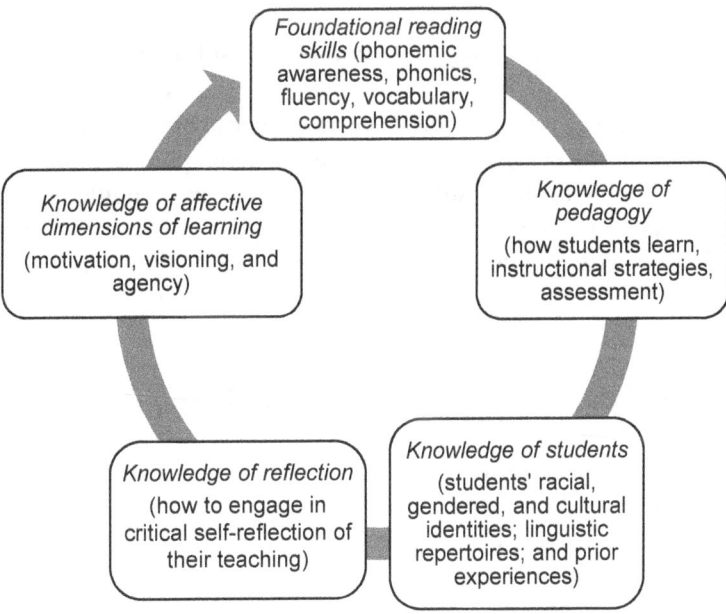

FIGURE 14.1. Characteristics of adaptive teachers of reading.

Adaptive teachers are in a constant mode of reflection and revising in their teaching as they take a variety of knowledge categories to structure adaptations in the moment. Adaptive teachers also possess a vision of what it is they wish to accomplish with their teaching. They ask themselves, "What is it that I want for my students to get as a result of reading this particular book, engaging in this lesson, and working on this particular task?" These teachers have a vision of themselves as a teacher and use their vision as a tool to work toward their ideal classroom (Duffy, 2002; Hammerness, 2001).

For example, Ms. Shelby, a fifth-grade teacher, shared that her vision was "to develop learners who can read what they want and use it to find out what they want to know—to connect to the real world." To align her instructional practices according to her vision, she structured literacy research projects as part of her daily reading instruction. Students selected a topic of interest, and Ms. Shelby helped students conceptualize a manageable topic to pursue. Prior to students working independently on their research project, Ms. Shelby taught targeted lessons on how to conduct research.

Lessons focused on explicitly teaching skills of navigating features of informational text, locating primary resources, and using digital platforms to find information, as well as how to analyze and synthesize texts to strengthen reading comprehension skills. Each day, Ms. Shelby, met with students in small groups to assess students' comprehension of their topic and the texts they were reading, and constructed mini-lessons based on students' instructional needs. In this way, her instructional practices connect with her overall vision of "develop[ing] learners who can read what they want and use it to find out what they want to know." Critical to adaptability is the role of teacher knowledge, visioning, and the reflection needed to modify instructional approaches to support the individual needs of students.

Adaptive teachers of reading apply knowledge of how to teach reading, along with an understanding of learning environments that supports student motivation and interest. Using foundational aspects of reading instruction, these teachers apply knowledge of the varying aspects of reading (e.g., phonics, fluency, decoding, vocabulary, comprehension) to support students as they struggle with concepts as they read. Adaptive teachers are continually assessing and revising their instruction as students' needs change, and use their knowledge of their students and pedagogy to adjust their instruction in support of their students' learning needs.

Implications for Future Research and Practice

Adaptive teachers consider student contributions as critical aspects of classroom literacy environments. Promising research has begun to explore national scales of teacher adaptability that have implications for future research and practice. For example, Vaughn and colleagues (2022), validated the Adaptive Teaching Inventory (ATI), a survey to measure teachers' perceptions of adaptability that can be used to strengthen the focus of adaptability in the teaching of reading. Administrators and policymakers can use inventories like this as a formative tool to enhance teacher adaptability across platforms. Additionally, Ankrum and colleagues (2020) developed the Adaptive Teaching Observational Protocol (ATOP), an observational protocol during literacy instruction to document the types of adaptations and materials used to adapt instruction, using the coding structures identified in Table 14.1.

Utilizing instruments such as the ATI and ATOP can support widespread implementation of adaptability in schools. Understanding more contextually the intersection between student achievement and teacher adaptability is vital, particularly in exploring how student variability intersects with supporting student reading difficulties in the upper grades. Widescale research is needed, specifically, in a variety of contexts (e.g., urban, rural, suburban), across student characteristics (e.g., racial, gendered, and cultural identities) that documents adaptability across measures. Additionally, a variety of methodological approaches are needed to examine the intersection of adaptability and reading instruction, particularly for students who are considered underperformers.

Future research should explore the relationship between adaptability and affective dimensions of effective literacy teaching (e.g., motivation, engagement, agency) to extend the field's understanding of how these dimensions may support and extend student literacy learning. For example, in their research on students in grades 3–5 across 11 Title I schools, Vaughn and colleagues (2024) found that students' sense of agency was related to higher levels of comprehension on state standardized assessments. Additional research documents consistently how reading motivation has the potential to increase and support student reading achievement (see Guthrie & Wigfield, 2023). Future studies of reading should investigate how adaptive teachers support affective dimensions of learning, in addition to outcomes on standardized literacy assessments.

Teacher preparation and professional development must work to make the metacognitive thought process of effective and adaptive reading teachers visible with in-school training opportunities with students who are experiencing reading difficulties. In these contexts, future teachers can learn how adaptability operates in real classrooms with real students. Without this intentionality in modeling how adaptive teachers modify their instruction to support students' individual needs, beginning teachers and professionals at all levels may inadvertently adopt a "one size fits all" approach to teaching reading rather than the specialized approach to teaching reading that is required to meet the variety of learner needs. As schools continue to face enormous pressures to support student reading achievement, a "one size fits all" approach will not support the increased, varied student needs.

Finally, the disparaging portrayals of teachers across the media and evidenced in policy approaches that aim to restrict teacher decision making must be countered with policies that uplift and empower teachers and the profession. Teachers are sophisticated professionals who are adaptive in their approach and meet a variety of learners' needs. They are vital. Without teachers, none of us would be reading this chapter. This chapter calls for advocacy in policy and across media outlets for highlighting teachers as professional decision makers and compels policy to embrace adaptability as a tool to effectively teach reading instruction, especially for students who are considered underperformers.

REFERENCES

Ackerman, P. T., & Dykman, R. A. (1996). The speed factor and learning disabilities: The toll of slowness in adolescents. *Dyslexia, 2,* 1–21.

Allington, R. L. (1977). If they don't read much, how they ever gonna get good? *Journal of Reading, 21*(1), 57–61.

Allington, R. L. (2009). If they don't read much . . . 30 years later. In E. H. Hiebert (Ed.), *Reading more, reading better* (pp. 30–54). Guilford Press.

Allington, R. L., & Johnston, P. (2002). *Reading to learn: Lessons from exemplary fourth-grade classrooms.* Guilford Press.

Ankrum, J. W., Morewood, A. L., Parsons, S. A., Vaughn, M., Parsons, A. W., & Hawkins, P. M. (2020). Documenting adaptive literacy instruction: The Adaptive Teaching Observation Protocol (ATOP). *Reading Psychology, 41*(2), 71–86.

Applegate, K. (2015). *Crenshaw.* Feiwel & Friends.

Athanases, S. Z., & de Oliveira, L. C. (2014). Scaffolding versus routine support for Latina/o youth in an urban school: Tensions in building toward disciplinary literacy. *Journal of Literacy Research, 46*(2), 263–299.

Borko, H., & Livingston, C. (1989). Cognition and improvisation: Differences in mathematics instruction by expert and novice teachers. *American Educational Research Journal, 26,* 473–498.

Coburn, C. E., Pearson, P. D., & Woulfin, S. L. (2011). Reading policy in the era of accountability. In M. L. Kamil, P. D. Pearson, E. B. Moje, & P. P. Afflerbach (Eds.), *Handbook of reading research* (Vol. 4, pp. 629–653). Routledge.

Dahl, R. (2013). *The magic finger.* Penguin.

Dewey, J. (1938). *Experience and education.* Touchstone.

Dozier, C. L., & Rutten, I. (2005). Responsive teaching toward responsive teachers: Mediating transfer through intentionality, enactment, and articulation. *Journal of Literacy Research, 37*(4), 459–492.

Duffy, G. G. (2002). Visioning and the development of outstanding teachers. *Literacy Research and Instruction, 41*(4), 331–343.

Duffy, G. G. (2005). Developing metacognitive teachers: Visioning and the expert's changing role in teacher education and professional development. In S. E. Israel, C. C. Block, K. L. Bauserman, & K. Kinnucan-Welsch (Eds.), *Metacognition in literacy learning: Theory, assessment, instruction, and professional development* (pp. 299–314). Erlbaum.

Duffy, G. G., Miller, S. D., Kear, K., Parsons, S. A., Davis, S., & Williams, B. (2008). Teachers' instructional adaptations during literacy instruction. In Y. Kim, V. Risko, D. L. Compton, D. K. Dickinson, M. K. Hundley, R. T. Jimenez, K. M. Leander, & D. W. Rowe (Eds.), *57th Yearbook of the National Reading Conference* (pp. 160–171). National Reading Conference.

Duffy, G. G., Miller, S. D., Parsons, S. A., & Meloth, M. (2009). Teachers as metacognitive professionals. In D. J. Hacker, J. Dunlosky, & A. C. Graesser (Eds.), *Handbook of metacognition in education* (pp. 240–256). Erlbaum.

Duffy, G. G., & Roehler, L. R. (1987). Improving reading instruction through the use of responsive elaboration. *Reading Teacher, 40*(6), 514–520.

Eccles, J. S., Wigfield, A., Midgley, C., Reuman, D., Iver, D. M., & Feldlaufer, H. (1993). Negative effects of traditional middle schools on students' motivation. *Elementary School Journal, 93*(5), 553–574.

Fairbanks, C. M., Duffy, G. G., Faircloth, B. S., He, Y., Levin, B. B., Rohr, J., & Stein, C.

(2010). Beyond knowledge: Exploring why some teachers are more thoughtfully adaptive than others. *Journal of Teacher Education, 61*(1/2), 161–171.

Flavell, J. H. (1976). Metacognitive aspects of problem solving. In L. B. Resnick (Ed.), *The nature of intelligence* (pp. 231–236). Routledge.

Gambrell, L. B., Malloy, J. A., & Mazzoni, S. A. (2011). Evidence-based best practices for comprehensive literacy instruction. In L. M. Morrow & L. B. Gambrell (Eds.), *Best practices in literacy instruction* (4th ed., pp. 11–36). Guilford Press.

Griffith, R., & Lacina, J. (2018). Teacher as decision maker: A framework to guide teaching decisions in reading. *Reading Teacher, 71*(4), 501–507.

Grossman, P. L. (1990). *The making of a teacher: Teacher knowledge and teacher education.* Teachers College Press.

Guthrie, J. T., & Wigfield, A. (2023). Roles of motivation and engagement in teaching the English language arts. In D. Fisher & D. Lapp (Eds.), *Handbook of research on teaching the English language arts* (5th ed. pp. 267–293). Routledge.

Hammerness, K. (2001). Teachers' visions: The role of personal ideals in school reform. *Journal of Educational Change, 2*(2), 143–163.

Hoberman, M. A. (2015). *Very short scary tales to read together.* Little, Brown Books for Young Readers.

Israel, B. A., Eng, E., Schulz, A. J., & Parker, E. A. (Eds.). (2005). *Methods in community based participatory research for health.* Jossey-Bass.

Johnston, P., Dozier, C., & Smit, J. (2016). How language supports adaptive teaching through a responsive learning culture. *Theory Into Practice, 55*(3), 189–196.

Kuhn, M. R., & Stahl, S. A. (2003). Fluency: A review of developmental and remedial practices. *Journal of Educational Psychology, 95*, 3–21.

National Center for Education Statistics. (2022). *Nation's report card: 2022 National Assessment of Educational Progress Reading Assessment.* Author.

National Reading Panel. (2000). *Report of the National Reading Panel: Teaching children to read: An evidence-based assessment of the scientific research literature on reading and its implications for reading instruction: Reports of the subgroups.* Author.

Parsons, S. A., Davis, S. G., Scales, R. Q., Williams, J. B., & Kear, K. (2010). How and why teachers adapt their literacy instruction. In S. Szabo, M. Sampson, M. Foote, & F. Falk Ross (Eds.), *31st Yearbook of the Association of Literacy Educators and Researchers* (pp. 221–236). Association of Literacy Educators and Researchers.

Parsons, S. A., Vaughn, M., Scales, R., Gallagher, M., Davis, S., & Ward-Parsons, A. (2018). Teachers' instructional adaptations: A research synthesis. *Review of Educational Research, 88*(2), 205–242.

Pearson, P. D., & Hoffman, J. V. (2011). Principles of practice for the teaching of reading. In T. V. Rasinski (Ed.), *Rebuilding the foundation: Effective reading instruction for 21st century literacy* (pp. 9–38). Solution Tree.

Pressley, M., Allington, R. L., Wharton-McDonald, R., Block, C. C., & Morrow, L. M. (2001). *Learning to read: Lessons from exemplary first-grade classrooms.* Guilford Press.

Purcell-Gates, V., Duke, N., & Stouffer, J. (2016). Teaching literacy: Reading. In D. H. Gitomer & C. A. Bell (Eds.), *Handbook of research on teaching* (5th ed., pp. 1217–1267). American Educational Research Association.

Russell, S. G., & Mantilla-Blanco, P. (2022). Belonging and not belonging: The case of newcomers in diverse US schools. *American Journal of Education, 128*(4), 617–645.

Sawyer, R. (2004). Creative teaching: Collaborative improvisation. *Educational Researcher, 33*(2), 12–20.

Schön, D. A. (1983). *The reflective practitioner: How professionals think in action*. Basic Books.

Shulman, L. (1987). Knowledge and teaching: Foundations of the new reform. *Harvard Educational Review, 57*(1), 1–23.

Shulman, L. S., & Shulman, J. H. (2004). How and what teachers learn: A shifting perspective. *Journal of Curriculum Studies, 36*(2), 257–271.

Taylor, B. M., Raphael, T. E., & Au, K. H. (2011). Reading and school reform. In M. L. Kamil, P. D. Pearson, E. B. Moje, & Afflerbach, P. P. (Eds.), *Handbook of reading research* (Vol. IV, pp. 594–628). Routledge.

Vaughn, M. (2019). Adaptive teaching during reading instruction: A multi-case study. *Reading Psychology, 41*(1), 1–33.

Vaughn, M. (2020). What is student agency and why is it needed now more than ever. Student agency: Theoretical implications for practice [themed journal issue]. *Theory Into Practice, 59*(2), 109–118.

Vaughn, M., Carrbonneau, K. J., Premo, J., Sotirovska, V. (2024). Exploring agency as a malleable factor related to literacy. *Elementary School Journal, 124*(4), 591–610.

Vaughn, M., Parsons, S. A., Gallagher, M. A. (2022). Challenging scripted curricula with adaptive teaching. *Educational Researcher, 51*(3), 186–196.

Vygotsky, L. S. (1978). *Mind in society: The development of higher psychological processes* (M. Cole, V. John-Steiner, S. Scribner, & E. Souberman, Trans.). Harvard University Press.

Wigfield, A., Muenks, K., & Eccles, J. S. (2021). Achievement motivation: What we know and where we are going. *Annual Review of Developmental Psychology, 3*, 87–111.

Williams, T., & Baumann, J. (2008). Contemporary research on effective elementary literacy teachers. In Y. Kim, V. J. Risko, D. L. Compton, D. K. Dickinson, M. K. Hundley, R. T. Jimenez, . . . D. W. Rowe (Eds.), *57th Yearbook of the National Reading Conference* (pp. 357–372). National Reading Conference.

Woulfin, S. L. (2015). Catalysts of change: An examination of coaches' leadership practices in framing a reading reform (2015). *Journal of School Leadership, 25*(3), 526–557.

CHAPTER 15

Reading Fluency for Struggling Readers

Melanie R. Kuhn

Educators tend to think of reading fluency as the purview of the primary grades (Kuhn & Stahl, 2022). However, disfluency is a problem for many readers in third grade and beyond (e.g., Stevens et al., 2017). In fact, it can affect both comprehension and the amount of reading that can be accomplished in a given amount of time. To address these issues effectively, it is important not only to consider reading fluency as a construct but also to identify the types of instruction and assessment that best scaffold its development. The goal of this chapter is a discussion of what it means to be a fluent reader and how to support students, especially those experiencing reading difficulties, as they develop their reading fluency.

What Is Reading Fluency?

Fluent reading incorporates both accurate, automatic word recognition and prosody, and it is often viewed as a bridge from decoding to comprehension (Kuhn & Stahl, 2003). As such, it is an integral aspect of students' reading development. And while automaticity is still the more familiar component of fluency, both automaticity and prosody contribute to text comprehension in unique ways (e.g., Schwanenflugel & Benjamin, 2016). It is critical to understand how both components aid comprehension if we are to utilize the most effective approaches for instruction and evaluation.

Accuracy and Automaticity

When considering fluency, most individuals initially think of automaticity, an essential component of fluent reading. To establish automaticity, word recognition must be accurate (Eunice Kennedy Shriver National Institute of Child Health and Human Development, 2000), since it is the case that skilled readers are capable of accurately recognizing the vast majority of the words they encounter in text (e.g., Foorman, 2023). For beginning readers, this process involves developing familiarity with the sound–symbol correspondences that occur regularly in written English (Kearns & Cooper Borkenhagen, 2024).

But accuracy is only part of the picture; unless readers learn to recognize words effortlessly, or automatically, their reading will continue to be slow and stilted (LaBerge & Samuels, 1974; Logan, 1997). Automatic word recognition is essential for skilled reading because individuals have a limited amount of attention available for processing information; this means that any attention expended on word identification is, by default, unavailable for comprehension. Until their word recognition becomes automatic, readers must expend a large amount of their attention on each word as they encounter it. Conversely, automaticity minimizes the attention required for word identification, allowing readers to focus on the text's meaning instead.

In addition to speed, automaticity incorporates effortlessness, both in terms of the ease with which a task is performed and the ability to perform two tasks simultaneously (Kuhn et al., 2010; LaBerge & Samuels, 1974; Logan, 1997), the latter occurring if one of the tasks requires little, if any, attention. Next, automatic processes occur without attention or conscious awareness; for example, when text is present during a newscast, you may find yourself reading it rather than attending to the story that is being presented orally. In terms of reading, these elements combine to allow readers to focus on meaning. There is a critical caveat here, however: It is possible for students to establish automatic word recognition in isolation and still have difficulty with it in their connected text reading (Kuhn & Stahl, 2003), a point that is discussed further in the section "Critical Elements of Fluency Instruction." This means that, while some students develop word recognition automaticity in isolation and transfer it to text reading on their own, others need guided practice for this to occur.

Prosody

The second component of reading fluency is prosody (Kuhn et al., 2010). Prosody includes those elements that comprise expression in oral reading (e.g., pitch, stress, and appropriate parsing). These characteristics are not just important for ensuring expressive reading, however. When applied correctly, they allow readers to determine shades of meaning that are not immediately apparent in written text (Kocaarsian, 2022; Wolters et al., 2022). Critically, while some aspects of oral expression are represented in text by punctuation, this is not always the case (e.g., where parsing or intonation should occur; Benjamin et al., 2013). Given the importance of automaticity (which assumes a high level of accuracy) *and* prosody in constructing meaning from text, the value of utilizing instructional approaches that integrate both elements becomes apparent.

Fluency as a Transition

When thinking about reading developmentally (e.g., Chall, 1995; Kuhn & Stahl, 2022), fluency is seen as a focus for late-first through third grades. However, it is important to remember that while students generally progress through stages of reading development in similar ways, these do not represent strict boundaries for your learners. It is entirely possible that students begin reading fluently either earlier or later than their peers, and it is essential that instruction is targeted accordingly. Further, students–or even adults–may be fluent with some material, but not with others; in other words, fluency can be situational, even for skilled readers (Kuhn & Schwanenflugel, 2019). For example, most literacy educators will find reading this chapter easier than they would an article in a legal journal, simply because they are familiar with the terminology and have the background knowledge required for comprehending one but not the other of these subjects. It is beneficial to keep this in mind for instruction, especially when working across genres or with challenging material.

Critical Elements of Fluency Instruction

There are several elements of fluency instruction that are consistent across approaches (Kuhn & Stahl, 2003) including increased opportunity for practice, support and modeling, and the use of challenging texts. These features are present whether the interventions are designed for students who are progressing at a developmentally appropriate pace or for students who are experiencing difficulty becoming fluent.

Opportunity for Practice

One of the most important aspects of fluency instruction is that it increases the amount of time students spend reading, or their opportunity for practice (Kuhn & Stahl, 2003). This is critical given that the amount of connected text reading in which students engage during the school day is quite limited. For example, Gambrell (1984) noted that, on average, elementary students spent 14 minutes per day on both in-school and out-of-school reading. Unfortunately, that number has not changed much in the four decades since. Brenner and colleagues (2009) found that over the course of a typical school day, third graders undertook only 9 minutes of in-school reading and another 9 minutes of reading on their own. In other words, students were reading about 4 minutes more per day than they had been during Gambrell's original observations. This is not nearly enough time for most children to become skilled readers. Given the importance of practice in the development of skills, from sports to music, it makes sense that increasing the amount of time students spend reading connected text will increase both their fluency and their overall reading ability (Cunningham & Stanovich, 1998; Kim, 2022).

One way in which fluency instruction supports students' transition to skilled reading is through its incorporation of the extensive reading of connected text (e.g., Kuhn & Stahl, 2003; Rasinski et al., 2011). Whether through short passages of approximately 100 words (e.g., repeated readings; Samuels, 1979) or through longer material (e.g., Chomsky, 1976), students are applying what they learned about word identification in context, a process that allows them to consolidate their knowledge. As Chomsky (1976) noted in her work, students are often competent at decoding, yet unable to integrate what they know about words in isolation to connected text reading. By providing them with extended opportunity to practice their reading of poems, magazines, and books (whether in print or electronically), students are given the opportunity to apply what they have learned to material that is likely to be engaging and simultaneously increases their reading stamina. Critically, however, simply assigning students to a text is unlikely to increase their reading ability; instead, it requires that the material is scaffolded (Kuhn & Stahl, 2003).

Support and Modeling

While fluency approaches increase the amount of connected text reading students undertake, they differ from much in-school reading, in that they all encompass some form of scaffolding (Dowhower, 1989). Dowhower classifies this scaffolding as either assisted or unassisted. In assisted approaches, students read texts with the support of a model or more skilled reader, whether in-person or recorded. Assisted approaches can be implemented with either a single text read multiple times or the reading of longer text(s) a single time. Unassisted approaches, on the other hand, involve the student independently reading a shorter text, usually ranging between 50 and 200 words, multiple times (i.e., repeated readings). However, even in unassisted approaches in which the student rereads the text between three and five times on their own, the initial and final readings are monitored by the teacher to ensure that the student's rendering is accurate and automatic. Ultimately, the importance of this scaffolding is that it allows students to work with material that is at the upper end of their zone of proximal development (Vygotsky, 1978). In other words, it allows them to work with texts with which they would be disfluent if they attempted to read them independently, a point that leads to the third trait, the use of challenging material.

Challenge

The third feature that emerged from our review of fluency interventions (Kuhn & Stahl, 2003) was that successful approaches use texts that are challenging for the students. This is accomplished through various instructional scaffolds, such as echo and choral reading, and is particularly important for learners who are unable to read the material that has been designated for whole-class instruction on their own. Without this extra support, it is unlikely that struggling readers will be able to keep up with their peers, a problem that will only increase as they move through the grades (Stanovich, 1986).

While the gap between texts that are assigned as grade level and those with which struggling readers are successful has always existed for some students, this gap has been amplified due to the adoption of the Common Core State Standards (National Governors Association Center for Best Practices & Council of Chief State School Officers, 2010) and other state standards. This is the outcome of the increase in lexile, or difficulty, level for texts required by these various standards, starting in the second grade and continuing through to the end of high school. This increase in difficulty has meant that some students who would have been reading at grade level under the old lexile levels are now reading texts that are considered below grade level under the new ones. As a result, there is an increase in the number of students who are viewed as struggling and who now require support. Luckily, the combination of opportunity for practice, support and modeling, and the use of challenging texts makes fluency instruction particularly effective in ensuring these students' success.

Wide versus Repeated Reading

The original approach to fluency instruction involved repeated readings (Chomsky, 1976; Samuels, 1979). It was based on the understanding that students' word recognition automaticity would best develop by practicing, or rereading, a given passage. The repetition helped students not only consolidate their orthographic knowledge but also determine the appropriate phrasing of the selection being read. In fact, for many years, repeated reading was the basis of all fluency instruction. However, a review of fluency undertaken by Steven Stahl and myself (Kuhn & Stahl, 2003) highlighted a surprising fact; while students made substantial gains in their fluency when repeatedly reading a text, if their peers read an equivalent amount of connected text once, the two groups made similar growth. Given this finding, we wondered whether it might not be the repetition, per se, that enhanced student fluency but rather the increased amount of time that students spent in the scaffolded reading of connected text. This led us to undertake a series of interventions that were intentionally designed to determine whether the two approaches might lead to equivalent gains in fluency.

Wide versus Repeated Reading in Small-Group Instruction

The first intervention designed to compare repeated reading with the equivalent amount of nonrepetitive, or wide, reading of connected text involved struggling second-grade readers (Kuhn, 2020). Twenty-four students identified as reading at a mid- to late-first-grade level participated. These students were placed into a repeated-reading, a wide-reading, a listening-only, or a control group. Fictional trade books were selected for the intervention. Since the material was meant to be somewhat challenging for the students, we used books identified as being between a late-first-grade and an early-third-grade (levels J–M) reading level according to Fountas and Pinnell (1999). The three intervention groups met for 15–20 minutes, three times per week, for 6 weeks. The repeated-reading group echo, choral, and partner read six books, the wide-reading group echo read a total of 18 books, and the listening-only group listened to an expressive reading of the same 18 books. Since the six students in each intervention group were all selected from the same classroom, the control group, which did not participate in any additional literacy activities beyond those taking place in their classrooms, comprised two students from each of the three second grades.

The pre- and posttests comprised the Sight Word Efficiency subtest of the Test of Word Reading Efficiency (TOWRE; Torgesen, Wagner, & Rashotte, 1999) and several measures from the Qualitative Reading Inventory–II (QRI-II; Leslie & Caldwell, 1995). The results indicated that both repeated-reading and wide-reading groups made greater gains on word recognition in isolation, correct words per minute, and prosody than either the control or the listening-only groups, but only the wide-reading group demonstrated substantial gains in comprehension. This finding is similar to repeated-reading research undertaken by O'Shea and colleagues (1985, 1987); they found that students who repeatedly read a text may need to be intentionally focused on comprehension for it to develop. Given that the study was relatively short and did not include comprehension instruction, it is possible that a more extensive intervention might show comprehension growth in both the repeated- and wide- reading groups. However, in terms of the original question, not only did the wide- and repeated-reading interventions show comparable growth in terms of comprehension, the wide-reading group outpaced its peers who undertook the repeated-reading approach. Furthermore, these results have been replicated (Ardoin et al., 2013; Schwebel, 2007), indicating that both approaches have the potential to increase students' overall fluency achievement.

Wide versus Repeated Reading in Whole-Class Settings

Fluency-Oriented Reading Instruction

The next study to evaluate the relative effectiveness of repeated and wide reading was a multiyear, multisite intervention. This approach built on work undertaken by Stahl and Heubach (2005). Fluency-Oriented Reading Instruction (FORI) was designed to improve the reading fluency of second graders attending school in a district that had mandated the exclusive use of grade-level material. Since many children in the district were reading below grade level, such selections were quite challenging for them. To help students access these texts, the researchers and teachers worked together to create an approach that would scaffold the weekly shared text; they decided to read the material several times over the course of a week. The weekly lesson plan began with the teacher reading aloud a selection from the school's basal or literature anthology; the students were expected to follow along in their own copies of the text. The class then undertook a discussion of the material to emphasize that a focus on meaning is the primary goal of reading. Over the next 3 days, the class undertook a choral, echo, and partner reading of the text. The final day of the week was designated as a time for extension activities.

The initial implementation of FORI (Stahl & Heubach, 2005) was undertaken with four classrooms, and 84 students participated in the full intervention. The weekly lesson plan served as the shared reading component of the literacy curriculum for the full school year, and the QRI (Leslie & Caldwell, 1988) was used as the pre- and posttest measure. The results showed that the students made an average of 1.88 years' growth. Given the unexpectedly positive results, the approach was scaled up with 10 classrooms the following year. Of the 180 students in the cohort who began the second grade, 125 students completed the intervention. These students made an average of 1.77 years' growth on the QRI. However, none of the students who were reading below the primer level made significant progress; this indicates that students need to have basic word recognition skills and other conceptual knowledge (e.g., concepts of print, phonemic awareness) in place for the approach to be effective.

Given the positive findings from the original interventions (Stahl & Heubach, 2005), we decided to use the FORI approach as the basis for the repeated-reading component of our intervention. However, we made one modification: Rather than having the students undertake a choral reading followed by an echo reading, we reversed the order. We felt the echo reading provided the students with a greater amount of support than did the choral reading. As such, we felt the weekly lesson plan better matched the gradual release of responsibility model (Pearson & Gallagher, 1983).

Wide Fluency-Oriented Reading Instruction

The second component of our intervention involved a wide-reading approach, Wide Fluency-Oriented Reading Instruction (Wide FORI). This paralleled FORI insofar as it increased the opportunity to read, incorporated scaffolding and modeling, and used challenging texts. However, rather than reading a single text repeatedly over the course of a week, the students in the Wide FORI classrooms read three texts: the required selection from the basal or literature anthology, along with two trade books. The selections were primarily fiction and identified as being at a late-first-grade and an early-third-grade (levels J–M) reading level according to Fountas and Pinnell (1999).

As a result, the Wide FORI lesson plan was designed to cover three complete stories each week. Since the main focus was the selection from the literature anthology, that text was covered over 3 days. Day 1 paralleled the first day of the FORI lesson plan; the teacher read the selection out loud while the students followed along. This was followed by a class discussion of the material to keep comprehension at the fore. Day 2 involved an echo reading of the story, and extension activities took place on Day 3. On Days 4 and 5 an echo reading of a second and third texts took place. This meant the Wide FORI and the FORI intervention differed in not only the number of texts read during the week but also the number of repetitions per text. Finally, both approaches were compared to a control condition that used a variety of literacy instruction, including shared reading, guided reading, and round-robin reading to cover the shared text from the literature anthology.

Results for the FORI and Wide FORI Intervention

The pre- and posttests included the TOWRE (Torgesen et al., 1999), a measure of word recognition in isolation, the Gray Oral Reading Test, 4th edition (Wiederholt & Bryant, 2001), a measure of oral reading of connected text, and the Wechsler Individual Achievement Test (Wechsler, 1992), a reading comprehension measure. The overall results indicated that both the FORI and Wide FORI approaches were effective at developing second graders' reading fluency, word-reading efficiency, and reading comprehension compared to the controls. Importantly, however, these gains emerged earlier for the students in Wide FORI classrooms, and these students, unlike those in the FORI condition, made greater gains in their reading fluency of connected text when compared to the controls. So, whereas both methods can be seen as effective at increasing the reading ability of second graders who are in the process of becoming fluent readers, the results for the Wide FORI were the better of the two. Given the study's design, we feel comfortable generalizing our findings to other schools serving low- to middle-socioeconomic-status populations that find their students experiencing difficulty with their reading of assigned texts. As was the case with the earlier research, while the use of grade-level material was initially challenging, the support or scaffolding provided helped to ensure it was accessible for the students. Finally, the participating teachers considered the approaches to be straightforward and easy to implement.

Fluency Instruction with Older Students

Fluency instruction for older students is generally meant for struggling readers (Kuhn & Stahl, 2003), so the approaches are designed for either individuals or small groups of learners. Furthermore, the bulk of this work has involved some form of repeated readings. In our review of fluency instruction, Steven Stahl and I looked at a total of 58 studies. Of these, 20 were undertaken with students in the fourth grade or above and another nine included at least some students who were in fourth grade or higher. As is often the case when attempting to review studies, there were variations in the type of intervention, the use of control groups, the type of material read, as well as other factors; however, much of what we found for students in second and third grade held for older students. For example, all of these studies extended students' opportunity to read, incorporated support and modeling, and, where noted, used material that was challenging for participants. In addition, if the control groups involved equivalent amounts of reading connected text without repetition, the students in both groups made comparable gains. And students who read material that was not challenging (i.e., material they were already able to read with reasonable fluency) failed to benefit from the intervention.

As noted earlier, fluency instruction helps older students consolidate their word knowledge as part of their reading of connected text (Chomsky, 1976; Kuhn & Stahl, 2003; Stahl et al., 2020). In fact, although older students may have specific difficulty with their word recognition, it is often the case that they are capable of decoding words in isolation but are not capable of transferring that knowledge to connected text reading. Given the growth that has been shown in studies of fluency approaches with older students, fluency difficulties should be considered when evaluating older struggling readers. And while they have not been directly evaluated with older students, it is also worth considering the potential of small-group approaches such as Fluency-Oriented Oral Reading and Wide Fluency-Oriented Oral Reading (Kuhn & Levy, 2015). Indeed, it seems likely that the scaffolded reading of conceptually rich texts with extensive vocabulary and content would be particularly beneficial for them. This is not to say that fluency instruction is all that is needed for older students experiencing difficulty with their academic reading, but that it has the potential to be an effective part of a broader literacy curriculum that incorporates a broad range of research-based instructional approaches (e.g., decoding, comprehension, writing).

Fluency Assessment

Since assessment plays an important role in determining whether a student needs instructional intervention, it is imperative to consider how best to evaluate reading fluency. When fluent reading and its assessment came to the fore in the early 2000s (i.e., Eunice Kennedy Shriver National Institute of Child Health and Human Development, 2000), there was a tendency to overemphasize the number of correct words read in a minute (cwpm or wcpm). To some extent, focusing primarily on reading rate defeats the purpose of becoming a fluent reader (Kuhn et al., 2010); in fact, many transitional readers began to think that the goal of skilled reading was speeded word recognition. While this led to an increase in their cwpm, it failed to lead to a corresponding improvement in comprehension (e.g., Applegate, Applegate, & Modla, 2009). One way to keep young readers from overvaluing rate is by assessing both of fluency's components—automaticity *and* prosody (Benjamin et al., 2013; Rasinski, 2004). This broader evaluation can better ensure students' focus on comprehension, since appropriate prosody incorporates pacing and expression, helping to moderate reading rate.

Evaluating Automaticity

It would be impossible to evaluate fluency without assessing a reader's automaticity (Rasinski, 2004). Luckily, there are resources available that provide educators with a sense of the range of appropriate cwpm for a given grade level (e.g., Hasbrouck & Tindal, 2017; Rasinski, 2004). The best known of these is the oral reading fluency (ORF) norms by Hasbrouck and Tindal (2017). These norms provide cwpm rates for students starting in the winter of first grade and continuing through the end of eighth grade. Prior to the midpoint of first grade, the majority of students work primarily on their decoding; as such, they are unlikely to be at the point where fluency is an instructional focus, although it is possible that some young learners are capable of reading connected text independently and fluently. However, it is at the midpoint of first grade that most learners are ready to begin fluency instruction. On the opposite end, reading fluency tends to asymptote in the seventh or eighth grade; as such, students' reading rate will no longer increase or will do so minimally.

Of the two ORF norms discussed here, Hasbrouck and Tindal's are the most detailed. They provide cwpm measures for students at the 90th, 75th, 50th, 25th, and 10th percentiles at three time points across the school year (fall, winter, and spring). When considering students' reading rate against these norms, however, it is critical to bear in mind that automaticity's importance lies in its connection to comprehension. In other words, the goal is not for all students to reach the 90th percentile of the fluency norms. Instead, students need to read quickly enough that their word recognition does not impede their understanding of the text. As a result, it is fine for students to be reading at the 40th or 50th percentile, so long as they are maintaining their comprehension. Rather than viewing particular rates as a standard all students need to achieve, these norms provide a useful guide for determining which students need to focus on increasing their reading rate (often those below the 30th percentile).

In addition to Hasbrouck and Tindal's most recent scale (2017), Rasinski (2004) created a set of ORF norms for the Pacific Resources for Education and Learning (PREL) regional center. As with the Hasbrouck and Tindal norms, the PREL ORF norms provide a target range for students at three time points over the school year (fall, winter, and spring). They also start at the midpoint of first grade and continue through the end of the eighth grade. However, if students' reading rate falls below *or* above a given range in these norms, their rate is likely to impede their comprehension; in these cases, students will probably benefit from some form of fluency instruction. For those students whose reading rates are substantially lower than their same-age peers, the instruction should focus on increasing their automaticity. On the other hand, if students are reading at rates above the norms, the instruction should focus on prosodic elements such as appropriate parsing. Again, what is important here is not the rate per se, but that students are not reading so slowly—or so quickly—that they impede their understanding. Just as some slower readers are able to construct meaning from text, some who read at a higher rate do so as well. Ultimately, whether an individual student needs fluency instruction depends not exclusively on their rate, but instead on their success in understanding the material being read. This leads to the second component of fluency assessment, prosody.

Evaluating Prosody

While determining students' cwpm provides a concrete measure of their fluency, measures of prosody are more subjective (Benjamin et al., 2013). For example, although prosody scales have high interrater reliability after training, it is rarely 100%. As with the ORF norms, there are two commonly used scales for determining prosody, the NAEP (National Assessment of Educational Progress) Oral Reading Fluency Expression Rubric (White et al., 2021) and the Multidimensional Fluency Rubric (Rasinski, 2016). Each of these has advantages and disadvantages. On the one hand, the NAEP rubric (White et al., 2021) is designed as a single measure that incorporates multiple aspects of prosodic reading. The categories range from word-by-word monotone reading to passage reading that incorporates appropriate expression and pacing (at least 80 cwpm). The Multidimensional Fluency Rubric (Rasinski, 2016), on the other hand, provides a unique measure for expression and volume, phrasing, smoothness, and pace. Each of these components is rated on a scale from one to four; therefore, this scale provides a more nuanced view of students' prosody. However, it is not as easy to implement as an evaluation tool, since each of the four areas requires attention. It is likely that this would require that a child's oral reading be recorded rather than evaluated as part of their classroom literacy lesson. The trade-off for the two scales is ease of use versus a more detailed composite of a student's oral reading prosody, and the choice between the two needs to be based on the time available, as well the goals for the specific groups of learners. For example, is it important to attend to each aspect of a learner's prosody to ensure effective prosody instruction, or is it sufficient to determine whether prosody needs to be incorporated in a series of lesson plans? Ultimately, whichever rubric is chosen, evaluating a student's prosody along with their cwpm increases the likelihood of choosing effective instructional approaches for students' fluency development.

Comprehensive Oral Reading Fluency Scale

Before leaving the topic of assessment, there is one scale that combines cwpm and prosody into a global measure of second and third graders' oral reading, the Comprehensive Oral Reading Fluency Scale (CORFS; Benjamin 2013). This scale is unique in that it provides a combined measure of reading rate with scores for both expressive intonation and natural pausing; the total score uses a point value for each of these three areas. Intonation and pausing were selected because they are the most salient components of prosody according to a spectographic analysis of the oral reading of 59 second graders and 60 third graders. While only evaluated for second and third grade, this scale has the potential to provide a more precise assessment for students beyond those grades.

So, What Does This Mean for Practice?

When thinking about fluency instruction in grades 3–8, students fall into two broad categories (Chall, 1995; Kuhn & Stahl, 2022). Third grade is generally considered to be a point when fluency instruction is appropriate for most of the class; alternatively, it is thought that most students in fourth grade and above will be fluent. As such, it is possible that only a small number of students will experience difficulty with their fluency development once they move out of the primary grades. Given this, it is useful to consider Tier 1, Tier 2, and Tier 3 interventions. As noted earlier in the chapter, certain components are found in most successful fluency approaches: opportunity for practice, support or scaffolding, and the use of challenging texts. To create effective routines for students, the approaches outlined here incorporate all of these. While I am only highlighting one approach in each of the following sections, there are many others that can be found both online (e.g., Reading Rockets, 2024; *readingrockets.org*) and in print (e.g., Kuhn & Levy, 2015; Rasinski & Cheesman Smith, 2018).

Whole-Class or Large-Group Instruction

Whole-class or large-group instruction (dividing the class approximately into half) is generally meant for Tier 1 and would be most appropriate for third-grade students (Jenkins et al., 2013). It is possible to use these fluency approaches with the primary or secondary texts for either an English language arts or content-area classes, such as science or social studies (Kuhn & Pigozzi, 2024). There are two options with these materials depending on the amount of reading that needs to be covered over the course of a week. Ideally, these lessons are meant for a selection that could be echo read in approximately 30 minutes; however, the range is somewhat flexible, between 20 and 40 minutes, depending on the lesson's goals and the other demands of the schedule. If the class is focusing on a single text that can be read repeatedly over the week, FORI can be used (Stahl & Heubach, 2005). Alternatively, if the selection is longer (a chapter book) or the goal is to cover multiple texts on the same subject (e.g., the rain forest, space exploration, or the Statue of Liberty), then Wide FORI is a better option (see Figure 15.1). However, even when

	Monday	Tuesday	Wednesday	Thursday	Friday
FORI	Teacher Introduces Story with prereading activities. T reads story to class; class discusses story.	Students practice story. T and Ss echo read story.	Students practice story. T and Ss choral read story.	Students practice story. Ss partner read story.	Ss do extension activities.

	Monday	Tuesday	Wednesday	Thursday	Friday
Wide FORI	Teacher Introduces Story with prereading activities. T reads story to class; class discusses story.	Students practice story. T and Ss echo read story. If time, students can choral or partner read again.	Ss do extension activities. If time, students can choral or partner read again.	Teacher and Ss echo or choral read trade book (Story 2). Option: Ss partner read story 2 Option: Ss do extension activities (writing, etc.)	Teacher and Ss echo or choral read trade book (Story 3). Option: Ss partner read story 3 Option: Ss do extension activities (writing, etc.)

FIGURE 15.1. FORI and Wide FORI lesson plan.

the material is unrelated to a particular subject, Wide FORI has been shown to lead to greater growth (Kuhn et al., 2010) and is therefore preferable.

Small-Group Instruction

Although small-group instruction is often thought of as a Tier 2 intervention, it is important to remember that it can—and should—be part of Tier 1 instruction as well (Jenkins et al., 2013). The two approaches outlined in Figure 15.2 can be used for either Tier 1 or Tier 2, depending on your goals and the material being covered (Kuhn & Pigozzi, 2024). Both approaches are appropriate for older struggling readers, as well as for third graders, and are designed for 20–30 minutes of connected text reading per session. If small-group fluency instruction is used for Tier 1, the primary material being covered that week can be used with those students who may experience some difficulty reading it independently. Alternatively, additional readings can be selected to expand a particular topic or theme to ensure any participating student is spending an extra 20–30 minutes engaging in classroom reading, at least doubling the average amount of time students spend on in-school reading (Brenner et al., 2009). Again, this instruction can be used in ELA or content-area classes.

Individual Instruction

There are multiple fluency interventions designed for individual learners that are appropriate for Tier 3 interventions (Kuhn & Stahl, 2003). As such, they are meant for any students experiencing difficulty with their reading fluency. For example, repeated reading is considered by many to be the seminal approach to fluency development for individual learners (LaBerge & Samuels, 1974). However, an alternative was introduced by Chomsky (1976) at around the same time. Reading-while-Listening used longer texts with third graders who were competent decoders yet still had trouble undertaking a fluent rendering of connected texts.

	Monday (20–30 minutes)	Wednesday (20–30 minutes)	Friday (20–30 minutes)
FOOR	Echo-read text and discuss the selected text.	Choral-read the material (if the students need additional support, you can echo-read instead).	Students partner-read the selection; if there is time, students can switch pages and begin a second partner reading.
	Monday (20–30 minutes)	Wednesday (20–30 minutes)	Friday (20–30 minutes)
Wide FOOR	Echo-read the first text and discuss the selection.	Echo-read the first text and discuss the selection.	Echo-read the first text and discuss the selection.

FIGURE 15.2. FOOR and Wide FOOR.

Chomsky (1976) considered extensive, scaffolded exposure to connected text to be the key to helping students consolidate their word recognition and ensure they became more skilled readers. As part of this process, she provided students with access to both print copies and recordings of two dozen books, allowing the children to select what they wanted to read from among these. After initially listening to the text in its entirety, the students read along with the recordings repeatedly until they were deemed fluent with the material. This approach, or modifications of it (e.g., Hollingsworth, 1978; Stevens et al., 2017), have been used successfully with older struggling readers as well. It is critical to note that this approach is not the equivalent of a listening center; instead, students need to read along with the recordings in their own copy of the material. And, while the procedure does require some monitoring on the part of the teacher, the internet provides access to a large number of texts that are likely to pique the interest of most students, eliminating the need to prepare recordings. Given the strong evidence for this approach, I strongly recommend it for students who need additional support for their fluency development.

Discussion

Looking across nearly three decades of fluency research, what are our primary takeaways? The first, and most obvious, is that fluency develops through practice. According to Logan (1997), each encounter with connected text lays down a trace or instance representation in memory that occurs at multiple levels (i.e., letters, words, phrases, higher-order propositional structures). When reading texts repeatedly, the traces are deepened. On the one hand, the repetition allows learners to determine the text's prosody and to overcome any difficulties they are experiencing with word recognition, and so forth. Furthermore, as a result of these encounters, readers are better able to solve these difficulties should they come across them in another text. On the other hand, when students read widely, they encounter a greater number of unique traces; this increases the likelihood that readers will come across specific aspects of those traces, for example, certain letter combinations or phrases, multiple times. When they do so, they will recognize them more easily. Additionally, such expanded context is likely to contribute to their expanded vocabulary and conceptual knowledge (Kuhn et al., 2010).

In terms of practice, it is necessary to develop automatic word recognition if students are to become fluent (Samuels, 1979), but decoding in isolation should only be part of this process. Indeed, it is critical that students, especially those who are struggling, are provided with extensive opportunities for the scaffolded reading of connected text as well (Kuhn & Stahl, 2003; Stahl & Huebach, 2005). It is also important to incorporate prosody into any fluency instruction rather than simply focusing on rate (Schwanenfluegel & Benjamin, 2016); while automaticity is a critical part of reading fluency, the goal is not simply to increase reading rate, but instead to read at an appropriate pace. Doing so will better ensure students' comprehension of what is being read. Next, while short texts, such as poems and paragraphs, can be used for fluency instruction and are the basis of traditional repeated readings approaches (Rasinski et al., 2011; Samuels, 1979), longer texts, including trade books, can be used for both repeated and wide fluency instruction (Chomsky, 1976; Kuhn & Levy, 2015). The use of longer selections also contributes to the expansion of students' vocabulary and contextual knowledge, especially when the material is carefully selected.

Finally, it is critical to remember that if students are to make substantial gains in their reading fluency, the material needs to be somewhat challenging (Kuhn & Stahl, 2003); in other words, if the goal is to improve reading fluency, choosing material with which the students are already fluent will not be beneficial. At the same time, the greater the challenge, the more support students will need. However, there will always be texts beyond a student's current capability, no matter how much scaffolding is provided, and it is best to save such material for a later time. The more the components and approaches addressed in this chapter are integrated into the literacy curriculum, as needed by your learners, the greater the chances that students will become fluent, skilled readers who are capable of reading—and understanding—the broad range of texts that they encounter as part of our modern lives.

REFERENCES

Applegate, M. D., Applegate, A. J., & Modla, V. B. (2009). "She's my best reader; she just can't comprehend": Studying the relationship between fluency and comprehension. *Reading Teacher, 62*, 512–521.

Ardoin, S. P., Morena, L. S., Binder, K. S., & Foster, T. E. (2013). Examining the impact of feedback and repeated readings on oral reading fluency: Let's not forget prosody. *School Psychology Quarterly, 28*(4), 391–404.

Benjamin, R. G., Schwanenflugel, P. J., Meisinger, E. B., Groff, C., Kuhn, M. R., & Steiner, L. (2013). A spectrographically grounded scale for evaluating reading expressiveness. *Reading Research Quarterly, 48*, 105–133.

Brenner, D., Hiebert, E. H., & Tompkins, R. (2009). How much and what are third graders reading?: Reading in core programs. In E. H. Hiebert (Ed.), *Reading more, reading better* (pp. 118–140). Guilford Press.

Chall, J. S. (1995). *Stages of reading development* (2nd ed.). Harcourt Brace.

Chomsky, C. (1976). After decoding: What? *Language Arts, 53*(3), 288–296.

Cunningham, A. E., & Stanovich, K. E. (1998). What reading does for the mind. *American Educator, 22*(1–2), 8–15.

Dowhower, S. L. (1989). Repeated reading: Theory into practice. *Reading Teacher, 42*, 502–507.

Eunice Kennedy Shriver National Institute of Child Health and Human Development. (2000). *Report of the National Reading Panel: Teaching Children to Read: Reports of the Subgroups* (00-4754). U.S. Government Printing Office.

Foorman, B. (2023). Learning the code. In S. Q. Cabell, S. B. Neuman, & N. P. Terry (Eds.), *Handbook on the science of early literacy* (pp. 73–82). Guilford Press.

Fountas, I. C., & Pinnell, G. S. (1999). *Matching books to readers: Using leveled books in guided reading, K–3*. Heinemann.

Gambrell, L. (1984). How much time do children spend reading during teacher-directed reading instruction? In J. A. Niles & L. A. Harris (Eds.), *Changing perspectives on research in reading/language processing and instruction. Thirty-Third Yearbook of the National Reading Conference* (pp. 193–198). National Reading Conference.

Hasbrouck, J., & Tindal, G. (2017). *An update to compiled ORF norms* (Technical Report No. 1702). Behavioral Research and Teaching, University of Oregon.

Hollingsworth, P. M. (1978). An experimental approach to the impress method of teaching reading. *The Reading Teacher, 31*, 624–626.

Jenkins, J. R., Schiller, E., Blackorby, J., Thayer, S. K., & Tilly, W. D. (2013). Responsiveness to intervention in reading: Architecture and practices. *Learning Disability Quarterly, 36*(1), 36–46.

Kearns, D. M., & Cooper Borkenhagen, M. J. (2024), Following the rules in an unruly writing system: The cognitive science of learning to read English. *Reading Teacher, 77*, 712–726.

Kim, Y. S. G. (2022). Co-occurrence of reading and writing difficulties: The application of the interactive dynamic literacy model. *Journal of Learning Disabilities, 55*(6), 447–464.

Kocaarsian, M. (2022). The relationships between oral reading fluency, sustained attention, working memory, and text comprehension in the third-grade students. *Psychology in the Schools, 59*(4), 744–764.

Kuhn, M. R. (2020). Whole class or small group fluency instruction: A tutorial of four effective approaches [Special issue]. *Education Sciences, 10*, Article 145.

Kuhn, M. R., & Levy, L. (2015). *Developing fluent readers: Teaching fluency as a foundational skill*. Guilford Press.

Kuhn, M. R., & Pigozzi, G. H. (2024, April). *Considering reading fluency: Scaffolding struggling readers with social studies texts*. Paper presented at the annual convention of the American Educational Research Association, Philadelphia.

Kuhn, M. R., & Schwanenflugel, P. J. (2019). Invited commentary, Prosody, pacing and situational fluency (or why fluency matters for older readers). *Journal of Adolescent and Adult Literacy, 61*(6), 363–368.

Kuhn, M. R., Schwanenflugel, P. J., & Meisinger, E. B. (2010). Aligning theory and assessment of reading fluency: Automaticity, prosody, and definitions of fluency. Invited review of the literature. *Reading Research Quarterly, 45*, 232–253.

Kuhn, M. R., & Stahl, K. A. D. (2022). Effective reading instruction: What we know now. In A. O'Donnell, J. Reeve, & N. Barnes (Eds.), *Oxford handbook of educational psychology*. Oxford University Press.

Kuhn, M. R., & Stahl, S. (2003). Fluency: A review of developmental and remedial practices. *Journal of Educational Psychology, 95*, 3–21.

LaBerge, D., & Samuels, S. J. (1974). Toward a theory of automatic information processing in reading. *Cognitive Psychology, 6*(2), 293–323.

Leslie, L., & Caldwell, J. (1988). *Qualitative reading inventory*. HarperCollins.

Leslie, L., & Caldwell, J. (1995). *Qualitative reading inventory-II*. Addison-Wesley.

Logan, G. D. (1997). Automaticity and reading: Perspectives from the instance theory of automatization. *Reading and Writing Quarterly, 13*(2), 123–146.

National Governors Association Center for Best Practices & Council of Chief State School Officers. (2010). *Common Core State Standards for English language arts & literacy in history/social studies, science, and technical subjects*. Authors.

O'Shea, L. J., Sindelar, P. T., & O'Shea, D. J. (1985). The effects of repeated readings and attentional cues on reading fluency and comprehension. *Journal of Reading Behavior, 17*(2), 129–142.

O'Shea, L. J., Sindelar, P. T., & O'Shea, D. J. (1987). The effects of repeated readings and attentional cues on the reading fluency and comprehension of learning-disabled readers. *Learning Disabilities Research, 2*(2), 103–109.

Pearson, P. D., & Gallagher, M. C. (1983). The instruction of reading comprehension. *Contemporary Educational Psychology, 8*, 317–344.

Rasinski, T. V. (2004). *Assessing reading fluency.* Pacific Resources for Education and Learning. https://eric.ed.gov/?id=ed483166.

Rasinski, T. V. (2016). *Timothy Rasinski.* https://timrasinski.com/resources.html.

Rasinski, T. V., & Cheesman Smith, M. (2018). *The megabook of fluency.* Scholastic.

Rasinski, T. V., Reutzel, C. R., Chard, D., & Linan-Thompson, S. (2011). Reading fluency. In M. L. Kamil, P. D. Pearson, E. B. Moje, & P. P. Afflerbach (Eds.), *Handbook of reading research* (Vol. IV, pp. 286–319). Routledge.

Reading Rockets. (2024). *Basics: Fluency.* www.readingrockets.org/reading-101/reading-and-writing-basics/fluency.

Samuels, S. J. (1979). The method of repeated readings. *Reading Teacher, 32*, 403–408.

Schwanenflugel, P. J., & Benjamin, R. G. (2016). The development of reading prosody and its assessment. In J. Thomson & L. Jarmulowicz (Eds.), *Linguistic rhythm and literacy* (pp. 187–213). Benjamins.

Schwebel, E. A. (2007). *A comparative study of small group fluency instruction: A replication and extension of Kuhn's (2005) study.* Unpublished master's thesis, Kean University, Union, NJ.

Stahl, K. A. D., Flanigan, K., & McKenna, M. C. (2020). *Assessment for reading instruction* (4th ed.). Guilford Press.

Stahl, S. A., & Heubach, K. M. (2005). Fluency-oriented reading instruction. *Journal of Literacy Research, 37*, 25–60.

Stanovich, K. E. (1986). Matthew effects in reading: Some consequences of individual differences in the acquisition of literacy. *Reading Research Quarterly, 21*(4), 360–407.

Stevens, E. A., Walker, M. A., & Vaughn, S. (2017). The effects of reading fluency interventions on the reading fluency and reading comprehension performance of elementary students with learning disabilities: A synthesis of the research from 2001 to 2014. *Journal of Learning Disabilities, 50*(5), 576–590.

Torgesen, J., Wagner, R., & Rashotte, C. (1999). *Test of Word Reading Efficiency.* PRO-ED.

Torgesen, J. K., Wagner, R. K., & Rashotte, C. A. (2012). *Test of Word Reading Efficiency* (2nd ed.) Pearson.

Vygotsky, L. (1978). *Mind in society.* Harvard University Press.

Wechsler, D. (1992). *Wechsler Individual Achievement Test.* Psychological Corporation.

White, S., Sabatini, J., Park, B. J., Chen, J., Bernstein, J., & Li, M. (2021). *The 2018 NAEP Oral Reading Fluency Study.* Institute of Education Sciences, National Center for Education Statistics. https://nces.ed.gov/nationsreportcard/subject/studies/orf/2021025_orf_study.pdf.

Wiederholt, J. L., & Bryant, B. R. (2001). *Gray Oral Reading Tests* (4th ed.). PRO-ED.

Wolters, A. P., Kim, Y. G., & Szura, J. W. (2022). Is reading prosody related to reading comprehension?: A meta-analysis. *Scientific Studies of Reading, 26*(1), 1–20.

PART IV
WHAT DOES THE RESEARCH SAY ABOUT WRITING INSTRUCTION?

CHAPTER 16

Changing Writing Instruction in the Middle Grades

Steve Graham

Writing is an essential tool today. It is everywhere (Graham & Kim, in press). We text, tweet, blog, email, and instant-message, to name just some of the ways we communicate through writing electronically. We use our signature to identify who we are, and we compose autobiographies, biographies, obituaries, and funerary inscriptions to describe who we were. We use writing to store and share information through a host of mediums including books, magazines, newspaper articles, scientific reports, travel guides, websites, product labels, encyclopedias, Power-Points, memos, blueprints, personal correspondences, faxes, multimodal presentations, religious texts, and government documents. Writing is a powerful tool for persuading others, exerting its influence through editorials, op-eds, advertisement, reviews, treatises, proposals, and written speeches. Even when it is not visible, writing can entertain and move us. It provides the words for the movies, plays, and songs we love so well. It is even therapeutic, as writing about the challenges we face increases our ability to cope physically and emotionally. Writing makes us smarter and better readers. Writing about new information increases understanding and make it more memorable. Teaching students to write, including students in the middle grades (3–8), makes them better readers.

Wow! Writing is really incredible when you think about all of its many and varied uses. So it begs the question: Why do so many teachers spend so little time teaching writing? In a review of 28 surveys and observational studies from around the world (Graham, 2019), I found that some teachers provided students with a solid writing program, as students wrote frequently and teachers invested considerable energy in teaching writing. This was not common. Writing instruction was generally characterized by little writing and even less instruction in some cases. For example, in a national survey study by Gilbert and Graham (2010), grade 4–6 teachers in the United States indicated they spent just 15 minutes a day teaching writing and engaged students in writing for only 25 minutes a day. This was also reflected in a national U.S. survey involving teachers in grades 6–8 (Graham et al., 2014). Across language arts, social studies, and science, students wrote for 26 minutes a day, and writing was taught for 16 minutes a day.

Our failure to provide students with the writing instruction they need has real consequences. In the last national assessment of students' writing in the United States (National Center for Education Statistics, 2012), grade 8 students writing scores were so low that two-thirds of them were at or below a basic level, indicating they had only partially mastered the writing skills needed for grade-level success. Such outcomes are not only evident in the United States but are also a global phenomenon (Graham & Rijlaarsdam, 2016). This means that too many students are not able to take full advantage of the affordances that writing provides for improved learning and better reading (Graham et al., 2020; Graham & Hebert, 2011). The relatively poor writing performance of students and lack of investment in teaching writing by schools prompted the National Commission on Writing (NCOW; 2003) to label writing as the neglected "R" (of reading, writing, and arithmetic).

It Is Time for a Change

Time is a slippery concept. As Carroll (1963) argued in his seminal model of school learning, instructional effectiveness depends on the time needed to learn and the actual time spent learning. This balance of time is not the same for every student, however, and time needed and spent learning depends on the quality of instruction provided.

Not surprisingly then, there is no empirical evidence that provides a definitive answer to the question of how much time should be devoted to teaching writing in middle grades or any grades for that matter (Graham, 2019). At the risk of incurring the criticism of others, I propose that a minimum of one hour a day needs to be devoted to teaching writing to students in grades 3–8. I did not pull this hour out of thin air or even a magician's hat. Rather, I based this recommendation on the consensus of the distinguished panel of writing experts who created the *Practice Guide for Elementary Writing* for the What Works Clearinghouse (Graham, Bollinger, et al., 2012). They agreed that students should write for at least 30 minutes a day and be taught to write for another 30 minutes each day. Undoubtedly, this is not enough time for every student to become a competent writer, and the equal balance between writing and teaching needs to be viewed with a skeptical eye. As a minimal requirement, though, it is a step in the right direction. As the NCOW (2003) indicated 20 years ago, the teaching of writing is a prisoner of time, and we must "ensure that curriculum in schools provides the necessary time for students to use writing to learn and to learn to write" (p. 6).

While change may be a natural feature of life, it must be realized that carving out more time for teaching writing in the middle grades will not be easy. The school curriculum is already bursting at its seams, and vested interests in other academic areas will resist a rebalancing of time. I base this last claim on my experiences with organizations that have placed considerable energy in promoting better reading instruction. I conducted a meta-analysis with Delores Perin to identify effective writing practices for students in grades 4–12 titled *Writing Next* (Graham & Perin, 2007). The Carnegie Corporation of New York and the Alliance for Excellence in Education supported this effort, and they were positive about improving writing instruction for adolescents in U.S. schools. Even so, they engaged in hand wringing more than once, worrying that the report would take attention away from their efforts to promote reading. I had a similar experience with the Southern Regional Educational Board (SREB) in developing a white paper for improving the teaching of writing (Graham et al., 2013). The hand wringing about the possible impact on reading in this case was serious enough that the report ended up focusing on a single state (Texas) instead of the 16 states represented by the SREB. I have also seen this reluctance to increasing time for writing when working with companies that develop programs for teaching literacy. This occurred even though all persons involved viewed writing as important.

If the bottleneck that currently constrains the time allocated to teaching writing to students in the middle grades is to be broken, we need to do a better job of making it clear why writing is so critical. This objective can be advanced by both local and national efforts (see Graham, 2019). At the local level, teachers and administrators can make a concerted effort to make sure parents know why writing is so valuable and why more time needs to be devoted to teaching it to students in the middle grades. While this may feel like a small step, the efforts of individual school personnel are a leap in the right direction. The more individuals involved in such a push, the greater the impact.

In order to reach a broader audience, however, concerted public campaigns aimed at informing policymakers, educators, and the public are needed (Graham, 2019). Such efforts can be led by parental and professional organizations, nonprofits, and even the Department of Education. These efforts are likely to be most successful when they are multifaceted, including social media, television, radio, and print materials.

Efforts to establish the value of writing and the importance of teaching it must go beyond describing the various ways we use writing, and make it crystal clear why writing is so essential to school success and reading. The more writing is tied to other school reform efforts, the more likely it will be viewed as indispensable. This includes promoting the idea that *writing is fundamental to learning.* As we found in several meta-analyses, writing improves learning in science, social studies, and math (Graham et al., 2020), and it makes information presented in text more comprehensible and memorable (Graham & Hebert, 2011). Writing does this by engaging students in productive thinking. As students write about information read, seen, or heard, they analyze the ideas presented, decide what is most important, integrate information, elaborate by connecting new and old ideas, reconsider information as it is transformed into their own words, and form a personal involvement with ideas as they decide how to treat them.

Establishing why writing is valuable and must be taught to students in the middle grades also involves making it clear that *writing is fundamental to reading.*

The evidence for this claim comes from three meta-analyses. Graham and Hebert (2011) found that when students in the middle grades write more or are taught to write, they become better readers who are more cable of understanding the text they read. Graham and Santangelo (2014) reported that teaching students in the middle grades to spell improved both word reading and reading comprehension. In Graham, Liu, Aitken, and colleagues (2018), teaching both writing and reading in equal proportions resulted in improved reading and writing outcomes. In many ways, it is unfortunate that the Report from the National Reading Panel (2000) did not examine the effects of teaching writing on reading, as the recommendations to improve reading through phonological awareness, phonics, vocabulary, reading fluency, and reading comprehension instruction would have been more comprehensive had they included the teaching of writing.

If reform efforts to improve reading and learning in key areas such as science and mathematics take up the call to make writing part of the solution, this provides one way to ease the bottleneck that constrains the time devoted to teaching writing. While it is important that dedicated time be provided for teaching writing to students in the middle grades (Graham, 2020), making writing a more integral part of teaching reading or learning in the content areas will increase the amount of time devoted to teaching writing across the school day. For example, if teachers of middle grade students use writing as a tool for thinking about scientific concepts and classrooms experiments, students will spend more time writing. It is also likely that when teaching subjects such as science or mathematics, teachers will provide instruction in how to engage in some of the types of writing activities they assign (see Graham & Hebert, 2011). Effective teachers recognize that defending a point of view in science calls for different evidence than defending a point of view in social studies. Consequently, they are likely to devote time to teaching students how to use argumentation in different subject areas.

Brick Walls

Improving how writing is taught in the middle grades is a formidable task, and there are a number of brick walls beyond the time issue that stand in the way. Particularly concerning are three barriers to good instruction that I would like to address here. One involves the preparation of teachers. In multiple surveys, teachers of students in the middle grades expressed concerns about their preparation to teach writing (Graham, 2019). To illustrate, 76% of the grade 3 and 4 teachers in a U.S. national survey indicated the college preparation they received to teach writing was inadequate. They further reported they were less prepared to teach writing than any other subject (Brindle et al., 2016). This was not surprising because their preparation to teach writing was mainly limited to a few classes in one or two courses. This is consistent with concerns expressed by literacy faculty in Schools of Education, who complained that there is little time to prepare preservice teachers on how to teach writing in their programs (Myers et al., 2016).

Of course, there are other ways that teachers learn how to teach. This includes the inservice preparation they receive from schools and the personal preparation they undertake. In a review by Graham (2019), teachers in the middle grades were not overly enthusiastic about the inservice preparation received, but were more positive about their own efforts to become better teachers of writing.

The issue of preparation to teach writing is not easily solvable. If college preparation programs are to improve, both bottom-up and top-down solutions are needed. This includes faculty systematically pushing for greater emphasis on teaching writing in their programs, as well as changes in state certifications requiring colleges to place greater emphasis on writing instruction. In the meantime, this leaves much of the burden on schools to ensure teachers of students in the middle grades are adequately prepared. Without additional state or national funding, what school districts can do is limited. The other avenue for increasing competence to teach writing is through personal efforts. One group that brings teachers together to teach each other is the National Writing Project, but much of their funding has evaporated in recent years. The problem of preparation is solvable, but until greater value is placed on teaching writing, it is unlikely to improve greatly unless individual teachers, schools, or districts make teaching writing a priority.

A second brick wall that stands in the way of making writing instruction better for students in the middle grades is an overreliance on teaching lore. As Cook and colleagues noted in 2012, a surprising reality in classrooms around the globe is that practices repeatedly shown to be effective in research are applied infrequently, but practices with little or no scientific backing are quite common. This is not to say that instructional practices acquired through experience teaching writing (e.g., using discussion to expand students' understanding of a writing topic), observing others teach writing (e.g., a teacher who has students write an argument from more than one perspective), and practices promoted by others (e.g., college faculty, developers of commercial materials) are ineffective, but basing writing instruction mostly or even solely on teaching lore is risky. The presumed effectiveness of such practices is commonly based on testimonials or purposefully selected examples of success (see Smagorinski, 1987). It is sometimes impossible to determine what aspects of teaching lore are responsible for presumed changes in students' writing, as teachers' writing instruction involves a host of activities. Further, some of the teaching lore applied in classrooms is based on a teacher's singular experiences, making it difficult to determine if it will be effective in other classrooms. In essence, teacher lore suffers from a lack of reliability, validity, and generalizability (Graham & Kim, in press).

Evidence-based practices (EBPs), on the other hand, provide clear and effective instructional models. There are writing practices tested with rigorous scientific methods and shown to reliably improve students' writing repeatedly in multiple contexts (Graham & Harris, 2014). EBPs need to become commonplace in teaching writing. I am not refuting the value of teachers or the knowledge they acquire as a result of teaching writing. The reset I am recommending here assumes teachers should apply the best evidence available to make conscious, informed, and judicious instructional decisions. The value of routinely using EBPs is that they have a proven track record of success established through rigorous testing. This is not to say that EBPs should be applied in an unquestioning manner or assumed to be effective in all situations. Rather, how EBPs are used should involve teachers' careful weighing of the benefits and limitations of these procedures within the context they are to be applied, and teachers' careful monitoring of their use to ensure that they obtain the desired outcomes. To make writing instruction better for students in the middle grades, I encourage teachers to contextualize knowledge gained from research with the knowledge they have acquired about their students, setting, and the teaching of writing.

Before moving to the third brick wall, it is worth considering why EBPs are not more ubiquitous in the teaching of writing to students in the middle grades. An obvious reason is that teachers receive little exposure to such procedures in their preservice and inservice preparation. But there are other, more subtle contributors, one of which is aptly illustrated in a chapter by Warshauer and colleagues (2016), who implied that the highly effective EBP, self-regulated strategy development (SRSD; Harris & Graham, 1999) is designed to make writing curricula teacher proof and exists to alleviate the pressures of national, state, and district timed-writing tests. With SRSD, students are taught strategies for planning, drafting, and revising text; self-regulation procedures for managing these strategies, the writing process, and their writing behaviors, and knowledge for how to use these strategies and self-regulation procedures successfully. If Warshauer and colleagues had examined the practice-based professional development model used to teach SRSD, they would have realized that teachers explore how to apply this approach specifically with students in their own classroom, designing their own lessons for how they will deliver SRSD instruction (see Graham & Harris, 2014). Furthermore, SRSD was never intended as an antidote for the wave of summative writing assessments that are now so prevalent. The first SRSD study was published by Harris and Graham in 1985, long before the current testing accountability movement. Attempts to undercut and devalue EBPs through misinformation are not in teachers' or students' best interests, as they decrease the likelihood that such practices will be applied, reducing the options middle grade teachers can draw on to provide the best writing instruction possible.

A third brick wall involves resistance to change. While individual teachers (as well as university faculty) can be resistant to changing their teaching practices, the problem can be much broader; it can be quite challenging to change a system. The problem of providing adequate writing instruction to students in the middle grades is primarily a systems problem. Individual teachers can and do make a difference (Ball & Cohen, 1999), but if writing is not viewed as a valuable and indispensable tool by the public, policymakers, school administrators, and teachers, then too many of our students in the middle grades will not receive the writing instruction they need and deserve. One useful way to address this brick wall is through the development of exemplars in which a school, school district, or state initiate successful systemic changes enhancing writing and writing instruction in the process. Such models make it clear that systems change is possible and provides blueprints that can be applied by others.

Writing Development Is Complex and Variable

In the writers-within-community model (Graham, 2018), I proposed that writing and writing development are interactively influenced by the communities in which the writing and writing instruction take place, and by the cognitive capabilities and resources of writers, collaborators, readers, mentors, and teachers who populate these communities. As teachers, administrators, and policymakers create their visions for how to teach writing effectively to students in the middle grades, it is important that they approach this endeavor with a multifaceted lens.

Next, while this is obvious, it should be remembered that learning to write is not limited to school settings. It starts before schooling begins. It occurs outside the classroom when school is in session. It continues after formal schooling ends. Learning to write is a lifelong process, with no set end point (Bazerman et al., 2018). While the writing instruction that students receive at schools in the middle grades is hugely important, it is not the only community that contributes to students' writing growth.

Just as importantly, there is no single or uniform path to writing development. It is variable and uneven (Graham, 2006b). It varies from one student to the next, and it is even variable within students. For example, a single student is typically better at some kinds of writing than other kinds (Graham et al., 2016). Students' writing growth can accelerate, plateau, and even regress, as there is no steady progression of writing from point A to point B. In fact, prespecified sequences of writing benchmarks, such as the Common Core State Standards (National Governors Association Center for Best Practices & Council of Chief State School Officers, 2010), are social norms of what might be expected or desired (Graham, 2019). Such norms can be useful because they provide guidelines for what students may be able to accomplish, but it must be kept in mind that whereas some students will exceed them, they will not be appropriate for other students.

The variability and uncertainty underlying writing development does not mean that growth as a writer is without form. It is shaped by participation in various writing communities and the cognitive processes and resources students bring to the tasks of writing and learning to write (Graham, 2019). While other factors such as genetics, gender, class, culture, race, ethnicity, language, and disability are related to students' writing growth, I focus on writing-community participation and individual cognitive processes here.

Students' writing success is determined in part by learning how to participate in the communities where they write and learn to write (Graham, 2019) For instance, middle school students entering a new language arts class must learn the classroom goals and purposes for writing, audiences and norms for writing, social writing practices, tools and methods used to support writing, motivations for writing, physical arrangement of the writing environment, and sanctioned actions for producing text and learning. While some of these elements may not be evident at the start of the class, and all of them can evolve over time, they ultimately result in a collective history that privileges certain writing purposes, tools, actions, and so forth, as well as a classroom writing identity (Graham, 2018). Students who are more familiar and committed to the writing goals and operation of the class are more likely to be successful writers in that context.

Writing growth of students is also driven by cognitive catalysts operating at the individual level. In a review of the literature (Graham, 2006b) and an examination of my own empirical work (Graham, 2022), I found compelling evidence that students' self-regulatory writing capabilities (e.g., planning and revising), knowledge of writing (e.g., writing discourse and topic knowledge), motivations for writing (e.g., self-efficacy) and foundational writing skills (e.g., handwriting, spelling, and sentence construction) impact their writing growth. While the evidence I examined provided the strongest support for writing self-regulation and writing foundational skills, all four catalysts play a role in determining students' growth as writers, including the growth of students in the middle grades.

Finally, individual growth in reading also serves as a catalyst for growth in writing. In a meta-analysis involving students in preschool to grade 12, Graham, Liu, Bartlett, and colleagues (2018) reported that teaching reading resulted in better writing. More specifically, teaching phonological awareness, phonics, and reading comprehension strengthened writing overall (e.g., spelling, number of words written, and text quality). Increasing students' interactions with words or text by reading, observing others read and interact with text, and reading and analyzing the text produced by other students resulted in qualitatively better writing. These findings, along with the findings that writing and writing instruction improve reading (Graham & Hebert, 2011), support the contention I made that *writing and reading connections* need to be brought more fully into the classroom (Graham, 2020). This is true for students in the middle grades, as well as students who are younger and older.

EBPs: Entrance Stage Right

Over the years, my colleagues and I have conducted many meta-analyses examining the effects of practices for teaching writing. This includes meta-analyses on the effects of instruction to teach writing strategies (Graham, 2006a), SRSD (Graham et al., 2013), writing self-regulation (Santangelo et al., 2016), handwriting (Santangelo & Graham, 2016), spelling (Graham & Santangelo, 2014), the process approach to writing (Sandmel & Graham, 2011), feedback (Graham, Hebert, et al., 2015; Scherer et al., 2024), and word processing (Morphy & Graham, 2012). We have also conducted a number of comprehensive analyses in which we examined any writing practice that had been tested in four or more investigations (Graham & Harris, 2018; Graham, McKeown, et al., 2012; Graham et al., 2022, 2023; Graham & Perin, 2007). So, what have we learned from these and other meta-analyses?

I recently summarized the findings from 36 meta-analyses of writing practices (including the meta-analyses cited earlier) in a book chapter (Graham, in press), producing a series of recommendations for teaching writing. These meta-analyses were not completely independent, as one or even many of the investigations present in one meta-analysis were evident in one or more of the other 35 reviews. As a result, I decided to treat each meta-analysis as if it were an informant, examining its findings in relation to the other reviews to determine what it revealed about effective writing instruction. Each of the resulting recommendations was based on findings from more than one meta-analysis. This analysis produced a set of nine EBP recommendations for teaching writing, including those that connect to the teaching of writing with students in the middle grades. EBP writing practices that can be used to address each recommendation were also generated. All of the identified EBPs practices were demonstrated to be effective repeatedly across different contexts.

I add a 10th recommendation in addition to the nine offered by Graham (in press). This recommendation was drawn from qualitative studies investigating the writing practices employed by exceptional literacy teachers. It was based on a meta-synthesis of such studies conducted mostly with grades 3–8 teachers (Graham, Harris, et al., 2015). Each of the obtained qualitative studies was read, and all writing practices used by participating teachers were described and catalogued. The information recorded for all studies were analyzed and themes that captured how exceptional teachers taught writing were identified. Then, studies were reread again, and writing practices that were consistent with each theme were identified. If a theme was evident in most of the investigations reviewed, it was considered a common writing practice among exceptional literacy teachers. While the data from this meta-synthesis did not establish a causal connection between exceptional teachers' practices and growth in students' writing, I think the practices of these teachers can inform best practices in teaching writing.

Table 16.1 presents the resulting 10 EBPs for teaching writing. All of the recommendations were based on evidence from investigations with students and teachers in the middle grades. For a few recommendations, some qualifications about grade-level applicability are needed. I provide these qualifications below when appropriate. It should be noted that collectively, these 10 recommendations are consistent with what we know about writing development (see earlier discussion).

The first recommendation is that students need to write. It is based on findings that increasing how much students' write resulted in small improvements in writing quality for students in grades 3–6. The average weighted effects sizes in the meta-analyses that provided evidence for this recommendation never exceed 0.30, indicating that writing is an important ingredient in learning to write, but by itself, it is not enough for students to make much progress as writers. In other words, good writing instruction must involve more than students writing.

The second recommendation also involved writing, but it focused on the use of writing as a tool for learning in science, social studies, and mathematics. Effective writing practices that support learning ranged from writing answers to questions about content to summarizing material, to writing a more extended paper (e.g., how to use the material, weaving the information into a story, or defending a particular position emanating from the content to be learned).

Much of the writing that occurs at school is done with paper and pencil or pen. When students compose text with a word processor, the quality and length

TABLE 16.1. Ten Evidence-Based Instructional Recommendations for Teaching Writing

EBP recommendations	EBP practices
1. Write	• Increase how much students' write
2. Write across the curriculum	• Use writing to support learning in science, social studies, and math
3. Employ 21st-century writing tools	• Use word processing programs to write • Use word processing plus programs to write (e.g., programs that include gaming features, planning and revising support, and/or multimodal composing options)
4. Support students as they write	• Provide clear goals for students' writing • Students engage in prewriting activities to gather and organize writing material • Students engage in inquiry to gather and evaluate data or ideas for writing • Students work together to plan, draft, and/or revise writing • Students receive feedback from teachers, peers, self, or computers
5. Teach foundational writing skills	• Teach students handwriting • Teach students spelling • Teach students sentence construction skills
6. Teach students to become more	• Engage students in a process approach to strategic writers • writing in which they plan, draft, revise, and edit what they write • Teach students strategies for planning, drafting, revising, and editing (this is most effective with the self-regulated strategy development [SRSD] model) • Teach students to use imagery to support their writing • Teach students to be more critical and creative when writing
7. Expand students' knowledge about writing	• Students analyze and emulate model text • Teach students the structures used to create text in different genres • Students observe others write or read and react to text
8. Bring computer-assisted instruction	• Use computer-assisted instruction to into the classroom • teach foundation writing skills • Use computer-assisted instruction to support students as they write
9. Take advantage of writing and reading	• Read to gather writing information connections • Write about material read • Read and write • Read to analyze text written by others • Teach writing and reading both • Balance amount of time spent teaching writing and reading
10. Create a motivating environment for writing	• Teacher demonstrates they enjoy writing and teaching it • Teacher creates a stimulating mood for writing • Teacher makes students' writing visible (e.g., displaying it on the wall, creating writing anthologies) • Teacher promotes positive writing interactions among students • Teacher encourages students to work hard; belief in what they are taught helps them write better, and attribute success to effort • Teacher adapts writing assignments and instruction to students' interests and needs • Teacher encourages students to do as much as they can on their own • Teacher sets high but realistic writing expectations for students, encouraging them to exceed previous accomplishments

Note. The last recommendation was based on an examination of the study of the writing practices of exceptional literacy teachers.

of their writing improves. The outcomes are even better when students compose with word processing plus programs. Such programs include software that goes beyond the typical features of word processing. This includes tools for planning a composition, providing feedback for text created, producing multimodal text, and increasing motivation (e.g., gaming features). The third recommendation brings attention to the need to move from 18th-century writing tools to 21st-century ones.

When students in the middle grades write, they benefit from support from other students or their teacher (recommendation 4). For example, the quality of students' writing can be enhanced when they compose text with their peers. This includes planning, drafting, and/or revising together. Writing quality is also enhanced when teachers provide students with clear goals about what they expect in students' papers. Plans for writing can be supported by engaging students in activities in which they gather, analyze, and/or organize information for writing (e.g., prewriting and inquiry activities). Finally, students' text can be improved by providing them with feedback. This feedback can come from teachers, peers, self, or a computer.

Teaching handwriting, spelling, and sentence construction skills has a positive impact on the writing of students in the middle grades (recommendation 5). The only exception to this contention was that evidence on teaching sentence construction was not available for students in grade 3. It must be noted that not all students need handwriting and spelling instruction in all middle grades. If they need such instruction in later grades, it can be effective though. I cannot make any claims about the effects of typing instruction, as this was rarely investigated. While the teaching of grammar was effective in a meta-analysis with students in grades 6–12 (Graham et al., 2023), the outcomes from grammar instructional studies across meta-analyses in Graham (in press) were too variable to provide any reliable recommendation for teaching grammar.

Multiple approaches designed to help students in the middle grades become more strategic writers improved writing quality (recommendation 6). This included designing writing routines in which students are expected to engage in the thinking processes involved in planning, drafting, revising, and editing. These production processes can be enhanced even further by teaching students strategies for carrying out these writing processes. The SRSD model (Harris & Graham, 1999) described earlier was especially effective at teaching such writing strategies. Teaching students to be more strategic by enhancing creativity (grades 3–8), critical thinking (grades 6–8), and learning how to create images (grades 3–6) can also improve writing.

The writing of students in the middle grades can be improved by helping them become more knowledgeable about writing (recommendation 7). Specifically, students become better writers by analyzing and emulating model text, learning the purposes and structural features of different types of writing (e.g., arguments), and observing others create or interact with text.

An underemployed tool in writing instruction for students in the middle grades is computer-assisted instruction. In the review by Graham (in press), it was an effective tool for improving students' foundational writing skills (e.g., handwriting) as well as a means of supporting writing production processes as students compose (recommendation 8).

Recommendation 9 focused on taking advantage of the reciprocal and positive relationships that exist between writing and reading. Each of these skills can be used to support and enhance the other. Since I discussed this earlier in the chapter, I only note here that actualizing this recommendation is particularly important for writing because it will surely increase the time devoted to teaching students to compose text.

The final recommendation stressed the importance of creating a motivating writing environment. While there is no direct evidence that the practices listed in Table 16.1 for this recommendation improved students' writing, I think they are important nonetheless. An often-overlooked outcome in our evaluation of students' success as writers is motivation. I believe it is critical that the teaching of writing produces both competent and motivated writers.

Concluding Comment

We have acquired a considerable amount of knowledge about the practice of writing instruction in schools today, the impediments to teaching writing effectively, how writing develops, and how writing can be taught effectively. The challenge we face in providing students with the writing instruction they need and deserve is not an issue of know-how. It is an issue of vision, commitment, and cooperation. Writing is essential, and we must make sure the public, policymakers, administrators, teachers, and even students know this. Changing the teaching of writing on a broad scale will be challenging. To accomplish such a goal, those interested in students' writing must pull together, regardless of our theoretical or practical orientations, to make sure writing maintains its place as one of our valued R's. It is also useful to remember that all changes leading to better writing instruction, no matter how small, are a part of the solution.

While it may be tempting to shrug writing off and assume it is no longer important because of innovations like ChatGPT, that would be a mistake. If students are not engaged in the thinking processes involved in composing when writing about content information, their learning will not be as deep. Furthermore, many of the purposes for writing identified at the start of this chapter cannot be achieved by having artificial intelligence (AI) write for us. While I have no doubt that the future of writing is humans using AI as a tool for writing, it is imperative that we not lose the affordances that writing provides to us in the process.

REFERENCES

Ball, D. L., & Cohen, D. K. (1999). Developing practice, developing practitioners: Toward a practice-based theory of professional education. In L. Darling-Hammond & G.

Sykes (Eds.), *Teaching as a learning profession: Handbook for policy and practice* (pp. 3–31). Jossey-Bass.

Bazerman, C., Berninger, V., Brandt, D., Graham, S., Langer, J., Murphy, S., . . . Schleppegrell, M. (2018). *The lifespan development of writing*. National Council of Teachers of English.

Brindle, M., Harris, K. R., Graham, S., & Hebert, M. (2016). Third and fourth grade teachers' classroom practices in writing: A national survey. *Reading and Writing, 29*, 929–954.

Carroll, J. B. (1963). A model of school learning. *Teachers College Record, 64*, 723–733.

Cook, B., Smith, G., & Tankersley, M. (2012). Evidence-based practices in education. In K. R. Harris, S. Graham, & T. Urdan (Eds.), *APA educational psychology handbook* (Vol. 1, pp. 495–527). American Psychological Association.

Gilbert, J., & Graham, S. (2010). Teaching writing to elementary students in grades 4 to 6: A national survey. *Elementary School Journal, 110*, 494–518.

Graham, S. (2006a). Strategy instruction and the teaching of writing. In C. MacArthur, S. Graham, & J. Fitzgerald (Eds.), *Handbook of writing research* (pp. 187–207). Guilford Press.

Graham, S. (2006b). Writing. In P. Alexander & P. Winne (Eds.), *Handbook of educational psychology* (pp. 457–478). Erlbaum.

Graham, S. (2018). The writer(s)-within-community model of writing. *Educational Psychologist, 53*, 258–279.

Graham, S. (2019). Changing how writing is taught. *Review of Research in Education, 43*, 277–303.

Graham, S. (2020). The sciences of reading and writing must become more fully integrated. *Reading Research Quarterly, 55*(Suppl. 1), S35–S44.

Graham, S. (2022). A walk through the landscape of writing: Insights from a program of writing research. *Educational Psychologist, 57*, 55–72.

Graham, S. (in press). What do meta-analyses tell us about the teaching of writing? In C. MacArthur, S. Graham, & J. Fitzgerald (Eds.), *Handbook of writing research* (3rd ed.). Guilford Press.

Graham, S., Bollinger, A., Booth Olson, C., D'Aoust, C., MacArthur, C., McCutchen, D., & Olinghouse, N. (2012). *Teaching elementary school students to be effective writers: A practice guide*. National Center for Education Evaluation and Regional Assistance, Institute of Education Sciences, U.S. Department of Education. http://ies.ed.gov/ncee/wwc/publications/practiceguides.

Graham, S., Cappizi, A., Harris, K. R., Hebert, M., & Morphy, P. (2014). Teaching writing to middle school students: A national survey. *Reading and Writing, 27*, 1015–1042.

Graham, S., & Harris, K. R. (2014). Conducting high quality writing intervention research: Twelve recommendations. *Journal of Writing Research, 6*(2), 89–123.

Graham, S., & Harris, K. R. (2018). Evidence-based writing practices: A meta-analysis of existing meta-analyses. In R. Fidalgo, K. R. Harris, & M. Braaksma (Eds.), *Design principles for teaching effective writing: Theoretical and empirical grounded principles* (pp. 13–37). Brill.

Graham, S., Harris, K. R., & McKeown, D. (2013). The writing of students with LD and a meta-analysis of SRSD writing intervention studies: Redux. In L. Swanson, K. R. Harris, & S. Graham (Eds.), *Handbook of learning disabilities* (2nd ed., pp. 405–438). Guilford Press.

Graham, S., Harris, K. R., & Santangelo, T. (2015). Research-based writing practices and the Common Core: Meta-analysis and meta-synthesis. *Elementary School Journal, 115,* 498–522.

Graham, S., & Hebert, M. (2011). Writing-to-read: A meta-analysis of the impact of writing and writing instruction on reading. *Harvard Educational Review, 81,* 710–744.

Graham, S., Hebert, M., & Harris, K. R. (2015). Formative assessment and writing: A meta-analysis. *Elementary School Journal, 115,* 524–547.

Graham, S., Hebert, M., Sandbank, M., & Harris, K. R. (2016). Credibly assessing the writing achievement of young struggling writers: Application of generalizability theory. *Learning Disability Quarterly, 39,* 72–82.

Graham, S., & Kim, Y. (in press). Introduction: Evidence-based practices for teaching writing. In S. Graham, C. Olson, T. Baker, H. Chung, U. Maamuujav, & J. Steiss (Eds.), *Writing instruction across the disciplines: Evidence-based practices in grades 6 to 12.* [AU: Provide inclusive page nos.]Guilford Press.[AU: Provide year and update information]

Graham, S., Kim, Y., Cao, Y., Lee, W., Tate, T., Collins, T., . . . Olson, C. (2023). A meta-analysis of writing treatments for students in grades 6 to 12. *Journal of Educational Psychology, 115*(7), 1004–1027.

Graham, S., Kiuhara, S., & MacKay, M. (2020). The effects of writing on learning in science, social studies, and mathematics: A meta-analysis. *Review of Educational Research, 90,* 179–226.

Graham, S., Liu, K., Aitken, A., Ng, C., Bartlett, B., Harris, K. R., & Holzapel, J. (2018). Effectiveness of literacy programs balancing reading and writing instruction: A meta-analysis. *Reading Research Quarterly, 53*(3), 279–304.

Graham, S., Liu, K., Bartlett, B., Ng, C., Harris, K. R., Aitken, A., Barkel, A., . . . Talukdar, J. (2018). Reading for writing: A meta-analysis of the impact of reading and reading instruction on writing. *Review of Educational Research, 88,* 243–284.

Graham, S., McKeown, D., Kiuhara, S., & Harris, K. R. (2012). A meta-analysis of writing instruction for students in the elementary grades. *Journal of Educational Psychology, 104,* 879–896.

Graham, S., et al. (2013). *Get it in writing: Making adolescent writing an immediate priority in Texas.* Southern Regional Educational Board. www.sreb.org/publication/get-it-writing-0.

Graham, S., & Perin, D. (2007). *Writing Next: Effective strategies to improve writing of adolescent middle and high school.* Alliance for Excellence in Education.

Graham, S., & Rijlaarsdam, G. (2016). Writing education around the globe. *Reading and Writing, 29,* 781–792.

Graham, S., & Santangelo, T. (2014). Does spelling instruction make students better spellers, readers, and writers?: A meta-analytic review. *Reading and Writing, 27,* 1703–1743.

Graham, S., Tavsanli, O., & Kaldirim, A. (2022). Improving writing skills of students in Turkey: A meta-analysis of writing interventions. *Educational Psychology Review, 34,* 889–934.

Harris, K. R., & Graham, S. (1999). Programmatic intervention research: Illustrations from the evolution of selfregulated strategy development. *Learning Disability Quarterly, 22,* 251–262.

Harris, K. R., & Graham, S. (1985). Improving learning disabled students' composition skills: Selfcontrol strategy training. *Learning Disability Quarterly, 8,* 27–36.

Morphy, P., & Graham, S. (2012). Word processing programs and weaker writers/readers: A meta-analysis of research findings. *Reading and Writing, 25,* 641–678.

Myers, J., Scales, R. Q., Grisham, D. L., Wolsey, T. D., Dismuke, S., Smetana, L., . . . Martin, S. (2016). What about writing: A national exploratory study of writing instruction in teacher preparation programs. *Literacy Research and Instruction, 55*, 309–330.

National Center for Education Statistics. (2012). *The nation's report card: Writing 2011* (NCES 2012-470). U.S. Department of Education, Institute of Education Sciences.

National Commission on Writing. (2003). *The neglected "R": The need for a writing revolution.* College Board.

National Governors Association Center for Best Practices & Council of Chief School Officers. (2010). *Common Core State Standards.* www.corestandards.org.

National Reading Panel. (2000). *Teaching children to read: An evidence-based assessment of the scientific research literature on reading and its implications for reading instruction: Reports of the subgroups.* National Institute of Child Health and Human Development, National Institutes of Health.

Rogers, L., & Graham, S. (2008). A meta-analysis of single subject design writing intervention research. *Journal of Educational Psychology, 100*, 879–906.[AU: Cite in text or delete here]

Sandmel, K., & Graham, S. (2011). The process writing approach: A meta-analysis. *Journal of Educational Research, 104*, 396–407.

Santangelo, T., & Graham, S. (2016). A comprehensive meta-analysis of handwriting instruction. *Educational Psychology Review, 28*, 225–265.

Santangelo, T., Harris, K. R., & Graham, S. (2016). Self-regulation and writing: An overview and meta-analysis. In C. MacArthur, S. Graham, & J. Fitzgerald (Eds.), *Handbook of writing research* (2nd ed., pp. 174–193). Guilford Press.

Scherer, S., Graham, S., & Busse, V. (2024). How effective is feedback for L1, L2, and FL learners' writing?: A meta-analysis. *Learning and Instruction, 93*(7), Article 101961.

Smagorinki, P. (1987). Graves revisited: A look at the methods and conclusions of the New Hampshire study. *Written Communication, 4*(4), 331–342.

Warshauer, S., Freedman, S. W., Hull, G. A., Higgs, J. M., & Booten, K. P. (2016). Teaching writing in a digital and global age: Toward access, learning, and development for all. In D. H. Gitomer & C. A. Bell (Eds.), *Handbook of research on teaching* (5th ed., pp. 1389–1450). American Educational Research Association.

CHAPTER 17

Effective Writing Instruction for Students with Learning Disabilities in Grades 3–8

Stephen Ciullo
Alyson A. Collins

This chapter takes a laser focus on writing instruction for students with learning disabilities (LD), as well as striving writers (i.e., students in general education who benefit from extra support in writing), in grades 3–8. Readers will learn why grades 3–8 are crucial for helping students with LD to become proficient writers, theories about how writing develops, research about the science of teaching writing, as well as suggestions for key stakeholders. Ultimately, the data-based information in this chapter can potentially improve the opportunities, experiences, and writing outcomes of students with LD.

In the first major section of this chapter, we explore why written expression is essential for students with LD, discuss challenges facing teachers and students, and describe theoretical models of writing instruction. In the second major section, we synthesize research that has been associated with improving students' writing outcomes. Topics include strategy instruction, integrating content-area knowledge and using both text-based evidence and high-leverage teaching practices. The final major section is devoted to implications. We provide suggestions for instruction, professional development, and teacher preparation, and preview exciting research on the horizon to support students with LD and striving writers.

Importance, Challenges, and Theoretical Models

Importance

Grades 3–8 are an important time for all students' writing development because the writing standards in these grade levels become more challenging. First, most standards in the United States promote writing for a variety of purposes and genres (e.g., narrative, informative) beginning in grade 3. The level of complexity for genre-based writing increases as students advance through each grade level. To illustrate, students must write across all genres with consideration of audience in grade 5 (Common Core State Standards [CCSS] ELA-LITERACY.W.5.2A; National Governors Association Center for Best Practices & Council of Chief State School Officers [NGA & CCSSO], 2010). By grade 8, students use text-based evidence to support their written ideas, write essays using the writing process, and evaluate the arguments of others (CCSS.ELA-LITERACY.W.8.1; NGA & CCSSO, 2010). Thus, upper elementary and middle school writing tasks include important writing activities.

Second, there are considerable "writing to learn" opportunities in grades 3–8 as students are exposed to interesting information in science, history, and well-designed English language arts (ELA) curricula. Consequently, key writing skills and effective strategies can be integrated while students write about content, simultaneously addressing students' writing development and promoting comprehension of content (Graham et al., 2020). Establishing the integration of reading and writing in these grade levels is essential for high school, college, and postsecondary writing (Shanahan & Shanahan, 2008). Examples include an argumentative writing assignment about a historical leader, writing an informational paragraph about a scientific experiment, or drafting a story. The second section of this chapter highlights emerging research that focuses on the integration of reading and writing in the content areas and disciplines.

Finally, writing can enrich students' lives and opportunities outside of school. By becoming a strong writer, students can become confident and empowered as they write for social, societal, personal, or health-related purposes (Graham, 2018). Our world is interconnected, and written expression in various forms (e.g., texting, emojis, commenting) promotes human connectivity and collaboration in the workplace. Thus, writing can expand learning opportunities both in and out of school for students with LD.

Challenges

There are some obstacles that students with LD and educators must overcome to advance written expression in grades 3–8. A meta-analysis comparing the writing performance of students with LD to their peers in general education was conducted to explore achievement gaps in writing (Graham et al., 2017). Students with LD who participated in intervention studies had lower outcomes than students without LD across all outcomes in the studies reviewed, including sentence writing fluency, grammar, and genre-based writing. Achievement gaps remind us that students with LD require specialized instruction, and educators must receive robust training experiences and quality resources for teaching writing.

The National Assessment of Educational Progress (NAEP) in writing assessment is another indicator suggesting that educational stakeholders should make concerted efforts to improve students' writing performance. Standardized NAEP writing measures, administered in grades 4, 8, and 12, suggest that the majority of students with disabilities score below the "basic" proficiency threshold (National Center for Education Statistics, 2015). To illustrate, only 5% of students with disabilities who took the eighth-grade NAEP writing test were "proficient." (Note that NAEP writing changed to an online computer-based format. Data from these newer measures are forthcoming.) Moreover, the need to reform how writing is taught in the United States is not exclusive to special education, as just 29% of students in general education were "proficient" on the aforementioned writing measure (U.S. Department of Education, 2011). Thus, there is a persistent need in U.S. schools to enhance the writing outcomes of all learners and to equip teachers with empirically based resources and strategies to address this challenge.

Educators in grades 3–8 are called upon to support specific issues that hinder the writing proficiency of students with LD. Skills that frequently require intervention include organizing or planning for essay writing, sentence writing proficiency, grammatical conventions, as well as students' self-efficacy about their writing (Graham et al., 2017). Additionally, some students with LD require explicit instruction to self-regulate their learning (Harris & Graham, 1999; Zimmerman & Risemberg, 1997). Compelling research on self-regulation, as well as strategy instruction interventions to boost self-regulatory skills, are provided later in this chapter.

Teacher-Specific Factors

Educators face obstacles that influence classroom writing instruction. Survey research with teachers has explored typical practice in writing, as well as educators' beliefs about writing. Two surveys with general educators revealed that evidence-based practices in writing were inconsistently implemented (Brindle et al., 2016; Gilbert & Graham, 2010). Teachers also reported using incidental learning methods (e.g., independent writing, inviting students to emulate exemplar writing models) in greater proportions than explicit instructional practices. Although providing students time to independently write affords engaging practice opportunities, students with LD also benefit from targeted explicit instruction to fortify skills and strategies to eventually use for independent writing.

We are currently conducting research aimed at understanding "typical practice" for teaching writing, as well as studying educators' beliefs about their preparation to teach writing. We conducted an exploration study to investigate the writing instruction provided to students with LD by sampling fourth-grade "dyads" (a special educator and a general educator who teach the same students with LD; Institute of Education Sciences [IES], Award R324A180137). Forthcoming publications from this project will illuminate which observed practices are associated with the writing performance of students with LD, as well as how teacher beliefs moderate these relationships. Survey studies from this research project have provided insights about the needs of educators related to teaching writing (Graham, Ciullo, & Collins, 2024; Graham et al., 2023). To illustrate, we surveyed 143 teachers ($n = 76$ general education; $n = 67$ special education) about their writing instruction for students with LD to understand teachers' beliefs, and the extent to which beliefs about writing instruction potentially vary among special educators and general educators. Both groups of teachers rated themselves as only moderately prepared to teach writing effectively. General education teachers' self-reported beliefs about their preparation were higher than those of special educators, with statistically significant differences between teacher groups (Graham et al., 2023). These findings are noteworthy because special educators will play a prominent role in future writing intervention, such as within multi-tiered systems of support.

Finally, key stakeholders should understand research pertaining to typical writing instruction in science and social studies classrooms. Thus, we are implementing a research project to document the extent to which writing instructional practices in inclusive science and social studies classrooms are responsive to the needs of students with LD (IES, Award R324A190028). This project also explores teachers' perceptions about their preparation and instruction, as well as statistical associations between teachers' instruction and students' writing performance. During an initial study from this project (Mason et al., 2022), we observed middle school science and social studies teachers and conducted focus groups and interviews to investigate challenges facing content-area teachers with infusing writing into these disciplines. First, science and social studies teachers in inclusive classroom settings reported receiving no or minimal preservice or inservice training focused on writing. For instance, 77% of science teachers and 85% of social studies teachers indicated the need for writing professional development. Second, observations and interviews revealed that graphic organizers and sentence stems were prevalent strategies, and that note taking (72% science, 68% social studies) was the most commonly observed activity. Thus, content-area teachers also require support with their classroom writing instruction. In the second major section, we describe interventions to enhance writing within science and social studies for students with LD.

Important Theoretical Models

Four theoretical models relate to how writing develops and how writing can be effectively taught to students with LD. These theories include the writers-within-community framework, the "not-so-simple view of writing," self-regulation, and explicit instruction. Each of these theories is briefly summarized in the following sections.

Writers-Within-Community Model

One framework that depicts how writing develops and the factors that play a role in who students are as writers is Graham's (2018) writers-within-community (WWC) model, which encapsulates the sociocultural aspect of how people convene as communities to write, with members of these communities sharing common purposes. Each community includes at least one writer who is surrounded by collaborators as they aim to accomplish their goals. This community may also include readers who serve as an audience and provide feedback toward progress in meeting assumed goals. In addition, teachers provide feedback to facilitate further growth. Within the writing community, members may write for different purposes, with specific goals, and from various perspectives. Writers use tools for carrying out writing tasks and engage in strategies and practices to produce written products.

A unique aspect of this model is that these communities may be situated within school settings or within contexts in which writers engage in everyday life. In the school environment, writing communities may involve teachers who serve as guides keenly focused on developing writers (see Graham, 2023). Outside of the school walls, writers may participate in communities in the workplace, on social media, or even peer-to-peer relationships. Given the breadth of these communities, the number of members varies within each, and the time frame for which they exist evolves across different groups. As such, this aspect of the WWC framework characterizes the sociocultural influence of communities in whom people are writers.

The WWC framework also portrays the cognitive mechanisms in which writers engage. Specific to students with LD, knowledge in oral language and reading have dynamic and interactive relations (Kim, 2022), with some students who have co-occurring challenges potentially needing intensive supports. Likewise, resources such as a students' beliefs and values influence their writing. Other mechanisms, such as attention, working memory, and executive control, also mediate writing production. Students with LD sometimes have difficulties in these areas, leaving them consistently striving, yet sometimes not successful, in reaching the same writing performance levels as their peers without disabilities (Graham et al., 2017). These control mechanisms have teaching implications because many students may need strategies for self-regulating behaviors while writing (see Graham et al., 2017). Moreover, production processes that guide conceptualization, ideation, translation, transcription, and reconceptualization are core components that depict the writer, and these are elements of the writing process for targeted instruction for students with LD (e.g., Troia et al., 2017). The interventions discussed in the second major section provide examples of effective supports to assist students with these complex processes.

Not-So-Simple View of Writing

The multidimensional nature of writing that is represented in the WWC framework is further supported in the "not-so-simple view of writing" (Berninger & Winn, 2006). This model originally depicted a simple view of writing in which spelling and handwriting contribute to text generation (Berninger et al., 2002). Although this initial iteration captured core cognitive mechanisms, over time, the theoretical model was expanded to incorporate skills such as keyboarding and a more comprehensive summary of executive and self-regulatory functions that together are enacted, with working memory facilitating interactions among the different components (Berninger & Winn, 2006). This view of writing is often depicted as a triangulation of transcription, executive function/self-regulation, and text generation with working memory at the core (Berninger & Winn, 2006). For students with LD, research has validated how higher-order abilities have direct effects on foundational skills (e.g., spelling; Ahmed et al., 2021). Moreover, foundational skills such as handwriting have direct effects on the quality and quantity students produce when writing, supporting the not-so-simple framework (Ahmed et al., 2021). As such, explicit instruction targeting multiple aspects of the writing abilities of students is critical given the interrelated nature of the components involved in text generation (Troia et al., 2017).

Self-Regulation

Self-regulated learning refers to specific processes that students use to guide themselves through a learning activity. Examples include setting goals, self-monitoring, using self-talk while working to enhance motivation, self-efficacy, as reflection after completing a task (Bandura, 1991; Zimmerman, 2002). Self-regulated learning strategies are powerful but sometimes underutilized. Educators play a role by teaching students how to regulate their learning. Providing this instruction through intentional strategies such as modeling, or demonstrating and thinking aloud, is key (Harris & Graham, 1999; Zimmerman, 2002). The goal of promoting self-regulation during writing is for students to understand the purpose of these learning mechanisms and to personalize them. For instance, a teacher first models self-talk while drafting an essay. With teacher facilitation, students develop their own self-talk (i.e., self-statements) and practice sharing self-regulated statements that are personally meaningful. Increasing awareness of how self-regulated learning supports writing is crucial for helping teachers, professional development providers, and education leaders to understand the science of writing. Examples of self-regulation from research for students with LD is included in the second major section.

Explicit Instruction (a "Writing Is Taught" Approach)

Explicit instruction is a structured way of teaching that includes modeling, examples, and guided practice. This is an effective approach with decades of research for teaching literacy skills, strategies, and concepts to students with LD (Hughes et al., 2017). Explicit instructional practices include setting measurable learning objectives, modeling (including metacognition) new strategies, providing examples and non-examples, and facilitating guided practice. After modeling and guided practice with a student, independent application of the strategy or skill occurs. Students are empowered to use these new strategies and tools with exciting, independent writing activities. These concepts of a "writing is taught, not caught" approach are also suggested for teachers working with students with disabilities across disciplines and are deemed as high-leverage practices (McLeskey et al., 2017). Examples of high-leverage practices are described later in this chapter in relation to implications for teaching and professional development. The following review of literature highlights writing interventions that have been associated with improved writing outcomes for students with LD in grades 3–8.

Interventions for Students with LD in Grades 3–8

The field of special education has access to informative reviews of literature, including meta-analyses that delineate interventions that have accelerated the writing performance of students with LD in grades 3–8. This section includes a synopsis of research that key stakeholders striving to strengthen and reform classroom writing instruction can consult. We address three topics: (1) systematic reviews of writing research, (2) intervention examples from empirical studies, and (3) teaching critical skills and strategies with high-leverage practices.

Determining What Works: Reviews of Research

Systematic reviews of intervention research are essential sources for determining which interventions work, under which conditions, and for whom (Therrien et al., 2020). These reviews of research are useful because they provide a comprehensive summary of research in a given area, and because recent guidance and innovations have enhanced the transparency and the rigor of these literature reviews. There are important reviews of research of writing that collectively inform key stakeholders about "what works" for students with LD. Their findings provide examples of reliable resources for understanding the science of teaching writing.

First, Graham and colleagues (2012) published a meta-analysis of writing interventions for grades K–5. This review included students in general education, as well as students with writing challenges and LD. The only outcomes measured in this review were defined as "writing quality," so spelling, grammar, and genre-based outcomes were not included. Examples of findings related to grades 3–5 include moderate to large effects on writing quality measures for strategy instruction (including self-regulation), goal-setting interventions, and peer assistance/support. The authors concluded that explicitly teaching and demonstrating writing skills, strategies, or processes was effective.

Next, Gillespie and Graham (2014) published a meta-analysis of writing interventions for students with LD. The researchers revealed several noteworthy findings from this review of experimental, quasi-experimental, and single-case design studies relevant to grades 3–8. Four intervention categories were associated with moderate to large effects in favor of students in the treatment conditions on writing quality measures (with statistically significant differences): strategy instruction (effect size [ES] = 1.09), goal-setting interventions (ES = 0.57), dictation interventions (ES = 0.55), and process writing interventions, such as drafting or revising essays (ES = 0.43). We describe several examples of these interventions later in this section when discussing strategy instruction that includes goal setting (e.g., self-regulated strategy development, Quick Writing).

Finally, there are two new federally funded meta-analyses with the potential to influence how writing is taught. First, we recently completed a meta-analysis for *all writing interventions*, for *all writing outcomes* (genre-based writing, quality, spelling, etc.), and for *all students* in grades K–5 (Collins, et al., 2024); IES Award R305A200363). Moreover, there is a recently published meta-analysis focusing on *all students, all interventions,* and *all writing outcomes* in grades 6–12 (Graham et al., 2023; IES Award R305C190007). These reviews of research collectively include hundreds of studies and over 6,000 unique effect sizes. The findings provide information about writing interventions for students with LD and striving writers.

We have synthesized several findings from the two aforementioned reviews of research. First, these two meta-analyses extended findings from previously published meta-analyses by demonstrating the effectiveness of strategy instruction. To illustrate, strategy instruction interventions were associated with a relatively large effect size (ES = 0.76) in the meta-analysis of secondary level writing (Graham, Yucheng, et al., 2024). The finding of statistically significant moderate to large effect sizes was further substantiated in the grade K–5 writing meta-analysis. Next, both meta-analyses demonstrated that providing students with time to write in itself was not sufficient for building writing proficiency (Graham, Collins, & Ciullo, 2024). Time for writing practice is important but should be accompanied by deliberate instruction for teaching planning strategies (e.g., graphic organizers), revising, and editing. Finally, there is evidence that writing across the curriculum can enhance both content learning and students' writing outcomes (Graham et al., 2020; Graham, Collins, & Ciullo, 2024). There are ample opportunities in grades 3–8 to write about key concepts or prior knowledge in content-rich subjects. Writing about text-based information occurs across genres and includes informative writing, persuasive writing, or argumentative writing.

Research for Self-Regulated Strategy Development

Self-regulated strategy development (SRSD) is an evidence-based practice. This intervention is distinguished because it has been replicated by research teams across the United States and in other countries. Furthermore, SRSD has been implemented with different student populations, including students with behavior disorders (e.g., Ennis & Jolivette, 2014) and numerous studies for students with LD (Gillespie & Graham, 2014). Importantly, independent reviews of SRSD have concluded that many SRSD studies were implemented with a high degree of methodological rigor (e.g., Baker et al., 2009), which strengthens our confidence in the findings. SRSD has been used to improve writing outcomes across all genres, including story writing, informational and expository writing, persuasive writing, and argumentative writing. These positive outcomes included studies that were stand-alone writing tasks (i.e., students writing not based on text), as well as recent studies in which students wrote about text-based sources and content that they previously read about or learned (Collins et al., 2021; Harris et al., 2019).

The SRSD instructional framework comprises six instructional stages:

1. *Develop and activate* background knowledge about the genre and topic.
2. *Discuss* the genre/topic and review exemplar models of writing.
3. *Model* the writing strategies (e.g., the graphic organizer used), as well as each self-regulation strategy (self-talk, positive self-statements, goal setting, etc.).

4. *Memorize* the strategies.
5. *Support* students' guided practice as they write with feedback.
6. Encourage *Independent* student performance.

These stages are each implemented regardless of the writing genre or grade level of the students. Any stage of SRSD can be revisited if students require additional support. This multicomponent intervention varies in length based on the grade level, or specific students' needs and progress. Examples of the self-regulation strategies that students learn is provided in Table 17.1.

As mentioned earlier, genre-based writing is commonplace in grades 3–8. Each genre is taught independently, as some research has indicated that effective writing does not inevitably generalize across different genre types (Olinghouse et al., 2012). Thus, while the self-regulation techniques (e.g., thinking aloud to emulate self-talk) are used regardless of genre, the graphic organizer–mnemonic used as a planning device varies. For instance, the mnemonic POW+TREE (POW: pick my idea, organize my notes, write, and say more; TREE: topic, reasons, explain

TABLE 17.1. Self-Regulation Strategies for Self-Regulated Strategy Development (SRSD)

Component	Description	Classroom example
Goal setting	Establishing specific, meaningful, and feasible writing goals based on previous writing performance and students' writing samples in a specific writing genre.	Four students and their teacher set a goal to remember to include important ideas from a text passage in their essays. "*By next Friday, we will write three complete sentences for our informational essays. We will write a topic sentence and two additional sentences that describe important details from the passage.*"
Self-monitoring	Students track their progress and monitor their performance. Students engage in self-assessment, as well as self-recording of their progress.	A small group of students using SRSD and their teacher (1) graph progress for informational writing, (2) sign a contract agreeing to use their new writing strategy, and (3) monitor their strategy use during and after writing using a checklist were used.
Self-talk	Teachers model, and students learn, how to use positive self-talk while taking notes and writing. Teachers model the entire process of using SRSD strategies, taking notes, and writing using a think-aloud and demonstration process.	Students share the self-talk statements that they developed for writing. These statements are written on a chart that students refer to. One student says the following statement when she becomes tired while writing: "*I can do this. I have my strategy to keep me focused. One step at a time!*"
Self-reinforcement	Students positively reinforce and reward themselves for meeting a specific writing criterion. This strategy can build confidence in students' writing and in the process of improvement.	Students attain the goal of writing a topic sentence and two supporting details from a text passage. The teacher and the class celebrate this accomplishment by giving each other high fives and listening to music after writing time.

reasons, and ending) is for persuasive writing (Harris et al., 2019). In the following paragraph, we discuss examples from our research focused on informational writing using social studies source text (utilizing the TIDE mnemonic [topic, important ideas, detailed explanation of ideas, and ending]).

Turning the TIDE: Text-Based Writing

We recently used SRSD to teach students how to write informational text about grade-aligned social studies concepts (Collins et al., 2021) using practice-based professional development to train teachers (e.g., Harris et al., 2012). Inclusive classrooms in grade 3 were randomized to treatment or control. Control classes engaged in typical practice, while the treatment classrooms used SRSD and TIDE to write about social studies topics. Phase 1 involved teaching students informational writing strategies using TIDE to practice writing in the informative genre without the use of text. In Phase 2, students were taught to write informative responses about text-based historical topics, key figures, and geography. Students wrote essays and used text evidence to support their ideas. Students and teachers also engaged in goal setting to improve their writing performance based on student or class need (e.g., "I will include at least two text details to support my topic sentence") and practiced self-regulation strategies including positive self-talk. Findings revealed that students in the treatment condition outperformed students in the control conditions with moderate to large effect sizes for genre-based elements (ES = 1.07) and writing quality (ES = 0.72). Students in the treatment condition also performed better on a norm-referenced writing measure (ES = 0.79). Our work with text-based writing in social studies using TIDE is currently being extended in a project that includes training special and general education co-teachers (IES Award R324X220101).

Quick Writing for Science and Social Studies

Research for students with LD has also included writing in science and in social studies. One such intervention is Quick Writing, which is characterized by brief spans of writing (10–15 minutes) in which students develop a plan, then draft a short passage in response to a prompt. Quick Writing studies have included students writing from source text (e.g., science or social studies text), as well as studies without the use of text, in which students write about topics on which they have background knowledge. For example, students in a history class could perform a Quick Write persuasive response to explain their position about whether there should be a law requiring automatic voter registration when U.S. citizens turn 18 years old. In this example, students convey their opinions for and against this position, using specific reasons to support their stance.

Studies that have tested Quick Writing for students with disabilities have included writing about scientific topics (Garwood et al., 2019), as well as social studies. Quick Writing studies typically employ an SRSD teaching plan to promote instruction in the strategies that students will use for independent writing.

To illustrate, we (Ciullo et al., 2021) conducted a persuasive Quick Writing study to investigate whether this intervention would be helpful for students with LD in grade 4. Students read social studies passages and were taught to apply a cognitive reading comprehension strategy. Next, students planned using the TREE mnemonic and composed a persuasive response. This study provides initial evidence that using Quick Writing with younger students with disabilities holds promise. Consistent with a systematic review of the Quick Writing literature (Mason & Basile, 2023), we urge other researchers to replicate Quick Writing in different subject areas. Ultimately, integrating reading, writing, and essential background knowledge can improve students' learning outcomes. As described in the third major section of this chapter, researchers should continue to investigate mechanisms for teaching writing across the curriculum.

Using High-Leverage Practices to Strategically Target Essential Skills

High-leverage practices (HLPs) in special education were developed through a collaboration between researchers, technical assistance centers, special educators, and other multidisciplinary team members (McLeskey et al., 2017). The HLPs provide recommendations that teachers who support students with disabilities can implement across content areas and settings. We encourage readers to review the full scope of HLPs, which includes video demonstrations and other key resources (*https://highleveragepractices.org*). Evidence-based practices, such as SRSD, include key HLPs such as setting specific learning goals, adapting materials, teaching cognitive and metacognitive strategies, and using explicit instruction. Thus, HLPs are included within the instructional and modeling phase of most evidence-based practices to promote scaffolded student learning that builds independence.

HLPs span four areas of practice: collaboration, assessment, social–emotional–behavioral, and instruction (McLeskey et al., 2017). We chose two HLPs from the "instruction" domain to highlight because they are commonly used when teaching writing. These HLPs can be applied to a broad range of instruction, such as foundational skills (e.g., sentence writing) or complex writing tasks, including writing with text evidence. Two HLPs key to writing intervention for students with LD are (1) explicit instruction (HLP #16) and (2) teaching cognitive and metacognitive strategies to support learning (HLP #14). The following brief examples illustrate how these HLPs are implemented within writing interventions.

Example 1: Sentence Complexity

Explicit instruction (HLP #16) is integral to an effective intervention that focuses on foundational writing called "sentence combining" for students with LD (Saddler et al., 2018). The purpose of sentence combining is to teach students to construct complete, complex, and syntactically correct sentences. Teachers utilize explicit instructional principles that include modeling, providing examples and non-examples, and using guided practice with feedback while teaching these strategies. For instance, a teacher explaining how to develop a compound sentence using a conjunction would first provide examples, a non-example, and then demonstrate (modeling) while thinking aloud. The teacher may demonstrate by making the following two sentences into a compound sentence during a social studies lesson: *The legislative branch of government makes laws. They also have the authority to declare war.* The teacher would model how to connect these sentences by writing, *The legislative branch of government makes laws and has the power to declare war.* In summary, sentence-combining interventions have used principles of explicit instruction such as modeling and providing examples to promote improved sentence writing for students with LD (Saddler et al., 2018).

Example 2: Cognitive Strategy Instruction Note Taking

Students with LD require support with prewriting skills, including making notes. The HLP of cognitive and metacognitive strategy instruction (HLP #14) can address this skill. Within the SRSD intervention using the TIDE strategy for writing in social studies that we previously described (Collins et al., 2021), teachers used cognitive strategy instruction to demonstrate taking notes from social studies passages. Teachers verbalized their thoughts as they made and organized notes. Within this study, teachers explained that notes should be brief, like sending a text message. For example, a teacher used a "think-aloud" when reading a passage about Thomas Edison and creating notes, saying, "OK, my passage says that Edison invented cool things like an electric light, an automatic telegraph machine, and a movie camera. That's a lot of words to write. I've got it! I'll pretend I'm sending a text message and write, 'Helped invent electric light, telegraph, and movie camera.' These quick notes will remind me about the important information from the passage." The teacher modeled in this way several times, reteaching if needed after students practiced.

In summary, HLPs make skills, strategies, and concepts accessible for students. We encourage professional development providers, educational advocates, as well as preservice teaching programs to utilize the HLP guidebook and video series (McLeskey et al., 2017). Key HLPs such as explicit instruction, cognitive strategy instruction, goal setting, or scaffolded instruction can be integrated within any writing intervention for students with LD to introduce the new strategy or skill, model it, and to cultivate student proficiency and confidence.

Example 3: Editing, Revision, and Grammatical Conventions

Students with LD typically need support throughout the writing process. Teachers can utilize HLPs such as explicit instruction and modeling cognitive strategies to teach editing, revision, or grammatical conventions. Regardless of the strategy, the tool introduced, or the topic, educators spend sufficient time modeling (demonstrating and thinking aloud) and breaking the process into small steps. For example, a review lesson about subject–verb agreement (e.g., *My friend Kate wants lunch*) would be modeled using the think-aloud, and both examples and non-examples would accompany the process. Educators can use strategies such as COPS (capitalization, organization, punctuation, spelling) as a procedure for editing and revision (e.g., Goldman et al., 2024) by breaking the process part into individual steps, providing guided practice, and reinforcing why the skill or strategy being taught is useful for improving the clarity of students' writing.

Implications and Future Directions

We began this chapter by discussing why writing is crucial in grades 3–8, challenges for students with LD, and theoretical frameworks germane to teaching writing. Next, we synthesized research that has been associated with improving the writing outcomes of students with LD. Our purpose is to provide knowledge for researchers, educators, educational leaders, and other key stakeholders to shape and improve writing instruction. Thus, the final section of the chapter is devoted to implications and future directions as we delineate future research priorities. The chapter concludes with a discussion of implications of the current research for teacher preparation policy and professional development to enhance classroom instruction.

Future Research to Support Writers with LD

One key line of research is to continue implementing exploratory studies to describe "typical practice" in writing. The two exploration studies discussed in the first section of this chapter investigated (1) associations between the instruction of special and general educators with the writing outcomes of grade 4 students with LD and (2) content and disciplinary writing instruction in inclusive middle school classrooms and relationships with students' writing outcomes. First, these studies should be replicated to provide a continuing account of classroom writing instruction, as well as the beliefs and perceptions of teachers to inform new research and reforms to practice.

Second, researchers should evaluate the efficacy of writing interventions within science and social studies. Moreover, we recommend studying the effects of knowledge rich English language arts curricula, which prioritize domain-specific knowledge for enhancing writing, as well as content learning outcomes for students with LD. These studies can include professional development for co-teachers (special educators and general educators working together) to strengthen teachers' capacity to deliver effective interventions and HLPs within content-area writing instruction.

Third, we anticipate an expansion of research studying how artificial intelligence (AI) can improve equity, access, and writing outcomes for students with LD. Research on automated essay scoring and feedback (e.g., Wilson et al., 2021) has already shown promise, while other innovative technology-based writing research is underway by researchers in the United States, including Dr. Adrea Truckenmiller. Thus, there are exciting opportunities for researchers to explore innovative uses of AI to improve students' written expression in and outside of the classroom.

Finally, there is a need for data-based instructional (DBI) interventions for co-teachers teaching writing in grades 3–8. There is a rationale for this line of research because the exploration research described in the first section of this chapter underscores that most educators do not perceive themselves as highly prepared to teach writing to students with LD. Useful interventions for teachers may include training and coaching in using writing assessment data to make DBI decisions for the implementation of evidence-based practices. These interventions may include ongoing instructional coaching based on observational data and student data sources to refine teachers' instruction, increase teacher self-efficacy, and improve the writing performance of students.

Implications for Teacher Preparation Leadership and Classroom Instruction

All teachers would benefit from additional teacher preparation coursework that focuses on writing intervention. Recent reforms to teacher preparation and state policy initiatives in response to a national science of reading movement demonstrates that advocacy efforts from parents, researchers, and other key stakeholders can produce systemic policy changes for teacher preparation (Neuman et al., 2023). Reform that is germane to teaching writing may include required coursework for special educators, as well as general education teachers focused on writing, and increased funding for research, professional development, and teacher preparation related to teaching writing. A deliberate effort by education policymakers, state education agencies, and institutions of higher education can shift how writing is taught.

Finally, school districts and educational assistance centers can begin offering professional development opportunities for all teachers in the use of HLPs within writing as well as evidence-based practices that are readily available but underutilized (Gilbert & Graham, 2010). Professional development in evidence-based interventions, including SRSD, can occur using a practice-based professional development model in which strategies are modeled by instructional coaches, followed by immediate teacher practice and constructive feedback (Harris et al., 2023). In closing, we can implement the evidence-based practices that currently exist to increase access to educational opportunities with improved written communication skills for students with LD.

REFERENCES

Ahmed, Y., Kent, S., Cirino, P. T., & Keller-Margulis, M. (2021). The not-so-simple view of writing in struggling readers/writers. *Reading and Writing Quarterly, 38*(3), 272–296.

Baker, S. K., Chard, D. J., Ketterlin-Geller, L. R., Apichatabutra, C., & Doabler, C. (2009). Teaching writing to at-risk students: The quality of evidence for self-regulated strategy development. *Exceptional Children, 75*(3), 303–318.

Bandura, A. (1991). Social cognitive theory of self-regulation. *Organizational Behavior and Human Decision Processes, 50*(2), 248–287.

Berninger, V. W., Abbott, R. D., Abbott, S. P., Graham, S., & Richards, T. (2002). Writing and reading: Connections between language by hand and language by eye. *Journal of Learning Disabilities, 35*(1), 39–56.

Berninger, V. W., & Winn, W. D. (2006). Implications of advancements in brain research and technology for writing development, writing instruction, and educational evolution. In C. A. MacArthur, S. Graham, & J. Fitzgerald (Eds.), *Handbook of writing research* (pp. 96–114). Guilford Press.

Brindle, M., Graham, S., & Harris, K. R. (2016). Third and fourth grade teacher's classroom practices in writing: A national survey. *Reading and Writing, 29*(5), 929–954.

Ciullo, S., Collins, A. A., & Graham, S. (2018–2023). *Exploring writing instruction delivered by educators providing services to students with disabilities* (Grant R324A180137). Institute of Education Sciences.

Ciullo, S., Mason, L. H., & Judd, L. (2021). Persuasive quick-writing about text: Intervention for students with learning disabilities. *Behavior Modification, 45*(1), 122–146.

Collins, A. A., Ciullo, S., & Graham, S. (2020–2023). *Comprehensive meta-analysis of writing interventions for students in grades K to 5* (Grant No. R305A200363). Institute of Education Sciences.

Collins, A. A., Ciullo, S., Graham, S., & Harris, K. (Co-Principal Investigator). (2022–2026). *Turning the TIDE: Building teacher capacity to accelerate text-based writing performance of students with and at-risk for disabilities* (Grant No. R324X220101). Institute of Education Sciences.

Collins, A. A., Ciullo, S., Graham, S., Sigafoos, L. L., Guerra, S., David, M., & Judd, L. (2021). Writing expository essays from social studies texts: A self-regulated strategy development study. *Reading and Writing, 34*, 1623–1651.

Ennis, R. P., & Jolivette, K. (2014). Existing research and future directions for self-regulated strategy development with students with emotional and behavioral disorders. *Journal of Special Education, 48*(1), 32–45.

Garwood, J. D., Werts, M. G., Mason, L. H., Harris, B., Austin, M. B., Ciullo, S., . . . Shin, M. (2019). Improving persuasive science writing for secondary students with emotional and behavioral disorders. *Behavioral Disorders, 44*(4), 227–240.

Gilbert, J., & Graham, S. (2010). Teaching writing to students in Grades 4–6: A national survey. *Elementary School Journal, 110*(4), 494–518.

Gillespie, A., & Graham, S. (2014). A meta-analysis of writing interventions for students with learning disabilities. *Exceptional Children, 80*(4), 454–473.

Goldman, S. R., Carreon, A., & Smith, S. J. (2023). Aligning an editing and revising writing strategy to technology supports for students with learning disabilities. *Journal of Special Education Technology, 39*(4), 567–575.

Graham, S. (2018). A revised writer(s)-within-community model of writing. *Educational Psychologist, 53*(4), 258–279.

Graham, S. (2023). Writer(s)-within-community model of writing as a lens for studying the teaching of writing. In R. Horowitz (Ed.), *The Routledge international handbook of research on writing* (2nd ed., pp. 337–350). Routledge.

Graham, S., Ciullo, S., & Collins, A. (2024). Do special and general education teachers' mindset theories about the malleability of writing predict their writing practices? *Journal of Learning Disabilities, 57*(2), 63–78.

Graham, S., Collins, A. A., & Ciullo, S. (2023). Special and general education teachers' beliefs about writing and writing instruction. *Journal of Learning Disabilities, 56*(3), 163–179.

Graham, S., Collins, A. A., & Ciullo, S. (2024). Evidence-based recommendations for teaching writing. *Education 3-13, 52,* 979–992.

Graham, S., Collins, A. A., & Rigby-Wills, H. (2017). Writing characteristics of students with learning disabilities and typically achieving peers: A meta-analysis. *Exceptional Children, 83*(2), 199–218.

Graham, S., Kiuhara, S. A., & MacKay, M. (2020). The effects of writing on learning in science, social studies, and mathematics: A meta-analysis. *Review of Educational Research, 90*(2), 179–226.

Graham, S., McKeown, D., Kiuhara, S., & Harris, K. R. (2012). A meta-analysis of writing instruction for students in the elementary grades. *Journal of Educational Psychology, 104*(4), 879–896.

Graham, S., Yucheng, C., Kim, Y. G., Lee, J., Tate, T., Collins, P., . . . Olson, C. B. (2024). Effective writing instruction for students in grades 6 to 12: A best evidence meta-analysis. *Reading and Writing.*

Harris, K. R., Camping, A., & McKeown, D. (2023). A review of research on professional development for multicomponent strategy-focused writing instruction: Knowledge gained and challenges remaining. In F. DeSmedt, R. Bouwer, T. Limpo, & S. Graham (Eds.), *Conceptualizing, designing, implementing, and evaluating writing interventions* (pp. 101–136). Brill.

Harris, K. R., & Graham, S. (1999). Programmatic intervention research: Illustrations from the evolution of self-regulated strategy development. *Learning Disability Quarterly, 22*(4), 251–262.

Harris, K. R., Lane, K. L., Graham, S., Driscoll, S. A., Sandmel, K., Brindle, M., & Schatschneider, C. (2012). Practice-based professional development for self-regulated strategies development in writing: A randomized controlled study. *Journal of Teacher Education, 63*(2), 103–119.

Harris, K. R., Ray, A., Graham, S., & Houston, J. (2019). Answering the challenge: SRSD instruction for close reading of text to write to persuade with 4th and 5th grade students experiencing writing difficulties. *Reading and Writing, 32*(6), 1459–1482.

Hughes, C. A., Morris, J. R., Therrien, W. J., & Benson, S. K. (2017). Explicit instruction: Historical and contemporary contexts. *Learning Disabilities Research and Practice, 32*(3), 140–148.

Kim, Y. S. G. (2022). Co-occurrence of reading and writing difficulties: The application of the interactive dynamic literacy model. *Journal of Learning Disabilities, 55*(6), 447–464.

Mason, L. H., & Basile, J. (2023). Building writing skills for summaries and quick writes. In X. Liu, M. Herbert, & R. A. Alves (Eds.), *The hitchhiker's guide to writing research: A festschrift for Steve Graham* (pp. 169–189). Springer International.

Mason, L. H., Berkeley, S., Ciullo, S., Collins, A. A., & Miller, A. (Co-Principal Investigator). (2019–2023). *Writing in middle school science and social studies: Exploring instruction and support for students with disabilities (Project Explore)* (Grant No. R324A190028). Institute of Education Sciences.

Mason, L. H., Ciullo, S., Collins, A. A., Brady, S., Elcock, L., & Owen, L. S. (2022). Exploring inclusive middle-school content teachers' training, perceptions, and classroom practice for writing. *Learning Disabilities: A Contemporary Journal, 20*(2), 111–128.

McLeskey, J., Barringer, M.-D., Billingsley, B., Brownell, M., Jackson, D., Kennedy, M., . . . Ziegler, D. (2017, January). *High-leverage practices in special education.* Council for Exceptional Children & CEEDAR Center.

National Center for Education Statistics. (2015). *NAEP data explorer*. Institute of Education Sciences.

National Governors Association Center for Best Practices & Council of Chief State School Officers. (2010). *Common Core State Standards for English language arts and literacy in history/social studies, science, and technical subjects*. Authors.

Neuman, S. B., Quintero, E., & Reist, K. (2023). *Reading reform across America: A survey of state legislation*. Albert Shanker Institute.

Olinghouse, N. G., Santangelo, T., & Wilson, J. (2012). Examining the validity of single-occasion, single-genre, holistically scored writing assessments. In E. Van Steendam, G. Rijlaarsdam, H. van den Bergh, & M. Tillema (Eds.), *Measuring writing: Recent insights into theory, methodology and practice* (pp. 55–82). Brill.

Saddler, B., Ellis-Robinson, T., & Asaro-Saddler, K. (2018). Using sentence combining instruction to enhance the writing skills of children with learning disabilities. *Learning Disabilities: A Contemporary Journal, 16*(2), 191–202.

Shanahan, T., & Shanahan, C. (2008). Teaching disciplinary literacy to adolescents: Rethinking content-area literacy. *Harvard Educational Review, 78*(1), 40–59.

Therrien, W. J., Cook, B. G., & Cook, L. (2020). Utilizing meta–analyses to guide practice: A primer. *Learning Disabilities Research and Practice, 35*(3), 111–117.

Troia, G. A., Graham, S., & Harris, K. R. (2017). Writing and students with language and learning disabilities. In J. M. Kauffman, D. P. Hallahan, & P. C. Pullen (Eds.), *Handbook of special education* (2nd ed., pp. 537–557). Routledge.

U.S. Department of Education, Institute of Education Sciences, National Center for Education Statistics, National Assessment of Educational Progress. (2011). *Writing assessment*. Authors.

Wilson, J., Huang, Y., Palermo, C., Beard, G., & MacArthur, C. A. (2021). Automated feedback and automated scoring in the elementary grades: Usage, attitudes, and associations with writing outcomes in a districtwide implementation of MI Write. *International Journal of Artificial Intelligence in Education, 31*(2), 234–276.

Zimmerman, B. J. (2002). Becoming a self-regulated learner: An overview. *Theory Into Practice, 41*(2), 64–70.

Zimmerman, B. J., & Risemberg, R. (1997). Becoming a self-regulated writer: A social cognitive perspective. *Contemporary Educational Psychology, 22*(1), 73–101.

CHAPTER 18

A Cognitive Strategies Approach to Teaching Text-Based Argument Writing to English Learners

Carol Booth Olson
Undraa Maamuujav
Huy Chung

Engaging students in text-based argument writing plays a pivotal role in developing their understanding of text, critical inquiry, reasoning, and analytical thinking, which are essential literacy skills for school success and civic participation. The Common Core State Standards (CCSS) for English Language Arts and Literacy in History/Social Studies, Science, and Technical Subjects describes argument literacy as "essential to both private deliberation and responsible citizenship in a democratic republic" (National Governors Association Center for Best Practices & Council of Chief State School Officers [NGA & CCSSO], 2010, p. 3). The significance of argument writing is also emphasized by Graham and Perin (2007), who assert that learning to write effective arguments is "not just an option for young people—it is a necessity," as it is "a predictor of academic success and a basic requirement for participation in civic life and in the global economy" (p. 3).

Given the curricular and instructional mandates for argument literacy development, U.S. secondary schools have placed a considerable emphasis on youths' argument writing, stressing the need for students to begin to develop proficiency in it from the elementary grades. Emphasizing the essential role of argument writing in school contexts, the CCSS explain:

> An argument is a reasoned, logical way of demonstrating that the writer's position, belief, or conclusion is valid. English Language Arts students make claims about the worth or meaning of a literary work or works. They defend their interpretations or judgments with evidence from the text(s) they are writing about. In history/social studies, students analyze evidence from multiple primary and

secondary sources to advance a claim that is best supported by the evidence, and they argue for a historically or empirically situated interpretation. In science, students make claims in the form of statements or conclusions that answer questions or address problems. (NGA & CCSSO, 2010, Appendix A, p. 23)

As stated in the CCSS (NGA & CCSSO, 2010), English language arts/literacy K–5, students as early as in grade 3 are expected to determine the main ideas, central message, theme, lesson, and/or moral of literary and informational texts and explain how these elements are conveyed, developed, and supported through key details. From grades 3–5, students are expected to "write opinion pieces on topics or texts, supporting a point of view with reasons" (NGA & CCSSO, 2010, p. 22). In grade 6, students progress to writing "arguments to support claims with clear reasons and relevant evidence" and in grades 7–8, students also must address and refute alternate or opposing claims.

While the expectations are high, the results of the National Assessment of Educational Progress (NAEP) present a bleak picture of students' writing performance. Although the writing assessment was not administered at grade 4 in 2011, only about one-fourth of students in eighth grade performed at or above the level of proficient in writing (U.S. Department of Education, National Center for Education Statistics, 2012). The NAEP reports (2012, 2019) suggest that the majority of the students, especially English learners (ELs), are challenged to meet the expectations set forth by rigorous national and state standards. Consistent with these reports, research shows that most students find argument writing challenging and have difficulty writing a clear, arguable claim and consistent supporting evidence (Perie et al., 2005; Salahu-Din et al., 2008). Several researchers (Biancarosa & Snow, 2004; Graham & Perin, 2007; Langer, 2002) have also noted the difficulties learners have in mastering the advanced reading skills necessary for analytical thinking and argument writing. Other researchers report that students are challenged by (1) developing reasoning that explains why or how their evidence supports their claims, (2) adapting writing to various purposes and audiences, and (3) acknowledging and refuting potential criticisms of their positions (Kuhn, 1991, 2005; Persky et al., 2003).

To meet the demands of text-based argument writing, students in the upper elementary and secondary levels are required to develop several advanced skills. They must closely read, analyze, and interpret complex texts of various genres, formulate an arguable claim, and support their claim with textual evidence and sound reasoning. These higher-order tasks are undoubtedly demanding for students in elementary grades and middle school. Furthermore, argument writing requires students to move beyond what Scardamalia and Bereiter (1987) referred to as "knowledge telling," a skill that relies primarily on retelling and summarizing. Instead, students need to reach an advanced level of "knowledge transformation." Transforming knowledge requires complex rhetorical problem solving as students analyze texts and extract evidence to construct their own arguments and interpretations. Writing at the level of knowledge transformation also requires language resources through which analytical thinking and reasoning are externalized. As summary and narrative writing are prioritized in elementary grades (Coffin,

2006), students develop linguistic repertoires to narrate, record, and retell stories, either real or imaginative. Students who have not developed language resources for construction of arguments and expression of reasoning tend to summarize or recount information as these language resources are readily accessible. Thus, to transition to knowledge transformation, students need language resources for argumentation.

The challenge of developing proficiency in argument writing is even greater for ELs. Meeting the rigorous grade-level standards can be especially demanding for these students. Even ELs with moderate to strong levels of English proficiency face particular challenges when learning argument writing. For many of these students, the conventions of argument writing and language resources needed may be obscure. As Bunch (2013) explains, the argument is "grounded in particular socially and culturally developed values and practices that may or may not align with those of students from different backgrounds" (p. 304). As a result, ELs may not recognize relevant information required to support their perspective, acknowledge or rebut viewpoints inconsistent with their own, or consider the merits of other views. Furthermore, many ELs face an additional cognitive load when writing in English as they are in process of learning the language features and rhetorical styles of English that have yet to be internalized (Fitzgerald, 2017; Scarcella, 2003). These factors may explain why only 1% of ELs in grade 8 scored proficient or above on the 2011 NAEP.

Given that ELs are the fastest-growing segment of the K–12 student population (Francis et al., 2006), the disparities in argument writing proficiency are especially worrisome. In a recent study, Steiss and colleagues (2022) found that ELs, compared to their English-fluent peers, had significantly lower performance in using evidence, developing and structuring their ideas, and using language to convey their ideas in their argument writing. ELs' exposure to and experience of literacy development is variable across the nation, with some who are "stuck" in designated English-language development programs while others are in mainstream classes (Olsen, 2010). A common thread, however, is that these students are not provided with adequate support or ample opportunities to develop argument literacy skills. They often receive instruction that places a premium on the "transmission of information, providing very little room for the exploration of ideas, which is necessary for the development of deeper understanding" (Applebee et al., 2003, p. 689). Without an effective instructional approach that attends to developing proficiency in argument writing, the gaps and disparity in ELs' argument writing will likely persist.

Why Take a Cognitive Strategies Approach to Text-Based Argument Writing?

Numerous reports from policy centers and blue-ribbon panels "implicate poor understandings of cognitive strategies as the primary reason why adolescents struggle with reading and writing" (Conley, 2008, p. 84; see also Graham, 2006; Snow & Biancarosa, 2003). Cognitive strategies are acts of mind, or thinking tools, such as planning and goal setting, tapping prior knowledge, making connections, monitoring, forming interpretations, reflecting and relating, evaluating, and so forth, that experienced readers and writers use to construct meaning from and with texts (Olson, 2012). Countless studies demonstrate the efficacy of cognitive strategy use in reading (Block & Pressley, 2002; National Institute of Child Health and Human Development, 2000; Paris et al., 1991; Pearson & Duke, 2002; Tierney & Pearson, 1983; Tierney & Shanahan, 1991). Similarly, Graham and Perin (2007) indicate that strategy instruction is the most effective of 11 key elements of writing instruction ($d = 0.82$) for all students and particularly for students who find writing challenging. Furthermore, in a recent meta-analysis, Graham and colleagues (2023) found that strategy instruction is the most common writing treatment tested in intervention research and it has one of the highest positive effects on overall writing quality. This is why in the What Works Clearinghouse Practice Guide *Teaching Secondary Students to Write Effectively* (Graham et al., 2016), an expert panel's number-one recommendation, with the highest level of statistical evidence, was "Explicitly teach appropriate writing strategies using a Model–Practice–Reflect instructional cycle" (p. 2). They concluded that "teaching students cognitive strategies is one way to develop their strategic thinking skills, ultimately helping them to write more effectively" (p. 7).

The preponderance of compelling research on the efficacy of cognitive strategy instruction at the secondary level may create the impression that this type of approach, which focuses on moving beyond decoding or encoding to interpreting, reflecting on, and creating and evaluating texts at a deeper level, might not be relevant in the elementary grades. However, nothing could be further from the truth. There is broad agreement among literacy scholars that along with decoding skills, students should be taught cognitive and metacognitive strategies in the early grades in order to become effective comprehenders and communicators. In fact, Block and colleagues (2002) pointed out that if students have not been taught "to wield comprehension processes enjoyably and profitably" by the third grade, "they will have fallen so far below their peers that they will never again regain lost ground, even if they have decoding skills that are on grade level" (p. 43). Traditionally, decoding was viewed as a primary-grade skill, with the development of comprehension through cognitive strategy use targeted for grades 3 and above. However, researchers have challenged this notion. For example, Pearson and Duke (2002) note that although there is a "widespread belief that it is not possible, or at least not wise, to teach comprehension to young children who are still learning to decode text," they advise that teaching strategy use to students in the primary grades "is not only possible but wise and beneficial" (p. 247). They make the case that comprehension and decoding can and should "exist side by side" in an exemplary and comprehensive literacy program (p. 251). Because of what Pearson calls the "synergistic relationship" of reading and writing, these two literacy skills should also be taught side by side from kindergarten on (National Writing Project & Nagin, 2003, pp. 29–30).

Although Graham and Perin (2007) note the dearth of experimental studies conducted with low-achieving writers from low-income families in inner-city settings, and especially with low English language proficiency, there is also evidence of the positive impact of cognitive strategy instruction on the literacy of ELs. Short and Fitzsimmons (2007) hypothesize that strategy instruction is especially effective for ELs with an intermediate level of English proficiency because it provides them with an explicit focus on language, increases their exposure to academic texts, makes the texts they read comprehensible, gives them multiple opportunities to affirm or correct their understanding and use of language, assists them in retrieving new language features and in using these features for academic purposes, and provides them with the means of learning language on their own, outside of class. In short, explicitly teaching strategic reading and writing behaviors to ELs can help them engage with complex texts and convey those interpretations in well-reasoned essays to meet the CCSS-ELA and other state-adopted standards (August & Shanahan, 2006; Bunch et al., 2012), enabling them to write compositions judged to be higher in quality and displaying more depth of interpretation, greater clarity of thesis, and better idea organization (Fitzgerald, 2017; Olson et al., 2023).

What Is the Pathway Project?

The Pathway Project is a literacy intervention developed by the UCI Writing Project at the University of California, Irvine, that takes a cognitive strategies approach to teaching text-based argument writing. The project provides ongoing, sustained professional development to prepare English language arts and English language development teachers to explicitly teach, model, and scaffold guided instruction in the cognitive strategies (or thinking tools) that research indicates experienced readers and writers access when they construct meaning. The primary goal is to prepare all students, but especially students in high-needs schools and mainstreamed ELs, to become strategic readers able to analyze and interpret complex texts and analytical writers capable of developing well-reasoned argument essays supported with textual evidence.

Research from the Pathway Project is cited in the What Works Clearinghouse Practice Guide *Teaching Academic Content and Literacy to English Learners in Elementary and Middle School* (Baker et al., 2014). Additionally, four of the fifteen research studies showcased in the What Works Clearinghouse Practice Guide *Teaching Secondary Students to Write Effectively* (Graham et al., 2016) are Pathway Project studies. Although, all of the Pathway research has been conducted with students in grades 6 and above, teachers from grades K–5 have successfully implemented the Pathway cognitive strategies approach in their classrooms (see *Thinking Tools for Young Readers and Writers: Strategies to Promote Higher Literacy in Grades 2–8*; Olson et al., 2018).

Evidence-Based Cognitive Strategy Instruction That Works

The Pathway Project draws from both cognitive and sociocultural theory by focusing on cognitive strategy use as a vehicle for higher-level thinking, using an apprentice model in which the teacher serves as a senior member of a learning community, providing a wide array of procedural tools to enhance cognitive strategy use, and promoting collaboration among teachers, between teachers and students, and among students to foster a community of writers. It is also grounded in a number of evidence-based practices that research has found to be effective, including strategy instruction, planning and goal setting, prewriting activities, emulating models, procedural facilitation (graphic organizers), sentence instruction, formative feedback, and revision instruction (Graham et al., 2023). In addition, it is a comprehensive writing program that takes a process approach to scaffolding activities before, during, and after reading and writing about texts (Graham et al., 2023). Provided below is a sample of pedagogical practices developed by the intervention that have been successfully implemented by both elementary and secondary teachers.

Cognitive Strategies Toolkit and Bookmarks

To conceptualize how readers and writers use cognitive strategies, or thinking tools, to construct meaning, the Pathway Project uses the model of a mental toolkit (see Figure 18.1). Teachers are given the following analogy to introduce the concept of the *cognitive strategies toolkit* to their students:

> "When we read, we have thinking-tools or cognitive strategies inside our heads that we access to construct meaning. When you think of yourself as a reader or writer, think of yourself as a craftsman, but instead of reaching into a metal tool kit for a hammer or a screwdriver to construct or build tangible or real objects you can actually touch, you're reaching into your mental tool kit to construct meaning from or with words."

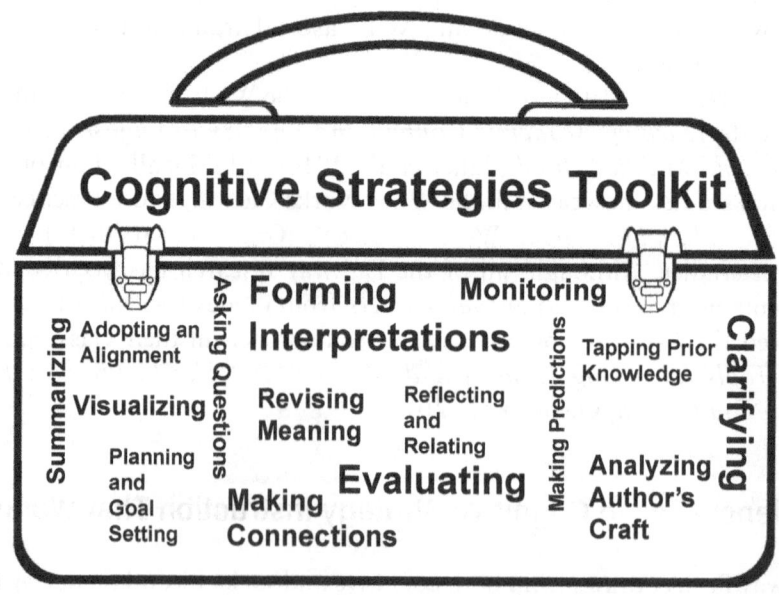

FIGURE 18.1. Cognitive strategies toolkit.

To make the concept of the toolkit more accessible to students, teachers give students laminated *cognitive strategies bookmarks* that they can use to annotate the texts they are reading. (see Figure 18.2). These bookmarks include sentence starters for each of the cognitive strategies that illustrate what goes on in the mind of a reader or writer in the act of meaning construction. For example, a sentence starter for revising meaning is "At first I thought but now I . . ." and a starter for reflecting and relating is "So, the big idea is. . . ."

In Emily McCourtney's second- and third-grade classroom, she created her own tangible readers' and writers' toolkit filled with objects to symbolize the cognitive strategies: puzzle pieces for making connections, a Slinky for summarizing, a crystal ball for making predictions, and so forth. Since Emily teaches in a blended learning school, she flipped her lesson by creating videos for students to watch at home to introduce each of the cognitive strategies. When they returned to her classroom, she gave them a quiz on the learning-game platform Kahoot! to review and assess their understanding of the cognitive strategies. To help her students annotate texts, she provided them with both paper and digital sticky notes with labels for each cognitive strategy that they could affix to the texts they were reading and make predictions, form interpretations, describe what they were visualizing, and so forth. Students then used these annotations to write up longer Lit Letters (Atwell, 1987) in response to texts to share with classmates in Book Clubs. Emily also engaged her students in metacognition by having them respond to a series of questions regarding what they were thinking as they annotated their text. Here are two responses from Jackson about the last book in Dustin Brady's *Trapped in a Videogame* series:

- *What did you notice? What made you stop and think?*
- "I noticed in the text that Jesse, Mark, and Sam are on a hovercraft as their escape vehicle to get away from a robot dragon. It made me wonder how they are going to use the hovercraft to escape."
- *What strategy did you use? What did it make you think?*
- "I used the strategy make a prediction. It made me think that they would be able to use the hovercraft to escape because it was rocket powered. I predicted that they would be able to get away from the robot dragon because the hovercraft is super fast."

DO/WHAT Chart

One of the first things the Pathway research team noticed when we analyzed students' writing, particularly in on-demand writing situations, was that their argument essays comprised retelling almost exclusively, often in one long, continuous paragraph, without a clear introduction, main body, and conclusion, which frequently failed to address what they were asked to do in the prompt. This was especially true for younger, inexperienced writers and for ELs. Graham and Perin (2007) note that "teaching adolescents strategies for planning, revising, and editing their compositions has shown a dramatic effect on the quality of students' writing" (p. 15). In our Pathway professional development, teachers were taught

Cognitive Strategies Sentence Starters

Planning and Goal Setting
- My purpose is...
- My top priority is ...
- I will accomplish my goal by...

Tapping Prior Knowledge
- I already know that...
- This reminds me of...
- This relates to...

Asking Questions
- I wonder why...
- What if...
- How come...

Making Predictions
- I'll bet that...
- I think...
- If _____, then...

Visualizing
- I can picture...
- In my mind I see...
- If this were a movie...

Making Connections
- This reminds me of...
- I experienced this once when...
- I can relate to this because...

Summarizing
- The basic gist is...
- The key information is...
- In a nutshell, this says that..

Adopting an Alignment
- The character I most identify with is...
- I really got into the story when...
- I can relate to this author because...

Cognitive Strategies Sentence Starters

Forming Interpretations
- What this means to me is...
- I think this represents...
- The idea I'm getting is...

Monitoring
- I got lost here because...
- I need to reread the part where...
- I know I'm on the right track because ...

Clarifying
- To understand better, I need to know more about...
- Something that is still not clear is...
- I'm guessing that this means _____, but I need to...

Revising Meaning
- At first I thought _____, but now I.....
- My latest thought about this is...
- I'm getting a different picture here because...

Analyzing the Author's Craft
- A golden line for me is...
- This word/phrase stands out for me because...
- I like how the author uses _____ to show...

Reflecting and Relating
- So, the big idea is...
- A conclusion I'm drawing is...
- This is relevant to my life because...

Evaluating
- I like/don't like _____ because...
- My opinion is _____ because...
- The most important message is _____ because...

FIGURE 18.2. Cognitive strategies bookmarks.

a planning and goal-setting strategy called the *DO/WHAT Chart* to help their students deconstruct the prompt.

In a classroom, to create a DO/WHAT Chart, students use green and blue highlighters and manually mark all of the verbs in the prompt that instruct a student to DO something in green and underline the task words that tell the student WHAT to do in blue (e.g., write [green] an essay [blue], and make [green] a claim [blue] about the main point, lesson, or message of the text). They then transfer those words onto a T chart below the prompt. Figure 18.3 illustrates a prompt and DO/WHAT Chart developed by Mary Widtmann for her fifth-grade classroom on analyzing theme. As mentioned previously, students are expected to determine the theme or central message of a text beginning at grade 3. Yet research indicates that, even at the high school level, theme is one of the most difficult of the story elements for students to grasp (Gurney et al., 1990). (Note that brackets represent the green DO verbs and underlining represents the blue WHAT task words in the prompt below.)

This strategy helps students attend to all of the requirements of the prompt, to create a road map for composing, and to introduce a claim or theme statement in the introduction to the essay rather than simply retelling what happened in the story. At grade 5, students cannot be expected to create a DO/WHAT Chart without support from the teacher. Mary broke each section of the prompt into manageable chunks and engaged her students in a whole-class activity of highlighting and making their T charts. She also provided a mini-lesson on the meaning of verbs such as *describe* versus *analyze*.

Argument Graphic Organizer

Using graphic organizers as a prewriting activity to brainstorm and to generate and organize ideas has been found to have a positive effect on writing outcomes (Graham et al., 2023). In our research, we found that many students were not familiar with the structure of an argument essay, and that when writing arguments of opinion, had an especially difficult time with where and how to address and refute a counterargument. The argument essay graphic organizer in Figure 18.4 can be used to plan, set goals, and create a structure for composing an argument essay. This organizer must be accompanied by guided support from the teacher. In fact, we recommend that the teacher conduct mini-lessons on each section of the graphic organizer, and that students write their essays in segments.

Using Sentence Stems to Acknowledge and Refute Counterarguments

George Hillocks (2011) points out, "Argument is not simply a dispute, as when people disagree with one another or yell at each other. Argument is about making a case in support of a claim in everyday affairs—in science, in policy making, in courtrooms, and so forth" (p. 1). Students often are uncertain about what type of tone and academic language is necessary to address and refute a counterargument

Writing Prompt: "They Don't Mean It!"
Background: We learned about cultural identity and thought deeply about how cultures mold someone's personal identity. In the text "They Don't Mean It!", the narrator of the story, Mary, a Chinese immigrant, and her best friend Kim, an American, learn about their different cultures. Although they have misunderstandings, the girls and their families learn to understand and appreciate each other's differences.
Writing Prompt: After reading "They Don't Mean It!", **select one important theme to write an essay about.** Create a specifically worded theme statement that expresses the author's main point, message, or lesson in the story. Your theme statement will be the thesis of your essay—the claim you make about the author's message or main idea. In your introduction: • Write a hook sentence to draw your reader into your essay. • Introduce text with a TAG (title, author, genre). • Briefly summarize the "conflict or problem" that Mary and Kim have as they are trying to understand each other's cultures. • Present the lesson that they learn about their cultures as your theme statement. In the body paragraphs use evidence from the text to explain: • Describe the relationship between the narrator, Mary, and her best friend, Kim, at the beginning of the story. What were their cultural similarities and differences? • Discuss why misunderstandings cause the relationship to change. • Analyze what lesson Mary and Kim learned as a result of their interaction. • Use quotes from the text to show how they are changing as they learn more about each other's cultures. In your conclusion: • Remind your reader of the author's message (your theme statement) and discuss how it related to the title of the story. • Explain how readers can use what Mary and Kim learn to improve their own lives. Best papers will: • Include strong evidence-based reasoning. • Use transitions to connect and move between events and ideas. • Use correct grammar, punctuation, and spelling.

DO	WHAT
Select	one important theme
Write	an essay
Create	a theme statement
Create	a hook
Summarize	the conflict
Present	the lesson
Describe	the relationship
Discuss	misunderstandings
Explain	how Mary and Kim learned to respect each other
Analyze	the lesson learned
Use	quotes
Remind	reader of author's message
Explain	how readers can use message

FIGURE 18.3. Prompt for "They Don't Mean It!"

Introduction
The background I provide about the text is:
The claim I want to make in response to the prompt is:

Main Body: Examples to support claim		
Main points/examples to support claim	Evidence (quote/paraphrase)	Commentary/Reasoning (How does this evidence support your claim?)

Main Body: Address counterargument		
A different claim in response to the prompt	Evidence and reasoning for opposing claim	Additional evidence and reasoning to refute the opposing claim

Conclusion
The main points of my argument are:
What we can learn from this text is:

FIGURE 18.4. Graphic organizer for argument writing essays.

diplomatically and with logical reasons. After developing their own claim, students can use the sentence stems in Figure 18.5 to acknowledge and refute a counterclaim to their position.

To scaffold this step in the writing process, it is helpful to pair up two students, each with a different claim, and have them practice respectfully acknowledging and then refuting each other's claims. This oral rehearsal is helpful for all students, but especially for younger students and ELs, as talk is an important precursor to writing. Additionally, it provides practice in the cognitive strategy of adopting an alignment or perspective taking. Research indicates that younger students are challenged by anticipating potential challenges to their own position (Kuhn, 1991).

Acknowledging and Refuting a Counterargument

Some people may argue that _____ [counterclaim]. However, _____ [reason to refute counterclaim].

Despite the argument that _____ [counterclaim], this evidence is not as convincing as _____ because _____ [reason to refute counterclaim].

Although _____ [counterclaim] is significant, the most compelling reason for _____ is _____ because _____ [reason to refute counterclaim].

Admittedly, _____ [counterclaim] was one reason that _____ is _____. Nevertheless, _____ is a more convincing reason because _____ [reason to refute counterclaim].

FIGURE 18.5. Counterargument sentence frames.

Color Coding for Revision

Another very common shortcoming in students' argument essays is the failure to provide evidence and commentary along with purposeful summary. As mentioned previously, inexperienced writers and ELs often use a simplified version of the idea-generation process called *knowledge telling*, which is retrieving information from long-term memory and converting the writing task into simply regurgitating what is known about a topic. More experienced writers, on the other hand, engage in a complex composing process known as *knowledge transformation*, in which they analyze the writing task and plan what to say and how to say it in accordance with rhetorical, communicative, and pragmatic constraints. One way to help students make their thinking visible is to use a visualizing strategy called *color coding* after they have composed an initial first draft of an essay. Teachers first designate four colors for the types of assertions that comprise a text-based argument essay (yellow for plot summary, green for evidence, blue for reasoning or commentary, and pink for counterargument) and say the following:

> "Summary is yellow because it's what is known and obvious. Like the sun, it's as plain as day. It is the background one shares to provide context for understanding the event or issue and the retelling of what happened. Reasoning is blue because it goes beneath the surface of things; it is deep, like the ocean. It includes your analysis, interpretation, insights, opinions, conclusions, etc. It is the 'So what?' of your paper. Evidence is green because it glues together your summary and your reasoning. It is your details supporting your claim, your

examples from the text, and your quotes and paraphrases. We will use pink for counterargument because it is not a primary color but a secondary color. It's not the main point of the essay which is to promote your argument. Pink is lighter than red because we are not engaging in an angry form of argument but, rather, considering and refuting another perspective. Not all argument essays need to address and refute a counterargument. But considering and rebutting an alternate point of view can add power to your claim." (See Figure 18.6.)

Noting that students whose text production corresponds to knowledge telling, Scardamalia and Bereiter (1987) suggest that they "need more than encouragement to revise" (p. 156) and should experience lessons in which the teacher models what is expected. To that end, students can be asked to read two sample argument essays written to a prompt, decide which one is more effective and which is less effective, and make a list of the attributes of each. Next, the teacher can guide them in color coding these essays, then setting them side by side to analyze the differences. They will notice that the less effective essay may consist primarily of yellow, include little green and blue, and may fail to include any pink, whereas the more effective paper will contain a balance of yellow, green, blue, and pink. After this practice step, students can work in pairs to color-code their own first drafts and then make a plan for revision.

Figure 18.7 includes a sample essay revised by a sixth grader in Angie Balius's classroom. Angie taught her students the text *The Hero and the Minotaur* by Robert Byrd (2005), which chronicles the many challenges Theseus faces as he journeys to Knossos to slay the minotaur and save the people of Athens. The prompt asks students to define what a hero is, describe what Theseus is attempting to prove, present a claim as to whether he is or is not a hero, provide at least three examples to support their claim, acknowledge and refute one counterclaim to their argument, and close with a lesson they learned from Theseus's journey.

As students repeatedly practice these pedagogical strategies, they are developing declarative, procedural, and conditional knowledge of cognitive strategy use (Paris et al., 1983) and becoming increasingly confident and competent readers and writers.

Summary	Evidence	Reasoning	Counterargument
Yellow	Green	Blue	Pink
Background to event/ issue; retelling what happened	Examples and details that support a claim; quotes from texts and paraphrases	Deeper thinking, interpretations, commentary, analysis; conclusions, the "So what?" insights, opinions	Acknowledgment of counterargument; reasons addressing and refuting counterargument

FIGURE 18.6. Color coding for revision.

> In the Greek myth "The Hero and the Minotaur" by Robert Byrd, we see that the main character Theseus shows that he is heroic by slaying the Minotaur and breaking the curse, being recognized for his great heroic deeds on the journey to the kingdom, and using his intelligence to not pick a fight with a god. And because of this, I believe that Theseus is in fact a hero. *Even if he caused some trouble,* **he still did what I think should be done to be portrayed as a hero.**
>
> One reason I think this is because he was able to do heroic deeds. <u>In the short story version of the myth by Robert Byrd, it is said that Aegeus asked, "Who performs these daring deeds? Let me meet the valiant champion."</u> [Aegeus decided to honor the stranger's bravery with a magnificent banquet in the Temple of Dolphins.] **What this means is that Theseus or, in this case, the stranger is being honored for his bravery when he takes a long path to the kingdom to meet his father, who is also known as Aegeus. Which just shows how much of a hero he is by getting recognized by the king himself.**
>
> Another reason why I think that Theseus is a hero is because he broke the curse by slaying the great minotaur inside of the labyrinth. <u>In the short story of the myth, it is said that "Theseus, angered by King Minos' cruelty replied, 'Let me go with those to be sacrificed. I will slay the Minotaur and end the curse that hangs over our city.'"</u> [Aegeus pleaded with him to stay in Athens, but Theseus remained steadfast and prepared for the voyage to Crete.] **What this shows is that Theseus is brave enough to venture through the labyrinth and slay the Minotaur whilst breaking the curse that hangs over the city. Showing that he is a hero by being brave.**
>
> *Some people might say that Theseus is disloyal, cowardly, and unheroic when he breaks his pledge to Ariadne and abandons her to Dionysus.* **But one last reason that I think Theseus is considered a hero is because he was smart enough to not pick a fight with a god.** <u>In the story, it is said that " Now Theseus had no choice but to leave, for he knew it would be foolish to challenge such a mighty god."</u> **This might not seem heroic but it can be in another way because instead of using his strength to fight a god he used his thinking to choose the smarter idea of leaving Ariadne for his own good.**
>
> In conclusion, while Theseus made some mistakes on the journey, he still proved himself to be a true hero with his strength, bravery, and smarts. This story also taught me a valuable lesson, that you can still succeed even with some mistakes along the way. You just have to keep on going.

FIGURE 18.7. Student essay on *The Hero and the Minotaur*. Bold typeface = blue; italics = pink; underline = green; brackets = yellow.

Research on the Efficacy of Pathway's Cognitive Strategies Approach

The Pathway Project began with an 8-year quasi-experimental longitudinal study in a large, urban district (98% Latinx, 84% receiving free and reduced-price lunch, 88% mainstreamed ELs) that yielded an average effect size of 0.34 for overall writing quality for students in grades 6–12 on a pre–post on-demand argument-writing assessment across the 8 years of implementation (Olson & Land, 2007). Middle school students (grades 6–8) received particular benefits from participating in the intervention because they had room to grow and had the highest needs. The project then received funding to conduct a cluster randomized controlled trial in the same district. Year 1 of that randomized controlled trial (Kim et al., 2011) yielded an effect size of 0.35. Year 2 of the randomized controlled trial for new, incoming students with teachers who received a second year of professional development yielded an effect size of 0.67 (Olson et al., 2012). In both years of the study, there were statistically significant effects on the writing subtest of the state Standards Test ($d = 0.10$).

The project received a grant to conduct a randomized controlled trial in a neighboring school district for students in grades 7–12 that yielded significant and positive results (Year 1, $d = 0.48$; Year 2, $d = 0.60$) (Olson et al., 2017). These results were attributed mainly to the growth seen in our seventh- and eighth-grade students (i.e., middle school students). When comparing middle school participants to high school participants, middle school students grew more than their high school peers across both years of the study, improving by nearly 2 points each year (e.g., Year 1 = 1.36; Year 2 = 1.96). Moreover, 10th-grade ELs in the treatment in Year 2 passed the state High School Exit Exam at 30 percentage points higher than ELs in the control and 20 percentage points higher than the state pass rate (treatment = 57.9%; state = 38%), indicating advantages for ELs as well.

This strong record positioned the project for a scale-up study that included four sites of the California Writing Project in the southern California region, all with large urban partner districts. Results were positive and significant for not only the holistic score ($d = 0.32$), but also all four of the analytic scores: content ($d = 0.31$), structure ($d = 0.29$), fluency ($d = 0.27$), and conventions ($d = 0.32$) (Olson et al., 2020). To date, five studies that were conducted to test the efficacy of Pathway have received approval from the What Works Clearinghouse of the Institute of Education Sciences, one without reservations (Kim et al., 2011) and four with reservations (Olson & Land, 2008; Olson et al., 2012, 2017, 2020).

In a more recent study using a subset of students from Olson and colleagues (2020), research team members qualitatively coded the pre- and posttest essays for 199 students using an analytical writing framework focused on 15 dimensions of argument essay writing. In this study, 32% of the students were designated as English only, 12% were designated as initially fluent English proficient, 25% were designated as redesignated fluent English proficient, and 28% were designated as ELs. When analyzing the essays of ELs in both the treatment and control condition at pretest, the research team found that students needed support across four main components of constructing argument essays: (1) presentation of ideas, (2) organization of literary arguments, (3) use of evidence and analysis, and (4) lexical and syntactic challenges. For example, the students tended to present unclear claims or failed to make claims, struggled with organizing ideas, and relied on retelling rather than including a balance of summary, evidence, and commentary. As a group, challenges in avoiding repetition and varying sentences were also present. However, analysis of the treatment students' posttest essays, after being exposed to Pathway strategies, revealed improvement across all four components, with particular growth seen in constructing introductions, presenting a clear claim, having distinct paragraphs, providing textual evidence, and diction (see Figure 18.8).

We attribute what resulted in significant gains in students' argument writing across the four components to particular aforementioned strategies from our previous section on evidence-based cognitive strategy instruction that works. For example, the fact that students were able to present better ideas in their writing

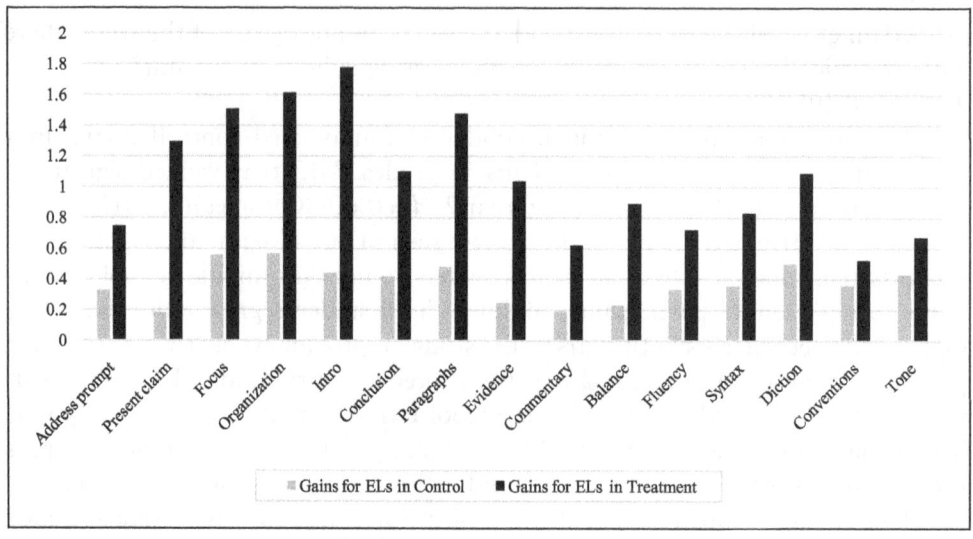

FIGURE 18.8. Mean score improvement for ELs (Olson et al., 2023).

and more nuanced claims can be attributed to the cognitive strategies toolkit and bookmarks, which help students to deepen their thinking and to move from literal comprehension to interpretation as readers (Conley, 2013; Langer, 2002; Tierney & Pearson, 1983). The DO/WHAT Chart was particularly useful in helping students improve on addressing the prompt and the organization of their essays. The argument graphic organizer can be linked to improved focus and use of evidence, and the color-coding strategy enhanced students' higher-level reasoning and commentary, helping to move them from knowledge telling to knowledge transformation. Finally, the use of sentence frames promoted syntactic and lexical growth in areas such as sentence fluency, diction, and tone, as the use of sentence frames are found to be effective in accelerating learners' development of the complex sentence structures in writing (Zwiers, 2008).

Conclusion

Given the demands of text-based argument writing and the few opportunities to practice, students from the early grades of their schooling need access to high-quality curricula and to receive explicit instruction and ongoing support to develop argumentation skills. Teachers can address the argument literacy needs of their diverse learners by adopting a comprehensive cognitive strategies approach that focuses on higher-level interpretive reading and text-based argument writing, alongside the development of language skills necessary to express their higher-level thinking effectively. Research on the efficacy of Pathway Project's teacher professional development demonstrates that all students, including ELs, benefit from rigorous instruction that prioritizes complex interpretive thinking and scaffolded instruction leading students to knowledge transformation. The robust effects of the Pathway intervention indicate the capacity for all students to grow as argument writers, regardless of language proficiency, if given the opportunity, time, and scaffolded strategy instruction.

REFERENCES

Applebee, A. N., Langer, J. A., Nystrand, M., & Gamoran, A. (2003). Discussion-based approaches to developing understanding: Classroom instruction and student performance in middle and high school English. *American Educational Research Journal, 40*(3), 685–730.

Atwell, N. (1987). *In the middle: Writing, reading, and learning with adolescents.* Heinemann.

August, D. E., & Shanahan, T. E. (2006). *Developing literacy in second language learners: Report of the National Literacy Panel on Language-Minority Children and Youth.* Erlbaum.

Baker, S., Lesaux, N., Jayanthi, M., Dimino, J., Proctor, C. P., Morris, J., . . . Newman-Gonchar, R. (2014). *Teaching academic content and literacy to English learners in elementary and middle school* (IES Practice Guide NCEE 2014-4012). What Works Clearinghouse.

Biancarosa, G., & Snow, C. E. (2004). *Reading next—A vision for action and research in middle and high school literacy: A report to Carnegie Corporation of New York* (2nd ed.). Alliance for Excellent Education.

Block, C. C., & Pressley, M. (Eds.). (2002). *Comprehension instruction: Research-based practices.* Guilford Press.

Bunch, G. C. (2013). Pedagogical language knowledge: Preparing mainstream teachers for English learners in the new standards era. *Review of Research in Education, 37*(1), 298–341.

Bunch, G. C., Kibler, A., & Pimentel, S. (2012, January). *Realizing opportunities for English learners in the Common Core English Language Arts and Disciplinary Literacy Standards.* Paper presented at the Understanding Language Conference at Stanford University, Stanford, CA.

Byrd, R. (2005). *The hero and the minotaur: The fantastic adventures of Theseus.* Dutton Children's Books.

Coffin, C. (2006). Mapping subject-specific literacies. *NALDIC Quarterly, 3*(3), 13–26.

Conley, D. T. (2008). *College knowledge: What it really takes for students to succeed and what we can do to get them ready.* Wiley.

Conley, D. T. (2013). *Getting ready for college, careers, and the Common Core: What every educator needs to know.* Jossey-Bass.

Fitzgerald, J. (2017). How practice-based research informs adolescent English language learners-composing and compositions. In K. A. Hinchman & D. Appleman (Eds.), *Adolescent literacies: A handbook of practice-based research* (pp. 357–378). Guilford Press.

Francis, D. J., Rivera, M., Lesaux, N., Kieffer, M., & Rivera, H. (2006). *Research-based recommendations for instruction and academic interventions.* Center on Instruction.

Graham, S. (2006). Exceptional children: Preview. *Exceptional Children, 72*(4), 391–396.

Graham, S., Bruch, J., Fitzgerald, J., Friedrich, L., Furgeson, J., Greene, K., . . . Smither

Wulsin, C. (2016). *Teaching secondary students to write effectively*. National Center for Education Evaluation and Regional Assistance, Institute of Education Sciences, U.S. Department of Education.

Graham, S., Kim, Y. S., Cao, Y., Lee, W., Tate, T., Collins, P., . . . Olson, C. B. (2023). A meta-analysis of writing treatments for students in grades 6 to 12. *Journal of Educational Psychology, 115*(7), 1004–1027.

Graham, S., & Perin, D. (2007). *Writing next: Effective strategies to improve writing of adolescents in middle and high schools—A report to Carnegie Corporation of New York*. Alliance for Excellent Education.

Gurney, D., Gersten, R., Domino, J., & Carnine, D. (1990). Story grammar: Effective literature instruction for high school students with learning disabilities. *Journal of Learning Disabilities, 23*, 335–348.

Hillocks, G. (2011). *Teaching argument writing, grades 6–12*. Heineman.

Kim, J., Olson, C. B., Scarcella, R., Kramer, J., Pearson, M., van Dyk, D., . . . Land, R. (2011). A randomized experiment of cognitive strategies approach to text-based analytical writing for mainstreamed Latino English learners in grades 6 to 12. *Journal of Research on Educational Effectiveness, 4*, 231–263.

Kuhn, D. (1991). *The skills of argument*. Cambridge University Press.

Kuhn, D. (2005). *Education for thinking*. Harvard University Press.

Langer, J. A. (2002). *Effective literacy instruction: Building successful reading and writing programs*. National Council of Teachers of English.

National Center for Education Statistics. (2012). *The Nation's Report Card: Writing 2011*. Institute of Education Sciences, U.S. Department of Education.

National Center for Education Statistics. (2019). *The Nation's Report Card: Writing 2017*. Institute of Education Sciences, U.S. Department of Education.

National Governors Association Center for Best Practices & Council of State School Officers. (2010). *Common core state standards for English language arts and literacy in history/social studies, science, and technical subjects*. Authors.

National Institute of Child Health and Human Development. (2000). Report of the National Reading Panel. *Teaching children to read: An evidence-based assessment of the scientific research literature on reading and its implications for reading instruction* (NIH Publication No. 00-4769). U.S. Government Printing Office.

National Writing Project & Nagin, C. (2003). *Because writing matters: Improving student writing in our schools*. Jossey-Bass.

Olsen, L. (2010). *Reparable harm. Fulfilling the unkept promise of educational opportunity for California's long term English learners*. California Together.

Olson, C. B., Balius, A., McCourtney, E., & Widtmann, M. (2018). *Thinking tools for young readers and writers: Strategies to promote higher literacy in grades 2–8*. Teachers College Press.

Olson, C. B., Kim, J. S., Scarcella, R., Kramer, J., Pearson, M., van Dyk, D., . . . Land, R. (2012). Enhancing the interpretive reading and analytical writing of mainstreamed English learners in secondary school: Results from a randomized field trial using a cognitive strategies approach. *American Educational Research Journal, 4*(2), 323–355.

Olson, C. B., & Land, R. (2007). A cognitive strategies approach to reading and writing instruction for English language learners in secondary school. *Research in the Teaching of English, 41*(3), 269–303.

Olson, C. B., & Land, R. (2008). Taking a reading/writing intervention for secondary

English language learners on the road: Lessons learned from the Pathway Project. *Research in the Teaching of English, 42*(3), 259–269.

Olson, C. B., Maamuujav, U., Steiss, J., & Chung, H. Q. (2023). Examining the impact of a cognitive strategies approach on the argument writing of mainstreamed English learners in secondary school. *Written Communication, 40*(2), 373–416.

Olson, C. B., Matuchniak, T., Chung, H. Q., Stumpf, R., & Farkas, G. (2017). Reducing achievement gaps in academic writing for Latinos and English learners in grades 7–12. *Journal of Educational Psychology, 109*(1), 1–21.

Olson, C. B., Woodworth, K., Arshan, N., Black, R., Chung, H. Q., D'Aoust, C., . . . Stowell, L. (2020). The pathway to academic success: Scaling up a text-based analytical writing intervention for Latinos and English learners in secondary school. *Journal of Educational Psychology, 112*(4), 701–717.

Paris, S. G., Lipson, M. Y., & Wixson, K. K. (1983). Becoming a strategic reader. *Contemporary Educational Psychology, 8*, 293–316.

Paris, S. G., Wasik, B. A., & Turner, J. C. (1991). The development of strategic readers. In R. Barr, M. Kamil, P. B. Mosenthal, & P. D. Pearson (Eds.), *Handbook of reading research* (Vol. II, pp. 609–640). Longman.

Pearson, P. D., & Duke, N. K. (2002). Comprehension instruction in the primary grades. In C. C. Block & M. Pressley (Eds.), *Comprehension instruction: Research-based best practices* (pp. 247–258). Guilford Press.

Perie, M., Grigg, W., & Donahue, P. (2005). *The Nation's Report Card: Reading, 2005*. National Center for Education Statistics.

Persky, H. R., Daane, M. C., & Jin, Y. (2003). *The Nation's Report Card: Writing, 2002*. National Center for Education Statistics.

Salahu-Din, D., Persky, H., & Miller, J. (2008). *The nation's report card: Writing, 2007*. National Center for Education Statistics.

Scarcella, R. (2003). *Academic English: A conceptual framework* (Technical Report 2003-1). University of California Linguistic Minority Research Institute.

Scardamalia, M., & Bereiter, C. (1987). Knowledge telling and knowledge transforming in written composition. In S. Rosenberg (Eds.), *Advances in applied psycholinguistics, Volume 2: Reading, writing and language learning* (pp. 142–175). Cambridge University Press.

Short, D., & Fitzsimmons, S. (2007). *Double the work: Challenges and solutions to acquiring language and academic literacy for adolescent English language learners—A report to Carnegie Corporation of New York*. Alliance for Excellent Education.

Snow, C., & Biancarosa, G. (2003). *Adolescent literacy and the achievement gap: What do we know and where do we go from here?* Carnegie Corporation of New York.

Steiss, J., Krishnan, J., Kim, Y. S. G., & Olson, C. B. (2022). Dimensions of text-based analytical writing of secondary students. *Assessing Writing, 51*, Article 100600.

Tierney, R. J., & Pearson, P. D. (1983). Toward a composing model of reading. *Language Arts, 60*(5), 568–580.

Tierney, R. J., & Shanahan, T. (1991). *Research on the reading–writing relationship: Interactions, transactions, and outcomes*. Erlbaum.

Zwiers, J. (2008). *Building academic language: Essential practices for content classrooms*. Jossey-Bass.

CHAPTER 19

Expansive Literacies for Middle Grade Learners

Jill Castek
Megan Goss
Aniqa Shah

>The symbiotic relationship between reading and writing is a cornerstone of our individual intellectual journey and our educational system. We write as an act of self-expression. We read because language renders unto us the vitality of real and imagined experience.
>—MARITA GOLDEN

We open this chapter with Golden's (2011, p. 5) quote because it represents important beliefs about the purposes of literacies, demonstrating their role in shaping our humanity and significance of the human experience. Literacies convey much more than connected meaning-making processes; enacting literacies allows learners to unlock meaning and express themselves. Throughout this chapter, we use literacies in the plural intentionally because literacies exchanged across spaces, contexts, languages, and modes are multiple (Forzani & Castek, 2022). Literacies make it possible for meanings to be exchanged across modes and forms and are fundamentally the way learners make sense of the world. Our views of literacies are closely linked to those of Freire and Macedo (1987), Muhammad (2020), and Tierney and Pearson (2024), who see literacies as inclusive of the multiple ways humans interact with each other. Viewed in this way, literacies are expansive, holistic, liberatory, and emancipatory.

The transformative potential of literacies involves much more than simply enacting reading, writing, listening, and speaking processes. Literacies signify connections that are more extensive than decoding words or accurately verbalizing connected text in a fluent manner, with proper phrasing and rhythmic intonations. Literacies engage individual cognition while connecting learners through social processes that make it possible to make sense of a complex and ever-changing world. Literacies are personal and individual, as well as universal and interconnected. We believe there is an urgent need for an expansive view of literacies that includes digital literacies and data literacies (Sheldon & Castek, 2023). Digital technologies have continually transformed literacies practices and instruction, which have in turn expanded how learners read texts, access information, create, and interact with one another.

For learners at all ages, digital literacies need to be an integral part of education to create wider access to texts and information, encourage creativity in self-expression, and support collaboration within a globally networked world. Digital literacies are self-directed or collaborative processes of constructing knowledge while engaged in at least five important online practices: (1) reading, discussing, and writing to define important questions; (2) locating relevant information; (3) critically evaluating information for accuracy, reliability, purpose, and perspective; (4) comparing, contrasting, and synthesizing information across multiple sources; and (5) communicating ideas with and for others (Leu et al., 2019). Digital literacies are essential for communication, information seeking, sharing of ideas, and self-expression in an era where platforms—digital apps, services, or infrastructures that facilitate social and economic exchange—shape the social practices of teachers and students. Platforms such as ChatGPT and other artificial intelligence (AI) create complex learning ecologies that affect literacies, writing practices, and writing instruction. Narrow approaches to AI and platforms serve to exacerbate inequities (Stornaiuolo et al., 2023).

This chapter explores literacies as meaningful educational connection points for all students in the middle years, ranging from age 8 to 14 years. When discussing literacies approaches, we differentiate expansive literacies from a narrow view of the science of reading (SOR). We advocate for the advancement of an expansive view of literacies as connected universal processes serving meaningful communicative purposes with transformative potentials. We adopt a critical stance toward some perceptions of the SOR because we believe they emphasize a simple view of reading that suggests Phonics First as the best way to teach early reading and extended phonics instruction as a means of promoting reading achievement for upper grade learners. This version of the SOR is most often thought about in the early grades (Cabell et al., 2024), pays little attention to writing and connected literacies, and lacks a view that encourages support for the literacy development of older students, especially regarding writing.

We begin this chapter by discussing central issues in literacy education today that provide a backdrop to understand the SOR. We address writing within our model of integrated literacies that highlights six essential components for nurturing, responsive and sustaining practices. Finally, we draw from our research working with teachers to provide vignettes showing connected research and practice.

Literacies Chanel Universal Human Experiences

> Literacy is a bridge from misery to hope. It is the road to human progress and the means through which every man, woman and child can realize his or her full potential.
> —Kofi Annan

Annan's quote reminds us that literacies tap into meaning making that represents human expression and the exchange of ideas. Literacies are personal and simultaneously social. Personal meaning making encourages an internalization and interpretation of what others are communicating. Social literacies connect learners through shared language, communication, and expressive meanings that include linguistic and other modes.

Literacies can be formal and rule-bound, expressed through sentence structures and word choices that conform to grammatical norms. At the same time, meaning-making processes can be loose and free, involving creativity in self-expression that cannot be contained (Vygotsky, 1978) by page or screen. Interpreting paintings, contemplating expressions captured in a sculpture, or engaging in a shared experience within a video game (Gee, 2009) are all ways we connect our thoughts with others to expand viewpoints that encourage a wider understanding of ourselves, and of the world (Moje, 2015).

Literacies Create Inclusive Classroom Culture

> The process of reading and writing and having arguments about ideas is valuable. I'm afraid it's something we're losing.
> —Haroon Moghul

Moghul's quote demonstrates that literacies make it possible to advance arguments that matter, but that learning through argumentation within a community for sharing ideas is taking a backseat to other forms of literacy instruction. We contend that within the culture of any given classroom, teachers can advance integrated literacies that foreground six essential components of culturally responsive and sustaining education, which include (1) co-creating classroom community, (2) growing independent learners, (3) centering and expanding culture and identity, (4) cultivating joy, (5) fostering criticality, and (6) building awareness and cultural competence. These six essential components stem from an extensive literature review (Roman et al., 2022) and identify insights from the field about how to support students who have been marginalized through the U.S. education system. The synthesis of this work offers a pathway supporting all students' literacies development, affect, motivation, and achievement. Figure 19.1 is our model of integrated literacies.

In the inner circle lies the interconnected processes of literacies learning. The outer circle informs our understanding of the contexts that are necessary for the rich literacy-driven model to work. The six essential components provide an important context for responsive and sustaining practices that encourage literacies and learning simultaneously.

Literacies Are Connected

> When we read, we are not looking for new ideas, but to see our own thoughts given the seal of confirmation on the printed page. The words that strike us are those that awake an echo in a zone we have already made our own—the place where we live—and the vibration enables us to find fresh starting points within ourselves.
> —Cesare Pavese

Pavese's words evoke a deep connection to the interconnectedness of literacies as a means of expressing ourselves in ways that are empowering and liberatory, awaking new connections, echoes, and vibrations. Yet, in many classrooms reading, writing, listening, speaking and creating are separate activities. Walking into a classroom, the day's agenda may indicate little to no overlap between language arts and science or math. It may be rare that any writing instruction is planned to support content and disciplinary learning.

Elementary students' report cards usually provide individual grades for reading, writing, listening, and speaking, which signals to the teacher, the students, and even the parents, that these processes are separate. In middle school, the siloing and separation are even more stark, with English being the only subject during which students consistently read and write. In English, writing is often about learning specific forms such as the five-paragraph essay or response to literature. Rather than viewing literacies as mutually supportive and holistic, time is spent considering the processes and products of reading, writing, listening, speaking, and creating as independent entities.

Allyn (2018) describes the relationship between reading and writing in this way: Reading is like breathing in; writing is like breathing out. One cannot exist without the other, and they recursively and reciprocally reinforce each other. To experience literacies in the most profound ways, students should have opportunities to experience integrated literacies rather than siloed literacy instruction. When

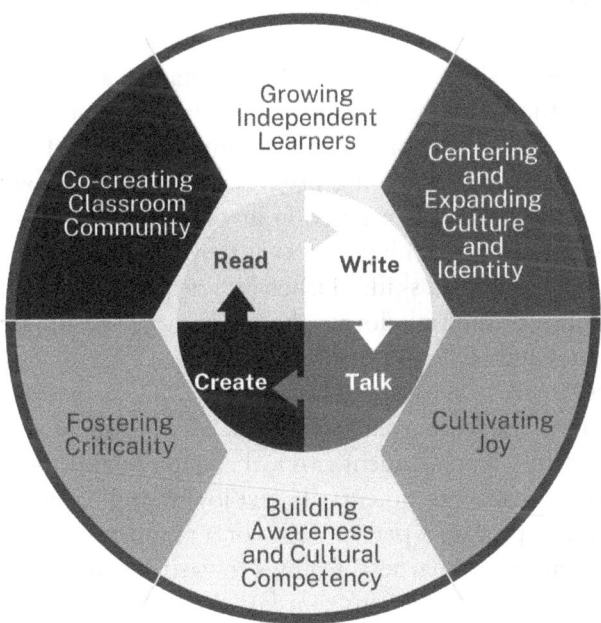

FIGURE 19.1. Integrated model of six essential components of culturally responsive and sustaining education, and interdependent literacies. The outer ring depicts the six essential components, and the inner circle represents connections across literacies, processes, and practices.

teachers and students see literacies as discreet skills, they inadvertently miss out on the multitude of opportunities to engage with the dynamic and emancipatory version of literacies that come from approaching learning and communication in a holistic way that extends the motivation to learn.

Literacies Are Inextricably Linked to Issues of Power, Equity, and Social Justice

> Reading is the sole means by which we slip, involuntarily, often helplessly, into another's skin, another's voice, another's soul.
> —Joyce Carol Oates

Oates's words demonstrate our humanity and the power of multiple perspectives. Literacies instruction can be a gatekeeper in schools, inviting some learners in while keeping others out (Whittingham et al., 2024). For example, if a learner comes into a science classroom knowing the discourse of science, they will be more successful in acquiring content. Learners who do not have a head start in those literacies are more likely to be marginalized and turned away. Literacies are rooted in access and tied to power (Macedo & Freire, 2018), and tied to issues of positionality, equity, and social justice (Jacobs & Castek, 2022). In formal schooling, literacy is organized through standards-based curricula, scope, sequence models, and assessment benchmarks that guide the instruction of literacies according to the mastery of targets and skills as demonstrated on classroom-based assessments.

Too much focus on skills can negate the true nature and purpose of literacies, the multiple ways that humans communicate with each other and allow learners to express themselves. Literacies instruction should yield differentiated outcomes, with each outcome indicating progress that adopts growth as a mindset (Dweck, 2019). When literacies instruction involves learners in ways that tap into their choice and interests, learning can occur by drawing in learners' desire to learn, incorporating literacies skills (Fisher & Frey, 2023). Learners can express their understandings in multiple forms that encourage the universal purposes of literacies—personal and collective meaning making.

When students are conceived of as unique, lifelong learners, literacies are understood as an endless set of avenues through which students can explore, learn, and express themselves. Each student can feel excited to express themself through literacies, and all students can potentially feel joyful and eager to choose the text they want to read, or pick up a pen to write, or a paintbrush, a tablet, or a microphone to express themself. Learners' feelings toward literacies should encourage a desire to learn and make connections that last throughout their lives. Researchers and practitioners across literacies research have demonstrated the importance of learning motivation and connected literacies instruction (Castek & Dwyer, 2018; Goss et al., 2016; Rainey et al., 2018; Spires et al., 2016) and have led the way with illustrative examples to encourage working toward these important goals.

In a literacies-rich learning context, learners have opportunities to experience literacies, to read, write, talk, create, and collaborate to unlock meanings by contributing understandings to the world (Castek & Manderino, 2020). Classroom time should be devoted to experiences that involve expansive opportunities to write, including writing to explore, writing to record, writing to make sense, writing to collaborate, and writing to make connections. Writing is an essential, multiperspectival literacy process that leads to more than just arriving at one right answer. Writing involves reflection, introspection, and building connections that serve as an invitation to jumping-off points for further exploration and discussion.

Yet there are always time constraints within school settings. The external pressures of standardized testing demand that state testing drive what is taught; teachers are isolated from each other, and students are pushed along from grade to grade, regardless of their unique needs and abilities—all contributing to pressures that help explain why our public school classrooms are less able to provide the "luxury" of time for students to use literacies for their own purposes. This is particularly true for lower-performing schools, in which the likelihood for students to have flexibility to choose what and how they learn is reduced, as these institutions and their teachers feel intensified pressure to raise test scores and prioritize remedial work (Darling-Hammond, 2001; Hammond, 2015; Paris & Alim, 2017).

For decades, the documented achievement gap has positioned many students in the United States as failures within the educational system (Hanushek et al., 2022). The term *achievement gap* has faced criticism for placing blame on students rather than acknowledging the circumstances in which they grow up. Additionally, the design of standardized tests often favors White, middle-class students, prompting educators to prefer the term *opportunity gap* to better reflect these systemic issues (Ladson-Billings, 2013). However, neither term fully captures the complexities of the issue, as recent research and national educational reports (Carnoy & García, 2017; Irwin et al., 2023; Quinn, 2020; Shukla et al., 2022) indicate that students who are Black, Indigenous, and People of Color (BIPOC) continue to face significant challenges in the educational system, underscoring the need for targeted interventions.

A narrow version of the SOR advances interventions that are skills-based in reading; for example, students may receive an overemphasis on practice with phonics, phonemic awareness and fluency, and may be provided with reading tasks that are determined and regulated by the teacher rather than being consulted about what they want to read and what interests them. The texts they read are often limited and fall below their interest level (Brown et al., 2020) and are meant to increase skills. Meanwhile, their more proficient peers who are seen as "good readers" gain more independence during their reading time and are encouraged to focus more on comprehension and responding creatively to their reading (Goss, 2006). This becomes even more problematic for BIPOC students, who are owed educational experiences as rich and emancipatory as possible, so that they can thrive (Gomez & Gomez, 2007; Love, 2019; Muhammad, 2020).

Literacies are deeply intertwined with power, equity, and social justice. Literacy instruction must go beyond skills acquisition to embrace an inclusive, holistic approach that values students' unique backgrounds and experiences. To foster meaningful engagement, literacies are best taught with interconnected, purposeful connections to gaining new knowledge in the forefront. Student choice and creativity must be prioritized, moving away from rigid curricula and standardized testing. By advocating for systemic changes that empower all learners, we can cultivate a generation of students capable of exploring and expressing their ideas freely. This transformation honors the essence of literacy as a tool for inquiry, empathy, and understanding in a diverse world.

Value Literacies as Opportunities for Growth and Connection

> If you want to learn something, go to the source. Just listen, read, and write. Little by little, you will come closer to what you need to say and express it through your voice.
> —Natalie Goldberg

Listening, reading, and writing, as referenced by Goldberg (2005, p. 11) are literacies that awaken individual meaning making yet also involve social processes through the exchange of perspectives. Writing is a medium that celebrates self-expression through the resonance of one's voice. When students are engaged in speaking and listening to each other in authentic ways, they are encouraged to evolve their understanding that can ultimately be represented in writing to communicate ideas and connections. Writing for an authentic purpose provides a reason to write and explain thinking for oneself and for others. Engagement in the modern world, whether in social, personal, academic, or work contexts, calls on learners to share ideas across cultures and involves building consensus and working together. Literacies instruction that encourages students to learn from each other provides opportunities to gain new perspectives. Listening is an important literacy process and invites reflection, and when learners engage in equitable talk, activity structures are more likely to invite all voices in rather than just a few "top" students' active engagement in learning.

Literacies are made up of a contextualized set of practices that are used within a domain or situation. The better a learner knows the practices associated with that domain, the more the learner will understand the epistemic rationale for what happens in that domain and, subsequently, the better they will be able to engage in the literacies within that domain. Likewise, the greater the engagement in the practices and literacies, the more potential there will be for increasing involvement, belonging, and understanding in the domain. However, not all skills are transferable between domains. Students are more likely to appreciate and value a domain if they feel they are willfully engaging in its practices. Lifelong learning involves the learner in choosing what is read, deciding what and how writing takes place, and encourages connections to the world around us. This type of inquiry-based learning is not a representation of academic achievement, nor is it learning to satisfy a standard, or earn a grade on a test. When students read and write as meaningful practices, they are more likely to find value in their learning experiences.

Culturally Responsive Teaching and Learning

> Because we are complex beings, we have racial, cultural, gender, environmental, and community identities, to name a few. Not only is it important to teach youths who they are, but educators should also teach students about the identities and cultures of others different from them. As learning takes place, one asks, 'How am I learning about who I am and about the lives of others?'
> —IVELISSE RAMOS AND GHOLDY MUHAMMAD

Ramos and Muhammad remind us that children of color require us to design instruction that is truly inclusive by addressing all facets of identity and culture as a means of connection with those who are alike and different from ourselves. Advocates for culturally and linguistically responsive–sustaining teaching and learning, many of whom are Black or Brown themselves, warn that too much focus on literacy skills and strategies is the wrong direction to take in literacy instruction. Emdin (2016), Hammond (2015), Love (2019), and Muhammad (2020), among others, demonstrate that BIPOC students are not the problem. For example, Brown (2019) explains that when taking an assets-based perspective toward BIPOC students, the teacher can use students' everyday language as an asset for acquiring academic language. Muhammad (2020) takes a similar stance, explaining that one of the most important purposes of literacy in the education of BIPOC students is to cultivate a critical stance while reading and writing—and that this can only happen when students read texts that have meaning in their lives. Despite policy reports that tend to draw our attention to deficits in BIPOC students themselves (National Center for Education Progress, 2023), authors and researchers who take up culturally and linguistically responsive–sustaining teaching and learning lenses remind us that this is not the case; rather it is the system, and the kinds of experiences BIPOC students have (or don't have) within this system, that is at fault (Ladson-Billings, 2014). Pedagogy for BIPOC students should work with students' own knowledge of their community, so that they can promote ideas for social change—it should not just be a tool to enhance test scores or grades (Love, 2019). Literacies should not be approached as a one-size-fits-all experience, nor should it be weaponized to "fix" students.

SOR Critiqued

> While our fact-checking attempts to touch on various facets of reading in more detail, meriting fuller consideration remain a host of key issues related to reading processes and pedagogy—including socio-cultural matters; multilingualism; and studies of comprehension, digital reading, and instructional approaches.
> —ROBERT J. TIERNEY AND P. DAVID PEARSON

Tierney and Pearson (2024) remind us that literacies are nested social and cultural practices, in contexts that extend to digital spaces, and are about sense-making rather than cognitively focused exercises. Students' experiences with text should involve engagement and encourage connections within and beyond school, including social, cultural, and aesthetic experiences that extend curiosity and spark new learning.

Approaches to literacies instruction championed by journalists (Hanford, 2022) and other columnists advocating for the SOR make claims that it will especially help students who struggle with reading. However, researchers who focus on supporting BIPOC students argue for a different path, especially as students leave the primary grades and begin to critically examine their own worlds and interests in the middle grades. There is power in integrated literacies that connect meaning making across reading, writing, talking, and creating; literacies can evoke change and build identity. There is therefore an urgent need to approach the teaching of literacies from a thoughtful stance that involves students as the central meaning makers who are capable in their abilities in reading, writing, talking, and creating for purposes that advance their interests and inquiries, and value their identities.

A special issue on the SOR (see Goodwin & Jiménez, 2021) examined many perspectives, including critiques. Aukerman and Chambers Schuldt (2021) argued that the SOR should be nested within a larger science of literacy that includes and connects to writing (Graham, 2020), oral language (Johnston, 2019), and meaning making, considering literacies habits that propel lifelong and whole-life learning (Cervetti et al., 2020; Pearson et al., 2020) across multiple modalities (Yaden et al., 2021). Since our focus is on ages 8–14, we argue that motivation, choice, and opportunities to expand knowledge and interests must be central to any approach that engages learners in the middle grades.

Our understanding of students' ideal literacy experiences can be expressed through nested models that demonstrate the importance of literacies as connected practices situated in a meaningful and empowering sociocultural contexts. This approach is consistent with Graham (2020), who asserts that classrooms and teachers who teach using an SOR approach need to appreciate that reading and writing must be seen as more fully integrated. We see literacies in all their forms as fully integrated approaches, intended to immerse students in interest-driven learning through meaning making.

Reading helps students to build background knowledge, explore widely, and inquire into topics of interest; and whenever possible, to make reading personally meaningful. Students need opportunities to make choices about which texts to read and how deeply to engage in those texts. Some texts are introductory and provide grounding, while others provide more detail, engaging readers in content in which they may be interested. There are many texts available across various reading levels, and each incorporates multiple modes and organizational means of conveying information.

Writing involves working through the development of ideas to refine thinking, engage in further inquiry, and making connections to other content. Vocabulary learning can be advanced through writing and inquiry. Learning the words that name concepts encourages specificity in thinking and connection. Additionally, oral literacies, known as talk, invites learners to respond to prompts and gives space to discussions that help learners develop different stances, connections, and associations. When learners engage in talk, they are invited to formulate ideas while also engaging in listening to others' perspectives, opinions, evidence, and reasoning. Talk is an exploratory way to sort through ideas, draw from information shared orally, and formulate arguments that can be represented in different ways.

Creation offers learners many forms for representing their ideas in expanded forms of writing. As learners create, they may connect drawing, diagramming, mapping within their writing, or they may create using a range of digital tools that incorporate modeling, integration of visuals, video, or other means to express understanding. Learners often take pride in creating, which encourages a personal form of meaning making that can be further advanced through writing, speaking, and further reading. Importantly, reading, writing, listening, speaking, and creating are mutually reinforcing processes that involve both receptive (reading, listening) and expressive (writing, talking, creating) ways of learning.

In the next section, we provide examples of integrated literacies in action to highlight how to conceive of instructional activities that encourage literacies development through interconnected reading, writing, talking, and creating. These examples come from research we have conducted with students in third through eighth grades, in partnership with their classroom teachers. We discuss how literacies instruction that takes these forms provides opportunities for literacies and the six essential components of culturally responsive and sustaining education to flourish.

Connections to Research and Practice

The examples that follow demonstrate important touchpoints that describe implementation. These vignettes provide concrete examples showing connections between research and practice that we address in our integrated literacies model (see Figure 19.1).

Example 1: Engaged Reading

Ms. Renoud's seventh-grade classroom is learning about evolution. The class begins by reading "Valley of the Whales"; she foregrounds a real-life example of an evolutionary discovery. Students perk up; a few students whisper excitedly, "Whoa! Where is that? Is it real?"

Ms. Renoud shares that this is a real place in Egypt. She pulls down a map, so students can see where Egypt is located. At their teacher's invitation, the class members share what they know about Egypt. Together, the students build an early conception of, and an excitement about, the text they will all read.

Ms. Renoud reads the first paragraph aloud, annotating as she uses a think-aloud protocol to reveal her thoughts. After reading the first paragraph and examining the accompanying image, she encourages her students to continue reading and annotating independently. Ms. Renoud reminds the students that annotating is like "having a personal conversation with the text" and reminds the students that they can choose whichever strategies they think are most useful to them.

Once pairs finish reading the article, Ms. Renoud signals that they should begin the next phase of reading, which involves partners discussing their annotations with each other. As students share their annotated questions and comments, they are learning from each other. Because these students are all unique people with different backgrounds, they have different questions and have noticed different aspects of the text. As they discuss, students help each other answer the questions they have. Ms. Renoud holds a whole-class discussion; going through the text together serves to summarize important ideas from the text. The rich and sophisticated conversation is another opportunity for shared interest building and meaning making to deepen comprehension as students learn from listening to each other.

Later that day, Ms. Renoud scans her class's written annotations. She is looking for several things: alternative conceptions; innovative annotations and ideas that she can bring forth; and, finally, annotations that come from students who could use more recognition by their peers. Because this first reading of the article is guided by the students themselves, their actual thinking is expressed through their annotations and includes what they know and with what they are struggling. Reading class annotations offers an opportunity for formative assessment for the teacher to determine what students need.

The next day, Ms. Renoud is prepared to talk about several important concepts she gathered from reading her students' annotations. She praises her students for their interesting and unique thinking, and their thoroughness. Ms. Renoud asks several students to explain more about their annotations. Students are all beaming excitedly and seem quite interested in hearing about their peers' annotations and thoughts.

Ms. Renoud then begins the portion of the reading sequence that she calls the "teacher-driven" read. Here, she uses a more traditional reading approach, providing students with the comprehension questions that she feels will help them understand essential concepts from the reading. Students engage in reading the text more than once because their own ideas are privileged and treated as valuable and important. Having a first reading that is student-directed provides opportunities for more student buy-in. The culture around reading is to promote student thinking first, which invites more student participation in subsequent readings. Working through the text twice, in two different ways, encourages a deeper engagement, connection, and understanding of the text.

This sequence of reading and writing annotations focuses on the importance of understanding the text together. In addition, the "reading" isn't just reading—it is surrounded by meaning making, writing and personal connection, and community discussions that involve talking and listening. Students are guided to write and create artifacts that make sense of the text. This rigorous approach to integrated literacies involves students in focused, close reading that also feels joyful. Students' ideas are important, and they are celebrated. Moreover, learners are accountable for difficult content.

Example 2: Socratic Seminar Sequence

Mrs. Rodriguez's sixth graders are conducting a science Socratic seminar sequence that involves the integration of literacies including reading, writing, talking, and creating. Socratic seminars are student-led, evidence-based conversations that help students to develop their argumentation skills. As students take on collective leadership to connect evidence to their argument, they learn to listen actively to others and gain a deeper understanding of the content under study. In this example, the science seminar sequence begins with students thinking about a complex science question, along with evidence that can be leveraged to answer that question. Students read and interpret evidence to respond to the question independently and in pairs. Next, they discuss their thinking with the class through student-led sharing that links claims, evidence, and reasoning. Finally, students independently write an argument based on their personal interpretations of the evidence, after listening to ideas from their peers. A science seminar sequence works best when it is placed at the end of a unit of study, so that all students can bring their accumulated knowledge about a topic to bear during the discussion.

Amid the typical social conversations found in a sixth-grade classroom, discussion of claims and previously researched evidence bubble up around the room, as students prepare for the science seminar sequence and whole-class discussion. They just finished a unit on weather and have spent a class period reading and annotating evidence about a new, weather-related science phenomenon. They also discussed the evidence with a small group of their peers, in preparation for the science seminar sequence. The students come together to discuss evidence with the class and make independent decisions regarding the novel science phenomenon: whether a large building that is situated far away from humans was damaged by a single storm or a series of several storms. After briefly reviewing the discussion guidelines, the teacher steps back to remove herself from the discussion. The students are eager to begin.

Adhira offers her thinking, "I thought it was one severe rainstorm." Students propel the discussion forward.

SELINA: I agree.

ALEX: I think it was multiple storms . . .

PEDRO: No, it's not, Alex!

ALEX: (*Consults evidence printed on cards in front of him.*) There is lots of evidence for multiple rainstorms . . .

SEVERAL STUDENTS: (*speaking at once*) There's lots of evidence for one storm!

ALEX: Listen—for the big storm there is an 8 Celsius degree change. 91 degrees and 77 degrees is a big difference [for multiple smaller storms]. I think that 91 degrees is enough. Even though there's strong winds, I don't think that wind is the biggest factor.

ADHIRA: (*Holds up a map; other students consult their own maps as she speaks*.) If you look at the map . . . the lake is probably pretty close to the Carson Wilderness Education Center and that would mean there is more evaporation and the clouds would be bigger, and if the clouds were bigger, the storm would probably last longer. And the smaller rainstorms would probably still be severe, but, if they were, like, going off and on, then it probably wouldn't cause the tree to fall.

JOHN: (*Consults a data table.*) There are two reasons why I think it could have been one rainstorm. First, on May 1–5, the wind was strong. The temperature might not be very high, but the pressure was also very high, which could give you a very high chance of one big storm. But also, May 16th through the 20th, the equipment was down, so maybe the rain could have caused that. So, there could have also been two . . .

ANTONIO: So then there could have also been two storms?

JOHN: Two storms—yeah . . .

CHARLIE: I thought it was one severe rainstorm, but now that I look at it, I think it was two because on May 11th, it can't really rain because the water vapor is low and the wind is very light and the temperature is really low, too.

This student-led discussion continues for over 30 minutes, during which students' knowledge from earlier reading is applied. The students' passion is evident as they share knowledge and create new knowledge together as they discuss. After the discussion, students are well prepared to write their own scientific arguments because of the deep engagement and thinking prompted by the discussion with their peers and the invitations to more thoroughly explain their thinking to others. These integrated literacies rely on student autonomy and encourage a classroom culture that respects students' ideas as they share their thinking equitably and respectfully as learners and knowers. As a culminating event, students advance their thinking by relying on integrated reading, writing, listening, speaking, and creating—all woven together in such a way that the need to use literacies is authentic and purposeful.

Example 3: Multimodal Writing

Ms. Aboud's fifth graders engage in an introductory activity that kicks off a unit focused on water resources. By drawing on the cultural and linguistic diversity of the class, the students are encouraged to make socioscientific and cultural connections to understand water resources by writing and sharing multimodal water stories. Through writing, learners connect their own knowledge with the perspectives of other learners as they make choices about their content focus and modes of self-expression. This approach emphasizes writing to engage in inquiry, promoting development of ideas, expansion of vocabulary, and refinement of thinking and scientific reasoning.

Instruction begins with the introduction of a digital video platform that threads multimodal discussion comments and encourages the use of voice integrated with gestures, visuals, and student-created texts. Students can record their voices alongside their digital writing and post to a shared digital space, so everyone can explore, examine, and appreciate each other's perspectives, word choices, and writing styles. Connecting in the social space of community is an important purpose of literacies instruction that builds community by getting all students involved in multimodal writing by sharing their in-progress drafts with one another as a jumping-off point for making further connections.

Ms. Aboud positions writing in her classroom as an exploratory and engaging activity; she herself engages in writing along with her students (Graves, 1983). Not only does she provide extended time for writing, but she also encourages motivation for the activity of writing by talking about decisions writers make based on their audience, genre, and opportunity for sharing writing with others in different forms and purposes. She also provides writing opportunities as ways to reflect, summarize, and document what has been learned. Writing is positioned as a higher form of thinking by Ms. Aboud; she helps her students to view writing not simply to fulfill an assignment that functions to assess what they have learned, but instead to enjoy the process of writing as a means of connecting their learning processes to interests and outcomes (Graham, 2020). By grounding literacies and scientific thinking about water, connections are made between writing and scientific understanding, while demonstrating cultural connections and respect for students' backgrounds, cultures, and linguistic resources.

In this writing activity, the topic of water offers many touchpoints to students' lives. An extended brainstorming phase involves viewing and exploring imagery and discussions that encourage connections across cultural, environmental, spiritual, and scientific realms. Engaging in imagery through discussion promotes speaking fluency, while composing using images, words, and personal connections creates the context to build word knowledge and vocabulary. Orally sharing a few water stories builds listening and speaking proficiencies. During these literacies processes, learners make connections across knowledge domains and create extended personal meaning. Deeper learning is born from pairing writing, with personal connections to content (Mintrop et al., 2022).

As students composed and created their stories, they made personal connections to the concept of water expressed and articulated using words, images, and their recorded narration. Instruction that draws in learners' personal connections can make learning more personal, connected, and meaningful, and can serve as an anchor for future learning. In the case of water, there are many kinds of connections to make: cultural, spiritual, scientific, environmental, and aesthetic or artistic to name a few (see Figure 19.2). During the composing and recording process, students connected many threads. A learners' story is part of a sociocultural context in which learning always lives, as students make connections to the content they are learning. As learners composed, they were enacting a meaningful activity of creating and writing, reading and talking to communicate a personal and universal message. Some of the vocabulary expressed cultural connection using

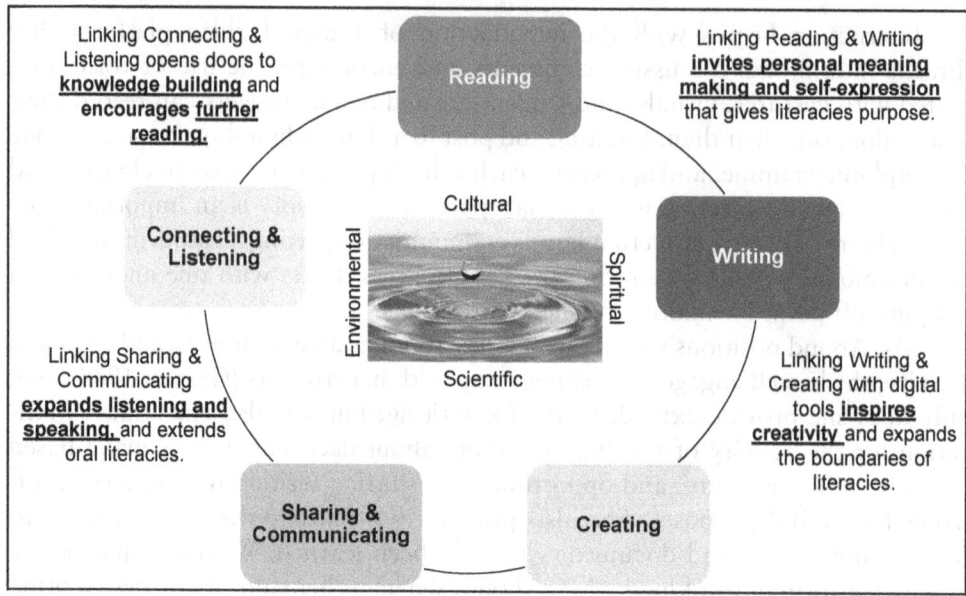

FIGURE 19.2. Connected literacies engaged during multimodal writing.

words specific to meanings that are representative of a learner's background and linguistic choices. Others incorporated scientific connections advocating for the environment when discussing clean water and protecting water sources. Writing and creation processes dovetail, which gives literacies learning unique purposes and meaning.

Example 4: Digital Inquiry Learning

Ms. Chow's eighth-grade students are exploring their connections to multiple meanings of sustainability. As native Hawaiian students studying literacies through a multidisciplinary approach, they employ inquiry learning for making connections, demonstrating their learning, and sharing their perspectives with a wider audience (Coiro et al., 2019). We observed two students working in a group to brainstorm personal connections to sustainability by creating a virtual field experience (VFE) from a native Hawaiian point of view. A VFE is an immersive digital experience that links customized graphics in visually based scenes the students design and create (Oguilve et al., 2022). Students decide to emphasize family and community sustainability, as well as environmental and resource sustainability, that honors the land and key components of their heritage.

They show connections visually in their work while they collaborate with one another to outline ideas for their digital inquiry, discussing together how to help their audience visualize, connect, and appreciate the concept of sustainability from their place-based lens. As a basis for their writing and digital creations, they take digital photos, draw, and capture 360 views of their school and community, organizing their ideas by brainstorming, providing each other feedback, and deciding on the scenes they will add to their VFE. They add written descriptions to their visual and immersive content to explain, demonstrate, and illustrate the ecologies of sustainable fishponds. They create scripts for audio integration, capturing images, and creating visuals. The collaborative writing processes advance writing skills with the goal of teaching the viewing audience about the specifics of native Hawaiian gardening and values of respect for the land and traditions. The resulting VFE demonstrates how creativity, together with digital tools for writing, provide strong illustrative potential to demonstrate the power of inquiry, collaboration, and stance toward the topic.

Literacies and Learning

The four vignettes demonstrate integrated literacies practices and illustrate connections to writing as part of meaning making. The examples offer both literacies process and products that can be assessed. The vignettes feature multiple opportunities for inquiry, self-expression, and meaning making. When literacies are integrated, the resulting instruction positions all learners as successful, capable, and agentive learners. The students were not engaged in remediation; instead, their work was differentiated and purposefully connected to aims they cared about and in which they were invested. The opportunity to engage in literacies practices advances their humanity, encouraging connections to learning content, learning through social engagement, and bettering their literacies development. Moreover, the examples show how teachers can both integrate literacies and attend to the nested context that connects these literacies to create a classroom community that grows independent learners, centers and expands culture and identity, cultivates joy, fosters criticality, and builds awareness and cultural competence.

Critical Implications and Future Directions

Integrating literacies involves research-based practices that encourage connections and build on what students need. It is important that teachers be critical of the evidence associated with any instructional method, including the SOR. As critical thinkers, we need to continue to develop healthy skepticism around what is considered "best practices" and question all methods by considering the students' needs and context of the classroom. Planning beyond the literacy block invites students' wider interests. It approaches literacies through multiple avenues to teach literacies, writing, and encourage writing engagement.

Gabriel (2020) reminds teachers, researchers, and literacy leaders that Science is both a body of knowledge generated through systematic inquiry and a *process* for generating such knowledge. As we respond to our students' needs, we must embrace the process of inquiry as we choose various instructional approaches. Implementing literacies instruction means being student centered. Connecting with what learners' interests are and building from what drives them, rather than what the curriculum guides, supports students' literacies in context, nesting skills into project-based approaches and disciplinary knowledge to encourage both literacies and content learning. Moreover, as educators, we need to play the long game in terms of student learning and the measure of its impact as students grow in their abilities over time and move across grades. Learning literacies cannot rely on any single summative assessment to explain strengths or to show where additional learning should be focused. Repeated practice with literacies needs to be meaningfully situated to encourage motivation and interest, as well as skills. After all, literacies are growth constructs that take time to develop. Students' proficiency can be demonstrated through meaningful, connected literacies and enacted in meaningful ways, through multiple experiences over time. Finally, within and outside the classroom, literacies are meant to create community among learners. Our charge is to provide the context for connection among learners as they engage literacies and use them flexibly.

REFERENCES

Allyn, P. (2018). *Reading is like breathing in; writing is like breathing out* [Blog]. www.literacyworldwide.org/blog/literacy-now/2015/07/16/reading-is-like-breathing-in-writing-is-like-breathing-out.

Aukerman, M., & Chambers Schuldt, L. (2021). What matters most?: Toward a robust and socially just science of reading. *Reading Research Quarterly, 56*(Suppl. 1), 85–103.

Brown, A. L., Palincsar, A. S., & Purcell, L. (2020). Poor readers: Teach, don't label. In U. Neisser (Ed.), *The school achievement of minority children* (pp. 105–143). Routledge.

Brown, B. (2019). *Science in the city: Culturally relevant STEM education*. Harvard Education Press.

Cabell, S., Neuman, S., Patton Terry, N. (Eds.). (2024). *Handbook on the science of early literacy*. Guilford Press.

Carnoy, M., & García, M. (2017). *Five key trends in U.S. student performance*. Economic Policy Institute. www.epi.org/publication/five-key-trends-in-u-s-student-performance-progress-by-blacks-and-hispanics-the-takeoff-of-asians-the-stall-of-non-english-speakers-the-persistence-of-socioeconomic-gaps-and-the-damaging-effect.

Castek, J., & Dwyer, B. (2018). Think globally, act locally: Teaching climate change through digital inquiry. *Reading Teacher, 71*(6), 755–761.

Castek, J., & Manderino, M. (2020). Teaching and learning in a digital world: Digital literacies for disciplinary learning. In M. Kuhn & M. Dreher (Eds.), *Developing conceptual knowledge through oral and written language*. Guilford Press.

Cervetti, G. N., Pearson, P. D., Palincsar, A. S., Afflerbach, P., Kendeou, P., Biancarosa, G., & Berman, A. I. (2020). How the Reading for Understanding initiative's research complicates the simple view of reading invoked in the science of reading. *Reading Research Quarterly, 55*(Suppl. 1), S161–S172.

Coiro, J., Dobler, E., & Pelekis, K. (2019). *From curiosity to deep learning: Personal digital inquiry in grades K–5*. Routledge.

Darling-Hammond, L. (2001). Inequality in teaching and schooling: How opportunity is rationed to students of color in America. In B. D. Smedley, A. Y. Stith, L. Colburn, & H. Evans (Eds.), *The right thing to do, the smart thing to do* (pp. 208–233). National Academies Press.

Dweck, C. S. (2019). The choice to make a difference. *Perspectives on Psychological Science, 14*(1), 21–25.

Emdin, C. (2016). *For white folks who teach in the hood. . . . and the rest of y'all too: Reality pedagogy and urban education.* Beacon Press.

Fisher, D., & Frey, N. (2023). Disciplinary literacy as social justice. *Educational Leadership, 80*(8), 74–75.

Forzani, E., & Castek, J. (2022). Expansive, dynamic, and critical new literacies: Widening views of digital and multimodal learning. In R. Tierney, F. Rizvi, & K. Ercikan (Eds.), *International encyclopedia of education* (4th ed., pp. 487–496). Elsevier.

Freire, P., & Macedo, D. (1987). *Literacy: Reading the word and the world.* Bergin & Garvey.

Gabriel, R. (2020). The future of the science of reading. *Reading Teacher, 74*(1), 11–18.

Gee, J. P. (2009). *A situated sociocultural approach to literacy and technology.* Arizona State University.

Goldberg, N. (2005). *Writing down the bones: Freeing the writer within* (2nd ed.). Shambhala.

Golden, M. (2011). *The word: Black writers talk about the transformative power of reading and writing.* Crown Books.

Gomez, L., & Gomez, K. (2007). Reading for learning: Literacy supports for 21st-century work *Phi Delta Kappan, 89*(3), 224–228.

Goodwin, A. P., & Jiménez, R. T. (2021). The science of reading: Supports, critiques, and questions. *Reading Research Quarterly, 56*(1), 7–16.

Goss, M. M. (2006). *An alignment of good intentions: Mandating basal curriculum.* ProQuest.

Goss, M., Castek, J., & Manderino, M. (2016). Disciplinary and digital literacies: Three synergies. *Journal of Adolescent and Adult Literacy, 6*(3), 335–340.

Graham, S. (2020). The sciences of reading and writing must become more fully integrated. *Reading Research Quarterly, 55*(Suppl. 1), S35–S44.

Graves, D. H. (1983). *Writing: Teachers and children at work* (20th anniversary ed.). Heinemann.

Hammond, Z. L. (2015). *Culturally responsive teaching and the brain: Promoting authentic engagement and rigor among culturally and linguistically diverse students.* Corwin Press.

Hanford, E. (2022, October–November). *Sold a story.* Podcast, APM Reports, American Public Media. https://features.apmreports.org/sold-a-story.

Hanushek, E. A., Light, J. D., Peterson, P. E., Talpey, L. M., & Woessmann, L. (2022). Long-run trends in the US SES–Achievement gap. *Education Finance and Policy, 17*(4), 608–640.

Irwin, V., Wang, K., Tezil, T., Zhang, J., Filbey, A., Jung, J., . . . Parker, S. (2023). *Report on the Condition of Education 2023* (NCES 2023-144). National Center for Education Statistics.

Jacobs, G., & Castek, J. (2022). Collaborative digital problem solving: Power, relationships, and participation. *Journal of Adolescent and Adult Literacy, 65*(5), 377–387.

Johnston, P. (2019). Talking children into literacy: Once more, with feeling. *Literacy Research: Theory, Method, and Practice, 68*(1), 64–85.

Ladson-Billings, G. (2013). Lack of achievement or loss of opportunity? In P. L. Carter

& K. G. Welner (Eds.), *Closing the opportunity gap: What America must do to give every child an even chance* (pp. 11–22). Oxford University Press.

Ladson-Billings, G. (2014). Culturally relevant pedagogy 2.0: a.k.a. the remix. *Harvard Educational Review, 84*(1), 74–84.

Leu, D. J., Kinzer, C. K., Coiro, J., Castek, J., & Henry, L. A. (2019). New literacies: A dual level theory of the changing nature of literacy, instruction, and assessment. In D. E. Alvermann, N. J. Unrau, & R. B. Ruddell (Eds.), *Theoretical models and processes of literacy* (7th ed., pp. 319–346). Routledge.

Love, B. (2019). *We want to do more than survive: Abolitionist teaching and the pursuit of educational freedom*. Beacon Press.

Macedo, D., & Freire, D. (2018). *Literacies of power: What Americans are not allowed to know* (exp. ed.). Routledge.

Mintrop, R., Zumpe, E., Jackson, K., Nucci, D., & Norman, J. (2022). *Designing for deeper learning as an equity approach: Schools and school districts serving communities disadvantaged by the educational system benefiting from deeper learning*. Carnegie Foundation for the Advancement of Teaching.

Moje, E. B. (2015). Doing and teaching disciplinary literacy with adolescent learners: A social and cultural enterprise. *Harvard Educational Review, 85*(2), 254–278.

Muhammad, G. (2020). *Cultivating genius: An equity framework for culturally and historically responsive literacy*. Scholastic.

National Assessment of Educational Progress. (2023). *The Nation's Report Card: Long-term trends in reading and mathematics assessments*. Author.

Oguilve, V., Wen, W., Castek, J., Sanderson, C., & Pineda, Z. (2022). Participatory learning: Educators designing media to expand global perspectives. In *Proceedings of EdMedia + Innovate Learning 2022*. www.learntechlib.org/primary/p/221406.

Paris, D., & Alim, H. S. (2017). *Culturally sustaining pedagogies: Teaching and learning for justice in a changing world*. Teachers College Press.

Pavese, C. (1980). *This business of living: Diaries, 1935–1950*. Quartet Books.

Pearson, P. D., Palincsar, A. S., Afflerbach, P., Cervetti, G. N., Kendeou, P., Biancarosa, G., . . . Berman, A. I. (2020). Taking stock of the Reading for Understanding initiative. In P. D. Pearson, A. S. Palincsar, G. Biancarosa, & A. I. Berman (Eds.), *Reaping the rewards of the Reading for Understanding initiative* (pp. 251–292). National Academy of Education.

Quinn, D. M. (2020). Experimental effects of "achievement gap" news reporting on viewers' racial stereotypes, inequality explanations, and inequality prioritization. *Educational Researcher, 49*(7), 482–492.

Rainey, E. C., Maher, B. L., Coupland, D., Franchi, R., & Moje, E. B. (2018). But what does it look like?: Illustrations of disciplinary literacy teaching in two content areas. *Journal of Adolescent and Adult Literacy, 61*(4), 371–379.

Ramos, I. & Muhammad, G. (n.d.). *Teaching toward genius: An equity model for pedagogy in action*. American Consortium for Equity in Education. www.ace-ed.org/teaching-toward-genius-an-equity-model-for-pedagogy-in-action.

Roman, N., Ryan, J., Goss, M., Vlasses, L., & Abbot, R. (2022, January). *From theory to practice: The six essential components of culturally responsive and sustaining science education*. Paper presented at the Learning Design Group at UC Berkeley's Lawrence Hall of Science, Science Educators for Equity, Diversity, and Social Justice Conference.

Sheldon, L., & Castek, J. M. (2023). New literacies: Expanding the conversation to include data literacies. In P. A. Schutz & K. R. Muis (Eds.), *Handbook of educational psychology* (pp. 579–602). Taylor & Francis.

Shukla, S. Y., Theobald, E. J., Abraham, J. K., & Price, R. M. (2022). Reframing educational outcomes: Moving beyond achievement gaps. *CBE—Life Sciences Education, 21*(2).

Spires, H. A., Kerkhoff, S. N., & Graham, A. C. K. (2016). Disciplinary literacy and inquiry: Teaching for deeper content learning. *Journal of Adolescent and Adult Literacy, 60*(2), 151–161.

Stornaiuolo, A., Higgs, J., Nichols, T. P., Leblanc, R. J., & de Roock, R. S. (2023). The platformization of writing instruction: Considering educational equity in new learning ecologies. *Review of Research in Education, 47*(1), 311–359.

Thompson, K. (2017, November 10). The story we have yet to tell: Talking with Haroon Moghul. *The Rumpus*. https://therumpus.net/2017/11/10/the-rumpus-interview-with-haroon-moghul.

Tierney, R. J., & Pearson, P. D. (2024). *Fact-checking the science of reading: Opening up the conversation*. Literacy Research Commons. https://literacyresearchcommons.org.

Tierney, R. J. & Pearson, P. D. (2024). *Executive Summary: Fact-checking the science of reading: Opening up the conversation*. Literacy Research Commons. https://literacyresearchcommons.org.

Vygotsky, L. S. (1978). *Mind in society: The development of higher psychological processes*. Harvard University Press.

Whittingham, C. E., Hoffman, E. B., & Paciga, K. A. (2024). Assessment, accountability, and access: Constrained skill mastery as instructional gatekeeper. *Journal of Early Childhood Literacy, 24*(1), 69–95.

Yaden, D. B., Jr., Reinking, D., & Smagorinsky, P. (2021). The trouble with binaries: A perspective on the science of reading. *Reading Research Quarterly, 56*(Suppl. 1), S119–S129.

PART V
TEACHER KNOWLEDGE AND PROFESSIONAL DEVELOPMENT

CHAPTER 20

Toward a Science of Professional Learning for Teachers of Grades 3–8

Sharon Walpole
John Z. Strong

Professional learning (PL) can be a waste of time and money. Ask any teacher. PL must be designed well if our aim is to improve instructional routines or interventions. Ask any intervention researcher. Poorly planned and executed PL can demoralize teachers. Ask any administrator. So why does a science of PL still elude us as a field?

Designing and providing effective PL opportunities for teachers in grades 3–8 is essential. We need to help teachers implement instruction aligned to the science of literacy and to move student achievement beyond the status quo. It is also essential to building the individual and collective efficacy that binds teachers together and promotes resilience and openness to new ideas (Tschannen-Moran & Johnson, 2011). There are two questions to answer: What do teachers of these grades need to know and be able to do in their classrooms, and how can they learn it most efficiently? We are pragmatists at our core. Teachers have no time to waste on learning that won't meet their needs and apply to their work. For researchers, PL work is also time consuming and expensive, so they, too, need to plan for efficiency. PL can actually cause increased student achievement, but not all PL efforts have that effect (Didion et al., 2020).

As we prepared to write this chapter, we brought several assumptions to our reading. First, we assumed that the knowledge and skills that teachers in grades 3–8 need are qualitatively different than what teachers in PreK–2 need, and that it would be useful to document PL targets in research implemented with teachers after second grade. For the sake of parsimony, we chose to refer to students in grades 3–8 as young adolescents. Second, we assumed that the PL targets would have to span reading, writing, and knowledge building. Third, we assumed PL efforts might include both English language arts and content-area instruction. We did not make any assumptions about the format of the PL, but we hypothesized that some formats might be used more often and/or have stronger evidence of effectiveness than others.

We found that not all research on PL, or research that includes PL, is easy to unpack as a set of knowledge and skills to target and a set of strategies for learning it (Kennedy, 2016). The reality of PL is messier than that. For example, Cantrell and Hughes (2008) took a step forward from teacher knowledge and skills. They positioned teacher beliefs and attitudes, expressed as personal and collective efficacy, as the core target of their PL efforts, and it was efficacy that undergirded their knowledge and skills targets. They also included students outside of our young adolescent range. They worked with 22 sixth- and ninth-grade teachers across content areas to learn and use a large set of content-area literacy routines. They employed institutes, planning, modeling, simulations, readings, and collaborations. Observations revealed that teachers did increase their use of these routines (knowledge and skills), and survey data indicated that their efficacy (beliefs) improved. In addition, teachers with higher initial efficacy implemented the routines more quickly.

But in this study and many others, there is no clear link between specific aspects of the PL and specific increases in instruction or efficacy; there is also no clear identification of which instructional routines were used more than others. Research has revealed causal effects of some PL strategies, such as coaching (Kraft et al., 2018). However, in the study by Cantrell and Hughes (2008), a broad focus on literacy instruction shared with a broad variety of PL strategies and supports was broadly associated with changes in implementation and efficacy. We can't isolate the effects of collaboration, modeling, coaching, or specific knowledge-building targets in this study to make future efforts more effective. But some studies we located did reveal PL targets for young adolescents and PL strategies worthy of emulation and further study. As we share what we learned from them, we start with a description of PL targets, move to PL processes, and finally end with limitations and implications for research and practice.

PL Targets: Knowledge and Skills

Effective PL strategies for increasing elementary teachers' knowledge, especially as measured with formal assessments and surveys, have long been sought and have proven practically elusive. Most available measures target knowledge related to early stages of reading development (e.g., phonological awareness, decoding and encoding), but some research teams are broadening their focus to include subscales for oral language, fluency, and comprehension (Davis, Samuelson, et al., 2022; Hall et al., 2024). This focus, though, is on what *elementary* teachers need to know and be able to do. Some of those teachers teach kindergarten; others teach third grade or fifth grade. It may be useful to consider knowledge for teaching in kindergarten through second grade separately from knowledge for teachers of young adolescents.

Some research teams are responding to this need. Hudson (2023), for example, recently tested a measure of knowledge for teaching reading comprehension with teachers in grades 3–6. She found that teachers with both high knowledge and strong implementation of comprehension and text structure instruction had higher student achievement on a standardized test and on a researcher-designed test of main idea generation. O'Byrne and colleagues (2021) developed a measure of teacher efficacy in content area reading and writing strategies and disciplinary literacy, attending to equity and critical literacy; analyzing and using text purposefully; engagement, interest, and relevance; differentiation; progress monitoring and assessment; instructional technologies; and strategies for teaching multilinguals. Savitz and colleagues (2024) used the instrument to gather initial efficacy estimates. This estimates work can help PL designers cater to potential differences in efficacy by content area. In addition, the instruments may help researchers target and/or measure the effects of PL for teachers of young adolescents.

PL does not always increase teachers' performance on formal knowledge assessments. Sometimes, initial teacher self-reports of knowledge can be higher before PL than after as teachers learn that there is more to teaching (Smith & Williams, 2020). Luckily, though, PL can change practice even without knowledge gains (Clark et al., 2018). Formal knowledge assessments are not the only strategy.

Researchers have used multiple strategies to gather information about what teachers of young adolescents know, so that they can target PL. A simple survey enhanced with interviews and observations identified specific aspects of writing standards, instruction, and assessment as targets (Howell et al., 2021). Think-aloud protocols, concept mapping, and a comprehension task with interview opportunities (Davis, Tenore, et al., 2022) revealed that a community of 62 teacher participants at these grades had a shared language about reading comprehension as a process of strategizing, working to establish coherence, using and creating knowledge, and connecting with others. Document analysis and observations (Clark et al., 2018) suggested an initial set of specific knowledge-building topics based on Kamil and colleagues' (2008) Institute of Education Sciences Practice Guide: how to teach comprehension strategies explicitly, how and why to provide explicit vocabulary instruction, how to provide opportunities for extended discussion, how to increase student motivation and engagement, and how to make intensive interventions available.

Customized PL designs to share already-validated instructional practices could also help us build a usable knowledge base. In Bryant and colleagues' (2001) school–university partnership, they first collected data on sixth-grade teacher's knowledge and beliefs. They chose three PL targets that matched teacher requests and would be new content for teachers: multisyllabic decoding, partner reading, and collaborative strategic reading (Klingner et al., 1998). They provided full-day workshops with lectures, modeling, and guided practice on each target several weeks apart. Multisyllabic decoding and collaborative strategic reading were implemented with partial fidelity. Partner reading was implemented with high fidelity. Teachers reported that collaborative strategic reading "fit" student needs and content goals, but time for instruction and preparation was still a barrier. Partner reading was viewed by fewer teachers as fitting student needs, and more than half of the teachers were concerned about students' lack of acceptance of the strategy, but it was implemented more often, and with better fidelity, potentially because it was easier to implement.

PL Processes

Once we know what knowledge and skills to target, choosing and using only the most effective PL processes is an idea whose time has come. Researchers (including us!) have used institutes, workshops, professional learning community (PLC) structures, modeling, video demonstrations, in-class coaching, virtual coaching, book clubs, and lesson study, alone and in combination. We've sometimes engaged in these high-cost interactions without systematic empirical reflection (Walpole et al., 2018). But many researchers have provided useful insights.

Comparing different PL designs could help us to understand which PL processes are more effective. Brownell and colleagues (2017) began with a 2-day knowledge-building institute targeting word study (multisyllabic decoding and structural analysis) and fluency. Participants were randomly assigned only to this institute or to a more comprehensive PL program. The PL program included monthly small-group meetings to analyze student data, set improvement goals, and make action plans for instruction. In addition, participants collected video of their instruction and watched it privately with a coach who provided feedback and engaged in discussion. Results of this study were mixed. Teachers in the PL program spent more time teaching word study and fluency. They had higher-quality instruction in word study but not fluency. Comprehensive PL built teachers' knowledge of fluency practices but not of word study. Finally, effects on achievement were mixed; students with teachers in the PL program achieved higher scores for word-level measures but not for oral reading fluency. The links between PL, teacher knowledge, teacher practice, and student achievement in this study were promising but not perfect.

Sailors and Price (2010) also compared two PL treatments targeting comprehension strategy instruction: a 2-day workshop and the workshop plus individual support through modeling and coaching. Both groups of teachers increased the number of chances they gave students to apply comprehension strategies during a lesson, but the teachers in the full PL treatment provided more opportunities. The full treatment was also associated with better student achievement. Coaching support for teachers was varied but included co-teaching, modeling, observation and feedback, and reflective discussions; unfortunately, we cannot unpack or make causal claims about the relative effects of each strategy.

Swanson and colleagues (2024) compared the effects of a PL model, Strategies for Teaching Reading, Information, and Vocabulary Effectively, supported by researchers or by school leaders. In both iterations, fourth-grade teachers participated in a 6-hour workshop delivered by the research team and two follow-up teacher study team meetings, with additional opportunities for practice, reflection, and problem solving. However, the research team led these meetings in the researcher-supported PL condition, while school leaders (e.g., assistant principals, instructional coaches) led these meetings in the school-supported condition. Both groups demonstrated improved student achievement on researcher-developed measures of content knowledge, vocabulary, and reading comprehension compared with a business-as-usual group that did not participate in the PL. There were no differences between the groups on a standardized measure of reading comprehension, but there was a small effect favoring the school-supported PL on a standardized measure of vocabulary. The researchers concluded that the school-supported PL was a promising approach for sustaining PL efforts after initial collaboration with researchers.

In 2009, Laura Desimone proposed a core framework for studying the effects of PL. Her article is widely cited (with over 7,000 citations according to Google Scholar). She argued that a focus on the features of the PL experience would allow us to bypass the noise produced by myriad PL delivery models and begin to generate stronger empirical evidence linking a theory of teacher change with a theory of instruction. The features she identified in the literature included content focus, active learning, coherence, sufficient duration, and collective participation; our adaptation of her conceptual framework, separating the teacher change components from the instructional components, is represented in Figure 20.1.

Desimone (2009) proposed that this framework, linking a theory of teacher change and a theory of instruction, would provide the PL research community the infrastructure to generate a stronger empirical knowledge base for identifying evidence-based PL practices. Researchers could use the framework to decide what to measure and when to measure it. Individual researcher decisions could then be combined and studied together more easily. That same year, Reed (2009) reviewed studies of PL for middle school teachers. Only four studies met her quality

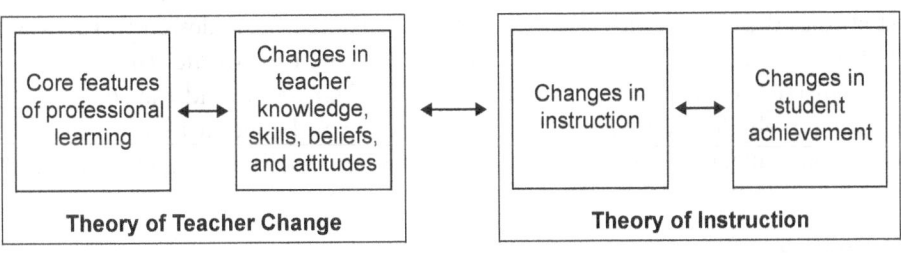

FIGURE 20.1. Conceptual framework for studying the effects of PL. Adapted from Desimone (2009).

standards. Across those studies, though, Reed traced characteristics consistent with Desimone's framework: She recommended that researchers target fidelity of implementation through teacher collaboration (active learning), plan based on teacher needs and with administrative support (coherence), build knowledge over time (duration), and plan schoolwide (collective participation).

Unfortunately, this charge to define and combine a PL knowledge base has not been taken up at large by researchers. For example, in a meta-analysis of 14 PL studies in middle school and high school reading that used randomized controlled trial or quasi-experimental designs (Basma & Savage, 2023) only one study measured change in teacher knowledge (de Kramer et al., 2012), none measured beliefs or attitudes, and none described the core features of the PL. However, we did find PL studies in our review that attended very specifically to Desimone's (2009) design charge (e.g., Brownell et al., 2017; Hall et al., 2021; Stevens et al., 2022; Traga Philippakos & MacArthur, 2021).

Recent meta-analyses of experimental and quasi-experimental studies have used Desimone's (2009) framework to unpack the content and effects of PL studies. One meta-analysis (Didion et al., 2020) reviewed studies of PL and reading achievement in kindergarten through eighth grade. While there were overall positive effects on achievement for teachers in PL treatments, moderator analyses did not identify specific design features associated with those effects. Another meta-analysis (Rice et al., 2024) reviewed studies of PL in reading comprehension on teacher and student outcomes in kindergarten through twelfth grade. The researchers found large effects of PL on teacher knowledge and small effects on student reading comprehension. However, none of the six potential moderators (coaching, format, content, provider, duration, or number of strategies taught) produced statistically significant differences. In a meta-analysis of studies of PL focused on data literacy training in K–12, Filderman and colleagues (2022) found that although active learning and collective participation moderated the effects of PL on teacher outcomes, content focus and coaching did not; however, reviewed studies did not report enough information about duration or coherence for moderator analyses to be conducted.

How these design features are interpreted by researchers and coded across studies may lead to different conclusions. A systematic review of studies of PL on PreK–12 teachers' implementation of intensive reading interventions found that most studies did not provide detailed descriptions of specific design features of PL (McMaster et al., 2021). Another systematic review of PL studies that focused on literacy instruction and intervention for English learners found that most studies most adequately described the PL's active learning and content focus, followed by its duration, collective participation, and coherence (Shelton, Hogan, et al., 2023).

This Review

For the purpose of this review, we chose to unpack Desimone's (2009) conceptual framework for PL in a broad set of studies with teachers of young adolescents, including studies not designed for causal inference. We selected studies by conducting a systematic review of the literature. We searched the Education Source full-text database for peer-reviewed academic journal articles published in English using the terms *professional development, professional learning, coaching,* or *teacher knowledge* paired with the Boolean terms AND *upper elementary,* or *intermediate,* or *middle school,* AND *reading* or *writing* or *literacy*. Our search yielded 551 articles, which we screened for inclusion in our review based on reading the title. We read the abstracts of 148 articles after excluding 403 that were not relevant based on title. We read 44 articles for this review after excluding 104 that were not relevant based on abstract. After reading, we excluded another 14 articles that were not relevant upon further review (e.g., researchers did not actually provide PL in the study). We reviewed the references list in two recent meta-analyses (Basma & Savage, 2023; Rice et al., 2024) and located an additional seven studies that examined the effects of PL in grades 3–8. In reading the final set of 37 articles, we coded the ways they enacted PL using Desimone's (2009) descriptors (i.e., content focus, active learning, coherence, sufficient duration, and collective participation). We hoped, then, to identify what researchers in grades 3–8 space have targeted for teachers to know and be able to do, and what methods they have used to build that understanding.

Content Focus

Desimone (2009) defined *content focus* to include both subject-matter content and how students learn that content (i.e., pedagogical content knowledge). All studies we located attended to content and pedagogy. They typically began with a content-focused institute, workshop, or seminar to introduce and define the focus, then followed up with other PL strategies. The content addressed instructional strategies for developing word recognition, comprehension, vocabulary, background knowledge, writing, and language.

We found evidence that word recognition still matters in some young adolescent PL efforts, but the targets differed from those of primary grades. Word recognition targets for young adolescents were multisyllabic decoding paired with morphology (Benedict et al., 2021), fluency (Brownell et al., 2017), or fluency and comprehension (Bryant et al., 2001). Studies that targeted multisyllabic decoding included both special educators and classroom teachers.

Researchers also targeted the broader set of before-, during-, and after-reading strategies commonly called content-area reading, including teachers of all content areas (Cantrell & Hughes, 2008). More specifically, researchers identified specific skill sets within the broad umbrella of comprehension strategies. They targeted inference, main idea identification, and summarization (Hall et al., 2021) and creation of gist-level summaries, and asking and answering questions in writing during reading across content areas (Stevens et al., 2022). Several research teams (Boardman et al., 2016; Moore et al., 2019; Vaughn et al., 2011) targeted collaborative strategic reading (Klingner et al., 1998, 2004) across content areas, a routine that has both a before–during–after reading sequence and a strategy focus. Sailors and Price (2010) focused on comprehension strategy instruction during reading across content areas. Still other research teams developed suites of instructional strategies for developing background knowledge, vocabulary knowledge, and comprehension (Simmons et al., 2010; Swanson et al., 2024; Vaughn et al., 2009, 2013, 2022; Wexler et al., 2022, 2023). In these cases, strategies could be applied to any content-area text, typically in social studies, but they were designed to work in a specific sequence before, during, and after student reading.

Researchers also targeted writing strategies in PL for young adolescents. Two teams added instructional strategies for writing to content-area reading strategies (Nichols et al., 2007; Smith & Williams, 2020). Writing informed by cognitive strategies (Kim et al., 2011; Traga Philippakos & MacArthur, 2021) or enhanced by digital tools and collaboration (Howell et al., 2021) were also content targets. Knecht and colleagues (2023) targeted sentence-level features in academic writing (connectives, anaphora, and appositives).

Some researchers targeted language more broadly. Castells and colleagues (2022) worked with eighth-grade history teachers to learn how to use discussion prompts to help students understand and make connections among multiple texts. They wanted teachers to use literal, intratextual inferential, and intertextual inferential questions intentionally to help students understand texts. Townsend (2015) targeted disciplinary academic vocabulary and morphology across content areas. Wilkinson and colleagues (2023) targeted students' ability to engage in text-based oral arguments.

Active Learning

Desimone (2009) defined *active learning* broadly, and researchers interpreted it broadly. Active learning included demonstration (lesson simulation, modeling, or co-teaching), observation, feedback, analysis of student work, and discussion. The active learning activities took place during initial institutes, during small-group interactions, and in one-on-one coaching.

Lesson Study is a promising practice for active learning. Benedict and colleagues (2021) employed formal Lesson Study in which groups of teachers co-plan, implement lessons, and observe one another. Then they meet to discuss what they have learned, potentially modifying their shared plan. Fourth- and fifth-grade special educators and classroom teachers collaborated in this study, implementing co-planned lessons across tiers of instruction. Researchers studied teacher participant discourse, describing phases of teacher learning about the content and about their students. Bryant and colleagues (2001) and Stevens and colleagues (2022) did not call their work Lesson Study, but it had many of the same features. Researchers modeled target practices in classrooms and then met with the participating teachers and their administrators to problem-solve every 2 weeks.

Small-group collaborative meetings were a means of active learning in multiple projects. Some teams used these meetings for goal setting and action planning (Brownell et al., 2017). Others used them for collaborative lesson planning (Castells et al., 2022; Hall et al., 2021; Kim et al., 2011). PLCs connected teachers to learn together and solve problems, sometimes with the leadership of a coach (Shelton, Swanson, et al., 2023; Simmons et al., 2010; Swanson et al., 2024). Although small-group collaborative meetings might include analysis of student work, some researchers targeted student work directly (Benedict et al., 2021; Brownell et al., 2017; Kim et al., 2011).

Engaging teachers in inquiry cycles was another structure to promote active learning among groups of teachers. Inquiry cycles were similar across studies. Knecht and colleagues (2023) used protocols for planning, teaching, and reflecting for four cycles. Stevens et al. (2022) engaged PLCs in sharing experiences, problem solving, and goal setting. Vaughn et al. (2022) used teacher team protocols to engage teachers in reflection, learning new practices, and identifying goals. Wexler and colleagues (2022) linked co-teaching teams with coaches to plan, implement, and reflect. Wilkinson et al. (2023) used study groups in which teachers watched and rated participant video, discussed it, and planned. Inquiry was also the heart of a formative experiment (Howell et al., 2021). Small-group meetings could also be used less formally to discuss a range of instructional strategies and commit to a specific classroom trial (Smith & Williams, 2021).

Coaches and coaching were active learning targets in PL studies, but their practices varied. Large-scale, state-funded access to coaches in middle school was associated with mixed results on student achievement (Lockwood et al., 2010). Site-based middle school coaches in the same state were generally well received as PL providers by English language arts and social studies teachers, and by administrators (Marsh et al., 2012). However, survey data with a nationally representative sample (Shelton, Swanson, et al., 2023) revealed that only 58% of middle school teachers had a coach designated in their building, and many of the coaches were also assistant principals. Many teachers with coaches in their buildings (42%) reported not having any support within a typical month; many coaches reported not providing support for literacy.

Despite problematic findings at scale, coaching (including one-on-one classroom observation and feedback in addition to co-teaching and modeling) was still prominent as one of several strategies in PL studies (Brownell et al., 2017; Cantrell & Hughes, 2008; Clark et al., 2018; Howell et al., 2021; Kim et al., 2011; Sailors & Price, 2010; Vaughn et al., 2011, 2013), as often as biweekly (Boardman et al., 2016; Moore et al., 2019) and sometimes weekly (Hall et al., 2021; Vaughn et al., 2009). Traga Philippakos and MacArthur (2021) provided individual coaching feedback to lesson videos. Townsend (2015) used participants' classroom videos and a reflection protocol to release reflection and coaching from PL providers to the content-area team. Wilkinson and colleagues (2023) added individual lesson demonstration to analysis of video in a coaching model. Wexler and colleagues (2023) provided structured, distributed coaching based on implementation data. After learning about each of three new practices, all teachers had coaching support to plan, implement, and reflect for 4 weeks. Coaches collected fidelity data. For the final 5 weeks of the quarter, teachers who had not reached acceptable implementation levels got additional intensive coaching support.

Coherence

Desimone (2009) defined *coherence* to include two characteristics that we saw as inseparable: the extent to which the PL processes are consistent with teachers' knowledge and beliefs, and the consistency of the PL target with the broader educational policies that influence their work (e.g., standards, curriculum). These coherence connections included intentional efforts to tap and connect to teachers' knowledge and beliefs, and efforts to build new uses for existing materials and assessments.

Researchers have made efforts to understand teacher knowledge and beliefs to target their PL efforts. Some teams used interviews (Bryant et al., 2001; Howell et al., 2021). Others have used needs assessment (Nichols et al., 2007) and entry surveys (Townsend, 2015). Still others collected social validity data (Stevens et al., 2022) or feasibility data (Traga Philippakos & MacArthur, 2021), or both (Wexler et al., 2023), toward the end of PL programs.

Efforts to establish coherence were clearly linked to materials. Many research teams used existing classroom instructional materials in PL (Boardman et al., 2016; Bryant et al., 2001; Cantrell & Hughes, 2008; Kim et al., 2011; Klingner et al., 2004; Knecht et al., 2023; Moore et al., 2019; Nichols et al., 2007; Stevens et al., 2022; Townsend, 2015; Wexler et al., 2022). Castells and colleagues (2002) and Hall et al. (2021) built new units, consistent with the curriculum. Other teams targeted specific units within the state social studies curriculum (Simmons et al., 2010; Swanson et al., 2024; Vaughn et al., 2009, 2011, 2013, 2022). Howell and colleagues (2021) targeted the text structures in PL on digital writing instruction to the curriculum scope and sequence.

Other strategies for coherence informed the underlying instructional design for the PL. Several studies connected to teacher beliefs through the use of a gradual release of responsibility model. In essence, researchers were modeling in the PL design a core tenet of the instruction. In Castells and colleagues' (2022) study of history teachers' text-based questioning, researchers first collected a set of initial questions that teachers proposed to use. They released responsibility in a sequence of collaborative co-planning seminars, so that teachers learned about questioning, analyzed their own initial questions, agreed on a common lesson frame, and co-planned new sets of questions. They then implemented the lessons they had co-constructed and met to reflect collaboratively on student learning. By the end of the intervention, teachers were designing their own questions. Students of the PL teachers demonstrated better question answering and content learning immediately after the unit, and the question-answering advantage was still evident 2 months later compared to a control group.

Howell and colleagues (2021) also released responsibility to teachers through inquiry. Their content focus was digital collaborative writing. After a pedagogy-focused institute, they helped teachers set inquiry goals and released responsibility. With the support of expert observation and coaching and support from preservice teachers, teachers implemented their inquiry cycles collaboratively. The research team, using a formative experiment design, documented some changes in practice but also saw teachers focusing more attention on technology tools and less attention on student collaborative writing. Based on their interactions with the teachers, the team proposed that they would add peer observation and online modules to enhance supports for teacher inquiry.

Hall and colleagues (2021) also investigated a gradual release of responsibility model. Their content target was instruction in inferencing, main idea identification, and summarization. They compared a fully scripted and a partially scripted version of the curriculum, with teachers randomly assigned. For the partially scripted condition, teachers transitioned from fully scripted models to partially scripted models, which required them to plan parts of the lessons themselves. Teachers in both conditions also transitioned to planning lessons independently. Students of teachers in the partially scripted condition outperformed those in the fully scripted condition on a standardized test. Although the partially scripted condition was associated with better student performance, teachers preferred the fully scripted lessons. Given the policy constraints of teacher planning time, completing and customizing the lesson scripts was too time consuming.

Wexler and colleagues (2022) released responsibility systematically across PL cycles and lesson planning templates. Teachers first studied new approaches, ending with a lesson planning frame. Then coaches (called "helpers" in the study) modeled how to plan and then implement a lesson in week 1, co-planned and co-taught in week 2, and released responsibility to plan and teach in week 3. A new cycle added content (and length) to the lesson planning frame and included the sequence of gradual release supports. Four cycles in all introduced the full lesson frame.

Moore and colleagues (2019) used a gradual release of responsibility in the final year of a 5-year study of collaborative strategic reading (Boardman et al., 2016; Klingner et al., 1998). They observed and interviewed teachers after the PL supports provided during the project were withdrawn. Such efforts at documenting teacher internalization and appropriation, or "sustainability" of a PL target get at the heart of coherence. If PL is effective and its content focus is consistent with teachers' beliefs and the real-life constraints of their work, teachers are likely to sustain those practices. They will incorporate the target into daily practice in ways that maintain and extend its intentions. The research team argued that fidelity to the core features of the target was important, but so was adaptation and integration.

Planning for gradual release and sustainment was also a characteristic of the PL plan in Wexler and colleagues' (2022) study over 2 years. The team attended to this coherence in two ways. First, they targeted fidelity in an intensive support year, including building administrators in PL and coaching meetings. That way, in the second year, they could release responsibility for maintaining the program to building staff for maintenance.

Duration

While none of the research teams used a single session, or even several sessions, there was no consistency in description of duration. Desimone (2009) suggested that sustained PL over the course of a semester, or at least 20 hours, might be sufficient for improving outcomes. In these studies, duration was described in number of hours, ranging from 16 to 50 (Benedict et al., 2021; Kim et al., 2011; Smith & Williams, 2020); number of weeks, ranging from 6 to 21 (Boardman et al., 2016; Castells et al., 2022; Simmons et al., 2010; Swanson et al., 2024; Vaughn et al., 2009, 2011, 2013, 2022); and number of months, ranging from 4 to 8 (Bryant et al., 2001; Howell et al., 2021; Knecht et al., 2023; Wexler et al., 2022). Cantrell and Hughes (2008) provided PL for an entire academic year. Frequency of specific types of PL events was also not consistently reported, and when it was reported, it varied. Frequency of PL activities such as coaching and support meetings ranged from weekly (Hall et al., 2021; Vaughn et al., 2009; Wexler et al., 2022) to biweekly (Boardman et al., 2016; Bryant et al., 2001) to monthly (Cantrell & Hughes, 2008; Nichols et al., 2007; Smith & Williams, 2021; Vaughn et al., 2011).

Collective Participation

Desimone (2009) defined *collective participation* as interaction and discourse between teachers in the same school, grade, or department as a feature of PL. Researchers have sought collective participation among different groupings of teachers. They have provided PL with regular education and special education teachers who served the same students (Benedict et al., 2021; Brownell et al., 2017; Bryant et al., 2001; Wexler et al., 2022) or teachers within grade levels but across content areas (Cantrell & Hughes, 2008; Moore et al., 2019; Nichols et al. 2007; Wexler et al., 2023). They have worked with teachers in the same content area and grade level in different schools, including social studies teachers in grades 4 and 5 (Boardman et al., 2016; Klingner et al., 2004; Simmons et al., 2010; Swanson et al., 2024; Vaughn et al., 2022) or grades 7 and 8 (Castells et al., 2022; Vaughn et al., 2009, 2011, 2013), as well as teachers in different schools and grade levels, including teachers of multilingual students (Kim et al., 2011) and monolingual English classrooms (Hall et al., 2021). Howell and colleagues (2021) also provided PL across grades and schools, but they leveraged specific group work purposefully to include similar or different settings and grades. Smith and Williams (2021) provided PL to English language arts teachers across middle school grades in the same school. We found only one study of individualized PL (Clark et al., 2018) that did not rely on teacher collaboration as a means of collective participation.

Limitations

We start our implications with important limitations. We set out to review PL work specific to teachers of young adolescents. We selected studies to read systematically, but different search strategies might reveal additional studies. Some of the studies we reviewed extended the range of grades to include teachers of younger children; some also included teachers of older children. We opted to include them, but including a smaller number of studies focusing exclusively on young adolescents might have led to different conclusions. We opted for a wide net rather than a narrow scope; different criteria for inclusion might yield different insights. Finally, we used Desimone's (2009) call to the field as a lens for our coding of the studies, but our own biases surely impacted our application of that lens.

Implications for Research

We were excited about the range of content targeted in these studies, especially because it did not replicate the overfocus on phonological awareness and phonics knowledge currently dominating PL for the early primary teachers (Tortorelli et al., 2021). There is surely room for better understanding of the relationship between language and literacy in instruction for young adolescents at large, and for multilingual learners and students with disabilities. We also need to better understand how to measure and develop teacher knowledge of these students' needs.

In our view, Desimone's (2009) framework has not yet produced the clarity she envisioned, but the work remains important. It would be useful to have clear guidance as we design PL to serve teachers and to advance knowledge. For now, we can say that researchers design content-focused PL initiatives with a range of strategies for active learning, coherence, duration, and collective participation. But we couldn't identify any specific combination that has been used multiple times across multiple settings with similar results.

When we tried to understand PL processes, we had one overarching insight. The details matter in PL, but academic journal guidelines may force researchers to gloss over details in writing for publication that they likely considered very carefully in real life. It may be that articles about the specific PL design of larger studies would be a welcome addition to our shared knowledge base as a field. A handful of studies we reviewed (Swanson et al., 2024; Vaughn et al., 2009, 2011, 2013, 2022; Wexler et al., 2022, 2023) are notable for the level of detail they provide about their PL design.

Many research teams are faced with a classic chicken-and-egg problem, and we see that as the most probable explanation for the continued lack of clarity about a science of PL. In order to test a new theory of instruction with adequate power, researchers must design PL—which requires a theory of teacher change. But either the theory of teacher change or the theory of instruction may be weak. We wonder whether researchers would be willing to hold their theory of teacher change constant at first, by adopting a specific PL design from a previous, successful study of teacher change. Then, if their student outcomes are positive, validating their theory of instruction, they could manipulate factors in the theory of teacher change. For example, it may be that replacing coaching with collaborative meetings would produce the same results but be more efficient. It may be that Lesson Study or co-planning would accelerate attainment of implementation fidelity and reduce the time needed to sustain the change. We cannot know that until we hold the theory of instruction constant and manipulate the theory of teacher change.

Castells and colleagues' (2022) study is a positive outlier. The researchers were able to document that both their theory of teacher change and their theory of instruction were sound in this targeted setting of one unit of history instruction in one grade level. They gradually released responsibility to teachers to plan the instruction. They documented their theory of teacher change by analyzing the questions teacher participants were able to write and through observations of instruction compared to a control group using the same texts without access to the questioning PL. They documented their theory of instruction by comparing student achievement on measures of question answering and on measures of content-area knowledge specific to the units immediately after the instruction and 2 months later. But a target audience of 10 teachers provided intense PL is not a scalable model to serve the needs of teachers of young adolescents.

We see the most important remaining work in defining the broad areas of active learning and coherence. Specifically, we would like to see experimental manipulations of active learning. For example, given an evidence-based theory of instruction, can we compare two or more theories of teacher change employing different strategies for active learning? Would one be associated with instructional fidelity or quality more quickly or more consistently across teachers? What would the results be with a less active version of teacher support?

For coherence, we read that many researchers do gather information about teacher knowledge and beliefs. Barring instances when that information was used to select the actual PL targets, what did researchers do with that information? How can teacher knowledge and beliefs consistent with a theory of instruction be leveraged in PL? When teacher knowledge and beliefs are inconsistent with the theory of instruction in a specific project (e.g., Smith & Williams, 2021), how can they be acknowledged and refuted? To what extent do teacher knowledge and beliefs influence instruction? Wijekumar and colleagues (2019) described an "ecological context of literacy instruction" (p. 17): preservice experiences, inservice PL, administrative practices, and instructional materials that influence teacher knowledge and skills. To what extent, and in what order, should researchers target each piece of the ecological puzzle?

We accept that the ecological context is real. A missing link in our literature review is studies of curriculum-specific PL. Slavin and colleagues' (2008) best-evidence synthesis found no research on middle school or high school textbooks but did find high-quality studies on what the team called "instructional-process programs" (p. 291). They applied this label to studies of approaches that targeted very specific changes in daily instruction coupled with extensive PL. Much has happened in curricula since that study was published. The push for high-quality instructional materials may yet influence the PL landscape and provide the context for authentic PL experiments. In essence, these materials are already a theory of instruction (though often an untested one). When they are adopted, they establish coherence and collective participation, at least in a target content area. The demand for adoption, training, and ongoing support of curriculum materials provides a potentially fertile ground for the design and testing of different types and amounts of active learning that could advance the science of PL, and then that science could be applied to a broader range of PL targets.

Implications for Practice

While we wait for research to more clearly specify a science of PL, there is no evidence that Desimone's (2009) descriptors are not important. Teachers of young adolescents deserve PL that builds their understanding of relevant content; is active, participatory, and ongoing; promotes collaboration with their colleagues; and is firmly embedded in the materials and policies with which they work. But without a clear science of PL, how these design features are interpreted in PL efforts will likely remain up to providers' interpretations. We urge building-level and district-level administrators to prevent any PL efforts that do not include these features.

REFERENCES

Basma, B., & Savage, R. (2023). Teacher professional development and student reading in middle and high school: A systematic review and meta-analysis. *Journal of Teacher Education, 74*(3), 214–228.

Benedict, A. E., Brownell, M., Bettini, E., & Sohn, H. (2021). Learning together: Teachers' evolving understanding of coordinated word study instruction within an RTI framework. *Teacher Education and Special Education, 44*(2), 134–159.

Boardman, A. G., Vaughn, S., Buckley, P., Reutebuch, C., Roberts, G., & Klingner, J. (2016). Collaborative Strategic Reading for students with learning disabilities in upper elementary classrooms. *Exceptional Children, 82*(4), 409–427.

Brownell, M., Kiely, M. T., Haager, D., Boardman, A., Corbett, N., Algina, J., . . . Urbach, J. (2017). Literacy learning cohorts: Content-focused approach to improving special education teachers' reading instruction. *Exceptional Children, 83*(2), 143–164.

Bryant, D. P., Linan-Thompson, S., & Ugel, N. (2001). The effects of professional development for middle school general and special education teachers on implementation of reading strategies in inclusive content area classes. *Learning Disability Quarterly, 24*(4), 251–264.

Cantrell, S. C., & Hughes, H. K. (2008). Teacher efficacy and content literacy implementation: An exploration of the effects of extended professional development with coaching. *Journal of Literacy Research, 40*(1), 95–127.

Castells, N., Minguela, M., Solé, I., Miras, M., Nadal, E., & Rijlaarsdam, G. (2022). Improving questioning–answering strategies in learning from multiple complementary texts: An intervention study. *Reading Research Quarterly, 57*(3), 879–912.

Clark, S. K., Schoepf, S., & Hatch, L. (2018). Exploring the use of personalised professional development to enhance teacher knowledge and reading instruction in the upper elementary grades. *Journal of Research in Reading, 41*, S30–S47.

Davis, D. S., Samuelson, C., Grifenhagen, J., DeIaco, R., & Relyea, J. (2022). Getting KnERDI with language: Examining teachers' knowledge for enhancing reading development in code-based and meaning-based domains. *Reading Research Quarterly, 57*(3), 781–804.

Davis, D. S., Tenore, F. B., McElhone, D., & DeIaco, R. (2022). What do upper-elementary and middle school teachers know about the processes of text comprehension? *Reading and Writing, 35*(9), 2257–2283.

de Kramer, R. M., Masters, J., O'Dwyer, L., Dash, S., & Russell, M. (2012). Relationship of online teacher professional development to seventh-grade teachers' and students' knowledge and practices in English language arts. *Teacher Educator, 47*(3), 236–259.

Desimone, L. M. (2009). Improving impact studies of teachers' professional development: Toward better conceptualizations and measures. *Educational Researcher, 38*(3), 181–199.

Didion, L., Toste, J. R., & Filderman, M. J. (2020). Teacher professional development and student reading achievement: A meta-analytic review of the effects. *Journal of Research on Educational Effectiveness, 13*(1), 29–66.

Filderman, M. J., Toste, J. R., Didion, L., & Peng, P. (2022). Data literacy training for K–12 teachers: A meta-analysis of the effects on teacher outcomes. *Remedial and Special Education, 43*(5), 328–343.

Hall, C., Solari, E. J., Hayes, L., Dahl-Leonard, K., DeCoster, J., Kehoe, K. F., . . . Vargas, I. (2024). Validation of an instrument for assessing elementary-grade educators' knowledge to teach reading. *Reading and Writing, 37*, 1955–1974.

Hall, C., Zucker, T. A., Montroy, J. J., & Dahl-Leonard, K. (2021). Pilot study of unlocking understanding professional development to support grade 3 reading comprehension. *Elementary School Journal, 122*(2), 278–313.

Howell, E., Perez, S., & Abraham, W. T. (2021). Toward a professional development model for writing as a digital, participatory process. *Reading Research Quarterly, 56*(1), 95–117.

Hudson, A. K. (2023). Upper elementary teachers' knowledge of reading comprehension, classroom practice, and student's performance in reading comprehension. *Reading Research Quarterly, 58*(3), 351–360.

Kamil, M. L., Borman, G. D., Dole, J., Kral, C. C., Salinger, T., & Torgesen, J. (2008). *Improving adolescent literacy: Effective classroom and intervention practices: A practice guide.* National Center for Education Evaluation and Regional Assistance, Institute of Education Sciences, U.S. Department of Education. https://ies.ed.gov/ncee/wwc/docs/practiceguide/adlit_pg_082608.pdf.

Kennedy, M. M. (2016). How does professional development improve teaching? *Review of Educational Research, 86*(4), 945–980.

Kim, J., Olson, C., Scarcella, R., Kramer, J., Pearson, M., van Dyk, D., Collins, P., & Land, R. (2011). A randomized experiment of a cognitive strategies approach to text-based analytical writing for mainstreamed Latino English language learners in grades 6 to 12. *Journal of Research on Educational Effectiveness, 4*(3), 231–263.

Klingner, J. K., Vaughn, S., & Arguelles, M. E. (2004). Collaborative strategic reading: "Real-world" lessons from classroom teachers. *Remedial and Special Education, 25*(5), 291–302.

Klingner, J. K., Vaughn, S., & Schumm, J. S. (1998). Collaborative strategic reading during social studies in heterogeneous fourth-grade classrooms. *Elementary School Journal, 99*(1), 3–22.

Knecht, R., Larson, L., & Townsend, D. (2023). Exploring teacher and student knowledge of sentence-level language features. *Journal of Adolescent and Adult Literacy, 66*(6), 344–354.

Kraft, M. A., Blazar, D., & Hogan, D. (2018). The effect of teacher coaching on instruction and achievement: A meta-analysis of the causal evidence. *Review of Educational Research, 88*(4), 547–588.

Lockwood, J. R., McCombs, J. S., & Marsh, J. (2010). Linking reading coaches and student achievement: Evidence from Florida middle schools. *Educational Evaluation and Policy Analysis, 32*(3), 372–388.

Marsh, J. A., McCombs, J. S., & Martorell, F. (2012). Reading coach quality: Findings from Florida middle schools. *Literacy Research and Instruction, 51*(1), 1–26.

McMaster, K. L., Baker, K., Donegan, R., Hugh, M., & Sargent, K. (2021). Professional development to support teachers' implementation of intensive reading intervention: A systematic review. *Remedial and Special Education, 42*(5), 329–342.

Moore, B. A., Boardman, A. G., Lasser, C. J., Schmidt, K. M., Smith, C. E., & Schwarz, V. S. (2019). Integrating evidence-based reading practices into middle-school content instruction: Exploring a facet of sustainability. *Teacher Development, 23*(3), 287–306.

Nichols, W., Young, C., & Rickelman, R. (2007). Improving middle school professional development by examining middle school teachers' application of literacy strategies and instructional design. *Reading Psychology, 28*(1), 97–130.

O'Byrne, W., Savitz, R. S., Morrison, J., Kane, B., Lilly, T., Ming, K. M., & Aldrich, C. (2021). Literacy across the disciplines: Development and validation of an instrument to assess literacy instruction in middle and high school classrooms. *Clearing House, 94*(2), 63–75.

Reed, D. K. (2009). A synthesis of professional development on the implementation of literacy strategies for middle school content area teachers. *Research in Middle Level Education Online, 32*(10), 1–12.

Rice, M., Lambright, K., & Wijekumar, K. (2024). Professional development in reading comprehension: A meta-analysis of the effects on teachers and students. *Reading Research Quarterly, 59*(3), 424–447.

Sailors, M., & Price, L. R. (2010). Professional development that supports the teaching of cognitive reading strategy instruction. *Elementary School Journal, 110*(3), 301–322.

Savitz, R. S., Morrison, J. D., Brown, C., Aldrich, C., Kane, B. D., & O'Byrne, W. I. (2024). Secondary teachers' adolescent literacy efficacy and professional learning considerations. *Reading Research Quarterly, 59*(1), 102–123.

Shelton, A., Hogan, E., Chow, J., & Wexler, J. (2023). A synthesis of professional development targeting literacy instruction and intervention for English learners. *Review of Educational Research, 93*(1), 37–72.

Shelton, A., Swanson, E., Wexler, J., Payne, S. B., & Hogan, E. (2023). An exploration of middle school literacy coaching: A study of teachers and instructional coaches. *Teacher Education and Special Education, 46*(4), 300–316.

Simmons, D., Hairrell, A., Edmonds, M., Vaughn, S., Larsen, R., Willson, V., . . . Byrns, G. (2010). A comparison of multiple-strategy methods: Effects on fourth-grade students' general and content-specific reading comprehension and vocabulary development. *Journal of Research on Educational Effectiveness, 3*(2), 121–156.

Slavin, R. E., Cheung, A., Groff, C., & Lake, C. (2008). Effective reading programs for middle and high schools: A best-evidence synthesis. *Reading Research Quarterly, 43*(3), 290–322.

Smith, N. L., & Williams, B. K. (2020). Supporting middle school language arts teachers through professional development. *Reading Psychology, 41*(5), 403–419.

Smith, N. L., & Williams, B. K. (2021). Content literacy PD: Middle grades language arts teachers' perceptions. *Reading Psychology, 42*(5), 504–516.

Stevens, E. A., Murray, C. S., Scammacca, N., Haager, D., & Vaughn, S. (2022). Middle school matters: Examining the effects of a schoolwide professional development model to improve reading comprehension. *Reading and Writing, 35*(8), 1839–1864.

Swanson, E., Stewart, A. A., Stevens, E. A., Scammacca, N. K., Capin, P., Bhat, B. H., . . . Vaughn, S. (2024). The efficacy of two models of professional development mediated by fidelity on fourth grade student reading outcomes. *Journal of Research on Educational Effectiveness, 17*(2), 288–317.

Tortorelli, L. S., Lupo, S. M., & Wheatley, B. C. (2021). Examining teacher preparation for code-related reading instruction: An integrated literature review. *Reading Research Quarterly, 56*(1), S317–S337.

Townsend, D. (2015). Who's using the language?: Supporting middle school students with content area academic language. *Journal of Adolescent and Adult Literacy, 58*(5), 376–387.

Traga Philippakos, Z. A., & MacArthur, C. A. (2021). Examination of genre-based strategy instruction in middle school English language arts and science. *Clearing House, 94*(4), 151–158.

Tschannen-Moran, M., & Johnson, D. (2011). Exploring literacy teachers' self-efficacy beliefs: Potential sources at play. *Teaching and Teacher Education, 27*(4), 751–761.

Vaughn, S., Klingner, J. K., Swanson, E. A., Boardman, A. G., Roberts, G., Mohammed, S. S., & Stillman-Spisak, S. J. (2011). Efficacy of collaborative strategic reading with middle school students. *American Educational Research Journal, 48*(4), 938–964.

Vaughn, S., Martinez, L., Linan-Thompson, S., Reutebuch, C., Carlson, C., & Francis, D. (2009). Enhancing social studies vocabulary and comprehension for seventh-grade English language learners: Findings from two experimental studies. *Journal of Research on Educational Effectiveness, 2*(4), 297–324.

Vaughn, S., Swanson, E., Fall, A.-M., Roberts, G., Capin, P., Stevens, E. A., & Stewart, A. A. (2022). The efficacy of comprehension and vocabulary focused professional development on English learners' literacy. *Journal of Educational Psychology, 114*(2), 257–272.

Vaughn, S., Swanson, E. A., Roberts, G., Wanzek, J., Stillman-Spisak, S. J., Solis, M., & Simmons, D. (2013). Improving reading comprehension and social studies knowledge in middle school. *Reading Research Quarterly, 48*(1), 77–93.

Walpole, S., Strong, J. Z., & Riches, C. B. (2018). Best practices in professional learning for improving literacy instruction in schools. In L. B. Gambrell & L. B. Morrow (Eds.), *Best practices in literacy instruction* (6th ed., pp. 429–446). Guilford Press.

Wexler, J., Kearns, D. M., Lemons, C. J., Shelton, A., Pollack, M. S., Stapleton, L. M., . . . Lyon, C. (2022). Improving literacy instruction in co-taught middle school classrooms to support reading comprehension. *Contemporary Educational Psychology, 68*, Article 102040.

Wexler, J., Swanson, E., Shelton, A., Kurz, L. A., Bray, L., & Hogan, E. (2023). Sustaining the use of evidence-based Tier 1 literacy practices that benefit students with disabilities. *Journal of Learning Disabilities, 56*(2), 145–160.

Wijekumar, K., Beerwinkle, A. L., Harris, K. R., & Graham, S. (2019). Etiology of teacher knowledge and instructional skills for literacy at the upper elementary grades. *Annals of Dyslexia, 69*(1), 5–20.

Wilkinson, I. A. G., Reznitskaya, A., & D'Agostino, J. V. (2023). Professional development in classroom discussion to improve argumentation: Teacher and student outcomes. *Learning and Instruction, 85*, Article 101732.

CHAPTER 21

Discourse, Positioning, and Agency
A Relational Perspective on Literacy Coaching in the Upper Elementary and Middle Grades

Dana A. Robertson
Jeanne R. Paratore

Over decades, studies have verified the importance of teacher knowledge in advancing students' literacy knowledge (Basma & Savage, 2018; Bond & Dykstra, 1967; Didion et al., 2020). Skillful teaching requires deep and sophisticated knowledge of foundational literacy skills and strategies (e.g., word study, fluency, text structure), along with a thorough understanding of how to both guide students to successfully comprehend and compose new and poignant texts and to use literacy actively to improve their lives and those of others. Yet despite the convergence of evidence, we still struggle to effectively enact teaching practices that support and sustain student learning. This problem is especially evident in upper elementary, middle, and secondary school classrooms, where students often fail to experience skillful evidence-based literacy instruction (Stark et al., 2024), and in schools that serve the nation's lowest-performing readers (Northrup & Kelly, 2019). Instead, instruction is often framed by a curriculum narrowed by scripted teaching, isolated skills, and inauthentic assignments, leaving little room for teachers to address the broader "ecosystem" (Reynolds, 2017) that influences how students use literacy in their daily lives. Furthermore, while there are several curricular programs available to teachers, alarmingly little trustworthy evidence validates such programs as effective (Slavin et al., 2008). In fact, studies have repeatedly shown that teachers' knowledge and implementation of evidence-based practices outweigh the influence of methods and curriculum (e.g., Bond & Dykstra, 1967; Hattie, 2015).

Such evidence supports a conclusion that enacting instruction grounded in the science of literacy demands not only evidence-based methods and curricula, but also skillful teachers who engage in intentionally responsive teaching, systematically leveraging their knowledge of their students' experiences and backgrounds; and collaborating with peers to refine and extend their knowledge to guide literacy curriculum choices and instructional practices. Accordingly, literacy reform policies have called for, and even mandated, professional development initiatives to support teachers' ability to orchestrate such instruction (Woulfin & Rigby, 2017). Many have included various literacy coaching models as a pathway toward improved teaching effectiveness. But evidence of the effectiveness of such models is murky, with some studies yielding positive, significant effects, while others indicating mixed or no effect (e.g., Kraft et al., 2018).

Our purpose in this chapter is to clarify the impact of literacy coaching on teaching and learning, with particular attention to understanding conditions that surround positive coaching outcomes. We begin with a brief review of related literature, summarizing what we know about literacy coaching with upper elementary and middle grade teachers and students. Then we turn to our own work, which examines the potential of relational coaching as a possible pathway to more consistent coaching outcomes. We conclude with an overall summary and discussion of collected findings and implications for research and practice.

Literacy Coaching: Knowns and Unknowns

Numerous studies have documented positive effects of literacy coaching on teachers' knowledge of and beliefs about literacy and implementation of more effective instruction. In particular, literacy coaching has been found to positively influence teachers' use of targeted instructional practices (Fisher et al., 2011; Marsh et al., 2015; Matsumura et al., 2009, 2010, 2012, 2013; Sailors & Price, 2010, 2015; Walsh et al., 2019); and teachers' use of assessment data to modify instruction (Marsh et al., 2010, 2015). It has also been found to result in significantly higher levels of performance on standardized literacy tests (Allen et al., 2015; Fisher et al., 2011; Lockwood et al., 2010; Marsh et al., 2010; Matsumura et al., 2009, 2010, 2013; Sailors & Price, 2010, 2015). Moreover, studies document that coaching can be delivered in varied contexts (e.g., face-to-face, web-mediated or video conferencing) and still yield positive outcomes (Allen et al., 2015; Walsh et al., 2020).

Positive outcomes notwithstanding, unevenness of coaching outcomes is clearly evident when findings are analyzed collectively through meta-analysis or meta-synthesis. In a meta-analysis of 60 studies (most, but not all, focused on literacy coaching), Kraft and colleagues (2018) found a medium effect size (0.49) on improving instruction, but a small effect size (0.18) on raising student achievement. Moreover, most of these positive outcomes are associated with early and elementary classroom instruction, and most are associated with small-scale efforts, with larger-scale coaching initiatives showing even smaller effects. In a meta-synthesis of 118 studies specific to literacy coaching and across all grade levels, Sailors and colleagues (2017) reported mixed findings related to changes in teachers' beliefs and concerns, teachers' instructional practices, and student outcomes, with some studies showing positive effects and others neutral effects. Relative to improving literacy instruction offered to upper elementary and middle grade students, Sailors and colleagues reported a dearth of research (7% of their studies) focused on coaching influences on reading comprehension.

Taken together, these findings suggest a need to better understand the precise nature of coaching initiatives that are likely to improve teaching and learning, within both small- and large-scale contexts.

Characteristics and Features of Positive Coaching Outcomes

Research describes several coaching characteristics and features: quantity and duration of coaching interactions; grouping contexts (i.e., whole class, small group, individual); and targeted instructional approaches, skills, or strategies. We briefly review existing evidence of effects of each on coaching outcomes.

First, relative to the relationship between coaching dosage and achievement outcomes, some studies confirm that more coaching opportunities yield greater outcomes than fewer opportunities (Matsumura et al., 2013; Sailors & Price, 2015), yet others have found no relationship (e.g., Kraft et al., 2018; Troyer, 2017). This may be because the frequency of coaching can be affected by multiple factors. For example, teachers may opt for more or fewer interactions based on the value they see in coaching (Smith, 2012); and these beliefs may be positively or negatively shaped by school leadership (Matsumura et al., 2009) or by teachers' perceptions of coaches' knowledge of teaching and coaching experience (e.g., Marsh et al., 2012).

Furthermore, the overall effectiveness of coaching may be affected by not only the quantity of coaching activities, but also by their distribution or duration. For example, Lockwood and colleagues (2010) found greater effects when coaching was sustained across years, but smaller or no effect after only 1 year. Relatedly, Harris and Sass (2011) examined professional development more generally and found no immediate effects, but that small significant effects emerged after 2 years in some cases. First, they speculated that the difference could be accounted for by several factors, including students' experiences with ineffective substitute teachers during the period of professional development (lessening their opportunities to learn, at least in the short term) and teachers' need to practice and integrate new strategies within their teaching repertoires to achieve intended outcomes. These differences suggest the complexity of both planning and measuring coaching outcomes, as quantity or frequency of coaching interactions may be confounded by distribution, duration, and implementation dips with new practices.

Second, the groupings for coaching and the types of coaching activities teachers engage in may make a difference in teachers' perceptions of coaching effectiveness and outcomes. Small-group and whole-class interactions have an important place in efficiently reaching more teachers with a common message (Bean & Ippolito, 2016). However, more opportunities to engage in individual coaching interactions that address an individual's understanding or implementation of a new practice or allows individuals to identify and pursue their own learning needs are associated with substantial improvements in teacher outcomes (Allen et al., 2015; Matsumura et al., 2013; Sailors & Price, 2015). Relative to types of coaching activities, Matsumura and colleagues (2010) found teacher participation in coaching increased when coaching activities emphasized planning and reflecting, enacting instructional practices with support, and building knowledge of the theoretical underpinnings of why the practices are effective and for whom. Similarly, Sailors and Price (2015) reported the efficacy of similar activities, as well as coteaching and opportunities for both the teacher and the coach to initiate topics for debriefing discussions. Teachers also improve instructional quality when coaching includes examining and using student data to plan instruction (e.g., Marsh et al., 2012).

Finally, the rationale or methods for identifying focal teaching strategies is important. In a review of 28 experimental studies of professional development in K–12 settings, Kennedy (2016) found that coaches who observed and evaluated teachers for compliance with predetermined practices were less effective than those who collaborated with teachers on solving their own problems of practice.

In summary, existing studies support a conclusion that coaching *can* have highly valuable outcomes, but the precise conditions for planning and implementing a coaching program that will achieve such outcomes, at least at present, defy clear definition. Some have argued this is because overall success or failure of a coaching program is dependent not only on broader activities or events but also on the very nature of the interpersonal interactions of coaches and teachers (e.g., Haneda et al., 2019; Jones & Rainville, 2014). In our own work, we have focused on these relational aspects, examining how, through discourse, coaches work with and support teachers in taking up and refining new understandings of teaching and learning. In the next two sections, we first present the theoretical framework that guides our thinking about relationship building and its potential impact on coaching outcomes; then we describe our own work related to relational coaching.

Reconceptualizing Literacy Coaching through a Relational Framework

Our work is grounded in a sociocultural view of learning (Vygotsky, 1934/1986) and situated cognition (Brown et al., 1989). These perspectives support the contention that when coaches and teachers interact through trusted and reciprocal relationships, each draws on the other's knowledge of and experiences. These collaborative contexts highlight the importance of the relational nature of coach and teacher beyond static roles (Davies & Harré, 1990; Robertson, Padesky, Ford-Connors, et al., 2020) given that the interactions create the possibility for uneven power relationships and positioning of the coach, the teacher, the students, the curricular resources, and the overall schooling context (Crafton & Kaiser, 2011).

Awareness that coaches are often positioned hierarchically within a school as a more knowledgeable other (Vygtosky, 1934/1986) is central to our thinking as we explore opportunities for and hindrances to co-constructed learning (Lysaker

& Furuness, 2012; Robertson, Padesky, Ford-Connors, et al., 2020). Like others (e.g., Cantrell et al., 2024), we theorize that in powerful learning contexts, meaning is negotiated dialogically and, more often, horizontally between the coach and teacher. This distributed expertise is demonstrably different from the vertical flow of knowledge that is evident when coaches are positioned or viewed as the sole expert with responsibility for "fixing" teachers. These co-constructed interactions build relational trust (Bryk & Schneider, 2003) in ways that support affirmative vulnerabilities (i.e., teachers and coaches willing to put their needs out in the open in ways that promote continuous learning) and lessen destabilizing vulnerabilities (i.e., fear, mistrust) that can derail teacher engagement with coaching (Robertson, Padesky, Ford-Connors, et al., 2020). They establish more equitable positioning as coaches and teachers jointly identify important problems related to the science of literacy, co-construct solutions that are perceived as mutually valued in supporting students' reading and writing needs, and then implement jointly planned instructional practices rather than predetermined practices that may be disconnected from teachers' situated learning needs.

Why Focus on Discourse Patterns as a Source for Understanding Coaching Outcomes?

The words teachers use have long been a focus for understanding and explaining learning outcomes (Cazden, 2002; Duffy et al., 1987; Johnston, 2004; Nystrand, 2006; Wolf et al., 2005). However, despite well-documented evidence, teacher talk remains both underutilized as an instructional tool and difficult to change (Elizabeth et al., 2012; Nystrand et al., 2003). Based on this evidence, a primary goal of our initial work coaching in both classroom and clinical contexts focused on helping teachers become more deliberate and strategic in their use of instructional talk. We conceptualized our coaching work as falling on a continuum of coaching intensity: discussing lesson observations, listening to audio or viewing video and discussing, reading and discussing lesson transcripts, and finally, teachers transcribing and analyzing their instructional talk with the support of a coach. Although our focus was intended to be on improving teachers' use of productive instructional talk, when we revisited the transcripts, we noticed that the coaches' talk, too, was likely consequential. In particular, the coaches' own use of elicitations seemed to promote teachers' own decision making, and this seemed to be associated with uptake of coaching suggestions (Robertson, 2012, 2013; Robertson et al., 2014).

Building from this work, we began to theorize that if teachers are having difficulty harnessing *their* instructional talk, perhaps the same could be said about coaches. Might examining the discourse between coaches and teachers help us understand the unevenness of coaching outcomes? To answer this question, we undertook investigations in contexts where we (university researchers and graduate students) served as coaches. Three types of coaching contexts served as settings for the various studies: (1) coaching with individual teachers in literacy clinics, (2) coaching with individuals and groups in classrooms, and (3) coaching for collective efficacy in schoolwide settings. In the next section, we share our work in each of these contexts.

Coaching with Individual Teachers in Literacy Clinics

The first undertaking was a multiple case study of five coach–teacher dyads in two university clinical contexts (Robertson, Ford-Connors, Frahm, et al., 2020). One was a practicum experience for a graduate licensure program in reading education. The second was a summer professional development opportunity for inservice teachers. One teacher was preservice; the remaining four teachers had teaching experience that ranged from 3 to 9 years.

In these two clinical contexts, coaches supported teachers through face-to-face meetings and "on-the-fly" interactions focused on literacy assessment and instructional practices as tutors worked one-on-one with students (first, third, and fifth grades). Coaches used many broad coaching practices (e.g., modeling, observing, co-teaching) and engaged in video coaching (van der Linden et al., 2021) as a process for co-viewing and discussing instruction.

Using an analytic replication process (Yin, 2014) of the video-recorded coach–teacher cases, Robertson, Ford-Connors, Frahm, and colleagues (2020) sought to develop an understanding of what coaches say and do that prompts teachers to consider or reconsider instructional practices or routines. Analyses explored types and frequencies of talk moves (e.g., elicitations, explanations, clarifications, expansions) and patterns of talk that surrounded teachers' uptake of instructional suggestions, both proximally and distally, that could be associated with coaching conversations. To account for teachers' prior knowledge and decision making, uptake was defined as instances in which teachers engaged in practices related to coaches' suggestions, whether it was enacted precisely as discussed or somewhat modified. These analyses also allowed for the examination of how the sequences of talk positioned the coach and the teacher within the interactions.

Across the five dyads, there was a fairly equitable exchange between coaches and teachers in dialogic sequences that surrounded teachers' uptake and maintenance of instructional practices. The most consistently used talk move by coaches was to *expand* or elaborate on a suggested practice, generally providing additional information to explain the practice and its implementation, and to describe when or why it would be useful based on student observations and data. Coaches also made *observations* and *elicitations*, and most offered *clarifications* by making statements or posing specific questions. Although teachers often *acknowledged* the coach's talk, their most prominent talk move was to *explain* their actions or decisions. In addition, teachers made *critical self-reflection* statements during their coaching sessions.

Data analyses showed three distinct discourse patterns. One was a joint problem identification framework, within which teachers and coaches first collaboratively identified predominant teaching and learning actions that contributed to either successful or unsuccessful outcomes (i.e., a coaching goal). Next, using as a starting point either an observation of an instructional segment in the lesson video or an elicitation prompting the teacher to make an observation or reflect, coaches and teachers engaged in collaborative problem solving. Observations and clarifications were voiced by both coaches and teachers. Notably, teachers' articulation of critical self-reflection, often believed to be indicative of a disposition that propels teacher growth, was neither consistently observed nor found to be related to teacher uptake.

A second framework was one dominated by redirection and reinterpretation. Most notable with the preservice teacher, this pattern occurred when the coach respectfully but persistently guided the teacher toward redirection and reinterpretation of teaching actions. Each incident involved substantial time discussing the coach's observations of teacher and student actions, and included the teacher's explanations and justifications for instructional actions. When the coach redirected, suggestions were typically situated within a larger framework of effective practice (e.g., providing elaborations of how teaching strategies such as context clues for vocabulary understanding can transfer to other texts and tasks), suggesting a macro-orientation to teaching and learning (Haneda et al., 2019), seemingly an attempt to guide the teacher to view the instructional instance in a broader light. As the coach continued to affirm and acknowledge the quality of the teacher's instruction, she also offered further expansions on the instructional suggestion as a refinement to the teacher's current practice. Throughout, even as elicitations and affirmations were used to redirect teaching actions, the coach consistently positioned the teacher as a valued contributor to the discussion (e.g., "So what do you attribute that to?"), perhaps allowing the teacher to view herself as a meaningful contributor to the solution to the teaching problem.

The third framework bore clear similarities to the familiar initiation–response–evaluation (IRE) pattern of classroom discourse (Cazden, 2002), in which teachers ask questions, students respond, and teachers evaluate. In the coaching context, the IRE pattern endured but with the roles flipped between "teacher" and "learner"; that is, the teacher (seemingly the learner), initiated questions or identified problems (67% of turns), thereby displaying a clear disposition toward collaborative problem solving, and the coach (seemingly the "teacher") responded with instructional suggestions, framed in talk that positioned the teacher as the decision maker (e.g., "You might try . . ."). The coach routinely expanded on the suggested practice with specific procedural and conditional knowledge relevant to effective implementation. The teacher then evaluated the idea and responded with affirmations or acknowledgments (e.g., "Yeah, I'll try that. I may like—I'll write this one, but you write the next one . . .").

Across these five cases, the intent was not to determine whether coaching made a difference, but rather, aligned with our pursuit of relational understanding, to identify instances of successful uptake of evidence-based practices and to determine whether common discourse patterns could be associated with those outcomes. Within the three common discourse patterns, Robertson, Ford-Connors, Frahm, and colleagues (2020) found coaches and teachers working within equitable partnerships as they exchanged ideas and seamlessly slipped in and out of the "leadership" role. Even in instances during which coaches explicitly redirected teachers, coaches used language in ways that allowed teachers, in time, to appropriate and "own" the instructional suggestions. Intentionally or not, coaches used talk moves to prompt teachers (who held differing dispositions toward coaching and presented varied instructional needs) to engage in discursive language that is clearly aligned with evidence of a relationship between teacher agency and teacher change (Bandura, 2001; Desimone & Stuckey, 2014).

Coaching with Individuals and Groups in Classrooms

Building on the idea that teachers' opportunities to exercise agency in their conversations with coaches may be associated with their uptake of new instructional practices, we next wondered whether agentic actions might differ when teachers were focused on more than one student or interacting with more than one person (e.g., a coach, peers, and an administrator). Might these conditions or contexts alter their disposition toward asserting agency? To gain insight into this question, Robertson, Padesky, Thrailkill, Frahm, and colleagues (2023) examined coaching conversations with veteran and novice teachers and a principal that occurred as part of a professional learning initiative in one rural, Title I elementary school. In-person literacy coaching interactions occurred across one school year with additional asynchronous interactions occurring monthly through a shared Google Doc. Teachers met individually with a coach and together as grade-level teams. A coaching cycle often included a premeeting (via Google Docs) to establish the focus of the school coaching visit and focal coaching goals. In-person coaching involved classroom observation and debriefing, modeling of instructional practices, or meetings to co-plan upcoming instruction, and included both individual and small-group interactions.

Video-recorded conversation transcripts and the Google Docs were coded first for agentive actions (e.g., autonomy, efficacy doubt, intentionality, principled resistance); and then for turn-by-turn talk moves (e.g., clarification, elaboration, explanation). Findings indicated that teachers exercised reflectivity, autonomy, and efficacy doubt as they questioned their past instructional practices and their emerging understandings of newly introduced practices. Teachers also made deliberate choices about ideas they wanted to know more about and how they thought they might integrate those ideas into their instructional routines. As in the previous study of clinical coaching, these instances of teacher agency occurred around instances of coach elicitations (e.g., "So, in terms of vocabulary integration, for this small-group lesson, what were you trying to accomplish?"), clarifications (e.g., "Could you tell me more about what you're thinking there?"), affirmations of teachers' ideas (e.g., "Right"), and expansions of procedural and conditional knowledge related to implementing the new instructional practices.

There were also instances when teachers exercised agency characterized as challenging or resisting suggested practices. Data analyses show that these instances seemed to be prompted by two different situations or circumstances that teachers perceived as problematic. One type focused on a *particular* recommended practice and took the form of questioning the worthiness of the practice or expressing efficacy doubt, at times comparing the new strategy to a familiar or long-held practice. Following a coach's affirmations and expansions related to the challenge, teachers often responded with an explanation (e.g., "That helps a lot. . . . I don't want to just do something because it's a process and just, here's the juicy word").

The second type related to teachers' perceptions that focal strategies or practices would disrupt well-established teaching routines and priorities or time management (e.g., "So we had to let some things go, and so that's always that fear of, OK, so now it's my guided reading time that I'm letting go so I have vocabulary . . . still finding all the time . . . it's really hard"); or a belief that the focal strategies or practices were indicative of ongoing (and largely ineffective) district-level attempts at change (e.g., "We can't put so much weight into it [district writing prompts for test preparation]"; "That's a conversation we've had over and over again").

Importantly, the ways coaches followed up on teachers' challenges mattered. In some instances, coaches did not acknowledge the challenge or resistance and continued with expansions of knowledge, citing supportive evidence as a justification for why the teachers should take up a recommended practice. When knowledge flowed vertically from coaches to teachers, coaches seemed to ignore, or maybe devalue, teachers' observations and reflections as the teachers grappled with how to bring new practices into their instructional routines. In other instances, coaches positioned teachers' challenges as valued contributions by acknowledging, revoicing, or elaborating teachers' comments (e.g., "So, I think the first consideration for you is to think about what writing do you want them to do for what purpose, and then that would dictate what the instruction looks like"). When this occurred, knowledge flowed horizontally, with coaches and teachers co-constructing an instructional path forward.

Coaching toward Collective Efficacy in Schoolwide Settings

The next set of studies looked beyond dyadic and small-group settings to understand how relational dynamics might play a role in the development of collective efficacy (Bandura, 2001; Hattie, 2015) across a school. Two analyses (Brock et al., 2021, 2024) provided the start of this work. Both were situated within a literacy professional development partnership that engaged university researchers and a private literacy agency that supported family engagement, after-school enrichment, and adult education. The purpose of the partnership was to provide quality professional development to teachers.

In the first analysis, Brock and colleagues (2021) focused specifically on the interactions between the agency-based leadership team and its university partners, and its efforts to promote a "culture of professional inquiry" (p. 856) around literacy. First, transcripts from face-to-face and Zoom meetings, field notes, and a monthly check-in email recapping each month's activities and verifying plans for upcoming activities, social task episodes were analyzed to identify "series of turns that focused on an overarching social task being accomplished" (p. 857). Next, these social task episodes were coded for discursive positioning moves, that is, instances in which speakers positioned themselves or others, explicitly or implicitly.

Findings indicated that the overall storyline across the school year changed, shifting from an early stage in which coaches dominated decision making, to a midpoint in which the two separate groups functioned as "viable partners" (p. 866), and, at year end, establishing a more equitable relationship in which both entities openly questioned themselves and others.

In a second analysis of the same data set, Brock and colleagues (2024) sought to better understand the factors associated with the shift in the collaborative nature of the relationship. Toward this end, they examined the precise nature of both the content and changes in decision-making discursive turns. They found that teachers gradually assumed a more substantive role by not only co-leading professional learning agendas, but also engaging in more conceptually rich discussions during coaching sessions (i.e., talking more about pedagogy and teacher–student learning interactions than surface-level talk about instructional practices). Although this outcome suggests that the design and implementation of the professional development effort eventually achieved its goal of a more democratic and co-constructed professional development process, the researchers speculated that the length of time it took to reach collaborative decision making may have resulted in diminished learning outcomes. Might more explicit and intentional talk about co-constructed learning hasten more equitably distributed decision making?

The next study (Padesky et al., 2023; Robertson, Padesky, Thrailkill, Kelly, et al., 2023), designed to answer that question, was grounded in a yearlong professional development initiative designed and implemented with the intent to bring explicit attention from the outset to the development of shared vision and distributed expertise. Focused on the collaboratively determined need for improving students' vocabulary and oral language abilities as a pathway toward improving overall reading achievement, coaches provided access to evidence-based practices, observed and modeled instruction, and debriefed with teachers, while teacher leaders worked with the coaches to co-design professional learning agendas and the collegial sharing of successes and challenges throughout the year (e.g., faculty meeting time in which teachers shared across grade levels, leading reflections during school leadership team meetings). Data analyses focused on the interactions of coaches *and* teacher leaders during monthly leadership team meetings. They first conducted a topical analysis of the monthly leadership team meetings to determine what coaches and teachers discussed and, generally, the overall nature of the conversations. They found that the faculty and coaches consistently focused their discussions on planning for future coaching activities and reflecting on their perceptions of the outcomes of the coaching that had already occurred.

Next, the researchers selected transcripts from three different months (representing the beginning, middle, and end of the yearlong experience) and conducted a fine-grained analysis of talk and agency within each. They found that over the course of the year, the teacher leaders worked to promote reflections and sustain autonomous teacher engagement in professional learning. The leadership team acted agentively in their interactions with the coaches, reflecting on how the professional learning was going and charting conversational topics for upcoming sessions in ways that built on observed successes while continuing to address challenges.

Coaches positioned teacher leaders to assume more control over leading the professional learning; in turn, teacher leaders invited participation from the other teacher representatives and coaches around next and future steps. Although the two teacher leaders held most of the conversational floor at the outset of the partnership (67% of talk turns), participation of the other teacher representatives increased over time as they critiqued and made principled decisions about their own (and their grade level) learning within the larger schoolwide focus on vocabulary (from 14% of talk turns to 27% of talk turns across the year). Coaches, on the other hand, maintained a facilitative stance, holding the conversational floor an average of only 25% of talk turns across the school year.

Through teachers' reflections, explanations, and elicitations, there was evidence of positive perceptions of the professional learning for themselves and that of their students that were intertwined with their instances of describing themselves as acting with autonomy, both individually and collectively. Within this sense of distributed expertise, coaches and the teacher leaders affirmed their expressed variability in their content knowledge and pedagogical knowledge related to vocabulary instruction, providing space for teachers to "stumble as they first experiment with new practices" (Desimone & Stuckey, 2014, p. 478) while feeling supported by the teacher leaders and coaches. Teachers and the principal reported teachers feeling empowered as they had opportunities to experience "narrow success" (Desimone & Stuckey, 2014, p. 479) in honing their pedagogical content knowledge within the context of their classrooms and curriculum. Furthermore, although student data were not collected formally, the faculty as whole repeatedly reported on the sense of excitement and engagement among their students with the curriculum as they had the vocabulary knowledge necessary to engage with the content.

Discussion, Critical Implications, and Future Directions

In this chapter, we set out to understand the mixed outcomes evident in coaching research and to deepen our understanding of conditions contributing to positive coaching outcomes. Toward that end, we theorized that relational dynamics play an important role in teachers' disposition toward uptake of a coach's instructional suggestions; and we presented our work focused on the relationship between coaches' discourse and teachers' agency and teaching actions.

Taken together, the case studies show that in instances when teachers take up coaching recommendations, the surrounding discourse consistently is marked by coaches' talk moves that, intentionally or not, position teachers as equitable partners in the learning enterprise. In such instances, coaches used elicitations to engage teachers in problem identification or question asking; elaborations in response to teachers' questions or queries to deepen teachers' knowledge of effective instruction; clarifications to prompt teachers' observations and reflections;

and affirmations of teachers' observed actions and reasoning. As coaches and teachers then work together to co-construct instructional plans, teachers' agency builds along with their commitment to refine their teaching practice.

When considered alongside the relational work of others (e.g., Bryk & Schneider, 2003; Cantrell et al., 2024; Crafton & Kaiser, 2011; Haneda et al., 2019; Jones & Rainville, 2014), we believe a search for productive coaching models cannot be reduced to factors such as frequency or duration of coaching, or presence of particular coaching actions (e.g., debriefing, modeling, co-planning). Our intent is not to diminish the importance of such factors. On the contrary, those are foundational for fostering meaningful learning opportunities. But without equal attention to relational dynamics, we are likely to continue to see the mixed outcomes evident in the current body of evidence.

So what must we do to heighten attention to relational aspects of coaching? Recognizing the importance of coach discourse and its relationship to teachers' opportunities to learn suggests that we need to reconsider how we prepare and support coaches. Just as teachers need support to harness their instructional talk with their students (Robertson et al., 2014), coaches also need to learn to harness their talk during coaching interactions (e.g., debriefing, co-planning, enacting practices with support) shown to be essential for positive coaching outcomes (e.g., Matsumura et al., 2013). Coach preparation and ongoing professional development should unpack these actions through video and transcripts and case studies to help coaches understand the potential consequential nature of how they frame their coaching discussions in how those discourse choices influence teachers' opportunities to exercise agency and sustain their collective professional growth as a school.

Importantly, to effectively enact relational coaching, schools must also reposition teachers and coaches as equitable partners. As we considered the coaching conversations that were marked by teachers asserting agentive behaviors, we found that these rarely occurred in connection with their willingness (or unwillingness) to maintain fidelity to predetermined instructional practices. Instead, these instances may be signs of rich teacher engagement with the professional learning ideas as they work to understand the new ideas in relation to their existing curriculum and planning, for which all participants' contributions were critical. With more equitable positioning of roles, coaches and teachers are poised to then focus on the co-construction of the instructional practices to adaptively consider how evidence-based practices will seamlessly integrate into teachers' instructional routines and address students' learning needs. Co-construction is central to the very idea of relational coaching.

Finally, even with coaches modeling, debriefing, and attending to their talk in ways that promote teacher agency, schools need to consider that implementation dips are undeniable as teachers work to integrate these new ideas into their schemas for teaching and learning (Desimone & Stuckey, 2014; Harris & Sass, 2011), which could, in reality, not fully appear until 1 or 2 years later. While increased attention to relational dynamics will not promise immediate results, it does offer promise as a pathway for teachers to invest in improving their craft in ways that stay grounded in the day-to-day realities of their experience in the classroom.

REFERENCES

Allen, J. P., Hafen, C. A., Gregory, A. C., Mikami, A. Y., & Pianta, R. (2015). Enhancing secondary school instruction and student achievement: Replication and extension of the MyTeachingPartner–Secondary intervention. *Journal of Research on Educational Effectiveness, 8*(4), 475–489.

Bandura, A. (2001). Social cognitive theory: An agentic perspective. *Annual Review of Psychology, 52*, 1–26.

Basma, B., & Savage, R. (2018). Teacher professional development and student literacy growth: A systematic review and meta-analysis. *Educational Psychology Review, 30*, 457–481.

Bean, R. M., & Ippolito, J. (2016). *Cultivating coaching mindsets: An action guide for literacy leaders*. Learning Sciences International.

Bond, G. L., & Dykstra, R. (1967). The cooperative research program in first-grade reading instruction. *Reading Research Quarterly, 2*(4), 5–142.

Brock, C. H., Robertson, D. A., Borti, A., & Gillis, V. G. (2021). Evolving identities: Exploring leaders' positioning in the birth of a professional literacy collaboration. *Professional Development in Education, 47*(5), 853–869.

Brock, C. H., Robertson, D. A., Borti, A., Thrailkill, L., Khasilova, D. (2024). Exploring the discursive positioning of members of a literacy professional learning community. *Professional Development in Education, 50*(5), 1034–1051.

Brown, J. S., Collins, A., & Duguid, P. (1989). Situated cognition and the culture of learning. *Educational Researcher, 18*(1), 32–42.

Bryk, A. S., & Schneider, B. (2003). Trust in schools: A core resource for school reform. *Educational Leadership, 60*, 40–44.

Cantrell, S. C., Perry, K. H., & Manion, B. (2024). "I'm pretty sure we did every idea": Teachers' experiences with external coaches and their relation to transformative learning. *Teacher Development, 28*, 397–417.

Cazden, C. (2002). *Classroom discourse.* (2nd ed.). Heinemann.

Crafton, L., & Kaiser, E. (2011). The language of collaboration: Dialogue and identity in teacher professional development. *Improving Schools, 14*(2), 104–116.

Davies, B., & Harré, R. (1990). Positioning: The discursive production of selves. *Journal for the Theory of Social Behavior, 20*(1), 43–63.

Desimone, L. M., & Stuckey, D. (2014). Sustaining teacher professional development. In L. E. Martin, S. Kragler, D. J. Quatroche, & K. L. Bauserman (Eds.), *Handbook of professional development in education: Successful models and practices, PreK–12* (pp. 467–482). Guilford Press.

Didion, L., Toste, J. R., & Filderman, M. J. (2020). Teacher professional development and student reading achievement: A meta-analytic review of the effects. *Journal of Research on Educational Effectiveness, 13*, 29–66.

Duffy, G. G., Roehler, L. R., Sivan, E., Rackliffe, G., Book, C., Meloth, M. S., . . . Bassiri, D. (1987). Effects of explaining the reasoning associated with using reading strategies. *Reading Research Quarterly, 22*, 347–368.

Elizabeth, T., Ross Anderson, T. L., Snow, E. H., & Selman, R. L. (2012). Academic discussions: An analysis of instructional discourse and an argument for an integrative assessment framework. *American Educational Research Journal, 49*, 1214–1250.

Fisher, D., Frey, N., & Lapp, D. (2011). Coaching middle-level teachers to think aloud improves comprehension instruction and student reading achievement. *Teacher Educator, 46*, 231–243.

Haneda, M., Sherman, B., Nebus Bose, F., & Teemant, A. (2019). Ways of interacting: What underlies instructional coaches' discursive actions. *Teaching and Teacher Education, 78*, 165–173.

Harris, D. N., & Sass, T. R. (2011). Teacher training, teacher quality and student achievement. *Journal of Public Economics, 95*, 798–812.

Hattie, J. (2015). The applicability of visible learning to higher education. *Scholarship of Teaching and Learning in Psychology, 1*, 79–91.

Johnston, P. H. (2004). *Choice words: How our language affects children's learning.* Stenhouse.

Jones, S., & Rainville, K. N. (2014). Flowing toward understanding: Suffering, humility, and compassion in literacy coaching. *Reading and Writing Quarterly, 30*, 270–287.

Kennedy, M. M. (2016). How does professional development improve teaching? *Review of Educational Research, 86*(4), 945–980.

Kraft, M. A., Blazar, D., & Hogan, D. (2018). The effect of teacher coaching on instruction and achievement: A meta-analysis of the causal evidence. *Review of Educational Research, 88*, 1–42.

Lockwood, J. R., McCombs, J. S., & Marsh, J. (2010). Linking reading coaches and student achievement: Evidence from Florida middle schools. *Educational Evaluation and Policy Analysis, 32*, 372–388.

Lysaker, J. T., & Furuness, S. (2012). Space for transformation: Relational, dialogic pedagogy. *Journal of Transformative Education, 9*, 183–197.

Marsh, J. A., Bertrand, M., & Huguet, A. (2015). Using data to alter instructional practice: The mediating role of coaches and professional learning communities. *Teachers College Record, 117*(4), 1–40.

Marsh, J. A., McCombs, J. S., & Martorell, F. (2010). How instructional coaches support data-driven decision making. *Educational Policy, 24*, 872–907.

Marsh, J. A., McCombs, J. S., & Martorell, F. (2012). Reading coach quality: Findings from Florida middle schools. *Literacy Research and Instruction, 51*, 1–26.

Matsumura, L. C., Garnier, H. E., Correnti, R., Junker, B., & Bickel, D. D. (2010). Investigating the effectiveness of a comprehensive literacy coaching program in schools with high teacher mobility. *Elementary School Journal, 111*, 35–62.

Matsumura, L. C., Garnier, H. E., & Spybrook, J. (2013). Literacy coaching to improve student reading achievement: A multi-level mediation model. *Language and Instruction, 25*, 35–48.

Matsumura, L. C., Sartoris, M., Bickel, D. D., & Garnier, H. E. (2009). Leadership for literacy coaching: The principal's role in launching a new coaching program. *Educational Administration Quarterly, 45*, 655–693.

Northrup, L., & Kelly, S. (2019). Who gets to read what?: Tracking, instructional practices, and text complexity for struggling middle school readers. *Reading Research Quarterly, 54*, 339–361.

Nystrand, M. (2006). Research on the role of classroom discourse as it affects reading comprehension. *Research in the Teaching of English, 40*(4), 392–412.

Nystrand, M., Wu, L. L., Gamoran, A., Zeiser, S., & Long, D. A. (2003). Questions in time: Investigating the structure and dynamics of unfolding classroom discourse. *Discourse Processes, 35*(2), 135–198.

Padesky, L. B., Robertson, D. A., Barney, A., & Clark, N. (2023). Using digital tools to promote teacher agency and enhance professional learning. In D. A. Robertson, L. A. Hall, & C. H. Brock (Eds.), *Innovation, equity, and sustainability in literacy professional learning* (pp. 191–212). Guilford Press.

Reynolds, D. (2017). Interactional scaffolding for reading comprehension: A systematic review. *Literacy Research: Theory, Method, and Practice, 66*, 135–156.

Robertson, D. A. (2012). *Teacher talk: Transcript analysis as a method of improving comprehension strategies instruction.* Unpublished doctoral dissertation, Boston University.

Robertson, D. A. (2013). Teacher talk: One teacher's reflections during comprehension strategies instruction. *Reading Psychology, 34*(6), 523–549.

Robertson, D. A., Ford-Connors, E., Frahm, T., Bock, K., Paratore, J. R. (2020). Unpacking productive coaching interactions: Identifying coaching approaches that supports instructional uptake. *Professional Development in Education, 46*, 405–423.

Robertson, D. A., Ford-Connors, E., & Paratore, J. R. (2014). Coaching teachers' talk during vocabulary and comprehension instruction. *Language Arts, 91*(6), 416–428.

Robertson, D. A., Padesky, L. B., Ford-Connors, E., & Paratore, J. R. (2020). What does it mean to say coaching is relational? *Journal of Literacy Research, 52*, 55–78.

Robertson, D. A., Padesky, L. B., Thrailkill, L. D., Frahm, T., & Brock, C. H. (2023). Reconsidering resistance and challenges: Teacher agency during joint instructional inquiry with literacy coaches. *Literacy Research and Instruction, 63*(3), 238–256.

Robertson, D. A., Padesky, L. B., Thrailkill, L. D., Kelly, A., & Brock, C. H. (2023). Exploring the role of instructional leaders in promoting agency in teachers' professional learning. *International Journal of Professional Development, Learners, and Learning, 6*(1), Article ep2402.

Sailors, M., Minton, S., & Villarreal, L. (2017). The role of literacy coaching in improving comprehension instruction. In S. E. Israel (Ed.), *Handbook of research on reading comprehension* (2nd ed., pp. 601–625). Guilford Press.

Sailors, M., & Price, L. R. (2010). Professional development that supports the teaching of cognitive reading strategy instruction. *Elementary School Journal, 110*(3), 301–322.

Sailors, M., & Price, L. (2015). Support for the Improvement of Practices through Intensive Coaching (SPIC): A model of coaching for improving reading instruction and reading achievement. *Teaching and Teacher Education, 45*, 115–127.

Slavin, R. E., Cheung, A., Groff, C., & Lake, C. (2008). Effective reading programs for middle and high schools: A best-evidence synthesis. *Reading Research Quarterly, 43*, 290–322.

Smith, A. T. (2012). Middle grades literacy coaching from the coach's perspective. *Research in Middle Level Education Online, 35*(5), 1–16.

Stark, K., Wexler, J., Shelton, A., Johnston, T. B., & Omohundro, K. (2024). Explicit and evidence-based literacy instruction in middle school: An observation study. *Reading and Writing, 37*, 2253–2274.

Troyer, M. (2017). Teacher implementation of an adolescent reading intervention. *Teaching and Teacher Education, 65*, 21–33.

van der Linden, S., van der Meij, J., & McKenney, S. (2021). Teacher video coaching, from design features to student impacts: A systematic literature review. *Review of Educational Research, 92*, 114–165.

Vygotsky, L. (1986). *Thought and language* (A. Kozulin, Trans.). MIT Press. (Original work published 1934)

Walsh, M., Matsumura, L. M., Zook-Howell, D., Correnti, R., & Bickel, D. D. (2020). Video-based literacy coaching to develop teachers' professional vision for dialogic classroom text discussions. *Teaching and Teacher Education, 89,* 1–14.

Wolf, M. K., Crosson, A. C., & Resnick, L. B. (2005). Classroom talk for rigorous reading comprehension instruction. *Reading Psychology, 26*(1), 27–53.

Woulfin, S. L., & Rigby, J. G. (2017). Coaching for coherence: How instructional coaches lead change in the evaluation era. *Educational Researcher, 46,* 323–328.

Yin, R. K. (2014). *Case study research: Design and methods* (5th ed.). SAGE.

CHAPTER 22

Upper Elementary Teachers' Specialized Knowledge of the Components and Processes of Reading Comprehension

Dennis S. Davis

Anyone who has taught upper elementary students (loosely defined in U.S. contexts as children ages 8–12 years in third through sixth grades) would likely agree that it can be challenging to help all students meet grade-level expectations spelled out in the literacy/English language arts (ELA) standards. For example, fifth-grade standards require teachers to prepare students to determine main ideas and themes; analyze texts for craft, structure, and argumentative reasoning; and to independently understand complex literary and informational texts (North Carolina Department of Public Instruction, 2017). Meeting this mandate would be difficult even in an ideal scenario in which students have already mastered foundational word-reading and language comprehension skills necessary for text comprehension. Unfortunately, this is not the case in many (perhaps most) upper grades classrooms. Despite expansive policies intended to improve foundational reading instruction in the initial elementary years, upper elementary teachers can safely assume that anytime they ask students to read and interact with a text as part of a lesson or assignment in any content area, many will need additional scaffolding to help them understand what they are reading. Teachers in these grade levels need extensive professional knowledge to support their instructional practices and decision making.

There has been tremendous interest in research on the discipline-specific knowledge educators use when teaching children to read. The logic underlying this body of research is straightforward. As summarized by Cunningham and

O'Donnell (2015), just as physics teachers must have deep knowledge of physics principles to guide students in learning their subject matter, reading teachers must have similarly deep knowledge of the content of reading. Specifying this content knowledge, however, has not been straightforward. Reading is different from disciplines such as physics. Reading is not a clearly defined discipline belonging to any one community of scholars (Phelps & Schilling, 2004). Moreover, reading is a tool used almost universally to support inquiry practices and learning across all disciplines and implicated in the work of all teachers. Despite agreement that teachers should know a lot about the content of reading, it has not been easy to precisely characterize the domains that make up this knowledge base.

Multiple lines of inquiry have addressed this topic. It is helpful to think of the teacher knowledge literature as a research genre motivated by four purposes. First, some study authors set out to report on new measurement tools (e.g., Binks-Cantrell et al., 2012; Hall et al., 2023; Phelps & Bridgeman, 2022). These studies are useful because they provide new resources to support research and professional development (PD) while shedding light on what experts in the field propose as the domains that make up teachers' specialized knowledge. Another common purpose in this literature is to characterize and evaluate the level of knowledge in samples of educators (e.g., Spear-Swerling & Cheesman, 2012; Washburn et al., 2011). A subset of this work also purports to examine variations in knowledge across different subgroups of teachers (e.g., Jordan et al., 2018). This research is informative for establishing conjectures about factors that might catalyze knowledge growth. A few studies go one step further and estimate the impact of PD opportunities on teacher knowledge (e.g., Folsom et al., 2017; McMahan et al., 2019). This research is useful for establishing claims about the teacher learning opportunities that lead to improved knowledge. Finally, a few studies are designed to examine how and whether teacher knowledge relates to teacher practice and student literacy outcomes (e.g., McCutchen et al., 2002; Piasta et al., 2009; Porter et al., 2023). These studies provide a rationale for why we should care about teacher knowledge as a focus of research. Not surprisingly, most of the teacher knowledge research has focused on early reading (grades K–2), dovetailing with persistent concerns about the scientific underpinnings of reading instruction in these grades.

The purpose of this chapter is to synthesize the smaller body of research that addresses the specialized knowledge base teachers have and need for effectively teaching reading comprehension in grades 3–6. I begin by explaining how I am conceptualizing reading comprehension. Because much of what we know about teacher knowledge in reading instruction in higher grades is extrapolated from research in lower grades, I give an overview of the typical research strategies and major findings from the research conducted primarily with early grades teachers before moving on to studies that focus directly on upper elementary teachers. Then I turn my attention to four questions, connected to the purposes (described earlier) that have motivated much of the teacher knowledge literature, to summarize what we know and still need to learn about teachers' knowledge in upper elementary contexts.

What Is Reading Comprehension, Anyway?

To interpret what research reveals about the requisite knowledge base for upper grades reading comprehension, we need to start with a shared definition of this construct. A useful way to define reading comprehension is to specify the processes involved in understanding a text. From this viewpoint, *reading comprehension* is the process of actively building a coherent mental representation of the ideas an author has written about by merging these ideas with one's knowledge and experiences. This definition aligns with a prominent theory of reading comprehension called the construction–integration model (Kintsch, 1991; Kucan & Palincsar, 2013). Mental representations are built in layers, starting at a surface level, that provides the raw linguistic material for kick starting the reader's meaning-making processes. The reader constructs an initial, mostly literal understanding of how the ideas in the surface layer fit together. This understanding is made possible by the reader's linguistic knowledge, which enables them to make local (small) inferences about how phrases and sentences hang together in meaningful ways. With this layer of mental representation established, the reader uses prior knowledge to make global (bigger) inferences to fill in gaps left unstated by the author. This produces a level of representation often called a *situation model*—a fleshed-out mental model of the whole situation described in the text. This mental model is the product of comprehension, and it includes not only what the text says but also what the text means. Inference making is the key driver of this process, and knowledge is the key resource allowing the process to unfold (Kendeou et al., 2016).

We can also explain reading comprehension by naming the components that serve as developmental prerequisites for meaning construction. There are a number of models that inform our understanding of these components (e.g., Kim, 2023; Scarborough, 2001). There is general agreement that two major clusters of components are essential for reading comprehension: *word recognition*, defined as the ability to recognize written words accurately and efficiently; and *language comprehension*, defined as the ability to construct meaning from spoken language (Hoover & Tunmer, 2022). Skilled reading comprehension is only possible when the components for automatic word reading (i.e., phonemic awareness and letter-sound knowledge) and language comprehension (i.e., vocabulary, semantic and syntactic knowledge, inferential reasoning, and world knowledge) can be flexibly orchestrated to construct a mental model of a text. Teaching the underlying components and processes of reading comprehension is the heart of upper elementary literacy instruction and requires extensive teacher knowledge.

Teacher Knowledge Research in Early Reading

I have selected a few influential studies of teacher knowledge of early reading that exemplify trends informing the research conducted with teachers of older children, which I detail in a later section. (See Cunningham et al., 2023, for a more comprehensive review of the research conducted with early elementary teachers.)

In a study that arguably served as a founding document for the ensuing inquiries on teacher knowledge in reading, Moats (1994) measured the knowledge of 89 educators on linguistic concepts such as phonemes, morphemes, syllables, and letter–sound correspondences. Low scores on the survey led Moats to argue that teachers' understanding of language structure was insufficient for teaching beginning reading. In the context of a multiyear study of reading instruction in high poverty schools, Moats and Foorman (2003) built on this work to iteratively design a teacher knowledge survey to examine teachers' "linguistic and disciplinary misunderstandings" (p. 30). Their measure included items on orthography, phonology, and morphology in the structure of English words and interpretation of student errors in oral reading and spelling. Based on responses from teachers of grades K–4, they concluded that many teachers lacked the knowledge needed for effectively teaching elementary children to read.

In another influential study, Cunningham and colleagues (2004) investigated teacher knowledge in three domains: children's literature, phonological awareness, and phonics. They found that teachers had difficulty correctly identifying the number of phonemes in words presented to them. On phonics items, overall performance was interpreted as inadequate. The researchers also measured the teachers' perceived knowledge and found that they overestimated their knowledge in all three domains. This led to the conclusion that teachers are often not well calibrated in their self-assessments of what they know about early reading constructs. This finding of low calibration has been found in other studies and is theorized to affect how teachers seek out and respond to PD (Cunningham et al., 2023).

Arguing that many previous measures of teachers' knowledge of foundational linguistic skills relied primarily on face validity, Binks-Cantrell and colleagues (2012) developed and tested the psychometric adequacy of a new measure called the Survey of Basic Language Constructs, which included items assessing explicit knowledge (e.g., defining concepts) and implicit skills (e.g., ability to perform a linguistic task) in four areas: phonemes, phonology, phonics, and morphology. They reported an internal consistency reliability of .90 for the full survey. They used the survey to evaluate K–5 teachers' knowledge and found that teachers had particular difficulty with explicit knowledge of phonics and items that asked them to count morphemes in words (Washburn et al., 2011).

Whereas previous studies assumed that teachers' knowledge, as evident on their survey measures, was specialized to the teaching profession, Phelps (2009) directly tested this claim with experienced elementary teachers and adults with no teaching experience. Respondents completed the Content Knowledge for Teaching Reading (CKTR) assessment. The CKTR instrument was an important advancement in this line of work because it expanded the domains and types of knowledge to be measured. In the development of the CKTR, Phelps and Schilling (2004) proposed a knowledge structure that included knowledge of content, knowledge of students and content, and knowledge of teaching and content. They measured each of these types of knowledge in the domains of reading comprehension and word analysis. Using this measure, Phelps reported differences in specialized knowledge in the domains of word analysis and comprehension between teachers and non-teachers, supporting the conclusion that teachers possess knowledge that is distinct from that of non-teachers, and that this knowledge is distinct from simply being a skilled adult reader.

Other studies have followed the tradition of including subscales assessing multiple components of reading (e.g., Carlisle et al., 2011; Hall et al., 2023). Much of this work proposes knowledge domains aligned with the five components of reading instruction attributed to the National Reading Panel (National Institute of Child Health and Human Development, 2000) report: phonological awareness, phonics, fluency, vocabulary, and reading comprehension. The idea behind these studies is that teachers need knowledge of all the components of reading including code-based and meaning-based domains.

Although terminology varies across the literature, there is general agreement that teachers' specialized knowledge for teaching reading includes both content knowledge and pedagogical content knowledge (König et al., 2022; Phelps & Schilling, 2004). Some researchers have tried to measure these knowledge types separately (e.g., Jordan et al., 2018), but often they are combined together in aggregate measures (e.g., Davis, Samuelson, et al., 2022). The first category includes explicit knowledge of terminology used in reading instruction (i.e., the metalanguage teachers use to name concepts they are teaching about, such as phonemic awareness and derivational morphology) and the ability to perform tasks or skills that children would be asked to perform during instruction (e.g., identifying the phonemes in a word). The second category, applied knowledge or pedagogical content knowledge, includes knowledge about instructional practices and difficulties that could arise when children are reading (Hall et al., 2023; Shulman, 1986). Newer measurement strategies have been proposed that would potentially yield more practice-situated understandings of teachers' knowledge (e.g., Phelps & Bridgeman, 2022), but to date, most of the available research with early elementary teachers relies on knowledge surveys that have not changed much in item format since the beginning of this genre.

Research on Teacher Knowledge with Direct Bearing on Upper Elementary Reading Comprehension Instruction

Against the backdrop of research on teachers' knowledge of early reading concepts, there is a growing body of research with direct implications for upper elementary reading comprehension instruction. A nonexhaustive sample of these studies and the domains of knowledge they included in their measurement strategies are listed in Table 22.1.

TABLE 22.1. Chronological Listing of Selected Teacher Knowledge Studies Addressing Components and Processes of Reading Comprehension Relevant for Upper Elementary Instruction

Study	Participants	Measurement strategy and knowledge domains
Moats & Foorman (2003)	103 third- and 4th-grade teachers (Phase 3 sample)	Multiple-choice Teacher Knowledge Survey
		Word structure at three levels: orthography, phonology, and morphology; interpreting student errors in oral reading and spelling (emphasis on not relying on context for word recognition); also includes item on definition of a sentence
McCutchen et al. (2009)	30 third- to fifth-grade teachers who participated in an intervention study to test the impact of a summer professional development (PD) institute	Informal Survey of Linguistic Knowledge (developed by Moats)
		Phoneme identification (counting), knowledge of morphemes, syllable structure, historical features of English language
Phelps (2009)	50 elementary teachers and 55 adult non-teachers	Content Knowledge for Teaching Reading; forced-choice questions embedded in teaching scenarios
		Knowledge in two domains (word analysis and comprehension) and three types of content knowledge ("pure" content without reference to teaching decisions or student work; content + students; content + teaching)
Kucan et al. (2009)	60 fourth- and fifth-grade teachers involved in a PD experience on reading comprehension instruction	Video viewing task with two short videos of classroom discussion-based comprehension instruction; teachers asked to write everything they noticed and to respond to reflection question prompts
		Teachers' understandings of specific approaches to discussion-based reading comprehension instruction
Kucan et al. (2011)	60 upper elementary teachers (28 fourth-grade teachers, 25 fifth-grade teachers, seven reading specialists)	Comprehension and Learning from Text Survey (CoLTS); teachers read an expository passage appropriate for 4th/5th grade students and answered constructed-response questions
		Specialized knowledge for discussion-based comprehension instruction, organized in two different subtasks: knowledge for analyzing a text to extract the most important ideas and identify potential challenges to students' comprehension; knowledge for analyzing student thinking and developing discourse moves to further their comprehension during discussion

(continued)

TABLE 22.1. (continued)

Study	Participants	Measurement strategy and knowledge domains
Spear-Swerling & Cheesman (2012)	142 elementary and special education teachers with a range of experience (some were pursuing licensure during the study)	Multiple-choice teacher knowledge survey and self-reported familiarity or experience with common assessments and intervention approaches
		Content and pedagogical content knowledge of the five pillars of reading from the National Reading Panel plus questions about reading assessment and response-to-intervention (RTI) practices; Items corresponded to three scales: phonemic awareness/phonics; fluency, vocabulary, comprehension; assessment and assessment/RTI
de Kramer et al. (2012)	80 seventh-grade English language arts (ELA) teachers in a study of the impact of online PD	Open-ended measure, with items asking teachers to identify words for instruction and explain why; list of strategies used by middle school readers for comprehension
		ELA knowledge, defined as content knowledge for teaching middle school vocabulary and reading comprehension
Duguay et al. (2016)	50 teachers (35 were middle school teachers and 15 were second-grade dual-language teachers)	Teacher Knowledge of Vocabulary Survey; list of true–false statements
		Vocabulary development and instruction; focus on teaching for language knowledge development for English learners
Kozak & Martin-Chang (2018)	106 preservice teachers in elementary education program	Instructional vignettes task; short description of a teaching scenario, followed by the question "What do you think of this teaching practice?"; a definitions task that asked teachers to define six concepts (e.g., Matthew effects, round-robin reading)
		Pedagogical knowledge for teaching 5th-grade language arts
Beerwinkle et al. (2018)	131 fourth- and fifth-grade teachers involved in a study of a text structure intervention in high-poverty schools	A survey item asking teachers to list all the text structures they teach
		Familiarity with five common expository structures: cause and effect, problem and solution, comparison, description, and sequence
Washburn & Mulcahy (2019)	350 preservice teachers from nine universities in multiple regions of the United States; seeking licensure in elementary, secondary, and special education	Selected items from Survey of Reading Related Knowledge and Perceptions, designed to test knowledge needed for teaching reading in grades 4+; 10 items related to morphology included morpheme counting and multiple-choice items
		Knowledge of morphology, with focus on explicit knowledge of morphemic analysis (evidenced by morpheme counting); familiarity with instructional practices for morphology

(continued)

TABLE 22.1. (continued)

Study	Participants	Measurement strategy and knowledge domains
Pittman et al. (2020)	150 elementary teachers in high-poverty schools, 69 of whom were in grades 4+	Multiple-choice Survey of Basic Language Constructs Concepts and teaching practices related to phonological and phonemic awareness, phonics, and morphology; plus two items defining basic and literal comprehension; included ability items, defined as those that required teachers to perform a task (e.g., counting the phonemes or morphemes in a word), and knowledge items (selecting the correct definition of a concept). Extracted factors identified as latent knowledge constructs; the five retained in their analyses were basic morpheme counting and knowledge, advanced morpheme counting, syllable counting, basic phoneme counting and knowledge, advanced phoneme skills and knowledge
Wijekumar et al. (2020)	155 teachers in general education (grades 3–5) and special education participating in a one-day PD session on a text structure reading comprehension strategy	Main idea task; teachers read a text and generated a main idea, which was scored on a rubric Competence in generating main idea statements, familiarity with evidence-based reading comprehension strategies
Davis, Tenore, et al. (2022)	62 upper elementary and middle school preservice and inservice teachers (grades 3–8), including elementary generalists, middle school ELA, science, and social studies	Multiple qualitative protocols individually administered in one-to-one interview format; including a think-aloud protocol, concept mapping activity, and the Kucan et al., (2011) CoLTS; analyzed to identify consistencies across the sample in their understandings of reading comprehension processes Knowledge of moment-to-moment comprehension processes during reading
Jakobson et al. (2022)	65 general education and special education teachers in Estonia; most in grades 1–4, and eight in grades 6–9	Semistructured interview focused on reading comprehension processes, transcribed and converted to frequency counts through content analysis Knowledge of reading comprehension processes, in particular teachers' familiarity with reading comprehension strategies; explicit knowledge elicited by asking what teachers understood about reading comprehension strategies; implicit knowledge elicited by asking what good readers do before, during, and after reading to understand a text; and a question that asked what teachers do to support struggling readers
Hudson (2022)	103 upper elementary teachers across grades 3–5 who were participating in a web-based text structure intervention	Teacher Knowledge of Reading Comprehension (TKRC) survey, with multiple-choice and fill-in-the-blank items Reading comprehension

(continued)

TABLE 22.1. *(continued)*

Study	Participants	Measurement strategy and knowledge domains
Davis, Samuelson, et al. (2022)	3,248 educators enrolled in an online PD course on teaching foundational reading; across a range of professional roles and grade levels	Multiple-choice survey instrument called the Knowledge for Enhancing Reading Development Inventory (KnERDI) Content and application (pedagogical content) knowledge in two domains: alphabetic code and word reading (which included decoding/phonics and phonological/phonemic awareness); and meaning and connected text processes (which included reading fluency, morphological awareness, vocabulary/semantics, syntactic awareness, text structure awareness, and mental model building)
Phelps & Bridgeman (2022)	59 preservice teachers in elementary education, 24% of whom also intended to eventually seek certification in grades 5–8	Performance assessment to measure what teachers do in moment-to-moment teaching practice Focus on measuring "doing" over "knowing"; measures performance skills for teaching reading and writing across the K–6 grade span; calls for new approach that situates items within performance scenarios; provides example of scenario describing a student who needs support in comprehension and fluency; respondent is asked to listen to an oral reading sample from the student, then submit a short audio clip to provide specific feedback to the student and to explain how the advice would lead to improved comprehension
Hall et al. (2023)	313 elementary teachers, mostly in grades K–2	Teacher Understanding of Literacy Constructs and Evidence-Based Instructional Practices (TULIP) survey Content and practice-related knowledge in areas of phonological awareness, phonics, fluency, oral language, and reading comprehension
Beachy et al. (2023)	Total of 303 teachers across two samples; most with elementary teaching license, about one-third teaching in grades 5+	Perceptions and Knowledge of Assessment in Literacy Survey (PKALS) Five components of reading and how they are assessed: phonological awareness (PA), phonics, fluency, vocabulary, and comprehension, organized in three subscales: perceived knowledge (Likert scale), assessment knowledge (multiple-choice), and knowledge of PA and phonics (multiple-choice)

Linguistic Concepts for Word Recognition

Some of this research directly prioritizes teacher knowledge of linguistic concepts with a direct connection to teacher knowledge measures used with early elementary teachers. For example, the previously described Moats and Foorman (2003) study culminated with a separate sample of around 100 third- and fourth-grade teachers. There was variation in these teachers' performance on the Teacher Knowledge Survey. The researchers interpreted their performance in three categories: high knowledge (34% of the sample), partial knowledge (43%), and very limited knowledge (21%). They used error rates from individual items to emphasize particular difficulties with identification of ending consonant blends, the magic-*e* syllable, the definition of a sentence, and interpreting oral reading errors that show overreliance on context for word recognition.

Underlying Components and Skills of Reading Comprehension

Other studies have taken a different approach, choosing to measure reading domains beyond linguistic constructs and early word reading. This research has resulted in the development of measures that zoom in on specific subdomains important for reading comprehension. For instance, Duguay and colleagues (2016) developed and validated a new measure focused specifically on teachers' specialized knowledge for vocabulary instruction, with a particular emphasis on language development for English learners (ELs). Their true–false Teacher Knowledge of Vocabulary Survey was piloted with a sample that comprised 35 middle school teachers and 15 second-grade dual-language teachers. The researchers interpreted subscores on the instrument to conclude that teachers had the most difficulty with items related to children's vocabulary development, fostering word consciousness, and instructional practices for ELs. Zooming in further to examine one aspect of meaning-based word learning, Washburn and Mulcahy (2019) conducted a study focused on preservice teachers' knowledge of English morphology. Morphology is included in several measures of teacher knowledge as a linguistic concept related to word-reading instruction (e.g., Moats, 1994; Moats & Foorman, 2003), but in this study, the researchers noted that morphology is also an important part of upper grades instruction. Teaching students about prefixes and suffixes can support vocabulary learning and comprehension. They selected items from an existing survey related to this domain, including items asking respondents to count morphemes in words and to answer multiple-choice questions on morphology instruction. They administered the survey to university teacher candidates from nine universities and found that respondents had difficulty identifying the number of morphemes in words.

In addition to vocabulary and morphology, other researchers have proposed that upper elementary teachers need to have deep knowledge of specific tasks that are prominently represented in standards and reading assessments in these grades. One such task is the ability to identify the structure of a text. In the context of a study of a text structure intervention with fourth- and fifth-grade teachers,

Beerwinkle and colleagues (2018) tested teachers' knowledge of common expository text structures using a simple survey item asking teachers to list the structures they teach. Responses were scored for alignment with the five structures identified by the researchers (cause and effect, problem and solution, comparison, description, and sequence). The researchers reported that many teachers did not accurately list these structures and often listed items that were not research-based. They concluded that upper elementary teachers may have inadequate knowledge to effectively model text structure identification for students.

Drawing from a related body of work, Wijekumar and colleagues (2020) proposed that upper elementary teachers should have competence in generating main idea statements and familiarity with evidence-based reading comprehension strategies. To examine the state of teachers' knowledge in this area, they administered a main idea task to general education (grades 3–5) and special education teachers involved in a 1-day PD session on text structure instruction. The mean rubric scores on the main idea task was 5.8 out of 8, with 72% of teachers generating a main idea statement that was deemed adequate by the researchers. They interpreted this trend as promising, but also noted that many teachers copied verbatim from the text rather than paraphrasing in their own words. Researchers concluded that these teachers would have difficulty properly modeling main idea processes to students when these processes require generating and synthesizing new logical connections between ideas.

Reading Comprehension

Other researchers have examined teachers' knowledge using measures that assess what they know about the broad construct of reading comprehension. This was the approach taken by Hudson (2022), who implemented the Teacher Knowledge of Reading Comprehension (TKRC) survey, comprising multiple-choice and fill-in-the-blank items, with 103 teachers in grades 3–5. These teachers were part of a web-based text structure intervention. The purpose of this study was not to make claims about the state of teachers' knowledge but rather to examine associations of knowledge with teachers' practices and student outcomes (as described in a later section). The researcher did, however, report that scores on the TKRC had a wide range (31% accuracy to 91%), with over half of the participants scoring 70% or higher on the measure.

My colleagues and I (Davis, Samuelson, et al., 2022) also emphasized reading comprehension with a teacher knowledge measure called the Knowledge for Enhancing Reading Development Inventory, or KnERDI (pronounced "nerdy"). The name pays homage to the "language nerd" identity that we hope teachers will embrace as they help children notice, manipulate, and reason about linguistic structures they encounter in school texts. This measure included multiple-choice items in two broad domains, corresponding to code-based word-reading and meaning-based comprehension (see Table 22.2). Both domains included a mixture of explicit content knowledge and applied or pedagogical content knowledge. A main purpose of our study was to propose a measurement scale that addressed

TABLE 22.2. Domains of Teacher Knowledge Included on the Knowledge for Enhancing Reading Development Inventory

Domain	Description
Phonology/phonemic awareness	Knowledge of phonological/phonemic awareness as an important prerequisite skill for efficient word reading, and how to support readers' abilities to identify and manipulate the sounds in language
Decoding/phonics	Knowledge of the correspondences of letters and sounds in the English alphabetic writing system; how to analyze and reason about orthographic patterns in words; how to systematically support children's development of automatic word reading
Morphology	Knowledge of how words are made up of units of meaning, including roots, prefixes, and suffixes; how awareness of morphemic structure can help children decode complex words and infer the meaning of unfamiliar academic words
Fluency	Knowledge of fluency as the ability to read a text with appropriate speed (automaticity), accuracy, and expression, which relies on the development of effortless word reading and language knowledge, and enables reading for understanding; how to support students' development of fluent reading
Vocabulary	Knowledge of how readers draw on their semantic knowledge of words to understand the meaning of a text; and how to help readers expand their vocabulary depth and breadth
Syntax	Knowledge of how connective words and cohesive devices signal relations among ideas within and across sentences/clauses; how to help readers develop syntactic awareness and use their expectations for sentence structure to understand complex sentences
Text structure	Knowledge of the organizational patterns in written text, particularly expository texts, which often include multiple organizational structures to connect ideas; how to help readers use their awareness of common organizational patterns to support their understanding of an author's message
Mental modeling	Knowledge of text comprehension as a process of building a coherent mental representation of a text by generating inferences that link ideas together across different parts of the text and with the reader's prior knowledge; how this process depends on the coordination of various linguistic skills and competencies (in the other facets on this inventory); how a reader's construction of a mental model can be supported by the use of metacognitive strategies, including comprehension monitoring

teachers' complex understanding of higher-level aspects of language structure used for meaning making. We also wanted to know how teachers' knowledge in this domain related to their foundational word-reading knowledge. We examined the reliability and validity of the KnERDI in multiple samples of educators enrolled in an online PD course (Ns = 1,393, 1,270, and 141). We found that the KnERDI measured both domains with acceptable reliability (exceeding 0.75 on all scales for all samples). Interestingly we found that although teachers generally performed better on the Meaning-Based Subscale (around 71% accuracy on average) compared to their Code-Based Subscale scores (around 65%), the two domains were highly correlated, such that virtually no one scored high in one domain and low in the other.

The items on our Meaning-Based Subscale emphasized components of comprehension that have rarely been addressed in the teacher knowledge literature and may be particularly important for upper elementary teachers. Our measure assumes that teachers need specialized knowledge to teach students about syntactic structure of complex sentences—that is, how connective words and cohesive devices signal relations among ideas within and across sentences and clauses. Also, our measure includes a facet called *mental modeling*, made up of items capturing teachers' knowledge of the process of building a coherent mental representation of a text by generating inferences that link ideas together across different parts of the text and with the reader's prior knowledge.

Assessment and Intervention Practices

Research has also been conducted on teachers' knowledge of assessment and intervention practices in reading (Al Otaiba et al., 2019; Washburn et al., 2023). This research highlights the critical need for teachers, particularly in the upper grades, to be able to identify and support a diverse range of difficulties that students may encounter with text comprehension. In one of the first studies to take on this topic, Spear-Swerling and Cheesman (2012) developed a teacher knowledge tool that included questions about reading assessment and response-to-intervention (RTI) practices. Their measure was organized in three scales: phonemic awareness/phonics; fluency/vocabulary/comprehension; and assessment/RTI. Analysis of individual items led to the conclusion that teachers had particular difficulty in several areas, including recognizing when a child was placed in a text that was too challenging for their word-reading abilities, and understanding the use of curriculum-based measures to keep track of students' reading progress. More recently, Beachy and colleagues (2023) developed and implemented a measure that included multiple-choice items on assessment strategies in reading along with items on phonemic awareness and phonics. They argued that content knowledge of reading is connected to the data-driven decision making at the heart of effective teaching. They administered their measure to around 300 teachers, about one-third of whom were teaching in fifth grade or higher. Overall performance on the assessment knowledge scale was interpreted as positive with a mean score of 65.7% correct and nearly two-thirds of the sample scoring above 66%.

Knowledge of Text Comprehension Processes Elicited through Alternative Methods

Despite the prominence of knowledge survey measures, there have also been influential studies using interviews and open-ended questions to bring upper elementary teachers' knowledge of comprehension processes to the surface. Kucan and colleagues (2011) introduced a novel measurement tool called the Comprehension and Learning from Text Survey (CoLTS). They proposed that upper elementary teachers need specialized knowledge for discussion-based comprehension instruction. Their CoLTS measure was designed to capture this knowledge. Teachers read a short expository text appropriate for fourth- or fifth-grade students and answered constructed-response questions. The questions required teachers to extract important ideas, identify potential challenges to students' comprehension, analyze the thinking evident in hypothetical student responses, and develop discourse moves that would advance students' understanding during classroom discussion. In an analysis of the responses provided by 60 teachers, the researchers found that most (85%) teachers did not sufficiently identify potential difficulties that the text could pose for upper elementary readers. Only about one-third generated adequate statements about the most important ideas in the text. They also noted limitations in the kinds of support teachers would provide to hypothetical student readers. They interpreted responses to show a tendency among teachers to prioritize personal connections and other common comprehension strategies rather than offering scaffolds to support ongoing construction of a coherent mental model of the text. Based on their findings, they argued for a conceptualization of specialized knowledge for teaching reading comprehension that emphasizes text analysis and an understanding of the contingent (flexible and responsive) nature of teacher discourse moves in facilitating text-based discussion.

Jakobson and colleagues (2022) used semistructured interviews with general and special education teachers in Estonia. Their interview elicited explicit knowledge by asking teachers to explain what they understood about reading comprehension strategies, and implicit knowledge by asking teachers to explain what good readers do before, during, and after reading to understand a text. They transcribed responses and created frequency counts of different categories of strategies. They determined that teachers showed knowledge of decoding and fluency, but few mentioned higher-level reading strategies such as inference making and comprehension monitoring. Their overall interpretation was that teachers in the sample had minimal explicit knowledge about reading comprehension strategies.

My colleagues and I (Davis, Tenore, et al., 2022) also examined teachers' knowledge of reading comprehension processes using in-depth interviews. We sampled 62 teachers of grades 3–8 with varying levels of experience. To improve generalizability of the findings from our small sample, we recruited teachers from three different areas of the United States. We interviewed teachers individually for 2–3 hours (across multiple sessions) using a set of semistructured protocols designed to elicit their knowledge of reading comprehension processes. We identified four concepts that cut across the data sources, representing the modal ways of understanding reading comprehension processes in the sample. Teachers had in-depth knowledge of a conventional repertoire of comprehension strategies. They understood text comprehension as a somewhat messy process of grappling with the challenges posed by the ideas in the text to achieve a sensible mental model. They knew about the central role of background knowledge as both a prerequisite and product of comprehending a text. Finally, teachers thought of reading as a process of social participation with authors and other readers. We argued that by starting with an in-depth description of what teachers already know about reading comprehension, rather than identifying gaps in their knowledge, we can better represent the knowledge assets held by a diverse group of teachers to identify starting points for continued professional learning. We also cautioned that methodological choices affect the knowledge assets or deficits researchers are able to surface.

What the Existing Research Teaches Us

In the sections that follow, I summarize key ideas from the existing research that inform our current understanding of upper elementary teachers' specialized knowledge in reading. I organize these ideas in response to four questions that have been central in the teacher knowledge research.

Does Teacher Knowledge Matter for Students' Literacy Learning in the Upper Elementary Grades?

Although it seems logical that students would benefit from more knowledgeable teachers, establishing this relationship is challenging, and very few studies conducted with upper grades students have attempted to do so. Relying in part on extrapolations from research conducted with younger children and from a few studies in the upper grades, there are three conclusions we can draw about this relationship.

First, there is evidence that teacher knowledge relates to the priorities teachers enact in their planning decisions. In one study using this approach, Spear-Swerling and Zibulsky (2014) examined associations between the content knowledge of elementary educators and the amount of time that these educators would devote to specific literacy activities during a hypothetical 2-hour literacy block. Educators' content knowledge specific to phonology and orthography was significantly and positively related to their self-reported quantities of instruction they planned to spend on letters, phonological awareness, and phonics. Other studies have used similar approaches, including one that specifically focused on time allocation when planning for fifth-grade students (Kozak & Martin-Chang, 2019). In that study, researchers asked preservice teachers to plan a week of fifth-grade ELA instruction. They assessed preservice teachers' knowledge in two ways. They gave them short vignettes describing teaching practices and prompted open-ended responses, which were scored on a knowledge rubric. They also asked teachers to define key ideas related to upper elementary reading instruction. The vignettes task did not correlate with any of the activities included in the planning measure. Scores on the definitions measure correlated modestly with the amount of planning time allocated to activities in which students were actively reading.

Research has also established that a relationship exists between teacher knowledge and observed teaching practice. Research on the early elementary grades has found noticeable but modest correlations between teachers' knowledge of language structure and ratings of their explicit code-focused instruction (McCutchen et al.,

2002). In a study closer to our age range of interest, van den Hurk and colleagues (2017) set out to determine whether teachers' fluency instruction was related to their pedagogical content knowledge in reading. This knowledge was assessed with a researcher-designed questionnaire that included items on oral language, phonemic awareness, decoding skills, and scaffolding fluent reading. The researchers observed and rated the quality of teachers' fluency instruction during their participation in a literacy-focused school improvement project. The researchers found a modest correlation between pedagogical content knowledge and instructional behavior; only 8% of the variance in instructional ratings was explained by teacher knowledge.

Finally, a small but important body of research has provided compelling evidence that teacher knowledge is indirectly associated with student literacy learning through a relationship with teaching practice. Two studies that focused on upper elementary contexts provide important insights regarding this dynamic relationship. In a study of third- through fifth-grade teachers who participated in an intervention study to test the impact of a summer PD institute, McCutchen and colleagues (2009) showed that teachers' linguistic knowledge predicted children's performance in vocabulary, spelling, word attack, and narrative composition for lower-performing students, and composition and spelling for all students. They concluded that teachers with more linguistic knowledge were able to intervene more precisely and effectively when upper elementary students show signs of difficulty. More recently, Hudson (2022) examined the knowledge–practice–outcomes relationship with 103 upper elementary teachers across grades 3–5. Student reading comprehension performance was measured on a standardized measure and a researcher-designed main idea task. Teacher knowledge was not directly correlated with students' outcomes. However, there was a significant interaction between teacher knowledge and quality of instruction (determined using a fidelity instrument from the text structure intervention the teachers were involved in) for both student measures. Students who received high-quality instruction from teachers who had more knowledge scored higher than students provided the same quality of instruction from less knowledgeable teachers. Hudson concluded that teachers with greater specialized knowledge of reading can provide better models and examples to students about main ideas and inferences and are better positioned to respond effectively to students' errors or intervention needs. This interactive hypothesis has found support in studies with younger children as well (Piasta et al., 2009).

Consensus has emerged that teacher knowledge predicts literacy learning indirectly and only to the extent that knowledge can be mobilized in classroom instruction (McElhone et al., 2017). This consensus aligns with literature advancing an ecological understanding of the multiple factors affecting student literacy learning in the upper grades. Teacher knowledge does not work alone. It is situated among other factors that affect student outcomes, including the quality of textbook content, the practices teachers choose to implement to structure students' practice with new content (Beerwinkle et al., 2018), and administrator decision making (Wijekumar et al., 2019).

What Should Upper Elementary Teachers Know to Teach Reading Comprehension Effectively?

We are far from establishing a complete characterization of everything that teachers of grades 3–6 should know. The studies identified in Table 22.1 provide useful conjectures for the domains of knowledge that have been highlighted as important in existing work. Collectively, this literature suggests that upper elementary teachers should have specialized content and pedagogical knowledge in the following areas:

- Linguistic concepts and structures at the word and subword levels, including the phonological (syllables and phonemes), orthographic, and morphological structures of words.
- Linguistic concepts and structures at the sentence (syntax) and text levels (e.g., expository text structure).
- Language development for ELs.
- Recognized components of reading instruction (namely, the pillars attributed to the National Reading Panel: phonemic awareness, phonics, fluency, vocabulary, and reading comprehension).
- Main idea, text structure, and summarization strategies commonly used in this grade band.
- Reading assessment practices for pinpointing students' needs in reading.
- Tiered intervention practices for supporting students in identified areas of need.
- Knowledge-driven and inference-driven text comprehension processes.
- Practices for facilitating text-based discussions to foster students' comprehension processes.

Expertise in all these areas could serve teachers well as they prepare young adolescents for increasingly complex texts, while shoring up foundational skills that should have been established in earlier grades. This list of proposed knowledge domains aligns closely with the comprehension-fostering practices identified in a recent synthesis for practitioners (Vaughn et al., 2022). That resource recommended the following practices for upper elementary and middle grades students experiencing reading difficulties: Explicitly teach decoding skills for multisyllabic and multimorphemic words; support fluency through purposeful reading activities; build knowledge of new concepts and words; teach students how to ask and answer literal and inferential questions; and teach students an explicit routine for constructing main idea/gist statements and for monitoring their ongoing comprehension.

It bears emphasizing that while this list of teacher knowledge domains aligns with theories of the major strands of reading that children need to develop, it represents only a portion of the many domains that teachers mobilize in effective reading instruction in grades 3–6. No study in this literature claims to propose everything that teachers should know. Each attends to a small slice of possible knowledge based on a particular research purpose or priority. Furthermore, this list only prioritizes the knowledge that enables teachers to support children in building a mental representation of a text. This does not include higher-level analytical, critical, and discipline-specific practices called for in educational standards. Teachers in the upper elementary grades are responsible for apprenticing children in these practices as they move into middle school, but they must do so in a way that complements and does not replace the support for foundational meaning construction that many students will need.

Do Upper Grades Teachers Possess Enough of the Proposed Requisite Knowledge?

At this point in the chapter, it should be clear that in the absence of consensus about what teachers should know, we will not be able to conclude whether they possess enough desired knowledge. One could certainly come away from reading the existing teacher knowledge literature with the impression that teachers do not know enough about reading to teach it well. This is the headline finding from much of the literature focused on early grades teacher knowledge since Moats first made this claim in the 1990s (e.g., Bos et al., 2001; Cohen et al., 2017; Pittman et al., 2020). In the studies of upper grades teachers listed in Table 22.1, there are echoes of this trend as well (Jakobson et al., 2022; Moats & Foorman, 2003; Wijekumar et al., 2020). For instance, Kucan and colleagues (2011) concluded that teachers in their sample would likely have trouble supporting children's active construction of meaning during an expository text discussion based on the patterns they observed in response to the CoLTS scenario. Beerwinkle and colleagues (2018) suggested that teachers in their study did not know enough about common text structures to effectively model this strategy for children. These are important fragilities to bring to the fore when designing professional learning opportunities for teachers. However, we should be careful about allowing these interpretations to coalesce into deficit-oriented characterizations of the general state of teachers' knowledge.

In my view, many studies in the teacher knowledge literature adopt the negative stance of finding gaps in knowledge rather than trying to unearth the nuanced knowledge assets that teachers bring to their instruction. Thus, much of what teachers know may go unnoticed. My colleagues and I directly addressed this concern in the aforementioned Davis, Tenore, and colleagues (2022) study of upper elementary and middle grades teachers' knowledge of reading comprehension processes. We started from the premise that teachers know a lot about their content that might not show up on knowledge survey measures. We also assumed that in the upper grades, many of the reading comprehension opportunities teachers facilitate occur in the context of content-area (science, social studies) learning. We wondered: What knowledge of reading comprehension might teachers demonstrate when given ample opportunity to explain what they know in relation to the work they do every day with their students? We created these opportunities using a multiple-methods approach. A concept map activity surfaced their explicit knowledge of the concepts, skills, and resources used in constructing meaning from a text. A think-aloud protocol gave us a window into their implicit understandings of reading processes and their explicit metalanguage for talking about those processes. A hypothetical teaching scenario interview elicited their pedagogical content knowledge for structuring text-based discussions to scaffold comprehension processes. We framed our findings around positive patterns in the data.

We certainly would not claim teachers in our sample knew everything we hoped they would know about reading comprehension processes, but they did know a lot. We were able to align the consistencies evident in their knowledge with identifiable research traditions, leading us to suggest that teachers might be "sampling and remixing" (Davis, Tenore, et al., 2022, p. 2277) from the available collective knowledge in the literature to inform their own customized knowledge base. We speculated that teachers' responses not only tell us about their individual knowledge, but they also give us a window into the perspectives on reading comprehension that have been sanctioned and circulated in the ecological system that affects their practice, including in their teacher preparation, PD opportunities, and in the assessments and curricula they have been required to implement in their schools. For example, the fact that teachers were quick to describe comprehension as a process of strategizing through a text using common strategies such as summarizing and questioning suggests to us that they have drawn some amount of knowledge from the vast literature on comprehension strategies instruction. This situative perspective (Collins & Greeno, 2010) offers a unique way to think about teachers' knowledge as both a possession that an individual has internalized and part of a shared set of resources distributed among the theories and models deemed acceptable in a professional community.

How Might Teachers Gain More of the Specialized Knowledge They Need?

Studies of teacher knowledge commonly seek to characterize the factors and experiences associated with improvements in knowledge. Often this has been done using cross-sectional comparisons—that is, measuring knowledge of a group of teachers and then taking advantage of variation in the sample to find out which characteristics are associated with higher knowledge (e.g., Hall et al., 2023; Jordan et al., 2018; Spear-Swerling & Cheesman, 2012). Two characteristics that have been of particular interest as potential sources of knowledge are teaching experience and master's degree attainment. One of the goals of our KnERDI study (Davis, Samuelson, et al., 2022) was to examine variation associated with these characteristics. We administered the instrument to three different samples of educators spanning the full range of experience levels (preservice to more than 30 years) and education level (pre-bachelor's through graduate degrees). We observed a consistent pattern of higher knowledge among more experienced teachers in all three samples. This might suggest that knowledge develops through time spent helping children learn to read and through practice-situated learning opportunities distributed across the career. Notably, we used teachers' self-reported years of experience teaching early reading in this analysis. We think this is a better indicator of domain-relevant experience than general teaching experience.

With regard to degree completion, our results were inconsistent across the three samples. In two of the samples, teachers with a master's degree or higher outperformed teachers with only a 4-year degree, who in turn outperformed teachers with a less than 4-year degree. In the third sample, however, teachers with advanced degrees and those with 4-year degrees had almost identical results on the KnERDI. We interpret the latter finding as aligning with an argument made in the broader literature that teachers are more likely to gain specialized knowledge when they participate in targeted learning opportunities that explicitly address desired content. Inconsistent relationships across samples could reflect differences in the quality or specificity of teachers' learning opportunities.

Cross-sectional studies like ours are limited because they cannot really tell us what caused changes in knowledge. This limitation is partially addressed in studies that observe or measure knowledge before and after targeted learning opportunities (Brady et al., 2009; Ehri & Flugman, 2018; McMahan et al., 2019). Results from studies with early grades teachers confirm that specialized knowledge of reading can develop over relatively short periods of time if the training is explicit and knowledge measures are closely aligned to the content of the training. In a pre–post study that directly targeted upper grades teachers, Kucan and colleagues (2009) examined changes in teachers' pedagogical content knowledge as a result of PD on Questioning the Author (Beck & McKeown, 2001) and Reciprocal Teaching (Palincsar & Brown, 1984). These two pedagogies were selected as key practices for structuring text-based discussions in upper elementary comprehension instruction. The researchers tracked knowledge using a video viewing task. Participants, who were fourth- and fifth-grade teachers, were shown short videos of classroom discussions and then responded to written reflection prompts. They completed this task before and after the PD sessions. The researchers noted increased attention to the teachers' discourse moves at posttest, along with a shift toward more analytical (rather than descriptive) comments. Differences were interpreted as evidence of improved understanding of the enactment and purposes of discussion-based comprehension instruction.

A more rigorous way of establishing a causal relation between PD and teacher knowledge growth is to measure knowledge in a sample of teachers randomly assigned to a targeted learning experience compared to teachers in a control condition. Much of this research has been conducted with teachers of younger children or with teachers across the elementary grade span. These studies have generally confirmed that targeted PD has positive effects on teacher knowledge. In a study of first- and second-grade teachers assigned to either a control condition or a treatment condition consisting of 4 days of PD and yearlong coaching, Goldfield and colleagues (2021) found that treatment teachers scored higher on a measure of specialized oral language content knowledge. Donovan and colleagues (2022) examined the impact of online and in-person PD on 86 K–5 educators on a measure assessing knowledge of phonology, decoding, spelling, fluency, morphology, vocabulary, and comprehension. They found that teachers in both training conditions outperformed teachers in a control condition on this measure. In a review of the group-comparison research, Hudson and colleagues (2021) identified 20 studies using experimental or quasi-experimental designs to test the impact of teacher preparation and PD on teachers' knowledge of foundational reading skills. They noted that they focused on foundational skills because there was not enough rigorous research on PD targeting teachers' knowledge of vocabulary and comprehension to warrant a systematic review. Nearly all the studies included samples of preservice teachers in university programs. Across the studies, preservice teachers improved their knowledge in the targeted areas, leading Hudson and colleagues to conclude that educators benefit from sustained, targeted learning opportunities, especially when they have a chance to apply newly formed knowledge under expert guidance.

A study of middle school ELA teachers provides some evidence that the benefits of PD on knowledge also extend to teachers in older grades. de Kramer and colleagues (2012) randomized seventh-grade teachers to either a control group or a treatment group that received over 100 hours of online PD on vocabulary, reading comprehension, and writing instruction. They tested the impact of the PD on ELA knowledge, defined as content knowledge for teaching vocabulary and reading comprehension. They used an open-ended measure of knowledge closely aligned to their PD focus. Items asked teachers to identify words for vocabulary instruction and explain their choices, and to list strategies used by middle school readers for comprehension. Accuracy means on their overall ELA knowledge measure were reported as 30 and 40% for the control and treatment groups, respectively. They interpreted the impact of the PD on teacher knowledge as a modest-sized effect.

Conclusion and Implications for Future Research

The bottom line from the existing research is that teachers' specialized knowledge of reading is malleable when teachers are provided well-designed professional learning experiences. If we knew definitively what upper grades teachers should know to meet the reading comprehension needs of all their students, positive learning experiences to build this knowledge could be deployed relatively easily. The research also suggests that once teachers develop this knowledge, we could expect to see modest changes in their teaching practice; and optimistically, this knowledge would interact with their practices to improve their students' literacy outcomes.

There is still much to be learned about the domains of specialized knowledge teachers need for upper grades reading comprehension instruction. One challenge in establishing an upper elementary specific research base is that teacher licensing and hiring practices do not make a clear distinction between teachers in these grade levels. Elementary teachers are typically licensed across the full elementary grade range. Today's fourth-grade teachers could be teaching first grade next year, and vice versa. Future research that seeks to understand the unique knowledge assets of upper elementary teachers will have to sample teachers who specialize in this grade band—for example, those who have taught in these grades for multiple years or who have sought out grade-specific PD.

Future research also needs to address the measurement issues evident in the extant literature. Across prior studies, claims about teachers' knowledge are inferred from single survey items or written prompts, qualitative protocols coded for themes/patterns in knowledge, and multi-item survey instruments. The survey instruments vary in their quality of design. Some are accompanied by basic information on internal consistency reliability. Others come with reports of factor-analytic methods to examine reliability, validity, and dimensionality, and some benefit from the use of measurement techniques (Rasch and item response theory models) to establish and validate performance scales. Each study measures teachers' knowledge relative to a somewhat idiosyncratic set of proposed knowledge. The variations in measurement tools and foci make it difficult to identify patterns across studies and to understand how different tools perform relative to each other. The literature would benefit from studies in which large samples of upper grades teachers (who are identified through a defensible sampling scheme to maximize generalizability) complete multiple preexisting knowledge surveys. This would allow researchers to examine how different tools relate to each other and to test theory-driven models of the structure and dimensionality of teacher knowledge not possible in individual measures. Not only would this kind of research produce generalizable knowledge to inform PD priorities, but it would also help establish normative information about typical levels of teacher knowledge. This information would also address another limitation observed in the current studies. There is a tendency to interpret teacher knowledge as low or inadequate when there is no evidence-based threshold of required knowledge for effective teaching or validated estimates of expected knowledge for teachers at different levels of experience.

Finally, studies that carefully consider the knowledge assets that teachers have access to and how knowledge is leveraged within the complex ecology of upper grades instruction would be particularly useful for advancing policy and practice. To address this need, researchers could conduct in-depth studies of the specialized reading comprehension knowledge that effective upper elementary teachers draw on in their planning and instruction. This might involve close analysis of the ecological factors affecting teachers' practices (see Wijekumar et al., 2019), coupled with observations, interviews, and video elicitation tools (see Kucan et al., 2009) to reveal how teachers' knowledge is applied and expanded in their work. This approach would be a radical departure from the typical strategy of measuring teachers' performance on proposed knowledge domains to identify gaps.

REFERENCES

Al Otaiba, S., Baker, K., Lan, P., Allor, J., Rivas, B., Yovanoff, P., & Kamata, A. (2019). Elementary teacher's knowledge of response to intervention implementation: A preliminary factor analysis. *Annals of Dyslexia, 69*, 34–53.

Beachy, R., Guo, D., Wright, K. L., & McTigue, E. M. (2023). The teachers' perceptions and knowledge of reading assessment survey: A validation study. *Reading and Writing Quarterly, 39*(6), 559–581.

Beck, I. L., & McKeown, M. G. (2001). Inviting students into the pursuit of meaning. *Educational Psychology Review, 13*(3), 225–241.

Beerwinkle, A. L., Wijekumar, K., Walpole, S., & Aguis, R. (2018). An analysis of the ecological components within a text structure intervention. *Reading and Writing, 31*, 2041–2064.

Binks-Cantrell, E., Joshi, R. M., & Washburn, E. K. (2012). Validation of an instrument for assessing teacher knowledge of basic language constructs of literacy. *Annals of Dyslexia, 62*(3), 153–171.

Bos, C., Mather, N., Dickson, S., Podhajski, B., & Chard, D. (2001). Perceptions and knowledge of preservice and inservice educators about early reading instruction. *Annals of Dyslexia, 51*(1), 97–120.

Brady, S., Gillis, M., Smith, T., Lavalette, M., Liss-Bronstein, L., Lowe, E., . . . Wilder, T. D. (2009). First grade teachers' knowledge of phonological awareness and code concepts: Examining gains from an intensive form of professional development and corresponding teacher attitudes. *Reading and Writing, 22*(4), 425–455.

Carlisle, J. F., Kelcey, B., Rowan, B., & Phelps, G. (2011). Teachers' knowledge about early reading: Effects on students' gains in reading achievement. *Journal of Research on Educational Effectiveness, 4*(4), 289–321.

Cohen, R. A., Mather, N., Schneider, D. A., & White, J. M. (2017). A comparison of schools: Teacher knowledge of explicit code-based instruction. *Reading and Writing, 30*, 653–690.

Collins, A., & Greeno, J. G. (2010). Situative view of learning. In V. G. Aukrust (Ed.), *Learning and cognition in education* (pp. 64–68). Elsevier.

Cunningham, A. E., Firestone, A. R., & Zegers, M. (2023). Measuring and improving teachers' knowledge in early literacy. In S. Cabell, S. Neuman, & N. P. Terry (Eds.), *Handbook on the science of early literacy* (pp. 211–223). Guilford Press.

Cunningham, A. E., & O'Donnell, C. R. (2015). Teachers' knowledge about beginning reading development and instruction. In A. Pollatsek & R. Treiman (Eds.), *The Oxford handbook of reading* (pp. 447–462). Oxford University Press.

Cunningham, A. E., Perry, K. E., Stanovich, K. E., & Stanovich, P. J. (2004). Disciplinary knowledge of K–3 teachers and their knowledge calibration in the domain of early literacy. *Annals of Dyslexia, 54*(1), 139–167.

Davis, D. S., Samuelson, C., Grifenhagen, J., Delaco, R., & Relyea, J. (2022). Getting KnERDI with language: Examining teachers' knowledge for enhancing reading development in code-based and meaning-based domains. *Reading Research Quarterly, 57*(3), 781–804.

Davis, D. S., Tenore, F. B., McElhone, D., & DeIaco, R. (2022). What do upper-elementary and middle school teachers know about the processes of text comprehension? *Reading and Writing, 35*(9), 2257–2283.

de Kramer, R. M., Masters, J., O'Dwyer, L. M., Dash, S., & Russell, M. (2012). Relationship of online teacher professional development to seventh-grade teachers' and students' knowledge and practices in English language arts. *Teacher Educator, 47*(3), 236–259.

Donovan, S. L., Odegard, T. N., Farris, E. A., & Flipse, J. L. (2022). Testing the impact of online training in areas of reading instruction on educator knowledge. *Reading and Writing, 35*, 199–221.

Duguay, A., Kenyon, D., Haynes, E., August, D., & Yanosky, T. (2016). Measuring teachers' knowledge of vocabulary development and instruction. *Reading and Writing, 29,* 321–347.

Ehri, L. C., & Flugman, B. (2018). Mentoring teachers in systematic phonics instruction: Effectiveness of an intensive year-long program for kindergarten through 3rd grade teachers and their students. *Reading and Writing, 31,* 425–456.

Folsom, J. S., Smith, K. G., Burk, K., & Oakley, N. (2017). *Educator outcomes associated with implementation of Mississippi's K–3 Early Literacy Professional Development Initiative* (REL 2017-270). Regional Educational Laboratory Southeast.

Goldfield, S., Snow, P., Eadie, P., Munro, J., Gold, L., Orsini, F., . . . Shingles, B. (2021). Teacher knowledge of oral language and literacy constructs: Results of a randomized controlled trial evaluating the effectiveness of a professional learning intervention. *Scientific Studies of Reading, 25*(1), 1–30.

Hall, C., Solari, E. J., Hayes, L., Dahl-Leonard, K., DeCoster, J., Kehoe, K. F., . . . Vargas, I. (2023). Validation of an instrument for assessing elementary-grade educators' knowledge to teach reading. *Reading and Writing, 37,* 1955–1974.

Hoover, W. A., & Tunmer, W. E. (2022). The primacy of science in communicating advances in the science of reading. *Reading Research Quarterly, 57*(2), 399–408.

Hudson, A. (2022). Upper elementary teachers' knowledge of reading comprehension, classroom practice, and student's performance in reading comprehension. *Reading Research Quarterly, 58*(3), 351–360.

Hudson, A., Moore, K. A., Han, B., Koh, P. W., Binks-Cantrell, E., & Joshi, R. M. (2021). Elementary teachers' knowledge of foundational literacy skills: A critical piece of the puzzle in the science of reading. *Reading Research Quarterly, 56*(Suppl. 1), S287–S315.

Jakobson, K., Soodla, P., & Aro, M. (2022). General and special education teachers' knowledge about reading comprehension processes and instructional practices. *Reading and Writing, 35,* 2229–2256.

Jordan, R. L. P., Bratsch-Hines, M., & Vernon-Feagans, L. (2018). Kindergarten and first grade teachers' content and pedagogical knowledge of reading and associations with teacher characteristics at rural low-wealth schools. *Teaching and Teacher Education, 74,* 190–204.

Kendeou, P., McMaster, K. L., & Christ, T. J. (2016). Reading comprehension: Core components and processes. *Policy Insights from the Behavioral and Brain Sciences, 3*(1), 62–69.

Kim, Y.-S. G. (2023). Simplicity meets complexity: Expanding the simple view of reading with the direct and indirect effects model of reading (DIER). In S. Cabell, S. Neuman, & N. P. Terry (Eds.), *Handbook on the science of early literacy* (pp. 9–22). Guilford Press.

Kintsch, W. (1991). The role of knowledge in discourse comprehension: A construction–integration model. *Advances in Psychology, 79,* 107–153.

König, J., Hanke, P., Glutsch, N., Jäger-Biela, D., Pohl, T., Becker-Mrotzek, M., . . . Waschewski, T. (2022). Teachers' professional knowledge for teaching early literacy: conceptualization, measurement, and validation. *Educational Assessment, Evaluation and Accountability, 34*(4), 483–507.

Kozak, S., & Martin-Chang, S. (2019). Preservice teacher knowledge, print exposure, and planning for instruction. *Reading Research Quarterly, 54*(3), 323–338.

Kucan, L., Hapgood, S., & Palincsar, A. S. (2011). Teachers' specialized knowledge for supporting student comprehension in text-based discussions. *Elementary School Journal, 112*(1), 61–82.

Kucan, L., & Palincsar, A. S. (2013). *Comprehension instruction through text-based instruction*. International Reading Association.

Kucan, L., Palincsar, A. S., Khasnabis, D., & Chang, C. (2009). The video viewing task: A source of information for assessing and addressing teacher understanding of text-based discussion. *Teaching and Teacher Education, 25*(3), 415–423.

McCutchen, D., Green, L., Abbot, R. D., & Sanders, E. A. (2009). Further evidence for teacher knowledge: Supporting struggling readers in grades three through five. *Reading and Writing, 22,* 401–423.

McCutchen, D., Harry, D. R., Cunningham, A. E., Cox, S., Sidman, S., & Covill, A. E. (2002). Reading teachers' knowledge of children's literature and English phonology. *Annals of Dyslexia, 52*(1), 207–228.

McElhone, D., Tenore, F. B., & Davis, D. S. (2017). How teachers mobilize and transform their conceptualizations of reading comprehension into representations of instructional practice. *Literacy Research: Theory, Method, and Practice, 66*(1), 232–247.

McMahan, K. M., Oslund, E. L., & Odegard, T. N. (2019). Characterizing the knowledge of educators receiving training in systematic literacy instruction. *Annals of Dyslexia, 69*(1), 21–33.

Moats, L. C. (1994). The missing foundation in teacher education: Knowledge of the structure of spoken and written language. *Annals of Dyslexia, 44,* 81–102.

Moats, L. C., & Foorman, B. R. (2003). Measuring teachers' content knowledge of language and reading. *Annals of Dyslexia, 53*(1), 23–45.

National Institute of Child Health and Human Development. (2000). *Report of the National Reading Panel: Teaching children to read: An evidence-based assessment of the scientific research literature on reading and its implications for reading instruction*. National Institutes of Health.

North Carolina Department of Public Instruction. (2017). *North Carolina Standard Course of Study: English language arts*. www.dpi.nc.gov/documents/files/ela-standard-course-study/open.

Palincsar, A. S., & Brown, A. L. (1984). Reciprocal teaching of comprehension fostering and comprehension-monitoring activities. *Cognition and Instruction, 1*(2), 117–175.

Phelps, G. (2009). Just knowing how to read isn't enough!: Assessing knowledge for teaching reading. *Educational Assessment, Evaluation and Accountability, 21*(2), 137–154.

Phelps, G., & Bridgeman, B. (2022). From knowing to doing: Assessing the skills used to teach reading and writing. *Reading and Writing, 35,* 2023–2048.

Phelps, G., & Schilling, S. (2004). Developing measures of content knowledge for teaching reading. *Elementary School Journal, 105*(1), 31–48.

Piasta, S. B., Connor, C. M., Fishman, B. J., & Morrison, F. J. (2009). Teachers' knowledge of literacy concepts, classroom practices, and student reading growth. *Scientific Studies of Reading, 13,* 224–248.

Pittman, R. T., Zhang, S., Binks-Cantrell, E., Hudson, A., & Joshi, R. M. (2020). Teachers' knowledge about language constructs related to literacy skills and student achievement in low socio-economic status schools. *Dyslexia, 26*(2), 200–219.

Porter, S. B., Odegard, T. N., Farris, E. A., & Oslund, E. L. (2023). Effects of teacher knowledge of early reading on students' gains in foundational skills and comprehension. *Reading and Writing, 37,* 2007–2023.

Scarborough, H. A. (2001). Connecting early language and literacy to later reading (dis) abilities: Evidence, theory, and practice. In S. Neuman & D. Dickinson (Eds.), *Handbook of early literacy research* (Vol. 1, pp. 97–110). Guilford Press.

Shulman, L. S. (1986). Those who understand: Knowledge growth in teaching. *Educational Researcher, 15*(2), 4–14.

Spear-Swerling, L., & Cheesman, E. (2012). Teachers' knowledge base for implementing response-to-intervention models in reading. *Reading and Writing, 25*(7), 1691–1723.

Spear-Swerling, L., & Zibulsky, J. (2014). Making time for literacy: Teacher knowledge and time allocation in instructional planning. *Reading and Writing, 27*(8), 1353–1378.

van den Hurk, H. T. G., Houtveen, A. A. M., & Van de Grift, W. J. C. M. (2017). Does teachers' pedagogical content knowledge affect their fluency instruction? *Reading and Writing, 30*, 1231–1249.

Vaughn, S., Gersten, R., Dimino, J., Taylor, M. J., Newman-Gonchar, R., Krowka, S., . . . Jayanthi, M. (2022). *Providing reading interventions for students in grades 4–9* (WWC 2022007). National Center for Education Evaluation and Regional Assistance, Institute of Education Sciences, U.S. Department of Education.

Washburn, E. K., Joshi, R. M., & Binks-Cantrell, E. S. (2011). Teacher knowledge of basic language concepts and dyslexia. *Dyslexia, 17*(2), 165–183.

Washburn, E. K., & Mulcahy, C. A. (2019). Morphology matters, but what do teacher candidates know about it? *Teacher Education and Special Education, 42*(3), 246–262.

Washburn, E. K., Pierce, A., Scott, C. E., & Waters, C. (2023). What does written reflection reveal about novice teachers' knowledge, beliefs, and skills related to literacy assessment? *Reading Horizons: A Journal of Literacy and Language Arts, 62*(1), 80–108.

Wijekumar, K., Beerwinkle, A. L., Harris, K. R., & Graham, S. (2019). Etiology of teacher knowledge and instructional skills for literacy at the upper elementary grades. *Annals of Dyslexia, 69*, 5–20.

Wijekumar, K., Beerwinkle, A., McKeown, D., Zhang, S., & Joshi, R. M. (2020). The "GIST" of the reading comprehension problem in grades 4 and 5. *Dyslexia, 26*, 323–340.

CHAPTER 23

Black Futures Matter
Reimagining Science of Literacy Instruction for Black Students

Jennifer D. Turner
Simone Gibson

As Black teacher educators, scholars, and literacy advocates, we frame our chapter to support *educators,* a broad term referring to teacher candidates, tutors, and other university students preparing to work with Black children in upper elementary and middle grade classrooms across the United States. At our respective institutions, we primarily work with White middle-class, monolingual women teacher candidates (JDT) and Black teacher candidates (SG), who together comprise more than 80% of the U.S. teacher workforce (National Center for Education Statistics, 2022). Given that 7.4 million Black children are attending U.S. public elementary and secondary schools (National Center for Education Statistics, 2023), we are committed to preparing equity-minded literacy educators who can *reach* and *teach* Black students. But what does it look like to reach and teach Black students, especially those who may have endured racial trauma when learning to read and write in schools? This question is at the heart of the introductory vignette that we now share:

> Through Literacy Brigade (LB), a tutoring program at the Historically Black College and University (HBCU) where I (SG) work, Black male college students are recruited and receive approximately 20 hours of training in the science of literacy and structured literacy (SL). The college tutors are paired with local Black middle school readers to provide weekly 90-minute individualized SL lessons. The LB program not only seeks to expose Black male college students to the field of teaching but also to create positive mentoring and tutoring relationships with Black middle school students.
>
> As the program director, I provide the SOL [science of literacy] and SL training for the tutors. They are often surprised to learn that reading proficiency is

based on exposure and repetition of skills rather than innate abilities, and that proficient readers have skills beyond simply memorizing the alphabet song. We spend significant time talking about the simple view of reading (Gough & Tunmer, 1986) and the Reading Rope (Scarborough, 2001). These models help tutors, who are often non-education majors, to expand their conceptualizations of the reading process and become familiar with the varying subskills involved with the teaching of reading and the importance of providing explicit instruction related to those subskills.

However, despite their training and the lesson template that guides each step of their instruction, tutors inevitably begin to recognize that the Reading Rope and the simple view of reading are missing some foundational and essential components: how to connect with and maintain the interest and focus of their Black tutees. The tutees who enroll in the LB program are typically Black middle school-age children with failing grades and a variety of experiences with and social–emotional responses to literacy instruction in schools. Some tutees have had significant challenges learning to read and write in schools, but they actively participate in the program because they hope that it will help them improve. Yet from my experience, I have found that tutees may carry "emotional baggage" related to reading that manifests itself in a variety of behaviors. For example, some students avoid eye contact and look down at their feet or the floor. Other students are quiet and reserved, limiting participation as they stare off from their work space or simply place their heads on their desks. Still others try to misdirect lessons through charming and witty conversation.

We talk openly and honestly about these behaviors and the reasons why learning to read and write in schools can be traumatizing for Black children, so that the tutors do not stereotype them (e.g., "They don't care about learning to read") or hold deficit views about them (e.g., "They are just bad kids"). We talk so that they understand that their tutees' behaviors are the result of years of negative literacy experiences in the classroom. Although tutors understand this, they still are quite taken aback by these behaviors. When we hold our debriefing sessions, they often ask questions like "How do I even start with a lesson when I can't get a child to tune in?"; "How do I get to know my kid so I can figure out how to catch him?" Others ponder, "How do I get [my tutee] to engage? I feel like I tried everything"; "When we were doing the games and stuff, it was fine. All smiles. As soon as I pulled out that assessment, it all just stopped." One tutor recently reflected, "I learned a lot about teaching reading but we needed more about how to make the lessons more interesting. I had to learn a lot about [name of student] before we could even get to the Reading Rope." In working with their Black middle school tutees, the tutors quickly recognize that they must extend beyond the Reading Rope and focus on the most foundational and immediate needs: building relationships with their tutees and ensuring a successful and engaging tutoring experience.

We offer this vignette as a starting point for thinking about what it means for educators to *reach and teach* older Black students through SOL in schools across the United States. SOL has become a popular reform effort for teaching foundational skills including phonemic awareness, phonics, vocabulary, fluency, comprehension, and writing (Duke & Cartwright, 2021; Petscher et al., 2020). SOL integrates research from the fields of psychology, reading, education, and cognitive science, and posits a view of reading and literacy that emphasizes the acquisition and mastery of the subskills related to reading and writing (National Institute of Child Health and Human Development, 2000).

While it is primarily focused on within K–2 classrooms, we acknowledge that foundational literacy instruction benefits Black students in the upper grade levels due to its focus on explicit and systematic instruction. Understanding that learning to read and write is a challenging task for students is crucial because some educators may mistakenly believe the following common myths:

- Black children will easily learn to read because they know the alphabet song.
- Black children learn to read from listening to books that are read aloud to them.
- Black children in the later elementary and middle school grades have already mastered foundational reading and writing skills (Learned, 2016; Moreau, 2014).

Given these challenges, we need educators who realize that their job is to make the process of reading and writing accessible for Black children by providing explicit and systematic instruction that targets subskills related to phonemic awareness, phonics, vocabulary, fluency, and comprehension (Scarborough, 2001). Foundational literacy instruction should also involve progress monitoring to determine whether the individualized lesson plan choices are impactful. Educators often think of assessments as being high-stakes summative tasks that evaluate student knowledge (Gray et al., 2012). However, studies suggest that educators assess the impact of lessons on learning every 4 weeks or so through progress monitoring, or brief formative assessments that target improvement relative to the specific concepts presented in the previous lesson(s). If students do not learn the content, it should be retaught before progressing to new content. As such, educators with this SOL-based knowledge of letter–sound relationships, who in turn use that knowledge to provide explicit and systematic classroom instruction and monitor skill acquisition and development, have the capacity to open access to school-based literacy skills, conventions, and practices for Black students (Delpit, 1992).

As the SB vignette clearly demonstrates, there are significant benefits in teaching foundational literacy skills to Black students. Yet the vignette also underscores a key area that is missing in the SOL discussion: race. Building with Milner's (2020) recent critique, we assert that the current SOL reform effort does not explicitly address the broader racialized issues related to teaching reading and writing to Black children. We must center race within the conversation of literacy to understand that anti-Black racism is pervasive in U.S. society because Blackness has long been a despised condition "in opposition to all that is pure, human(e), and white" (Dumas & Ross, cited in Coles, 2019, p. 3). For centuries, Black people in the United States were denied equal access to literacy and education through enslavement, Jim Crow, as well as more current forms of systemic racism and anti-Black violence (e.g., police brutality). These racist systems work not only to mitigate Black people's literacy development and educational attainment, but also to destroy their bodies, minds, and spirits through limited access to health and education, low generational wealth (e.g., home ownership), incarceration, poverty, and premature death (Matthew, 2018; McGhee, 2021; Smith, 2021; Taylor, 2019). Within this anti-Black society, literacy for Black children is not only about access and skills acquisition, but it also involves liberation, justice, and empowerment (Ladson-Billings, 2016; Muhammad, 2020).

As a result of the enduring and pervasive anti-Blackness in U.S. society, Black students' opportunities to learn literacy are inequitable (Milner, 2017). For instance, deficit-oriented perceptions of language differences can have devastating implications for Black children and their literacy education. When teachers view Black Language as "improper speech," they are more likely to negatively perceive Black children's intellectual capacities (Day, 2018) and reading abilities (Washington & Seidenberg, 2021). Moreover, when teachers perceive Black Language to be a barrier to Black students' literacy education and development, they incessantly correct, silence, and police students as a means of fixing and eradicating Black Language (Baker-Bell, 2020; Washington & Seidenberg, 2021). These deficit framings reflect anti-Black linguistic racist practices that promote "the linguistic violence, persecution, dehumanization, and marginalization that Black Language (BL) speakers endure when using their language in schools and in everyday life" (Baker-Bell, 2020, p. 9). We are especially concerned about these harmful practices and mindsets because of race-neutral approaches that use White Mainstream English as the standard for "acceptable" ways to talk and write (Hankerson, 2017).

Relatedly, literacy studies (e.g., Turner, 2022) have consistently demonstrated how schools circulate and reproduce persistent stereotypes that (mis)characterize Black children as

- Illiterate, unintelligent, and unmotivated
- Violent, aggressive, and undisciplined
- Lacking support for reading and writing because their caregivers and community members do not value education
- Having "limited" futures focused on athletic or entertainment careers, or life trajectories that will eventually end in prison or death.

Current SOL-related instructional practices (i.e., SL) do not mitigate these intractable stereotypes, nor do they address the importance of race in learning to read and write for Black students. In fact, current instruction often reflects Western logic that touts decontextualized and deculturalized approaches as "best practices" that transcend race and therefore promotes literacy learning for all children (Milner, 2020). The reality, however, is that decontextualized and deculturalized approaches to literacy instruction privilege White middle-class behaviors, literacies, and knowledge while marginalizing and devaluing Black children's cultural identities, language, literacies, and knowledges (Griffin & Turner, 2021). As such, decontextualized and deculturalized instructional approaches cause Black children to experience racial trauma and psychosocial harm from curricular violence (Jones, 2020) that includes invisibility and stereotypical renderings of their lives, experiences, and values, as well as a denigration of their home and community-based literacy traditions. Moreover, decontextualized and deculturalized instructional practices that overemphasize skill and drill instruction mitigate Black children's development by limiting "their access to texts with more complex concepts, syntax, and vocabulary, and impedes their acquisition of higher-level comprehension and critical thinking skills" (Turner, 2019, p. 445).

In this chapter, we advocate for teaching SOL from a racialized instructional approach that we call the *Black Futures approach*. We use this term to center race in the identities, literacies, and lives of Black children, and to describe how foundational literacy skills might be taught in racialized ways that are more responsive to and equitable for Black students. We believe that a Black Futures approach is important for teacher candidates and tutors, like those in our introductory vignette, who are providing skills instruction for Black children. Although presented with a lesson template that establishes a routine for presenting content and skills, the tutors recognized that they needed to adapt and supplement the template based on knowledge about their tutees. This is where cultural knowledge becomes essential. We know that educators' knowledge about their students' cultural values, interests, and experiences significantly inform their instructional choices and assessment decisions. Unfortunately, many educators either lack knowledge about Black communities, Black Language, and Black Culture or they lack the empowerment to leverage culturally relevant materials and instructional perspectives that improve Black students' literacy outcomes (Edwards et al., 2010). Based on decades of literacy research (e.g., Willis, 2015), we assert that a racially centered, culturally grounded approach to literacy instruction would be most beneficial and equitable for Black students.

Therefore, in this chapter, we explore a Black Futures approach as a reimagining of literacy instruction for Black students. For us, the opening vignette does not ask, "How do educators (e.g., tutors, teacher candidates) effectively teach the subskills represented by the Reading Rope?" but instead raises the question "How do educators effectively teach Black students in ways that affirm their literacy assets, connect with their racial identities, and promote the learning of foundational skills?" This shift is crucial because it radically refocuses conversations about literacy from *teaching foundational skills* to *teaching Black children*. As such, we reimagine SOL from a Black Futures approach that articulates an equity-centered, future-forward perspective that centralizes race and the humanity of Black children, while simultaneously emphasizing evidence-based strategies and practices within the classroom. Within a Black Futures approach, Black children are uplifted as fully human—worthy of the futures they determine for themselves through the rich language and literacy practices in their families, friendship groups, and communities (Albro & Turner, 2019; Gibson & Terrell Shockley, 2018; Griffin & Turner, 2021; Turner, 2019, 2022). Toward that end, we invite readers to reimagine literacy instruction with us using a Black Futures approach. We first theorize what literacy might look like through a Black Futures approach through four vignettes. As such, we hope to make visible the instructional mindsets, understandings, and practices that educators can mobilize for teaching literacy through a Black Futures approach. We conclude with implications for educator preparation programs.

Freedom Dreaming: Toward a Black Futures Approach for SOL Instruction

Our perspectives on Black Futures are derived from our collaborative *freedom dreaming* or what Bettina Love (2019) described as imaginative and creative thinking about making systems (e.g., schools) equitable that were never designed for the benefit of Black children. Our freedom dream has centered on one key question: *What do we want literacy instruction to look like for Black children?* Together, we dreamed of literacy instruction that unapologetically does the following:

- Centers Black children in literacy curricula, teaching, and learning. Literacy instruction should purposefully center on the foundational questions of who Black children are and who they want to become. Educators can then integrate their students' current interests and cultural histories, as well as their future goals and aspirations, into literacy lesson plans.

- Cultivates inviting and safe classroom environments not only for Black children but also for the families, caregivers, and communities that cherish and support them.

- Demands the identification of educators who love and care for Black children and demonstrate considerable care and investment in who Black children are and what they desire to be in the world. We dream of educators who understand that Black children have beautiful, brilliant, and literate Black futures.

To further manifest our freedom dreams for Black literacy learners, we created Black Futures as a race-centered approach to teaching literacy. Two types of educator mindset shifts are integral to the Black Futures approach. First, educators must shift from myopic conceptions of literacy toward more expansive perspectives related to Black literacies. We define *Black literacies* as racialized practices of reading, writing, speaking, listening, viewing, and creating that are "grounded in Black liberatory thought, which supports and empowers the emotional, psychological, and spiritual conditions of Black people throughout the Diaspora" (Johnson et al., 2017, p. 63). Black literacies move beyond conventional literacy as reading and writing print to include multimodal forms of communication (i.e., visual, gestural, aural, linguistic) situated within Black communities and social networks (Griffin & Turner, 2021). Black literacy is also a powerful form of critical literacy that provides Black youth (and adults) with the ability to create, comprehend, and critique texts, as well as disrupt and dismantle anti-Black racism in society that negatively impacts their life outcomes. Building with these understandings, we recognize that

Black children already have rich Black literacies cultivated through relationships with family members, friends, and community members. Through their Black literacies, Black children learn to build and sustain their own self-knowledge, ancestral strength, and advocacy for more equitable systems and outcomes in society. A Black Futures instructional approach, then, helps educators capitalize on existing literacy strengths of Black children to humanize their schooling experiences (Dunn & Love, 2020).

Second, we assert that a Black Futures approach honors the language traditions of Black students and therefore can align with scientific theories of literacy that address the ways that the brain responds to sound and language. Research has shown that a primary function of the brain involves maintaining a feeling of safety (Park & Huang, 2010). Familiar social and community-based exposures, such as engaging through the varying languages spoken at home and in home-based communities, help the brain to feel safe. When it feels safe, the brain is able to process new learning (Muthukrishna et al., 2018). When new learning takes place, the brain essentially builds and activates neural pathways through a process called *myelination*, in which neurons work together both more quickly than normal and produce more powerful outputs known as "firing and wiring together" (Hammond, 2015, p. 31). On the contrary, when our brains feel unsafe and potentially threatened, due in part to an unfamiliarity or feeling rejected, they fight against making connections (Hammond, 2015). The amygdala, which processes emotions, will remain alert and release cortisol to prepare for defense. Cortisol is aligned with the shrinking of the working memory, which in turn impacts the retention of information and learning (Perfetti et al., 2007). Capitalizing on existing home literacies in schools is a strategy that helps emerging readers to feel safe and spark a brain-based reaction that supports the acquisition of new information and skills, such as skills aligned with reading foundations (Perfetti et al., 2007). This feeling of safety in turn supports the way that the brain processes phonemes and graphemes, and varying subskills aligned with phonemic awareness, and reinforces the ways that students hear sounds. Acknowledging the rich language traditions and repertoires of Black students fosters supportive environments in which they feel safe and experience more meaningful engagements that will foster learning (Hammond, 2021).

Informed by these two key shifts, we further articulate a Black Futures approach to literacy instruction through a series of vignettes: (1) Centering Black Children and Black Futures, (2) Valuing Black Language and Dialects as Assets, (3) Progress Monitoring as Fuel for Cultural Responsiveness, and (4) Partnering with Black Caregivers and Communities. In sharing these brief stories, we begin to envision what literacy instruction for Black students may look like from a Black Futures approach.

Vignette 1: Centering Black Children and Black Futures

I (JDT) work at a Historically White University (HWU) in which the majority of elementary teacher candidates are White, middle-class, young women. In my methods courses, teacher candidates complete a project with a "striving" reader from their internship classrooms in local elementary schools. The assignment requires candidates to give traditional oral reading fluency, comprehension, and spelling assessments to identify their striving reader's strengths and areas of growth. In addition to these traditional literacy assessments, the candidates also give a career dream drawing assessment that I developed (Turner, 2022). The career dream drawing assessment invites children to create a drawing, using crayons, colored pencils, and/or markers, about their career goals and life aspirations. Through this assessment, teacher candidates have the opportunity to work one-on-one with a child and talk with them about their dreams for the future.

Many teacher candidates select Children of Color, especially Black boys, as their striving readers for this project. In describing what they've learned from the career dream drawing assessments, some teacher candidates begin confronting their own prejudices based on their "surprise" that Black and Brown students have "big dreams" such as becoming U.S. President, a doctor, or a computer engineer. We discuss how "low" literacy scores at one point in a child's educational career do not determine their future trajectories. Others note how their perceptions change, from initially seeing their Black boys (and girls) as "unmotivated" to "thoughtful" "smart" and "engaged" after hearing them talk about their futures. More importantly, some candidates begin to realize that the only time they talked to their striving reader was to reprimand them, and the career dream drawing assessments helped them develop more affirming points of contact and connection with these students.

Building with the information elicited from the career dream drawings, the candidates and I work together to transform the literacy curriculum and instruction (e.g., choices in materials, activities) by intentionally connecting to their striving readers' postsecondary desires, interests, and goals. As we select and read books connected to Black students' futures, candidates begin to include biographies about Black inventors, authors, photographers, and entertainers in their interactive read-alouds. Some invite the entire class to create career dream drawings, while others have included drawings and other multimodal responses in their literacy lessons, so that students can leverage their own critical skills to express meaning and communicate their knowledge.

As the vignette suggests, a Black Futures approach suggests that teacher candidates must first believe in the dreams and aspirations of Black children. Before they even begin to teach literacy skills, teachers must learn to listen to Black children, respect their dreams and aspirations, and affirm the goals that they set for themselves. It is important for teachers to recognize that many Black children experience schools, and even English language arts classrooms, as sites of curricular violence and harm (Jones, 2020), where their dreams, aspirations, and spirits are crushed (Love, 2019). Through a Black Futures instructional approach, teachers see the potential of Black children and therefore create spaces in the literacy curriculum for them "to imagine, dream, create, resist, take up space, and be . . . [and] to define themselves on their own terms, free from interruption and prescriptive identity markers placed on Black folx" (Dunn & Love, 2020, p. 191). We have encountered many educators who think that they "know" their Black students because they have assessed their Lexile levels, writing scores, or fluency rates. Yet these educators frequently have no idea about *who their Black students are and who they want to become.* Knowing what Black students desire in their professional and personal futures helps teachers to "see" Black students in their full humanity and to build more meaningful and personal relationships with them (Griffin & Turner, 2021).

In addition, teachers using a Black Futures approach contextualize foundational skill instruction within the life goals and aspirations of Black children. This requires that teachers center students' career interests, aspirations, and hopes in the teaching of reading and writing. For example, a veteran literacy teacher and I (JDT) co-designed and co-taught a career-centered unit for African American/Black, Latine/x, and White children (ages 10–12 years) in a 4-week summer reading program (Albro & Turner, 2019). Throughout the unit, we invited the children to think about, discuss, artistically express (e.g., drawings, collage) and research their career aspirations. When children engaged in career research, they were eager to learn the vocabulary connected to their aspirations. During our classes, we discussed the pronunciations and meanings of words like *salary, resume,* and *college* because the children encountered these words in the pages of nonfiction books about different professions, on career websites, and in conversations with community speakers. By using these words in their own digital nonfiction writing about their career dreams and aspirations, the children had multiple opportunities to practice reading and writing words within connected text, which supports skills acquisition, including fluency, word recognition, and comprehension.

Finally, this vignette further reminds us that motivational and affective aspects must be considered when using a Black Futures approach for literacy instruction. While motivation is not an aspect of literacy learning typically addressed in SOL reforms, it is a vital aspect of literacy learning and development for Black children (Jones, 2022). Rather than presuming that Black children are unmotivated to learn literacy, a Black Futures approach helps teachers reimagine literacy instruction that deeply connects to the joy, intellect, curiosity, and criticality of Black children. One way that teachers can connect literacy instruction to the brilliance of Black children is to cherish, celebrate, and support the liberatory futures that Black children envision for themselves and for society (Griffin & Turner, 2021). For us, a Black Futures approach toward literacy instruction underscores the reality that the *futures that Black readers bring to a text* are a key determinant of whether they will *want* to understand that text.

Vignette 2: Valuing Black Language and Dialect as Learning Assets

I (SG) work at an HBCU where the vast majority of my teacher candidates are young Black women. Ironically, most of my students come from New Jersey, Pennsylvania, Virginia, or DC, with a sprinkling from Ohio. Interestingly, although my university is located in Maryland, very few teacher candidates are from Baltimore or other parts of Maryland. In light of these regional differences, I want my teacher candidates to conscientiously attend to differences in the manners in which we enunciate words and make sense of the varying sounds in words. Communication and especially language differences take center stage in my literacy methods courses. My Black teacher candidates come from diverse speaking backgrounds, and I have learned to capitalize on these differences to help them to be more mindful, first, of their lack of knowledge about Baltimorese and, second, to fully absorb how dialect plays such a vital role in our work with teaching reading, especially for foundational reading and literacy.

In my quest to help ensure that teachers acknowledge and affirm regional-based speaking traditions of Black children, particularly the Baltimorean dialect spoken in the local communities near my university, I have begun to help candidates to be intentional regarding listening for, acknowledging, exploring, and uplifting dialectical differences. Beginning the first day of class, I emphasize differences in the ways that we say words as we introduce ourselves. My speech, for instance, tends to be more aligned with a light southern accent, where I sing my vowels, holding the vowel sounds longer than my friends who are from other places in the U.S. North. Beyond serving as an effective ice breaker that helps students to become more comfortable with me and their peers, candidates tend to enjoy laughing at differences in how we enunciate words such as *water*, *dog*, *Maryland*, and *mother*, among many others. While I tend to always introduce myself first and invite students to then model their introductions after my own, I repeat words they say that sound different than my own. Candidates often tend to critique one another while laughing during this process, making comments like "Why do you say it like that?" and "That's wild."

We begin a process of both acknowledging differences in the ways we enunciate and how many of our sounds, even for those from the same parts of the same city, tend to differ. I encourage my students to explore how words are enunciated differently on account of regional differences and often refer to family and friends who accentuate certain words in different ways but ways that also reflects their communities. One student commented how she says "git" while her mother says "get" as in "I am going to get [pick up] the trash." We recognize and normalize these differences, acknowledging how what is normed as an appropriate enunciation in one community may sound very different from appropriate ways of speaking in other communities.

These introductory conversations commence an evolving dialogue that continues over the course of the semester, in which we return to the notional concepts of speech differences and norms from those communities. In addition, we return to the notional concepts of speech differences and the speaking norms established within those communities. These conversations are significant because speech differences become particularly meaningful for SOL teaching and assessing phonemic awareness and phonics. For instance, in Northeast Baltimore, you may have children who say words that reflect vowel fronting, which involves shifting of back vowels to a more forward position in the mouth (Jeremiah, 2000). So, the long *u* vowel, for instance, fronts to [ʉu]. I continue to emphasize a collective cognizance of these differences with all of my teacher candidates, in furtherance of the goal to (1) ensure that candidates are trained to hear and understand those enunciation differences; (2) ensure that they do not penalize students on assessments based on these differences; (3) uplift enunciation differences heard in class; and (4) concurrently discern, share, and incorporate other ways the same grapheme may sound in places other than Baltimore. To accomplish these goals, candidates must conduct informal research about Baltimorese within the community. Beyond the goal of validating regional-based speaking traditions of Black children, this undertaking (and attending evaluation) is important because teachers who are unaware of the differences might mistakenly assume students are struggling with aspects of phonemic awareness and phonics. For example, initially, candidates observe notable differences in words like *dog* and *frog*. Many children in the schools where we engage in practicum-based tutoring experiences in Northeast Baltimore enunciate /o/ like /u/. So, *dog* sounds like *dug*, as in "I dug a hole in the ground yesterday." Candidates hear *dug* and may initially want to identify the enunciation of /o/ as a problem to be rectified through intervention. However, through intentional observations, candidates quickly learn to not only acknowledge this local speaking tradition but will often say "good" when they hear kids enunciate using the fronted /u/. So, rather than correct Black students in Baltimore who enunciate sounds in ways that reflect community affiliations and traditions, candidates are trained to take time to explain differences in how sounds may vary based on where you travel. We avoid mandating that our Black students learn what the teacher candidates perceive as "correct forms" of enunciating different sounds as they begin to recognize that misperceptions of correct pronunciation often vary based on region.

This language-inspired vignette offers key insights to teaching literacy from a Black Futures approach. First, a Black Futures approach acknowledges that Black Language, or what some scholars call African American Language, *is* a language. We agree with Smitherman (1999) that it is "starkly clear that the speech of Africans in America is so fundamentally different, in so many ways, from the speech of European Americans that it seems to get right up in yo face and *demand* that you address it as 'language'" (p. 14). Consequently, we assert that Black students have the right to speak their native language (i.e., Black Language) and to use their rich linguistic repertoires as resources to learn literacy in schools. Black Language is important because it reflects the communicative practices of enslaved African ancestors, as well as those in Black families and communities (Baker-Bell et al., 2020). While not all Black students speak Black Language, it is critical that teachers respect, celebrate, and affirm all the languages that Black students bring with them to school, with the understanding that "multiple languages can coexist" (Baker-Bell et al., 2020). Respect may evidence itself in varying forms but should also include an exploration of the richness of the historical roots of Black English (Woodson, 2023).

Relatedly, teachers must be aware that Black children have a wide range of rich linguistic repertoires and they may speak with different pronunciations based on regional variations. The vignette underscores the fact that while the Mid-Atlantic region has some of the highest variations in dialect in the United States, little scholarship exists about Baltimorese, the dialect often spoken in Baltimore (Jeremiah, 2000). Dialect includes pronunciation, grammar, and vocabulary, and serves as an indication of social identity, signaling where a person is from and the phonological facts about who they are (Jeremiah, 2000). Even when Black students speak Black Language, it may sound different depending on their neighborhood, community, or region. A Black Futures orientation helps teachers understand that these language variations are part of everyday life for Black youth that should not be ignored or corrected (Diehm & Hendricks, 2021; Gibson & Terrell Shockley, 2018; Washington & Seidenberg, 2021). Inquiry projects like the one that I (SG) describe in the vignette support educators in *acknowledging* and *understanding* Black students' speech differences rather than intuitively making negative assumptions about those differences. The goal in teaching reading, and sound variance in enunciation of words read, should not be to correct Black children but rather to educate their teachers. Correcting vowel fronting, or any community-based variations, reflects the denigrated status of Black Language in U.S. society and negatively impacts Black children's self-awareness, self-value, self-confidence, feelings of safety, and ultimately engagement with foundational reading and writing.

Finally, the vignette suggests that a Black Futures approach opens new possibilities for (re)positioning Black students' language as an essential resource for developing reading *and* writing skills (O'Gilvie et al., 2011). Johnson and Sullivan (2020) contend that Black students need instruction that enables them to "read and write themselves into the context and content of their literacy learning" (p. 420). We argue, then, that teaching Black students is not only about helping them leverage their language to flexibly employ reading and writing subskills, but to also understand their place in the legacy of intellectuality, advocacy, and liberation of Black people (Baker-Bell, 2020). Without knowledge about the ways that language, culture, and reading intersect, students' literacy knowledge can become pathologized as ignorance. For example, teachers can teach voice by inviting Black students to read and write about Black literature and popular Black multimodal texts (e.g., memes, song lyrics) that employ Black linguistic devices, study their own everyday Black languages and Black literacies in spoken and written forms, and experiment with language for authentic communication with intended audiences (Hankerson, 2017). A Black Futures approach to literacy opens new spaces for educators to leverage Black language as they teach Black students to read and write in schools.

Vignette 3: Progress Monitoring as Fuel for Cultural Responsiveness

Drawing on SOL research, tutors in the LB program monitored the progress of their middle school tutees, most of whom were reading around a second-grade level. Tutors assessed their tutees every third session for about 5–10 minutes. Although typically given to K–2 students, I (SG) opted for tutors to give the Dynamic Indicators of Basic Early Literacy Skills (DIBELS) assessment to understand tutees' foundational reading proficiency levels. Tutors were presented with the DIBELS assessment packet, and we worked through each subsection of the test. Tutors also practiced administering and scoring the DIBELS while I pretended to be a tutee/student. Because I wanted the tutors to understand the relationship between assessment and instruction, we also discussed how the reading subskills contributed to proficient reading using the Reading Rope, and identified where the subskills would be taught and assessed within the lesson plan template.

During the LB program, tutors began to understand the power of progress monitoring as a means of promoting cultural responsiveness. One tutor offered an inspirational example in their written reflections. After assessing the tutee, he (the tutor) realized that his student had not understood the "doubles spelling rule," or doubling the final letter in spelling one-syllable consonant–vowel–consonant words that end in /l/, /s/, /z/, or /f/. The tutor was stuck. For LB tutors, revisiting lessons tended to cause some stress because they had to work to ensure the lesson being presented was more relevant and interesting than the original. While we worked together to think about how the lesson might be retaught, the tutor decided to just talk with the student. After the conversation, the student responded, "I know them twins." The student understood the doubles rule as "them twins." Once the tutor retaught the lesson using the rule of "them twins," the tutee earned a proficient score on the assessments.

At the end of the LB program, the tutors began to fully recognize the importance of progress monitoring. While reflecting, tutors were reminded to review their tutees' data to evaluate the impact of the tutoring. When revisiting the DIBELS progress chart, many tutors were able to identify areas of growth. Tutors often commented that they "feel really proud" of their tutees' progress. One tutor spoke at length, noting, "I had no idea. It feels like we are in a routine. I'm so used to the routine. You get in the groove of what you are doing. Sometimes it feels like 'I don't know if this is working or if you are just here, like every week.' When I looked at his chart [scores]), it was like, 'OK. I see it. We have been doing stuff. He has been learning. I gave those tests. So, I know it's real.' I did something with this kid."

In this vignette, LB tutors learned to see the significance of using the data that they regularly collected to modify foundational skills instruction. Although they received limited training, the tutors regularly administered literacy assessments and used student data to teach, reflect on, and reteach skills lessons. We know that educators might administer literacy assessments, and some may even analyze the data, but many do not reteach lessons based on those outcomes (Sach, 2012). Like the LB tutors, educators who enact a Black Futures approach understand not only the purposes for assessing reading and spelling skills, but also the value of using that formative data to make sound instructional decisions.

Relatedly, LB tutors had a great deal of agency to create individualized and culturalized lessons for their tutees. Too often, literacy instructional practices are overly restrictive and confined by the structure of the lesson plan templates. As the vignette suggests, the literacy structure helps LB tutors, as non-education majors, to teach the lesson elements in an explicit and systematic manner. However, the LB program also provided support for tutors to integrate cultural knowledge of the students into their lessons to ensure that their foundational skills instruction was relevant and meaningful. No two tutoring lessons looked the same, despite their use of the standardized template. Tutors were encouraged to design lessons with activities aligned with foundational reading and writing skills that were intimately connected to students' cultural interests and knowledge. In this example, the phrase "them twins" uses Black Language and signifies "twin vibes" popularized in Black music and Black social media (Smoot, 2023). Both the tutor and tutee shared this cultural knowledge, which promoted the successful reteaching of the "double spelling rule" lesson. We believe that this exemplifies a Black Futures approach in which foundational skills instruction for Black students is driven by data and fuels cultural responsiveness.

Vignette 4: Partnering with Black Caregivers and Communities

In the LB tutoring program, we met with caregivers on a biweekly basis to provide additional support around various topics:

- Various subskills of reading
- Language-based learning differences (e.g., honoring your home speech at school)
- Reading assessments (e.g., DIBELS, state assessment), their purposes and their outcomes
- Strategies for advocating for their children in school.

A survey was conducted at the beginning of LB to identify best days, times, and formats for caregiver sessions. To ensure more active participation, caregiver session formats and days rotated on a biweekly basis. Sessions were led by myself (SG) and another Black female educator, who specializes in working with Black males who are dyslexic. Sessions spanned around 30 minutes and were intended to be more practical than theoretical. For example, we discussed reading subskills with caregivers by sharing the Reading Rope, while concurrently exploring ways that those subskills are already supported at home and/or considering how families might support them at home.

Feedback collected through surveys at the end of each session was positive. Many caregivers stated that they "didn't know" this information and the sessions were "helpful because no one talks about this." Several parents followed up with me to obtain the progress monitoring data from the LB program to help support conversations with their child's school. One caregiver inquired, "Can I tell a friend about this, even though her child isn't in the program?" Another asked, "Do you [and the LB program] come to schools? Can you help my school with these talks also? We don't have this at my school."

As this vignette demonstrates, working with Black caregivers is important. Too often, educators privilege schools as the primary site where reading and writing skills are learned and mistakenly believe that Black families and community members don't care about school literacy. Black caregivers are frequently misperceived as a "barrier" to school literacy learning due to persistent stereotypes that denigrate the culture, literacies, and language of Black homes and communities (Rommell, 2024). As such, caregivers are not welcomed at schools in ways that support meaningful engagement or collaboration (Bolgatz et al., 2020).

Reenvisioning literacy through a Black Futures instructional approach (re) positions Black caregivers as assets because they are their children's first teachers. Moreover, Black homes and communities are crucial sites for Black children's literacy learning because caregivers cultivate the oral and written language skills that undergird proficient reading and writing (Edwards & Turner, 2009). Recognizing the important role of Black caregivers, a Black Futures approach builds literacy instruction on meaningful home and school connections. For example, teachers can unearth caregivers' home-based literacy experiences and activities through storytelling and use that information to transform classroom instruction (Edwards & Turner, 2010). Informing Black caregivers about strategies for building on and reinforcing school-based lessons at home can also support children's literacy development, provided that Black caregivers and their home literacy practices are respected and validated.

Moving Forward

For Black people, literacy has never been just about skills; it is about our freedom, self-worth, and joy, as well as our histories, present realities, and desired futures. In this chapter, we recognize this more holistic definition of literacy and how it informs the learning of Black children through a Black Futures approach to literacy. Specifically, we have shared four vignettes to articulate a Black Futures approach to teaching Black children foundational skills. Through these powerful vignettes, we have illuminated the knowledge, dispositions, and skills that educators need to teach foundational reading and writing skills in ways that are relevant and meaningful for Black students.

We are excited about the practical implications of this work. As faculty involved with educator preparation programs, we recognize that extending the science of literacy beyond the Reading Rope is critically important. As the LB tutors in the introductory vignette have reminded us, skills-based models are necessary but not sufficient for teaching Black students because they do not address race. Hence, our Black Futures approach centers on race by teaching reading and writing within the context of Black students' dreams, interests, and cultures, ensuring that learning environments are safe, caring, and affirming. While we realize that a Black Futures approach is not the only way to modify literacy instruction, we believe that it holds promise for teaching foundational skills and strategies to Black students.

In writing this chapter, we realized that the power of the Black Futures approach was manifested through our collaborative conversations. We teach at very different institutions, yet as Black women in the literacy faculty, we were able to come together and integrate key insights from our work in literacy into a rich instructional model. Thus, we utilize this chapter as a "call to action" for other Black educators, including educator preparation program faculty at HWUs, HBCUs, as well as Black educators in public elementary and middle schools, to come together to reimagine literacy for Black students. Our collective power is imperative for the freedom dreaming that we need to do, and the work that it takes to make literacy learning more equitable and joyful for Black students. We live with an abundance and not a scarcity of knowledge. Coming together helps us see how reading and literacy instruction can be both embedded within the cultures of Black students and also be explicit and systematic. We can be relentless advocates of reading and literacy for Black children while also challenging structural racism and historic inequities. Toward that goal, we conclude with additional questions that may help Black teachers and Black faculty in education preparation programs to *reach and teach* Black students through the Black Futures approach:

- How can university faculty use the Black Futures approach to decenter Whiteness in education preparation programs?
- How can educators use the Black Futures approach and the science of literacy as tools to challenge the anti-Black racism in the schooling system and in literacy classrooms?
- What do educators need to know about Black Language and Black literacy practices to teach literacy through a Black Futures approach?
- How can university faculty and educators work together, using a Black Futures approach, to modify literacy and make learning more engaging and joyful for the Black students in their classrooms?
- How can a Black Futures approach promote healing and thriving for Black students who have been stigmatized and traumatized by literacy instruction in schools?

REFERENCES

Albro, J., & Turner, J. D. (2019). Six key principles: bridging students' career dreams with literacy standards. *Reading Teacher, 73*(2), 161–172.

Baker-Bell, A. (2020). Dismantling anti-black linguistic racism in language arts classrooms: Toward an anti-racist black language pedagogy. *Theory Into Practice, 59*(1), 8–21.

Baker-Bell, A., Williams-Farrier, B., Jackson, D., Johnson, L. L., Kynard, C., & McMurty, T. (2020). *This ain't another statement! This is a DEMAND for Black linguistic justice*. https://cccc.ncte.org/cccc/demand-for-black-linguistic-justice.

Bolgatz, J., Crowley, R., & Figueroa, E. (2020). Countering White dominance in an independent elementary school: Black parents use community cultural wealth to navigate "private school speak." *Journal of Negro Education, 89*(3), 312–327.

Coles, J. A. (2019). The Black literacies of urban high school youth countering antiblackness in the context of neoliberal multiculturalism. *Journal of Language and Literacy Education, 15*(2), 1–35.

Day, M. (2018). Speech and intelligence: Does my use of colloquiums label me incompetent? *Virginia English Journal, 68*(1), 16–34.

Delpit, L. D. (1992). Acquisition of literate discourse: Bowing before the master? *Theory Into Practice, 31*(4), 296–302.

Diehm, E. A., & Hendricks, A. E. (2021). Teachers' content knowledge and pedagogical beliefs regarding the use of African American English. *Language, Speech, and Hearing Services in Schools, 52*(1), 100–117.

Duke, N. K., & Cartwright, K. B. (2021). The science of reading progresses: Communicating advances beyond the Simple View of Reading. *Reading Research Quarterly, 56,* S25–S44.

Dunn, D., & Love, B. (2020). Antiracist language arts pedagogy is incomplete without Black joy. *Research in the Teaching of English, 55*(2), 190–191.

Edwards, P., McMillon, G. T., & Turner, J. D. (2010). *Change is gonna come: Transforming literacy education for African American students.* Teachers College Press.

Edwards, P. A., & Turner, J. D. (2009). Family literacy and comprehension. In S. Israel & G. Duffy (Eds.), *Handbook of research on reading comprehension* (pp. 622–641). Routledge.

Edwards, P. A., & Turner, J. D. (2010). Do you hear what I hear?: Using parent stories to listen to and learn from African American parents. In M. L. Dantas & P. Manyak (Eds.), *Home–school connections in a multicultural society: Learning from and with culturally and linguistically diverse families* (pp. 137–155). Routledge.

Gibson, S., & Terrell Shockley, E. (2018). Walking the tightrope between advocacy and knowledge: An appeal from teacher educators to speech-language pathologists regarding African American English. *Perspectives of the ASHA Special Interest Groups, 3*(1), 147–158.

Gough, P. B., & Tunmer, W. E. (1986). Decoding, reading, and reading disability. *Remedial and Special Education, 7*(1), 6–10.

Gray, K. E., Webb, D. C., & Otero, V. K. (2012). Effects of the learning assistant experience on in-service teachers' practices. *AIP Conference Proceedings, 1413*(1), 199–202.

Griffin, A. A., & Turner, J. D. (2021). Toward a pedagogy of Black livingness: Black students' creative multimodal renderings of resistance to anti-Blackness. *English Teaching: Practice and Critique, 20*(4), 440–453.

Hammond, Z. (2015). *Culturally responsive teaching and the brain: Promoting authentic engagement and rigor among culturally and linguistically diverse students.* Corwin Press.

Hammond, Z. (2021). Liberatory education: Integrating the Science of Learning and culturally responsive practice. *American Educator, 45*(2), 4–11.

Hankerson, S. (2017). Black voices matter. *Language Arts Journal of Michigan, 32*(2), 7–14.

Jeremiah, M. A. (2000). Baltimore speech: Evidence from phonology. *CLA Journal, 44*(2), 231–242.

Johnson, L. L., Jackson, J., Stovall, D. O., & Baszile, D. T. (2017). "Loving Blackness to death": (Re)Imagining ELA classrooms in a time of racial chaos. *English Journal, 106*(4), 60–66.

Johnson, L. P., & Sullivan, H. (2020). Revealing the human and the writer: The promise of a humanizing writing pedagogy for Black students. *Research in the Teaching of English, 54*(4), 418–438.

Jones, S. (2022). Turning away from anti-blackness: A critical review of adolescent reading motivation research. *Reading Research Quarterly, 57*(4), 1107–1127.

Jones, S. P. (2020). Ending curriculum violence. *Teaching Tolerance, 64,* 47–50.

Ladson-Billings, G. (2016). #Literatelivesmatter: Black reading, writing, speaking and listening in the 21st century. *Literacy Research: Theory, Method, and Practice, 65,* 1–11.

Learned, J. E. (2016). "Feeling like I'm slow because I'm in this class": Secondary school contexts and the identification and construction of struggling readers. *Reading Research Quarterly, 51*(4), 367–371.

Love, B. (2019). *We want to do more than survive: Abolitionist teaching and the pursuit of educational freedom*. Beacon Press.

Matthew, D. B. (2018). *Just medicine: A cure for racial inequality in American health care*. New York University Press.

McGhee, H. (2021). *The sum of us: What racism costs everyone and how we can prosper together*. One World.

Milner, H. R. (2017). Race, talk, opportunity gaps, and curriculum shifts in (teacher) education. *Literacy Research: Theory, Method, and Practice, 66*(1), 73–94.

Milner, H. R. (2020). Disrupting racism and whiteness in researching a science of reading. *Reading Research Quarterly, 55*(Suppl. 1), S249–S253.

Moreau, L. K. (2014). Who's really struggling?: Middle school teachers' perceptions of struggling readers. *RMLE Online, 37*(10), 1–17.

Muhammad, G. (2020). *Cultivating genius: An equity framework for culturally and historically responsive literacy*. Scholastic.

Muthukrishna, M., Doebeli, M., Chudek, M., & Henrich, J. (2018). The cultural brain hypothesis: How culture drives brain expansion, sociality, and life history. *PLoS Computational Biology, 14*(11), Article e1006504.

National Center for Education Statistics. (2022). *Fast Facts: Teacher characteristics and trends*. U.S. Department of Education, Institute of Education Sciences. https://nces.ed.gov/fastfacts/display.asp?id=28.

National Center for Education Statistics. (2023). *Racial/ethnic enrollment in public schools: The condition of education*. U.S. Department of Education, Institute of Education Sciences. https://nces.ed.gov/programs/coe/indicator/cge.

National Institute of Child Health and Human Development. (2000). *Report of the National Reading Panel: Teaching children to read: Reports of the subgroups* (00-4754). Author.

O'Gilvie, H. O., Turner, J. D., & Hughes, H. L. (2011). Teaching through language: Using multilingual tools to promote literacy achievement among African American elementary students. In P. Schmidt & A. Lazar (Eds.), *Practicing what we teach: How culturally responsive literacy classrooms make a difference* (pp. 141–155). Teachers College Press.

Park, D. C., & Huang, C. M. (2010). Culture wires the brain: A cognitive neuroscience perspective. *Perspectives on Psychological Science, 5*(4), 391–400.

Perfetti, C. A., Liu, Y., Fiez, J., Nelson, J., Bolger, D. J., & Tan, L. H. (2007). Reading in two writing systems: Accommodation and assimilation of the brain's reading network. *Bilingualism: Language and Cognition, 10*(2), 131–146.

Petscher, Y., Cabell, S. Q., Catts, H. W., Compton, D. L., Foorman, B. R., Hart, S. A., . . . Wagner, R. K. (2020). How the science of reading informs 21st-century education. *Reading Research Quarterly, 55*(Suppl. 1), S267–S282.

Rommell, E. (2024). Family composition, race, and teachers' perceptions of parent–teacher alliance. *Social Problems*, spae017.

Sach, E. (2012). Teachers and testing: An investigation into teachers' perceptions of formative assessment. *Educational Studies, 38*(3), 261–276.

Scarborough, H. S. (2001). Connecting early language and literacy to later reading (dis)abilities: Evidence, theory, and practice. In S. B. Neuman & D. K. Dickinson (Eds.), *Handbook of early literacy research* (Vol. 1, pp. 97–110). Guilford Press.

Smith, C. (2021). *How the word is passed: A reckoning with the history of slavery across America*. Hachette UK.

Smitherman, G. (1999). *Talkin that talk: Language, culture, and education in African America*. Routledge.

Smoot, D. (2023, September 7). *What is the 'In the cut with my twin' sound on TikTok and where does it come from?* Yahoo!life. www.yahoo.com/lifestyle/cut-twin-sound-tiktok-where-204537825.html?fr=sycsrp_catchall.

Taylor, K. Y. (2019). *Race for profit: How banks and the real estate industry undermined black homeownership*. University of North Carolina Press Books.

Turner, J. D. (2019). Improving Black students' college and career readiness through literacy instruction: A Freirean-inspired approach for K–8 classrooms. *Journal of Negro Education, 88*(4), 443–453.

Turner, J. D. (2022). Freedom to aspire: Black children's career dreams, perceived aspirational supports, and Africentric values. *Race Ethnicity and Education, 25*(1), 128–153.

Washington, J. A., & Seidenberg, M. S. (2021). Teaching reading to African American children: When home and school language differ. *American Educator, 45*(2), 26–33.

Willis, A. I. (2015). Literacy and race: Access, equity, and freedom. *Literacy Research: Theory, Method, and Practice, 64*, 23–55.

Woodson, C. G. (2023). *The mis-education of the Negro*. Penguin.

CHAPTER 24

Beyond Words
Multimodal and Digital Literacies, Culture, and Identity in Learners' Lives

Cheryl A. McLean

> At times, I observe groups of 9–10-year-old students, sometimes huddled over their Chromebooks, and at other times fluidly moving over to view their neighbors' screens. I watch silently as the blur of hands and fingers swiping and scrolling across digital screens is matched only by the steady buzz of chatter and laughter punctuated by barely controlled squeals of excitement at a particular image or video. Along with the Chromebooks, strewn across their wooden desks are notebooks and worksheets that contain feverishly scribbled notes gathered from the screens....
> —McLean (2020, p. 538)

As a literacy teacher educator and researcher, my ongoing work with K–12 learners, teachers, and preservice teachers has fostered my heightened awareness and growing understanding of the diverse literacy practices, modalities, and multimodal resources young people use to make meaning, navigate sociocultural spaces, and develop their identities as learners and individuals. Reflecting on our contemporary educational literacy landscape, I have found that young people are strategically using digital technology and multimodal tools and texts to communicate, create, and (re)present themselves and their social worlds. What is more, given its current predominance in students' lives, the digital screen has now become central to their literacy practices: Children and young people are increasingly using the screen as a primary mode with which to read, write/compose, view, speak, listen, and make meaning. Whether this screen is found in the palm of their hands, whether it is mobile or fixed on a desk or wall, or even located in the home or classroom, the communicative resources of digital and electronic media afford multiple opportunities for social and academic engagement.

In this chapter, I offer a praxis-oriented conception of digital and multimodal literacies and share some of the ways that these literacies show up in learners' communicative practices and lived experiences. Then, drawing on my research in

K–12 schools and higher education, I go on to consider what such modes, texts, and tools might mean for teachers and students in the contemporary classroom. Finally, after highlighting key challenges for teachers and teacher educators, I offer some overarching implications for teaching and learning and consider how these might influence future research directions.

Multimodal and Digital Literacies

The term *multimodality* implies a disposition toward the inclusion of modes of communication *beyond* the printed word. Whether print, visual/images, oral, aural, kinesthetic/gestural, these modes are signs/semiotics. It is helpful to think of each mode as a language of communication with its own grammar or structures that, when taught, learned, and applied—formally and informally—allows the user to convey and interpret meaning. In our daily lives, we generally use a *combination* of these modes to "read" the world around us, to communicate and interact with others, and to learn and grow. However, whereas as literacy educators and researchers we are certainly aware that learning involves multiple modes, I would argue that it is the proliferation of these digitally mediated, multimodal forms of communication and children's facility with engaging with such modes, texts, and tools that has highlighted its educational value and prompted the push for its meaningful use in the classroom.

With the growing variety and influence of digital texts, tools, and social networks, young learners are now increasingly developing and harnessing communicative dispositions and skills beyond the traditionally valued print-based reading and writing. Simply put, the meaning-making practices that our students overwhelmingly use, prefer, and value are multimodal (oral, aural visual, tactile, spatial, gestural etc.). This is evinced in our contemporary communicational landscape, where meaning making and communication through reading, writing, speaking, listening, moving/performing, and thinking occur primarily through the digital screen. In 2024, the screen (with its digital applications and social media platforms) has become a source of entertainment (e.g., games, YouTube, movies/television, ebooks, TikTok), information and education (e.g., Wikipedia, Google, TED Talks), communication (e.g., websites, texting, Instagram, Snapchat, Skype, Zoom, WhatsApp, X, Facebook), social positioning (e.g., Instagram, Facebook, X), and community and affinity groups (e.g., chat/message groups, X, Instagram, Facebook, WhatsApp). Through such digital tools and texts, children are required to engage with a combination of modes to engage with content, to communicate with others, and to express themselves. For example, a typical video game or even a short-form video involves the player or viewer *in real time*, simultaneously navigating and interpreting the multiple languages or grammatical structures of colors, animation, sounds, words (printed, spoken, typed), symbols, and tactile (screen, keyboard, controller). Yet these children are often required to shift from such multimodal interactive spaces to classrooms that often privilege the printed text as the primary mode of communication and meaning making.

I would argue that children's modal and semiotic skills and dispositions are developing *because* of the digital screen, and *despite* some of our more traditional current teaching/learning contexts. When comparing the communicative processes of traditional print-centric reader–writer relationship versus that of electronic media, Miller (2015) notes that print is characterized by isolation, distance, and slow publication time, while electronic media's network-centric character is built on connectedness through the immediacy of access, production, and dissemination. Indeed, the primacy of digital texts, tools, and social networks that our students access, consume, engage with, and produce as a source of communication, entertainment, information, community relations, means that the screen now functions as a central part of students' identities influencing their relationships with reading, writing, speaking, listening, viewing, as well as their relationships with each other. As I have stated previously, "Unlike with the traditional print book, the modern reader is no longer relegated to consuming information after the fact; instead, the reader often becomes an interactive participant who responds to the word by digitally reproducing (reposting/sharing), responding (commenting), remixing (making memes), coproducing/creating (editorializing), and archiving (memorializing) this information" (McLean, 2020, p. 537). It is this social aspect—the interconnectedness between reader and writer, the interactive nature of the internet's virtual worlds and communities that challenged me to consider how the nature and properties of children's digital screen reading might be influencing their identities as readers, and their meaning-making processes. In seeking to determine students' access to digital texts and their attendant digital literacy competencies, I have found that the collaborative and social nature of social media and their digital applications, platforms, and communities lend themselves to opportunities for play and the exploration of modal literacies to read, write, comprehend, and communicate.

The number and formats of these different genres of digital and social media texts, as well as the range of modalities they combine, reminds us that the concept and practice of literacy is layered, nuanced, and multidimensional, in that literacy is often *defined* and *confined* by the individuals, the available tools/resources (modal and digital, linguistic), funds of knowledge (Moll, 1992), the environments (physical, virtual, ideological, relational etc.), and the user's purpose/intent. What this means is that when attempting to conduct literacy research and/or design literacy instruction, one must consider (1) who the learners are (i.e., identities, abilities, interests, sociocultural histories); (2) the forms of engagement and types of skills the learners acquire and use; (3) the types of texts with which learners currently engage and/or are to engage; (4) the spaces/contexts (physical, virtual, cultural, academic etc.); (5) the communities in which they occur; and (6) the situated modalities (i.e., how modes are used to produce meaning). In acknowledging the value of semiotic resources in supporting students' engagement and meaning making, educators and researchers are then able to expand opportunities for students' learning by using multiple forms of representation and formats of communication.

Because multimodality converges in digital literacy practices and spaces and, given the ubiquitous nature of digital screens in our daily lives, there is growing need to purposefully leverage these modalities in learning and teaching. What the works of researchers in the field of literacy research, and my own research have shown over the past two decades is that semiotics plays a pivotal role in the literacy development and practice (see Jewitt, 2005; Kress, 2010, 2003; McLean, 2024, 2020; McLean & Rowsell, 2020b; Pahl & Rowsell, 2010; Rowsell et al., 2012). Such research has shown that the primary way in which learners make meaning and communicate is through a combination of modes: images/visuals, printed words/writing, oral/speech, sound/music, moving image/movement, touch, spatial, and so forth. As the extensive body of literature on the topic in the past decades illustrates, the integration of multimodality in classroom instruction is not new given that it increases options for communication and meaning making. In my own research, I have argued that whether it is through modes such as visual, oral, aural, tactile, and movement, as well as related formats (e.g., print, digital screen, speech, audio, video), for effective learning and teaching to occur, both teachers and students must have the necessary dispositions toward these modalities. Underlying the need and efforts to understand and harness students' digital and multimodal literacy mindsets and practices is the overarching goal of improving student learning and performance through teacher knowledge and professional development that are more responsive to students' contemporary literacies, sociocultural backgrounds, and interests.

Contextualizing Teaching and Learning

Effective and responsive teaching creates and supports opportunities for meaningful and engaged learning. For literacy teaching and learning to be more effective and responsive, there must be a holistic approach that intentionally accounts for the students' *and* teachers' multimodal literacy practices, knowledge, skills, and dispositions alongside related instructional approaches, and curricula tools, texts, and content. Viewing both students and teachers as learners, and multimodal and digital spaces as learning contexts opens a range of learning opportunities.

Student Learners

In my ethnographic research on students' multimodal and digital literacies, I discovered that the screen of the digital mobile device such as a tablet or laptop better allowed *me* to "see" modern/digital reading in action in the classroom. What I mean here is that through my participant observations in my role as teacher-researcher in English language arts classrooms, the relational dimensions of digital/screen reading showed up in the modal and sensory-driven practices that included visual, oral, ludic, aural, verbal, tactile, and physical. For example, in the opening vignette of this chapter, the social and modal nature of learning through screens is evident in students' active participation in the assigned task, as well as their interactions and collaboration with each other. What is more, in their one-on-one and focus group interviews about their digital literacies, these students shared that collaboration was their *preferred* form of engagement. As such, they sought out opportunities to do so online, and when not available, (i.e., as part of the designed lesson structure or formal learning activity) created these collaborative opportunities through physical movement, talk, conferring, direct messaging, choral singing, showing, and so forth. Reading in such classrooms where digital technologies are used becomes a social process that is (1) participatory, in that it was interactive and involved sharing of content; (2) tactile, involving semiotic resources like touch repertoire to navigate texts (e.g., scroll, swipe, type, tap); (3) accommodating of the interactions of material, physical, digital, virtual, texts, tools, and spaces; and (4) fun, playful, and unpredictable (see Wohlwend et al., 2018).

Using multimodal tasks and instructional approaches allows teachers to *see* the learning shifts and "aha" moments as the students use their funds of knowledge, their lived experiences, and academic knowledge to (1) think critically about and analyze the academic text (e.g., via close reading, textual evidence, and details to first understand the plot and character, vocabulary, tone, voice, imagery); (2) move across efferent and aesthetic responses by tapping into their emotional responses to the text (e.g., via compositions involving visuals, performance, and music); and (3) do cross-modal work in which they move from words to visuals and back to words. Provision of a more enabling, modally rich learning framework that supported digital and modal dispositions in a practice-driven learning environment gave learners creative, interactive, collaborative, and communicative opportunities, freedom, and flexibility. Attending to learners' semiotic literacy resources helps facilitate authentic transactional and transformational learning processes.

Cultural and Identity Mediation

Over the past two decades, my research has consistently shown that outside the classroom, children and young people are actively participating in social networks and online platforms (e.g., YouTube, Instagram, and TikTok) to create, consume, and/or interact with content. Whether the format is music videos, short-form videos, videogames, podcasts, photostories, and so forth, children are engaging with a range of literacy skills that include reading, writing, speaking, listening, and viewing, be it through talk (podcasts), writing (comments), images (videos, demos, photos, visuals, vlogs), or performance and movement (dance demos and challenges). These online social networks and communities can serve a variety of needs and interests—from affinity groups-based social trends to cultural and ethnic spaces. For example, in some cases, children may choose to follow, like, and/or subscribe to their favorite musical entertainers or popular social media influencers. In other cases, they create and engage in cultural- and affinity-based social media networks and communities as an identity mediation tool. Whether it is on social media platforms and messaging applications such as Instagram or WhatsApp, these young people participate in and/or design communities in which they can connect, interact, collaborate, and create through language/linguistic expressions, social identity groups, and even cultural practices. Exploring the literacy practices in which children engage within these online social spaces helps to expand our conceptions of literacy beyond the traditional written word and print-based reading to include multimodal, multimedia texts, and artifacts. Of greater import is the fact that it is within these spaces are opportunities to discover not only the multimodal literacies (i.e., the practices, compositions, or products) but also the development of their identities (i.e., the agency and creative confidence) that defines the act and experience of (re)making in formal and informal environments (McLean & Rowsell, 2020a).

As literacy educators who are charged with teaching diverse children (ethnoculturally, linguistic, neurologically, racially, cognitively, etc.), we must continue to learn how our young people use digital media as resources to negotiate multiple social and cultural systems. Reconceptualizing classroom practice requires a contemporary view of literacy that is broad and inclusive enough to accommodate and value children's diverse ways of being, and flexible enough to afford them the opportunities and resources needed to thrive. Perhaps, one of the key things that my research has shown is that multiple modal tools and digital spaces create *opportunities* for marginalized and minoritized youth to harness and develop their communicative dispositions and skills, and more importantly, to have these become a valued part of the broader educational and societal narrative.

Teachers as Learners

My research on digital and multimodal literacies has also highlighted how *teachers'* modal and design dispositions have shaped their pedagogical practices (McLean & Rowsell, 2013). In seeking to better understand how educators were thinking about and using multimodal logic in their classrooms to create learning and teaching opportunities, our findings showed that when a design-oriented approach to instruction is premised on the social practice of *shared knowledge* between teacher and students, this shifted the traditional and narrow mindset of teacher as "knowledgeable other." What we found was that while these K–12 educators reported that using multimodal texts and tools enhanced their own learning, these were still seen as discrete from traditional print texts in their classroom instructional practice. In attempting to shift from a monomodal print-centric mindset to instruction incorporating multimodal literacies and logic of design, research participants acknowledged the challenges placed on the teacher to create/design, facilitate, and model these literacies. They reported that to teach using multimodal instruction, they themselves first needed to become familiar and *comfortable* with the modes, conventions, and design grammar. Modal choice and variety, particularly for a learner who feels more comfortable with words and traditional forms of instruction, proved intimidating for teachers who were still grappling with their own learning styles and preferences for the logic of written language and printed text. However, these teachers' modal learning experiences show that developing teachers' digital and modal knowledge and dispositions would allow them to be more proactively responsive to students' literacies, thereby enhancing students' investment and engagement in the classroom.

If we are to harness students' digital and multimodal literacies in our schools and classrooms, then *teachers* need to have the necessary skills, dispositions, and tools to do so, namely, the discourse/language, the space to practice/try out, and the knowledge base about design and the use of technology to foster their own learning and critical thinking. For teachers' mindsets, and by extension, their instructional planning and practices to reflect digital and multimodal literacies, the teachers must embrace a multimodal logic. Thus, to leverage any real change in literacy teacher education, there needs to be a meaningful shift from a print-centric and static approach to teaching reading and writing—one that purposefully integrates multiple modes such as sound, animation, visuals, moving images, spatial dimensions, and so forth, into the instructional design and delivery and assessment. For this to occur, teacher preparation programs, as well as teachers' knowledge, dispositions, and skills, must be grounded in an expanded notion of literacy, and promote their *comfort* with these diverse modes, and multimodal texts and tools of representation and assessment, that is, all teaching (i.e., preparation/education, planning, instruction, and assessment) must be framed by a design framework that applies the multimodal contexts, tools, language, and mindsets to better support learners.

Content and Context

My research has consistently shown that to achieve increased student engagement and improved performance, educators need *intentional* instructional practices designed around a multimodal logic. For this to occur, there must be a pedagogical focus on design, technology, and multimodality that shapes not only the instructional approaches, but also curricular content, texts, tasks/activities, and assessment methods. Given that curriculum and assessment are closely tied to formal teaching and learning, to argue for pedagogies that meaningfully attend to students' multimodal and digital literacies is not enough; digital and multimodal curricular texts, content, and assessment practices must simultaneously accompany such pedagogical practices.

In the recent decade, the K–12 classroom practice and attendant K–12 curricular content have been responsive to these realities of students' engagement with digital texts and tools by integrating information and communications technology, print and digital sources for reading and writing, and informational text features (e.g., charts, graphs, diagrams) into the "domain-specific knowledge, skills, and abilities" connected to language, reading, writing, and speaking and listening (New Jersey Department of Education, 2024a). For example, included in the New Jersey K–12 state standards is a standard on "Computer Science and Design Thinking," designed to produce "computationally literate creators" who can "ethically produce and critically consume technology," "engage as collaborators, innovators, and entrepreneurs," and "navigate the dynamic digital landscape" (New Jersey Department of Education, 2024b). Such curricular considerations and emphases illustrate policymakers' and educators' efforts to shift teaching and learning, and classroom instruction, away from a print-centric approach to one that is broader and more multimodal and digital. Taken further, these shifts signal the acknowledgment that digital technologies, skills, and dispositions are central to how our young learners communicate and make meaning.

Yet the challenge of multimodal instruction often lies in the range of modes that can be used to compose a product or text, the levels of students' and teachers' expertise and experience with such modes, the forms of assessing students' multimodal texts and products, and the state-mandated forms of assessment (McLean & Rowsell, 2015). Over a decade ago, based on an international study across the United Kingdom, the United States, and Canada, my colleagues and I argued for assessments for learning through multimodality that includes (1) purpose and audience, (2) text structures, (3) technical features used for effect, and (4) reflection (McLean et al., 2012). In the classroom, for example, a digital story, website, podcast, vlog or short-form video might be used as a practical model for the design of an assignment that is *guided* by a relevant rubric(s) for application of principles of design. Nonetheless, the challenge of finding and applying systematic and formalized ways in which to assess such modal practices persists. Here, I reiterate that for multimodality to really take hold in policy and practice, there need to be relevant assessment frameworks and ways of evaluating and interpreting these frameworks that are built around multimodal design principles and digital literacies. Assessing multimodal texts, compositions, and practices using one-dimensional and/or print-centric approaches is counter to the authentic and innate ways in which one learns, and it negates learners' contemporary knowledge, skills, and dispositions.

Going Beyond Words

Students' identities as learners and individuals are inextricably tied to their experiences with classroom teachers, instruction approaches, and the curriculum. Therefore, as teachers, teacher educators, and researchers, it is important to consider the contemporary and evolving practices and ways of knowing of young people. Any efforts to promote student engagement and learning must value their dynamic literacy practices. For such an approach to be meaningful, educators must adopt approaches to teaching and learning that are reciprocal and responsive to students' diverse knowledge, skills, experiences, and sociocultural realities.

Critical Implications

What does it mean to go *beyond words* in literacy teaching and learning? For me, *beyond words* means shifting from a narrow and constraining print- and word-based mindsets and pedagogies; it also means moving past the *talk* about engaging students to meaningfully enacting appropriate approaches (i.e., practicing responsiveness in terms of our harnessing of multimodal digital texts and tools in the preparation of teachers, to the curriculum content, to teachers' instructional modes, as well as our mindsets as educators and policymakers). Going beyond words requires us to firmly frame our policies, pedagogies, curriculum, and research around our contemporary *learners*. In fact, my own approaches to literacy pedagogy and research are now directly informed by my awareness of the pervasiveness of young people's digitized worlds and literacies, and the knowledge that students' reading processes and text interactions with digital and multimodal literacies–practices–texts are often dependent on the purpose/task, the time, the text, the audience, the context, the modalities, and the medium. I would argue that filling the gap between *what we know* and *what we need to know* requires a both/and approach that embraces depth *and* breadth—that is, (1) the depth that is attained through critical reflection of and the revisiting of literacy research via new and different lenses (theoretical and methodological) and (2) the breadth or plurality that is achieved only when we disrupt traditionally default Euro-normative literacies to make equitable space for the diversity of literacy practices and the communities that use them.

Taking a holistic approach to literacy research and instruction—*who, what, where, why, and how*—has been particularly useful in providing a more nuanced view of the development of children's multimodal literacy practices and related learning processes. Such a praxis-oriented approach strives to bring together research, teaching, and learning in a way that is designed to help educators reconceptualize meaning making and consider contemporary practices to equitably support diverse learners. As literacy researchers, teachers, and teacher educators, we must recognize and promote the importance of reimagining literacy pedagogy and shaping our mindsets and policies around digital reading. Screen logic and dispositions are modally and socially playful and multidimensional. When thinking about the learners with whom I have worked, the multiple modes that they use—in physical and virtual worlds, in classrooms and in digital spaces,

1. Play becomes a form of making real and imagined social worlds: Learners creatively try on, try out, and play around with artifacts, objects, materials, spaces, and so forth, and even to remake or create artifacts, new meanings, and social groups.
2. The community aspects of digital media and its social networks offer opportunities to make, create, and compose in interactive and collaborative ways.
3. Semiotic tools and spaces foster identity construction, creative thinking, and agency.

Our approach to the field of literacy instruction and research can only come from a multipronged *praxis-oriented* one that attends to the learners/teachers, knowledge claims, tools/resources, and modes of representation. However, any changes and disruptions can only be meaningful if we, as educators, truly consider what it means to read, write, speak, listen, and view in these modern times.

• *Reading.* In thinking about the global, plural, and modal nature of digital reading and literacy, we are reminded of the need to make our own approach to reading culturally sensitive, multimodal and ideological (Street, 1984). No longer can we rely solely on Eurocentric, middle-class approaches that have defined the field of literacy research and practice. Instead, the digitized tools and spaces highlight that reading is about different and plural types of genres, texts, modes, and perspectives/experiences.

- *Writing.* Our concept of writing and grammar needs to shift to one that is contextual, modal, and plural. The seeming rigidity and one-dimensionality of "standard" academic writing and grammar of English must now accommodate a language of design and an understanding of modal grammar.

- *Speaking.* We must recognize plurality of speech. Just as there are many languages and bilingual, multilingual, and emergent bilingual learners in our classrooms and society, so too are there many cultural identities that need to be given a voice in and out of the classroom. Even further, considering our digital landscape, a balanced approach to literacy instruction now requires us to be as comfortable with printed page and digital screen to the point that teachers can shift seamlessly from teacher–student read-alouds from a storybook to artificial intelligence (AI) read-alouds.

- *Listening.* While it is somewhat common to include audio devices and music in the curriculum, the use of sound and audio devices in students' learning is often limited to audio clips and podcasts that accompany written text. There is much room for growth in terms of developing sonic literacy and understanding that sound is still a very hidden or underexplored aspect of our curriculum.

- *Viewing/visuals.* As my ongoing research has shown, there are untapped opportunities for learning through visuals. This requires us to truly understand what multimodality does and is in terms of the grammar of visual design and deploying it in meaningful ways the classroom and the curriculum.

Future Directions

Across the research on multimodality, culture, and identity, the process of learning (i.e., the "how"), the contexts (i.e., the "where"), the content (i.e., the "what"), the learners/teachers (i.e., the "who") one cannot but consider new frontiers in terms of AI and critical literacy. The increasing presence of AI in our everyday literacy practices—from search engines, speech-to-text applications to writing/text and video generators—signal not only challenges in effectively assessing students' comprehension and learning but also the ethical issues of representation and voice. Certainly, teachers and teacher educators would benefit from developing their own comfort with AI and knowing ways in which to include digitized literacies, texts, and tools that would engage students while developing their critical thinking and problem-solving skills, particularly in terms of the accuracy and "truth" of content they consume, produce, and are exposed to. Given the contemporary communicational landscape, what our approach to literacy teaching/learning really needs is the development of learners' capacity to problem-solve—to do the critical thinking that would allow for more ethical choices, logical and discerning reasoning when engaging with all texts, content, and artifacts, and a deeper valuing of our diverse experiences and ways of knowing.

REFERENCES

Jewitt, C. (2005). Multimodality, "reading, and "writing" for the 21st century. *Discourse: Studies in the Cultural Politics of Education, 26*(3), 315–331.

Kress, G. (2003). *Literacy in the new media age.* Routledge.

Kress, G. (2010). *Multimodality: A social semiotic approach to contemporary communication.* Routledge.

McLean, C. (2020). The shallows or hidden depths?: Wrestling with the nature and depth of screen reading. *Reading Teacher, 73*(4), 535–542.

McLean, C. (2024). Making an influence: Sponsorship and creolization on social media. *Reading Research Quarterly, 59,* 228–256.

McLean, C., & Rowsell, J. (2013). (Re)designing literacy teacher education: A call for change. *Teaching Education, 24*(1), 1–26.

McLean, C., & Rowsell, J. (2015). Imagining writing futures: Photography, writing and technology. *Reading and Writing Quarterly, 31,* 102–118.

McLean, C., & Rowsell, J. (2019). Digital literacies in Canada. In J. Lacina & R. Griffith (Eds.), *Preparing globally minded literacy teachers: Knowledge, practices, and case studies* (pp. 177–197). Routledge.

McLean, C., & Rowsell, J. (Eds.). (2020a). *Maker literacies and maker identities in the digital age: Learning and playing through modes and media.* Routledge.

McLean, C., & Rowsell, J. (2020b). Turning the page and swiping the screen on reading in the English classroom. In B. Marshall, J. Manuel, L. Pasternak, & J. Rowsell (Eds.), *The Bloomsbury handbook of reading perspectives and practices* (pp. 79–90). Bloomsbury.

McLean, C., Rowsell, J., & Lapp, D. (2012). Tupaq, Katy Perry, and *Schindler's List*, in the Secondary English secondary classroom: Assessing English in new times. *English in Australia, 46*(3), 9–20.

Miller, R. (2015). On digital reading. *Pedagogy, 16*(1), 153–164.

Moll, L. (1992). Funds of knowledge for teaching: Using a qualitative approach to connect homes and classrooms. *Theory Into Practice, 31*(2), 132–141.

New Jersey Department of Education. (2024a). *New Jersey Student Learning Standards.* www.nj.gov/education/standards.

New Jersey Department of Education. (2024b). *New Jersey Student Learning Standards: Computer Science & Design Thinking.* www.nj.gov/education/standards/compsci/index.shtml.

Pahl, K., & Rowsell, J. (2010). *Artifactual literacy: Every object tells a story.* Teachers College Press.

Rowsell, J., McLean, C., & Hamilton, M. (2012). Visual literacy as a classroom approach. *Journal of Adolescent and Adult Literacy, 55*(5), 444–447.

Street, B. V. (1984). *Literacy in theory and practice.* Cambridge University Press.

Wohlwend, K. E., Buchholz, B. A., & Medina, C. L. (2018). Playful literacies and practices of making in children's imaginaries. In K. A. Mills, A. Stornaiuolo, A. Smith, & J. Z. Pandya (Eds.), *Handbook of writing, literacies, and education in digital cultures* (pp. 136–147). Routledge.

Author Index

Aaron, P. G., 117
Abbott, R., 160
Abu-Rabia, S., 70
Ackerman, P. T., 242
Adams, G. L., 232
Adams, M. J., 2, 38
Adlof, S. M., 117, 118
Ahmed, Y., 128, 295
Ahn, S., 32, 33, 35, 47, 52, 54, 56, 144
Aitken, A., 278
Al Dahhan, N. Z., 186, 187
Al Otaiba, S., 194, 395
Albro, J., 413, 417
Alexander, R., 14, 20, 23
Alfieri, L., 232
Alim, H. S., 331
Allen, A. S., 208
Allen, J. P., 368, 370
Allen, L. K., 110
Allington, R. L., 190, 192, 242
Alloway, T. P., 31
Allyn, P., 329
Aloe, A. M., 231
Amendum, S. J., 3, 141
Anderson, R. C., 12, 48, 52, 53, 159, 169, 172
Andreev, L., 88
Anglin, J. M., 51, 52, 55, 86
Ankrum, J. W., 245, 251
Apel, K., 32, 33, 125
Applebee, A. N., 309
Applegate, A. J., 263

Applegate, K., 246
Applegate, M. D., 263
Archer, A. L., 31, 33, 41, 231
Ardoin, S. P., 137, 260
Arner, T., 108, 110
Asadi, I. A., 122
Ascenzi-Moreno, L., 63, 74
Assor, A., 162
Asterhan, C. S. C., 11, 12
Athanases, S. Z., 244
Atteberry, A., 188
Atwell, N., 313
August, D. E., 73, 311
Augustine, C. H., 193
Aukerman, M., 334
Azevedo, R., 80, 169

B

Bailey, T. R., 216
Baixeries, J., 82
Baker, L., 153, 154, 161
Baker, S. K., 297, 311
Baker-Bell, A., 412, 419, 420
Ball, D. L., 280
Balyan, R., 108
Bandura, A., 154, 295, 374, 375
Bao, R., 209
Barker, E., 187, 188
Baron, J., 52

Barquero, L. A., 189
Barr, C. D., 88
Bartholomew, C. C., 234
Bartlett, B., 282
Barzilai, S., 11
Basile, J., 300
Basma, B., 354, 355, 367
Baumann, J., 241
Bayer, N., 4
Bazerman, C., 281
Beachy, R., 391, 395
Bean, R., 215
Bean, R. M., 369
Beck, I. L., 64, 80, 82, 89, 402
Becker, W. C., 231
Beeman, K., 73
Beers, A., 119
Beerwinkle, A. L., 389, 393, 398, 400
Bell, S. M., 191
Benedict, A. E., 208, 355, 356, 357, 360
Benjamin, R. G., 136, 137, 141, 255, 256, 263, 264, 265, 268
Benson, S., 66
Bereiter, C., 308, 319
Berninger, V. W., 294
Bhabha, H., 66
Bhattacharya, A., 32
Bialystok, E., 70, 71
Biancarosa, G., 3, 308, 309
Biber, D., 86
Bidell, T. R., 189
Biemiller, A., 85
Billings, L., 19
Binks-Cantrell, E., 384, 386
Bishop, R. S., 73
Block, C. C., 310
Boardman, A. G., 355, 357, 358, 359, 360
Bolgatz, J., 422
Bollinger, A., 276
Bond, G. L., 367
Bondie, R. S., 208
Bonifacci, P., 122
Booton, S. A., 86
Borko, H., 243
Borman, G. D., 190
Bos, C., 400
Bouton, E., 12
Bowers, P. N., 52, 197
Brady, S., 402
Brasseur-Hock, I. F., 30
Bråten, I., 16
Brenner, D., 257, 267
Bridgeman, B., 384, 387, 391
Brindle, M., 278, 292
Britain, M., 52

Brock, C. H., 375, 376
Brown, A. L., 159, 331, 402
Brown, B., 333
Brown, C., 215
Brown, J. S., 370
Brown, P. C., 33
Brownell, M., 208, 352, 354, 355, 356, 357, 360
Bryant, B. R., 262
Bryant, D. P., 351, 355, 356, 358, 360
Bryant, P., 85
Bryk, A. S., 371, 378
Buehl, M. M., 22
Bunch, G. C., 309, 311
Burchinal, M., 42
Burgess, S. R., 125
Burkam, D. T., 190
Burns, M. K., 102, 128, 129, 136, 139
Butterfuss, R., 108
Byrd, R., 319

C

Cabell, S., 327
Cabell, S. Q., 1
Cadime, I., 122
Cain, K., 86, 101, 120, 122
Caldwell, J., 260, 261
Calvin, G., 208
Cantrell, S. C., 350, 355, 357, 358, 360, 371, 378
Capin, P., 211
Carlisle, J. F., 47, 51, 52, 87, 144, 387
Carlo, M. S., 64, 90
Carlson, S. E., 107, 110, 174
Carnoy, M., 331
Carroll, J. B., 276
Carter, E. W., 234
Cartwright, K. B., 115, 120, 121, 125, 128, 138, 139, 410
Carver, R. P., 125
Castaneda, R., 89
Castek, J., 6, 326, 330, 331
Castells, N., 356, 358, 360, 362
Castles, A., 31
Catts, H. W., 124
Cazden, C., 371, 373
Cervetti, G. N., 4, 53, 89, 115, 168, 169, 172, 174, 176, 178, 211, 226, 334
Chall, J. S., 1, 2, 257, 265
Chambers Schuldt, L., 334
Chandler, B., 2
Chapman, J. W., 118, 119, 154, 160
Chard, D. J., 36
Cheesman, E., 215, 384, 389, 395, 401
Cheesman Smith, M., 266

Chen, R. S., 124, 129
Cheng, C., 70
Chinn, C. A., 11, 12, 22, 159
Chiu, Y. D., 125, 126
Cho, E., 160
Cho, S. J., 56
Choi, S., 100, 215
Chomsky, C., 258, 259, 262, 267, 268, 269
Chomsky, N., 48
Chow, J. C., 215
Christodoulou, J. A., 4, 187, 188, 194
Chung, H., 6
Church, J. A., 189
Cirino, P. T., 30
Ciullo, S., 5, 292, 297, 300
Clark, A. M., 73
Clark, S. K., 351, 357, 360
Clay, A., 205, 207
Cobb, P., 22
Coburn, C. E., 241
Coffin, C., 308
Cohen, D. K., 280
Cohen, R. A., 400
Coiro, J., 340
Cole, A. M., 121
Coles, J. A., 411
Collins, A., 5, 292, 401
Collins, A. A., 296, 297, 299, 301
Compton, D. L., 101, 142
Conklin, K., 86, 87
Conley, D. T., 309, 322
Conner, C. M. D., 129
Conners, F. A., 120, 125
Connor, C. M., 170, 207, 208
Conradi, K., 153, 160
Contesse, V. A., 190, 195
Cook, B., 279
Cook, L., 215, 225
Cook, S. C., 225
Coolong, C. M., 194
Cooper, H. M., 194
Cooper Borkenhagen, M. J., 256
Côté, M. F., 70
Cox, K. E., 161
Coxhead, A., 82, 89
Crafton, L., 370, 378
Crenshaw, K., 65
Cromley, J. G., 80, 169
Crone, D. A., 213
Crosson, A. C., 88
Crowell, A., 12
Cummins, J., 67, 71, 73
Cunningham, A. E., 257, 383, 386
Cunningham, J. W., 137, 141
Cutting, L. E., 117, 119, 120, 124, 125

D

Daane, M. C., 30
Dahl, R., 247
Dakin, K., 186
Daley, S., 69
Daniel, J., 195
Darling-Hammond, L., 331
David, M. D., 144
Davies, B., 370
Davies, M., 84
Davis, C. J., 83
Davis, D. S., 6, 168, 350, 351, 387, 390, 391, 393, 396, 400, 401
Dawes, L., 14
Dawson, N., 230
Day, M., 412
De Bot, K., 189
De Glopper, K., 175
de Kramer, R. M., 354, 389, 403
De La Paz, S., 23
De Naeghel, J., 156
de Oliveira, L. C., 244
Deacon, S. H., 52, 87
Deci, E. L., 153, 157, 161, 162
Delpit, L. D., 411
Denton, C. A., 194
Desimone, L. M., 353, 354, 355, 356, 358, 359, 360, 361, 363, 374, 377, 378
Dewey, J., 11, 241
Dewitz, P., 205
Didion, L., 349, 354
Diehm, E. A., 420
Diliberto, J. A., 32
Dixon, L. Q., 70
Domitrovich, C. E., 234
Donegan, R. E., 194, 195, 196
Donnelly, P. M., 194
Donovan, S. L., 402
Dowhower, S. L., 258
Dowling, N. M., 190
Downey, C., 208
Dozier, C. L., 242
Driver, R., 11
Duffy, G. G., 241, 242, 243, 250, 371
Duguay, A., 389, 392
Duke, N. K., 115, 120, 128, 138, 139, 176, 310, 410
Dunn, D., 415, 416
Durgunoğlu, A. Y., 64
Durlak, J. A., 233, 234
Dweck, C. S., 152, 330
Dwyer, B., 330
Dykman, R. A., 242
Dykstra, R., 367
Dynarski, M., 30

E

Ebert, K. D., 124
Eccles, J. S., 157, 161, 162, 242
Ecker, U., 99
Edmonds, M. S., 197
Edwards, O. V., 11
Edwards, P. A., 73, 413, 423
Ehri, L. C., 32, 38, 402
Elizabeth, T., 371
Elleman, A. M., 226
Emdin, C., 333
Engelmann, S., 232
Engeström, Y., 66
Ennis, R., 18
Ennis, R. P., 297
Erduran, S., 11
Ericsson, K. A., 104

F

Fairbanks, C. M., 242
Falkum, I. L., 86, 87
Faller, E., 90
Feinn, R., 215
Fellbaum, C., 89
Ferrer-i-Cancho, R., 81
Fien, H., 211
Filderman, M. J., 37, 100, 213, 354
Fischer, F., 23
Fischer, K. W., 189
Fisher, C. W., 87
Fisher, D., 135, 137, 330, 368
Fisher, J., 207
Fitzgerald, J., 63, 65, 137, 309, 311
Fitzsimmons, S., 311
Fixsen, D. L., 215, 233
Flavell, J. H., 243
Fletcher, J. M., 215
Flores, N., 67, 72, 73
Florit, E., 119, 122, 125
Flugman, B., 402
Flynn, L. J., 195, 196
Folsom, J. S., 193, 194, 384
Foorman, B. R., 31, 119, 126, 127, 129, 215, 256, 386, 388, 392, 400
Ford, M., 23
Ford-Connors, E., 370, 371, 372, 373
Forzani, E., 326
Fountas, I. C., 135, 136, 169, 259, 261
Frahm, T., 372, 373, 374
Francis, D. J., 30, 120, 125, 128, 227, 309
Franke, M. L., 208
Fredricks, J. A., 156
Freebody, P., 172
Freeman, J., 208
Freire, D., 330
Freire, P., 326
Frey, N., 137, 330
Freyd, P., 52
Friend, M., 215, 225
Fuchs, D., 225
Fuchs, L. S., 215, 216
Fulmer, S. M., 146
Furuness, S., 371

G

Gabriel, R. E., 235, 341
Gallagher, M. C., 261
Galloway, E. P., 88
Gambrell, L. B., 241, 257
García, M., 331
García, O., 62, 67, 72, 73
Gardner, S., 15, 16
Garwood, J. D., 299
Garza, R., 207
Gates, C., 193, 194
Gatlin-Nash, B., 42
Gaultney, J. F., 171
Gay, G., 207
Gee, J. P., 64, 66, 328
Georgiou, G. K., 123, 129
Gersten, R., 211, 212, 213
Geva, E., 67, 70
Giazitzidou, S., 32
Gibson, S., 7, 413, 420
Gilbert, J. K., 51, 54, 56, 275, 292, 303
Gillespie, A., 296, 297
Gilmour, A. F., 100
Goldberg, N., 332
Golden, M., 326
Goldfield, S., 402
Goldman, S. R., 91, 302
Gomez, K., 331
Gomez, L., 331
Gong, X., 4
Goodman, K. S., 115
Goodwin, A. P., 2, 32, 33, 35, 47, 48, 50, 51, 52, 54, 55, 56, 57, 144, 145, 146, 334
Gorard, S., 12
Gore, J., 208
Gore, J. M., 208
Goss, M., 6, 330
Goss, M. M., 331
Goswami, U., 85
Gotwals, A. W., 82, 176
Gough, P. B., 30, 52, 53, 55, 68, 69, 86, 115, 116, 117, 124, 125, 128, 129, 139, 410
Govier, T., 14, 18, 23

Graesser, A. C., 135, 136, 140, 141
Graham, S., 5, 39, 275, 276, 277, 278, 279, 280, 281, 282, 283, 285, 291, 292, 293, 294, 295, 296, 297, 303, 307, 308, 309, 310, 311, 312, 313, 315, 334, 339
Graves, D. H., 339
Gray, K. E., 411
Greeno, J. G., 66, 401
Gregory, M., 2, 12, 14, 15, 19
Griffin, A. A., 412, 413, 414, 417
Griffith, R., 244
Grills-Taquechel, A. E., 197
Grissom, J. A., 208
Grossman, P. L., 243
Gurney, D., 315
Guryan, J., 190, 191
Gustafson, S., 117, 122
Guthrie, J. T., 139, 153, 154, 155, 156, 157, 158, 159, 160, 161, 162, 163, 178, 249, 251
Gutiérrez, K., 66, 72, 73, 74

H

Hagen, Å., 3
Hall, C., 350, 354, 355, 357, 358, 359, 360, 384, 387, 391, 401
Halle, M., 48
Halliday, M. A. K., 88
Hallinger, P., 207
Hamilton, 213
Hamm, D. N., 142
Hammer, D., 13
Hammerness, K., 250
Hammerschmidt-Snidarich, S., 36
Hammond, Z. L., 331, 333, 415
Haneda, M., 370, 373, 378
Hanford, E., 334
Hankerson, S., 412, 420
Hanna, P. R., 31
Hanushek, E. A., 331
Harackiewicz, J. M., 157
Harn, B., 233
Harré, R., 370
Harris, D. N., 369, 378
Harris, K. R., 174, 279, 280, 282, 283, 285, 292, 295, 297, 299, 303
Hart, L., 30, 80
Hasan, R., 88
Hasbrouck, J., 263, 264
Hattie, J., 367, 375
Hebert, M., 276, 277, 278, 282
Hemsley, G., 70
Henderson, J. B., 13, 22
Hendricks, A. E., 420
Hennessy, S., 12

Henrichs, L. F., 82
Henry, M. K., 48, 52
Herrera, S., 212, 213
Heubach, K. M., 144, 261, 266, 268
Hidi, S., 157
Hiebert, E. H., 31, 53, 87, 89, 137, 140, 144
Hillocks, G., 315
Hjetland, H. N., 122, 126, 127
Ho, A. N., 155, 160
Hoberman, M. A., 247
Hodgkinson, T., 143
Hodgkiss, A., 86
Hoffman, J. V., 241, 244
Hoffmeister, R., 70
Hogan, E., 354
Hollingsworth, P. M., 268
Hoover, W. A., 52, 53, 55, 68, 69, 86, 116, 117, 127, 129, 385
Howe, C., 12, 13, 23
Howell, E., 351, 356, 357, 358, 360
Huang, C. M., 415
Huckin, T., 64
Hudson, A. K., 143, 215, 351, 390, 393, 398, 403
Hughes, C. A., 33, 231, 295
Hughes, H. K., 350, 355, 357, 358, 360
Hulme, C., 186
Humphrey, N., 186
Huo, M. R. Y., 123
Hwang, H., 168
Hyland, K., 86

I

Ibrahim, R., 122
Inhelder, B., 11
Ippolito, J., 91, 369
Irwin, V., 331
Israel, B. A., 243

J

Jackson, J. G., 108, 110
Jacob, R., 208
Jacobs, G., 330
Jacobson, M. G., 170
Jakobson, K., 390, 396, 400
Jang, H., 162
Jared, D., 31
Jenkins, J. R., 52, 266, 267
Jeremiah, M. A., 418, 419
Jewitt, C., 431
Jiménez, R. T., 48, 64, 71, 72, 73, 334
Johnson, A., 187, 188
Johnson, D., 349

Johnson, E. S., 209
Johnson, L. L., 414
Johnson, L. P., 420
Johnson, V., 99
Johnston, P., 16, 242, 248, 249, 334
Johnston, P. H., 371
Johnston, T. C., 117
Jolivette, K., 297
Jones, R. L., 62, 65, 66, 72
Jones, S., 47, 50, 57, 370, 378, 417
Jones, S. M., 170
Jones, S. P., 413, 416
Jordan, R. L. P., 384, 387, 401
Joshi, R. M., 117, 122
Joyce, B. R., 208
Junker, B. W., 20

K

Kaefer, T., 169, 170
Kaiser, E., 370, 378
Kamil, M. L., 226, 227, 351
Katz, L. A., 51
Katzir, T., 155
Kavanagh, J., 11
Kazemi, E., 208
Ke, S., 123
Kearns, D. M., 31, 34, 51, 215, 256
Keenan, J. M., 142
Kelley, J., 90
Kelly, A., 376
Kelly, S., 135, 367
Kendeou, P., 3, 99, 100, 102, 108, 110, 122, 126, 385
Kennedy, A., 226
Kennedy, M. M., 226, 350, 370
Kershaw, S., 118, 120, 124, 125
Kershaw-Herrera, S., 143
Kieffer, M. J., 69, 90, 123, 125
Kim, J., 210, 320, 321, 356, 357, 358, 360
Kim, J. S., 155, 158, 159, 170, 190, 191, 192, 194
Kim, M. K., 36
Kim, Y., 275, 279
Kim, Y. S., 70
Kim, Y.-S. G., 30, 41, 118, 125, 128, 257, 294, 385
King, P. M., 21
Kintsch, W., 69, 100, 102, 139, 169, 385
Kirby, J. R., 52, 117, 197
Kitchener, K. S., 21
Klauda, S. L., 156, 157, 159, 160
Klingner, J. K., 158, 159, 229, 233, 351, 355, 358, 359, 360
Knecht, R., 356, 357, 358, 360
Knoph, R. E., 3, 84

Kocaarsian, M., 256
Köder, F., 86, 87
König, J., 387
Kozak, S., 389, 397
Kraal, A., 174
Kraft, M. A., 186, 234, 350, 368, 369
Kress, G., 431
Kretlow, A. G., 234
Kubina, R. M., Jr., 36
Kucan, L., 82, 144, 385, 388, 390, 395, 400, 402, 404
Kuhn, D., 12, 14, 16, 21, 308, 317
Kuhn, M. R., 1, 5, 144, 246, 255, 256, 257, 258, 259, 262, 263, 265, 266, 267, 268, 269
Kuperman, V., 83

L

LaBerge, D., 39, 256, 267
Lacina, J., 244
Ladson-Billings, G., 65, 331, 333, 412
Lammert, C., 143
Land, R., 320, 321
Landauer, T. K., 86
Lane, H. B., 144
Langer, J. A., 308, 322
Lara-Cinisomo, S., 194
LaRusso, M., 125
Lawrence, J. F., 3, 84, 89, 90, 91
Learned, J. E., 411
Lee, A. J., 65, 73
Lee, A. Y., 65, 73
Lee, H., 123
Lee, J., 36, 230
Lee, J. W., 70, 71
Leider, C. M., 70
Lemons, C. J., 214, 215
Lesaux, N. K., 72, 88, 90
Leseman, P. P. M., 82
Leslie, L., 176, 260, 261
Leu, D. J., 327
Levesque, K. C., 87, 230
Levorato, M. C., 86, 121, 122
Levy, L., 263, 266, 269
Levy, R., 66
Lewis, W. E., 145
Licealde, V. R. T., 143
Lillenstein, J., 215
Lin, A. R., 91
Lin, Y. C., 186
Lipman, M., 14, 18
Liu, K., 278, 282
Livingston, C., 243
Livingston, E. M., 235
Lo, M., 170

Lockwood, J. R., 357, 368, 369
Logan, G. D., 256, 268
Lonigan, C. J., 119, 120, 125
López, F. A., 71, 72
Louick, R., 70
Love, B., 331, 333, 414, 415, 416
Lovett, M. W., 41
Löweke, S., 161, 162
Luh, H. J., 233
Lukianoff, G., 14, 15
Lupo, S. M., 1, 145, 230
Lyon, G. R., 186
Lysaker, J. T., 370

M

Maamuujar, U., 6
MacArthur, C. A., 354, 356, 357, 358
Macedo, D., 326, 330
Magliano, J. P., 108
Mahony, D., 52
Maki, K. E., 36
Maloney, A., 4
Maloney, E., 31
Mancilla-Martinez, J., 126, 127
Manderino, M., 331
Mandinach, 213
Mantilla-Blanco, P., 242
Marks, R., 187
Marsh, J. A., 357, 368, 369, 370
Martin-Chang, S., 389, 397
Martínez, R. A., 66, 87
Mason, L. H., 293, 300
Massonnie, J., 122
Mateos-Aparicio, P., 189
Matsumura, L. C., 368, 369, 370, 378
Matthew, D. B., 412
Matthews, J. S., 71, 72
May, H., 145, 147
McCarthy, K. S., 107, 108, 110
McClung, N. A., 89
McCombes-Tolis, J., 215
McCombs, J. S., 190, 193, 194
McCutchen, D., 384, 388, 397, 398
McDuffie-Landrum, K. A., 225
McEachin, A., 188
McElhone, D., 398
McGhee, H., 412
McGill-Franzen, A., 190, 192
McKenna, M., 4
McKeown, D., 282
McKeown, M. G., 80, 82, 227, 402
McLean, C., 7, 428, 430, 431, 433, 435
McLeskey, J., 295, 300, 301
McMahan, K. M., 384, 402

McMaster, K. L., 3, 100, 102, 105, 106, 107, 174, 354
McNair, J. C., 73
McNamara, D. S., 104, 107, 108, 110, 176
Meece, J. L., 154
Meisler, S. L., 189
Menard, J., 198
Mercer, N., 12, 23
Mesmer, H. A. E., 138, 139, 140, 141
Metsala, J. L., 144
Michaels, S., 12, 14
Milburn, T. F., 119, 120
Miller, R., 430
Milner, H. R., 411, 412
Mintrop, R., 339
Mitchell, M. E., 189
Mo, E., 71
Moats, L. C., 186, 215, 386, 388, 392, 400
Modla, V. B., 263
Moje, E. B., 66, 328
Moll, L., 66, 137, 430
Montesinos, M. M. T., 122
Moore, B. A., 355, 357, 358, 359, 360
Moore, W., 12
Morales, P. Z., 66
Moreau, L. K., 411
Morgan, P. L., 186
Morphy, P., 282
Morris, B. M., 120
Mounk, Y., 14, 15
Muhammad, G., 326, 331, 333, 412
Mulcahy, C. A., 389, 392
Mullins, P. M., 186
Murawski, W. W., 215
Murphy, V. A., 87
Muthukrishna, M., 415
Myers, J., 278

N

Nagin, C., 310
Nagy, W., 38, 47, 48, 52, 53, 55, 82
Nakamoto, J., 71
Nation, K., 31, 86
Neuman, S. B., 30, 303
Newton, N., 108
Nguyen, C. T., 15
Nguyen, T. D., 235
Nguyen, T. Q., 142, 143
Nichols, W., 356, 358, 360
Nickow, A., 186
Nicula, B., 110
Nilsson, K., 121, 122, 129
Nippold, M. A., 86, 186, 195
Nomanbhoy, D. M., 52

Northrop, L., 135
Northrup, L., 367
Nouwens, S., 120
Novicoff, S., 186
Numeroff, L. J., 101
Nussbaum, E. M., 11, 23
Nystrand, M., 19, 371

O

Oakhill, J., 101
O'Byrne, W., 351
O'Connor, C., 12
O'Connor, R. E., 35, 142, 225, 231
O'Donnell, C. R., 384
O'Gilvie, H. O., 420
Ogle, D. M., 169
Oguilve, V., 340
Olinghouse, N. G., 298
Oliverira, M., 122, 125
Olsen, L., 309
Olson, C. B., 6, 310, 311, 320, 321, 322
Omanson, R. C., 80
Omohundro, K., 4
O'Reilly, T., 91, 108, 176
Osborne, J., 15, 23
O'Shea, L. J., 260
Ossa Parra, M., 67, 68, 74
Ouellette, G., 119

P

Pacheco, M. B., 55, 56
Packer, M. J., 71
Padeliadu, S., 32
Padesky, L. B., 370, 371, 374, 376
Pagan, S., 191, 192
Pahl, K., 431
Paige, D., 120, 125
Palincsar, A. S., 159, 385, 402
Paratore, J. R., 6
Paris, D., 331
Paris, S. G., 142, 310, 319
Park, D. C., 415
Park, Y., 70
Parks, R., 84
Parsons, S. A., 241, 245
Pasquarella, A., 70
Passmore, S., 81
Patall, E. A., 162
Patel, L., 62
Pearson, P. D., 1, 89, 137, 140, 142, 168, 169, 211, 241, 244, 261, 310, 322, 326, 333, 334
Peng, P., 121, 122, 124, 171, 177, 210, 227

Pennell, C., 197
Perazzo, D., 187
Perdue, M. V., 189
Perfetti, C. A., 30, 31, 55, 80, 119, 415
Perie, M., 308
Perin, D., 277, 282, 307, 308, 310, 313
Perkins, J., 47, 50, 56
Perry, C., 32
Persky, H. R., 308
Petscher, Y., 47, 50, 52, 55, 57, 410
Phelps, G., 384, 386, 387, 388, 391
Piaget, J., 11
Piasta, S. B., 384, 398
Pigozzi, G. H., 266, 267
Pinnell, G. S., 135, 136, 169, 259, 261
Pintrich, P. R., 153, 154
Pitre, C. C., 41
Pittman, R. T., 390, 400
Poch, A. L., 216
Podhajski, B., 215
Poortman, C., 215
Porter, B. M., 189
Porter, S. B., 384
Potter, J., 217
Pouscoulous, N., 87
Pressley, M., 174, 241, 310
Prevoo, M. J., 70, 71, 73
Price, L., 369
Price, L. R., 352, 356, 357, 368, 370
Prochnow, J. E., 160
Proctor, C. P., 62, 65, 66, 67, 68, 69, 70, 71, 72, 73, 74
Proctor, P., 3
Protopapas, A., 119, 122
Pulido, D., 172
Purcell-Gates, V., 241

Q

Quinn, D. M., 190, 192, 331
Quinn, J. M., 69, 80

R

Rademaker, F., 234
Rainey, E. C., 330
Rainville, K. N., 370, 378
Rapanta, C., 13, 22
Rapp, D. N., 101, 103
Rashotte, C., 260
Rasinski, T. V., 258, 263, 264, 265, 266, 269
Rauch, J., 14, 15
Rayner, K., 103
Recht, D. R., 176

Redding, C., 235
Reed, D. K., 4, 143, 190, 193, 194, 223, 224, 231, 232, 234, 235, 353
Reeve, J., 156, 162
Reichle, E. D., 55
Resnick, L. B., 12
Retelsdorf, J., 155
Rettig, 161, 162
Reynolds, D., 50, 52, 55, 57, 145, 146, 367
Reznitskaya, A., 2, 12, 13, 17, 18, 19, 22, 73
Rice, M., 354
Rich, M. D., 11
Richardson, V., 16
Rigby, J. G., 368
Rijlaarsdam, G., 276
Risemberg, R., 292
Roberts, G., 215, 223, 227, 228, 233
Roberts, T., 19
Robertson, D. A., 6, 370, 371, 372, 373, 374, 376, 378
Roch, M., 121, 122
Rodríguez-Moreno, A., 189
Roe, M. A., 189
Roehler, L. R., 243
Roman, N., 328
Romeo, R. R., 190
Rommell, E., 422
Rosenblatt, L. M., 12, 139
Rowsell, J., 431, 433, 435
Rozendaal, J. S., 158
Russell, S. G., 242
Rutten, I., 242
Ryan, R. M., 153, 157, 161, 162

S

Sabatini, J., 142
Sach, E., 421
Saddler, B., 300, 301
Sailors, M., 352, 356, 357, 368, 369, 370
Salahu-Din, D., 308
Samuels, S. J., 39, 256, 258, 259, 267, 268, 269
Samuelson, C., 350, 387, 391, 393, 401
Sanchez-Vincitore, L. V., 122
Sandmel, K., 282
Sanetti, L. M. H., 233
Santangelo, T., 39, 278, 282
Sass, T. R., 369, 378
Savage, R., 129, 354, 355, 367
Savitz, R. S., 351
Sawyer, R., 243
Scammacca, N., 30, 196, 197
Scarborough, H. S., 69, 117, 119, 120, 124, 125, 128, 385, 410, 411
Scarcella, R., 309

Scardamalia, M., 308, 319
Schaffner, E., 161, 162
Schallert, D. L., 70, 71
Schatschneider, C., 118, 120, 124, 125
Scherer, S., 282
Schiefele, U., 153, 161, 162
Schifter, D., 13
Schilling, S., 384, 386, 387
Schlott, R., 14, 15
Schmitt, N., 86, 87
Schneider, B., 371, 378
Schön, D. A., 244
Schunk, D. H., 154, 160
Schwanenflugel, P. J., 36, 141, 255, 257, 268
Schwarz, B. B., 11
Schwebel, E. A., 260
Scott, C. M., 124
Scott, J. A., 89
Sedova, K., 12
Seidenberg, M. S., 31, 42, 412, 420
Sénéchal, M., 191, 192
Shah, A., 6
Shanahan, C., 210, 291
Shanahan, T., 73, 177, 210, 291, 310, 311
Sharp, A. M., 12, 14, 18, 19
Sheehan, K. M., 136, 140, 141
Sheldon, L., 326
Shelton, A., 354, 357
Short, D., 311
Showers, B., 208
Shukla, S. Y., 331
Shulman, J. H., 243
Shulman, L. S., 243, 387
Siegel, L. S., 32, 67, 70
Silverman, R. D., 69, 72, 73, 118, 125
Simmons, D., 227, 356, 357, 358, 360
Simon, H. A., 104
Slavin, R. E., 362, 367
Slonim, N., 85
Smagorinki, P., 279
Small, D., 143
Smith, A. T., 369
Smith, C., 412
Smith, K. C., 3
Smith, M., 137
Smith, N. L., 351, 356, 357, 360, 362
Smitherman, G., 419
Smoot, D., 422
Snow, C. E., 63, 64, 65, 66, 72, 90, 91, 100, 124, 125, 308, 309
Snowling, M. J., 186
Solé, R. V., 81
Soter, A., 12, 19
Sparapani, N., 138
Spear-Swerling, L., 215, 384, 389, 395, 397, 401
Spencer, M., 121, 143

Spichtig, A., 89
Spillane, J. P., 207
Spires, H. A., 330
Splitter, L. J., 12, 14, 19
Stadthagen-Gonzalez, H., 83
Stafura, J., 31
Stahl, K. A. D., 1, 255, 257, 262, 265
Stahl, S., 255, 256, 257, 258, 259, 262, 267, 268, 269
Stahl, S. A., 144, 170, 247, 260, 261, 266, 268
Stalega, M., 4
Stanovich, K. E., 188, 210, 257, 258
Stark, K., 367
Stauffer, R. G., 169
Stein, M. L., 191
Steiss, J., 309
Stevens, E. A., 36, 194, 211, 224, 226, 232, 233, 255, 268, 354, 355, 356, 357, 358
Stipek, D. J., 16
Stone, C. A., 51, 87
Stormont, M., 215
Stornaiuolo, A., 327
Stout, J., 207
Street, B. V., 436
Strong, J. Z., 6, 137
Stuckey, D., 374, 377, 378
Sullivan, H., 420
Sunstein, C. R., 15
Swanborn, M. S., 175
Swanson, E., 224, 227, 228, 229, 232, 2233, 34, 353, 356, 357, 358, 360, 361
Swanson, H. L., 215

T

Taboada, A., 156
Taboada Barber, A., 4, 120, 123, 155, 157, 158, 159, 163
Tappan, M. B., 71
Tate, W., 65
Taylor, B. M., 241
Taylor, C. L., 86
Taylor, K. S., 88
Taylor, K. Y., 412
Templeton, S., 52
Tenore, F. B., 351, 390, 396, 400, 401
Terrell Shockley, E., 413, 420
Terry, N. P., 100
Therrien, W. J., 36, 296
Thomas, E. E., 65
Thrailkill, L. D., 374, 376
Tierney, R. J., 310, 322, 326, 333
Tilstra, J., 118
Tindal, G., 263, 264
Tobia, V., 122
Tock, J., 57

Todaro, S., 101
Tomlinson, C. A., 205, 207
Tong, X., 87
Topolka-Jorissen, K., 208
Topping, K. J., 142
Torgesen, J. K., 37, 195, 196, 260, 262
Torppa, M., 122, 126
Tortorelli, L. S., 136, 142, 361
Toste, J. R., 2, 30, 32, 33, 37, 40, 41, 144, 146, 155, 160, 161, 197, 227
Tourangeau, K., 187
Townsend, D., 55, 80, 82, 356, 357, 358
Traga Philippakos, Z. A., 354, 356, 357, 358
Troia, G. A., 294, 295
Trottier Brown, L., 143, 144
Troyer, M., 369
Tschannen-Moran, M., 349
Tulis, M., 146
Tunmer, W. E., 30, 68, 69, 115, 116, 117, 118, 119, 124, 127, 128, 139, 154, 160, 385, 410
Turner, J. D., 7, 137, 412, 413, 414, 416, 417, 423
Tyler, A., 52

U

Uccelli, P., 88
Urow, C., 73

V

Valencia, S. W., 135, 136, 139, 141
van den Broek, P., 100, 101
van den Hurk, H. T. G., 398
van der Linden, S., 372
Van Dijk, T. A., 100
van Garderen, D., 216
van Wingerden, E., 120, 121, 122, 125
Vaughn, A., 216
Vaughn, M., 5, 243, 245, 247, 250, 251
Vaughn, S., 30, 31, 41, 145, 195, 196, 197, 210, 211, 212, 213, 215, 216, 223, 224, 227, 228, 230, 231, 233, 355, 356, 357, 358, 360, 361, 399
Vellutino, F. R., 124, 129
Venezky, R. L., 32
Verhoeven, L., 125
Von Hippel, E., 234
Vygotsky, L. S., 11, 66, 243, 258, 328, 370

W

Waggoner, M. A., 14, 19, 159
Wagner, D., 194

Wagner, R., 260
Wagner, R. K., 41, 69, 118, 119, 120, 124
Walpole, S., 6, 145, 352
Walsh, M., 368
Walton, D., 15, 23
Wang, J. H. Y., 155
Wang, M., 70, 157
Wantchekon, K., 155
Wanzek, J., 30, 186, 194, 195, 196, 197, 210, 212, 213, 216, 224, 228, 229
Warshauer, S., 280
Washburn, E. K., 384, 386, 389, 392
Washington, J. A., 42, 412, 420
Watanabe, M., 108
Wauters, L., 121
Wawire, B. A., 70, 122
Webster-Stratton, C., 233, 234
Wechsler, D., 262
Wei, L., 62, 67, 73
Weippert, T. L., 67
Wells, G., 11
Welsch, D. M., 69
Wexler, J., 4, 223, 225, 226, 228, 229, 234, 235, 356, 357, 358, 359, 360, 361
White, S., 264, 265
White, T. G., 52, 190, 191
Whittingham, C. E., 330
Wiederholt, J. L., 262
Wigfield, A., 153, 154, 155, 156, 157, 161, 162, 163, 227, 242, 249, 251
Wijekumar, K., 362, 390, 393, 398, 400, 404
Wilkinson, A. I. G., 12
Wilkinson, I. A. G., 2, 13, 17, 18, 19, 21, 22, 356, 357
Williams, B. K., 351, 356, 357, 360, 362
Williams, T., 241
Williamson, G. L., 141
Willis, A. I., 413
Wilson, A. M., 198
Wilson, J., 302

Windschitl, M., 14
Winn, W. D., 294
Wissinger, D. R., 23
Wohlwend, K. E., 432
Wolf, M., 156, 157, 161, 163, 185, 371
Wolters, A. P., 256
Wonnacott, E., 86
Woodson, C. G., 419
Woulfin, S. L., 235, 242, 368
Wright, B. A., 189
Wright, T. S., 4, 168, 172, 173, 176, 226
Wysocki, K., 52

X

Xu, M., 170

Y

Yaden, D. B., Jr., 334
Yan, E. F., 107, 110
Yarkoni, T., 84
Yin, R. K., 372
Yoon, S. Y., 36, 230
Yucheng, C., 297

Z

Zecker, S. G., 189
Zeno, S. Z., 31, 84
Zhang, D., 123
Zhang-Wu, Q., 70
Zibulsky, J., 397
Zimmerman, B. J., 160, 292, 295
Zipf, G. K., 81
Zuilkowski, S. S., 70
Zwiers, J., 322

Subject Index

Note. *f* or *t* following a page number indicates a figure or table.

Academic knowledge, 177. *See also* Knowledge
Academic vocabulary, 3, 82, 83–90, 83*t*, 85*f*, 92. *See also* Vocabulary knowledge
Acceptability, 19, 19*f*, 234
Accountability reform, 241–242
Accuracy, 118, 141, 255–256. *See also* Reading fluency
Achievement gaps, 186, 187–188, 331
Active learning, 356–357, 362. *See also* Learning
Active view of reading, 139
Adaptive teaching
   characteristics of reading instruction and, 248–250, 249*f*
   common adaptations and rationales, 244–248, 245*t*
   future directions, 250–251
   overview, 241–243
   theories and, 243–244
Adaptive Teaching Inventory (ATI), 5, 250–251
Adaptive Teaching Observational Protocol (ATOP), 251
Administrators, 207–208, 215
Adolescent literacy, 66–67, 196–197
Affective dimensions of learning, 249*f*, 251
Affective engagement, 156. *See also* Reading engagement
Affixes, 35–36, 38–39, 39*f*, 55. *See also* Prefixes; Suffixes
Age of Acquisition (AoA), 83–84, 83*t*. *See also* Developmental processes
Agency, 249*f*, 251, 374–375, 378

AIM Coaching, 229–230, 234. *See also* Coaching
Alphabetic principle, 185
Anti-Black racism, 411–412, 414–415
Anti-Black violence, 412
Apprentice model, 311–312
Argumentation
   development of, 2
   future directions, 22–23
   overview, 11–13
   progress evaluation and, 21–22
   tools and activities for, 16–20, 18*f*, 19*f*, 20*f*, 21*f*
   See also Classroom dialogue; Text-based argument writing
Argumentation Rating Tool (ART), 19–20, 19*f*, 20*t*, 21–23, 21*t*
Artificial intelligence (AI)
   overview, 327
   reading comprehension and, 110
   reading motivation and, 163
   writing instruction and, 286, 302–303
   See also Digital literacies; Expansive literacies; Technology-based instruction
Assessment
   adaptive teaching and, 243, 249
   artificial intelligence (AI) and, 110
   fluency instruction and, 260, 262, 263–265
   morphology and, 49–50, 52, 57–58
   multimodal literacies and, 434–435
   multi-tiered systems of supports (MTSS) and, 102–103, 204–205, 206*t*, 208–210, 209*f*
   professional learning and, 351

Assessment *(cont.)*
  reading comprehension and, 103, 109–110
  summer reading programs and, 194
  teacher knowledge and, 386–387, 395, 399, 401
  writing instruction for students with learning disabilities, 291–292
Assisted approaches, 258. *See also* Scaffolding
Attention-deficit/hyperactivity disorder (ADHD), 121, 186
Autism spectrum disorder, 186–187
Automaticity, 255–256, 263–264, 268–269. *See also* Reading fluency
Autonomy, 158, 162, 374

B

Background knowledge
  adaptive teaching and, 242, 249f
  critique of SOR and, 334
  overview, 177
  professional learning and, 355–356
  writing instruction for students with learning disabilities, 297
  See also Knowledge
Behavioral engagement, 156. *See also* Reading engagement
Beliefs, 154–155
Bilingualism, 65, 123–124. *See also* Multilingual literacy
Black, Indigenous, and People of Color (BIPOC) students
  achievement and opportunity gaps and, 331
  critique of SOR and, 334
  culturally responsive practices and, 207, 333
  future directions, 423–424
  literacy instruction and, 7, 414–423
  overview, 409–414
  See also Race
Black caregivers and communities, 422–423
Black Futures approach
  future directions, 423–424
  overview, 413–414
  science of literacy (SOL) and, 414–423
Black Language, 412, 415, 417–420, 424
Black literacy, 414–423, 424

C

CALI (Content-Area Literacy Instruction). *See* Content-Area Literacy Instruction (CALI) intervention
Caregivers, 191–192, 422–423
Challenging texts, 258–259, 265–266
Change, 334, 361–362

Chatbot systems (ChatGPT etc.). *See* Artificial intelligence (AI)
Choice
  critique of SOR and, 334
  literacies and, 332
  literacy coaching and, 374, 378
  reading motivation and, 162
Choral reading, 39, 40f, 145
Clarity, 19, 19f, 21t
Classroom community, 329f
Classroom dialogue
  future directions, 22–23
  language and vocabulary development and, 2
  overview, 12–13
  progress evaluation and, 21–22
  theoretical assumptions and, 13–16
  See also Argumentation; Discussions
Classroom environment, 243, 328, 334, 414
Classroom practice, 16–20, 18f, 19f, 20f, 21f. *See also* Classroom dialogue; Instructional approaches
Classwide peer tutoring protocol, 105
Coaching
  in-class coaching, 374–375
  outcomes from, 369–370
  overview, 377–379
  professional learning and, 350, 352, 356–357
  Promoting Adolescents' Comprehension of Text Plus (PACT Plus), 229–230
  relational framework and, 370–377
  in schoolwide settings, 375–377
Cognitive engagement, 156. *See also* Reading engagement
Cognitive skills, 142–143
Cognitive strategies toolkit, 312–313, 312f, 314f
Cognitive strategy instruction
  Pathway Project and, 311–323, 312f, 314f, 316f, 317f, 318f, 319f, 320f, 322f
  text-based argument writing and, 309–311
  writing instruction for students with learning disabilities, 301
  See also Strategy instruction
Cognitive theories, 101–102, 146, 311–312
Cognitive-behavioral anxiety management techniques, 197
Coherence, 101, 358–359, 362
Coh-Metrix, 136
Collaboration, 157–159, 350, 432
Collaborative lesson planning, 356–357
Collaborative problem solving, 216, 218
Collaborative strategic reading, 352, 355–356
Color coding for revision, 318–319, 319f, 320f, 322
Common Core State Standards (CCSS)
  fluency instruction and, 259
  text complexity and, 135, 136–137, 139–141

Subject Index

text-based argument writing and, 307–308, 311
writing instruction for students with learning disabilities, 291
See also Standards
Communities, 422–423
Community of inquiry, 13–15, 16–20, 18f, 19f, 20f, 21f. *See also* Classroom dialogue; Inquiry
Compensatory word identification strategies, 31
Complete view of reading (CVRi), 128
Complexity, 84–85, 85f. *See also* Text complexity
Comprehension
  knowledge-building and, 169–175, 176–178
  multilingual reading and, 70–71
  overview, 3
  professional learning and, 350–351, 355–356
  research on, 168
  science of literacy (SOL) and, 410–411
  simple view of reading (SVR) and, 69–70, 118–120
  supplemental intervention classes and, 231
  teacher knowledge and, 395–397, 399–400, 403
  text-based argument writing and, 310
  theoretical and empirical models of knowledge and, 169
  vocabulary knowledge and, 29–30
  See also Reading comprehension
Comprehension and Learning from Text Survey (CoLTS), 395–397, 400
Comprehensive Oral Reading Fluency Scale (CORFS), 265
Computer-assisted instruction, 285–286
Conceptually coherent (CC) texts, 172–175, 176, 177–178
Connection, 332, 334, 338–340, 340f
Construction–integration (CI) model, 69
Constructivist theories, 11–12
Content knowledge
  argumentation and, 12
  early reading and, 385–387
  overview, 2, 169, 383–384
  reading comprehension and, 393–395
  schoolwide literacy models and, 232–233
  text-based discussions and, 227
  writing and, 278
  See also Knowledge; Teacher knowledge
Content Knowledge for Teaching reading (CKTR) assessment, 386–387
Content-area instruction
  future directions, 234–235
  knowledge-building and, 176–178
  overview, 224–225, 226–230
  professional learning and, 355–356
  reading difficulties/disabilities (RD) and, 185
  supplemental intervention classes and, 230–231
  writing and, 283, 293, 299–300, 302
  See also Instructional approaches

Content-Area Literacy Instruction (CALI) intervention, 170, 225–226
Content-based reading, 158
Core reading programs, 205. *See also* Curriculum
Correct words per minute, 260, 264
Critical developmental curriculum framework, 73–74
Critical literacy perspectives, 62–63, 65–68, 72–74
Critical perspectives, 3, 64–65
Critical race theory (CRT), 65, 73
Critical thinking, 120, 329f
Critical-analytic stance, 12–13
Cross-linguistics, 70–71
Cultivating Linguistic Awareness for Voice and Equity in Schools (CLAVES) curriculum, 3, 72–73
Cultural competency, 329f
Cultural factors
  adaptive teaching and, 249f
  Black Futures approach, 413
  interconnectedness of literacies and, 329f
  multimodal literacies and, 432–433, 436–437
  See also Culturally responsive practices
Cultural-historical activity theory, 66
Culturally responsive practices, 207, 333, 420–422. *See also* Cultural factors
Curiosity, 153–154
Curriculum
  adaptive teaching and, 241–242
  Black Futures approach, 414
  fluency instruction and, 269
  literacies and, 332
  literacy coaching and, 368
  multilingual literacy and, 71–74
  multimodal literacies and, 434–435
  multi-tiered systems of supports (MTSS) and, 205
  professional learning and, 358, 362
  reading difficulties/disabilities (RD) and, 185–186
  schoolwide literacy models and, 232
  teacher knowledge and, 401
  See also Instructional approaches
Curriculum-based measurement (CBM), 206t. *See also* Assessment

D

Data collection and data analysis, 4, 208–210, 209f, 216–217
Data literacies, 326–327. *See also* Expansive literacies
Data-based decision making, 102, 208–210, 209f, 213, 214–217, 217f, 218

Subject Index

Data-based individualization (DBI), 214–216, 214f, 218
Data-based instructional (DBI) interventions, 303
Deafness, 121
Decoding
  morphology instruction and, 53–55
  multilingual reading and, 70–71
  multisyllabic word reading (MWR) and, 31–32, 34–35
  overview, 2
  professional learning and, 352
  self-efficacy and, 160
  simple view of reading (SVR) and, 3, 69–70, 115, 116, 117–118, 119, 120–121, 124, 126–129, 129n
  teacher knowledge and, 394t, 398, 399, 402–403
  text-based argument writing and, 310
  vocabulary knowledge and, 87
  word reading efficiency and, 31
Deep reading, 156, 157. *See also* Reading engagement
Developmental disorders, 186–187. *See also* Disabilities
Developmental literacy perspectives, 62–63, 68–71, 72–74. *See also* Simple view of reading (SVR)
Developmental processes
  language of learning and, 82
  learning to read well, 152–153
  literacy development, 51–53, 155, 187–188, 244
  multilingual literacy and, 63–64
  reading trajectories during school and vacation and, 187–188
  vocabulary knowledge and, 83–90, 83t, 85f
  writing development, 5–6, 281–282
Diagnostic assessment, 206t. *See also* Assessment
Dialogic instruction, 74
Dialogue, 15–16, 73. *See also* Argumentation; Classroom dialogue; Discussions
Differentiation, 244. *See also* Instructional approaches
Difficulty of text, 138–139, 138f, 258–259. *See also* Text complexity
Digital literacies
  contextualizing teaching and learning, 431–435
  future directions, 437
  going beyond words and, 435–437
  overview, 7, 326–327, 428–431
  professional learning and, 358
  See also Artificial intelligence (AI); Expansive literacies; Multimodal literacies
Direct and indirect effect model of reading (DIER), 128–129
Direct and inferential mediation model (DIME) of reading comprehension, 128

Direct inferential mediation model, 169
Direct reading instruction, 185
Directed reading–thinking activity, 169
Disabilities
  interventions and, 223–224
  Promoting Adolescents' Comprehension of Text Plus (PACT Plus), 228
  schoolwide literacy models and, 223–224, 232
  simple view of reading (SVR) and, 116, 121–122, 124
  special education services and, 186–187
  See also Developmental disorders; Learning disabilities; Reading difficulties/disabilities (RD); Struggling readers
Disciplinary knowledge, 2, 12, 88
Discourse, 66–67, 371–372, 373–374, 378
Discussions
  adaptive teaching and, 247–248
  connections between research and practice and, 337–338
  critique of SOR and, 334–335
  interconnectedness of literacies and, 329f
  literacies and, 332
  teacher knowledge and, 396
  text-based discussions, 226–227
  vocabulary knowledge and, 90–91
  See also Classroom dialogue
District-level leadership, 215
Diversity, 84–85, 85f
Do SMILE (deep reading-oriented instruction; sharing; me; importance; liking; engagement) acronym, 157–163
Domain knowledge, 168. *See also* Knowledge
DO/WHAT Chart, 313, 315, 316f, 322
Dynamic skills framework, 189
Dyslexia, 116, 186–187. *See also* Disabilities; Reading difficulties/disabilities (RD)

E

Ecological context, 362
Editing, 301–302. *See also* Writing instruction
Educational psychology, 71–72
Efficacy doubt, 374–375
Efficiency in word reading, 30–32, 41–42
Electronic media. *See* Digital literacies; Multimodal literacies
Empathy, 332
Engagement
  adaptive teaching and, 251
  critique of SOR and, 334
  literacies and, 332
  multimodal literacies and, 434–435
  overview, 4
  reading comprehension and, 156–163

text-based discussions and, 227
writing instruction and, 275–276
See also Reading engagement
English language arts (ELA) instruction
  knowledge-building and, 176–178
  Pathway Project and, 311–323, 312*f*, 314*f*, 316*f*, 317*f*, 318*f*, 319*f*, 320*f*, 322*f*
  writing instruction for students with learning disabilities and, 291, 302
English learners (ELs)
  cognitive strategies approach and, 310–311
  overview, 62
  Pathway Project and, 311–323, 312*f*, 314*f*, 316*f*, 317*f*, 318*f*, 319*f*, 320*f*, 322*f*
  text-based argument writing and, 6, 308–309
  See also Multilingual literacy
Epistemic stance, 16, 63
Equity, 330–332, 412, 414–423
ESHALOV (Every Syllable Has At Least One Vowel) strategy, 35
Ethnic backgrounds
  achievement and opportunity gaps and, 331
  critique of SOR and, 334
  culturally responsive practices and, 207, 333
  simple view of reading (SVR) and, 123–124
  See also Black, Indigenous, and People of Color (BIPOC) students
Evidence-based practices
  multi-tiered systems of supports (MTSS) and, 205, 207–217, 209*f*, 214*f*, 217*f*
  schoolwide literacy models and, 225–226, 233
  writing instruction and, 279–280, 282–286, 284*t*, 292, 296–297
  See also Instructional approaches; *individual practices*
Executive function, 69, 139, 143, 294–295
Expansive literacies
  connections between research and practice and, 335–341, 340*f*
  critique of SOR and, 333–335
  future directions, 341–342
  human experiences and, 327–328
  interconnectedness of literacies and, 328–330, 329*f*
  issues of power, equity, and social justice and, 330–332
  learning and, 341
  as opportunities for growth and connection, 332
  overview, 6, 326–327
  See also Multimodal literacies
Expectancy–value theory (EVT), 161, 162
Explicit instruction
  content-area classes and, 226
  morphology instruction and, 50
  multilingual literacy and, 66

multi-tiered systems of supports (MTSS) and, 210, 212
overview, 226–228
schoolwide literacy models and, 231–232
teacher knowledge and, 397–398
writing instruction for students with learning disabilities, 295, 300–302
See also Instructional approaches
Extrinsic motivation, 161–162. *See also* Motivation
Eye-tracking methodology, 103–104

F

Feasibility, 210, 212–213, 234
Fidelity of implementation, 233–234, 351–352, 362
Fixed mindsets, 152
Flexibility, 34, 243
Fluency
  adaptive teaching and, 249*f*
  assessment and, 263–265
  multisyllabic word reading (MWR) and, 32, 36
  overview, 268–269
  professional learning and, 350, 352
  reading theories and, 69
  science of literacy (SOL) and, 410–411
  simple view of reading (SVR) and, 117–118, 120–121, 123
  summer reading programs and, 191–192
  supplemental intervention classes and, 231
  teacher knowledge and, 387, 394*t*, 395, 398, 402–403
  text complexity and, 144–145, 147
  See also Reading fluency
Fluency instruction
  assessment and, 263–265
  overview, 257–259, 265–269, 266*f*, 267*f*
  wide versus repeated reading and, 259–263
  See also Fluency; Reading fluency
Fluency-Oriented Reading Instruction (FORI), 144–145, 260–263, 265–267, 266*f*
Formative assessment, 206*t*, 208. *See also* Assessment
Freedom dreaming, 414–423
Freedom of speech, 14–15
Frequency, 84–85, 85*f*
Funds of knowledge, 137

G

Gender, 249*f*
Goal setting, 301, 310

Goals, 153–154, 243, 298t
Grade-level text, 138, 259. *See also* Text complexity
Gradual release of responsibility, 232, 358–359, 362
Grammar, 80–81, 119, 301–302. *See also* Writing instruction
Graphemes, 34, 418–419
Graphic organizers, 315, 317f, 322
Gray Oral Reading Test, 4th edition, 262
Grouping of students, 194, 243. *See also* Small-group instruction
Growth, 332
Growth mindsets, 152–153, 330
Guided practice, 232, 295
Guided reading, 261

H

Hearing problems, 121
Higher-level processing, 174–175, 176, 308–309
Higher-leverage practices (HLPs), 300–302, 303
Holistic approach, 436
Home-based summer reading programs, 190–192. *See also* Summer instruction/intervention
Human experience, 327–328
Hyperlexia, 116

I

Idea sharing, 157–159
Identity, 329f, 334, 432–433, 435
Idioms, 86
IES Practice Guide, 227, 228, 230–231
In-class coaching. *See* Coaching
Inclusivity, 327–328, 331
Independent practice, 232, 257–258
Individualized education program/plan (IEP), 187, 187t
Inference
  inference-making instruction and intervention and, 103–110
  knowledge-building and, 172, 175
  professional learning and, 359
  reading comprehension and, 101–102, 385
Information processing, 256
Initiation–response–evaluation (IRE) pattern of discourse, 374. *See also* Discourse
Inquiry
  classroom dialogue and, 13–16
  digital inquiry learning, 340–341
  inquiry dialogue, 15–16
  literacies and, 332
  professional learning and, 357
  teacher knowledge and, 384

Inservice preparation, 279. *See also* Professional development
Instructional approaches
  Black Futures approach, 413–423
  Black students and, 411–414
  contextualizing teaching and learning, 431–435
  fluency and, 257–259
  going beyond words in, 435–437
  issues of power, equity, and social justice and, 330
  knowledge-building and, 169–175
  literacy coaching and, 368
  multimodal literacies and, 431–435
  multisyllabic word reading (MWR) and, 32–41, 39f, 40f
  multi-tiered systems of supports (MTSS) and, 102–103
  professional learning and, 351–352
  reading comprehension and, 100–102, 103–110
  reading difficulties/disabilities (RD) and, 186
  reading engagement and, 156–157
  reading motivation and, 176–178
  schoolwide literacy models and, 231–234
  summer reading programs and, 191–198
  teacher knowledge and, 387–398, 388t–391t, 394t
  text complexity and, 143–147
  tier 2 supports, 210–213
  See also Classroom practice; Content-area instruction; Curriculum; Differentiation; Evidence-based practices; Explicit instruction; Multi-tiered systems of supports (MTSS); Strategy instruction; *individual approaches*
Instructional assessment, 206t. *See also* Assessment
Instructional blocks, 207
Instructional design, 358
Integrated literacies model
  connections between research and practice and, 335–341, 340f
  critique of SOR and, 334
  future directions, 341–342
  learning and, 341
  overview, 328–330, 329f
  See also Expansive literacies; Literacies
Integration of information, 102. *See also* Inference; Reading comprehension
Intellectual disabilities (ID), 121, 122. *See also* Disabilities
Intelligent tutoring systems (ITSs), 107–109. *See also* Technology-based instruction
Intensive interventions, 214f, 217f, 223–226, 232–234. *See also* Interventions; Multi-tiered systems of supports (MTSS)
Intensive summer reading interventions, 195–196. *See also* Summer instruction/intervention

Subject Index

Interdependence continuum, 71
Intervention blocks, 207
Interventions
    fluency instruction and, 259–260, 263–268, 266f, 267f
    knowledge-building and, 169–175
    multi-tiered systems of supports (MTSS) and, 102–103
    overview, 223–226
    Pathway Project and, 311–319, 312f, 314f, 316f, 317f, 318f, 319f, 320f
    Promoting Adolescents' Comprehension of Text Plus (PACT Plus), 228–230
    reading comprehension and, 103–110
    reading difficulties/disabilities (RD) and, 186
    schoolwide literacy models and, 232–234
    summer reading programs, 189–198
    supplemental intervention classes and, 230–231
    teacher knowledge and, 395
    text complexity and, 143–146
    tier 2 supports, 210–213
    vocabulary knowledge and, 90–91
    writing instruction for students with learning disabilities, 296–302, 298t
    See also Multi-tiered systems of supports (MTSS)
Intrinsic motivation for reading, 53–54, 161–162. *See also* Reading motivation
iSTART and iSTART–Early (Interactive Strategy Training for Active Reading and Thinking), 107–109, 110

J

Joint problem identification framework, 373–374

K

Knowledge
    adaptive teaching and, 250
    argumentation and, 11–12
    critique of SOR and, 334
    fluency instruction and, 262–263
    knowledge-building and, 169–175, 176–178
    multimodal literacies and, 430
    research on, 168
    text-based discussions and, 227
    theoretical and empirical models of, 169
    See also Content knowledge; Vocabulary knowledge
Knowledge for Enhancing Reading Development Inventory (KnERDI), 393–395, 401–402
Knowledge telling, 318, 322
Knowledge transformation, 318, 322
K-W-L (Know, Want to Know, Learned), 169

L

Language
    adaptive teaching and, 249f
    Argumentation Rating Tool (ART), 11–12, 19
    Black Futures approach, 413, 415, 417–420, 424
    Black students and, 412
    comprehension and, 52, 55–57, 385
    language development and, 2–3, 63–64, 88
    multi-tiered systems of supports (MTSS) and, 207
    professional learning and, 355–356
    simple view of reading (SVR) and, 122–124
    teacher knowledge and, 397–398
    translanguaging and, 67–68
    See also Multilingual literacy
Language of learning, 80, 81–82. *See also* Academic vocabulary; Vocabulary knowledge
Large-group instruction, 243, 266–267, 266f
Leadership, 207–208, 215
Learning
    adaptive teaching and, 249f
    argumentation and, 11–12
    Black students and, 412, 414
    contextualizing teaching and learning, 431–435
    critique of SOR and, 334–335
    expansive literacies and, 341
    going beyond words in, 435–437
    literacies and, 329f, 332
    overview, 1
    reading comprehension and, 100
    teacher knowledge and, 397–398
    from text, 169–175
Learning communities, 311–312. *See also* Community of inquiry
Learning disabilities, 5–6, 216. *See also* Disabilities; Reading difficulties/disabilities (RD); Writing instruction for students with learning disabilities
Lesson planning, 359, 361–362
Lesson Study, 352, 356–357, 361
Letter identification skills, 160
Letter–sound correspondence knowledge, 115. *See also* Decoding
Lexical dimensions, 84–85, 85f
Lexile Early Literacy Indicators, 137
Lexile Framework for Reading, 136–137
Lexile scores, 136–137, 140, 259
Linguistic backgrounds, 123–124
Linguistic comprehension, 69–71, 116, 118–121, 124, 126–129, 129n. *See also* Comprehension
Linguistic interdependence hypothesis, 71
Linguistic knowledge, 398
Linguistic responsive practices, 207
Listening comprehension, 119, 173–174, 437. *See also* Comprehension

Literacies
    Black literacy, 413, 414–423
    classroom culture and, 327–328
    critique of SOR and, 333–335
    human experiences and, 327–328
    interconnectedness of literacies and, 328–330, 329f
    issues of power, equity, and social justice and, 330–332
    as opportunities for growth and connection, 332
    See also Expansive literacies; Multilingual literacy; Multimodal literacies
Literacy clinics, 372–374
Literacy coaching
    outcomes from, 369–370
    overview, 367–369, 377–379
    Promoting Adolescents' Comprehension of Text Plus (PACT Plus), 229–230
    relational framework and, 370–377
    See also Coaching; Teacher knowledge
Literacy development, 51–53, 155, 187–188, 244. *See also* Developmental processes
Literacy instruction
    Black Futures approach, 413–423
    Black students and, 7, 411–414
    developmental processes and, 63–64
    multimodal literacies and, 430
    supplemental intervention classes and, 230–231
    See also Adaptive teaching
Literature circles, 247–248

M

Main idea identification, 359
Mastery measurement, 206t. *See also* Assessment
Matthew effect (ME), 188–189
Meaning making
    critique of SOR and, 334
    expansive literacies and, 327–328, 332
    morphological assessment and, 58
    multimodal literacies and, 429
    opportunities for growth and connection and, 332
    self-efficacy and, 160
Metacognition, teacher, 243–244
Metacognitive strategy instruction, 301. *See also* Strategy instruction
Mindsets, 152–153, 330
Model of Reading Engagement (MORE) intervention, 170–171
Modeling
    adaptive teaching and, 244–245
    fluency instruction and, 258
    literacy coaching and, 378
    professional learning and, 350, 352
    schoolwide literacy models and, 232
    teacher knowledge and, 394t
    writing instruction for students with learning disabilities, 295, 297
Model–Practice–Reflect instructional cycle, 310
Monitoring, 175, 298t
Morphemes, 32, 87, 244
Morphological analysis, 87
Morphological awareness, 51, 123
Morphological decoding, 87. *See also* Decoding
Morphological development, 1
Morphology
    assessment and, 57–58
    instruction and, 2–3, 49–58
    language comprehension and, 55–57
    literacy and, 51–53
    multisyllabic word reading (MWR) and, 32, 35–36
    overview, 2–3, 47–48, 58
    research on, 48–49, 51–58
    simple view of reading (SVR) and, 119
    teacher knowledge and, 386, 392–393, 394t, 399, 402–403
    text complexity and, 144
    vocabulary knowledge and, 87
    word reading and, 53–55
    See also Multisyllabic word reading (MWR)
Motivation
    active view of reading and, 139
    adaptive teaching and, 242, 249f, 251
    critique of SOR and, 334
    overview, 4
    reading theories and, 69
    simple view of reading (SVR) and, 128–129
    text complexity and, 147, 152–153
    text-based discussions and, 227
    See also Reading motivation
Multidimensional Fluency Rubric, 264–265
Multilingual literacy
    critical literacy perspective and, 65–68
    curriculum and, 71–74
    developmental literacy perspective and, 68–71
    history of, 63–71
    multilingual reading and, 70–71
    multi-tiered systems of supports (MTSS) and, 207
    overview, 3, 62–63
    simple view of reading (SVR) and, 123–124
    See also English learners (ELs); Language; Literacies
Multimodal literacies
    contextualizing teaching and learning, 431–435
    future directions, 437
    going beyond words and, 435–437

Subject Index

overview, 7, 428–431
See also Digital literacies; Expansive literacies; Literacies
Multimodal writing, 338–340, 340f
Multimodality, 74, 429. *See also* Multimodal literacies
Multimorphemic words, 399
Multisyllabic word reading (MWR)
   adaptive teaching and, 244–245
   instruction and, 32–41, 39f, 40f
   morphology instruction and, 50
   overview, 2–3, 29–30, 41–42
   professional learning and, 352
   supplemental intervention classes and, 230
   teacher knowledge and, 399
   Word Connections program, 37–41, 39f, 40f
   word reading efficiency and, 31–32
   See also Morphology; Word reading; Word recognition
Multi-tiered systems of supports (MTSS)
   assessment and, 205, 206t
   fluency instruction and, 265–266
   key components of, 204–205
   overview, 3, 102–103, 204, 205, 217–218
   reading comprehension and, 103–110
   schoolwide literacy models and, 232–234
   struggling readers and, 4
   tier 1 practices, 205, 207–210, 209f, 218
   tier 2 supports, 210–213, 218
   tier 3 supports, 213–217, 214f, 217f, 218
   See also Instructional approaches; Interventions

N

National Assessment of Educational Progress (NAEP), 291–292, 308, 309
National Writing Project, 279
Nested models, 334
Nonconceptually coherent (NCC) reading, 172
Northwest Evaluation Association's (NWEA) Measures of Academic Progress (MAP), 187
Note taking, 301
Not-so-simple view of writing model, 294–295

O

Observations, 374
Opportunity gaps, 41–42, 331
Oral comprehension, 119. *See also* Comprehension
Oral language
   critique of SOR and, 334
   literacy coaching and, 376
   multimodal literacies and, 437
   professional learning and, 350

   teacher knowledge and, 398
   writing instruction for students with learning disabilities, 294
Oral literacies, 334–335. *See also* Literacies; Oral language
Oral Reading Fluency Expression Rubric, 264–265
Oral reading fluency (ORF), 36, 117–118, 263–264, 265. *See also* Fluency; Processing speed; Reading fluency
Orthographic awareness, 70
Orthographic processing, 87, 185
Orthographies, 122–123, 126
Outcome measures, 206t. *See also* Assessment

P

PACT and PACT Plus, 228–230, 233
Parents, 191–192, 422–423
Partner reading, 352
Pathway Project, 311–323, 312f, 314f, 316f, 317f, 318f, 319f, 320f, 322f
Pedagogy, 249f
Peer attitudes, 159
Peer-based work, 285
Perspectives, 19, 19f, 332
PHAST program, 41
Phonemic awareness
   adaptive teaching and, 249f
   multilingual reading and, 70
   science of literacy (SOL) and, 410–411
   self-efficacy and, 160
   simple view of reading (SVR) and, 116
   teacher knowledge and, 386, 394t, 395, 398
Phonics
   adaptive teaching and, 249f
   science of literacy (SOL) and, 410–411
   simple view of reading (SVR) and, 116
   teacher knowledge and, 386, 387, 394t, 395
Phonics First, 327
Phonological awareness
   multilingual reading and, 70
   teacher knowledge and, 386, 387, 394t, 402–403
   vocabulary knowledge and, 87
Phonological representations, 81
Planning, 309–310
Pleasure of reading, 161–162
Policy, 146–147
Polysemy, 84–85, 85f
Power, 330–332
Practice, independent, 232, 257–258
Pragmatic processing, 185
Predicting, 175
Prefixes, 35–36, 38–39, 39f, 55

Preservice preparation
  adaptive teaching and, 251
  morphology and, 47
  teacher knowledge and, 401
  third space theory and, 67
  writing instruction and, 5–6, 278, 303
  See also Professional learning (PL)
Preteaching, 170
Prewriting skills, 301. *See also* Writing instruction
Prior knowledge, 169, 310. *See also* Background knowledge; Knowledge
Processing speed, 117–118. *See also* Oral reading fluency (ORF)
Professional development
  adaptive teaching and, 251
  argumentation and, 16–20, 18f, 19f, 20f, 21f
  literacy coaching and, 377, 378
  overview, 6–7, 12
  Project CALI and, 225
  research on, 352–360, 353f
  school-led, 227–228
  teacher knowledge and, 401, 402–403, 404
  writing instruction and, 5–6, 279, 303
  See also Professional learning (PL); Teacher knowledge
Professional learning communities, 208, 352, 357
Professional learning (PL)
  active learning, 356–357, 362
  coherence, 358–359, 362
  collective participation, 360
  content focus, 355–356
  duration, 359–360
  increasing teachers' knowledge and skills and, 350–351
  limitations, 360–361
  multi-tiered systems of supports (MTSS) and, 208
  overview, 6, 349–350, 363
  PL processes, 352–360, 353f
  research on, 361–362
  See also Professional development; Teacher knowledge
Progress monitoring, 102, 204–205, 206t, 213, 214, 216–217, 217f, 218, 420–422. *See also* Assessment
Project CALI (Content-Area Literacy Instruction). *See* Content-Area Literacy Instruction (CALI) intervention
Promoting Adolescents' Comprehension of Text Plus (PACT Plus), 228–230, 233
Prosody
  assessment and, 263, 264–265
  instruction and, 260
  multisyllabic word reading (MWR) and, 36
  overview, 256

text complexity and, 141–142
  See also Fluency; Oral reading fluency (ORF); Reading fluency
Proximity, 84–85, 85f
Purposes for reading and writing, 158, 308–309, 332. *See also* Writing

Q

Quad Text Sets, 145–146
Qualitative features, 140
Qualitative Reading Inventory–II (QRI-II), 260
Quality Teaching Framework, 208
Quantitative characteristics, 140–141
Questioning, 105–107, 175
Quick Writing, 299–300

R

Race
  achievement and opportunity gaps and, 331
  adaptive teaching and, 249f
  critical race theory (CRT) and, 65
  critique of SOR and, 334
  culturally responsive practices and, 207, 333
  simple view of reading (SVR) and, 123–124
  See also Black, Indigenous, and People of Color (BIPOC) students
Racial trauma, 409–410, 413. *See also* Black, Indigenous, and People of Color (BIPOC) students
Racism, 411–412, 414–415
RAND model of comprehension, 139
Rapid word identification, 31
Rate, reading, 117–118, 141, 264
Readability, 136–137, 140–141. *See also* Text complexity
Read-alouds, 173–174
Reader-task considerations, 141–142
Reading comprehension
  bridging theory and teaching practices and, 100–102
  future directions, 109–110
  inference-making instruction and intervention and, 103–110
  knowledge-building and, 169–175
  multilingual reading and, 70–71
  multisyllabic word reading (MWR) and, 32
  multi-tiered systems of supports (MTSS) and, 102–103
  overview, 99–100, 110, 152–153, 385
  professional learning and, 350–351
  Promoting Adolescents' Comprehension of Text Plus (PACT Plus), 228–230

reading engagement and, 156–163
reading theories and, 69
self-efficacy and, 160
simple view of reading (SVR) and, 69–70, 115, 123, 126
summer reading programs and, 191–192
teacher knowledge and, 7, 387–397, 388t–391t, 394t, 399–400
text complexity and, 141, 142, 144–145, 147
text-based discussions and, 227
vocabulary knowledge and, 29–30, 80–81, 87, 92, 226–228
See also Comprehension; Strategy instruction
Reading difficulties/disabilities (RD)
overview, 185–187, 187t
simple view of reading (SVR) and, 116, 124
summer reading programs, 187–198
See also Disabilities; Struggling readers
Reading engagement
connections between research and practice and, 335–336
knowledge-building and, 169–175, 176–178
overview, 152–153, 156, 162–163
reading comprehension and, 156–163
science of, 155–156
See also Engagement
Reading fluency
assessment and, 263–265
multisyllabic word reading (MWR) and, 36, 39, 41
overview, 255–256, 268–269
text complexity and, 141–142
as a transition, 257
See also Fluency
Reading instruction, 248–250, 249f
Reading motivation
knowledge-building and, 169–175, 176–178
overview, 152–153, 156, 163
science of, 153–155
See also Motivation
Reading performance and outcomes, 155, 160–161, 232–233
Reading rate, 117–118, 141, 264
Reading Rope, 410, 422, 423
Reading skills, 1, 249f, 277–278, 392–393
Reading wars, 2
READS for Summer Learning, 191
Reasoning
argumentation and, 12, 23
Argumentation Rating Tool (ART), 19, 19f
small-group collaborations and, 159
text-based argument writing and, 308
Reciprocal teaching groups, 159, 402
Reflection, 249f, 250
Reinforcement, 298t
Relational framework, 370–377, 378

Relativism, 15–16
Repeated reading, 36, 41, 259–263, 269
Response to intervention (RTI), 204, 395. *See also* Multi-tiered systems of supports (MTSS)
Revision, 301–302, 318–319, 319f, 320f. *See also* Writing instruction
REWARDS program, 41
Root words, 55–56
Round-robin reading, 261

S

Scaffolding
adaptive teaching and, 243, 244, 246
fluency instruction and, 258, 265–266
knowledge and, 169, 177
summer reading programs, 191–192
supplemental intervention classes and, 231
teacher knowledge and, 398
text complexity and, 145, 146
text-based argument writing and, 317
writing instruction for students with learning disabilities, 301
Scheduling, 207, 276–278, 331
School-based summer programs, 190, 192–194. *See also* Summer instruction/intervention
Schoolwide literacy models
content-area classes and, 226–230
future directions, 234–235
implementing practices, 231–234
literacy coaching and, 375–377
overview, 223–226
Promoting Adolescents' Comprehension of Text Plus (PACT Plus), 228–230
Science of literacy (SOL), 1, 409–411, 412–413, 414–423
Science of reading (SOR)
critique of, 333–335
expansive literacies and, 327
human experiences and, 327–328
interventions and, 331
overview, 1, 48–49
reading engagement and, 155–156
reading motivation and, 153–155
schoolwide literacy models and, 235
word reading and, 54
Screening, 102, 206t, 208–210, 209f, 218. *See also* Assessment
Self-determination theory (SDT), 157, 162
Self-efficacy beliefs, 154–155, 158–161. *See also* Beliefs
Self-monitoring, 298t
Self-reflection, 249f, 373, 374
Self-regulated strategy development (SRSD), 280, 282, 285, 297–299, 298t, 303

Self-regulation, 294–295
Self-reinforcement, 298t
Self-talk, 298t
Semantic complexity, 143. *See also* Text complexity
Sentence stems, 315, 317, 318f, 322
Shared knowledge, 433–434. *See also* Knowledge
Shared reading, 145, 261
Sight-word recognition, 116
Simple view of reading (SVR)
  applicability of, 121–125
  Black students and, 410
  complicating, 117–125
  implications of, 116
  language comprehension and, 55–57
  literacy and, 52
  long view of, 125–129
  multilingual reading and, 70–71
  overview, 3, 68, 69–70, 115–116, 117–121, 124–125
  word reading and, 53–55
  See also Developmental literacy perspectives
Situation model, 100–101, 385
Skills instruction, 249f, 285–286, 392–393
Small-group instruction
  adaptive teaching and, 243
  fluency instruction and, 259–260, 267
  reading engagement and, 157–159
  summer reading programs and, 195–196
SMILE (sharing; me; importance; liking; engagement) acronym, 157–163
Social constructivism, 243–244
Social engagement, 156, 159. *See also* Reading engagement
Social justice, 330–332
Social media networks. *See* Digital literacies; Multimodal literacies
Sociocultural theories, 146, 311–312, 334, 370
Socratic seminar sequence, 337–338
Sounding out words, 115. *See also* Decoding
Special education services, 186–187. *See also* Disabilities
Specific learning disability (SLD), 186–188, 187t. *See also* Disabilities
Spelling, 39, 50, 402–403
Standardized testing, 332
Standards, 139–141, 434–435. *See also* Common Core State Standards (CCSS)
Strategies for Teaching Reading, Information, and Vocabulary Effectively (STRIVE), 227
Strategy instruction
  efficacy of, 320–322, 322f
  English learners (ELs) and, 311
  knowledge-building and, 171
  overview, 226–228
  professional learning and, 351–352, 355–356
  reading comprehension and, 107–109
  self-regulated strategy development (SRSD), 280, 282, 285, 297–299, 298t, 303
  text-based argument writing and, 310–311
  writing instruction and, 282
  writing instruction for students with learning disabilities, 296, 300–302
  See also Cognitive strategy instruction; Instructional approaches
Struggling readers
  adaptive teaching and, 242–243
  fluency instruction and, 259–260, 262–263
  knowledge-building and, 171
  multi-tiered systems of supports (MTSS) and, 210–213
  schoolwide literacy models and, 232–233
  self-efficacy and, 160
  simple view of reading (SVR) and, 116
  summer reading programs, 187–198
  supports for, 4–5
  vocabulary knowledge and, 87
  See also Reading difficulties/disabilities (RD)
Student factors
  achievement and opportunity gaps and, 331–332
  adaptive teaching and, 243, 244, 249f
  text complexity and, 142–143
  writing instruction for students with learning disabilities, 294
Student-to-student sharing, 157–158
Suffixes
  morphology instruction and, 51–52, 55, 58
  multisyllabic word reading (MWR) and, 35–36, 38–39, 39f
Summative assessment, 206t, 208. *See also* Assessment
Summer instruction/intervention
  Black Futures approach, 417
  literacy instruction for older struggling readers and, 196–197
  overview, 185–186, 197–198
  reading outcomes during, 187–188
  summer reading programs, 188–198
Supplemental interventions
  future directions, 235
  overview, 223–226, 230–231
  Promoting Adolescents' Comprehension of Text Plus (PACT Plus), 229–230
  schoolwide literacy models and, 232–234
  See also Interventions
Survey of Basic Language Constructs, 386
Sustained reading engagement, 156–157. *See also* Reading engagement
Syllabication, 34–35. *See also* Multisyllabic word reading (MWR)
Syntax, 50, 51–52, 55–57, 119, 244, 394t
Systematicity, 210, 211
Systemic racism, 411–-412

Subject Index

T

Teacher education, 67. *See also* Preservice preparation; Professional development
Teacher knowledge
 adaptive teaching and, 251
 Black Futures approach, 413, 415–417, 419–420, 423–424
 early reading and, 385–387
 future directions, 403–404
 increasing, 350–351
 multimodal literacies and, 433–434
 overview, 6–7, 367–368, 383–384
 research on, 397–403
 text complexity and, 143–144, 147
 upper elementary reading comprehension instruction and, 387–397, 388t–391t, 394t
 writing instruction and, 278–280, 292–293, 303
 See also Content knowledge; Literacy coaching; Preservice preparation; Professional development; Professional learning (PL)
Teacher Knowledge of Reading Comprehension (TKRC), 393
Technology-based instruction, 103, 107–109, 110, 302–303. *See also* Artificial intelligence (AI)
Test of Word Reading Efficiency (TOWRE), 260, 262
Text complexity
 building teacher knowledge on, 143–144
 future directions, 146–147
 instructional supports and, 143–146
 measuring, 136–137, 140–141
 morphological assessment and, 58
 operationalizing, 137–139, 138f
 overview, 3–4, 29–30, 135–136
 reading fluency and comprehension and, 141–142, 258–259, 265–266
 research on, 139–143
 standards and, 139–141
 supplemental intervention classes and, 231
 teacher knowledge and, 399
 theoretical frameworks, 139
Text difficulty, 138–139, 138f, 146. *See also* Text complexity
Text selection, 73, 172–175, 258–259
Text structure, 394t
Text-based argument writing
 cognitive strategies approach and, 309–311
 English learners (ELs) and, 6
 overview, 307–309
 Pathway Project and, 311–323, 312f, 314f, 316f, 317f, 318f, 319f, 320f, 322f
 See also Argumentation; Writing; Writing instruction
Text-based discussions. *See* Discussions
Text-based writing, 299. *See also* Text-based argument writing; Writing
TextEvaluator, 136, 140–141
Textual information, 169. *See also* Knowledge
Think-aloud protocols
 knowledge-building and, 175
 reading comprehension and, 103–104, 105
 schoolwide literacy models and, 232
 writing instruction for students with learning disabilities, 295, 301
Think-pair activities, 159
Third space theory, 66–67, 73
TIDE mnemonic (topic, important ideas, detailed explanation of ideas, and ending), 299
Tiered instruction, 102–110. *See also* Multi-tiered systems of supports (MTSS)
Topic knowledge, 168. *See also* Knowledge
Translanguaging, 67–68, 73
Tutoring, 186, 243, 247, 410, 420–423

U

Universal screening, 206t, 208–210, 209f, 218. *See also* Assessment
Usability, 234
USHER (United States History for Engaged Reading) program, 155

V

Vacation, summer. *See* Summer instruction/intervention
Validity, logical, 19, 19f
Value of reading, 161
Varied practice reading (VPR) approach, 230–231
Video demonstrations, 352
Virtual coaching. *See* Coaching
Virtual field experience (VFE), 340
Vocabulary instruction
 morphology instruction and, 50, 55–57
 multilingual literacy and, 64
 overview, 47–48, 90–91, 92, 226–228
 Promoting Adolescents' Comprehension of Text Plus (PACT Plus), 228–230
 reading comprehension and, 80–81
 supporting in schools, 90–91
 text complexity and, 145
 See also Vocabulary knowledge
Vocabulary knowledge
 adaptive teaching and, 242
 critique of SOR and, 334–335
 developmental processes and, 2–3, 51–52, 83–90, 83t, 85f, 91–92
 knowledge-building and, 172–175, 176–178
 language of learning and, 81–82
 literacy coaching and, 376
 morphology instruction and, 2–3, 52

Vocabulary knowledge *(cont.)*
  overview, 1, 2, 47–48, 80–81, 91–92
  professional learning and, 355–356
  reading comprehension and, 29–30, 80–81, 87, 92, 226–228
  research on, 168
  schoolwide literacy models and, 232–233
  science of literacy (SOL) and, 410–411
  simple view of reading (SVR) and, 121, 123, 124
  summer reading programs and, 191–192
  supplemental intervention classes and, 231
  supporting in schools, 90–91
  teacher knowledge and, 387, 392–393, 394*t*, 395, 403
  text complexity and, 29–30
  vocabulary comprehension and, 118–120, 249*f*
  See also Academic vocabulary; Knowledge; Vocabulary instruction

W

Walk-throughs, administrative, 207–208
Wechsler Individual Achievement Test, 262
White Mainstream English, 412
Whole-class instruction, 243, 266–267, 266*f*
Wide Fluency-Oriented Reading Instruction (Wide FORI), 261–262, 265–267, 266*f*. *See also* Fluency-Oriented Reading Instruction (FORI)
Wide reading, 259–263
Word Connections program, 37–41, 39*f*, 40*f*
Word Generation program, 90–91, 92
Word identification strategies, 31
Word knowledge, 83–90, 83*t*, 85*f*, 244. *See also* Vocabulary knowledge; Word reading; Word recognition
Word processing, 282, 283, 285. *See also* Writing
Word reading
  instruction and, 47–48
  knowledge and comprehension and, 169
  morphology instruction and, 50, 51–52, 53–55
  multilingual reading and, 70
  reading comprehension and, 30
  self-efficacy and, 160
  teacher knowledge and, 395
  word reading efficiency and, 30–32, 41–42
  See also Multisyllabic word reading (MWR); Word recognition
Word recognition
  fluency and, 255–256, 260, 268–269
  fluency instruction and, 262–263
  multisyllabic word reading (MWR) and, 32
  overview, 2–3, 115
  professional learning and, 355–356
  reading comprehension and, 100, 385
  teacher knowledge and, 392
  See also Decoding; Multisyllabic word reading (MWR); Word knowledge; Word reading
Working memory, 120–121, 294–295
Writers-within-community (WWC) model, 293–294
Writing
  critique of SOR and, 334–335
  importance of, 277–278
  interconnectedness of literacies and, 329–330, 329*f*
  multimodal literacies and, 338–340, 340*f*, 437
  opportunities for growth and connection and, 332
  overview, 275–276, 331
  professional learning and, 355–356
  science of literacy (SOL) and, 410–411
  writing development, 5–6, 281–282
  See also Text-based argument writing; Writing instruction
Writing communities, 293–294
Writing instruction
  barriers to, 278–280
  evidence-based practices and, 282–286, 284*t*
  overview, 275–276, 286
  professional learning and, 358
  research on, 5–6
  teacher knowledge and, 403
  time for, 276–278
  See also Text-based argument writing; Writing; Writing instruction for students with learning disabilities
Writing instruction for students with learning disabilities
  challenges with, 291–293
  future directions, 302–303
  importance of, 290–291
  interventions and, 296–302, 298*t*
  overview, 290
  theories and, 293–295
  See also Learning disabilities; Writing instruction

Z

Zone of proximal development, 66, 258